THE U.S.
INTELLIGENCE COMMUNITY

THIRD EDITION

THE U.S.
INTELLIGENCE COMMUNITY

Jeffrey T. Richelson

WESTVIEW PRESS
BOULDER • SAN FRANCISCO • OXFORD

Published in 1995 in the United States of America by Westview Press, Inc., 5500 Central Avenue, Boulder, Colorado 80301-2877, and in the United Kingdom by Westview Press, 12 Hid's Copse Road, Cumnor Hill, Oxford OX2 9JJ

Second edition published in 1989 by HarperBusiness, a division of HarperCollins Publishers. First edition published in 1985 by Ballinger Publishing Company.

Library of Congress Cataloging-in-Publication Data
Richelson, Jeffrey.
  The U.S. intelligence community / Jeffrey T. Richelson.—3rd ed.
    p.   cm.
  Includes index.
  ISBN 0-8133-2355-6.—ISBN 0-8133-2376-2 (pbk.)
  1. Intelligence service—United States.   I. Title.   II. Title: U.S.
intelligence community.   III. Title: United States intelligence
community.
JK468.I6R53   1995
327.1273—dc20   94-48474
                                                                         CIP

Printed and bound in the United States of America

The paper used in this publication meets the requirements
of the American National Standard for Permanence of Paper
for Printed Library Materials Z39.48-1984.

10   9   8   7   6   5   4   3   2

CONTENTS

FIGURES

TABLES

PHOTOGRAPHS

PREFACE

This book represents an attempt to accomplish in one volume what requires several volumes. It attempts to provide a comprehensive and detailed order of battle of the U.S. intelligence community—to describe its collection and analysis organizations, their activities, and the management structure that is responsible for directing and supervising those organizations and activities.

Given the purpose of the book, I do not, until the concluding chapter, seek to evaluate the intelligence community's effectiveness in performing its varied tasks or comment on the acceptability, wisdom, or morality of its activities. In the concluding chapter I address some of the issues facing the intelligence community and the general public.

The data used in this book come from a variety of sources—interviews; official documents (many of which were acquired under the Freedom of Information Act); books written by former intelligence officers, journalists, and academics; trade and technical publications; newspapers; and magazines. The public literature on intelligence is vast and of varying quality, and I have done my best to sort the wheat from the chaff. I have also sought to identify sources to the maximum extent possible while protecting those sources who wished to remain anonymous.

Two groups of individuals were instrumental in helping me to write this book. The work of the Freedom of Information officers who responded to my many hundreds of requests is greatly appreciated. Some may have been frustrated to find that providing one set of requested documents only led to additional requests.

In addition, various journalists, researchers, and others have provided information, documents, suggestions, corrections, and assistance. Those who can be acknowledged publicly are: William Arkin, Desmond Ball, Robert Bolin, William Burrows, Duncan Campbell, Seymour Hersh, David Morison, Jay Peterzell, John Pike, Joseph Pittera, John Prados, Owen Wilkes, Marshall Windmiller, Robert Windrem, and several members of the National Security Archive—Tom Blanton, Bill Burr, Kate Doyle, and Peter Kornbluh.

Jeffrey T. Richelson

1

INTELLIGENCE

Informed policymaking and decisionmaking require adequate information and analysis. Only if policymakers and decisionmakers are sufficiently informed about the state of the world and the likely consequences of policies and actions can they be expected to make intelligent decisions. If their responsibilities have foreign aspects, the acquisition of foreign intelligence information will be essential.

The individuals with the most prominent need for foreign intelligence are those concerned with national security policymaking and decisionmaking. Hence, the President, the National Security Council (NSC), the Secretary of State, the Secretary of Defense, and the Joint Chiefs of Staff are the most visible consumers of foreign intelligence.

However, policymakers with responsibilities in the areas of technology transfer and trade, energy, the environment, and public health may also require foreign intelligence. In the 1970s it became evident that foreign actions with respect to oil could have a dramatic impact on U.S. security. In his role as Chairman of the House Permanent Select Committee on Intelligence, Edward Boland noted that "many believe ... that energy and related economic problems can threaten us more deeply and affect our national security more rapidly than any change in the military picture short of war itself."[1]

Clearly, the availability of foreign energy resources as well as the stability of the dollar can be influenced by the actions of foreign governments or groups. Likewise, the environmental policies of foreign governments can threaten the health of individuals outside their borders. For example, the Soviet Union engaged in extensive dumping of nuclear waste into the oceans.[2] Thus, the Environmental Protection Agency requires intelligence regarding environmental accidents, foreign government compliance with international environmental obligations, and the status of environmentally sensitive areas. With respect to compliance, the EPA is interested in the disposal of nuclear wastes, illegal ocean dumping, and the smuggling of prohibited animals and animal products. Environmentally sensitive topics of concern to the EPA include tropical rain forest destruction, Antarctic pollution sources, and Arctic ice conditions.[3]

INTELLIGENCE

Intelligence can be defined as the "product resulting from the collection, processing, integration, analysis, evaluation and interpretation of available information concerning foreign countries or areas."[4] Collection can be defined as the purposeful acquisition of any information that might be desired by an analyst, consumer, or operator. Collection activity can take any of several overlapping forms: open source collection, clandestine collection, human source collection, and technical collection.

Open source collection includes the acquisition of material in the public domain: radio and television broadcasts, newspapers, magazines, technical and scholarly journals, books, government reports, and reports by foreign service officers and defense attachés concerning public activities. The extent to which open source collection yields valuable information will vary greatly with the nature of the targeted society and the subject involved. The information might be collected by human sources—individuals who buy books and journals or observe military parades—or by technical means—recording television and radio programs.

Clandestine collection involves the acquisition of data that are not publicly available. As with open source collection, both human and technical resources may be employed. The traditional human spy may be employed to provide sensitive political, military, or economic information. Alternatively, technical collection systems can be used to photograph military installations or intercept a wide variety of communications and electronic signals.

Great secrecy and sensitivity characterize human source clandestine collection. Although much technical collection is also clandestine, secrecy is not always as vital in technical collection as it is in human collection. Foreign nations are well aware that the United States operates an extensive space reconnaissance program. Even those nations capable of tracking the movements of U.S. spacecraft can take only limited denial and deception measures. As a result, the ability to effectively collect the required data does not, in general, depend on clandestine operation. In contrast, a human "asset" whose identity becomes known to a foreign security service will soon be arrested or become the channel for disinformation.

Analysis involves the integration of collected information—that is, raw intelligence from all sources—into finished intelligence. The finished intelligence product might be a simple statement of facts, an estimate of the capabilities of another nation's military forces, or a projection of the likely course of political events in another nation.

Strictly speaking, intelligence activities involve only the collection and analysis of information and its transformation into intelligence; however, counterintelligence and covert action are intertwined with intelligence activity. Counterintelligence encompasses all information acquisition and activity designed to assess foreign intelligence and security services and neutralize hostile services. These activities involve clandestine and open source collection as well as analysis of information concerning the structure and operations of foreign services. Such collection and analysis, with respect to the technical collection activities of hostile services, can be employed to conduct denial operations. Counterintelligence may also involve the direct penetration and disruption of hostile services.

Covert action, also known as "special activities," includes any operation designed to influence foreign governments, persons, or events in support of the sponsoring government's foreign policy objectives while keeping the sponsoring government's *support* of the operation secret. Whereas in clandestine collection the emphasis is on keeping the activity secret, in covert action the emphasis is on keeping the sponsorship secret.

There are several distinct types of covert action: black propaganda (propaganda that purports to emanate from a source other than the true one); gray propaganda (in which true sponsorship is not acknowledged); paramilitary or political actions designed to overthrow or support a regime; support (aid, arms, training) of individuals and organizations (newspapers, labor unions, and political parties); economic operations; disinformation; and assassination.

THE INTELLIGENCE CYCLE

It is important to put the collection and analysis activities conducted by various intelligence units into proper perspective—that is, to relate those activities to the requirements and needs of the decisionmakers and the use made of the finished intelligence product. This objective is achieved through the concept of the "intelligence cycle." The intelligence cycle is the process by which information is acquired, converted into finished intelligence, and made available to policymakers. Generally, the cycle comprises five steps: planning and direction, collection, processing, analysis and production, and dissemination.[5]

The planning and direction process involves the management of the entire intelligence effort, from the identification of the need for data to the final delivery of an intelligence product to a consumer. The process may be initiated by requests or requirements for intelligence based on the needs of the President, the Departments of State, Defense, and Treasury, or other consumers. In some cases, the requests and requirements become institutionalized. Thus, the President does not need to remind the intelligence community to collect information on nuclear proliferation.

Collection, as indicated above, involves the gathering of raw data from which finished intelligence will be produced. The collection process involves open sources, clandestine agents, and technical systems. Processing is concerned with the conversion of the vast amount of information coming into the system to a form suitable for the production of finished intelligence. It involves language translation, decryption, and sorting by subject matter as well as data reduction—interpretation of the information stored on film and tape through the use of photographic and electronic processes.

The analysis and production process entails the conversion of basic information into finished intelligence. It includes the integration, evaluation, and analysis of all available data and the preparation of various intelligence products. Because the "raw intelligence" that is collected is often fragmentary and at times contradictory, specialists are needed to give it meaning and significance. The final step in the cycle, dissemination, involves the distribution of the finished intelligence to the consumers—the policymakers (and operators) whose needs triggered the process.

Like any model, this outline of the intelligence cycle is a simplification of the real world. As noted above, certain requirements become standing requirements. Similarly, policymakers do not specify, except in rare cases, particular items of information. Rather, they indicate a desire for reports on, for example, Chinese strategic forces or the political situation in Egypt. The collectors are given the responsibility of determining how to obtain the information necessary to prepare such reports. In addition, the collection agencies have certain internal needs to acquire information to provide for their continued operation—information related to counterintelligence and security and information that will be useful in potential future operations.

It should also be noted that decisionmakers, particularly in the midst of a crisis, may require only processed intelligence instead of fully analyzed intelligence. Thus, in the midst of the Cuban Missile Crisis, the most important intelligence was the purely factual reporting concerning Soviet activities in Cuba and on the high seas.

THE UTILITY OF INTELLIGENCE

The utility of intelligence activity, here narrowly construed to mean collection and analysis, depends on the extent to which it aids national, departmental, and military service decisionmakers. Two questions arise in this regard: In what ways does intelligence aid decisionmakers, and what attributes make intelligence useful? With respect to the first question, five distinct areas exist in which intelligence can be useful to national decisionmakers: policymaking, planning, combat and other conflict situations, warning, and treaty verification.

In their policymaking roles, national decisionmakers set the basic outlines of foreign, defense, and international economic policy. Their need for intelligence in order to make sound decisions is summed up in the report of the Rockefeller Commission:

> Intelligence is information gathered for policymakers which illuminates the range of choices available to them and enables them to exercise judgement. Good intelligence will not necessarily lead to wise policy choices. But without sound intelligence, national policy decisions and actions cannot effectively respond to actual conditions and reflect the best national interests or adequately protect … national security.[6]

In addition to its value in policymaking, intelligence is vital to the specific decisions needed to implement policy and decisions that might be labeled planning decisions. Some planning decisions may be concerned with the development and deployment of new weapons systems. It has been noted that "timely, accurate, and detailed intelligence is a vital element in establishing requirements and priorities for new systems. Intelligence provides much of the rationale for planning and initiating RDT&E [Research, Development, Test, and Evaluation] efforts and continues to impact these efforts throughout the development and system life cycle."[7]

One incident illustrating the role of intelligence in weapons development occurred in 1968 when U.S. intelligence monitored a submarine belonging to the oldest class of Soviet nuclear submarines traveling faster than 34 miles per hour, with apparent power to spare. That speed exceeded previous Central Intelligence Agency estimates for the submarine and led the CIA to order a full-scale revision of speed estimates for Soviet submarines. The revised estimates also provoked one of the largest construction programs in the history of the Navy—the construction of the SSN 688 attack submarine.[8]

Another set of planning decisions involve the development of war plans. In the months between the Iraqi invasion of Kuwait (August 1990) and the beginning of Operation Desert Storm (January 1991), the United States collected a massive quantity of intelligence about Iraqi nuclear, chemical, and biological weapons programs, electrical power networks, ballistic missiles, air defense systems, ground forces, and air forces. The data collected allowed for development of a war plan based on the most up-to-date information that could be gathered.

Other decisions aided by intelligence include the suspension or resumption of foreign aid, the employment of trade restrictions or embargoes, and attempts to block the transfer of commodities related to nuclear or ballistic missile proliferation. Intelligence might be able to tell the decisionmaker(s) the likely effects of such actions, including the reactions of those nations targeted by the decision. The Carter administration went ahead with the planned sale of planes to Saudi Arabia in part as a result of intelligence indicating that if the United States backed out of the deal the Saudis would simply buy French planes.[9]

More recently, the United States, based on intelligence concerning a "suspicious procurement pattern" by Iran, has acted to prevent the sale of equipment that would have allowed that nation to begin manufacturing nuclear weapons. Argentina halted certain sales to Iran after the United States expressed concern that the equipment in question would have allowed Iran to convert natural uranium into precursor forms of highly enriched uranium. Similarly, the United States successfully lobbied the government of the People's Republic of China to halt the sale of a large nuclear reactor that would have included a supply of enriched fuel and would have permitted Iran to conduct research related to the nuclear fuel cycle.[10]

Intelligence is also useful in a variety of conflict situations, most prominently combat. Regardless of how well developed a war plan is, combat forces require intelligence on the movements and actions of enemy forces as well as on the impact of air and other attacks against enemy facilities and troops. Thus, even after months of intense collection prior to Operation Desert Storm, the United States still needed to conduct an intense intelligence collection campaign during the conflict.

Conflict situations in which intelligence is of value need not be exclusively of a military nature, however. Any situation where nations have at least partially conflicting interests, such as in arms control negotiations, trade negotiations, or international conferences, would qualify. Intelligence can indicate how far the other negotiator can be pushed and the extent to which a position must be modified to be adopted. In 1969 the United States intercepted Japanese communications concerning the negotiations then taking place between the United States and Tokyo over the reversion of Okinawa to Japanese control.[11]

Intelligence can also provide warning of upcoming hostile actions. Warning might concern military, terrorist, or other action to be taken against the decisionmaker's own government or nation or against another country that the decisionmaker is interested in protecting. With advance notice, defenses can be prepared, responses considered and implemented, and preemptive actions (diplomatic or military) taken to forestall or negate the action. Thus, in 1980, on the basis of intelligence from a human source, President Jimmy Carter warned Soviet General Secretary Leonid Brezhnev of the danger of invading Poland. In March 1991, on the basis of communications intelligence indicating Iraqi intentions to use gas against rebel forces, the United States warned the Iraqis that such an action would not be tolerated.[12]

Intelligence is also necessary to assess whether other nations are in compliance with various international obligations. The United States is concerned with whether Russia and other Soviet successor states are complying with arms control agreements currently in force, for example. Intelligence also ensures the compliance of all signatories to the treaties limiting nuclear proliferation and nuclear testing. In 1993 it was reported that the United States was concerned with China's apparent violation of its pledge not to sell M-11 missiles to Pakistan. At times the United States is also concerned about whether an allied nation is complying with terms of an economic agreement. One subject of contention in 1987 was whether Japan was violating the Semiconductor Arrangement established with the United States in 1986. The arrangement was intended to avoid the below-cost dumping of semiconductors and permit greater foreign semiconductor sales in the Japanese market.[13]

The overall utility of intelligence in regard to military matters was concisely summarized by the Eisenhower administration's Technological Capabilities Panel:

If intelligence can uncover a new military threat, we may take steps to meet it. If intelligence can reveal an opponent's specific weakness, we may prepare to exploit it. With good intelligence we can avoid wasting our resources by arming for the wrong danger at the wrong time. Beyond this, in the broadest sense, intelligence underlies our estimate of the enemy and thus helps guide our political strategy.[14]

For maximum utility, intelligence must not only address relevant subjects but also possess the attributes of quality and timeliness. Unless all relevant information is marshaled when assessing intelligence on a subject, the quality of the finished product may suffer. Covertly obtained intelligence should not be assessed in isolation from overtly obtained intelligence. As Professor H. Trevor-Roper observed:

> Secret intelligence is the continuation of open intelligence by other means. So long as governments conceal a part of their activities, other governments, if they wish to base their policy on full and correct information, must seek to penetrate the veil. This inevitably entails varying methods. But, however the means may vary, the end must still be the same. It is to complement the results of what for convenience, we may call "public" intelligence: that is, the intelligence derived from the rational study of public or at least available sources. Intelligence, in fact, is indivisible.[15]

In addition to being based on all relevant information, the assessment process must be objective. As former Secretary of State Henry Kissinger told the U.S. Senate in 1973: "Anyone concerned with national policy must have a profound interest in making sure that intelligence guides, and does not follow, national policy."[16]

Further, intelligence must reach decisionmakers in good time for them to act decisively. Intelligence as foreknowledge has always had particular relevance in military matters. It can give the military commander the great advantage of not being taken by surprise. Chinese philosopher Sun Tzu recognized the value of this advantage 2,500 years ago: "The reason the enlightened prince and the wise general conquer the enemy whenever they move and their achievements surpass those of ordinary men is foreknowledge."[17]

TYPES OF INTELLIGENCE

To understand how specific varieties of foreign intelligence can be useful to government officials, one need only consider the components of intelligence. To begin, one might identify several categories of intelligence—political, military, scientific and technical, sociological, economic, and environmental.

Political intelligence encompasses both foreign and domestic politics. Clearly, the foreign policies of other nations have an impact on the United States. A variety of issues might be involved: support for the United States on a U.N. issue, a nation's relations with North Korea or Cuba, attitudes and policies concerning the Middle East, the support of revolutionary groups, and perceptions of U.S. leadership.

The domestic politics of other nations—whether friendly, neutral, or hostile—are also of significant concern to the United States since the resolution of domestic political conflict—whether by coup, election, or civil war—can affect the orientation of that nation in the world, the regional balance of power, the accessibility of critical resources to the United States, or the continued presence of U.S. military bases.

Thus, the outcome of elections in Russia or Israel can have a dramatic impact on U.S. relations with those nations. Likewise, the resolution of the internal conflict in Iran in 1979 deprived the United States of several assets: oil, a military ally, and critical intelligence bases from which Soviet missile telemetry could be intercepted. And the course of events within China can have a major impact on the state of U.S.-Chinese relations.

Military intelligence is useful and required for a variety of reasons. In order to determine its own military requirements—whether nuclear, conventional, or special operations—the United States must know the capabilities of potential adversaries. In addition, military intelligence is also required to assess the need and impact of any military aid the United States may be asked to provide. Further, military intelligence is required to assess the balance of power between pairs of nations (e.g., India-Pakistan, Iran-Iraq, North Korea–South Korea) whose actions can affect U.S. interests.

Scientific and technical intelligence includes both civilian- and military-related scientific and technical development. A nation's ability to produce steel or oil may influence both that country's stability and U.S. fortunes. In many cases, technological developments that occur in the civilian sector have military applications. Examples include computer technology, ball bearing production, mirrors and optical systems, and lasers. Hence, intelligence concerning a nation's progress in those areas or its ability to absorb foreign-produced technology in those areas is relevant to its potential military capability.

One aspect of scientific and technological intelligence that has been of constant concern for more than thirty years is atomic energy intelligence. Whether the announced purpose of a nation's atomic energy activities has been civilian or military, those activities have received a high intelligence priority. In addition to the obvious need to determine whether various foreign governments are developing nuclear weapons, there has also been a perceived need to acquire secret intelligence in support of decisionmaking concerning applications for nuclear technology exports. Thus, the first Director of Central Intelligence (DCI) noted in 1947 that the United States "cannot rely on information submitted by a licensee" and that it was necessary to the United States to "determine actual use, [to] endeavor to discover secondary diversions."[18]

Sociological intelligence concerns group relations within a particular nation. Such relations can have a significant impact on a nation's stability as well as on the nature of its foreign policy. India has been subject on numerous occasions to the acts of Sikh terrorists who seek to turn India's Punjab state into the independent

Sikh nation of "Khalistan." Most recently, it has become apparent how ethnic and other group conflicts can threaten the stability of regions. Such intelligence can be essential in regard to areas that are of great interest to the United States, such as Canada and Europe.

Economic intelligence is also of great importance. The activities of the Organization of Petroleum Exporting Countries (OPEC) and the European Community (EC), for example, are matters of concern to U.S. national security and economic policy officials. In 1975 the DCI noted that economic intelligence of value to U.S. policymakers included "such topics as the activities of multi-national corporations, international development programs, regional economic arrangements and the workings of international commodity markets."[19] Specific areas of interest included:

- rates of production, consumption, pricing of raw materials and energy sources, and international commodity arrangements as a means to sharing the burden of price fluctuation between producers and consumers of primary commodities;
- price and nonprice restrictions on international trade; and
- the international payments mechanism and the coordination of national fiscal monetary policies.[20]

With regard to any one country, U.S. officials may have a need for intelligence concerning all aspects of domestic and foreign affairs. In the case of Russia, intelligence of value includes (but is by no means limited to) Boris Yeltsin's health; the status of the Russian nuclear arsenal and its general-purpose forces; the state of the Russian economy; government subsidization of industry and agriculture; the size, power, and intentions of groups opposed to Yeltsin; Russian compliance with arms reduction treaties; Russian relations with other former Soviet republics, and Russian sales of advanced weapons.[21]

THE INTELLIGENCE COMMUNITY

The U.S. intelligence community has been precisely defined in a number of government directives and regulations. One of those regulations stated that:

The CIA, the NSA, DIA, the [National Reconnaissance Office], the Bureau of Intelligence and Research of the Department of State, the intelligence elements of the military services, the FBI, the Department of the Treasury, the DOE, the Drug Enforcement Administration, and the staff elements of the Director of Central Intelligence constitute the intelligence community.[22]

Recent additions to the community are the Central Imagery Office and the Defense HUMINT Service. Also worthy of consideration are the Defense Mapping Agency, the intelligence components of the unified commands, and the intelligence elements of the Department of Commerce. These intelligence elements, along with those mentioned directly above, can be grouped into five categories:

- national intelligence organizations,
- Department of Defense intelligence organizations,
- military service intelligence organizations,
- the intelligence components of the unified commands, and
- civilian intelligence organizations.

NOTES

1. U.S. Congress, House Permanent Select Committee on Intelligence, *Intelligence on the World Energy Future* (Washington, D.C.: U.S. Government Printing Office, 1979), p. 2.

2. William J. Broad, "Russians Describe Extensive Dumping of Nuclear Waste," *New York Times,* April 27, 1993, pp. C1, C8; Fred Hiatt, "Russians Set to Dump Nuclear Waste at Sea," *Washington Post,* October 17, 1993, p. A25.

3. Environmental Protection Agency, "EPA NSR-29 Intelligence Requirements," May 14, 1992.

4. Joint Chiefs of Staff, *U.S. Department of Defense Dictionary of Military Terms* (New York: Arco Publishing, 1988), p. 183.

5. Central Intelligence Agency, *Intelligence: The Acme of Skill* (Washington, D.C.: CIA, n.d.), pp. 6–7; Central Intelligence Agency, *Fact Book on Intelligence* (Washington, D.C.: CIA, 1993), pp. 10–11.

6. Commission on CIA Activities within the United States, *Report to the President* (Washington, D.C.: U.S. Government Printing Office, 1975), p. 6.

7. HQ USAF, ACS, I, INOI 80-1, "The Intelligence Role in Research, Development, Test and Evaluation (RDT&E)," January 18, 1985.

8. Patrick Tyler, "The Rise and Fall of the SSN 688," *Washington Post,* September 21, 1986, pp. A1, A18.

9. Zbigniew Brzezinski, *Power and Principle: Memoirs of the National Security Adviser, 1977–1981* (New York: Farrar, Straus & Giroux, 1983), p. 248.

10. Steve Coll, "U.S. Halted Nuclear Bid by Iran," *Washington Post,* November 17, 1992, pp. A1, A30.

11. Seymour Hersh, *The Price of Power: Kissinger in the Nixon White House* (New York: Summit, 1983), p. 103.

12. Benjamin Weiser, "A Question of Loyalty," *Washington Post Magazine,* December 13, 1992, pp. 9ff.; Patrick E. Tyler, "U.S. Said to Plan Bombing of Iraqis If They Gas Rebels," *New York Times,* March 10, 1991, pp. 1, 15.

13. Ann Devroy and R. Jeffrey Smith, "U.S. Evidence 'Suggests' China Breaks Arms Pact," *Washington Post,* May 18, 1993, p. A9; Douglas Jehl, "China Breaking Missile Pledge, U.S. Aides Say," *New York Times,* May 6, 1993, pp. A1, A6; John M. Goshko, "U.S. Warns China of Sanctions for Missile Exports to Pakistan," *Washington Post,* July 26, 1993, p. A10; "Psst! Want to Buy a Missile?" *Newsweek,* September 6, 1993, p. 28; R. Jeffrey Smith, "Ukraine Begins to Dismantle Nuclear Missiles Aimed at U.S.," *Washington Post,* July 28,

1993, p. A13; "Japan Counters Dumping Charges with Position Paper," *Defense Electronics*, June 1987, p. 18.

14. James J. Killian, Jr., *Sputnik, Scientists, and Eisenhower: A Memoir of the First Special Assistant to the President for Science and Technology* (Cambridge: MIT Press, 1977), p. 80.

15. Hugh Trevor-Roper, *The Philby Affair—Espionage, Treason and Secret Services* (London: Kimber, 1968), p. 66.

16. U.S. Congress, Senate Committee on Foreign Relations, *Nomination of Henry A. Kissinger* (Washington, D.C.: U.S. Government Printing Office, 1973). For evidence that Kissinger did not always follow his own advice, see Hersh, *The Price of Power*, pp. 529–60.

17. Samuel Griffith, trans., *Sun Tzu, The Art of War* (London: Oxford Press, 1963), p. 144.

18. Sidney Souers, "Atomic Energy Intelligence," RG 218 (Joint Chiefs of Staff), File 131, July 1, 1947, Military Reference Branch, National Archives and Record Administration.

19. "Director of Central Intelligence: Perspectives for Intelligence, 1976–1981," *Covert Action Information Bulletin* 6 (October 1979): 13–24 at 19.

20. Ibid., p. 20.

21. R. James Woolsey, "Threats to the U.S. and Its Interests," Opening Statement before the U.S. Senate Select Committee on Intelligence, January 25, 1994, pp. 10–15; Bill Gertz, "Yeltsin in Control of Nuclear Arsenal," *Washington Times*, September 24, 1993, p. A17; Fred Hiatt, "Russia Shifts Doctrine on Military Use," *Washington Post*, November 4, 1993, pp. A1, A33; Steven Zaloga, "Russia Exporting Top-of-the-Line Weapons," *Armed Forces Journal International*, December 1992, pp. 45–46; Michael R. Gordon, "Moscow Is Selling Weapons to China, U.S. Officials Say," *New York Times*, October 18, 1992, pp. A1, A4; Michael R. Gordon, "Russia Selling Submarines to Tehran's Navy," *New York Times*, September 24, 1992, p. A9; Henrik Bering-Jensen, "Wrestling with the Arms of Russia," *Insight*, April 25, 1979, pp. 14ff.; Don Oberdorfer, "Russian Strife Seen Straining Arms Controls," *Washington Post*, February 4, 1993, p. A11.

22. DIA Regulation 50-17, "Release of Classified DOD Intelligence to Non-NFIB U.S. Government Agencies," July 26, 1978.

2
NATIONAL INTELLIGENCE ORGANIZATIONS

The activities of the U.S. intelligence community are similar to those of many other nations—collection, analysis, counterintelligence, and covert action. However, the extent of those activities and the methods employed, especially with respect to technical collection, far surpass those of every other nation except Russia.

The United States collects information via reconnaissance satellites, aircraft, ships, signals and seismic ground stations, radar, and undersea surveillance as well as through the traditional overt and clandestine human sources. The total cost of these activities is approximately $28 billion per year.

Given this wide range of activity and the large number of intelligence consumers, it is not surprising that a plethora of organizations are involved in intelligence activities. Of these organizations, four are considered to be national intelligence organizations in that they perform intelligence functions for the entire government (rather than just a department). Their activities provide intelligence for national-level policymakers, and they are responsive to direction by supra-departmental authority. The four organizations are: the Central Intelligence Agency (CIA), the National Security Agency (NSA), the National Reconnaissance Office (NRO), and the Central Imagery Office (CIO).

CENTRAL INTELLIGENCE AGENCY

In the aftermath of World War II, the U.S. central intelligence organization that had been created for the conflict—the Office of Strategic Services (OSS)—was disbanded. Several branches of the organization were distributed among other departments of the government. The X-2 (Counterintelligence) and Secret Intelligence Branches were transferred to the War Department to become the Strategic Services Unit, and the Research and Analysis Branch was relocated in the State Department.[1]

Shortly afterward, however, President Harry S. Truman authorized consideration of postwar intelligence organization, which resulted in the establishment of the National Intelligence Authority and its operational element, the Central Intelligence Group (CIG), to coordinate and collate intelligence reports. The CIG served as a coordinating mechanism as well as having some responsibility for intelligence collection.[2]

As part of the general consideration of national security needs and organization, the question of intelligence organization was addressed in the National Security Act of 1947. The act established the CIA as an independent agency within the Executive Office of the President to replace the CIG. According to the act, the CIA was to have five functions:

1. to advise the National Security Council in matters concerning such intelligence activities of the government departments and agencies as relate to national security;
2. to make recommendations to the National Security Council for the coordination of such intelligence activities of the departments and agencies of the government as relate to the national security;
3. to correlate and evaluate the intelligence relating to the national security, and to provide for the appropriate dissemination of such intelligence within the Government using, where appropriate, existing agencies and facilities;
4. to perform for the benefit of the existing intelligence agencies such additional services of common concern as the National Security Council determines can be more effectively accomplished centrally; and
5. to perform other such functions and duties related to intelligence affecting the national security as the National Security Council may from time to time direct.[3]

The CIA was to have no domestic investigative role or powers of arrest.

The provisions of the act left a great deal of room for interpretation. Thus, the fifth and final provision has been cited as authorizing covert action. In fact, the provision was intended only to authorize espionage.[4]

Whatever the intentions of Congress in 1947, the CIA developed in accord with a maximalist interpretation of the act. Thus, the CIA has become the primary U.S. government agency for intelligence analysis, clandestine human intelligence collection, and covert action. It has also played a major role in the development of overhead reconnaissance systems—both aircraft and spacecraft—used for gathering imagery and signals intelligence. In addition, the Director of the CIA is also the Director of Central Intelligence and is responsible for managing the activities of the entire intelligence community.

Under President Reagan's 1981 Executive Order 12333, which is still in effect, the CIA is permitted to collect "significant" foreign intelligence secretly within the United States if that effort is not aimed at learning about the domestic activities of U.S. citizens and corporations. The order also gives the CIA authority to conduct, within the United States, "special activities" or covert actions approved by the President that are not intended to influence U.S. political processes, public opinion, or the media.[5]

CIA headquarters is in Langley, Virginia, just south of Washington, and twenty-two other CIA offices are scattered around the Washington area. Among its newer facilities may be a 2,500-square-foot building complex in Reston, Virginia, that appears to be connected with satellite reconnaissance operations. As of 1991 the CIA had approximately 20,000 employees in the Washington area and a budget of approximately $3 billion.[6]

The agency is divided into four directorates, each headed by a Deputy Director; an Arms Control Intelligence Staff; and four offices directly subordinate to the Director and Deputy Director. The four directorates are the Directorate of Administration, the Directorate of Operations, the Directorate of Science and Technology, and the Directorate of Intelligence.* The offices are those of General Counsel, Inspector General, Congressional Affairs, and Public and Agency Information. The general structure of the CIA is depicted in Figure 2-1.

Day-to-day management of the agency is generally the responsibility of the Deputy Director of Central Intelligence, with the DCI handling community-wide issues and representing the intelligence community to the President and the NSC.

Within the Directorate of Administration are nine offices that perform a wide variety of administrative services: the Office of Communications, the Office of Logistics, the Office of Security, the Office of Financial Management, the Office of Medical Services, the Office of Personnel, the Office of Training and Education, the Office of Information Technology, and the Office of General Administration.[7]

The Office of Communications, with more than 2,000 employees in 1973, maintains facilities for secret communications between CIA headquarters and overseas bases and agents. Presumably, this duty includes control over any CIA agent communications satellites. Its personnel install and maintain communications equipment (including transmitters and receivers ranging from high-frequency to microwave) and install and operate high-speed data transmission equipment. The Office of Logistics operates warehouses in the United States for weapons and other equipment and supplies office equipment.[8]

The Office of Security is responsible for the physical protection of CIA installations at home and abroad. It also administers polygraph tests to CIA applicants and contractor personnel. The Office of Financial Management is responsible for developing and maintaining accounting systems; establishing and supervising financial regulations and procedures; performing administrative, internal, and industrial audits; and disbursing funds. The office maintains field units in Hong Kong, Buenos Aires, and Geneva with easy access to money markets.[9]

The Office of Medical Services plans and directs the CIA's medical programs. The office is responsible for medical examinations and immunizations for employees and dependents traveling overseas, health education and emergency

---

*A Directorate of Planning and Coordination was created in September 1989 to conduct strategic planning activity that would identify long-term priorities, determine the resources required to support those priorities, and monitor annual progress against the strategic plan. (William Webster, "Establishment of the Position of Deputy Director for Planning and Coordination," CIA document, September 11, 1989.) The directorate was abolished after a short and unhappy existence. (Interview with CIA official.)

Figure 2-1. Organization of the Office of the DCI/CIA.

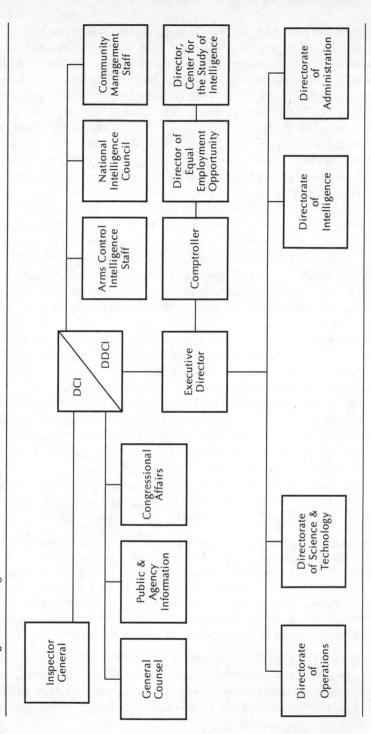

health care, and psychiatric services. It also helps develop the Psychological Assessment Program to determine which individuals are best suited for the agency and is involved in psychiatric and medical intelligence production. The Office of Personnel is responsible for recruitment and maintenance of personnel files. With the Office of Training and Education it operates CIA training facilities—including the main facility, the Armed Forces Experimental Training Facility at Camp Peary, Virginia. Along with the Office of Medical Services and the Office of Security it shares responsibility for screening agency applicants. In response to the statement of personnel needs from agency components, the Office of Personnel prepares an Advanced Staffing Plan for the following fiscal year, listing the total personnel requirements by category of personnel and job titles.[10]

The Office of Training and Education conducts courses on operations, intelligence analysis, management, languages, information science, and executive leadership. The Office of Information Technology operates the CIA's computer facilities. It is also responsible for the agency's domestic communications and computer security. In 1994, subsequent to the revelations concerning Aldrich Ames, DCI R. James Woolsey announced that the CIA would establish an Office of Personnel Security, which will presumably be located in the Directorate of Administration.[11]

The Directorate of Operations (formerly the Directorate of Plans) is responsible for clandestine collection and covert action (special activities). The directorate, with about 5,000 personnel, is organized into various staffs and divisions and also contains two DCI Centers, an Office of Military Affairs, and a HUMINT Requirements Tasking Center, as shown in Figure 2-2. The staffs, which perform supervisory, planning, and evaluative functions, are the Foreign Intelligence Staff, the Covert Action Staff, Staff D, and the Evaluation, Plans and Design Staff.

The Foreign Intelligence Staff is responsible for checking the authenticity of sources and information; screening clandestine collection requirements; and reviewing the regional division projects, budget information, and operational cable traffic.[12] The responsibilities and authority of the Foreign Intelligence Staff were summarized by a former head of the staff, Peer de Silva:

> The Foreign Intelligence Staff had a continuing responsibility for monitoring intelligence-collection projects and programs carried out abroad. These operations and collection programs were of course controlled and directed by the area divisions concerned; the FI Staff simply read the progress charts on the various projects (or the lack of progress) and played the role of determining which intelligence-collection programs should be continued, changed or terminated. With the exception of a few individual operations of special sensitivity, this FI Staff function was worldwide.[13]

The Covert Action Staff, in cooperation with the area divisions, develops plans for covert action operations, considers plans proposed by area divisions, and evaluates the implementation of the plans. Its covert action operations include: (1) political advice and counsel; (2) subsidies to individuals; (3) financial support

Figure 2-2. Organization of the Directorate of Operations.

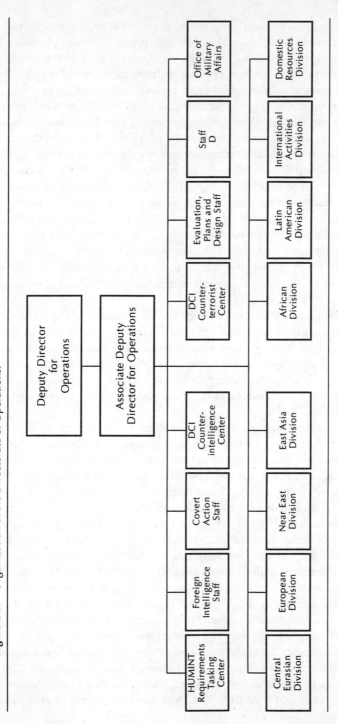

and "technical assistance" to political parties; (4) support to private organizations, including labor unions and business firms; (5) covert propaganda; (6) private training of individuals; (7) economic operations; and (8) paramilitary or political action operations designed to overthrow or support a regime. Thus, during the presidency of Salvador Allende, the Covert Action Staff might have devised an article uncomplimentary to Allende in cooperation with the Chilean desk of what was then the Western Hemisphere Division. A CIA front, such as Forum World Features in London, would then be used to write and transmit the article.[14]

Staff D is in charge of bugging, wiretapping, and some Communications Intelligence (COMINT) activities—some in support of other government agencies. Thus, the U.S. Secret Service regularly tasks the CIA with providing real-time communications intelligence and close support to the Secret Service when the President is traveling in foreign countries. In 1973, at the request of NSA, the staff monitored telephone conversations between the United States and Latin America for several months in an effort to identify narcotics traffickers. On another occasion, Staff D apparently gave money to a code clerk working in the Washington embassy of a U.S. ally for supplying information that assisted in breaking the ally's code.[15]

The Evaluation, Plans and Design Staff does much of the bureaucratic planning and budgeting for the Directorate of Operations. The staff also assesses the effectiveness of operations, attempting to assign dollar values to the information acquired. It also has served as a home for unwanted elements of other staffs and offices. The International Communism Branch of the Counterintelligence Staff was transferred to the evaluation staff as a result of the downgrading of the Counterintelligence Staff.[16]

Actual implementation of staff-planned activities is generally the responsibility of the area divisions, of which there are eight: Central Eurasian, Latin American, European, East Asia, African, Near East, International Activities, and Domestic Resources. Each of the regional area divisions has its own support, covert action, counterintelligence, and foreign intelligence staffs. In addition, each of the area divisions is broken down into branches and desks representing ever more specific geographical areas.[17] The International Activities Division, previously known as the Special Operations Division, handles paramilitary activities such as those that were directed against the Sandinista government of Nicaragua in the 1980s.[18]

The Domestic Resources Division (DRD) was created in 1991 with the merger of two formerly independent divisions—the Foreign Resources Division and the National Collection Division—which became branches under the new division. The Foreign Resources Division (FRD) was created in 1963 as the Domestic Operations Division and given responsibility for "clandestine operational activities of the Clandestine Services conducted within the United States against foreign targets."[19] The present function of the Foreign Resources Branch (FRB) is to locate foreign nationals of special interest who are residing in the United States and recruit them to cooperate with the CIA abroad. As a means of identifying such individuals the FRB has relationships with scores of individuals in U.S. academic institutions, including faculty. These individuals do not attempt to recruit students but assist by providing background information and occasionally by brokering introductions.[20]

The National Collection Branch (NCB), known previously as the Domestic Collection Division and the Domestic Contact Service, openly collects intelligence from U.S. residents who have traveled abroad, including scientists, technologists, economists, and energy experts returning from foreign locations of interest. Among those interviewed are academics—in 1982 the Domestic Collection Division was in touch with approximately 900 individuals on 290 campuses in the United States.[21]

The Chief of the DRD (and probably the chiefs of the NCB and the FRB) can approve the use of individuals who are employees or invitees of an organization within the United States to collect important foreign intelligence at fairs, workshops, symposia, and similar types of commercial or professional meetings that are open to those individuals in their overt roles but closed to the general public.[22]

There are also two DCI Centers in the Directorate of Operations—the Counterintelligence Center (CIC) and the Counterterrorist Center (CTC). These centers were established during William Webster's tenure as DCI in order to give heightened status to the missions as well as to bring together representatives of different intelligence community components, including analysts, involved in the counterintelligence and counterterrorism missions. The CIC consolidated the Counterintelligence Staff, the Foreign Intelligence Capabilities Unit (established in 1983 to look for attempts by foreign intelligence agencies to manage perceptions of U.S. intelligence), elements of the CIA Office of Security, and other intelligence community elements. The Director of the CIC was given the status of Associate Deputy Director for Operations for Counterintelligence.[23]

An Office of Military Affairs, directed by the Associate Deputy Director of Operations for Military Affairs, was established in 1992 to improve the CIA's responsiveness to military Human Intelligence (HUMINT) requirements.[24]

The Directorate of Science and Technology (DS&T), with about 5,000 employees in 1991, was created in 1962 to consolidate various CIA offices dealing with technical intelligence. Originally designated the Directorate of Research, it became the Directorate of Science and Technology in 1963. The DS&T has undergone several reorganizations and has gained and lost responsibilities in the twenty years since it was created. Both the Directorate of Intelligence and the Directorate of Operations have at times disputed actual or planned DS&T control of various offices and divisions. Thus, at various times the DS&T has been assigned scientific intelligence analysis functions, to the dismay of the Directorate of Intelligence. At one time, the directorate controlled the Office of Weapons Intelligence (formed by merging the Foreign Missile and Space Analysis Center with certain functions of the Office of Scientific Intelligence).[25]

In 1973 the National Photographic Interpretation Center (NPIC) was transferred to the DS&T from the Directorate of Intelligence. The NPIC is the successor to a series of CIA photographic interpretation units first established in 1953 as the Photographic Intelligence Division (PID). The original division had thirteen interpreters. In 1958 the PID merged with a statistical analysis division of the Office of Current Intelligence to form the PIC. Under the provision of National Security Council Intelligence Directive (NSCID) 8 of 1961 and its successors, the NPIC is run by the CIA as a "service of common concern" serving the entire intelligence community. It presently has several thousand interpreters and is located in Building 213 of the Washington Navy Yard at 1st and M Streets.[26]

In 1991 the Senate Select Committee on Intelligence directed that the Director and Deputy Director positions be rotated between CIA and Defense Department officials every three years. Previously the NPIC Director was always a CIA official. The rationale for the new requirement was that it would represent "a first step toward making the Center more responsive to military requirements."[27]

In addition to the NPIC, the components of the DS&T include the Office of Development and Engineering, the Office of Technical Collection, the Office of Research and Development, the Office of Technical Services, and the Foreign Broadcast Information Service (FBIS). The Office of Development and Engineering is the successor to a long line of CIA components involved in overhead reconnaissance. The first such CIA component was created in 1954 to develop the U-2 aircraft and was named the Development Project Staff. It subsequently became known as the Office of Special Activities, the Office of Special Projects, and, in 1973, the Office of Development and Engineering.[28]

The Office of Development and Engineering is involved in the development of major technical collection systems such as the KH-11 imaging satellite. The office "provides total systems development for major systems—from requirements definition through design, engineering, and testing and evaluation, to implementation, operation and even support logistics and maintenance." Specific areas of research in developing such systems include laser communications, digital imagery processing, real-time data collection and processing, electro-optics, advanced signal collection, and advanced antenna design.[29]

The Office of Technical Collection was created by merging the Office of SIGINT Operations (OSO) and the Office of Special Projects. OSO "develop[ed], operat[ed] and maintain[ed] sophisticated equipment required to perform collection and analysis tasks with maximum efficiency." The OSO was heavily involved in the development of the RHYOLITE/AQUACADE series of signals intelligence satellites. Through its Special Collection Service, and in conjunction with the NSA, the office operated covert listening posts in a large number of U.S. embassies. It has also been involved in the construction of Signals Intelligence (SIGINT) facilities operated by foreign nations (such as China), the training of their personnel, and the maintenance of the equipment at the site.[30]

The Office of Special Projects was involved in the development and operational support of systems, possibly emplaced sensor systems, to collect measurement and signatures intelligence, signals intelligence, and nuclear intelligence. According to a CIA document, the office "develops collection systems tailored to specific targets."[31]

The Office of Research and Development (OR&D) conducts research in the areas of communications, sensors, semiconductors, artificial intelligence, image recognition, process modeling, database management, and high-speed computing. The OR&D also conducts research for all directorates of the CIA, attempting to go beyond the state of the art in order to anticipate and answer the future technology needs of the intelligence community. The office's Advanced Concepts Staff provides a place for experienced researchers to conduct individual research projects aimed at identifying future intelligence issues and problems.[32]

The Office of Technical Services (OTS) was previously the Technical Services Division (TSD) of the Directorate of Operations. It was absorbed by the DS&T in 1973 in an acquisition that took more than ten years. When the DS&T was formed its leadership argued that the TSD should be brought under its control, but the leaders of the Operations (then Plans) Directorate resisted this suggestion, arguing that the division should be close to its consumers, the operators in Plans. The TSD was transferred to the DS&T as part of a series of transfers and changes initiated by DCI William Colby.[33] The technical services provided by OTS involve secret writing methods, bugging equipment, hidden cameras, coding and decoding devices, video and image enhancement, and chemical imagery.[34]

The Directorate of Science and Technology operates two services of common concern—one is the NPIC, and the other is the Foreign Broadcast Information Service (FBIS). The FBIS monitors the public radio and television broadcasts of foreign nations as well as the broadcasts of "black" or clandestine radio stations and prepares summaries and analyses of broadcasts of interest for use by intelligence analysts and officials. The FBIS dates back to 1941, when the Federal Communications Commission (FCC) established, at the request of the State Department, the Foreign Broadcast Monitoring Service. From that point on the U.S. government had an organization to "record, translate, analyze and report to other agencies of the government on broadcasts of foreign origin." FBIS reports include *China's Evolving Arms Control Policy* (1988), *After Vladivostok: China's Response to Gorbachev's Overture* (1987), and *Chinese Views of Soviet Reform* (1987).[35]

The Directorate of Intelligence is the primary U.S. government organization for intelligence analysis. As shown in Figure 2-3, the present structure of the directorate includes two staffs (Management Planning Services and Collection Requirements and Evaluation), five regional offices, six functional offices, and two independent centers.[36]

Prior to a 1981 reorganization, research offices were formed along purely functional lines to handle economic research, political analysis, geography and cartography, and strategic research. The present regional offices—the Office of Slavic

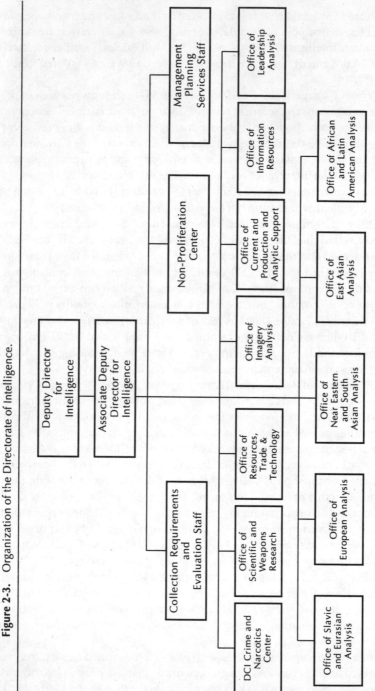

22

Figure 2-3. Organization of the Directorate of Intelligence.

and Eurasian Analysis, the Office of African and Latin American Analysis, the Office of East Asian Analysis, the Office of European Analysis, the Office of Near Eastern and South Asian Analysis—were established to increase multidisciplinary output and thus provide better support to policymakers.[37]

The functional offices—the Office of Resources, Trade and Technology, the Office of Imagery Analysis, the Office of Current Production and Analytic Support, the Office of Information Resources, the Office of Leadership Analysis, and the Office of Scientific and Weapons Research—make up the remainder of the Directorate of Intelligence.[38]

The Office of Resources, Trade, and Technology (ORTT), operating from both a technical and a policy perspective, conducts sanctions monitoring, supports economic negotiations, investigates foreign efforts to unfairly aid business and questionable foreign financial practices, keeps abreast of international arms market trends, devises defense industry strategies, conducts energy resource analysis, and studies geographic and demographic issues and environmental trends.[39]

The Office of Imagery Analysis (OIA) was created in 1961 as the Imagery Analysis Service to give the CIA an imagery analysis capability to supplement the CIA-run NPIC. OIA analysts examine overhead photography to extract information on the deployment of military forces, industrial production, and the development, testing, and production of new weapons systems. As of October 1993 OIA was staffed and managed by NPIC.[40]

The Office of Current Production and Analytic Support (CPAS) publishes all Directorate of Intelligence reports and produces CIA maps, charts, and specialized graphics for use in CIA reports and briefings for the President. It also manages the CIA's twenty-four-hour Operations Center. The Operations Center maintains watch over incoming data from a variety of collection assets and can inform authorities if incoming intelligence indicates that a crisis situation is developing somewhere in the world. In addition, the CPAS is responsible for production of the *National Intelligence Daily* and the *President's Daily Brief.*[41]

In 1986 the Office of Central Reference was split into two new offices: the Office of Information Resources (OIR) and the Office of Leadership Analysis (OLA). The OIR provides library and reference support, computer-based applications development, and training and consulting in automated data processing. The OLA produces reports on foreign leaders and organizations for all levels of the government.[42]

The Office of Scientific and Weapons Research (OSWR) was formed by merging the Office of Scientific Intelligence and the Office of Weapons Research. The OSWR is responsible for determining the scope and nature of foreign scientific and technical activities and programs as well as the performance characteristics of foreign weapons and space systems. The OSWR's analysts study science policy, the physical sciences, civil and military technology, nuclear energy and weapons, nuclear proliferation, offensive and defensive weapons systems, general-purpose weapons, antisubmarine warfare, and space systems.[43]

The DCI's Crime and Narcotics Center (CNC) is also assigned to the Directorate of Intelligence. It is staffed by analysts and operators from the CIA, the Federal Bureau of Investigation, the Defense Department, the National Security Agency, the State Department, and the Treasury Department.[44]

Also housed in the Directorate of Intelligence is the Non-Proliferation Center (NPC), which was established in September 1991 after disclosures about Iraq's capabilities to produce nuclear and other weapons of mass destruction. The NPC consists of about 100 intelligence analysts and clandestine operators, about a third of whom come from agencies other than the CIA. The center monitors the worldwide development and acquisition of production technology, designs, components, or entire military systems in the area of nuclear, chemical, and biological weapons and advanced conventional weapons. The NPC's Transfer Network Groups analyze and identify international suppliers of technologies and the trade mechanisms used to transfer goods.[45]

An analytic unit outside the Directorate of Intelligence is the Arms Control Intelligence Staff (ACIS), headed by the DCI's Special Assistant for Arms Control. The present ACIS can trace its origins to the creation in the mid-1970s of a four-person staff within the Directorate of Intelligence to coordinate CIA arms control–related activities and positions on pivotal verification and monitoring issues. The staff expanded in the 1980s in concert with negotiations on intermediate nuclear forces, strategic arms reduction, and the verification protocols to the Peaceful Nuclear Explosions Treaty and the Threshold Test Ban Treaty. In 1989 the ACIS was further expanded when it absorbed the DCI's Treaty Monitoring Center and the conventional forces component of the Office of Soviet Analysis. At that time ACIS was transferred from the Directorate of Intelligence to the office of the DCI.[46]

NATIONAL SECURITY AGENCY

The National Security Agency (NSA) is one of the most secret (and secretive) members of the U.S. intelligence community. The predecessor of NSA, the Armed Forces Security Agency (AFSA), was established within the Department of Defense on May 20, 1949, when Secretary of Defense Louis Johnson signed JCS Directive 2010. Johnson made AFSA subordinate to the Joint Chiefs of Staff. AFSA had little power to direct the activities of the military service SIGINT units; rather, its functions were defined in terms of the activities not performed by the service units.[47]

On or before October 24, 1952—the day that President Truman sent a top secret eight-page memorandum (now declassified) entitled "Communications Intelligence Activities" to the Secretary of State and the Secretary of Defense—the Department of Defense established, by directive, the NSA in place of the AFSA. The creation of NSA had its origins in a December 10, 1951, memo sent by Walter Bedell Smith to National Security Council Executive Secretary James B. Lay stating that "control over, and coordination of, the collection and processing of Communications Intelligence have proved ineffective" and recommending a survey of communications intelligence activities. This proposal was approved on December 13, 1951, and the study was authorized on December 28, 1951. The report was completed by June 13, 1952. The report, known as the "Brownell Committee Report" after committee chairman Herbert Brownell, surveyed the history of U.S. communications intelligence activities and suggested the need for a much greater degree of coordination and direction at the national level. As the change in the security agency's name indicated, the role of the NSA was to extend beyond the armed forces. The NSA is considered to be "within but not part of DOD."[48]

Although the agency was created in 1952, it was not until 1957 that its existence was officially acknowledged in the *U.S. Government Organization Manual* as a "separately organized agency within the Department of Defense" that "performs highly specialized technical and coordinating functions relating to national security." Despite the lack of official acknowledgment, the NSA's existence was a matter of public knowledge from at least mid-1953. In that year Washington newspapers ran several stories concerning the construction of the NSA's new headquarters at Fort George G. Meade, Maryland. In late 1954 the NSA was again in the news when an NSA employee was caught taking secret documents home.[49]

The charter for the NSA is National Security Council Intelligence Directive (NSCID) 6. In its most recently available form, NSCID 6 of January 17, 1972 ("Signals Intelligence"), directs the NSA to produce SIGINT "in accordance with the objectives, requirements and priorities established by the Director of Central Intelligence Board." The directive also authorizes the Director of NSA "to issue direct to any operating elements engaged in SIGINT operations such instructions and assignments as are required" and states that "all instructions issued by the Director under the authority provided in this paragraph shall be mandatory, subject only to appeal to the Secretary of Defense."[50]

NSCID 6 defines the scope of SIGINT activities—which can be divided into Communications Intelligence (COMINT) and Electronics Intelligence (ELINT)—as follows:

> COMINT activities shall be construed to mean those activities which produce COMINT by interception and processing of foreign communications by radio, wire, or other electronic means, with specific exception stated below and by the processing of foreign encrypted communications, however transmitted. Interception comprises range estimation, transmitter operator identification, signal analysis, traffic analysis, cryptanalysis, decryption, study of plain text, the fusion of those processes, and the reporting of the results.
>
> COMINT and COMINT activities as defined herein shall not include (a) any intercept and processing of unencrypted written communications, press and propaganda broadcasts, or (b) censorship.
>
> ELINT activities are defined as the collection (observation and recording) and the processing for subsequent intelligence purposes, of information derived from foreign

non-communications electro-magnetic radiations emanating from other than atomic detonation or radioactive sources. ELINT is the technical and intelligence information product of ELINT activities.[51]

Signals intercepted include diplomatic, military, scientific, and commercial communications as well as the electronic emanations of radar systems and the signals sent by weapons systems while being tested. The intercepted signals may be transmitted by telephone, radio telephone, radio, and cables.

The responsibilities of the NSA Director are specified by DOD Directive S-5100.20, "The National Security Agency and the Central Security Service." According to this document, the Director is to perform the following functions:

- Exercise SIGINT operational control over SIGINT activities of the U.S. Government to respond most effectively to military and other SIGINT requirements. ...
- Provide technical guidance to all SIGINT or SIGINT-related operations of the U.S. Government.
- Produce and disseminate SIGINT in accordance with the objectives, requirements and priorities established by the Director of Central Intelligence. ...
- In relation to the Department of Defense SIGINT activities, prepare and submit to the Secretary of Defense a consolidated program and budget, and requirements for military and civilian manpower, logistic and communications support, and research, development, test, and evaluation, together with his recommendations pertaining thereto.
- Prescribe within his field of authorized operations requisite security regulations covering operating practices, including the transmission, handling, and distribution of SIGINT material within and among the elements under his control.[52]

The NSA has a second major mission. Until recently that mission was known as Communications Security (COMSEC) but it has been broadened to Information Security (INFOSEC). In its INFOSEC role NSA performs the same COMSEC functions as it did in the past. It creates, reviews, and authorizes the communications procedures and codes of a variety of government agencies—including the State Department, the DOD, the CIA, and the FBI. This role includes development of secure data and voice transmission links on such satellite systems as the Defense Satellite Communications System (DSCS) and the Satellite Data System (SDS). Likewise, for sensitive communications FBI agents use a special scrambler telephone that requires a different code from NSA each day. The NSA's COMSEC responsibilities also include ensuring communications security for strategic weapons systems such as the Minuteman missile so as to prevent unauthorized intrusion, interference, or jamming. In addition, the NSA is responsible for developing the codes by which the President must identify himself in order to authorize a nuclear strike. In fulfilling these responsibilities, the NSA has produced documents such as *Communications Security—The Warsaw Pact COMINT Threat* (1975), *National COMSEC Plan for Fixed Point and Strategic Communications* (1977), and *National COMSEC Plan for Space Systems and Nuclear Weapons Sys-*

Figure 2-4. Organization of the National Security Agency.

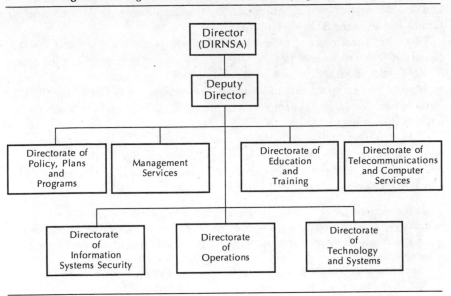

tems (1982).[53] As part of its INFOSEC mission the NSA is also responsible for protecting intelligence community and military data banks and computers from unauthorized access by individuals or governments.

NSA headquarters at Fort Meade houses somewhere between 20,000 and 24,000 employees in three buildings. The NSA budget is approximately $3.5 billion. As indicated in Figure 2-4, it is divided into several directorates, the three most prominent being the Directorate of Operations, the Directorate of Information Systems Security, and the Directorate of Technology and Systems (formerly the Directorate of Research and Engineering).*

The Directorate of Operations, headed by the Deputy Director of Operations, traditionally had three groups responsible for regional operations and the analysis of data from those operations. The A Operations Analysis Group, commonly known as A Group, was responsible for the Soviet Union and Eastern European nations. B Group was responsible for China, Korea, Vietnam, and the rest of Communist Asia, and G Group was responsible for all other nations, both Third World and allied.[54] In the aftermath of the demise of the Soviet Union this system

---

*NSA has sought to obscure its organizational structure by referring in public documents to "organizations"—for example, the "Operations Organization." This labeling is used with respect to a large number of units in NSA regardless of their place in the hierarchy. The actual hierarchy is directorate, group, office, division, and branch. See Inspector General, Department of Defense, *Review of Hiring Practices at the National Security Agency,* 1994, p. 3.

was apparently reduced to two groups—one dealing with all European nations and another focusing on all other nations (the non-European nations from G Group and all of the B Group nations).[55]

Two other Directorate of Operations components are W Group and the National SIGINT Operations Center (NSOC). W Group is responsible for space SIGINT—the interception and processing of all communications and signals emitted by foreign spacecraft and missiles. Subordinate to W Group are the Defense Special Missile and Astronautics Center (DEFSMAC) and the National Telemetry Processing Center (NTPC).[56]

DEFSMAC was established as a joint operation of the NSA and the Defense Intelligence Agency (DIA) by Department of Defense Directive S-5100.43, "Defense Special Missile and Astronautics Center" of April 27, 1964.[57] According to a former Deputy Director of NSA, DEFSMAC

> is a combination of the DIA with its military components and the NSA. It has all the inputs from all the assets and is a warning activity. They probably have a better feel for any worldwide threat to this country from missiles, aircraft or overt military activities, better and more timely, at instant fingertip availability than any group in the United States. So DEFSMAC is an input to NSA, but it also [is] an input to DIA and the CIA and the White House Situation Room and everybody else.[58]

DEFSMAC receives data bearing on Soviet, Chinese, and other nations' space and missile launches. It in turn warns other assets that a launch or test is imminent so that they can prepare to monitor the event.

The National Telemetry Processing Center processes the electronic signals radioed back to earth by Soviet, Chinese, and other nations' missiles during their test flights.

The National SIGINT Operations Center's function is to oversee and direct the SIGINT coverage of any crisis event. NSOC operates around the clock and is in instantaneous touch with every major NSA facility in the world. In the event that a facility intercepts signals that employees believe to be significant, facility personnel file a CRITIC intelligence report with NSOC, which may immediately pass the message on to the Director of NSA. If NSOC authorities feel that the event is really not of sufficient importance, they may revoke the report's CRITIC status.[59]

The Directorate of Information Systems Security is responsible for INFOSEC with respect to the communications and signals discussed above. The Directorate of Technology and Systems has responsibility for developing the techniques and equipment necessary for conducting intercept operations, breaking codes, and ensuring secure U.S. codes. The directorate explores codebreaking possibilities, develops the equipment required for the NSA's COMINT and ELINT intercept programs, and seeks to develop secure coding machines.[60]

In addition to the three main directorates there are several others of importance. The Directorate of Telecommunications and Computer Services is responsible for computer support, computer security, and the functioning of the NSA's

communications network—the Digital Network/Defense Special Security Communications System (DIN/DSSCS). Information transmitted on this system, via the Defense Satellite Communications System (DSCS), includes intercepts from overseas stations. The Directorate of Support Services (formerly the Directorate of Installations and Logistics) is responsible for overseas housing, disposal of classified waste, construction of facilities at Fort Meade, and the procurement of computers. The Office of Administration has a variety of functions including personnel matters, training, employment, and security.[61] The Directorate of Plans, Policy, and Programs is charged with the management and allocation of SIGINT/COMSEC resources, especially the preparation of the Consolidated Cryptographic Program (discussed in Chapter 17).[62]

In addition to directing activities at NSA headquarters and the NSA's few overseas facilities, the Director of NSA (DIRNSA) is responsible for supervising the SIGINT activities of Service Cryptological Elements (SCEs). In this role the Director serves as the head of the Central Security Service (CSS). The CSS function of the NSA, with the Director of the NSA serving simultaneously as Chief of the CSS, was established in 1971 in order "to provide a unified, more economical and more effective structure for executing crypotologic and related operations presently conducted under the Military Departments." There is, however, no separate CSS staff.[63]

NATIONAL RECONNAISSANCE OFFICE

The National Reconnaissance Office (NRO) manages satellite reconnaissance programs for the entire U.S. intelligence community. These programs involve the collection of photographic and signals intelligence and ocean surveillance data.

The NRO has a broad range of functions. It has participated in various policy committees, such as the NSAM 156 committee established by President Kennedy in 1962 to review the political aspects of U.S. policy on space reconnaissance,[64] and it played a significant role in drawing a curtain of secrecy around the reconnaissance program. Thus, in a memorandum to President Kennedy concerning the launch of the SAMOS II (the Air Force's initial photographic reconnaissance satellite), Assistant Secretary of Defense for Public Affairs Arthur Sylvester noted that the material to be made available to news reporters concerning the launch and the program "represents a severe reduction from what had been previously been issued." Sylvester further stated that "Dr. Charyk [Director of NRO] has reviewed those changes and is satisfied that they meet all his security requirements and those of his SAMOS Project Director, Brigadier General [Robert] Greer."[65] The NRO has also been heavily involved in developing security regulations concerning the release of information on military satellite payloads to be placed in orbit by the Space Transportation System (STS). The NRO is responsible for the routine operation of the satellites, including maneuvers such as turning them on and off and facing them toward or away from the sun.[66]

Although the NRO Director has always been an Air Force official, the NRO is, as its name indicates, a national-level organization. In fact, it is directly supervised by one of two executive committees chaired by the Director of Central Intelligence—the National Reconnaissance Executive Committee.[67]

The decision to establish the NRO was made on August 25, 1960, after several months of debate at the White House, the Department of Defense, the Air Force, and the CIA concerning the nature and duties of such an organization. Its creation was a response to various problems plaguing the early missile and satellite programs as well as to the May 1, 1960, incident in which a U-2 was shot down over the Soviet Union. As a result of this event, the Office of the Secretary of Defense and the Air Force sought a revised program to exploit, as early as possible, any reconnaissance data that could be obtained from SAMOS test flights. On June 10, President Eisenhower asked Secretary of Defense Thomas S. Gates, Jr., to reevaluate the program and brief the National Security Council on intelligence requirements, the technical feasibility of meeting those requirements, and the DOD's plans.[68]

Gates, in turn, appointed a panel of three—Dr. Joseph Charyk, Undersecretary of the Air Force; John J. Rubel, Deputy Director of the Defense Directorate of Research and Engineering; and Dr. George B. Kistiakowsky, the President's science adviser. The eventual product of their work was their briefing of August 25, which was followed, according to an official Air Force history, by a "key decision by the NSC and the President which, eliminating previous uncertainties, signaled the start of a highest priority program reminiscent of the wartime Manhattan Project effort"—the creation of the NRO. The NRO replaced an office (the Directorate of Advanced Technology) that coordinated satellite development for the Air Force Chief of Staff.[69]

The national scope of the organization was a major point of importance to those involved in its formation. Thus, George Kistiakowsky noted that it was important "that the organization should have a clear line of authority and that on the top level direction be of a national character, including OSD [Office of the Secretary of Defense] and CIA and not the Air Force alone." One reason such a framework was desired was to be certain that the utilization of the photographic "take" not be left solely in the hands of the Air Force.[70]

At its inception, and until September 1992, NRO's existence was classified. Thus, in August 1960 the Air Force quickly moved to establish a cover organization for the NRO within the Office of the Secretary of the Air Force. On August 31, 1960, Secretary of the Air Force Dudley C. Sharp established, via Order 115.1, the Office of Missile and Satellite Systems. The Director of the office was to be responsible "for assisting the Secretary in discharging his responsibility for the direction, supervision and control of the SAMOS Project." On the same day, Order 116.1 established the Director of the SAMOS Project, located at El Segundo, California, who would be directly responsible to the Secretary of the Air Force.[71]

As the entire reconnaissance program fell under a veil of secrecy, the connection of both offices with reconnaissance was obscured. The Office of Missile and Satellite Systems became the Office of Space Systems, with subsequent versions of Order 115.1 making no mention of reconnaissance. The Office of the Director of the SAMOS Project became the more euphemistic Office of Special Projects, with the Director and his personnel being described only as a "field extension" of the Office of the Secretary of the Air Force.[72]

The first public revelation of the NRO's existence came in 1973 as the result of an error made in a Senate report. The Special Select Committee on Secret and Confidential Documents accidentally included the NRO in a list recommending which intelligence agency budgets should be subject to public disclosure. The slip led to a fairly extensive article in the *Washington Post* a few months later in which the NRO's functions, budget, and cover were discussed. The following year the CIA lost in its attempt to have a similar discussion deleted from Victor Marchetti and John Marks's *The CIA and the Cult of Intelligence.*

However, the NRO's existence remained officially classified. Official documents, such as the *Department of Defense Annual Report* and Executive Orders, omitted the NRO's name and referred only to offices charged with "the collection of specialized foreign intelligence through reconnaissance programs." The closest an executive branch document came to admitting the existence of NRO was the report of the Murphy Commission, which referred to a "semi-autonomous office within the Defense Department with the largest budget of any intelligence agency and that operates overhead reconnaissance programs for the entire intelligence community."[73] At the same time, the CIA's Publication Review Board cleared for publication two books by former high CIA officials, including former Director William Colby, that referred to the NRO. However, the board would not permit former DCI Stansfield Turner to refer to the NRO in his 1985 memoirs.[74]

The NRO's existence was declassified on September 18, 1992. A "Memorandum to Correspondents" stated that "there is a National Reconnaissance Office (NRO) organized as an agency of the Department of Defense and funded through a program known as the National Reconnaissance Program (NRP)." The memorandum also stated, inter alia:

> The mission of the NRO is to ensure that the U.S. has the technology and spaceborne and airborne assets needed to acquire intelligence worldwide, including to support such functions as monitoring of arms control agreements, indications and warning and the planning and conduct of military operations. The NRO accomplishes this mission through research and development, acquisition, and operation of spaceborne and airborne data collection systems.[75]

During the NRO's first thirty years, its Director was generally the Undersecretary of the Air Force—a custom that began with Joseph Charyk. There have been exceptions to the rule. Alexander Flax served as Director while Assistant Secretary of the Air Force for R&D in the 1960s. Robert J. Hermann served in the position during the Carter administration while he was Assistant Secretary of the Air Force for Research, Development and Logistics—apparently because the individual who served as Undersecretary at the time knew little about reconnaissance satellites. During the Reagan administration the Undersecretary once again served as NRO Director until Undersecretary Edward Aldridge was promoted to Secretary. Aldridge proceeded to take the NRO job with him.[76]

In 1990 the position of Assistant Secretary of the Air Force for Space was established. The Assistant Secretary also became Director of the NRO. The responsibilities of the NRO Director are specified in DOD Directive TS-5105.23, "National Reconnaissance Office," the most recent version of which is dated March 27, 1964. Those responsibilities include establishing, managing, and conducting the National Reconnaissance Program and establishing "the security procedures to be followed for all matters of the National Reconnaissance Program."[77]

In 1991 NRO's structure consisted of a Director, a Deputy Director (who also serves as Director of the Defense Support Project Office, which is discussed in Chapter 16), a Deputy Director for Military Support, an NRO Staff, and three programs—Program A (Air Force), Program B (CIA), and Program C (Navy). The Air Force component of NRO, Program A, was the El Segundo–based Office of Special Projects, which had responsibility for Air Force reconnaissance satellite development and coordination with contractors. The CIA component of NRO was headed by the CIA's Deputy Director for Science and Technology. It has been responsible for the most significant advances in U.S. satellite development—such as the KH-11 and RHYOLITE satellites. This program existed more as a concept than a physical entity—it consisted simply of whatever work the CIA's DS&T was doing in the area of satellite reconnaissance. The naval component of NRO, responsible for the Navy's ocean surveillance satellites, used to be the Navy Space Project of the Naval Electronics System Command (NAVALEX). With the disestablishment of NAVALEX it became part of the Space and Sensor Systems Program Directorate of the Naval Space and Air Warfare Command (NAVSPAWAR) and then part of the SPAWAR's Space Technology Directorate.[78]

In 1992 the NRO underwent a "far reaching restructuring," according to DCI Robert Gates. The restructuring altered NRO's structure from an organizational one (Air Force, CIA, Navy) to a functional one. Under the new framework, virtually all NRO governmental personnel are to be located in the Washington area. The functional structure seems to involve directorates for imagery and signals intelligence/ocean surveillance, with Air Force and CIA personnel working together on imagery and SIGINT satellite projects. Figure 2-5 shows the probable organizational structure of the NRO.[79] NRO's annual budget appears to be in the area of $6 billion.[80]

CENTRAL IMAGERY OFFICE

In April 1992 testimony before a joint session of the House Permanent Select Committee on Intelligence and the Senate Select Committee on Intelligence, DCI

Figure 2-5.   Probable Organization of the National Reconnaissance Office.

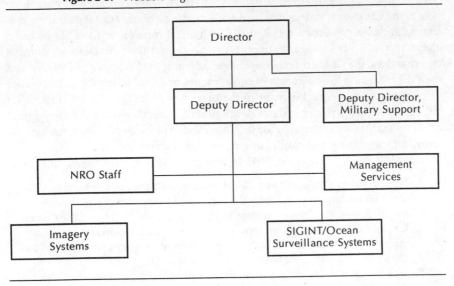

Robert Gates noted that the Imagery Task Force he had established upon becoming DCI had recommended the creation of a National Imagery Agency, which would absorb the CIA's National Photographic Interpretation Center as well as the Defense Mapping Agency.[81]

The task force's vision for a National Imagery Agency was not as broad as that which had been recommended by some in congressional hearings and written into proposed legislation by both the House and Senate intelligence committees. The broader vision would have created a National Imagery Agency (NIA) responsible for virtually the entire range of imagery functions—decisions on spacecraft and aircraft capabilities, research and development to support those decisions, tasking, collection operations, and analysis.[82]

During his testimony Gates rejected the recommendations of both his task force and the congressional committees. Within months it was announced, however, that a Central Imagery Office was being established within the Department of Defense. Its creation was due to some of the same factors that produced suggestions for the establishment of an NIA—congressional frustration with a lack of coherent imagery management, imagery collection and dissemination problems that surfaced during Desert Shield and Desert Storm, budgetary constraints, and changing requirements for the support of military operations.[83]

Thus, the Central Imagery Office (CIO) was established on May 6, 1992—both by Department of Defense Directive 5105.56 and a Director of Central Intelligence Directive. Under the terms of the DOD Directive, the CIO is designated a DOD Combat Support Agency and is supervised by the Assistant Secretary of Defense for Command, Control, Communications, and Intelligence, or ASD (C³I).[84]

In contrast to the alternative national imagery agencies that had been proposed, the CIO was not designed to absorb existing agencies or take on their collection and analysis functions. Rather, the general mission of the CIO includes ensuring responsive imagery support to the Department of Defense, combat commanders, the CIA, and other agencies; advising the Secretary of Defense and the DCI regarding future imagery requirements, and evaluating the performance of imagery components. Pursuant to the provision of imagery support, the CIO has been assigned a role in systems development—specifically, establishing imagery architectures and standards for interoperability of imagery dissemination systems and supporting and conducting research and development.[85]

According to DOD Directive 5105.26, the Director of the CIO shall, inter alia:

1. Manage the establishment of national imagery collection requirements consistent with guidance received from the Director of Central Intelligence ... ;

2. Ensure responsive imagery support to the Department of Defense, the Central Intelligence Agency, and, as appropriate, other Federal Government departments and agencies, including by coordination of imagery collection tasking, collection, processing, exploitation, and dissemination;

3. Task imagery collection elements of the Department of Defense to meet national intelligence requirements, including requirements established by the Director of Central Intelligence ... except that the Director of the CIO shall advise an imagery collection element on collection of imagery to meet such national intelligence requirements when the collection element both (a) is assigned to or under the operational control of the Secretary of a Military Department or a commander of a unified and specified command and (b) is not allocated by the Secretary of Defense to meet national intelligence requirements;

4. Advise imagery collection elements of the Department of Defense on the collection of imagery to meet non-national intelligence requirements;

5. Establish, consistent to the maximum practicable extent with the overall functional architectures of the Department of Defense, the architectures for imagery tasking, collection, processing, exploitation, and dissemination within the Department of Defense, and to the extent authorized by the heads of other departments or agencies with imagery tasking, collection, processing, exploitation, and dissemination functions establish the architectures for imagery tasking, collection, processing, exploitation, and dissemination within those departments or agencies;

6. Establish, in coordination with the Director of the Defense Information Systems Agency as appropriate, standards for imagery systems for which the Department of Defense has responsibility and ensure compatibility and interoperability for such systems, and, to the extent authorized by the heads of other departments and agencies with imagery systems, establish standards and ensure compatibility and interoperability with respect to the systems of those departments or agencies;

7. Serve as the functional manager for a Consolidated Imagery Program within the National Foreign Intelligence Program consistent with applicable guidance received from the Director of Central Intelligence ... ;

Figure 2-6. Organization of the Central Imagery Office.

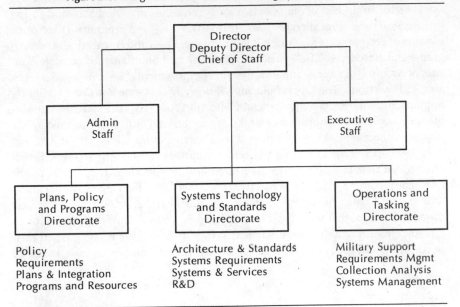

Source: Central Imagery Office, *CIO Briefing Slides,* 1992.

8. Serve as the functional manager for the Tactical Imagery Program within the budget aggregation known as the Tactical Intelligence and Related Activities;

9. Evaluate the performance of imagery components of the Department of Defense in meeting national and non-national intelligence requirements, and to the extent authorized by the heads of other departments or agencies with imagery tasking, collection, processing, exploitation, and dissemination functions, evaluate the performance of the imagery components of those departments or agencies in meeting national and non-national intelligence requirements;

10. Develop and make recommendations on national and non-national imagery policy, including as it relates to international matters, for the approval of appropriate Federal Government officials;

11. Support and conduct research and development activities related to imagery tasking, collection, processing, exploitation, and dissemination, consistent with applicable law and Department of Defense directives;

12. Advise the Secretary of Defense and the Director of Central Intelligence on future needs for imagery systems;

13. Ensure that imagery systems are exercised to support military forces.[86]

DOD Directive 5105.26 authorizes the CIO to make maximum use of facilities and personnel assigned to the Defense Mapping Agency, the Defense Intelligence Agency, the National Security Agency, and, to the extent authorized by the DCI, the Central Intelligence Agency.[87]

The organization of the CIO is shown in Figure 2-6. Under the Director, Deputy Director, and Chief of Staff are two staffs (an Administration Staff and an Executive Staff) and three directorates. The Plans, Policy and Programs Directorate consists of components for Policy, Requirements, Plans and Integration, and Programs and Resources. The Systems Technology and Standards Directorate consists of Architecture and Standards, Systems Requirements, Systems and Services, and R&D sections. The Operations and Tasking Directorate consists of Military Support, Requirements Management, Collection Analysis, and Systems Management sections. It also houses a central imagery tasking authority "to execute the imagery collection tasking authority of the Director of the CIO."[88]

In 1993, the House Permanent Select Committee on Intelligence (HPSCI) recommended that the CIO be disestablished and its functions transferred to the DIA. The recommendation was based on the belief that if the Defense Department was to coordinate photographic collection and distribution, the DIA was best suited to perform that task. The House Armed Services Committee argued, however, that it was premature to conclude that the CIO could not accomplish its mission. Ultimately, the HPSCI backed off its recommendation for at least a year.[89]

NOTES

1. For a history of the OSS, see R. Harris Smith, *OSS: The Secret History of America's First Central Intelligence Agency* (Berkeley: University of California Press, 1972); and Bradley F. Smith, *The Shadow Warriors: O.S.S. and the Origins of the C.I.A.* (New York: Basic Books, 1983).

2. U.S. Congress, Senate Select Committee to Study Governmental Operations with Respect to Intelligence Activities, *Final Report, Book 4, Supplementary Detailed Staff Reports on Foreign and Military Intelligence* (Washington, D.C.: U.S. Government Printing Office, 1976), pp. 4–6; Thomas F. Troy, *Donovan and the CIA: A History of the Establishment of the Central Intelligence Agency* (Frederick, Md.: University Publications of America, 1981), pp. 325–49.

3. U.S. Congress, House Permanent Select Committee on Intelligence, *Compilation of Intelligence Laws and Related Laws and Executive Orders of Interest to the National Intelligence Community* (Washington, D.C.: U.S. Government Printing Office, 1983), p. 7.

4. Lawrence Houston, Memorandum for the Director, Subject: CIA Authority to Perform Propaganda and Commando Type Functions, September 25, 1947.

5. Ronald Reagan, "Executive Order 12333: United States Intelligence Activities," December 4, 1981, in *Federal Register* 46, 235 (December 8, 1981): 59941–54 at 59950.

6. Paul Hodge, "CIA Plans Major New Building," *Washington Post,* October 2, 1981, p. B1; Leah Y. Latimer, "Reston Mystery: Is the CIA Planning to Set Up Shop Downtown?" *Washington Post,* September 12, 1986, p. C5; Gregory Treverton, *Covert Action: The Limits of Intervention in the Postwar World* (New York: Basic Books, 1987), p. 14; Ronald Kessler, *Inside the CIA: Revealing the Secrets of the World's Most Powerful Spy Agency* (New York: Pocket Books, 1992), pp. xxvii, 144; Walter Pincus, "CIA Struggles to Find Identity in a New World," *Washington Post,* May 9, 1994, pp. A1, A9; Private information.

7. Central Intelligence Agency, *Fact Book on Intelligence* (Washington, D.C.: CIA, 1991), p. 9; Hans Moses, "The Clandestine Service of the Central Intelligence Agency," *American Intelligence Journal* (Autumn/Winter 1992–1993): 81–85.

8. Victor Marchetti and John Marks, *The CIA and the Cult of Intelligence* (New York: Knopf, 1974), p. 74; David Atlee Phillips, *Careers in Secret Operations: How to Be a Federal Intelligence Officer* (Frederick, Md.: University Publications of America, 1984), p. 28; Jeffrey Lenorovitz, "CIA Satellite Data Link Study Revealed," *Aviation Week & Space Technology,* May 2, 1977, pp. 25–26; Arnaud be Borchgrave, "Space-Age Spies," *Newsweek,* March 6, 1978, p. 37.

9. Phillips, *Careers in Secret Operations,* p. 26; Marchetti and Marks, *The CIA and the Cult of Intelligence,* p. 73; Commission on CIA Activities in the United States, *Report to the President* (Washington, D.C.: U.S. Government Printing Office, 1975), p. 91.

10. *Directorate of Administration, Central Intelligence Agency* (Washington, D.C.: CIA, n.d.), unpaginated; Phillips, *Careers in Secret Operations,* p. 27; Marchetti and Marks, *The CIA and the Cult of Intelligence,* p. 74; U.S. Congress, House Permanent Select Committee on Intelligence, *Pre-Employment Security Procedures of the Intelligence Agencies* (Washington, D.C.: U.S. Government Printing Office, 1980), p. 31.

11. Commission on CIA Activities Within the United States, *Report to the President,* p. 92; *Directorate of Administration, Central Intelligence Agency*; Address by R. James Woolsey to Center for Strategic and International Studies, Washington, D.C., "National Security and the Future Direction of the Central Intelligence Agency," July 18, 1994, p. 12.

12. U.S. Congress, Senate Select Committee to Study Governmental Operations with Respect to Intelligence Activities, *Final Report, Book 4, Supplementary Detailed Staff Reports,* p. 46, n4.

13. Peer de Silva, *Sub Rosa: The CIA and the Uses of Intelligence* (New York: Times Books, 1978), p. 291.

14. Marchetti and Marks, *The CIA and the Cult of Intelligence,* p. 72.

15. Department of Justice, *Report on CIA-Related Electronic Surveillance Activities* (Washington, D.C.: Department of Justice, 1976), pp. 4, 13; James Bamford, *The Puzzle Palace: A Report on NSA, America's Most Secret Agency* (Boston: Houghton Mifflin, 1982), p. 131.

16. Author's interview; Kessler, *Inside the CIA,* p. 29.

17. Marchetti and Marks, *The CIA and the Cult of Intelligence,* pp. 70–75; David Wise, *The American Police State* (New York: Vintage, 1976), pp. 188–92; "Aides Disciplined by CIA Are Irked," *New York Times,* November 15, 1984, pp. A1, A8; Robert Parry, "Latin Manual Is Linked to 'Psy-War' Plan," *Washington Post,* December 3, 1984, p. A10; Kessler, *Inside the CIA,* p. 18.

18. Robert Parry, "CIA Manual Producers Say They're Scapegoats," *Washington Post,* November 15, 1984, p. A28; "Aides Disciplined by CIA Are Irked"; Parry, "Latin Manual Is Linked to 'Psy-War' Plan."

19. Wise, *The American Police State,* p. 188.

20. U.S. Congress, Senate Select Committee to Study Governmental Operations with Respect to Intelligence Activities, *Final Report, Book 1, Foreign and Military Intelligence* (Washington, D.C.: U.S. Government Printing Office, 1976), p. 439; Ralph E. Cook, "The CIA and Academe," *Studies in Intelligence* (Winter 1983): 33–42 at 38–39; Kessler, *Inside the CIA,* p. 18.

21. U.S. Congress, Senate Select Committee to Study Governmental Operations with Respect to Intelligence Activities, *Final Report, Book 1, Foreign and Military Intelligence*, p. 439; Cook, "The CIA and Academe," p. 38; Wise, *The American Police State*, p. 189.

22. Central Intelligence Agency, *Appendices to Guidance for CIA Activities Within the United States and Outside the United States* (Washington, D.C.: CIA, November 30, 1982), p. 20.

23. Loch Johnson, "Smart Intelligence," *Foreign Policy* (Winter 1992–1993): 53–69; David Wise, *Molehunt: The Secret Search for Traitors That Shattered the CIA* (New York: Random House, 1992), pp. 298–99; Angelo Codevilla, *Informing Statecraft: Intelligence for a New Century* (New York: Free Press, 1992), p. 155.

24. Central Intelligence Agency, *Fact Book on Intelligence* (Washington, D.C.: CIA, 1993), p. 11.

25. U.S. Congress, Senate Select Committee to Study Governmental Operations with Respect to Intelligence Activities, *Final Report, Book 4, Supplementary Detailed Staff Reports*, pp. 77–78.

26. U.S. Congress, House Select Committee on Intelligence, *U.S. Intelligence Agencies and Activities: Intelligence Costs and Procedures* (Washington, D.C.: U.S. Government Printing Office, 1976), p. 543; John Prados, *The Soviet Estimate: U.S. Intelligence Analysis and Russian Military Strength* (New York: Dial, 1982), p. 156; NSCID No. 8, "Photographic Interpretation, February 17, 1972," *Declassified Documents Reference System (DDRS)* 1976-253G; George Wilson, "N-PIC Technicians Ferret Out Secrets Behind Closed Windows," *Los Angeles Times,* January 12, 1975, p. 25; Curtis Peebles, "Satellite Photographic Interpretation," *Spaceflight,* October 1982, pp. 161–63.

27. Senate Select Committee on Intelligence, *Report 102-117: Authorizing Appropriations for Fiscal Year 1992 for the Intelligence Activities of the U.S. Government, the Intelligence Community Staff, the Central Intelligence Agency Retirement and Disability System, and for Other Purposes* (Washington, D.C.: U.S. Government Printing Office, 1991), p. 7.

28. Central Intelligence Agency, *A Consumer's Guide to Intelligence* (Washington, D.C.: CIA, 1993), p. 12; U.S. Congress, House Select Committee on Intelligence, *U.S. Intelligence Agencies and Activities*, pp. 537–44.

29. *Directorate of Science and Technology, Central Intelligence Agency* (Washington, D.C.: CIA, n.d.), unpaginated.

30. *Office of SIGINT Operations* (Washington, D.C.: CIA, n.d.), n.p.; Desmond Ball, *A Suitable Piece of Real Estate: American Installations in Australia* (Sydney: Hale & Iremonger, 1980), p. 73; Bob Woodward, *Veil: The Secret Wars of the CIA, 1981–1987* (New York: Simon & Schuster, 1987), pp. 313–14.

31. CIA document fragment, released under the FOIA; Kessler, *Inside the CIA*, p. 168.

32. *Office of Research and Development* (Washington, D.C.: CIA, n.d.), unpaginated.

33. Thomas Powers, *The Man Who Kept the Secrets: Richard Helms and the CIA* (New York: Knopf, 1979), p. 340, n38.

34. *Directorate of Science and Technology, Central Intelligence Agency* (Washington, D.C.: CIA, n.d.), unpaginated.

35. Central Intelligence Agency, *Fact Book on Intelligence*, p. 9; Ray S. Cline, *Secrets, Spies and Scholars* (Washington, D.C.: Acropolis, 1976), pp. 11–12; U.S. Congress, Senate Select Committee to Study Governmental Operations with Respect to Intelligence Activities, *Final Report, Book 4, Supplementary Detailed Staff Reports*, p. 236; Air University Library,

China: Military Capabilities (Maxwell AFB, Ala.: AUL, February 1988), p. 31; Air University Library, *China: Military Capabilities* (Maxwell AFB, Ala.: AUL, August 1990), p. 25.

36. Central Intelligence Agency, *Fact Book on Intelligence,* p. 9; Private information.

37. "Shifting CIA Production from Topical to a Geographic Base," April 1982 (CIA memo); Elaine Sciolino, "C.I.A. Casting About for New Missions," *New York Times,* February 4, 1992, pp. A1, A8; David W. Overton, "The DI 10 Years After Reorganization," *Studies in Intelligence* 36, 5 (1992): 45–54 at 45; John A. Gentry, *Lost Promise: How CIA Analysis Misserves the Country* (Lanham, Md.: University Press of America, 1993), p. 94. The last reference suggests there were drawbacks to the reorganization plan, whereas Overton has a more positive view.

38. Central Intelligence Agency, *Fact Book on Intelligence,* p. 9.

39. Central Intelligence Agency, *A Consumer's Guide to Intelligence,* p. 13. Also see Gentry, *Lost Promise,* pp. 8, 10.

40. Central Intelligence Agency, *Fact Book on Intelligence,* p. 5; *Office of Imagery Analysis, Directorate of Intelligence, Central Intelligence Agency* (Washington, D.C.: CIA, n.d.), n.p.; Central Intelligence Agency, *A Consumer's Guide to Intelligence,* p. 13.

41. *Directorate of Intelligence, Central Intelligence Agency,* p. 4; Gentry, *Lost Promise,* p. 39.

42. *Directorate of Intelligence, Central Intelligence Agency,* p. 5.

43. Ibid., p. 5; Phillips, *Careers in Secret Operations,* p. 24.

44. Robin Wright and Ronald J. Ostrow, "Webster Unites Rival Agencies to Fight Drugs," *Los Angeles Times,* August 24, 1989, pp. 1, 27; Michael Isikoff, "CIA Creates Narcotics Unit to Help in Drug Fight," *Washington Post,* May 28, 1989, p. A12.

45. "Bush Approved Covert Action by CIA to Halt Spread of Arms," *Los Angeles Times,* June 21, 1992, p. A20; Bill Gertz, "CIA Creates Center to Monitor Arms," *Washington Times,* December 3, 1991, p. A5; "Intelligence Will Be Key Tool in Proliferation Battle," *Defense Week,* December 9, 1991, p. 3; Johnson, "Smart Intelligence"; Paula L. Scalingi, "Intelligence Community Cooperation: The Arms Control Model," *International Journal of Intelligence and Counterintelligence* 5, 4 (Winter 1991–1992): 402–3; Barbara Starr, "Woolsey Tackles Proliferation as the Problem Gets Worse," *Jane's Defence Weekly,* November 13, 1993, p. 23.

46. Scalingi, "Intelligence Community Cooperation," pp. 405–6.

47. Brownell Committee, *The Origin and Development of the National Security Agency* (Laguna Hills, Calif.: Aegean Park Press, 1981), pp. 30–31; The National Cryptologic School, *On Watch: Profiles from the National Security Agency's Past 40 Years* (Ft. Meade, Md.: NCS, 1986), p. 17.

48. Walter Bedell Smith, "Proposed Survey of Communications Intelligence Activities," December 10, 1951; Brownell Committee, *The Origin and Development of the National Security Agency,* pp. 1, 81; U.S. Congress, Senate Select Committee to Study Governmental Operations with Respect to Intelligence Activities, *Final Report, Book 3, Foreign and Military Intelligence* (Washington, D.C.: U.S. Government Printing Office, 1976), p. 736; National Security Agency/Central Security Service, *NSA/CSS Manual 22-1* (Ft. Meade, Md.: NSA, 1986), p. 1.

49. *United States Government Organization Manual, 1957–1958* (Washington, D.C.: U.S. Government Printing Office, 1957), p. 137; "Washington Firm Will Install Ft. Meade Utilities," *Washington Post,* January 7, 1954, p. 7; "U.S. Security Aide Accused of Taking Secret Documents," *New York Times,* October 10, 1954, pp. 1, 33.

50. NSCID No. 6, "Signals Intelligence," February 17, 1972 (Sanitized), 1976-168A; Department of Justice, *Report on CIA-Related Electronic Surveillance Activities*, pp. 77–78.

51. NSCID No. 6, "Signals Intelligence."

52. Department of Defense Directive S-5100.20, "The National Security Agency and the Central Security Service," December 23, 1971.

53. U.S. Congress, Senate Select Committee to Study Governmental Operations with Respect to Intelligence Activities, *Final Report, Book 1, Foreign and Military Intelligence*, p. 354; U.S. Congress, House Committee on Appropriations, *Department of Defense Appropriations for 1983, Part 3* (Washington, D.C.: U.S. Government Printing Office, 1981), pp. 824–29; Leslie Maitland, "FBI Says New York Is a 'Hub' of Spying in U.S.," *New York Times*, November 14, 1981, p. 12; Patrick E. Tyler and Bob Woodward, "FBI Held War Code of Reagan," *Washington Post*, December 13, 1981, pp. 1, 27.

54. Bamford, *The Puzzle Palace*, p. 91; Private information.

55. Bill Gertz, "Electronic Spying Reoriented at NSA," *Washington Times*, January 27, 1992, p. A4.

56. Private information.

57. Department of Defense, *Defense Special Missile and Astronautics Center: Organization, Mission, Functions and Concept of Operations*, September 27, 1982, p. 1.

58. Raymond Tate, "Worldwide C³I and Telecommunications," Harvard University, Center for Information Policy Resources, Seminar on C³I, 1980, p. 30.

59. Seymour Hersh, *"The Target Is Destroyed": What Really Happened to Flight 007 and What America Knew About It* (New York: Random House, 1986), pp. 52–53, 67–69.

60. Bamford, *The Puzzle Palace*, pp. 96–97.

61. Ibid., pp. 97–112.

62. Ibid., pp. 112–13.

63. Melvin Laird, *National Security Strategy of Realistic Deterrence: Secretary of Defense Melvin Laird's Annual Defense Department Report, FY 1973* (Washington, D.C.: U.S. Government Printing Office, 1972), p. 135; Bamford, *The Puzzle Palace*, p. 157.

64. National Security Action Memorandum 156, "Negotiation on Disarmament and Peaceful Uses of Outer Space," May 26, 1962; Raymond Garthoff, "Banning the Bomb in Outer Space," *International Security* 5, 3 (1980/1981): 25–40 at 26.

65. Arthur Sylvester, Assistant Secretary of Defense for Public Affairs, Memorandum for the President, Subject: SAMOS II Launch, 1961, *DDRS* 1979-364B.

66. Philip Taubman, "Secrecy of U.S. Reconnaissance Office Is Challenged," *New York Times*, March 1, 1981, p. 10.

67. William Colby and Peter Forbath, *Honorable Men: My Life in CIA* (New York: Simon & Schuster, 1978), p. 370.

68. George B. Kistiakowsky, *A Scientist in the White House: The Private Diary of President Eisenhower's Special Assistant for Science and Technology* (Cambridge: Harvard University Press, 1976), pp. 378–79; Carl Berger, *The Air Force in Space, Fiscal Year 1961* (Washington, D.C.: USAF Historical Liaison Office, April 1966), p. 34.

69. Berger, *The Air Force in Space, Fiscal Year 1961*, pp. 35, 42; Larry Booda, "New Capsule to Be Developed for SAMOS," *Aviation Week*, September 12, 1960, pp. 26–27.

70. Kistiakowsky, *A Scientist in the White House*, pp. 382, 394.

71. Dudley C. Sharp, Secretary of the Air Force Order 115.1, "Organization and Functions of the Office of Missile and Satellite Systems," August 31, 1960; Dudley C. Sharp, Secretary of the Air Force Order 116.1, "The Director of the SAMOS Project," August 31, 1960.

72. Verne Orr, Secretary of the Air Force Order 115.1, "Office of Space Systems," March 10, 1983; Verne Orr, Secretary of the Air Force Order 116.1, "The Office of Special Projects," March 10, 1983.

73. U.S. Congress, Senate Special Select Committee on Secret and Confidential Documents, "Questions Related to Secret and Confidential Documents" (Washington, D.C.: U.S. Government Printing Office, 1973), p. 16; Laurence Stern, "$1.5 Billion Secret in the Sky," *Washington Post,* December 9, 1973, pp. 1, 9.

74. *Report of the Commission on the Organization of the Government for the Conduct of Foreign Policy* (Washington, D.C.: U.S. Government Printing Office, 1975), p. 95; Colby and Forbath, *Honorable Men,* p. 370; Theodore Shackley, *The Third Option* (New York: McGraw-Hill, 1981); Stansfield Turner, *Secrecy and Democracy: The CIA in Transition* (Boston: Houghton Mifflin, 1985).

75. Department of Defense, *Memorandum for Correspondents, No. 264-M,* September 18, 1992; Barton Gellman, "Remember, You Didn't Read It Here," *Washington Post,* September 19, 1992, p. A4.

76. Bamford, *The Puzzle Palace,* pp. 191–92; James Canan, *War in Space* (New York: Harper & Row, 1982), pp. 110–11; "Aldridge Seeks Shift of USAF Space Program Responsibilities," *International Tech Trends,* May 19, 1986, p. 7.

77. Department of Defense Directive TS-5105.23, "National Reconnaissance Office," March 27, 1964.

78. John Pike, *The NRO, NSA & DIA Budgets: Everything You Always Wanted to Know But Weren't Cleared to Ask* (Washington, D.C.: Federation of American Scientists, 1993), p. 8; Ralph Vartabedian, "Air Force Spy Satellite Unit Leaving Calif.," *Los Angeles Times,* October 16, 1992, pp. A1, A5.

79. Remarks by Robert M. Gates, Director of Central Intelligence, to the Association of Former Intelligence Officers, November 14, 1992, Boston; Vincent Kiernan, "NRO Streamlines to Cut Intelligence Bureaucracy," *Space News,* December 7–13, 1992, pp. 1, 29; Vartabedian, "Air Force Spy Satellite Unit Leaving Calif."

80. Pike, *The NRO, NSA & DIA Budgets,* p. 8.

81. Robert M. Gates, Director of Central Intelligence, *Statement on Change in CIA and the Intelligence Community,* April 1, 1992, p. 28.

82. H.R. 4165, "National Security Act of 1992," 1992; S.2198, "Intelligence Reorganization Act of 1992," 1992.

83. Central Imagery Office, *Briefing Slides,* 1992.

84. Department of Defense Directive 5105.26, "Central Imagery Office," May 6, 1992; Central Imagery Office, *Briefing Slides,* p. 4.

85. Central Imagery Office, *Briefing Slides,* p. 2.

86. Department of Defense Directive 5105.26, "Central Imagery Office," pp. 2–3.

87. Ibid.

88. Central Imagery Office, *Briefing Slides,* p. 8; Department of Defense Directive 5105.26, "Central Imagery Office," p. 4.

89. U.S. Congress, House Committee on Armed Services, *Intelligence Authorization Act, Fiscal Year 1984* (Washington, D.C.: U.S. Government Printing Office, 1993), pp. 2–3; Neil Munro, "Central Imagery Office Seeks Funds," *Defense News,* August 9–15, 1993, p. 26; Joseph Lovece, "Pentagon Backs House Panel on Central Imagery Office," *Defense Week,* November 1, 1993, p. 9.

3
DEFENSE DEPARTMENT INTELLIGENCE ORGANIZATIONS

In addition to the national intelligence organizations within the Department of Defense (DOD)—the National Reconnaissance Office (NRO), the National Security Agency (NSA), and the Central Imagery Office—there are several department-level agencies with the primary function of satisfying the intelligence requirements of the Secretary of Defense, DOD components, and the military services.

Two of these agencies—the Defense Intelligence Agency (DIA) and the Defense Mapping Agency (DMA)—can trace their origins to the centralization trend that began at the end of the Eisenhower administration and continued through the early 1970s. Another, the Defense HUMINT Service, is part of the extensive organizational changes that have taken place since 1991.

DEFENSE INTELLIGENCE AGENCY

The Defense Intelligence Agency (DIA) was one manifestation of the trend toward centralization that began in the Eisenhower administration and reached its peak in the Kennedy administration. The Eisenhower administration concluded in the late 1950s that a consolidation of the military services' general intelligence activities (defined as all non-SIGINT, nonoverhead, nonorganic intelligence activities) was needed.[1] This belief was, according to one analyst, a by-product of the missile gap controversy of the time: "Faced with the disparate estimates of Soviet missile strength from each of the armed services which translated into what have been called self-serving budget requests for weapons for defense, the United States Intelligence Board created a Joint Study Group in 1959 to study the intelligence producing agencies."[2]

The Joint Study Group, chaired by the CIA's Lyman Kirkpatrick, concluded that there was a considerable overlap and duplication in defense intelligence activities and a resulting maldistribution of resources. The consequence was that the "overall direction and management of DOD's total intelligence effort becomes a very difficult if not impossible task. Indeed, the fragmentation of effort creates 'barriers' to the free and complete interchange of intelligence information among the several components of the Department of Defense."[3]

The study group thus recommended that the Secretary of Defense "bring the military intelligence organization within the Department of Defense into full consonance with the concept of the Defense Reorganization Act of 1958."[4] How to do this was a subject of controversy.

The study group's report noted that it had been suggested that a single intelligence service be established for the entire Defense Department, reporting directly to the Secretary of Defense. The study group concluded, however, that "on balance it would be unwise to attempt such an integration of intelligence activities so long as there are three military services having specialized skills and knowledge."[5]

Despite the study group's conclusion, in a February 8, 1961, memorandum to the Joint Chiefs of Staff (JCS), Defense Secretary Robert McNamara observed:

> It appears that the most effective means to accomplish the recommendations of the Joint Study Group would be the establishment of a Defense Intelligence Agency which may include the existing National Security Agency, the intelligence and counterintelligence functions now handled by the military departments, and the responsibilities of the Office of the Assistant to the Secretary, Special Operations.[6]

McNamara requested the JCS to provide, within thirty days, a concept for a defense intelligence agency, a draft DOD directive for its authorization, and a time-phased implementation schedule. He also provided some preliminary guidelines for developing a plan that included the complete integration of all defense intelligence requirements and the elimination of duplication in intelligence collection and production.[7]

On February 9 the JCS Joint Staff suggested that the JCS direct the staff to develop a concept for the DIA that would be consistent with McNamara's memo and place the new agency under the control of the JCS.[8]

On March 2, 1961, the Joint Chiefs sent McNamara recommendations, including an organizational concept for the establishment of a Military Intelligence Agency (MIA) under the JCS. On April 3 McNamara requested advice on several basic issues concerning the proposed agency, including its proposed placement under the JCS and its specific functions. Ten days later the JCS approved a Joint Staff draft memorandum for the Secretary of Defense. The memo justified placing the DIA/MIA under the JCS on the grounds that the DOD Reorganization Act of 1958 specifically assigned the Joint Chiefs the responsibility of strategic planning and operational direction of the armed forces, and the fulfillment of such responsibilities required control of appropriate intelligence assets. In contrast, placing the DIA/MIA in OSD would "concentrate military intelligence assets at a level above, and isolated from, the organization charged with strategic planning and operational direction of the armed forces."[9]

The Joint Staff memo also suggested placing NSA under the authority of the JCS. In addition, it argued that total integration of all military intelligence activities might not be a sound concept but that if any intelligence activities were left with the services, the DIA/MIA Director should be charged with closely monitoring them. Further, the Director would be authorized to eliminate duplication, review all service intelligence programs and budgets, and assign priorities to military intelligence collection requirements.[10]

The agency that resulted was a compromise but was close to the JCS viewpoint. On July 5, 1961, McNamara decided to establish a DIA reporting to the Secretary of Defense through the JCS. On August 1, McNamara formally established the DIA, via DOD Directive 5105.21, as a DOD agency and made it responsible for: (1) organization, direction, management, and control of all DOD intelligence resources assigned to or included within the DIA; (2) review and coordination of those DOD intelligence functions retained by or assigned to the Military Departments; (3) supervision over the execution of all approved plans, programs, policies, and procedures for intelligence functions not assigned to the DIA; (4) exercise of maximum economy and efficiency in allocation and management of DOD intelligence resources; (5) response to priority requests by the United States Intelligence Board; and (6) fulfillment of intelligence requirements of major DOD components.[11]

As a result of the DIA's creation, the Joint Staff Director for Intelligence (J-2) was abolished, as was the Office of Special Operations, the small intelligence arm of the Secretary of Defense.[12]

On December 16, 1976, the Secretary of Defense issued a new charter for the DIA (i.e., a new version of DOD 5105.21), limiting the operational control of the JCS over the DIA to (1) obtaining the intelligence support required to perform their statutory function and assigned responsibilities and (2) assuring that adequate, timely, and reliable intelligence support was available to the unified and specified commands. In all other matters, the Director of the DIA would report to the Secretary of Defense through the Assistant Secretary of Defense (ASD) for Intelligence. The mission of the·DIA was also stated more concisely as being "to satisfy, or to ensure the satisfaction of, the foreign intelligence requirements of the Secretary of Defense, the Joint Chiefs of Staff, DOD components and other authorized recipients, and to provide the military intelligence contribution to national intelligence."[13]

About five months later, on May 19, 1977, the Secretary of Defense signed a new version of DOD Directive 5105.21 that slightly altered the organization and administration of the agency. Under the revised charter the Director would report to the Secretary of Defense and the Chairman of the JCS. In addition, the Director of the DIA would be under the operational control of the JCS for purposes of: (1) obtaining intelligence support required to perform the statutory and assigned responsibilities of the JCS and (2) ensuring adequate, timely, and reliable intelligence support for the unified and specified commands. Staff supervision of the DIA would be exercised by the ASD for Command, Control, Communications, and Intelligence (C³I) with respect to resources and by the ASD for International Security Affairs with respect to policy.[14]

According to the May 1977 DOD Directive, the DIA's responsibilities were to:

1. satisfy or insure the satisfaction of the foreign intelligence requirements of the Secretary of Defense and DOD components;
2. participate in the Defense Systems Acquisition Review Council process by providing threat evaluations and validations based on information from coordinated intelligence;
3. coordinate all Defense intelligence collection and production requirements and validate, register, assign and recommend priorities for evaluating the satisfaction of DOD collection and production requirements;
4. serve as Program Manager for the General Defense Intelligence Program and manage such other programs as may be designated by the Secretary of Defense;
5. manage all aspects of Defense intelligence production within the General Defense Intelligence Program;
6. manage and operate a facility for the timely and the interactive tasking of collection systems and capabilities in response to time-urgent needs of the Department of Defense;
7. manage the Defense Attaché System;
8. manage all DOD intelligence information systems except those dedicated to signals intelligence operations;
9. participate in joint national and Defense intelligence activities such as the National Photographic Interpretation Center, the Defense Special Missile and Astronautics Center and other such activities as may be developed by mutual interagency agreement and approved by the Secretary of Defense;
10. in coordination with other intelligence agencies concerned, recommend plans for intelligence operations and coordinate the execution of approved intelligence operations plans;
11. provide the focal point for relationships with foreign intelligence services;
12. review, coordinate and evaluate the effectiveness of career development for general military personnel; establish a DOD career development program for civilian general intelligence personnel;
13. recommend changes in the application of current and new collection systems or improvements in DOD intelligence systems and related collection systems;
14. operate the Defense Intelligence School;
15. supervise a DOD-wide intelligence dissemination program and provide centralized dissemination services in support of DOD and other authorized recipients;
16. establish, maintain, and operate facilities for DOD imagery indexing, processing, duplication, evaluation and central repository services in support of DOD and other authorized recipients;
17. provide guidance to DOD components concerning the release of Defense intelligence information to foreign governments, international organizations and the public;
18. administer DOD security policies and programs to protect intelligence and intelligence sources and methods, including direction of the Defense Special Security System;
19. serve as the intelligence staff officer (J-2) of the Joint Chiefs of Staff;
20. ... [coordinate] intelligence requirements and considerations for space, less C^3 systems. Collaborate with appropriate Joint Staff Directorates—with respect to intelligence activities and procedures and development of intelligence require-

ments and considerations for space systems. Maintains cognizance over all space systems which have military intelligence utility;

21. in collaboration with J3 [Operations Directorate], JCS, represent the OJCS and unified and specified commands in intelligence issues and efforts relating to the exploitation of current national capabilities.[15]

On February 22, 1990, the ASD (C³I) established a Steering Group of senior officers in DOD intelligence organizations to review the readiness of the defense intelligence system to meet the changing international security environment. The effort, which would be labeled "Defense Intelligence in the 1990s," was intended to identify the potential issues, risks, and opportunities expected to emerge in the 1990s.[16]

In June 1990 the group prepared a fairly brief TOP SECRET/CODEWORD draft interim executive summary of issues that had been raised by the participants in the effort and appended a listing of "issues" suggesting alternative ways of addressing individual topics.[17]

The draft summary was intended to be a forerunner of the final review. However, because of a shift in thinking at the senior level of DOD, no final review study was completed—although the results of the review were presented to the Secretary of Defense, the Deputy Secretary of Defense, and other senior defense officials in September–December 1990. And on December 14, 1990, Undersecretary of Defense Donald J. Atwood issued a memorandum entitled "Strengthening Defense Intelligence Functions" that noted that senior-level DOD officials had reviewed the department's intelligence activities and requested from the memo's addressees detailed plans to achieve a variety of objectives, including strengthening "the role and performance of the Defense Intelligence Agency in the intelligence requirements, production, and management processes."[18]

The memo resulted in the March 15, 1991, ASD (C³I) *Plan for Restructuring Defense Intelligence.* With respect to the DIA the plan called for:

- strengthening the role and performance of DIA as a Combat Support Agency
- improving the quality of the Defense Intelligence product through streamlining and reconfiguring DIA to improve its estimative capability with emphasis on quality analysis and reporting strategically important intelligence
- strengthening DIA's management of intelligence production and analysis
- assigning DIA the responsibility to perform/oversee basic encyclopedic data production
- establishing within DIA a capability to validate threat information to ensure an independent intelligence input to the acquisition process
- establishing within DIA a Policy Issues Office to improve support to the Office of the Secretary of Defense.[19]

The plan also noted that a November 27, 1990, memorandum from the Deputy Secretary of Defense entitled "Assistant Secretary of Defense for Command, Control, Communications, and Intelligence" had assigned authority, direction, and control over the DIA and the General Defense Intelligence Program (GDIP) Staff to the ASD (C^3I). Prior to this, responsibility for the GDIP Staff had belonged to the Director of the DIA.[20]

Although the plan was generally consistent with the direction of the congressional intelligence oversight committees, the proposals to increase the ASD (C^3I)'s authority over the DIA and the GDIP Staff ran into congressional opposition. The Senate Armed Services Committees took strong exception, believing that the result would be to make the DIA overly subordinate to politically appointed officials in the DOD. The committee also observed that increasing the authority of the ASD (C^3I) would run "the risk of poor management of DIA when the appointed official has little experience in intelligence" and would do "nothing to solve DIA's real problems—a lack of authority to manage defense intelligence." As a result, the DOD authorization bill included language specifying the DIA's responsibilities and the individuals to whom the Director of the DIA would report. Thus, the bill noted, "The committee intends that ASD (C^3I) shall not exercise day-to-day operational authority, and shall have no role in analysis, dissemination of analyses, and civilian and military personnel actions of DIA."[21]

In response to the Senate action and in anticipation of the upcoming House-Senate conference, Secretary of Defense Dick Cheney wrote to Senate Armed Services Committee Chairman Sam Nunn addressing a number of areas that would be discussed in the conference. In his letter Cheney noted, "The Administration strongly opposes provisions in the Senate amendment to establish ill-advised organizational arrangements for defense intelligence activities."[22]

Possibly as a result of Cheney's letter, the House-Senate conference on the DOD authorization bill produced a compromise that somewhat circumscribed the role of the ASD (C^3I) and enhanced the independence of the DIA. Specifically, the National Defense Authorization Act for Fiscal Years 1992 and 1993 (Public Law 102-190) authorized the ASD (C^3I) to be assigned a supervisory role, but not "day-to-day operational control," over the DIA for 1992.[23]

During the 1960s and early 1970s the DIA underwent several extensive reorganizations. Although subsequent years were not without occasional organizational changes, they were not as frequent or of such a dramatic nature. However, between 1991 and 1993 the DIA underwent two extensive reorganizations designed to improve performance, deal with mandated personnel and budget reductions, adapt to changing international realities, and better coordinate military intelligence activities.

As shown in Figure 3-1, the DIA now includes three directorates—Planning and Administration, Policy Support, and Intelligence—and three main centers—National Military Intelligence Production, National Military Intelligence Collection, and National Military Intelligence Support.

The Directorate for Intelligence serves as the Joint Chiefs of Staff J-2. Subordinate to its Director are Deputy Directors for Crisis Operations; Crisis Management; the National Military Joint Intelligence Center; Joint Staff Support; Intelli-

48

Figure 3-1. Organization of the Defense Intelligence Agency.

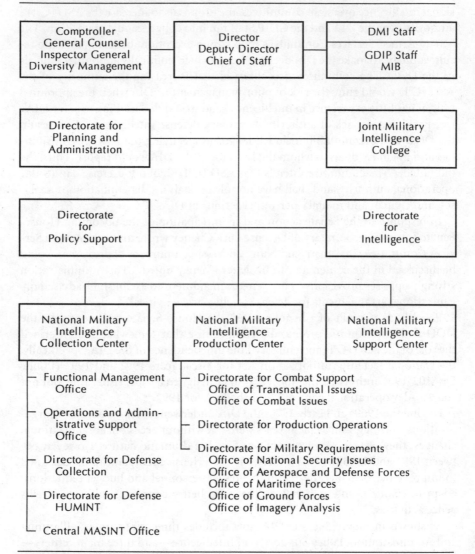

Source: *Department of Defense Telephone Directory, April 1994* (Washington, D.C.: U.S. Government Printing Office, 1994), pp. D-24 to D-25.

gence Doctrine, Plans, Policy and Systems Requirements; and Unified Command Support.[24]

The directorate provides current and warning intelligence to the Secretary of Defense, the Chairman of the JCS, and other DOD officials. It also assesses, coordinates, produces, and integrates all-source current and indications and warning intelligence; provides daily briefings on current intelligence to the Secretary of Defense, the Chairman of the JCS, and other DOD officials; produces a Morning Summary, daily Defense Intelligence Notices, Warning Reports, and Intelligence Appraisals; and contributes to the *National Intelligence Daily.*[25]

The National Military Joint Intelligence Center, operated under the supervision of one of the directorate's Deputy Directors, is an indications and warning center that "operates 24 hours a day and is responsible for providing time-sensitive intelligence to the National Military Command Center, the Secretary of Defense, Joint Chiefs of Staff, military commands, and military services.[26]

The National Military Intelligence Production Center (NMIPC) consists of three main directorates—Combat Support, Production Operations, and Military Requirements. The Directorate for Combat Support consists of two offices—Transnational Issues (e.g., narcotics trafficking, terrorism, proliferation) and Combat Issues. The Directorate for Military Requirements produces assessments through five offices—National Security Issues, Aerospace and Defense Forces, Maritime Forces, Ground Forces, and Imagery Analysis.[27]

Attached to the NMIPC are two subordinate centers that were transferred to the DIA from the Army. In its 1991 report, *Intelligence Authorization Act, Fiscal Year 1992,* the House Permanent Select Committee on Intelligence strongly recommended that "the Armed Forces Medical Intelligence Center [and] the [Army] Missile and Space Intelligence Center ... be transferred in their entirety to DIA and become designated Field Production Activities of DIA." By early 1992 the DIA had developed a plan for transfer of the centers to its control and the transfer orders were issued.[28]

In 1982 the Armed Forces Medical Intelligence Center (AFMIC) was established, replacing the Army's Medical Intelligence and Information Agency (MIIA), which provided medical intelligence for the entire defense community. AFMIC's formation was possibly the result of unhappiness with the medical intelligence efforts of the MIIA. Discussions of Defense Audit Service personnel with the Director of the General Defense Intelligence Program Staff in 1981 indicated intelligence community concern about a lack of adequate medical intelligence in Southwest Asian and Third World countries, "where casualties from unusual diseases and environmental conditions could occur."[29]

Medical intelligence is particularly vital in planning for combat operations, particularly in areas significantly different from the United States in terms of environment and prevalence of disease. One aspect of AFMIC's activities consists of producing general medical intelligence on health and sanitation, epidemiology, environmental factors, and military and civilian medical care capabilities—as in

Figure 3-2.   Organization of the Armed Forces Medical Intelligence Center.

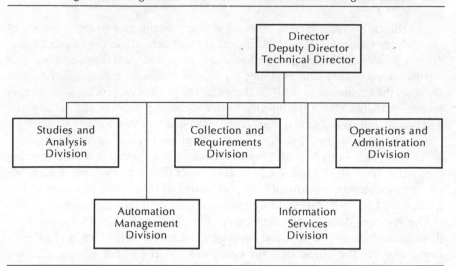

Source: DOD 6240.1R, "Organization and Functions of the Armed Forces Medical Intelligence Center (AFMIC)," April 1986.

AFMIC's "Medical Capabilities Study: Democratic People's Republic of Korea." A second aspect of its work involves the production of medical scientific and technical intelligence concerning all basic and applied biomedical phenomena of military importance, including biological, chemical, psychological, and biophysical. The AFMIC report entitled "Medical Effects of Non-Ionizing Electromagnetic Radiation—LASER" represents one example of such an effort.[30]

AFMIC is also certainly responsible for assessing foreign biomedical R&D and its impact on the physiological effectiveness of medical forces as well as for the exploitation of foreign medical materiel obtained under the DOD Foreign Materiel Exploitation Program (FMEP).[31]

Subordinate to the Director, Deputy Director, and Technical Director of AFMIC are five divisions, as shown in Figure 3-2. The Studies and Analysis Division produces all foreign medical intelligence for AFMIC. The Collection and Requirements Division coordinates all aspects of medical intelligence collection and the acquisition and exploitation of medical materiel for DOD. The Operations and Administration Division is responsible for the budget, fiscal reports, personnel, and security. The Automation Management Division provides data processing services, and the Information Services Division provides translation support, develops user-interest profiles, and acquires, controls, and disseminates intelligence documents.[32]

The Missile and Space Intelligence Center, the second subordinate center attached to the NMIPC, had about 400 personnel in 1982 and is located at Redstone

Figure 3-3. Organization of the Missile and Space Intelligence Center.

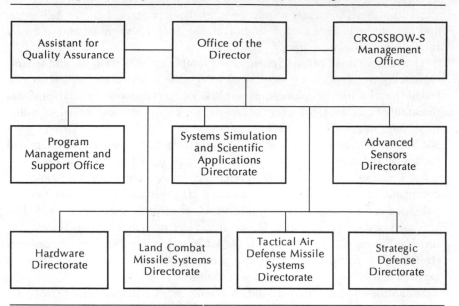

Source: U.S. Army Missile and Space Intelligence Center, "Organization and Functions, U.S. Army Missile and Space Intelligence Center" (Redstone Arsenal, Ala.: AMSIC, June 9, 1986), p. III-1.

Arsenal, Alabama. In June 1956 the Special Security Office of the Army Ballistic Missile Agency (ABMA) was established to procure missile and space intelligence data for the Commander of the ABMA. To analyze the data, a Technical Intelligence Division (TID) was established. This division was subordinate to the ABMA's Assistant Chief of Staff for Research and Development. Subsequent to the March 1958 consolidation of all Army activities at Redstone Arsenal into the Army Ordnance Missile Command (AOMC), the fifty-person TID was redesignated the Office of the Assistant Chief of Staff for Missile Intelligence. When the AOMC was absorbed in 1962 by the Army Missile Command (itself subordinate to the U.S. Army Materiel Command) the AOMC was redesignated the Directorate of Missile Intelligence, and in September 1970 it became the Missile Intelligence Agency. On August 1, 1985, it was redesignated the U.S. Army Missile and Space Intelligence Center (AMSIC).[33]

The center's mission is to "acquire, produce, maintain, and disseminate scientific and technological intelligence pertaining to missile and space weapons systems, subsystems, components, and activities; related sciences and technologies representing state-of-the art to support ... DOD requirements."[34]

The structure of the AMSIC is shown in Figure 3-3. The Systems Simulation and Scientific Applications Directorate provides data processing and scientific and technical computations to all units of the AMSIC. It also develops computational models, simulations, and data processing systems for the AMSIC. The Advanced Sensors Directorate acquires and analyzes imagery, signals intelligence, and human intelligence data in support of the AMSIC's scientific and technical intelligence production effort.[35]

The Land Combat Missile Systems Directorate produces scientific and technical intelligence concerning single and integrated short-range ballistic missile (SRBM) and antitank guided missile (ATGM) weapons systems and provides threat support to the Department of Defense for projected intercontinental ballistic missiles and precision guided weapons systems. The Tactical Air Defense Missile Systems Directorate produces the same intelligence for single and integrated tactical air defense weapons systems, including projected systems and modifications. This directorate also studies foreign tactical weapons systems technologies; command, control, and communications; R&D organizations; personalities; capabilities; and programs that may affect present or projected systems needed by U.S. tactical air defense forces. The Strategic Defense Directorate is responsible for determining the foreign state of the art in strategic ballistic missile defense, strategic air defense, and command, control, and communications as well as for examining R&D organizations and personalities.[36]

Subordinate to the National Military Intelligence Collection Center (NMICC) of the DIA are five components, the three most significance being the Directorate for Defense Collection, the Directorate for Defense HUMINT, and the Central MASINT Office (CMO). The center was formed by placing under one component the functions of the old Directorates for Attachés and Operations and for Collection and Imagery Activities (minus the Imagery Activities) and the CMO.[37]

The Directorate for Defense Collection is intended to provide collection support to the NMIPC and the National Military Joint Intelligence Center. The Directorate for Defense HUMINT directed attaché and DIA clandestine collection operations and will supervise the activities of the Defense HUMINT Service (see next section).[38]

The third element of the collection group is the newly created Central MASINT (Measurement and Signature Intelligence) Office. The office is "a joint combat support directorate, [which] serves a dual role as the Director of Central Intelligence's Executive Agent for MASINT and as the DoD MASINT Manager." It is "responsible for end-to-end management of current collection activities and future sensor/technology development in direct support of National and DoD consumers." The organization of the CMO is shown in Figure 3-4.[39]

As of 1978 the DIA had 4,300 to 5,500 employees (including 1,000 attachés) and a budget in the $200 million to $250 million range. It presently has about 6,500 employees and a budget of $622 million.[40] Main headquarters for the DIA is the Defense Intelligence Analysis Center at Bolling AFB in Washington, D.C. The DIA also conducts some of its operations from other locations, namely the Pentagon, the Washington Navy Yard, and the Plaza West.

Figure 3-4.   Organization of the Central MASINT Office.

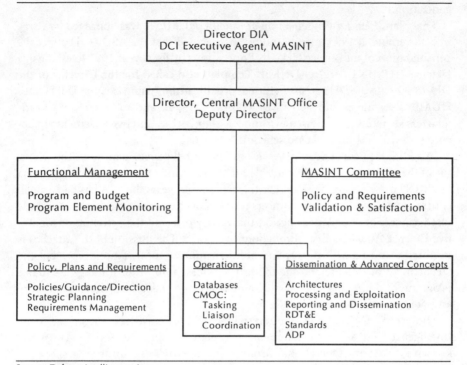

Source: Defense Intelligence Agency.

DEFENSE HUMINT SERVICE

Early in the Reagan administration, Deputy Undersecretary of Defense (Policy) Richard Stillwell sought to establish a DOD HUMINT agency. His effort, codenamed MONARCH EAGLE, partially resulted from DOD and military service dissatisfaction with CIA collection priorities. The project was vetoed by Congress, however, on the grounds that it would overlap with CIA HUMINT collection efforts and make control of sensitive operations more difficult.[41]

In December 1992 DOD Directive 5200.37, "Centralized Management of DOD Human Intelligence (HUMINT) Operations," centralized HUMINT decision-making under the DOD HUMINT Manager, established the concept of HUMINT Support Elements at combatant commands, and required consolidation of HUMINT Support Services.[42]

In June 1993, in response to discussions with DCI James Woolsey during the annual Joint Review of Intelligence Programs, Deputy Secretary of Defense William J. Perry requested that the ASD (C³I) develop a plan to consolidate the separate human intelligence components of the Defense Department into a single organization.[43]

That plan, *Plan for Consolidation of Defense HUMINT,* was approved by Perry in a November 2, 1993, memorandum. It specified that the ASD (C³I) effect the consolidation of the service HUMINT operations by fiscal year 1997 to establish a Defense HUMINT Service (DHS).[44] The plan also called for the Director of the DIA to activate the DHS as a provisional organization, "using existing DoD GDIP HUMINT resources and structures within FY 1994," and to "establish a headquarters structure ... followed by support, clandestine, and overt elements in accordance with [a] time-phased schedule."[45]

In addition to consolidating service human intelligence operations, the Director of the DIA will also be responsible for transferring DIA clandestine and overt HUMINT activities to the DHS. For the past several years the DIA has had a small contingent of clandestine case officers responsible for recruiting agents to provide intelligence. For a far longer period the agency directed the activities of ninety-five Defense Attaché offices throughout the world. The mission of the attachés is to observe and report military and politico-military information, represent the Department of Defense and the military services, administer military assistance programs and foreign military sales, and advise the U.S. ambassador on military and politico-military matters.[46]

The Army HUMINT contribution to DHS will primarily come from the Army Intelligence and Security Command's Foreign Intelligence Activity (formerly known as the Army Operational Group). The activity's organization is shown in Figure 3-5.

In 1966 the Navy established an organization—first known as the Naval Field Operations Support Group and then as Task Force 157—to conduct clandestine collection operations. That organization was disestablished in 1977. At the same time, Task Force 168 was assigned the task of overt collection. The Navy contribution to the DHS will include Task Force 168's overt collection activities, which were absorbed by the Office of Naval Intelligence in 1992, as well as a contingent of one hundred clandestine case officers to be recruited over the next five years. Liaison between the Navy and the DIA concerning HUMINT matters will be performed by the Navy HUMINT Element DIA.[47]

The Air Force contribution to the DHS will come from the transfer of personnel from the former Air Force Intelligence Command's 696th Intelligence Group (IG), which will be disbanded. This group, which conducts clandestine collection activities and debriefs defectors, was previously known as the Air Force Special Activities Center, the 7612th Air Intelligence Group, and the 1127th Field Activities Group. The 1127th was described as "an oddball unit, a composite of special intelligence groups who 'conducted worldwide operations to collect intelligence from human sources.' The men of the 1127th were con artists. Their job was to get people to talk—Russian defectors, North Vietnamese soldiers taken prisoner."[48]

Figure 3-5.   Organization of the Foreign Intelligence Activity.

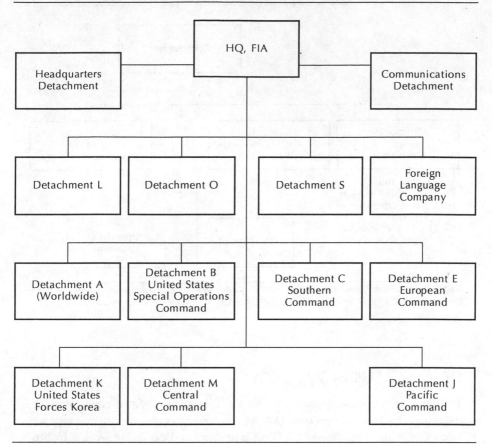

Source: USAINSCOM Regulation 10-44, "United States Army Foreign Intelligence Activity," September 1, 1989.

The organization of the 696th IG is shown in Figure 3-6. The Directorate of Operations is the key component, both at headquarters and at the operating locations. The directorate has eighteen operating locations and five detachments in the United States and overseas, as shown in Table 3-1. Detachment 4's personnel were involved in the Defense Liaison Program, Project SHOTGUN, and Projects SEEK/LADEN.[49]

Air Force HUMINT General Defense Intelligence Program positions will be transferred to the DIA over a period of three years, with clandestine collection programs to be transferred first, followed by positions assigned to overt collection programs. An Air Force HUMINT Office, established at DIA/DHS, will provide liaison on HUMINT matters with the new service.[50]

Figure 3-6.   Organization of the 696th Intelligence Group.

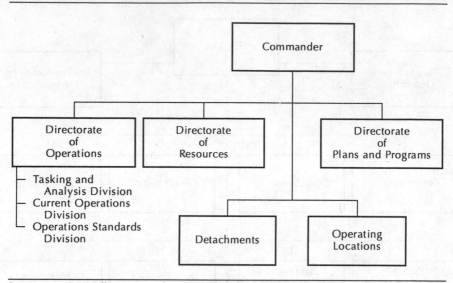

Source: *American Intelligence Journal* (Autumn/Winter 1992–1993): 19; *Department of Defense Telephone Directory,* August 1993 (Washington, D.C.: U.S. Government Printing Office, 1993), pp. O-172 to O-173.

DEFENSE MAPPING AGENCY

The Defense Mapping Agency (DMA) was created in 1972 to consolidate the mapping, charting, and geodesy (MC&G) functions of the various military services. The primary mission of the DMA is to support the military services by providing mapping, charting, and geodesy products and services that are critical to successful military operations. Specifically, the DMA is responsible for producing strategic and tactical maps, charts, geodetic information, databases, and specialized products to support current and advanced weapons and navigation systems. It is also responsible for establishing DOD mapping, charting, and geodetic requirements and providing them to the ASD (C³I).[51]

In many instances, DMA operations involve the processing of data acquired by technical intelligence systems—as indicated by the fact that 80 percent of DMA's 9,500 employees hold Sensitive Compartmented Information (SCI) clearances. SCI data is employed in producing the data that allow the targeting of cruise missiles by Terrain Contour Matching (TERCOM). Such data are also required for precise specification of target location in the Single Integrated Operational Plan (SIOP) and for accurate targeting of U.S. warheads.[52]

Table 3-1.   696th Intelligence Group Detachments and Operating Locations.

Detachment/Operating Location	Base
Det. 1	Yokota AB, Japan
Det. 2	Wright-Patterson AFB, Ohio
Det. 3	Lindsey AS, Germany
Det. 4	Ft. Belvoir, Virginia
Det. 5	Homestead AFB, Florida
OL BE	Berlin, Germany
OL CZ	Camp Zama, Japan
OL DU	Düsseldorf, Germany
OL EG	Eglin AFB, Florida
OL FH	Ft. Huachuca, Arizona
OL FR	Frankfurt, Germany
OL GI	Giessen, Germany
OL HM	Hamburg, Germany
OL HI	Hickam AFB, Hawaii
OL KO	Seoul, Korea
OL LA	Los Angeles, California
OL MU	Munich, Germany
OL NU	Nuernberg, Germany
OL NY	New York
OL PI	Pirmasens, Germany
OL PT	Patrick AFB, Florida
OL ST	Stuttgart, Germany
OL TO	Tokyo, Japan

Source: "Joint Department of Defense Plain Language Address Directory," in United States Military Communications-Electronics Board, USMCEB Publication No. 6, Issue 25, *Message Address Directory* (Washington, D.C.: U.S. Government Printing Office, January 30, 1993), p. 71.

Under the Director for the DMA, as shown in Figure 3-7, are twelve independent offices, six directorates, and six centers. The Directorate for Plans and Requirements establishes DMA mapping, charting, and geodesy objectives, prepares plans, and develops policy to provide MC&G products throughout the government. The Naval Warfare Systems, Land Combat Systems, and Aerospace Warfare Systems Divisions of the directorate define standard and new hydrographic, topographic, and aeronautical products for emerging weapons and C^3I systems.[53]

The Directorate for Programs, Production and Operations programs resources and assigns tasks to subordinate DMA elements. It reviews and evaluates utilization of resources and execution of production and support task assignments and establishes policy for DOD participation in national, interagency, and international MC&G activities as well as MC&G data collection requirements and priorities.[54]

The DMA has two principal production facilities providing MC&G products. Among its functions, the DMA Aerospace Center in St. Louis, Missouri:

58

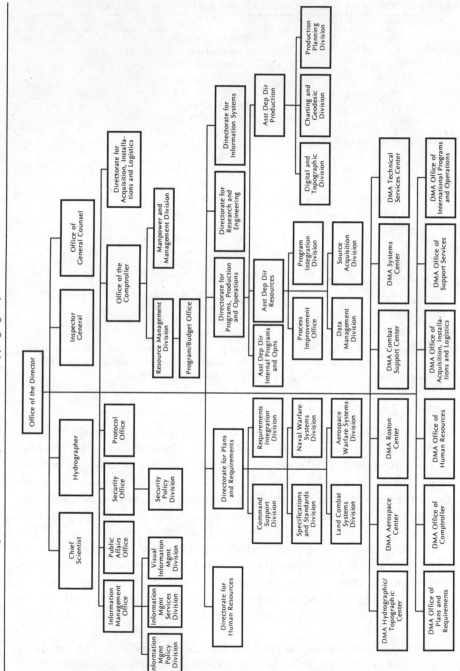

Figure 3-7. Organization of Headquarters, Defense Mapping Agency.

Source: Defense Mapping Agency.

1. produces, distributes and maintains aeronautical, extraterrestrial, and astronautical charts, air target materials, and special products in support of aerospace and missile weapon systems;
2. operates and maintains the Department of Defense centralized libraries for aeronautical charts, free world air facilities and flight information, point positioning databases, gravity data and installation/positional data;
3. produces and maintains flight information publications, flight control aids and evaluated information on air facilities to satisfy the daily operational requirements of the Armed Forces;
4. provides geodetic and geophysical studies and data in support of various weapons systems;
5. produces and maintains digital and point positioning databases in support of aerospace weapons delivery systems;
6. produces cultural and terrain information for use in radar simulators, terminal guidance, en route navigation, and [Air Combat Command] penetration routes.[55]

The geodetic and geophysical studies (item 4) are partially based on data acquired by military and civilian geodetic satellites (SEASAT-1, GEOSAT, GOES) and allow compensation for force fields that might throw missiles off their intended path. Thus, the data are crucial to U.S. missile accuracy.[56]

The DMA Hydrographic/Topographic Center at Brookmont, Maryland, produces topographic and hydrographic charts (including bottom contour maps) and related material for surface and subsurface navigation, topographic maps for land forces, Digital Terrain Evaluation Data for cruise missiles, and some products for air operations. The Hydrographic/Topographic Center produces Precise Bathyspheric Naval Zone Charts, which are required by submarines in order to obtain location fixes without surfacing. The Charting Division of the center's Mapping and Charting Division provides support to special Navy projects, such as submarine reconnaissance operations, by producing Special Support Graphics based on hydrographic, bathymetric, and navigational data.[57]

The DMA Combat Support Center (DMACSC) is responsible for providing timely and tailored MC&G support to military services, unified and specified commands, and other government agencies. The DMA Systems Center (DMASC) is responsible for research, development, installation, and maintenance of the DMA production line to ensure responsiveness to MC&G requirements. The center's Modernization Development Group, first established in 1982 as the Special Program Office for Exploitation Modernization (SPOEM), develops and implements the Digital Production Systems (DPS) capability to produce DMA products using data produced by "advanced collection systems" (i.e., the KH-11 and Advanced KH-11 imagery satellites). The DMA Reston Center (DMARC) "produce[s] and maintain[s] MC&G products in direct support of DoD combat forces and weapons systems."[58]

NOTES

1. U.S. Congress, Senate Select Committee to Study Governmental Operations with Respect to Intelligence Activities, *Final Report, Book 1, Foreign and Military Intelligence* (Washington, D.C.: U.S. Government Printing Office, 1976), p. 325.

2. U.S. Congress, Senate Select Committee to Study Governmental Operations with Respect to Intelligence Activities, *Final Report, Book 6, Supplementary Reports on Intelligence Activities* (Washington, D.C.: U.S. Government Printing Office, 1976), p. 266.

3. Secretary of Defense Robert S. McNamara, Memorandum for the President, Subject: The Establishment of a Defense Intelligence Agency, July 6, 1961, *DDRS* 1986-000085.

4. Joint Study Group, *The Joint Study Group Report on Foreign Intelligence Activities of the United States Government,* December 15, 1960, p. 31.

5. Ibid., p. 23.

6. Robert McNamara, Memorandum for the Chairman, Joint Chiefs of Staff, Subject: Establishment of a Defense Intelligence Agency, February 8, 1961, NA, MRB, RG 218, CCS 2010 (Collection of Intelligence), 1960 Box, 20 Dec 1960 Folder, p. 1127.

7. McNamara, Memorandum for the Chairman, Joint Chiefs of Staff, Subject: Establishment of a Defense Intelligence Agency, February 8, 1961, p. 1129.

8. Joint Staff, DJSM-156-61, Memorandum for General Lemnitzer et al., Subject: Establishment of a Defense Intelligence Agency, 9 February 1961, NA, MR, RG 218, CCS 2010 (Collection of Intelligence), 1960 Box, 20 Dec 1960 Folder.

9. JCS 2031/166, Joint Chiefs of Staff Decision on JCS 2031/166, Memorandum by the Director, Joint Staff, on Establishment of a Defense Intelligence Agency, 13 April 1961; JCS 2031/166, Memorandum by the Director, Joint Staff, for the Joint Chiefs of Staff on Establishment of a Defense Intelligence Agency, 7 April 1961, with Enclosure (Revised Draft Memorandum [April 12, 1961] for the Secretary of Defense, Subject: Establishment of a Defense Intelligence Agency (DIA), both in NA, MRB, RG 218, CCS 2010 (Collection of Intelligence), 1960 Box, 20 Dec 1960 Folder.

10. Draft Memorandum for the Secretary of Defense, Subject: Establishment of a Defense Intelligence Agency (DIA).

11. Historical Division, Joint Secretariat, Joint Chiefs of Staff, *Development of the Defense Agencies,* November 3, 1978.

12. Ibid.

13. Ibid., citing Department of Defense Directive 5105.21, "Defense Intelligence Agency," December 16, 1976.

14. Historical Division, Joint Secretariat, Joint Chiefs of Staff, *Development of the Defense Agencies,* Tab B.

15. Joint Chiefs of Staff, *JCS Pub 4: Organization and Functions of the Joint Chiefs of Staff* (Washington, D.C.: JCS, August 1, 1985), pp. VII-3-3 to VII-3-5.

16. William K. O'Donnell, Memorandum for W. M. MacDonald, Director, Freedom of Information and Security Review OASD (PA), Subject: Freedom of Information Act (FOIA) Appeal—Jeffrey T. Richelson, July 31, 1991.

17. Ibid.

18. Ibid.; Assistant Secretary of Defense (Command, Control, Communications, and Intelligence), *Plan for Restructuring Defense Intelligence,* March 15, 1991, p. 1; Donald J. Atwood, Memorandum for Secretaries of the Military Departments et al., Subject: Strengthening Defense Intelligence Functions, December 14, 1990.

19. Assistant Secretary of Defense (Command, Control, Communications, and Intelligence), *Plan for Restructuring Defense Intelligence,* p. 3.

20. Ibid.; Donald J. Atwood, Memorandum for Secretaries of the Military Departments et al., Subject: Assistant Secretary of Defense for Command, Control, Communications and Intelligence, November 27, 1990.

21. Richard A. Best, Jr., "Reforming Defense Intelligence," *Congressional Research Service 92-91F,* January 22, 1992, p. 22; Neil Munro, "Pentagon Fights Move to Alter Oversight of DIA," *Defense News,* September 23, 1991, p. 28; U.S. Congress, Senate Committee on Armed Services, *National Defense Authorization Act for Fiscal Years 1992 and 1993, Report 102-113* (Washington, D.C.: U.S. Government Printing Office, 1991), pp. 271–73.

22. Letter, Secretary of Defense Dick Cheney to Honorable Sam Nunn, Chairman, Committee on Armed Services, September 20, 1991.

23. Best, "Reforming Defense Intelligence," p. 22.

24. *Department of Defense Telephone Directory, August 1993* (Washington, D.C.: U.S. Government Printing Office, 1993), p. O-24.

25. Defense Intelligence Agency, *Organization, Mission, and Key Personnel,* 1984, pp. 43–46.

26. Central Intelligence Agency, *A Consumer's Guide to Intelligence* (Washington, D.C.: CIA, 1993), p. 42.

27. *Department of Defense Telephone Directory, August 1993,* p. O-24; "Structure Set for New Production Center," *Communique,* May 14, 1993, pp. 4, 5, 7.

28. House Permanent Select Committee on Intelligence, *Report 102-65, Part 1 on Intelligence Authorization Act, Fiscal Year 1992* (Washington, D.C.: U.S. Government Printing Office, 1991), p. 8; Letter, John W. Shannon, Acting Secretary of the Army, to Lt. General James R. Clapper, Jr., Director, Defense Intelligence Agency, February 4, 1992; Defense Intelligence Agency, *Plan for the Transfer of the Armed Forces Medical Intelligence Center and the Missile and Space Intelligence Center to the Defense Intelligence Agency,* n.d.

29. Defense Audit Service, *Semiannual Audit Plan, First Half, Fiscal Year 1982* (Washington, D.C.: DAS, 1981), p. 32.

30. Armed Forces Medical Intelligence Center, *Organization and Functions of the Armed Forces Medical Intelligence Center* (Ft. Detrick, Md.: AFMIC, April 1986), p. vi; Defense Audit Service, *Semiannual Audit Plan, First Half, Fiscal Year 1982,* p. 32.

31. Defense Audit Service, *Semiannual Audit Plan, First Half, Fiscal Year 1982,* p. 32.

32. Armed Forces Medical Intelligence Center, *Organization and Functions of the Armed Forces Medical Intelligence Center,* pp. 1–3.

33. *Organization, Mission and Functions: U.S. Army Missile and Space Intelligence Center, Redstone Arsenal, Alabama* (Redstone Arsenal, Ala.: AMSIC, n.d.), pp. 4–6.

34. AR 10-86, "United States Army Intelligence Agency," February 27, 1986, pp. 3–4.

35. *Organization, Mission and Functions: U.S. Army Missile and Space Intelligence Center,* pp. 8–13.

36. Ibid., pp. 14–20.

37. "New Collection Center Forming," *Communique,* May 14, 1993, p. 3.

38. Ibid.

39. Defense Intelligence Agency, "Mission Description" [Central MASINT Office], n.d.

40. "Shaping Tomorrow's CIA," *Time,* February 6, 1978, pp. 10ff.; "Pruning the Pentagon's Spreading Tree," *National Journal,* October 31, 1987, p. 2737; Tony Capaccio and Eric Rosenberg, "Deutsch Approves $27 Billion for Pentagon Spy Budgets," *Defense Week,* August 29, 1994, pp. 1, 13.

41. Raymond Bonner, "Secret Pentagon Intelligence Unit Is Disclosed," *New York Times,* May 11, 1983, p. A13; Robert C. Toth, "U.S. Spying: Partnership Re-Emerges," *Los Angeles Times,* November 14, 1983, pp. 1, 12.

42. Office of the Assistant Secretary of Defense (Command, Control, Communications, and Intelligence), *Plan for the Consolidation of Defense HUMINT,* 1993, p. 1.

43. Ibid.

44. William J. Perry, Memorandum for Secretaries of the Military Departments et al., Subject: Consolidation of Defense HUMINT, November 2, 1993.

45. Office of the Assistant Secretary of Defense (Command, Control, Communications, and Intelligence), *Plan for Consolidation of Defense HUMINT,* p. 7.

46. Private information; U.S. Congress, House Committee on Armed Services, *Hearings on H.R. 4181 to Authorize Certain Construction at Military Installations for Fiscal Year 1987, and Other Purposes* (Washington, D.C.: U.S. Government Printing Office, 1986), pp. 199–200; Defense Intelligence Agency, *Organization, Mission, and Key Personnel,* pp. 22–23; Joint Chiefs of Staff, *JCS Pub 1.1,* pp. III-10-14 to III-10-15.

47. Jeffrey Richelson, "Task Force 157: The Navy's Secret Intelligence Service, 1966–1977," 1994; Private information; Office of Naval Intelligence, "ONI-65 Mission Statement," n.d.

48. Benjamin Schemmer, *The Raid* (New York: Harper & Row, 1975), pp. 26–27.

49. Diane T. Putney, *History of the Air Force Intelligence Service, 1 January–31 December 1984, Volume 1, Narrative and Appendices* (Ft. Belvoir, Va.: AFIS, n.d.), pp. 250–52.

50. Col. Clarence Fairbrother, "Air Force HUMINT—To Be or Not to Be?" *Spokesman,* October 1993, p. 2; HQ, Air Force Intelligence Command, HQ AFIC Programming Plan 93-01, *Establishment of the Air Force Intelligence Field Operating Agency,* August 17, 1993, Basic-IV-1.

51. U.S. Congress, House Committee on Armed Services, "Written Statement of Maj. Gen. Richard N. Wells," *Hearings on Military Posture and HR 5968, Part 5* (Washington, D.C.: U.S. Government Printing Office, 1982), pp. 1231–34; Department of Defense Directive 5105.40, "Defense Mapping Agency," December 6, 1990.

52. David C. Morrison, "You Are Here," *National Journal,* October 31, 1987, pp. 2735–38.

53. Defense Mapping Agency, *FY 93–97 Joint Manpower Program—Headquarters* (Washington, D.C.: DMA, 1992), Part 1, Organizational Chart, pp. 22–23, 93–97.

54. Ibid., Part 1, pp. 24, 97.

55. Defense Mapping Agency, *FY 93–97 Joint Manpower Program—Aerospace Center* (Washington, D.C.: DMA, 1992), Part 1, p. 3.

56. U.S. Congress, Senate Committee on Appropriations, "Prepared Statement of Brigadier General Donald O. Aldridge," *Department of Defense Appropriations for 1982, Part 5* (Washington, D.C.: U.S. Government Printing Office, 1981), p. 262.

57. Defense Mapping Agency, *FY 93–97 Joint Manpower Program—Hydrographic/Topographic Center* (Washington, D.C.: DMA, 1992), Part 1, p. 83.

58. Defense Mapping Agency, *FY 93–97 Joint Manpower Program—Combat Support Center* (Washington, D.C.: DMA, 1992), Part 1, p. 2; Defense Mapping Agency, *FY 93–97 Joint Manpower Program—Systems Center* (Washington, D.C.: DMA, 1992), Part 1, pp. 1, 40; Defense Mapping Agency, *FY 93–97 Joint Manpower Program—Reston Center* (Washington, D.C.: DMA, 1992), Part 1, p. 1.

4
MILITARY SERVICE
INTELLIGENCE ORGANIZATIONS

Unlike the United Kingdom and Canada, which abolished their military service intelligence organizations with the creation of defense intelligence organizations, or Australia, which restricts its service intelligence organizations to the production of purely tactical intelligence, the United States has maintained elaborate service intelligence organizations.

The continued major role of U.S. service intelligence organizations is partly a function of bureaucratic politics and partly a function of U.S. military requirements. A military force with large service components, each with wide-ranging functional and geographical responsibilities, may be better served in terms of intelligence support by organizations that are not too detached from the service components. Additionally, some strategic intelligence and collection functions may be best performed by service organizations. Thus, some intelligence tasks—such as producing information about foreign aerospace or submarine technology—may be carried out most efficiently by the services most directly affected, in this case the Air Force and Navy, benefiting both the services involved as well as national policymakers.

Until recently, it could be said that each of the major services has maintained an intelligence community of its own—a number of distinct intelligence organizations directed by the service's intelligence chief. However, the past several years has seen the disestablishment and/or consolidation of formerly separate intelligence organizations in each of the major services. Among the factors producing these changes are growing budgetary constraints (which will result in a 20 to 25 percent cut in service intelligence budgets by the 1997 fiscal year as well as a substantial cut in civilian personnel) and the pressure exerted by congressional oversight committees. A 1990 report of the Senate Select Committee on Intelligence observed that:

> While new requirements and the increasing cost of collection systems have driven a share of the increase in intelligence, the cost of maintaining large numbers of intelligence organizations internal to the Department of Defense has also contributed. Every echelon from the Office of the Secretary of Defense, to the Service Departments, to the CINCs [Commanders-in-Chief] and below have their own organic intelligence

Figure 4-1. Army Intelligence Organizations.

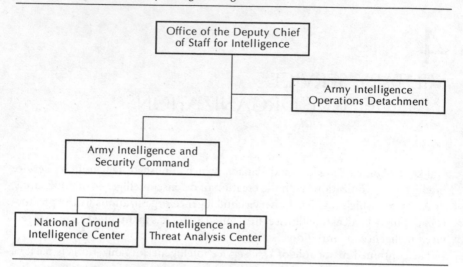

arms. For each organization, we need separate buildings, separate administration, separate security, separate communications, and separate support services.

The existence of these multiple organizations raises other important concerns. Over the years, numerous individuals and reports ... have criticized the Defense Department for significant duplication of effort; insufficient integration and sharing of information; uneven security measures and regulations; pursuit of parochial service, CINC, [and] other interests rather than joint intelligence interests; and gaps in intelligence support and coverage, despite the number of intelligence organizations.[1]

As a result, the committee, along with the Senate Armed Services Committee, directed the Secretary of Defense to review all of the Defense Department's intelligence activities and "to the maximum degree possible, consolidate or begin consolidating all disparate or redundant functions, programs, and entities."[2]

The next year, on March 15, the Assistant Secretary of Defense (C³I) issued his *Plan for Restructuring Defense Intelligence*. The plan instructed each military service to "consolidate all existing intelligence commands, agencies, and elements into a single intelligence command within each Service."[3] Although that objective has not been completely met, each of the major services has undertaken partial consolidations of their intelligence communities.

ARMY INTELLIGENCE ORGANIZATIONS

U.S. Army intelligence organizations, as depicted in Figure 4-1, are directed by the Office of the Deputy Chief of Staff for Intelligence. The major operational agency is the Army Intelligence and Security Command (INSCOM), which is responsible for human intelligence, counterintelligence, and SIGINT/COMSEC. Other Army intelligence organizations are the National Ground Intelligence Center (NGIC) and the Intelligence and Threat Analysis Center (ITAC), which are supervised by INSCOM.

The Army intelligence community used to have three additional members—the Intelligence Support Activity (ISA), the Army Missile and Space Intelligence Center (AMSIC), and the Army Intelligence Agency. However, in spring 1989 the ISA (also known as the ROYAL CAPE and GRANTOR SHADOW Special Access Programs) was disestablished and its assets absorbed by INSCOM. ISA's disestablishment in 1989 came seven years after Secretary of Defense Frank Carlucci first ordered it closed, and after recommendations in 1986 and 1988 that it be disestablished. As noted in Chapter 3, the AMSIC was transferred to control of the Defense Intelligence Agency in 1992. With the transfer of AMSIC to the DIA, and the assignment to INSCOM of responsibility for supervising the operations of the ITAC and the NGIC (then the Foreign Science and Technology Center, FSTC), much of the rationale for the Army Intelligence Agency—which was established in 1984 to direct the production of Army scientific and technical as well as general military intelligence—disappeared. It was disestablished at the end of the 1993 fiscal year.[4]

The Office of the Deputy Chief of Staff for Intelligence (see Figure 4-2) consists of two offices (Resource Management, and Intelligence Programs and Budget) and five directorates—Foreign Liaison, Foreign Intelligence, Counterintelligence and Security Countermeasures, Intelligence Policy and Operations, and Intelligence Plans and Integration. Each of the directorates determines policy in its respective area, oversees implementation, and represents the Army in interagency intelligence forums.[5]

The Foreign Liaison Directorate conducts liaison with other army intelligence organizations—such as Australia's Military Intelligence Directorate. It also coordinates the activities of the Foreign Liaison Office of the U.S. Army Intelligence Operations Detachment (AIOD)—with its Attaché Coordination and Tours Divisions simultaneously serving as elements of the AIOD. In addition, the directorate develops and coordinates the Foreign Intelligence Assistance Program.[6]

The Foreign Intelligence Directorate (with Intelligence, Threat Intelligence, and Intelligence Production Management Divisions) is concerned with current intelligence, long-term assessment, and threat intelligence.[7]

The Directorate of Counterintelligence and Security Countermeasures is concerned with counterintelligence operations, signals security, and operations security as well as personnel, physical, and information security. It formulates policy for the Army's cryptologic effort, including Communications Intelligence Security Standards. Its Technology Transfer Division is simultaneously an element of the AIOD. The directorate represents the Army on several interagency counterintelligence and security committees, including the Defense Counterintelligence

Figure 4-2. Organization of the Office of the Deputy Chief of Staff for Intelligence.

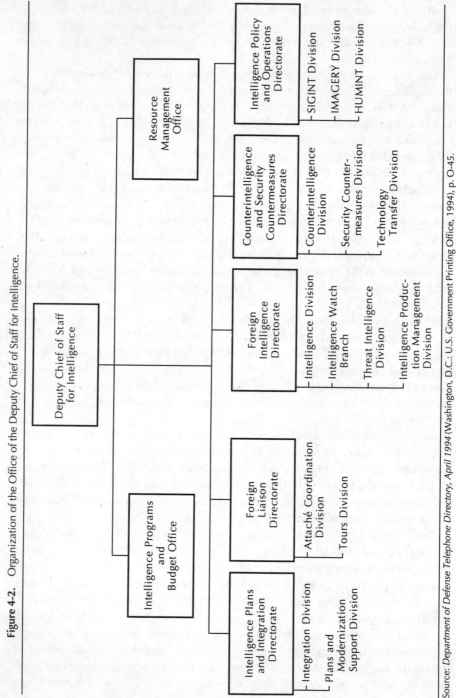

Source: Department of Defense Telephone Directory, April 1994 (Washington, D.C.: U.S. Government Printing Office, 1994), p. O-45.

Board and the NSC's interagency groups on counterintelligence and countermeasures.[8]

The Intelligence Policy and Operations Directorate is concerned with intelligence collection by space systems, signals intelligence platforms, human resources, and the integration of collection methods.[9]

The Army Intelligence Operations Detachment is a field-operating agency under the supervision and control of the Deputy Chief of Staff for Intelligence (DCSI). Each element of the detachment is authorized to communicate directly with the Office of the Secretary of Defense, the Office of the JCS, and the headquarters of the Department of the Army.[10]

The detachment's Office of Foreign Liaison administers foreign military attaché tours, Department of the Army VIP tours, and foreign counterparts visits. It also processes identification and applications for foreign attachés. The Intelligence Command and Control Office monitors and inspects all Army-wide intelligence activities to ensure compliance with Executive Orders and DOD and Army directives. The Watch Office monitors global situations to provide Indicators and Warning (I&W) support to the Army's Operations Center and provides I&W briefings to members of the Army Staff. The Current Intelligence Division provides a daily written current intelligence "Black Book" for distribution to the Army Secretariat or Army Staff.[11]

The Army Intelligence and Security Command, headquartered at Fort Belvoir, Virginia, was established on January 1, 1977, when the U.S. Army Security Agency (ASA) was redesignated as the U.S. Army Intelligence and Security Command and absorbed the (then) U.S. Army Intelligence Agency (AIA), the Forces Command Intelligence Group, the Intelligence Threat Analysis Detachment, and the Imagery Interpretation Center. The latter three organizations had been field operating activities of the Assistant Chief of Staff for Intelligence.[12] The ASA was the successor to the variously named Army signals intelligence agencies of World War II. The Commanding General of INSCOM is therefore responsible both to the Army's DCSI and to the Chief (i.e., the Director of NSA). INSCOM personnel staff SIGINT collection facilities at numerous overseas bases. In addition, INSCOM conducts clandestine human intelligence and counterintelligence operations. And, as noted earlier, in 1992 INSCOM was assigned responsibility for supervising the activities of the FSTC and the ITAC, as well as the intelligence production activities that had formerly been performed by the AIA.[13]

In INSCOM a number of Deputy Chiefs of Staff (DCS) are responsible for different areas of activity. Thus, as illustrated in Figure 4-3, in addition to the Chief of Staff there are DCSs for: Resource Management, Personnel, Logistics, Information Management, Security, and Operations. The Deputy Chief of Staff, Operations, is the principal coordinating officer responsible for current intelligence collection, production, electronic warfare, and counterintelligence and security support operations.[14]

68

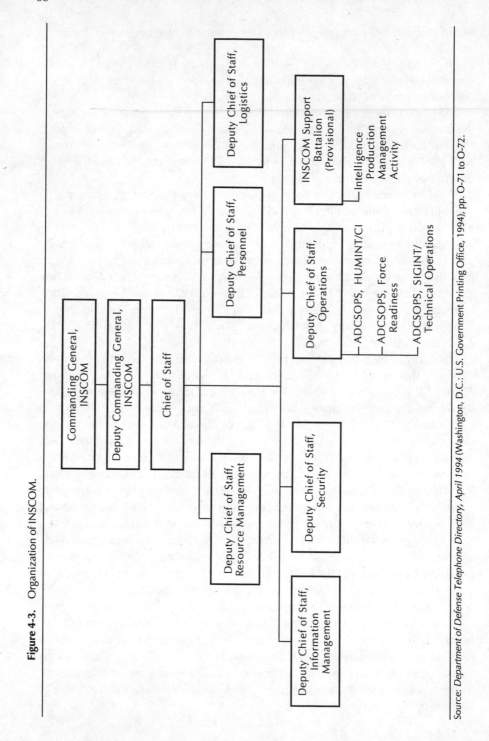

Figure 4-3. Organization of INSCOM.

Commanding General, INSCOM

Deputy Commanding General, INSCOM

Chief of Staff

Deputy Chief of Staff, Logistics

Deputy Chief of Staff, Personnel

INSCOM Support Battalion (Provisional)

Intelligence Production Management Activity

Deputy Chief of Staff, Resource Management

Deputy Chief of Staff, Operations

ADCSOPS, HUMINT/CI

ADCSOPS, Force Readiness

ADCSOPS, SIGINT/ Technical Operations

Deputy Chief of Staff, Security

Deputy Chief of Staff, Information Management

Source: *Department of Defense Telephone Directory, April 1994* (Washington, D.C.: U.S. Government Printing Office, 1994), pp. O-71 to O-72.

Subordinate to the DCS, Operations, are Assistant Deputy Chiefs of Staff, Operations (ADCSOPS), for HUMINT/Counterintelligence (CI), Force Readiness, and SIGINT and Technical Operations. Reporting to the ADCSOPS (HUMINT/CI) are three divisions: HUMINT, CI, and Plans, Policies, and Programs. Within the HUMINT Division, the Collection Management Division prepares the INSCOM HUMINT Plan, maintains the HUMINT target system, oversees the preparation of Mission Target Analysis for HUMINT collection units, and provides guidance on collection emphasis, changing priorities, and new collection objectives. The other branches initiate, plan, develop, and execute Department of the Army strategic HUMINT collection programs—including Project LANDMARK CAPER—pending transfer of such assets to the Defense HUMINT Service.[15]

The CI Division develops and disseminates guidance to implement Army policy concerning technical surveillance countermeasures, Special Access Program support, offensive counterintelligence operations, and operations security support.[16]

The ADCSOPS, SIGINT/Technical Operations, directs the activities of four divisions: SIGINT, Support to Military Operations (SMO), TROJAN, and IMINT. The SIGINT Division conducts liaison with NSA, conducts long-range SIGINT planning, and reviews and validates SIGINT architectures and concepts for future SIGINT operations. The SMO Division serves as the point of contact for INSCOM SIGINT support to military operations. The IMINT Division administers and/or coordinates imagery collection, exploitation, processing, and dissemination in support of Army requirements at the Echelon Above Corps level.[17]

Actual operational activities are performed by two types of INSCOM units—those headquartered in the Washington area and those operating in the field. One key operational unit headquartered in the Washington area is the U.S. Army Foreign Intelligence Activity, previously designated the U.S. Army Operations Group Activity and before that the Army Operational Group, which conducts HUMINT operations. Its organizational structure is shown in Figure 3-5. Another is the U.S. Army Foreign Counterintelligence Activity, responsible for planning, coordinating, and executing counterespionage and offensive counterintelligence operations. Finally, the U.S. Army Foreign Materiel Intelligence Group conducts foreign materiel exploitation operations from the Washington area.[18]

Units in the field include the SIGINT collection units, which operate under NSA/INSCOM tasking. (In the past the INSCOM units conducting these activities were designated "U.S. Army Field Stations." However, on January 1, 1988, most INSCOM field stations were redesignated as numbered military intelligence units.) Present SIGINT collection activities are located at Kunia, Hawaii; Key West, Florida; San Antonio, Texas; Pyong Taek, South Korea; Misawa, Japan; and Okinawa, Japan. A SIGINT activity at Augsburg, Germany, with 1,700 personnel was disestablished in early 1993. Also disestablished since the end of the Cold War are Field Station Sinop and Field Station Berlin.[19]

Other numbered military intelligence units (such as the 470th MI Brigade at Fort Clayton, Panama) have human intelligence and counterintelligence operations as their primary function. Those units' activities are significantly influenced by the theater commander rather than INSCOM headquarters.

As of December 31, 1990, INSCOM had more than 16,000 personnel, as shown in Table 4-1. That number is expected to shrink to 12,000 over the next five years.

The U.S. Army Intelligence and Threat Analysis Center, now a subordinate command of INSCOM, has about 300 employees and is located in the Washington Navy Yard. The ITAC is responsible for:

- providing intelligence assessments of near-term to twenty-year projected capabilities and vulnerabilities of those foreign forces which represent either potential threats to US Army operations, or potential allies in support of US operations;
- providing intelligence assessments of current military capabilities and vulnerabilities as well as military aspects of the political, economic, sociological, demographic and geographic environment of those non-allied, non–Warsaw Pact countries in which the US Army may operate;
- producing intelligence assessments, current and projected, of foreign force doctrinal, organizational, operational, and tactical concepts;
- producing counterintelligence and international assessments of the current projected organizations, capabilities and methods of foreign intelligence and security services and terrorist groups;
- producing imagery intelligence on foreign ground force equipment and weapons systems according to the National Tasking Plan and provide national-level imagery exploitation support to the US Army;
- providing direct analytic exchange between the Army Intelligence Agency and the National Security Agency in support of Army requirements for SIGINT.[20]

As indicated in Figure 4-4, ITAC is organized into a Personnel/Administrative Office and three directorates: Information Management, Research and Analysis, and Imagery.

The regional divisions of the Research and Analysis Directorate produce comprehensive studies on the military capabilities of selected countries in which the U.S. Army may be deployed as well as on many political, sociological, economic, demographic, cultural, and geographic aspects of those countries. They also produce near-term, mid-term (ten years) and long-term (twenty years) forecasts of conflict environments, military capabilities, and vulnerabilities of selected countries.[21]

The Counterintelligence and Terrorism Division of the Research and Analysis Directorate produces assessments of the organization and functions of foreign intelligence and security services, worldwide terrorist activity, international technology transfer, and the efficiency of Army Special Access Programs.[22]

The Imagery Directorate produces imagery and photogrammetric analysis of ground force weapons, electronic systems (e.g., radars), support systems (e.g., remotely piloted vehicles, river-crossing equipment, mine warfare equipment), and

Table 4-1. INSCOM Personnel Distribution as of December 31, 1990.

		Personnel	
Unit	Station	Military	Civilian
HQINSCOM	Arlington Hall Station	234	312
USA Military Spt Office	Arlington Hall Station	291	4
ACTUSAINSCOM Main	Arlington Hall Station	16	0
Act Auto Systems	Arlington Hall Station	86	59
USA Intel Exec	Arlington Hall Station	35	31
ACTUSA INSCOM FORC MOD	Arlington Hall Station	23	41
ACTUSA STU ANALYSIS	Arlington Hall Station	33	22
ACTUSAINSCOM FAA	Arlington Hall Station	0	7
Contract Support Activity	Arlington Hall Station	0	30
INSCOM CONUS MI Group	Ft. Meade, Md.	1221	22
USA Element NSA	Ft. Meade, Md.	46	0
USA Program Analysis Group	Ft. Meade, Md.	2	17
USA Field Support Center	Ft. Meade, Md.	492	416
USA Operations Group Acty	Ft. Meade, Md.	111	37
USA Central Security Facility	Ft. Meade, Md.	13	91
USA Fgn Area Off Detachment	Ft. Meade, Md.	11	1
USAINSCOM MI Battalion	Ft. Meade, Md.	129	63
USA Special Security Group	Pentagon	452	25
ACTINSCOM	Ft. Belvoir, Va.	44	16
ACTUSAINSCOMLAN EI&CM	VHFS, Va.	68	41
USA Theater Intelligence Center	Ft. Shafter, Hawaii	40	3
3 MI Center EAC	Ft. Shafter, Hawaii	33	0
USA Field Station Sinop	Sinop, Turkey	291	0
USA Field Station Berlin	Berlin, Germany	845	66
USA Field Station Korea	Camp Humphreys, ROK	257	64
USA Field Station Kunia	Kunia, Hawaii	1121	32
701 MI Brigade	Augsburg, Germany	1667	122
750 MI Battalion	Misawa, Japan	129	1
748 MI Battalion	San Antonio, Tex.	275	5
747 MI Battalion	Galeta Island, Panama	127	0
749th MI Company	Key West, Fla.	64	0
66 MI Brigade EAC, HHC	Munich, Germany	107	0
66 MI Brigade EAC, Aug	Munich, Germany	157	43
18 MI Battalion I&E, HHC	Munich, Germany	69	0
18 MI Battalion, I&E, Aug	Munich, Germany	40	84
204 MI Battalion SIGINT	Augsburg, Germany	456	0
204 MI Battalion, Aug	Augsburg, Germany	6	3
527 MI Battalion CI	Kaiserslautern, Germany	204	0
527 MI Battalion CI, Aug	Kaiserslautern, Germany	248	103
5 MI Company Interrogation	Munich, Germany	113	0
5 MI Company Interrogation, Aug	Munich, Germany	13	24
581 MI Company Imagery, Aug	Zweibrucken, Germany	31	0
766 MI Detachment CI	Berlin, Germany	33	0
766 MI Detachment CI, Aug	Berlin, Germany	6	5
584 MI Detachment CI	Vicenza, Italy	26	0
584 MI Detachment CI, Aug	Vicenza, Italy	0	2
581 MI Detachment Imagery	Zweibrucken, Germany	128	0

Table 4-1.   INSCOM Personnel Distribution as of December 31, 1990. (*continued*)

Unit	Station	Personnel Military	Personnel Civilian
Institute for Advanced Russian/East European Studies	Garmisch, Germany	11	29
USA Crypto Spt Activity	Heidelberg, Germany	18	1
INSCOM Language Center	Munich, Germany	12	11
USA Intelligence Support Detachment	Munich, Germany	44	9
500 MI Brigade EAC, HHC	Camp Zama, Japan	53	0
500 MI Brigade EAC, Aug	Camp Zama, Japan	54	54
181 MI Detachment CI	Camp Zama, Japan	20	0
181 MI Detachment CI, Aug	Camp Zama, Japan	0	11
USA Asian Studies Institute	Camp Zama, Japan	8	96
470 MI Brigade EAC, HHC	Ft. Clayton, Panama	53	0
470 MI Brigade EAC, Aug	Ft. Clayton, Panama	67	8
2 MI Center EAC	Ft. Clayton, Panama	44	0
2 MI Center EAC, Aug	Ft. Clayton, Panama	6	0
Collection Evaluation Company	Ft. Clayton, Panama	140	12
29 MI Battalion CEWI	Ft. Davis, Panama	265	0
501 MI Brigade EAC, HHC	Yongsan, S. Korea	85	0
501 MI Brigade EAC, Aug	Yongsan, S. Korea	20	16
524 MI Battalion C&E	Yongsan, S. Korea	194	0
524 MI Battalion College, Aug	Yongsan, S. Korea	97	53
532 MI Battalion Operations	Yongsan, S. Korea	445	0
3 MI Battalion AE	Camp Humphreys	412	0
3 MI Battalion AE, Aug	Camp Humphreys	0	0
513 MI Brigade EAC, HHC	Ft. Monmouth, N.J.	125	0
513 MI Brigade EAC, Aug	Ft. Monmouth, N.J.	60	9
201 MI Battalion SIGINT	Vint Hills Farm Station	354	0
202 MI Battalion I&E	Ft. Monmouth, N.J.	160	0
202 MI Battalion I&E, Aug	Ft. Monmouth, N.J.	13	0
MI Battalion (LI)	Ft. Monmouth, N.J.	481	4
17 MI Company Imagery Ex	Ft. Monmouth, N.J.	111	0
164 MI Company CI	Ft. Monmouth, N.J.	94	0
174 MI Center EAC	Ft. Monmouth, N.J.	201	0
11 MI Company Technical Intelligence	Aberdeen Proving Ground	91	0
USA Foreign MA Group	Aberdeen Proving Ground	103	3
902 MI Group CI, HHC	Ft. Meade, Md.	64	0
902 MI Group CI, Aug	Ft. Meade, Md.	3	36
CI SS Support Battalion	Ft. Meade, Md.	166	72
USA Foreign CI Activity	Ft. Meade, Md.	39	17
INSCOM MI CI Detachment	Pentagon	20	1
Act MI Battalion CI/CE	Presidio, San Francisco, Calif.	180	17
Det INSCOM MI (CI)	Alexandria, Va.	9	3

Note: Total authorized INSCOM personnel as of December 31, 1990, was as follows: 1,696 officers, 755 warrant officers, 11,667 enlisted men and women, and 2,254 civilians, for a total of 16,372 men and women.

Source: Department of the Army, MOFI-ZB-I, *Department of the Army Force Accounting System Active Army Troop List*, December 31, 1990.

Figure 4-4.   Organization of the Intelligence and Threat Analysis Center.

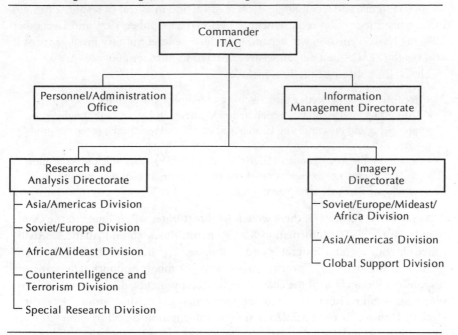

Source: *Department of Defense Telephone Directory, April 1994* (Washington, D.C.: U.S. Government Printing Office, 1994), pp. O-74 to O-75.

installations (e.g., nuclear weapons depots). The directorate also conducts imagery exploitation in support of contingency planning, military operations, special operations, training, and exercises—identifying geographical features that can provide cover for special operations infiltrators or impediments to the advance of a brigade.[23]

One ITAC project, the Army Intelligence Survey (AIS), started around 1985, centers on producing a six-volume study on each of thirty-one countries. The AIS will provide operational commanders with basic data to use in contingency planning. An earlier ITAC effort, *Combat Elements of the North Korean Army,* was credited by ITAC with influencing President Carter's decision to halt the withdrawal of U.S. troops from South Korea.[24]

The National Ground Intelligence Center (NGIC), located in Charlottesville, Virginia, was established in 1962 as the Foreign Science and Technology Center (FSTC) by consolidating the intelligence offices of the individual Army technical services—among them Signal, Ordnance, Quartermaster, Engineering, and Chemical services. It was redesignated as the NGIC during 1994. As of 1982 it had a total of 570 personnel and a budget of more than $20 million. As noted above, it now operates as a subordinate command of INSCOM. The NGIC's mission is to "produce scientific and technical intelligence concerning sciences, ground force weapon systems, and technologies (less medical and missiles) in response to valid intelligence production requirements." Between September 1994 and December 1995 the NGIC's mission will expand to include general military intelligence as it absorbs the ITAC. Total personnel are expected to number 800.[25]

The NGIC's specific functions include:

- identifying and projecting the scientific and technical threat to the U.S. Army;
- forecasting foreign military research, development, and acquisition trends;
- producing and disseminating all-source scientific and technical intelligence products;
- managing the Army Foreign Materiel Program (FMP) to include the acquisition and exploitation of foreign materiel and the dissemination of the resulting data;
- producing Foreign Target Signatures data.[26]

As shown in Figure 4-5, there were four directorates subordinate to the Commander of the FSTC: Information Management, Research and Analysis, Intelligence Operations, and Programs and Resources. The Research and Analysis Directorate, through its Combat Arms and Combat Support Divisions, is responsible for analysis of the characteristics, components, deployment, and employment of all combat arms and support systems. The directorate's Electronic Systems Division is responsible for similar information on all operational electronic systems and for advanced electronic technologies, and the Science and Technology Division is responsible for assessing foreign science and technology and their potential impact on future ground force weapons systems. The Integration Division assesses foreign chemical warfare capabilities and research and development activities as well as processing current intelligence products. The Signatures Division is responsible for providing intelligence on the signatures of foreign military systems.[27]

The main function of the Intelligence Operations Directorate involves foreign materiel. The directorate's Foreign Materiel Division develops and executes activities related to the acquisition and exploitation of foreign materiel, whereas the Foreign Systems Division maintains the Army's inventory of foreign systems as well as acquired materiel, which it refurbishes as required and exploits to provide technical data reports. The directorate's Collection Management Division registers, validates, prioritizes, and levies information collection requirements as well as monitoring the extent to which they are fulfilled.[28]

NAVY INTELLIGENCE ORGANIZATIONS

Of all the military services, the Navy saw the most dramatic changes in its intelligence structure in the early 1990s. On September 30, 1991, the Navy had seven distinct intelligence organizations. On January 1, 1993, it had two.

Figure 4-5. Organization of the Foreign Science and Technology Center.

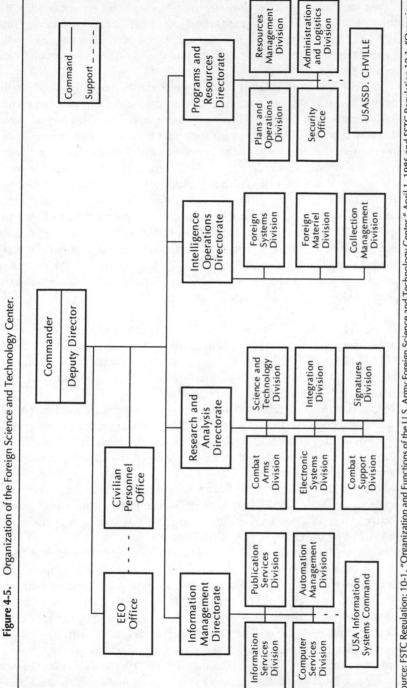

Source: FSTC Regulation: 10-1, "Organization and Functions of the U.S. Army Foreign Science and Technology Center," April 1, 1986 and FSTC Regulation 10-1, "Organization and Functions, U.S. Army Foreign Service and Technology Center," February 1, 1990.

The seven naval intelligence organizations that existed on September 30, 1991, were: the Office of Naval Intelligence, the Naval Intelligence Command, Task Force 168, the Naval Technical Intelligence Center, the Navy Operational Intelligence Center, the Naval Intelligence Activity, and the Naval Security Group Command.

The Office of Naval Intelligence (ONI) represented the apex of the naval intelligence community and was responsible for management and direction and some intelligence production. The Naval Intelligence Command (NIC), a second-echelon command, performed significant management functions. The remaining organizations, with the exception of the Naval Security Group Command, were third-echelon commands and reported to NIC. Task Force 168 engaged in overt human source collection as well as providing support to fleet technical collection operations. The Naval Technical Intelligence Center (NTIC) was the Navy scientific and technical (S&T) intelligence organization, its primary focus being the Soviet Navy. The Navy Operational Intelligence Center (NOIC) monitored naval movements, relying heavily on signals intelligence acquired by national and Navy collection systems. The Naval Intelligence Activity was responsible for providing automatic data processing support to naval intelligence organizations. Finally, the Naval Security Group Command (NSGC) performed SIGINT and COMSEC missions.

On October 1, 1991, Task Force 168, NOIC, and NTIC were all disestablished as separate organizations and their functions and personnel assigned to a newly created Naval Maritime Intelligence Center (NAVMIC). Under the new arrangement the analytical functions previously performed by NTIC and NOIC were integrated into NAVMIC's Intelligence Directorate.[29]

The consolidation was designed to achieve several objectives, including satisfying congressional and OSD instructions to consolidate and reorganize the service intelligence structures and adjusting "to current and anticipated future changes in the threat to maritime forces and to an expected redefinition of requirements levied upon naval intelligence."[30]

On January 1, 1993, an even more drastic consolidation took place. The Naval Intelligence Command, Naval Maritime Intelligence Center, and Naval Intelligence Activity were all disestablished and their functions and most of their personnel absorbed by the Office of Naval Intelligence.[31]

Although it was intended, as of fall 1991, to merge the NSGC with the Naval Intelligence Command, no such merger took place.[32] Thus, the Navy remains the only major service that has not merged its Service Cryptologic Element with one or more of its other intelligence components. However, the Navy consolidation still represents, overall, the most complete consolidation among the services—with all other intelligence functions being part of the new ONI, with no subordinate commands, and consolidation of all activities at a single location.

According to the ONI's *Strategic Planning for the Office of Naval Intelligence*, "ONI's ongoing intelligence role is now defined as providing basic and background maritime intelligence for the JICs; providing support to Department of the Navy RDT&E, acquisition and training functions; providing maritime S&T and general military intelligence support to many branches of the Government; and support for certain unique national-level programs."[33]

In accordance with its absorption of the functions of disestablished units, ONI was radically reorganized. The new ONI structure consists of the Director of Naval Intelligence (DNI), a Deputy DNI, a Chief of Staff, an Assistant DNI, nine special assistants, and eight directorates, as shown in Figure 4-6. The two key directorates are the Intelligence Directorate and the Collection Directorate.

The ONI Intelligence Directorate performs functions that were previously the responsibility of the NAVMIC Intelligence Directorate. The Intelligence Directorate, with its five departments and Newport Detachment, conducts regional studies of relevance to the Navy, produces scientific and technical intelligence on foreign naval systems, and monitors military and civil maritime activities.

The directorate's Civil Maritime Analysis Department monitors the movements of merchant ships of all nations. It also maintains a technical characteristic database of the world's merchant and fishing ships. In addition, it reports on merchant ships possibly associated with arms deliveries, counternarcotics, or terrorism. The Integration and Regional Analysis Department assesses advances in foreign naval-related science and technology, technology proliferation, and weapons systems transfers. The department also conducts analyses of foreign maritime-related doctrine and strategy that emphasize the integration of warfare disciplines. Further, it analyzes foreign geopolitical and economic developments to determine their impact on other countries' abilities to conduct maritime defense operations.[34]

The Intelligence Directorate's Strike and Air Warfare Department establishes and directs scientific and technical analysis programs to determine the technical capabilities, performance, and vulnerabilities of foreign, air, surface, and space warfare platforms and systems. The Undersea Warfare Department's functions include:

- assessing current and projected foreign acoustic and nonacoustic ASW systems capabilities;
- processing, exploiting, and reporting acoustic signals produced by foreign ships, submarines, underwater weapons, and detection systems;
- monitoring foreign submarine order-of-battle, readiness, production, and acquisition; and
- assessing foreign submarine operations and tactics.[35]

The ONI Collection Directorate, depicted in Figure 4-7, consolidated the collection units of NIC and NAVMIC. It consists of four departments (Collection Operations; Collection Requirements; Collection Policy, Plans, and Programs; Special Operations) and the Navy HUMINT Element DIA.

Figure 4-6. Organization of the Office of Naval Intelligence.

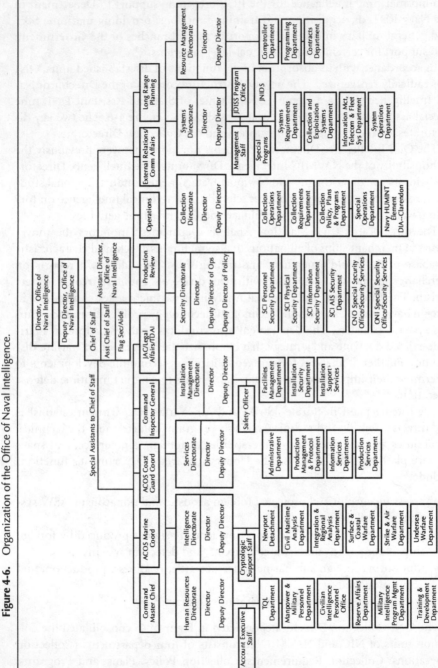

Source: Office of Naval Intelligence.

Figure 4-7. Organization of the Collection Directorate, ONI.

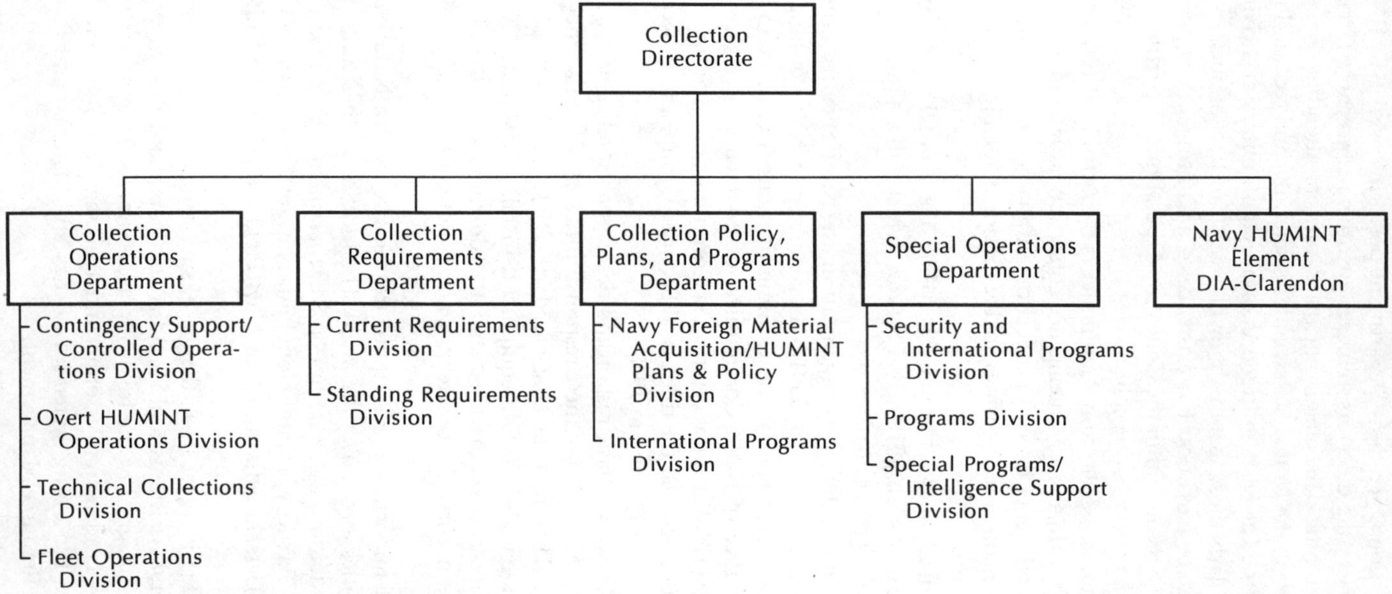

```
                          Collection
                          Directorate
                              |
  -----------------------------------------------------------------
  |                    |                    |                      |
Collection        Collection          Collection Policy,    Special Operations
Operations        Requirements        Plans, and Programs   Department
Department        Department          Department                  |
  |                   |                    |               Security and
Contingency      Current             Navy Foreign Material  International Programs
Support/         Requirements        Acquisition/HUMINT     Division
Controlled       Division            Plans & Policy
Opera-                               Division              Programs Division
tions Division   Standing
                 Requirements        International Programs  Special Programs/
Overt HUMINT     Division            Division                Intelligence Support
Operations                                                   Division
Division

Technical
Collections
Division

Fleet
Operations
Division

                                        Navy HUMINT
                                        Element
                                        DIA-Clarendon
```

Source: Office of Naval Intelligence.

The Collection Operations Department performs overt HUMINT operations, such as interviewing defectors, refugees, or others concerning targets of interest; collects biographic data on foreign naval officers attending Navy and Marine Corps schools in the United States; collects scientific and technical intelligence in Europe and the Far East; and reports on foreign military and civil naval activities—particularly those that might involve the transport of nuclear weapons, ballistic missiles, or narcotics. The existence of a Contingency Support/Controlled Operations Division within the Collection Operations Department indicates the Navy's return to clandestine collection.

The directorate's Collection Requirements Department is responsible for identifying and prioritizing key intelligence collection issues and gaps, targeting priority Navy intelligence issues for collection emphasis, and presenting Navy collection requirements and priorities to the national intelligence community and tasking authorities.[36]

As noted in Chapter 3, the Navy HUMINT Element DIA will serve as the ONI contact with the Defense HUMINT Service, which will assume control of present Navy HUMINT operations.

The other naval intelligence organization, the Naval Security Group Command (NSGC), is headquartered at 3801 Nebraska Avenue, NW, Washington, D.C. The NSGC is the descendant of the Communications Security Group (OP-20-G) within the Office of Naval Communications, which was established in March 1935. After World War II it was renamed Communications Supplementary Activities. In 1950 it adopted the title Naval Security Group, and it became the Naval Security Group Command in 1968.[37]

The NSGC has two basic responsibilities: signals intelligence and communications security. As a result of these responsibilities, NSGC personnel perform a variety of tasks. They staff the land-based HF-DF CLASSIC BULLSEYE collection sites, run sea-based collection equipment, install SIGINT and COMSEC equipment on ships and submarines, staff the downlinks for the Navy's CLASSIC WIZARD ocean surveillance satellites, and conduct COMSEC monitoring operations.

The most important NSGC units are the twenty-five Naval Security Group (NSG) activities spread over the world. The location of these units is listed in Table 4-2. In addition, there are five NSG Departments (Diego Garcio, British Indian Ocean Territory; Guam; Honolulu, Hawaii; Rota, Spain; and San Diego), seven NSG Detachments, and four NSG Field Offices in the United States and abroad.[38]

As indicated in Figure 4-8, there are, subordinate to the Commander of the NSGC, several Assistants and six Assistant Commanders. The Assistant Commanders are assigned to the following areas: Special Operations (i.e., SIGINT); Total Quality Leadership; Personnel and Training; Telecommunications and Automatic Data Processing Systems; Logistics and Material; and Plans, Programs, Budget, and Resource Management.[39]

Table 4-2. NSGC Activities and Detachments.

NSGC Activities	NSGC Detachments
Adak, Alaska	Yokosuka, Japan
Anchorage, Alaska	Barbers Point, Hawaii
Winter Harbor, Maine	Brunswick, Maine
Augsburg, Germany	Crane, Indiana
Charleston, South Carolina	London, United Kingdom
Edzell, United Kingdom	Norfolk, Virginia
Fort Meade, Maryland	Monterey, California
Galeta Island, Panama	
Groton, Connecticut	
Guantanamo Bay, Cuba	
Hanza, Japan	
Homestead, Florida	
Kamiseya, Japan	
Keflavik, Iceland	
Key West, Florida	
Kunia, Hawaii	
Medina Annex, Lackland AFB, Texas	
Misawa, Japan	
Naples, Italy	
Northwest, Virginia	
Pearl Harbor, Hawaii	
Pyong Taek, Republic of Korea	
Sabana Seca, Puerto Rico	
Terceira, Portugal	

Source: "United States Navy Plain Language Address Directory," in United States Military Communications-Electronics Board, USMCEB Publication No. 6, Issue 25, *Message Address Directory* (Washington, D.C.: U.S. Government Printing Office, January 30, 1993), pp. 41–42.

Subordinate to the Assistant Commander for Special Operations are the Shore Operations, Fleet Support Ocean Surveillance, Ocean Surveillance Systems, and Special Technology Divisions. The Shore Operations Division manages fixed systems such as the various circularly disposed antenna arrays for ocean surveillance. The Fleet Support Division directs Navy SIGINT operations based on ships, such as the CLASSIC OUTBOARD operations. The Ocean Surveillance Systems Division manages the Navy's High Frequency Direction Finding system in support of ocean surveillance programs. The Special Technology Division manages the CLASSIC WIZARD/PARCAE/Advanced PARCAE ocean surveillance satellite program.[40]

AIR FORCE INTELLIGENCE ORGANIZATIONS

Two Air Force organizations perform departmental intelligence functions: the Office of the Assistant Chief of Staff, Intelligence (OACS, I), and the Air Intelli-

Figure 4-8.   Organization of the Naval Security Group Command.

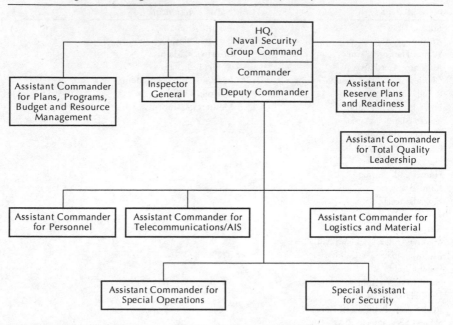

Source: *Department of Defense Telephone Directory, April 1994* (Washington, D.C.: U.S. Government Printing Office, 1994), p. O-146.

gence Agency (AIA). A third Air Force intelligence unit, the Air Force Technical Applications Center (AFTAC), serves the entire intelligence community.

OACS, I, at the apex of the Air Force intelligence community, directs and reviews the activities of the AIA. Subordinate to the Assistant Chief of Staff for Intelligence and his Deputy are, as shown in Figure 4-9, two directorates—Plans and Requirements and Resource Management.[41]

The Directorate of Plans and Requirements evaluates, validates, and prioritizes intelligence requirements levied on the U.S. Air Force (USAF) and national technical collection systems; validates requirements for developing, acquiring, integrating, and applying intelligence collection systems; and manages special reconnaissance and collection operations.[42]

The OACS, I, is primarily a management organization aimed at directing the work of the Air Intelligence Agency with respect to collection and analysis, with the Assistant Chief of Staff for Intelligence representing the Air Force in dealings with the rest of the U.S. intelligence community. This framework was dictated by a 1971 directive issued by the Secretary of the Air Force mandating reassignment of Air Staff operating and support functions to other organizations. In response to this directive the Air Force Intelligence Service (AFIS) was established on June

Figure 4-9. Organization of the Assistant Chief of Staff, Intelligence, U.S. Air Force.

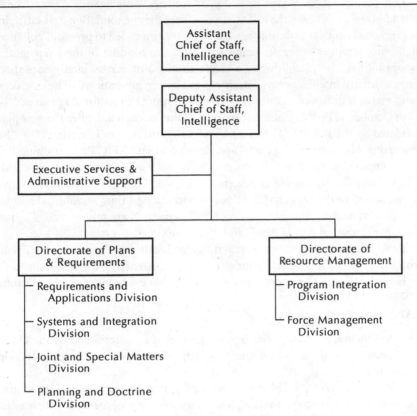

Source: *Department of Defense Telephone Directory, April 1994* (Washington, D.C.: U.S. Government Printing Office, 1994), pp. O-168 to O-169.

27, 1972. In 1988 the AFIS's status was upgraded, and it became the Air Force Intelligence Agency (AFIA). On October 1, 1991, as part of a reorganization of Air Force intelligence activities, it became the Air Force Intelligence Support Agency (AFISA).[43]

A second part of that October 1 reorganization involved the establishment of the Air Force Intelligence Command (AFIC) by merging the Electronic Security Command, the Foreign Technology Division of the Air Force Systems Command, the Air Force Special Activities Center and other elements of the AFIA, and (apparently) the Air Force Technical Applications Center. The result was the creation of an Air Force equivalent of INSCOM that combined SIGINT functions with intelligence production and HUMINT functions in the same organization. And, like INSCOM, the AFIC had a center located a significant distance from head-quarters that had its own identity and produced S&T intelligence.

In addition to fulfilling the ASD C^3I's mandate for consolidation and satisfying congressional oversight committees, the AFIC was intended to provide "enhanced intelligence support to theater commanders in the conduct of their warfighting responsibilities" by establishing "a single focal point across intelligence disciplines to satisfy intelligence requirements to support operations." The new command was also designed to improve Air Force support to national agencies.[44]

On October 1, 1993, yet another reorganization occurred. Under the new plan, mandated by the June 15, 1993, HQ USAF Program Action Directive 93-8, "Restructuring Air Force Intelligence," and detailed in HQ AFIC Programming Plan 93-01, *Establishment of the Air Force Intelligence Field Operating Agency*,[45] the AFIC became the Air Intelligence Agency (AIA) and HUMINT operations were to be transferred to the Defense HUMINT Service. In addition, an internal restructuring and renaming of the remaining AFIC elements were undertaken. The present organization of AIA is shown in Figure 4-10.

The AIA has major units at several different locations. The 497th Intelligence Group (IG) at Bolling AFB, Washington, D.C., is essentially the successor to the Air Force Intelligence Support Agency (AFISA) that existed just prior to October 1, 1993.

AFISA functions included:

- monitoring, analyzing, and reporting on hostile actions against the United States or its allies and on trends and implications of worldwide developments;
- preparing current and long-range intelligence assessments related to arms control and military, political, and economic developments in [Russia, Europe,] the Middle East, Africa, Asia, and the Western Hemisphere;
- providing intelligence support to the weapons systems acquisition process;
- monitoring, coordinating, and providing guidance on U.S. Air Force scientific and technical intelligence production;
- handling matters concerning the full range of targeting issues, including target development, weaponeering, target materials, and mapping, charting, and geodesy; and
- managing all U.S. Air Force Sensitive Compartmented Information (SCI) security functions.[46]

The AFISA, which had about 425 employees, consisted—as is shown in Figure 4-11—of several administration and support offices and six directorates.[47]

The Directorate of Assessments consisted of nine divisions. The Acquisition Support Division provided threat support to the Air Force Acquisition Executive. The Special Tasking Division reviewed and validated requirements to be placed on U.S. space imagery systems and exploitation organizations on behalf of the Air

85

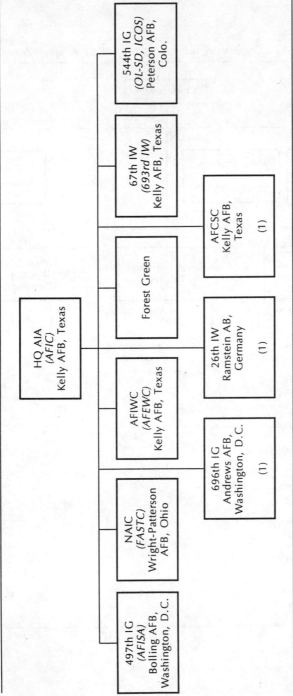

Figure 4-10. Organization of the Air Intelligence Agency.

Note: The chart indicates the basic structure for the newly formed Air Intelligence Agency. Organization names are shown followed by their former designations. (1) indicates proposed inactivation.

Source: Gabriel Marshall, "FOA Becomes Fact," *Spokesman,* November 1993, p. 8.

Figure 4-11. Organization of the Air Force Intelligence Support Agency.

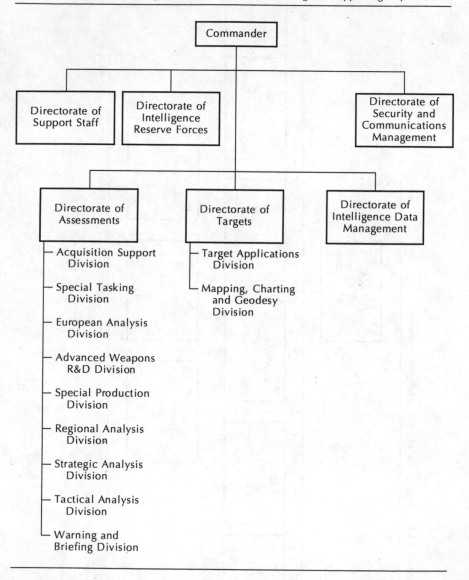

Force and represented the Air Force to the Central Imagery Tasking Authority (CITA) and its subcommittees.[48]

The European Analysis Division monitored, analyzed, and reported on hostile intent or actions against the United States or its allies and on trends and implications of European political and military doctrinal developments. It also analyzed European economic, military, and political affairs and represented the Air Force during the preparation of national intelligence documents dealing with European political, military, economic, and arms control issues.[49]

The Advanced Weapons R&D Division was responsible for assessments concerning foreign aircraft and missiles, radars, C^3 systems, basic and applied research, and technologies with "weaponization potential." The Special Production Division's responsibilities were classified, but they probably were the same as those of the AFIA's Special Studies Division, which in 1984 presented briefings and participated in discussions with the purpose of "resensitizing" the U.S. intelligence community and policymakers to foreign denial and deception activity. In that year the division also continued to fund research projects on denial and deception. One of those studies, performed by the Federal Research Division of the Library of Congress, focused on Soviet concepts of camouflage, concealment, and deception. A second study—carried out by the Arnold Engineering Development Center—analyzed camouflage, concealment, and deception activity at a classified facility in the Soviet Union.[50]

The Regional Analysis Division prepared current and estimative intelligence assessments on military, air, and air defense forces as well as on political, economic, and cultural developments in the Asia Pacific, the Middle East, Africa, and Latin America. The Strategic Analysis Division monitored and validated Air Force intelligence production on strategic missiles and bombers, space systems, nuclear weapons, and directed energy weapons. It also provided memos and briefings to the Secretary of the Air Force and the Air Force Chief of Staff on current trends and projections in strategic systems and their threat. In addition, it provided technical intelligence on strategic systems to arms control policymakers, acquisition program managers, and operational commands.[51]

The Tactical Analysis Division reported on the technical characteristics, capabilities, and employment strategies for all foreign tactical weapons systems. It examined chemical and biological weapons developments, air base operability issues, and Russian Air Force capabilities, tactics, and training. The Warning and Briefing Division provided around-the-clock Air Force indications and warning representation at the National Military Intelligence Center. The representative was responsible for satisfying Air Force requirements for intelligence pertinent to crises or potential crises.[52]

The Directorate of Targets (with a Target Applications Division and a Mapping, Charting and Geodesy Division) provided input to forces structure planning and reviews RDT&E, acquisition, and operational effectiveness of weapons systems and munitions. It also established, validated, and maintained MC&G requirements and assessed MC&G data utility for satisfying current and future weapons system needs.[53]

Under the October 1, 1991, restructuring of Air Force intelligence, the Air Force Systems Command Foreign Technology Division became the Foreign Aerospace Science and Technology Center (FASTC) and was placed under AFIC supervision. On October 1, 1993, the National Air Intelligence Center (NAIC) was formed by the functional (although not geographic) consolidation of the FASTC with the Air Combat Command's 480th Air Intelligence Group, which performed imagery interpretation tasks.[54]

The Foreign Aerospace Science and Technology Center was first established in 1917 as the Foreign Data Section of the Airplane Engineering Department and was soon transferred from Washington, D.C., to Dayton, Ohio. It was subsequently renamed the Technical Data Section (1927), the Technical Data Laboratory (1942), T-2 (Intelligence) of the Air Technical Service Command (1945), the Air Technical Intelligence Center (1951), and the Foreign Technology Division (FTD).[55]

In 1947 all nonintelligence functions were removed from FASTC's mission statement. The FASTC's major areas of technical intelligence activity included the prevention of technological surprise, the advancement of U.S. technology by use of foreign technology, the identification of weaknesses in foreign weapons systems, and the use of certain design traits of foreign weapons systems as indicators of strategic intent.[56]

As indicated in Figure 4-12, the main body of the FASTC consisted of four directorates: Data Exploitation, Mission Support, Technical Services, and Technical Assessments. The Directorate of Data Exploitation (with MASINT Exploitation, Imagery Exploitation, Data Integration, Literature Exploitation, Foreign Materiel, and Signals Exploitation Divisions) "acquires, processes, analyzes, and integrates intelligence data and information on foreign weapons systems, subsystems and technologies into products and services required to support the Technical Assessments Directorate and selected external S&TI [Scientific and Technical Intelligence] community customers."[57]

The Directorate of Technical Assessments (with Aerodynamic Systems, Ballistic Missile, C³, Electronic Systems, Customer Interaction, Engineering, Space Systems, and Technology Divisions and Proliferation and Threat Modeling Research Offices) "plans, directs, and manages the production of S&T intelligence on the characteristics, capabilities, limitations, and vulnerabilities of foreign offensive aerospace systems, foreign technology development, and command, control, and communications."[58] As a result of an internal reorganization two new directorates were established—Global Threat and Customer Interaction.[59]

FASTC detachments included Detachment 3 at Lindsey Air Station, Germany, and Detachment 4 at Yokota Air Base, Japan. In addition to exploitation of international air shows, trade fairs, and exhibits, the detachments were, as of 1982, in-

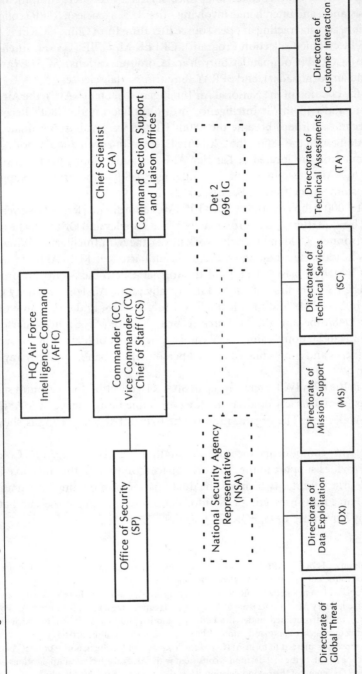

Figure 4-12. Organization of the National Air Intelligence Center.

HQ Air Force Intelligence Command (AFIC)

Commander (CC) Vice Commander (CV) Chief of Staff (CS)

Chief Scientist (CA)

Command Section Support and Liaison Offices

Office of Security (SP)

Det 2 696 IG

National Security Agency Representative (NSA)

Directorate of Global Threat

Directorate of Data Exploitation (DX)

Directorate of Mission Support (MS)

Directorate of Technical Services (SC)

Directorate of Technical Assessments (TA)

Directorate of Customer Interaction

Sources: HQ FASTC, *Mission and Organization Pamphlet* (Wright-Patterson AFB, Ohio: FASTC: July 1992), p. 1; Bruce Ashcroft, "National Air Intelligence Center Emerges from FASTC, 480th IG," *Spokesman*, November 1993, p. 12.

volved in a variety of other collection projects: HAVE THEORY (equipment, technical assistance, and interchange involving other U.S. agencies), STEP (collection, translation, and abstracting of open source literature from China), CREEK ARCH (USAFE Electronic Collection Program), CREEK MAGPIE (USAFE Intelligence Program), COOK (Command, Control, and Communications), SCALE (ground-based and airborne radar), and SPRAY (environmental sciences).[60]

With the creation of the National Air Intelligence Center (NAIC), the Air Combat Command's 480th Air Intelligence Group (previously the 480th Reconnaissance Technical Group) became the 480th IG and was made subordinate to the NAIC. Along with the 480th, the 27th Intelligence Squadron and the 36th Intelligence Squadron are located at Langley AFB, Virginia. Both squadrons provide support to NAIC customers. The 20th Intelligence Squadron provides support to NAIC customers at Offutt AFB, Nebraska.[61]

About 2,000 people work for NAIC and its subordinate elements—over 1,600 at NAIC headquarters and approximately 350 at Langley and Offutt.[62] The bulk of AIA's personnel, 9,600 individuals, work under the 67th Intelligence Wing (IW), which is headquartered along with AIA headquarters at Kelly AFB, Texas. The 67th IW largely consists of units of the former Electronic Security Command (ESC). The ESC was first established informally as the Air Force Security Group (AFSG) in May 1948 and then formally on July 1, 1948, under the same title. In October 1948 it became the Air Force Security Service (AFSS), headquartered at Arlington Hall Station, Arlington, Virginia. The AFSG of May 1948 consisted of eleven officers and some enlisted clerical personnel on loan from the Army Security Agency.[63]

Units in the 67th IW largely engage in SIGINT collection from ground stations as well as from a variety of aircraft. However, some units engage in MASINT or imagery collection. The organization of the 67th Intelligence Wing is shown in Figure 4-13.

Other AIA components include the 544th IG at Peterson AFB, Colorado (which provides support to the Air Force Space Command), the Air Force Information Warfare Center (which has the dual mission of providing information to U.S. Air Force units protecting U.S. information from compromise), and at least as of early November 1993, FOREST GREEN.[64*]

---

*The definition of FOREST GREEN is officially classified. It has generally been believed to be a program related to the enhancement of nuclear detonation detection. However, according to the official AFIC/AIA unclassified newsletter, FOREST GREEN is an AFIC/AIA *center*. In this regard it should be noted that the January-March 1992 issue of *Insight*, the classified magazine of the former Air Force Intelligence Command (obtained under the FOIA by another author), contains an article entitled "AFIC" on the intelligence command. Among the sanitized portions of the article are paragraphs listing the organizations merged to form AFIC and the locations where the majority of AFIC personnel are located. The length of the first deletion is consistent with "Air Force Technical Applications Center" (AFTAC) and the length of the second deletion is consistent with "Patrick AFB, Fla.," the location of

Along with the rest of the military intelligence community, AIA will experience personnel cuts over the next several years. Its personnel authorization is expected to decline from 16,329 in 1993 to about 14,686 in 1996.[65]

The Air Force Technical Applications Center, the third member of the trio forming the Air Force intelligence community, was first established in 1948 as the Special Weapons Squadron and subsequently became known as AFOAT-1 (the 1st Section of the Office of the Assistant Secretary of the Air Force for Atomic Energy). It received its present name in 1958. Until the 1970s its mission was classified and was described in sanitized congressional hearings only as "Project CLEAR SKY." [66]

With about 1,200 personnel, and headquartered at Patrick AFB, Florida, the AFTAC operates the U.S. Atomic Energy Detection System (AEDS). AEDS is a worldwide system with operations in more than thirty-five countries. The system uses scientific means to obtain and evaluate technical data on the nuclear energy activities of foreign powers—especially those activities covered by the Limited Test Ban Treaty of 1963, the Non-Proliferation Treaty of 1968, the Threshold Test Ban Treaty of 1974 (which limits the yield of underground tests to 150 kilotons), and the Peaceful Nuclear Explosions Treaty of 1976. The AFTAC was responsible for tracking debris from the Chernobyl disaster of 1986.[67]

In pursuit of its mission AFTAC has an extensive network of U.S. and foreign sites, including more than seventeen manned detachments, five operating locations, and seventy unmanned equipment locations.[68] In addition to those seismic and hydroacoustic sites, AFTAC collects data via airborne and space operations.

AFTAC worldwide operations are managed through its headquarters organization (see Figures 4-14 and Figure 4-15). At the next level are Direct Reporting Units and two operations areas—the HQ Pacific Technical Operations Area (at Wheeler AFB, Hawaii) and the HQ European Technical Operations Area (at Lindsey AS, Germany). In addition, the McClellan Central Laboratory (MCL) located at McClellan AFB in California plays a role in AFTAC operations. MCL is divided into three sections:

- Applied Physics Laboratory: responsible for sample preparation, optical characterization, instrumental analysis, identification of samples, and precision isotopic measurement of samples.
- Radiation Analysis Laboratory: responsible for managing the flow of samples through chemical processing techniques and the measurement of

AFTAC's headquarters. Further, the article lists "nuclear intelligence" and "USAEDS" (U.S. Atomic Energy Detection System) among the activities that AFIC manages. Additionally, the May 1993 issue of the *Spokesman* listed a dispatch from AFTAC in its "Unit News" section. It would seem reasonable to conclude that FOREST GREEN is AFTAC. At the same time, there is a direct link between AFTAC and higher Air Force authorities. A November 30, 1993, letter to the author from the Vice Commander of AFTAC stated that "AFTAC reports directly to AF/XO, Deputy Chief of Staff, Plans and Operations."

Figure 4-13. Organization of the 67th Intelligence Wing.

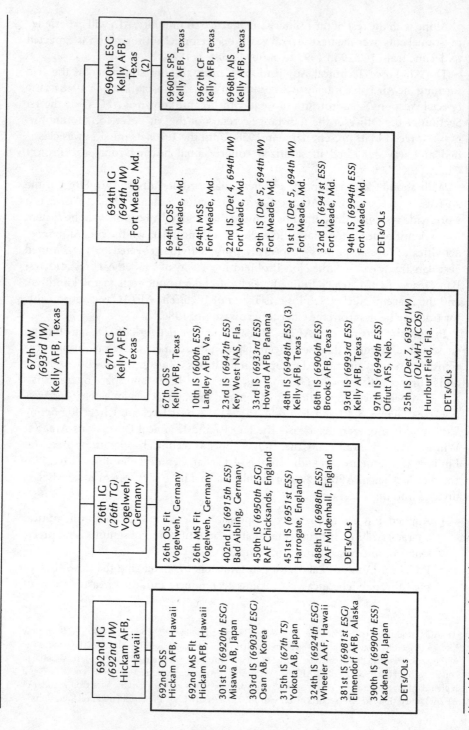

67th IW
(693rd IW)
Kelly AFB, Texas

692nd IG
(692nd IW)
Hickam AFB,
Hawaii

26th IG
(26th TG)
Vogelweh,
Germany

67th IG
Kelly AFB, Texas

694th IG
(694th IW)
Fort Meade, Md.

6960th ESG
Kelly AFB,
Texas
(2)

692nd OSS
Hickam AFB, Hawaii

692nd MS Flt
Hickam AFB, Hawaii

301st IS *(6920th ESG)*
Misawa AB, Japan

303rd IS *(6903rd ESG)*
Osan AB, Korea

315th IS *(67th TS)*
Yokota AB, Japan

324th IS *(6924th ESG)*
Wheeler AAF, Hawaii

381st IS *(6981st ESG)*
Elmendorf AFB, Alaska

390th IS *(6990th ESS)*
Kadena AB, Japan

DETs/OLs

26th OS Flt
Vogelweh, Germany

26th MS Flt
Vogelweh, Germany

402nd IS *(6915th ESS)*
Bad Aibling, Germany

450th IS *(6950th ESG)*
RAF Chicksands, England

451st IS *(6951st ESS)*
Harrogate, England

488th IS *(6988th ESS)*
RAF Mildenhall, England

DETs/OLs

67th OSS
Kelly AFB, Texas

10th IS *(600th ESS)*
Langley AFB, Va.

23rd IS *(6947th ESS)*
Key West NAS, Fla.

33rd IS *(6933rd ESS)*
Howard AFB, Panama

48th IS *(6948th ESS)* (3)
Kelly AFB, Texas

68th IS *(6906th ESS)*
Brooks AFB, Texas

93rd IS *(6993rd ESS)*
Kelly AFB, Texas

97th IS *(6949th ESS)*
Offutt AFS, Neb.

25th IS *(Det 7, 693rd IW)*
(OL-MH, ICOS)
Hurlburt Field, Fla.

DETs/OLs

694th OSS
Fort Meade, Md.

694th MSS
Fort Meade, Md.

22nd IS *(Det 4, 694th IW)*
Fort Meade, Md.

29th IS *(Det 5, 694th IW)*
Fort Meade, Md.

91st IS *(Det 5, 694th IW)*
Fort Meade, Md.

32nd IS *(6941st ESS)*
Fort Meade, Md.

94th IS *(6994th ESS)*
Fort Meade, Md.

DETs/OLs

6960th SPS
Kelly AFB, Texas

6967th CF
Kelly AFB, Texas

6968th AIS
Kelly AFB, Texas

Note: Information in parentheses is former designation.

Source: *Spokesman,* November 1993, p. 9.

Figure 4-14. Organization of the Air Force Technical Applications Center, Worldwide Operations.

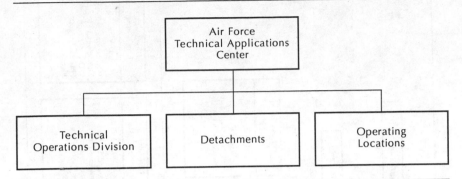

Source: Air Force Technical Applications Center.

chemically separated radioactive samples using alpha, beta, and gamma detection systems.

- Gas Analysis Laboratory: performs separation, purification, and measurement of all radioactive gases of interest to AFTAC. In particular, it supports the Nuclear Debris Collection and Analysis and PONY EXPRESS gas analysis efforts.[69]

AFTAC activities are aided by the U.S. Geological Survey (USGS) Military Geology Project, which "conducts research toward the basic understanding of geological, geophysical and hydrologic parameters of foreign sites, including those related to nuclear testing, the peaceful applications of nuclear explosions, and the geological characteristics at the sites of critical military facilities." The project's goals include determining the effects of local geologic conditions on the shock wave propagation and teleseismic yield determination of nuclear explosions; evaluating the capability of monitoring the Limited Test Ban Treaty, the Threshold Test Ban Treaty, the Peaceful Nuclear Explosions Treaty, and the Comprehensive Test Ban Treaty; and evaluating the potential for clandestine nuclear testing.[70]

MARINE CORPS INTELLIGENCE ORGANIZATIONS

Management of Marine Corps intelligence activities is the responsibility of the Assistant Chief of Staff for Command, Control, Communications, and Computer, Intelligence and Interoperability, who also serves as Director of Intelligence. There are four intelligence branches subordinate to the Director and Deputy Director of Intelligence. In addition, the Special Activities Support Office is subordinate to the Director and the Special Assistant for Intelligence.[71]

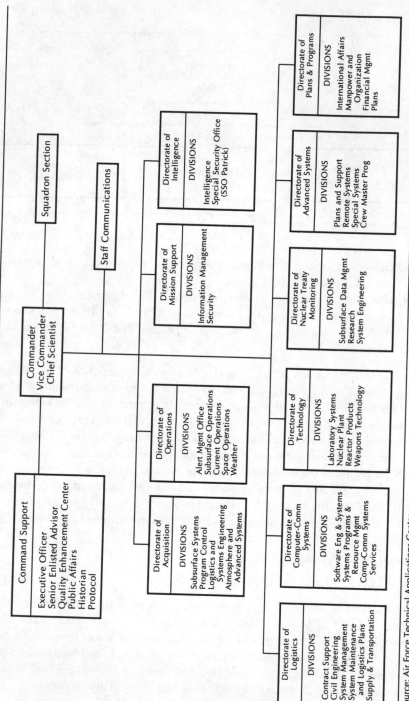

Figure 4-15. Organization of Headquarters, Air Force Technical Applications Center.

Command Support
Executive Officer
Senior Enlisted Advisor
Quality Enhancement Center
Public Affairs
Historian
Protocol

Commander
Vice Commander
Chief Scientist

Squadron Section

Staff Communications

Directorate of Acquisition
DIVISIONS
Subsurface Systems
Program Control
Logistics and
Systems Engineering
Atmosphere and
Advanced Systems

Directorate of Operations
DIVISIONS
Alert Mgmt Office
Subsurface Operations
Current Operations
Space Operations
Weather

Directorate of Mission Support
DIVISIONS
Information Management
Security

Directorate of Intelligence
DIVISIONS
Intelligence
Special Security Office
(SSO Patrick)

Directorate of Logistics
DIVISIONS
Contract Support
Civil Engineering
System Management
System Maintenance
and Logistics Plans
Supply & Transportation

Directorate of Computer-Comm Systems
DIVISIONS
Software Eng & Systems
Systems Programs &
Resource Mgmt
Comp-Comm Systems
Services

Directorate of Technology
DIVISIONS
Laboratory Systems
Nuclear Plant
Reactor Products
Weapons Technology

Directorate of Nuclear Treaty Monitoring
DIVISIONS
Subsurface Data Mgmt
Research
System Engineering

Directorate of Advanced Systems
DIVISIONS
Plans and Support
Remote Systems
Special Systems
Crew Master Prog

Directorate of Plans & Programs
DIVISIONS
International Affairs
Manpower and
Organization
Financial Mgmt
Plans

Source: Air Force Technical Applications Center.

Table 4-3. Marine Support Battalion Company Locations.

Company	Location
A	Fort Meade, Md.
B	Edzell, U.K.
C	Guam
D	Galeta Island, Panama
E	Misawa, Japan
F	Rota, Spain
G	Pyong Taek, Korea
H	Homestead, Fla.
I	Adak, Alaska
K	Pensacola, Fla.
L	Guantanamo Bay, Cuba

Source: "United States Navy Plain Language Address Directory," in United States Military Communi-cations-Electronics Board, USMCEB Publication No. 6, Issue 25, *Message Address Directory* (Washington, D.C.: U.S. Government Printing Office, January 30, 1993), p. 145.

The Counterintelligence and Human Intelligence Branch (with Plans and Policy, Terrorist Threat, and Special Project sections) functions as the focal point for coordination of counterintelligence and HUMINT matters with commands, agencies, and offices external to the Marine Corps. The Intelligence Plans and Estimates Branch participates in the formulation of JCS papers containing current and estimative intelligence. It also conducts liaison with the JCS, the DIA, the NSA, the CIA, the Department of State, and other intelligence organizations in matters pertaining to intelligence estimates.[72]

The Signals Intelligence/Electronic Warfare and C^3 Countermeasures Branch (with Plans and Policy, Manpower and Training, Electronic Warfare, and Command, Control, Communications Countermeasures [C^{3}CM] sections) functions as the focal point for coordination of cryptologic/signals intelligence matters with commands, agencies, and offices outside of the Marine Corps.[73]

Subordinate to both the Deputy Director for Intelligence and the Deputy Director for C4 is the Operational Intelligence Interoperability Branch, which is responsible for Marine Corps participation in the Tactical Exploitation of National Capabilities (TENCAP) program. The branch develops concepts and feasibility demonstrations to tactically exploit national systems capabilities and conducts operations to exploit current national systems. It also represents the Marine Corps to the Defense Reconnaissance Support Program, CITA, and the SIGINT Overhead Reconnaissance Subcommittee of the SIGINT Committee.[74]

Analysis for the Marine Corps is conducted by forty-seven Marines serving with the Marine Corps Intelligence Center (MCIC) at the National Maritime Intelligence Center (NMIC) complex at Suitland, Maryland. The center was created as a result of a 1987 study on Marine Corps intelligence requirements. The analysts conduct studies of other countries' abilities to counter amphibious landings and supply intelligence analyses relevant to weapons procurement, training, and doctrine.[75]

The Marine Support Battalion provides for Marine Corps participation in Naval Security Group Command activities. The battalion is headquartered in Washington, D.C., with lettered companies assigned to NSGC field sites throughout the world, as shown in Table 4-3.[76]

NOTES

1. U.S. Congress, Senate Select Committee on Intelligence, *Report 101-358: Authorizing Appropriations for Fiscal Year 1991 for the Intelligence Activities of the U.S. Government, the Intelligence Community Staff, the Central Intelligence Agency Retirement and Disability System, and for Other Purposes* (Washington, D.C.: U.S. Government Printing Office, 1990), pp. 4–5.

2. Ibid., p. 5.

3. Assistant Secretary of Defense (Command, Control, Communications, and Intelligence), *Plan for Restructuring Defense Intelligence,* March 15, 1991, p. 7.

4. Letter, Jane B. Sealock, INSCOM Chief, Freedom of Information/Privacy, to the author, September 21, 1992; History Office, INSCOM, *Annual Historical Review: United States Army Intelligence and Security Command, Fiscal Year 1989* (Ft. Belvoir, Va.: INSCOM, 1990), p. 9; Frank C. Carlucci, Memorandum to the Deputy Undersecretary for Policy, May 26, 1982; U.S. Army Intelligence Support Activity, Memorandum for Commander, U.S. Army Intelligence and Security Command, Subject: ROYAL CAPE (U), March 24, 1988; U.S. Army Intelligence Support Activity, Subject: Deactivation of USAISA [deleted], January 16, 1986; Msg. from CDR USAISA, Subject: Termination of USAISA and "Grantor Shadow," March 31, 1989; U.S. Army Intelligence and Security Command, Permanent Order 24-3, March 16, 1989; U.S. Army General Order No. 18, "U.S. Army Intelligence Agency," June 15, 1984; Maj. Gen. Paul E. Menoher, Jr., "INSCOM Faces Changes," *INSCOM Journal,* December 1993, pp. 2, 22.

5. *Department of Defense Telephone Directory, April 1994* (Washington, D.C.: U.S. Government Printing Office, 1994), p. O-45.

6. AR 10-5, "Department of the Army," November 1978, pp. 2-29 to 2-31; Chief of Staff Regulation No. 10-27, "Department of the Army, Office of the Chief of Staff, Organization and Functions, Office of the Assistant Chief of Staff for Intelligence," September 11, 1986, p. 21.

7. AR 10-5, "Department of the Army," pp. 2-29 to 2-31; Chief of Staff Regulation No. 10-27, "Department of the Army, Office of the Chief of Staff, Organization and Functions, Office of the Assistant Chief of Staff for Intelligence," p. 21; *Department of Defense Telephone Directory, April 1994,* p. 0-45.

8. AR 10-5, "Department of the Army," pp. 2-29 to 2-31; *Department of Defense Telephone Directory, April 1994,* p. O-45; Chief of Staff Regulation No. 10-27, "Department of the Army, Office of the Chief of Staff, Organization and Functions, Office of the Assistant Chief of Staff for Intelligence," p. 6.

9. *Department of Defense Telephone Directory, April 1994,* p. O-45.

10. AR 10-61, "Organization and Functions, United States Army Intelligence Operations Detachment," March 1, 1983, p. 3.

11. Ibid., pp. 2–3.

12. Memorandum to correspondents, undated.

13. Letter, Paul D. Sutton, INSCOM, to the author, November 20, 1992; INSCOM, Permanent Order 41-1, "United States Army Intelligence and Security Command, Intelligence Production Management Activity (Provisional), Falls Church, Virginia, 22041," April 9, 1992; INSCOM Permanent Order 41-2, "United States Army Foreign Science and Technology Center (WOKPAA), Charlottesville, Virginia 22901, United States Army Intelligence and Threat Analysis Center (W3YDAA), Washington, D.C. 20370," April 9, 1992.

14. USAINSCOM Regulation 10-2, "Organization and Functions: United States Army Intelligence and Security Command," June 25, 1989, p. 2-7-1.

15. USAINSCOM Regulation 10-2, "Organization and Functions, United States Army Intelligence and Security Command," pp. 2-7-23 to 2-7-29; *Department of Defense Telephone Directory, April 1994*, pp. O-71 to O-75.

16. USAINSCOM Regulation 10-2, "Organization and Functions: United States Army Intelligence and Security Command"; *Department of Defense Telephone Directory, April 1994*, p. O-72.

17. USAINSCOM Regulation 10-2, "Organization and Functions: United States Army Intelligence and Security Command," pp. 2-7-14 to 2-7-21; *Department of Defense Telephone Directory, April 1994*, p. O-72.

18. USAINSCOM Regulation 10-44, "United States (US) Foreign Intelligence Activity," December 11, 1992; USAINSCOM Regulation 10-43, "United States Army Foreign Counterintelligence Activity," September 1, 1989; USAINSCOM Regulation 10-62, "United States Army Intelligence and Security Command, Foreign Materiel Intelligence Group," January 16, 1989.

19. History Office, USAINSCOM, *Annual Historical Review: U.S. Army Intelligence and Security Command, Fiscal Year 1988* (Arlington, Va.: INSCOM, 1989), p. 10; T. K. Gilmore, "The 701st MI Brigade and Field Station Augsburg's Discontinuance and Farewell Ceremony," *INSCOM Journal*, March 1993, pp. 8–10.

20. USAITAC Regulation 10-1, "Organization and Functions Manual," October 15, 1986, p. 2-1.

21. Ibid.

22. Ibid., pp. 4-8 to 4-9.

23. Ibid., pp. 4-10 to 4-12.

24. Captain John Arbeeny, "ITAC: The Unique Organization," *INSCOM Journal*, February 1982, pp. 3–4.

25. *U.S. Army Foreign Science and Technology Center Unit History, FY 63–FY 77* (Charlottesville, Va.: FSTC, n.d.), p. 3; Donald B. Dinger, "U.S. Army Foreign Science and Technology Center," *Army Research, Development and Acquisition Magazine*, July–August 1982, p. 40; Paul E. Menoher, "INSCOM Thrives Despite Changes," *INSCOM Journal*, September 1994, p. 1.

26. FSTC Regulation 10-1, "Organization and Functions, U.S. Army Foreign Science and Technology Center," April 1, 1986, p. 3; FSTC Regulation 10-1, "Organization and Functions, U.S. Army Foreign Science and Technology Center," February 1, 1990, p. 3.

27. *U.S. Army Foreign Science and Technology Center*, pp. 10–11; FSTC Regulation 10-1, "Organization and Functions, U.S. Army Foreign Science and Technology Center" (1986),

Appendix D; FSTC Regulation 10-1, "Organization and Functions, U.S. Army Foreign Science and Technology Center" (1990), Appendix D.

28. FSTC Regulation 10-1, "Organization and Functions, U.S. Army Foreign Science and Technology Center" (1986), pp. G-3, G-5, G-7; Al Minutolo, "Army Foreign Materiel Program Supports DOD," *INSCOM Journal*, March 1993, pp. 28–29.

29. R. M. Walsh, Assistant Vice Chief of Naval Operations, Memorandum for the Secretary of the Navy, Subject: Disestablishment and Establishment of Certain Naval Intelligence Command Shore Activities, July 31, 1991; OPNAV Notice 5450, Subject: Disestablishment and Establishment of Commander, Naval Intelligence Command Shore Activities, and Modification of Detachments, September 13, 1991; Naval Intelligence Command, *Organization, Mission, and Key Personnel: Naval Intelligence Command, HQ, Naval Maritime Intelligence Center, Naval Intelligence Activity,* October 1991, pp. 59–80.

30. "Fact and Justification Sheet: COMNAVINTCOM Claimancy Reorganization," attachment to R. M. Walsh, Assistant Vice Chief of Naval Operations, Memorandum for the Secretary of the Navy.

31. Memorandum for the Secretary of the Navy, Subject: Disestablishment of Three Shore Activities and Establishment of One Consolidated Shore Command, December 1, 1992; *Office of Naval Intelligence, Consolidating the Naval Intelligence Command, Naval Maritime Intelligence Center, Naval Intelligence Activity* (Suitland, Md.: ONI, January 7, 1993).

32. Maj. Herbert M. Strauss, *Status Report: Strengthening Defense Intelligence* (Washington, D.C.: OASD [C³I], 1991), p. 4.

33. Office of Naval Intelligence, *Strategic Planning for the Office of Naval Intelligence: Vision and Direction for the Future,* July 1992, p. 2.

34. Naval Intelligence Command, *Organization, Mission, and Key Personnel,* October 1991, pp. 60, 62.

35. Naval Intelligence Command, *Organization, Mission, and Key Personnel,* p. 68.

36. Ibid., p. 90.

37. HQNSGINST C5450.2D, *Naval Security Group Command Headquarters Organizational Manual,* September 17, 1986, pp. v–vi.

38. United States Military Communications-Electronics Board, USMCEB Publication No. 6, Issue 25, *Message Address Directory* (Washington, D.C.: U.S. Government Printing Office, January 30, 1993), pp. 41–42.

39. *Department of Defense Telephone Directory, April 1994,* p. O-146.

40. HQNSGINST C5450.2D, *Naval Security Group Command Headquarters Organizational Manual,* pp. G50-4 to G50-8.

41. *Department of Defense Telephone Directory, April 1994,* p. O-168.

42. U.S. Air Force, *Headquarters Publication 2-1: Organization and Functions Chartbook,* March 1986, pp. 6-22 to 6-24.

43. "Air Force Intelligence Service," *Air Force Magazine,* May 1982, p. 126.

44. Department of the Air Force, "Air Force Creates New Intelligence Command," June 6, 1991.

45. HQ USAF, "Basic Plan to HQ USAF Program Action Directive (PAD) 93-8, Restructuring Air Force Intelligence," June 15, 1993; Headquarters, Air Force Intelligence Command, HQ AFIC Programming Plan 93-01, *Establishment of the Air Force Intelligence Field Operating Agency,* August 17, 1993.

46. HQ USAF, AFR 23-45, "Air Force Intelligence Support Agency," March 31, 1992.

47. "Air Force Intelligence Service," *Air Force Magazine*, May 1987, p. 145; *Department of Defense Telephone Directory, August 1993* (Washington, D.C.: U.S. Government Printing Office, 1993), pp. O-162 to O-163; "USAF Personnel Strength by Commands, FOAs, and DRUs," *Air Force Magazine*, May 1993, p. 30.

48. AFISAR 23-1, "Organization and Functions: Air Force Intelligence Support Agency (AFISA)," June 18, 1992, p. C-3.

49. Ibid., p. C-4.

50. Ibid., p. C-5; Diane T. Putney, *History of the Air Force Intelligence Service, 1 January–31 December 1984, Volume 1, Narrative and Appendices* (Ft. Belvoir, Va.: AFIS, n.d.), pp. 38, 44.

51. AFISAR 23-1, "Organization and Functions: Air Force Intelligence Support Agency (AFISA)," pp. C-5 to C-6.

52. Ibid., p. C-7.

53. Ibid., p. F-2.

54. Bruce Ashcroft, "National Air Intelligence Center Emerges from FASTC, 480th IG," *Spokesman*, November 1993, p. 12.

55. *FTD 1917–1967* (Dayton, Ohio: FTD, 1967), pp. 8, 10, 12, 22, 26.

56. Col. Robert B. Kalisch, "Air Technical Intelligence," *Air University Review* 12 (July–August 1971): 2–11 at 7, 9.

57. Foreign Aerospace Science and Technology Center, FASTCP 23-4, *HQ FASTC Mission and Organization Pamphlet*, July 1992, p. 4.

58. Ibid., p. 27.

59. Ashcroft, "National Air Intelligence Center Emerges from FASTC, 480th IG."

60. Bill Stacy, *History of the Foreign Technology Division (AFSC), 1 October 1986–30 September 1987, Fiscal Year 1987, Volume 1, Narrative* (Wright-Patterson AFB, Ohio: FTD, 1988), p. 2; HQ FTD, FTD Regulation 200-5, "Detachments 3 and 4 Reporting," June 4, 1982, Attachment 1.

61. Ashcroft, "National Air Intelligence Center Emerges from FASTC, 480th IG."

62. Ibid.

63. Gabriel Marshall, "FOA Becomes Fact," *Spokesman*, November 1993, p. 8; *Electronic Security Command: Master of the Electronic Battlefield* (San Antonio, Tex.: ESC, n.d.), p. 1; "USAF Personnel Strength by Commands, SOAs and DRUs," *Air Force Magazine*, May 1987, p. 81.

64. Marshall, "FOA Becomes Fact"; Dave Doenges and Christy Leader, "AFIWC Combines AFEWC, AFCSC," *Spokesman*, November 1993, pp. 10–11; Dave Doenges, "FOA Structure Outlined," *Spokesman*, August 1993, pp. 6, 13.

65. Doenges, "FOA Structure Outlined."

66. U.S. Congress, Senate Committee on Appropriations, *Department of Defense Appropriations, FY 1973, Part 4* (Washington, D.C.: U.S. Government Printing Office, 1972), pp. 364–65; "Air Force Technical Applications Center," *Air Force Magazine*, May 1987, pp. 165–66.

67. "Air Force Technical Applications Center," pp. 165–66; "USAF Personnel Strength by Commands, FOAs, and DRUs."

68. "Air Force Technical Applications Center."

69. 3400 Technical Training Wing, *Introduction to Detection Systems* (Lowry AFB, Colo.: 3400 TTW, October 18, 1984), p. 16; Air Force Technical Applications Center, CENR 23-1, *Organization and Functions ChartBook (U)*, July 31, 1991, p. 34.

70. U.S. Geological Survey, "The USGS Military Geology Project," December 1992. On the USGS-AFTAC relationship, see *Memorandum of Agreement Between the Air Force Technical Applications Center and the United States Geologic Survey*, April 6, 1990.

71. MCO P5400.45, *Headquarters Marine Corps Organization Manual (HQMCORGMAN)*, May 15, 1989, p. 7-5.

72. Ibid., p. 7-47.

73. Ibid, pp. 7-51 to 7-55.

74. Ibid., p. 7-13.

75. Neil Munro, "Center Will Spearhead Marines' Data Analysis," *Defense News*, January 20, 1992, p. 12.

76. "Marine Corps Intelligence," *Military Intelligence*, July–September 1983, pp. 12ff.

5
UNIFIED COMMAND
INTELLIGENCE ORGANIZATIONS

In addition to the intelligence functions performed by organizations reporting to the headquarters of the Department of Defense and the military services, a substantial intelligence capability is maintained within the unified military commands.

The unified commands consist of forces drawn from all the military services. Some unified commands focus on a specific region of the world. The regional unified commands are the Atlantic Command, Central Command, European Command, Pacific Command, and Southern Command. Unified commands not based on specific regions include the U.S. Space Command, the U.S. Special Operations Command, the U.S. Strategic Command, and the U.S. Transportation Command. The present unified command structure is shown in Figure 5-1, and the geographic responsibilities of the relevant unified commands are shown in Figure 5-2.

Until 1991, intelligence analytical functions were often distributed across several unified and component command organizations.* Additionally, components of the commands were assigned management responsibilities for the on-scene aspects of national reconnaissance and other sensitive collection operations.

However, as part of the overall streamlining mandated by the *Plan for Restructuring Defense Intelligence,* the ASD (C³I) specifically required that the analysis centers of the Atlantic, Pacific, and European Commands and their components be consolidated into joint intelligence centers that would be under the control of the unified command's Commander-in-Chief. That other commands would be expected to follow this lead was clear. It was believed that such action would "not only yield resource savings through elimination of duplicative efforts but ... strengthen support to the CINC and components through improved efficiency."[1]

The plan allowed for the retention of intelligence staffs in the form of J-2 Intelligence Directorates at both the unified and component command levels in order

---

*A component command of a unified command is a particular service command. Thus, the Pacific Fleet is a component command of the Pacific Command.

to "support planning for and conduct of current military operations and to provide focused intelligence requirements statements."[2]

The formation of such joint intelligence centers meant the disestablishment of organizations such as the Fleet Intelligence Center, Pacific (FICPAC), the European Defense Analysis Center (EUDAC), and the Fleet Intelligence Center, Europe and Atlantic (FICEURLANT), and the assignment of their functions and personnel to larger joint intelligence organizations.[3] The unified command Operations Directorates were unaffected by the changes and are still responsible for monitoring reconnaissance activities in specific geographic areas.

ATLANTIC COMMAND

The U.S. Atlantic Command (USACOM, formerly LANTCOM) is primarily responsible for U.S. naval activities in the Atlantic Ocean.* The USACOM Intelligence Directorate serves as the point of contact between USACOM and external intelligence agencies and supervises USACOM intelligence analysis activities. Those activities are concentrated in the Atlantic Intelligence Command.

On August 9, 1990, the Atlantic Joint Intelligence Center (LANTJIC) was renamed the Atlantic Intelligence Command. The command combines the functions performed in earlier years by the Fleet Intelligence Center, Europe and Atlantic (FICEURLANT); the Altantic Defense Analysis Center (LANTDAC); the Fleet Ocean Surveillance Information Center (FOSIC) Detachment, Norfolk; the Atlantic Forward Area Support Team (LANTFAST), and components of the LANTCOM Intelligence Directorate.

In addition to indications and warning and current intelligence, LANTDAC responsibilities included intelligence support to joint planning, theater technical ELINT (TECHELINT) and operational ELINT production, and support to the Navy's Electronic Warfare Reprogrammable Library Program.[4]

The FICEURLANT, staffed by 388 full-time personnel, was

> responsible for gathering and analyzing a wide variety of intelligence data. Aircraft and satellite photographic data [were] studied, ship and aircraft transmissions [were] recorded and analyzed, and all other inputs from a wide variety of human and electronic sources [were] gathered and studied. This information [was] used by Atlantic Fleet ... planners in developing tactics and strategies for a range of potential enemies and contingencies. The information produced by FICEURLANT [was employed by] the fleet and many other national intelligence organizations in keeping track of potential enemy activities, weapons development and deployment, and information regarding submarines, ships and electronic transmissions.[5]

---

*In 1993 LANTCOM became USACOM with an expanded mission, including the training of U.S. military forces based in the continental United States. (Barbara Starr, "Joint Force Training Is Key Role for USACOM," *Jane's Defence Weekly*, October 9, 1993, p. 18.)

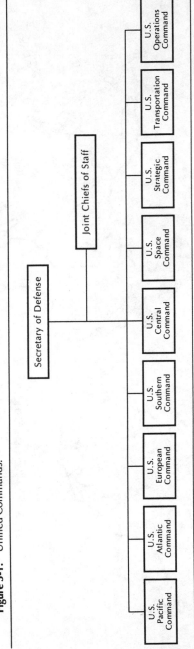

Figure 5-1. Unified Commands.

Figure 5-2. Unified Commands: Areas of Responsibility.

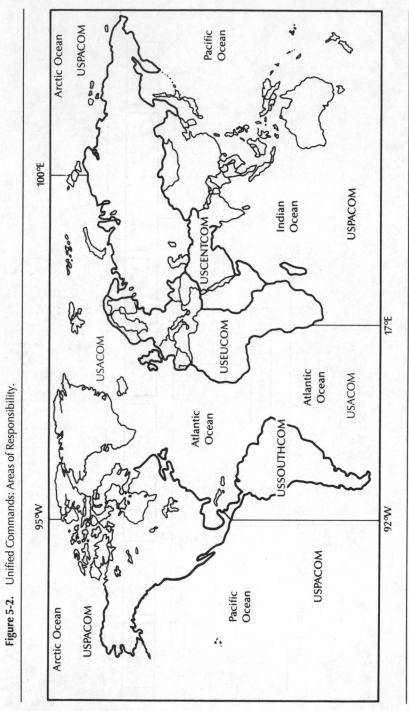

Alaska, Antarctica, Canada, Conus, and Mexico are not assigned for normal operations; JCS has cognizance over Russia.

The Fleet Ocean Surveillance Information Center Detachment at Norfolk (FOSIC), created on January 1, 1972, as the Ocean Surveillance Information Processing Center, supervised the analysis and near-real-time reporting of Soviet, Warsaw Pact, and Cuban naval, air, and aerospace activity to Commander-in-Chief, Atlantic (CINCLANT) and Commander-in-Chief, Atlantic Fleet (CINCLANTFLT) consumers. FOSIC tracked Soviet/Warsaw Pact naval activities in the CINCLANTFLT area of responsibility and conducted all-source analysis of Soviet and other Communist surface and submarine operations in the CINCLANTFLT area of responsibility. The FOSIC also analyzed Soviet aerospace operations for inclusion in the daily "Soviet Satellite Activity Message."[6]

As indicated in Figure 5-3, the Commander of the Atlantic Intelligence Command (AIC) supervises a support staff and five directorates: Direct Joint/Fleet Support, Production, Intelligence Analysis, Information/Communications Systems, and Technical Services.

The Direct Joint/Fleet Support Directorate (with Current Intelligence, Ocean Surveillance, TECHELINT, and LANTFAST Divisions) combines functions previously performed by LANTDAC, FOSIC, and Task Force 168's Atlantic Forward Area Support Team. The Ocean Surveillance Division performs the functions of FOSIC; the TECHELINT Division performs the technical ELINT production functions that were formerly LANTDAC's responsibility; the Current Intelligence Division performs the current intelligence and indications and warning functions previously performed by LANTDAC; and the LANTFAST Division provides support to the Atlantic Fleet in acoustic, imagery, and nuclear intelligence collection operations.

The AIC Production Directorate (see Figure 5-4) performs functions that were formerly the responsibility of the LANTCOM Intelligence Directorate and FICEURLANT—that is, providing products in direct support of particular types of operations—amphibious landings and air strikes.

The AIC Intelligence Analysis Directorate (see Figure 5-5) focuses on issues that may have a less direct connection with specific military operations. Its Multisource Exploitation Division focuses on regional issues. Other analytic divisions focus on counterintelligence, counterterrorism, and narcotics trafficking.

CINCUSACOM's Operations Directorate, which is not part of the AIC, is responsible for active intelligence collection operations employing submarines, surface ships, fixed arrays, and aircraft. Management responsibility is assigned to the Director of Special Surveillance Operations. The Assistant Director is responsible for reviewing USCINCLANT/CINCLANTFLT operational policy and directives concerning: (1) ocean surveillance, (2) antisubmarine warfare, (3) installation and repair of the Sound Surveillance System (SOSUS), and (4) special submarine operations.[7]

As of late 1991 a total of 559 people worked at AIC.[8]

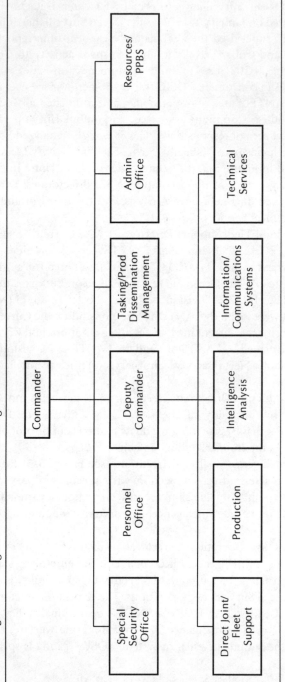

Figure 5-3. Organization of the Atlantic Intelligence Command.

Figure 5-4. Organization of the AIC Production Directorate.

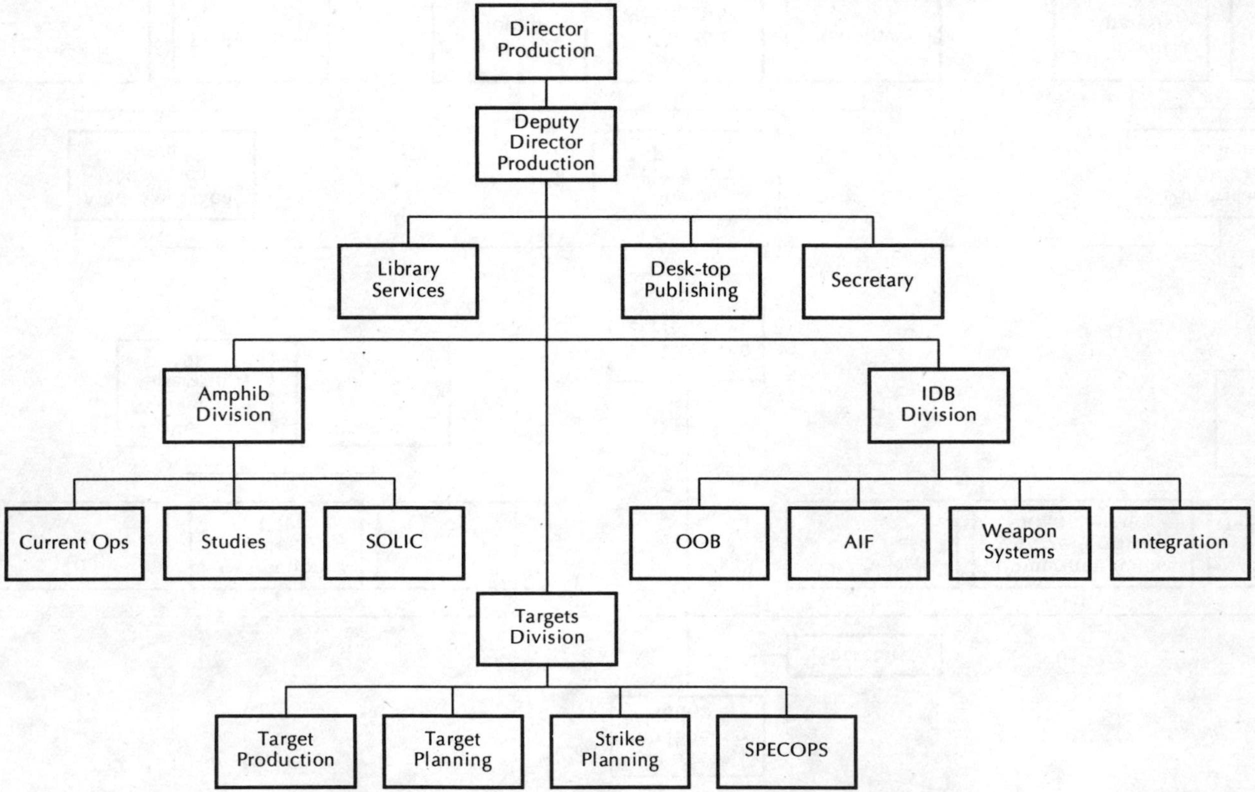

Source: Atlantic Intelligence Command.

Figure 5-5. Organization of the AIC Intelligence Analysis Directorate.

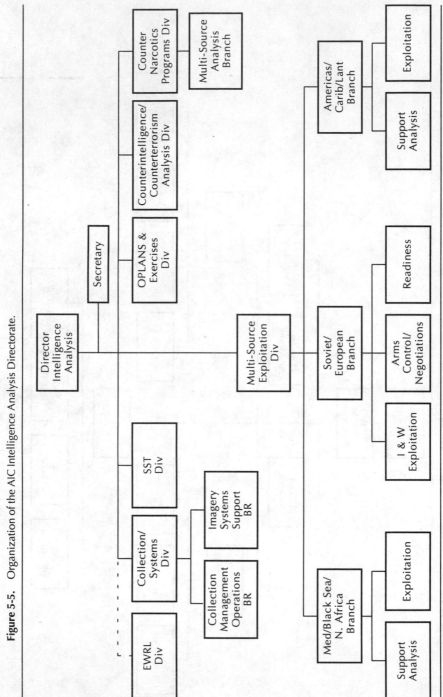

Source: Atlantic Intelligence Command.

CENTRAL COMMAND

The Central Command (CENTCOM) was formed on January 1, 1983, as a successor to the Rapid Deployment Force. It assumed responsibility for the general southwest Asia region, including the countries of the Middle East and the Persian Gulf area (Iran, Iraq, Jordan, Saudi Arabia, and Kuwait), Northeast Africa (Egypt, Somalia, Kenya, Ethiopia, and Sudan), and Southwest Asia (Pakistan and Afghanistan).[9]

The Intelligence Directorate (J-2) of the Central Command "conducts intelligence collection, targeting, planning systems development, and international exchanges to support combined exercises, contingencies, and the command's warfighting mission."[10]

The organization of the CENTCOM Joint Intelligence Center, which grew out of Operation Desert Storm, is shown in Figure 5-6. The JIC's mission is to:

- provide a deployable, all-source indications and warning, operational intelligence, and assessments capability to [the Commander-in-Chief, CENTCOM,] to meet wartime and peacetime needs
- provide mission-oriented intelligence support to component commanders
- serve as the theater collection manager
- produce finished intelligence.[11]

In the event of a war in which CENTCOM is a participant, several additional components would be established under the JIC: a Joint Intelligence Production Complex, a Joint Interrogation Facility, a Joint Debriefing Center, and a Joint Captured Material Exploitation Center.[12]

The J-2 Directorate has an authorized strength of 263, while the JIC has an authorized strength of 287.[13]

EUROPEAN COMMAND

The European Command's (EUCOM's) Intelligence Directorate, depicted in Figure 5-7, is responsible for:

- providing intelligence support to European Command headquarters, component commands, and Allied Command Europe (ACE);
- coordinating intelligence planning, collection, analysis, targeting, and dissemination activities throughout the European theater in support of U.S. and allied requirements; and
- planning, programming, and budgeting for resources necessary to conduct the European Command's peacetime and wartime missions.[14]

The directorate's Intelligence Operations Division is responsible for twenty-four-hour Indications and Warning, including near-real-time warning of terror-

Figure 5-6. Organization of the Joint Intelligence Center, CENTCOM.

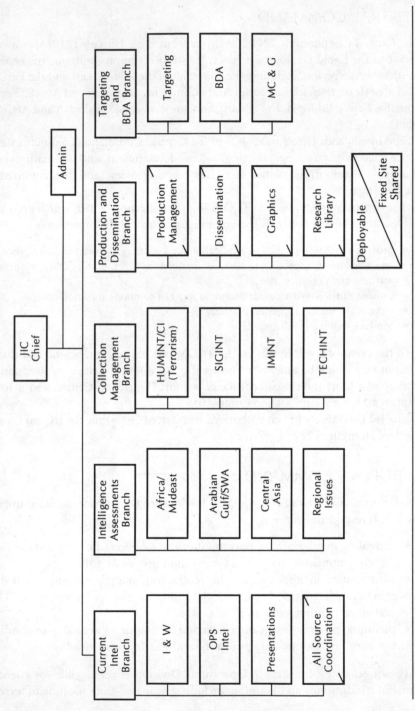

Source: Central Command, "The CENTCOM Perspective: CENTCOM/SOCOM Joint Intelligence Support Concept, 1992," n.d.

Figure 5-7. Organization of the EUCOM Intelligence Directorate.

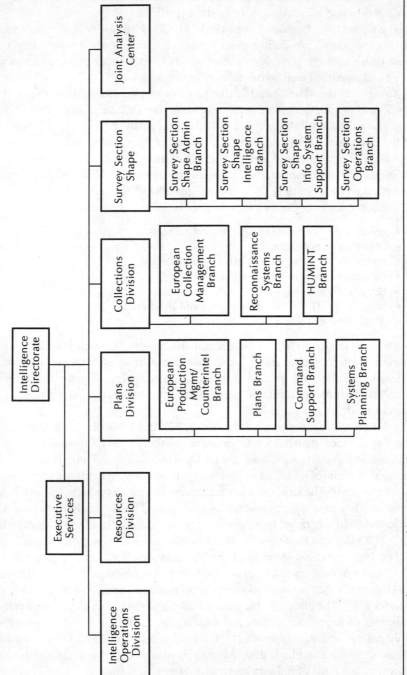

Source: ED20-1, *Headquarters United States European Command Organization and Functions*, February 8, 1993, p. O-2.

ist attack, as well as policy and planning direction for theater intelligence support to detection and monitoring of illicit drug trafficking.[15]

The Collections Division is the single EUCOM authority responsible for receiving, reviewing, validating, prioritizing, assigning, and/or forwarding European Command imagery, signals intelligence, human intelligence, and measurement and signature intelligence collection requirements.[16]

Along with the Atlantic and Pacific Commands, the European Command was specifically required by the *Plan for Restructuring Defense Intelligence* to develop plans for a joint intelligence center, called a Joint Analysis Center (JAC) in the case of the European Command. The JAC, located at RAF Molesworth, combines the functions of the European Defense Analysis Center (EUDAC), the 497th Reconnaissance Technical Group, the European component of FICEURLANT, and the analytical portions of the EUCOM Intelligence Directorate.

The Joint Analysis Center's functions include:

- theater-wide, all-source analyses and assessments;
- collection management;
- multisource processing/exploitation/dissemination;
- indications and warning (I&W) support;
- target intelligence support;
- support to NATO multinational forces and U.S. joint task forces;
- distributed production.[17]

The Joint Analysis Center's products include theater current intelligence summaries; theater regional assessments; theater threat assessments; electronic, air, defensive missile, and ground orders of battle; topical reports; I&W reports; counterterrorism, counterintelligence, and counternarcotics events reports; and exercise analyses and support.[18]

JAC operations, as shown in Figure 5-8, fall under the direct control of either the Deputy Commander for Operations or the Deputy Commander for Resources. The primary functional area is Operations, which consists of eight divisions, all but one of which are at least partially involved in intelligence production and/or analysis. The Crisis Act Team/Exercise Division conducts JAC-wide planning for crisis, contingency, and wartime support. The Target Division's functions include developing target intelligence, support databases, and target materials for JAC, EUCOM, and the Supreme Allied Commander Europe (SACEUR).[19]

The Imagery Division oversees the JAC imagery intelligence process and the production of imagery intelligence to satisfy consumer requirements. The Analysis Division is the "primary all source intelligence analysis and production division for JAC." The division's Terrorism Analysis Branch provides assessments and estimates of terrorist activities and capabilities through estimates and through daily current intelligence products. The S&T Branch of the Collection and Production Division conducts detailed analysis in support of scientific and technological assessments of military materiel, systems, or facilities.[20]

Figure 5-8. Organization of the EUCOM Joint Analysis Center.

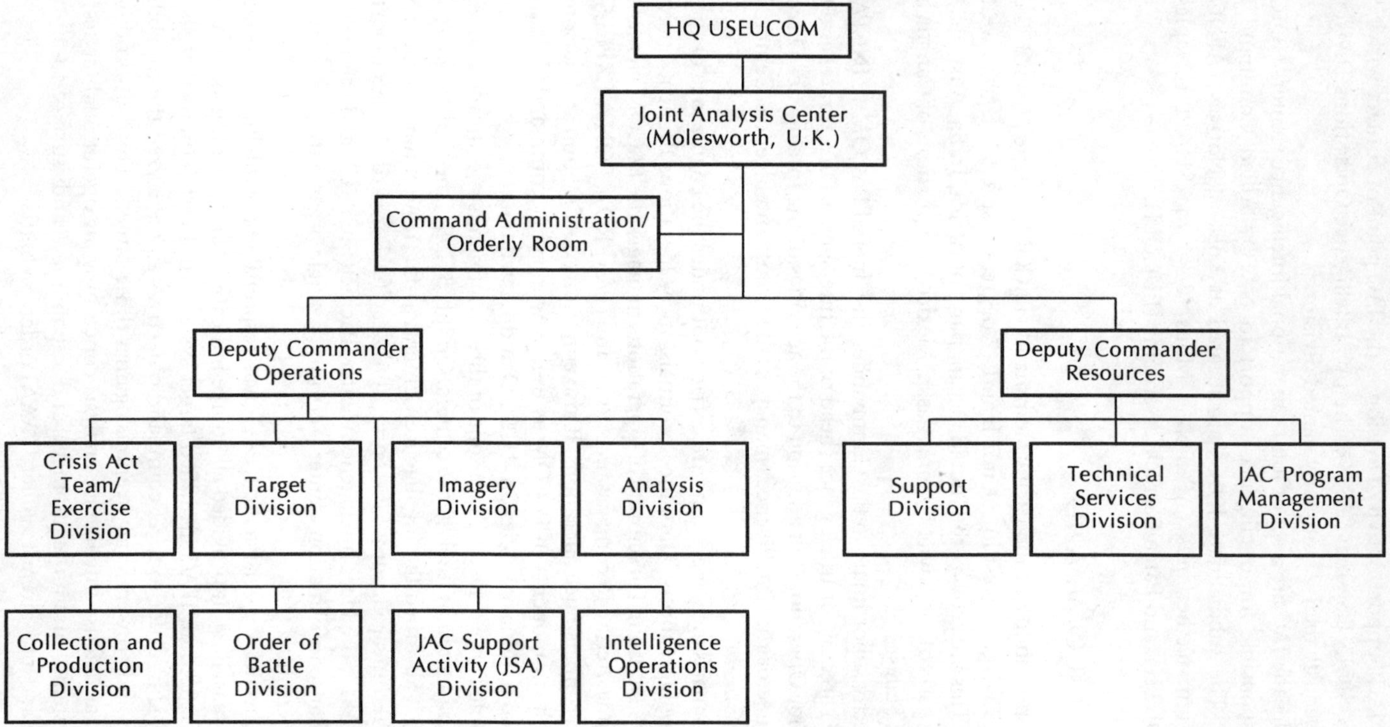

Source: ED 20-1, *Headquarters United States European Command Organization and Functions*, February 8, 1993, p. J-4-2.

The JAC Support Activity Division is the JAC point of contact with NSA and the U.S. SIGINT System (USSS). The JAC Intelligence Operations Division is simultaneously the J-2's similarly named division.[21]

Under the JAC are a set of Joint Operational Intelligence Centers (JOICs) that are responsible for intelligence support to NATO's Allied Command Europe (ACE). The subordinate JOICs are located at Kolsaas, Norway (AFNORTH); Brunssum, Netherlands (AFCENT); Mons, Belgium (SHAPE); Naples, Italy (AFSOUTH); and Patch Barracks, Germany (EUCOM).[22]

PACIFIC COMMAND

The responsibility of the Pacific Command (PACOM) extends from 100 degrees east to 95 degrees west in the north and 17 degrees east to 92 degrees west in the south. This area covers the Indian Ocean, parts of Africa, India, Australia, Japan, China, parts of the Soviet Union, Alaska, Mexico, and portions of Canada and the United States.

Directly subordinate to the Commander-in-Chief of PACOM (CINCPACOM) are the Director for Intelligence (head of the Intelligence Directorate) and the Director for Operations. In addition to the activities of the Intelligence Directorate, the Director of Intelligence manages the Joint Intelligence Center, Pacific (JICPAC).

Reconnaissance operations are carried out under the cognizance of the Directorate of Operations. Thus, the Reconnaissance Operations Branch, Current Operations Division, Directorate of Operations manages the PACOM element of the Peacetime Aerial Reconnaissance Program (PARPRO), PONY EXPRESS, and space reconnaissance operations. It also conducts coordination and liaison activities with components of PACOM as well as with other commands (U.S. and allied) and national agencies on PARPRO and related matters.[23]

As noted above, PACOM was one of three commands specifically designated to establishment joint intelligence centers. On July 3, 1991, the JICPAC was commissioned. It absorbed the Intelligence Center, Pacific (IPAC); the 548th Reconnaissance Technical Group; Task Force 168's Pacific Forward Area Support Team (PACFAST); the Fleet Intelligence Center, Pacific (FICPAC); and the Fleet Ocean Surveillance Information Center—creating a single organization with more than 1,200 personnel.[24]

Intelligence Center Pacific (IPAC) was responsible for intelligence production in six areas. First, it provided all-source indications and warning and intelligence analysis. Second, IPAC identified target systems and installations that should be destroyed in order to meet command objectives and analyzed the capabilities of nuclear and conventional weapons against those targets. Third, it produced all-source air defense intelligence analysis concerning air operational tactics, weapons systems, aircraft equipment and capabilities, and surface-to-air missile (SAM) and anti-aircraft artillery (AAA) orders of battle.[25]

IPAC's fourth responsibility was producing Ground Order of Battle files, which included information changes in combat unit dispositions, personnel, weapons systems and equipment strengths, and combat unit tactics. Fifth, the center performed electronic intelligence production functions, such as maintaining an Electronic Order of Battle for the countries in its domain and conducting operational ELINT exploitation in crisis situations, and conducted imagery interpretation.[26] Finally, it produced "all-source intelligence pertaining to the ... internal security, political, economic, sociological and scientific and technological situations in all PACOM countries."[27]

The Fleet Ocean Surveillance Information Center (FOSIC), Pacific, located at Pearl Harbor, was one of six FOSIC facilities. Others were located at Rota, Spain; Norfolk, Virginia; London; San Francisco; and Kamiseya, Japan.[28] FOSIC facilities received data from underwater sensors, satellites, ships, land stations, and ocean surveillance aircraft and processed the data to obtain a picture of naval movements in their areas of responsibility. Of particular interest before 1992 was any indication of buildups in Soviet or other hostile naval activity. The data were transmitted to both the Navy Operational Intelligence Center (NOIC) and the area Commander-in-Chief.

The FOSIC, Pacific, was responsible for analyzing navies in the Soviet Union, China, North Korea, and the allied and neutral countries in the PACOM region. The intelligence produced concerned the mission, organization, personnel, tactics, training, aircraft, missiles, space systems, naval forces, electronic systems, equipment, naval facilities, and seaborne infiltration activities of those navies.[29]

Among the products provided by the FOSIC located at Pearl Harbor were two types of reports concerning foreign shipping activities relevant to naval operations. Contact Area Summary Position Reports (CASPERs) provided information on shipping in a particular area of operations or in the vicinity of a U.S. ship or aircraft as well as on ships that could provide medical assistance. CASPERs came in four varieties. One variety gave such information about shipping in a circular area with a radius of up to 9,999 nautical miles, and a second reported on areas covering a series of circular patterns with radii as requested. A third variety of CASPER covered a polygonal area with a minimum of three and a maximum of twenty-three points defined by latitude and longitude; the fourth reported on a rectangular corridor defined by two endpoints and a corridor width in nautical miles. The Daily Estimated Position Locator (DEPLOC) provided detailed underway and in-port shipping information on specified geographic areas over an extended period of time.[30]

Whereas the FOSIC was responsible for providing intelligence on naval movements, FICPAC was responsible for providing intelligence on the naval forces of Pacific and Indian Ocean countries and on attributes of those countries relevant to PACOM naval operations. FICPAC produced intelligence related to both conventional and nuclear weapons mission planning as well as amphibious warfare intelligence materials, including Transportation, Ports and Harbors, Coastal

Landing Beaches and Helicopter Landing area studies, Amphibious Contingency Support Briefs, and Pacific Ocean and Indian Port directories.[31]

FICPAC also supervised preliminary and second-phase imagery analysis of all Soviet Pacific Fleet (SOVPACFLT) bases and deployment locations as well as supervising studies on SOVPACFLT capabilities, operations, and related matters of intelligence interest. FICPAC also produced studies, such as the Naval Special Warfare Target Intelligence Studies, in support of PACOM naval special warfare forces.[32]

The 548th Reconnaissance Technical Group, which had subordinate Technical Squadrons at Yokota AB, Japan, and possibly at Yongsan AB, Korea, was responsible for providing photo interpretation services for PACOM, Pacific Air Forces, and national agencies. The Yokota squadron served as a primary site for interpretation of SR-71 photos provided by flights from Kadena AB, Japan.[33]

Task Force 168's PACFAST was a seventeen-person unit with headquarters at Pearl Harbor, Hawaii, three detachments (Kamiseya, Japan; Subic Bay, Philippines; and San Diego, California), and representatives at Moffett Field, California; Misawa, Japan; and Ford Island, Pearl Harbor, with expertise in fleet intelligence collection, photography, and acoustic intelligence. Its specific responsibilities included monitoring Pacific Fleet photographic intelligence resources and managing the Acoustic Characteristics Analysis Program, the Portable Acoustic Collection Equipment (CLUSTER PACE), and the SUNFLYER collection programs for the Commander-in-Chief, Pacific Fleet (CINCPACFLT).[34]

The JICPAC, as shown in Figure 5-9, essentially consists of two directorates—the Directorate of Resources and the Directorate of Operations. The principal components are the two cells (the Exercise Support Cell and the Command Support Cell) and five departments (North Asia, South Asia, Trans-Regional, Combat Applications, and Operations Intelligence).

The Command Support Cell serves as the direct link between JICPAC and CINCPAC headquarters for intelligence support. It provides rapid response intelligence support and prepares intelligence briefings, summaries, and point papers. The Exercise Support Cell is responsible for coordinating analytical support for Pacific Command exercises.[35]

The North Asia Department's primary focus is the Russian Far East and Korea. Its Russian Far East and Korean Analysis Divisions conduct studies concerning the Russian and Korean geopolitical situation as well as producing air order-of-battle (AOB), ground order-of-battle (GOB), naval order-of-battle (NOB), and defensive missile order-of-battle (DMOB) documents. It also analyzes the C^3 structure, doctrine, strategy, tactics, readiness, and other aspects of the former Soviet states and Korean military organizations. The department's North Asia Division produces similar studies on China, Taiwan, Mongolia, and Japan.[36]

The South Asia Department's divisions produce similar reports on nations in South Asia, Southwest Asia/Indian Ocean, and Oceania.[37] The Trans-Regional Department, through its Collection Requirements Division, develops, reviews,

Figure 5-9. Organization of the Joint Intelligence Center, Pacific.

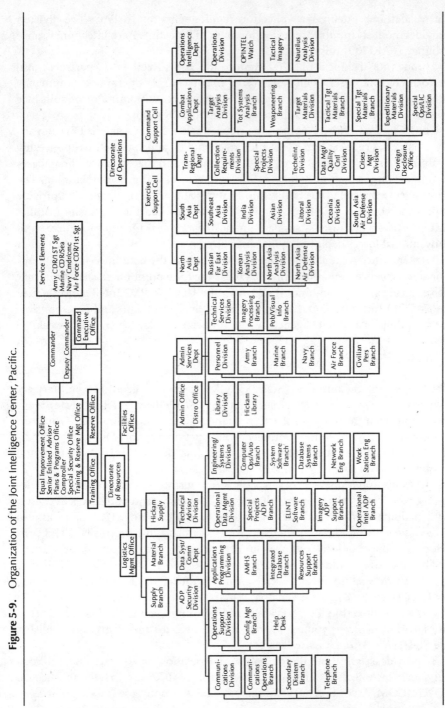

Source: Joint Intelligence Center, Pacific.

and validates all intelligence collection requirements for JICPAC. The division provides monthly inputs for the development of Peacetime Aerial Reconnaissance Program (PARPRO) missions.[38]

Through its Technical ELINT Division, the Trans-Regional Department also performs technical ELINT analysis in support of PACOM operational commanders as well as processing, analyzing, and reporting on submarine reconnaissance matters in support of the Naval Activities Support Program.[39]

The JICPAC's Combat Applications Department's Target Analysis Division analyzes targets, produces target lists and target studies, and conducts weaponeering analysis. It also is responsible for the development and maintenance of databases to support target analysis, target lists, weaponeering, and mission planning. The department's Special Projects Division analyzes all-source intelligence to provide support to counter-drug forces, and its Special Ops and Low Intensity Conflict (LIC) Division performs a similar function for Special Operations Forces and conventional forces deployed in LIC environments.[40]

The Operations Intelligence Department directs the activities of the Operational Intelligence Center (OIC). The OIC is the focal point for crucial, time-sensitive intelligence. It combines the FOSIC, the USCINCPAC Intelligence Watch, the PACOM Indications and Warning Center, and other units and is responsible for providing current intelligence twenty-four hours a day, seven days a week.[41]

SOUTHERN COMMAND

The U.S. Southern Command (SOUTHCOM) is responsible for U.S. military activities in Central and South America. The J-2 (Intelligence Directorate) is divided into four sections—Collection Management, Indications and Analysis, Plans and Security, and the Contingency Production Support Division—and directs intelligence production as well as managing the SOUTHCOM Automatic Ground Order of Battle System for Panama.[42]

The Collection Management Division is responsible for determining and delegating intelligence requirements throughout the command and serves as liaison with national agencies and the Joint Reconnaissance Center. The division also provides collection planning guidance and develops and reviews plans and programs in support of local, national, and DOD intelligence collection activities.[43]

The Indications and Analysis Division produces a variety of SOUTHCOM products—Special Intelligence Briefs, Annual Intelligence Briefs, and the Country Intelligence Study (CIS), Panama. It maintains the Travelers in Panama (TIP) File as well as operating the Indication and Warning Center. The Plans and Security Division manages command walk-in and defector programs and publishes the *SOUTHCOM Intelligence Plan*.[44]

To provide a significant photographic interpretation capability, a 480th Reconnaissance Technical Group, now part of the NAIC, was first established in SOUTHCOM. According to 1987 congressional testimony, the "tasking of the 480

RTG has changed significantly, new programs have been assigned and others expanded; the geographic area of responsibility was expanded and numerous state-of-the art equipment/systems added."[45]

The SOUTHCOM Joint Intelligence Center consists of two main subdivisions: the Indications and Analysis Center (IAC) and the Counternarcotics Division. The IAC consists of three branches: Indications and Warning, Collection Management, and Analysis. The Counternarcotics (CN) Division consists of the CN Analysis/Watch Branch, the CN Support Branch, the CN Operations/Intelligence Branch, and the Counternarcotics Branch.[46]

U.S. SPACE COMMAND

The Air Force Space Command was established on September 1, 1982, to bring responsibilities for the Air Force's space-related research, development, and acquisition and operational activities under one managerial roof. The Deputy Commander of the Air Force Space Command is the head of the Air Force's Space Division—the space research, development, and acquisition organization at El Segundo, California.[47] The Navy followed suit by establishing a Naval Space Command in 1983, and the Army established the Army Space Command, which has become the Army Space and Strategic Defense Command. To provide overall direction of U.S. and military service space activities, a U.S. Space Command (USSPACECOM) was established in 1985.

Subordinate to the Commander-in-Chief of USSPACECOM is the Directorate of Intelligence. The Director's responsibilities include:

- providing direct support to intelligence organizations of subordinate commands;
- providing threat estimates and intelligence on foreign space systems;
- formulating intelligence and counterintelligence plans, policies, and operational procedures; and
- providing advice in support of the command's Tactical Exploitation of National Capabilities (TENCAP) role.[48]

Subordinate to the Director are three Deputy Directors for Intelligence Plans, Programs and Systems; Intelligence Collection; and Foreign Military Intelligence. The Deputy Directorate for Intelligence Plans, Programs and Systems (with Intelligence Plans, Resources, Strategic Concepts, and Systems Divisions) "defines, develops, and coordinates intelligence plans, programs, and requirements." Its functions include serving as the USSPACECOM point-of-contact with respect to the acquisition of intelligence systems.[49]

The Deputy Directorate for Intelligence Collection (with Collection Management, Collection Planning, and Counterintelligence Divisions) oversees and coordinates sensitive intelligence collections for USSPACECOM and USSPACECOM component commands, manages intelligence collection planning, determines collection system requirements, and seeks to shield USSPACECOM from espionage, sabotage, and terrorism.[50]

The Deputy Director for Foreign Military Intelligence also serves as the Director of the Combined Intelligence Center (CIC) and is responsible for all substantive intelligence produced by the CIC. The deputy directorate consists of an Intelligence Operations Center (IOC) and four divisions: Integrated Threat, Space Forces, Exploitation, and CIC Operations (see Figure 5-10).

The Intelligence Operations Center, through its Current Intelligence Cell, is responsible for providing all-source operational intelligence on foreign space, missile, and air threat platforms and weapons. The center's Integrated Warning Division manages the NORAD/USSPACECOM I&W Center.

The Integrated Threat Division is responsible for intelligence analysis on foreign missile and strategic aerospace forces. The functions of the division's Missile Analysis Branch include analyzing the current and historical status of former Soviet mobile ICBM forces. The Space Forces Division maintains the Defense Intelligence Space Order of Battle documents for both Commonwealth of Independent States (CIS) and non-CIS space systems. Its Detection/SATRAN Branch analyzes foreign antisatellite systems (including directed energy and electronic warfare systems) as well as foreign intelligence satellites. The Exploitation Division assesses the day-to-day status of foreign spacecraft and aerospace and missile-related ground sites.[51]

The ground-based sensors run by the Air Force Space Command provide information to the USSPACECOM Space Defense Operations Center (SPADOC), which is responsible for:

- detecting, tracking, and providing COMBO information for space objects by employing all-source input data;
- providing real-time coordination for status and alert of U.S. and allied space assets to owners, operators, and users of interference, attack, malfunctions, and damage assessment;
- providing space object identification data for all satellites; and
- generating alert, warning, and verification of potentially hostile space-related events that affect space systems' survivability by employing all-source data.[52]

Real-time operational control of the Space Surveillance Center (SSC), which was integrated into SPADOC in December 1985, is the responsibility of the Deputy Director of Space Control, Directorate of Operations, USSPACECOM. The SSC also tasks and alerts sensors for tracking support of routine catalog maintenance, space object identification support, space launches and maneuvers, and decays and deorbits. Finally, it maintains a catalog of orbital characteristics of all observable human-made space objects that can be used to predict their position. This activity involves more than 20,000 space observations daily to monitor the status of more than 5,400 space objects.[53]

Figure 5-10. Organization of the Deputy Directorate for Foreign Military Intelligence, USSPACECOM.

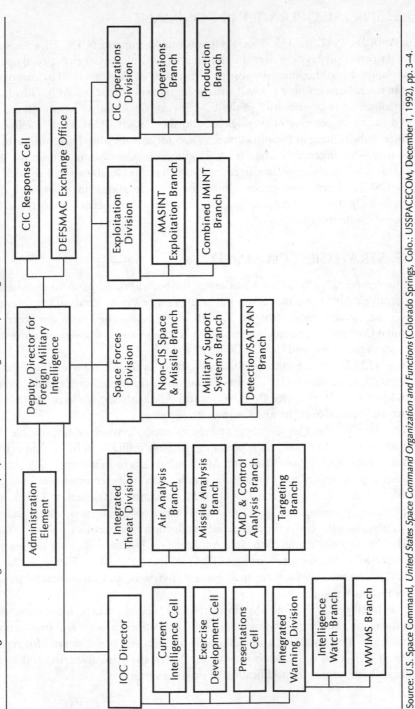

Source: U.S. Space Command, *United States Space Command Organization and Functions* (Colorado Springs, Colo.: USSPACECOM, December 1, 1992), pp. 3–4.

U.S. SPECIAL OPERATIONS COMMAND

On April 16, 1987, the U.S. Special Operations Command (USSOC) was established to exert supervision over the activities of the military service special operations units, which became component commands of the USSOC. The command began operations on June 1, 1987, with headquarters at MacDill AFB, Florida.[54]

Intelligence responsibilities in the U.S. Special Operations Command are located in the Directorate of Intelligence and the USSOCCOM Joint Intelligence Center. Subordinate to the directorate's Director and Deputy Director are three divisions—Intelligence Management; Intelligence Architecture, Programs and Systems; and Operational Intelligence—with branches as shown in Figure 5-11. The USSOC Joint Intelligence Center began operations in 1994 with five branches: Operations, Analysis, Imagery/Targeting, Intelligence Support, and Intelligence Systems Operations.[55]

U.S. STRATEGIC COMMAND

On September 27, 1991, President George Bush announced plans to disestablish the Strategic Air Command (SAC) and create two new commands to take over the SAC's functions. Operation of SAC aircraft would be assigned to the Air Force Air Combat Command, and nuclear strategic planning would be assigned to the new U.S. Strategic Command (STRATCOM).[56]

The STRATCOM's Senior Intelligence Officer is the Director of Intelligence. The Intelligence Directorate consists of four divisions: Intelligence Plans, Policy and Resources; Intelligence Production and Applications; Collection Management; and Special Security and Counterintelligence.[57]

The Intelligence Plans, Policy and Resources Division is responsible for STRATCOM intelligence policy, planning, programming, and budgeting activities. The Intelligence Production and Applications Division is responsible for intelligence production and application policy, planning, requirements management, and staff oversight. The STRATCOM Collection Management Division is responsible for managing STRATCOM intelligence collection, processing, and exploitation and establishes the command's collection management policy.[58]

The Intelligence Production and Applications Division also supervises the Strategic Joint Intelligence Center (STRATJIC). As shown in Figure 5-12, the STRATJIC has two staffs, three independent divisions, and three directorates. It employs about 900 people.

The Intelligence Systems Division's responsibilities include identifying and documenting requirements for intelligence collection, processing, production, application, data handling, and dissemination systems. The division also represents STRATCOM in its dealings with the NRO, the CIA, the DIA, and other agencies with respect to modification of existing systems.[59]

Figure 5-11.   Organization of the U.S. Special Operations Command, Directorate of Intelligence.

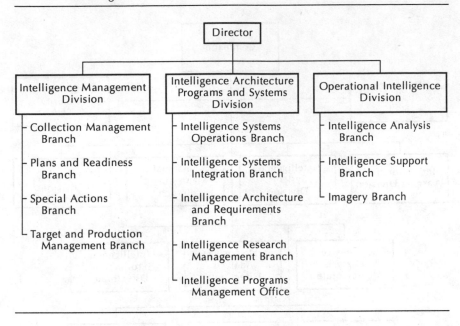

The Indications and Warning Division provides crisis management support to STRATCOM headquarters. It presents command intelligence briefings, disseminates STRATCOM daily intelligence messages, and produces Defense Intelligence Network items on topics of interest to STRATCOM. It also provides priority imagery exploitation and reporting of targets.[60]

The Trajectory Division generates all-source intelligence and related material to support the STRATCOM's military planning responsibilities, particularly the Single Integrated Operational Plan (SIOP). In addition, it performs studies of current and future U.S. ICBM capabilities.[61]

The Offensive Analysis Directorate produces intelligence assessments—based on imagery, SIGINT, and other collection methods—of foreign offensive aircraft, fixed and mobile missiles, fixed and mobile C^3 systems, and associated installations. The Defensive Analysis Directorate performs a similar function for defensive aircraft, missiles, and C^3 systems and associated installations.[62]

U.S. TRANSPORTATION COMMAND

On October 1, 1987, the U.S. Transportation Command (TRANSCOM) was activated at Scott AFB, Illinois. TRANSCOM is responsible for consolidating all U.S.

Figure 5-12.   Organization of the U.S. Strategic Command Strategic Joint Intelligence Center.

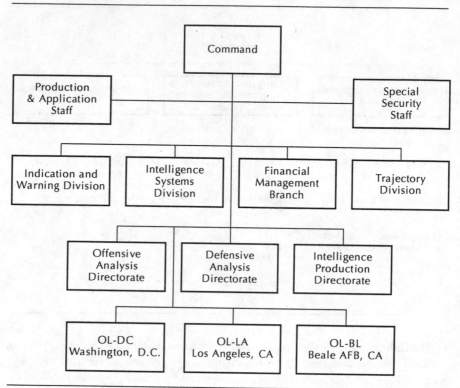

Source: U.S. Strategic Command, "Command and Relationships," August 17, 1992, p. 10.

strategic air, sea, and land transportation during war or a buildup to war and for exercising centralized control. TRANSCOM components include the Navy's Military Sealift Command, the Army's Military Traffic Management Command, and the Air Force Military Airlift Command.[63]

The Transportation Command's Intelligence Directorate develops and implements TRANSCOM intelligence policy, programs, doctrine, and organizational concepts.[64] TRANSCOM's Joint Intelligence Center (JIC) is subordinate to the Intelligence Directorate. The JIC has two divisions.

The Intelligence Production Division (with Atlantic, Pacific, Functional, Mapping, Charting, and Geodesy Branches and an Imagery Analysis Detachment) provides, along with DIA, functional management of worldwide port facility production. The Atlantic and Pacific Branches are responsible for producing intelligence on the capabilities, limitations, and vulnerabilities of transportation networks in their respective areas—including port and airfield studies, lines of communications studies, and logistic facilities studies.[65] The Functional Branch is responsible for production of intelligence on scientific and technical developments in the transportation industry, medical intelligence to support evacuation, and intelligence on threats to transportation systems.[66]

Intelligence Operations Division activities are conducted by three branches. The Indications and Warning Branch maintains intelligence indications and warning activity twenty-four hours per day, seven days per week. The Intelligence Estimates Branch produces and delivers foreign weapons system analysis for the command's aircraft and tactics development programs. It provides threat and weapons systems capability information for command, control, and communications countermeasures, electronic combat, tactical deception, and psychological operations programs. The Current Analysis Branch receives, collates, analyzes, produces, and disseminates current intelligence to the Transportation Command—particularly with regard to regional and terrorist matters.[67]

NOTES

1. Assistant Secretary of Defense (Command, Control, Communications, and Intelligence), *Plan for Restructuring Defense Intelligence,* March 15, 1991, p. 4.

2. Ibid.

3. On the disestablishment of the Fleet Intelligence Centers, see Arthur D. Baker III, "Farewell to the FICs," *Naval Intelligence Professionals Quarterly* (Winter 1992): 7–9.

4. LANTDAC msg. 25205 OZ, April 1986, Subject: Establishment of Atlantic Command Defense Analysis Center (LANTDAC).

5. U.S. Congress, House Committee on Appropriations, *Military Construction Appropriations for 1987, Part 2* (Washington, D.C.: U.S. Government Printing Office, 1986), pp. 261–62.

6. CINCLANT Instruction C5450.75, "Fleet Ocean Surveillance Information Center, Detachment (FOSIC DET), CINLANTFLT," May 7, 1986, Encl (1): Missions, Tasks and Functions Assigned to Fleet Ocean Surveillance Information Center Detachment, CINCLANTFLT.

7. USCINCLANT/CINCLANTFLT/CINCWESTLANT/COMOCEANLANT Staff Instruction 5200.1Q, "Promulgation of Commander in Chief, U.S. Atlantic Command, Commander in Chief, U.S. Atlantic Fleet, Commander in Chief, Western Atlantic Area, and Commander, Ocean Sub-Area Staff Organization and Regulations Manual," pp. 2-3-41 to 2-3-42.

8. Information supplied by Atlantic Intelligence Command.

9. U.S. Congress, House Committee on Armed Services, *Hearings on HR 1816* (Washington, D.C.: U.S. Government Printing Office, 1983), p. 955.

10. "Intelligence Community Notes," *Defense Intelligence Journal* 1 (1992): 105–12.

11. Central Command, "The CENTCOM Perspective: CENTCOM/SOCOM Joint Intelligence Support Concept," 1992.

12. Ibid.

13. Ibid.

14. European Command, ED 20-1, *Headquarters United States European Command Organization and Functions,* February 8, 1993, p. O-1.

15. Ibid., p. O-4.

16. Ibid., p. O-14.

17. European Command, *USEUCOM Plan for Theater Intelligence,* July 1, 1991, p. 2-3.

18. Ibid., p. 2-4.

19. European Command, ED 20-1, *Headquarters United States European Command Organization and Functions,* pp. U-4-7 to U-4-8.

20. Ibid., pp. U-4-9, U-4-13, U-4-27.

21. Ibid., pp. U-4-33 to U-4-34.

22. European Command, *USEUCOM Plan for Theater Intelligence,* p. 2-1.

23. Commander-in-Chief, U.S. Pacific Command, *Organization and Functions Manual, FY 86/87,* pp. 81–82.

24. Letter from K. Kibota, Chief, Administrative Support Division, Joint Secretariat, U.S. Pacific Command, to author, October 8, 1991; "The New Boy on the Block," *Naval Intelligence Professionals Quarterly* (Spring 1991): 2; "West Coast Intelligence Consolidations," *Naval Intelligence Bulletin* (Fall/Winter 1990): 22–23.

25. Enclosure (1) to CINCPAC Instruction 5400.22, "Intelligence Center Pacific (IPAC) Augmentation Support," July 23, 1979.

26. Ibid.

27. Information provided by U.S. Pacific Command.

28. U.S. Congress, Senate Committee on Appropriations, *Department of Defense Appropriations, FY 1972, Part 3* (Washington, D.C.: U.S. Government Printing Office, 1971), p. 487; U.S. Congress, Senate Committee on Appropriations, *Department of Defense Appropriations, FY 1973, Part 3* (Washington, D.C.: U.S. Government Printing Office, 1972), p. 475; Paul Bracken, *The Command and Control of Nuclear Forces* (New Haven, Conn.: Yale University Press, 1983), p. 38.

29. CINCPACFLT Instruction 5400.3M, Ch-5, "United States Pacific Fleet Regulations," March 9, 1984, pp. A 2-13 to A 2-14; A 2-18 to A 2-21.

30. CINCPACFLT Instruction 3130.6F, "Pacific Area Ocean Surveillance Report Services," November 8, 1982, p. 1-2.

31. Ibid., pp. 2-36, 2-37, 2-39.

32. Ibid., pp. 2-41, 2-43, 2-45.

33. PACAF Regulation 23-4, "Organization and Functions—Headquarters Pacific Air Forces," September 24, 1986, p. 62; PACAF Regulation 23-17, "548th Reconnaissance Technical Group," June 8, 1987; Benjamin Schemmer, *The Raid* (New York: Harper & Row, 1975), p. 254.

34. CINCPACFLT C3880.4F, "Letter of Instruction of Commander, Task Group 168.1/ Pacific Forward Area Support Team (PACFAST)," August 8, 1986, p. 1, and Enclosure 1, "Pacific Area Support Team Functions."

35. Joint Intelligence Center Pacific, *Organization and Functions Manual (JMP—Part 1),* 1993, pp. 68–69.

36. Ibid., pp. 98–106.

37. Ibid., pp. 108–17.

38. Ibid., pp. 118–25.

39. Ibid., pp. 126–28, 133.

40. Ibid., pp. 71, 125.

41. Ibid., p. 90; "The New Boy on the Block."

42. Headquarters, U.S. Southern Command Regulation 10-1, "Organization and Functions Manual," October 1, 1983, p. 7-1.

43. Ibid., p. 7-3.

44. Ibid., p. 7-4.

45. U.S. Congress, House Committee on Appropriations, *Military Construction Appropriations for 1988, Part 2* (Washington, D.C.: U.S. Government Printing Office, 1987), p. 510.

46. Joint Staff, Memorandum for Chief of Staff, U.S. Army, Subject: FY 1993 JMP for USSOUTHCOM Joint Intelligence Center, August 5, 1992, pp. B-2 to B-7.

47. "Space Command," *Air Force Magazine*, May 1983, pp. 96–97.

48. U.S. Space Command (USSPACECOM), *United States Space Command Organization and Functions* (Colorado Springs, Colo.: USSPACECOM, December 1, 1992), p. 3-5.

49. Ibid., pp. 3-2, 3-8.

50. Ibid., pp. 3-3, 3-9.

51. Ibid., pp. 3-11 to 3-14.

52. Headquarters, U.S. Space Command, *Initial Manning Document, FY 1986/87*, 1985.

53. Ibid.; "Space Defense Operations Center Upgrades Assessment Capabilities," *Aviation Week & Space Technology*, December 9, 1985, pp. 67–73.

54. Ronald Reagan, Memorandum for the Honorable Caspar W. Weinberger, Secretary of Defense, Subject: Establishment of Combatant Commands, April 13, 1987; Caspar Weinberger, Memorandum for the President, Subject: Establishment of the U.S. Special Operations Command and the Specified Forces Command, April 6, 1987.

55. Letter from Robert C. Mabry, USSOC Deputy Chief of Staff, to author, April 15, 1993; U.S. Special Operations Command, "Draft of JIC Structure," February 2, 1994.

56. "Intelligence Community Notes."

57. U.S. Strategic Command, "Command and Relationships," August 17, 1992, pp. 6, 30.

58. Ibid., p. 31.

59. Ibid., p. 62.

60. Ibid., p. 64.

61. Ibid., p. 66.

62. Ibid., pp. 63–64, 66–68.

63. James W. Canan, "Can TRANSCOM Deliver?" *Air Force Magazine*, October 1987, pp. 40–46.

64. U.S. Transportation Command, USTRANSCOM Pamphlet 20-2, "Organization and Functions," February 6, 1992, p. 12.

65. Ibid., p. 13.

66. Ibid., p. 13.

67. Ibid.

6
CIVILIAN INTELLIGENCE ORGANIZATIONS

The bulk of U.S. intelligence resources, whether in terms of personnel or dollars, lies in the hands of the national intelligence organizations and the military services. Some intelligence activities, however, are carried out by various branches of the civilian executive departments. These offices in the Departments of State, Energy, Treasury, Commerce, Justice, and Transportation collect and/or analyze intelligence on foreign political and military affairs, economic affairs, or narcotics.

DEPARTMENT OF STATE INTELLIGENCE

With the dissolution of the Office of Strategic Services (OSS) after World War II, its research and analysis functions were transferred to the State Department. Those functions were carried out by the Interim Research and Intelligence Service. Since that time there have been two name changes and many more reorganizations. The service has been designated the Bureau of Intelligence and Research (INR) since 1957.[1]

The bureau does not engage in clandestine collection, although it receives reports through normal diplomatic channels and conducts open source collection. However, it performs a variety of functions concerning operational matters, serving as liaison between the Department of State and the intelligence community, to ensure that the actions of other intelligence agencies, such as the Central Intelligence Agency, are in accord with U.S. foreign policy.[2]

In terms of production, the INR faces in two directions. One direction is outward, where it is involved in interagency intelligence production efforts such as National Intelligence Estimates (NIEs) and Special National Intelligence Estimates (SNIEs). The second direction is inward—toward the State Department's internal organization. In this role the INR prepares a variety of intelligence products. The Secretary of State's *Morning Intelligence Summary* is designed to inform the Secretary of State and his principal deputies of current events and current intelligence. INR also prepares a variety of regional and functional summaries as well as single subject Intelligence Research Reports.[3]

The Director of INR holds a rank equivalent to an Assistant Secretary and, as shown in Figure 6-1, is assisted by three Deputy Assistant Secretaries who directly

Figure 6-1. Organization of the Bureau of Intelligence and Research.

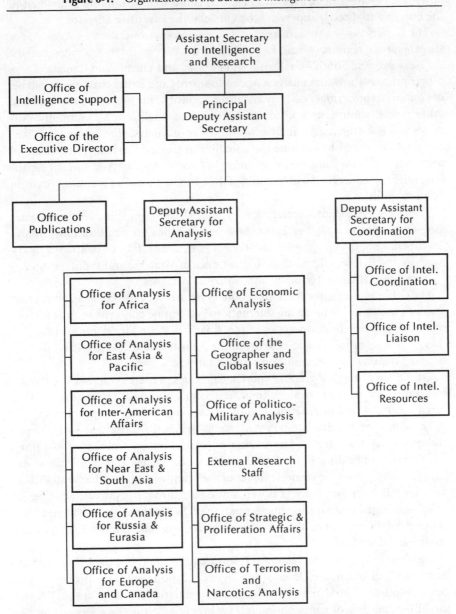

Sources: Bureau of Intelligence and Research, *INR: Intelligence and Research in the Department of State* (Washington, D.C.: Department of State, n.d.); *United States Department of State Telephone Directory* (Washington, D.C.: U.S. Government Printing Office, Spring/Summer 1994), pp. State 12–13.

supervise the INR's seventeen offices and one staff. The Principal Deputy Assistant Secretary for Intelligence and Research is the second-ranking individual in the bureau and directly supervises the Office of the Executive Director.[4]

The Deputy Assistant Secretary for Analysis supervises Offices of Analysis for six geographic regions: Africa; East Asia and the Pacific; Inter-American Affairs; the Near East and South Asia; Russia and Eurasia; and Europe and Canada. These offices primarily produce analyses of developments and issues that are, or will be, of concern to policymakers. They are also responsible for preparing regional and other special summaries and for contributing to intelligence community estimates and assessments. An analyst for the Office of Analysis for Europe and Canada might be asked to examine the situation in unified Germany, the future of democracy in Turkey, and/or the situation in Cyprus. An East Asia and Pacific analyst might be concerned with the role of the Chinese People's Liberation Army in domestic politics.[5]

The Deputy Assistant Secretary for Analysis is also responsible for the bureau's long-range analytical studies. He or she supervises the Office of Economic Analysis, the Office of the Geographer and Global Issues, the Office of Politico-Military Analysis, the External Research Staff, the Office of Strategic and Proliferation Affairs, and the Office of Terrorism and Narcotics Analysis.[6]

The Office of Economic Analysis produces reports for policymakers on current and long-range issues involving international economic concerns such as foreign economic policies, business cycles, trade, financial affairs, food, population and energy, and economic relations between the industrialized countries and the developing nations and between Communist nations.[7]

The Office of the Geographer and Global Issues prepares studies of policy issues associated with physical, cultural, economic, and political geography, U.S. maritime issues, and international boundaries and jurisdictional problems.[8]

The Office of Politico-Military Analysis is primarily concerned with theater and regional military forces. The External Research Staff commissions those projects that cannot be done in the INR. The Office of Strategic and Proliferation Affairs focuses on both the strategic forces of the acknowledged nuclear states (Russia, China, Britain, and France) as well as the nuclear/ballistic missile activities of unacknowledged and aspiring nuclear nations. The Office of Terrorism and Narcotics Analysis examines the structure, operations, and linkages of terrorist groups and drug cartels.[9]

The Deputy Assistant Secretary for Coordination supervises the Office of Intelligence Coordination, the Office of Intelligence Liaison, and the Office of Intelligence Resources. The Office of Intelligence Coordination works with the DIA and the FBI on matters of common interest and represents the State Department in community coordination of human and technical intelligence collection and production priorities. The Office of Intelligence Liaison coordinates proposals for covert action programs. Its basic responsibility in connection with such programs is to ensure "thorough consideration of their support of and implications for U.S. foreign policy."[10]

The Office of Intelligence Resources provides staff support, representation, and coordination for the department's interests in the National Foreign Intelligence Program and budget. It works with other intelligence community agencies and other branches of the department and overseas missions in planning, tasking, deploying, and evaluating technical collection activities. It also advises department officers on the use of intelligence produced by major technical collection systems.[11]

INR employs approximately 360 individuals.[12]

DEPARTMENT OF ENERGY INTELLIGENCE

The Department of Energy's intelligence role can be traced to July 1946, when the National Intelligence Authority decided that the Atomic Energy Commission (AEC) had an appropriate foreign intelligence role and authorized AEC representation on the Intelligence Advisory Board. On December 12, 1947, the AEC's intelligence role was affirmed by National Security Council Intelligence Directive No. 1.[13]

The Energy Reorganization Act of 1974 transferred the AEC's intelligence responsibilities to the Energy Research and Development Administration, and the Department of Energy Organization Act of 1977 transferred them to the newly created Department of Energy. In April 1990 the Energy Department consolidated its intelligence functions by establishing an Office of Intelligence to bring under one roof the Offices of Foreign Intelligence, Threat Assessment, and Counterintelligence. A 1994 reorganization resulted in the redesignation of the office as the Office of Energy Intelligence within the Office of Nonproliferation and National Security.[14]

As shown in Figure 6-2, the Office of Energy Intelligence has four subordinate components: the Data Requirements Staff, the Energy Assessment Division, the Nuclear Nonproliferation Division, and the Intelligence Support Division. As a result of the reorganization, the threat assessment and security functions were transferred to units outside the intelligence office. The Nuclear Nonproliferation Division (with sections for Nuclear Proliferation Intelligence and Weapons Intelligence) studies and reports on foreign military atomic and nuclear weapons programs for both intelligence and treaty monitoring purposes. During Operations Desert Shield and Desert Storm, the division provided the Joint Chiefs of Staff and the DIA with assessments of the Iraqi nuclear weapons program and its capabilities. It is also concerned with issues such as the command, control, and security of tactical and strategic nuclear weapons in Russia and other former Soviet states, the dismantlement of nuclear weapons in the former Soviet Union, the disposition of the nuclear materials removed from those weapons, and the proliferation potential (via a "brain drain") of the former Soviet republics.[15]

Figure 6-2.   Organization of the Office of Energy Intelligence.

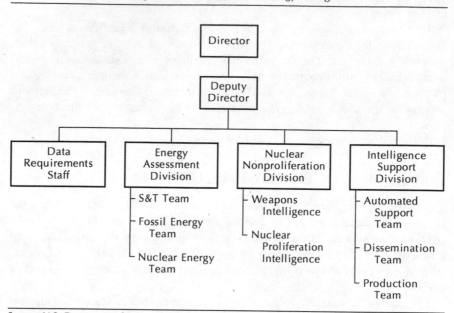

Source: U.S. Department of Energy, *National Telephone Directory* (Washington, D.C.: U.S. Government Printing Office, July 1994), p. 46.

The Energy Assessment Division focuses on international developments that could affect the overall U.S. energy posture and the Strategic Petroleum Reserve. Special studies produced by the office examine the prospects for disruption of energy supplies due to worldwide political, economic, and social instabilities. In addition, the division analyzes overall energy balances within Russia and other nations, focusing on total energy needs that might influence supply and demand. It also examines energy technologies that may have dual uses (civil and military) in support of foreign availability studies related to the DOE Military Critical Technologies List.[16]

The Department of Energy is also responsible for the Lawrence Livermore Laboratory's intelligence program, which is conducted by the International Assessments Program, or Z Division, of Livermore's Nonproliferation, Arms Control, and International Security Directorate. Z Division was established in 1965 to analyze the Soviet nuclear weapons program, and, shortly thereafter, the Chinese program. In the mid-1970s, Z Division began analyzing the proliferation of nuclear weapons to smaller nations.[17]

As indicated in Figure 6-3, Z Division consists of three groups—the Science and Technology Group, the Weapons States Assessments Group, and the Nuclear

Figure 6-3.   Organization of Z Division.

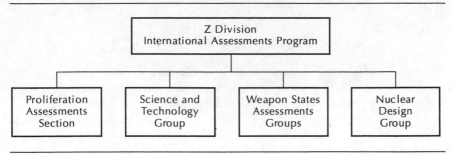

Source: U.S. Department of Energy.

Design Group—and one Proliferation Assessments Section. These organizations provide:

- national capability assessments of potential proliferant countries;
- analyses of state-of-the-art fuel cycle technologies, such as enrichment and reprocessing, that proliferants could use to acquire fissile material;
- assessments of worldwide availability of nuclear weapons technology that could enable a proliferant to build the physics package of a weapon;
- assessments of worldwide availability of related but nonnuclear weapons technology such as safety, arming, firing, and fusing systems; and
- assessments of the activities and behavior of nuclear supplier states and international organizations involved in nuclear commerce, safeguards, and physical security.[18]

DEPARTMENT OF THE TREASURY INTELLIGENCE

The Office of Intelligence Support, which is subordinate to the Executive Secretary of the Department of the Treasury, overtly collects foreign economic, financial, and monetary data in cooperation with the Department of State. It also disseminates foreign intelligence relating to U.S. economic policy as required by the Secretary of the Treasury and other Treasury officials. Additionally, it develops intelligence requirements and informs the remainder of the intelligence community of them and generally represents the department in intelligence community deliberations.[19]

The office is headed by the Special Assistant to the Secretary (National Security) and includes a Senior National Intelligence Adviser, five National Intelligence Advisers, two Technical Librarians, a Watch Office (with eight Watch Officers), and a Special Projects unit. The National Intelligence Advisers are responsible for a variety of areas: various countries and regions, trade, energy, monetary affairs, National Foreign Intelligence Board (NFIB) support, and National Security Agency support.[20]

DEPARTMENT OF COMMERCE INTELLIGENCE

Department of Commerce participation in intelligence activities has been heightened in the past fifteen years by many factors—first owing to concern over technology transfer to the Soviet bloc and, more recently, to concern over the spread of advanced weapons technology. Intelligence is required concerning (1) those who wish to acquire such technology, (2) those who may attempt or are attempting to provide it, and (3) its accessibility from foreign sources.

Neither the concern over technology transfer nor an intelligence role for the Department of Commerce in that area is new. For a brief period in the 1950s, U.S. efforts to regulate the flow of information and goods to the Soviet Union and other potential adversary nations involved the Commerce Department in an intelligence role. At the urging of the National Security Council, the Office of Strategic Information (OSI) was established within the Department of Commerce in 1954.[21]

The OSI was not established by legislation but created by presidential directive on November 1, 1954, in response to the NSC recommendation—a recommendation that resulted from concern about Soviet efforts to obtain U.S. industrial and military information. The OSI tried to create "prepublication awareness" concerning the perceived danger resulting from the availability of certain unclassified scientific and technical information. Particular concern focused on aerial photography, resulting in the creation of an OSI Task Force on Aerial Photography. The task force recommended a specific educational program through government and industry "to alert producers and users of the strategic intelligence value of aerial photographs."[22] The OSI clashed with the DOD and Congress. The DOD considered the OSI's security role redundant; Congress was concerned about the OSI's negative impact on scientific projects. As a result, the OSI was disestablished in June 1957.[23]

At present, the Department of Commerce has three units with intelligence functions: the Office of Intelligence Liaison, the Office of Export Enforcement (OEE), and the Office of Foreign Availability. The Office of Intelligence Liaison, which is subordinate to the Office of the General Counsel, serves as the liaison between the Department of Commerce and the intelligence community, particularly with respect to technology transfer issues. The office receives all information transmitted from the intelligence community to the Department of Commerce and distributes it to the appropriate components.[24]

The office also provides day-to-day intelligence support to key Department of Commerce officials having international policy or program responsibilities. This support includes preparation of a daily department foreign intelligence summary covering major international developments. Support also includes intelligence information for key departmental officials traveling abroad.[25] Additionally, the office is responsible for reviewing and assessing Department of Commerce intelligence requirements. Based on the results of such assessments, it tasks the intelligence community to provide the necessary data.[26]

The OEE, formerly the Compliance Division of the Office of Export Administration, is subordinate to the Assistant Secretary for Trade Administration. Its function is to ensure that the proper approvals have been obtained for the export of sensitive technology and to prevent unauthorized shipments of such technology. The functions of the OEE's Intelligence Division include:

- receiving, interpreting, and analyzing intelligence and trade data to determine whether preventive, deterrent, or some other type of enforcement action [is] required or appropriate;
- providing leads for ongoing investigations and assisting investigative personnel in the conduct of investigations;
- disseminating intelligence information and analysis to agents of the OEE and other appropriate federal agencies;
- applying qualitative and quantitative methodologies to establish patterns and profiles of diversion and acquisition; and
- collecting intelligence to assist in the conduct of prelicense checks and postshipment verifications.[27]

In 1984, a Foreign Availability Assessment Division, subsequently renamed the Foreign Availability Division and then the Office of Foreign Availability (OFA), was established under the Office (now Bureau) of Export Administration (which is, in turn, subordinate to the Assistant Secretary for Trade Administration). The office was established to assess the foreign availability of high-technology products to the Soviet bloc and the People's Republic of China, with a view to ensuring that U.S. companies were not placed at a needless competitive disadvantage by being prohibited by U.S. export controls from selling their goods to the Soviet bloc and China. Today, much of the OFA's effort is related to questions concerning the proliferation of nuclear and ballistic missile technology and chemical/biological weapons.[28]

Foreign availability for a national security item exists when a foreign-made item of comparable quality is available to controlled countries in quantities sufficient to satisfy their needs such that U.S. exports of the item would not contribute significantly to the military potential of such countries. Foreign availability assessments influence U.S. decisions concerning the export of U.S. high-technology products and may lead to discussions with allied governments in attempts to eliminate availability.[29]

The office consists of three divisions: the Capital Goods and Materials Assessment Division; the Computers, Electronics, and Instrumentation Assessment Division; and the Operations and Strategic Analysis Division. The first two divisions study the foreign availability of machine tools; biotechnology, chemicals, and

Table 6-1. Activities and Impact of the Office of Foreign Availability.

	FY86	FY87	FY88
Classified Reports Reviewed	55,000	65,000	65,000
Foreign Availability Studies Completed	26	28	28
Decontrol Actions Initiated	4	10	10

Note: FY87 and FY88 figures are estimated.

Source: U.S. Congress, House Committee on Appropriations, *Departments of Commerce, Justice and State, the Judiciary and Related Agencies, Appropriations for 1988, Part 6* (Washington, D.C.: U.S. Government Printing Office, 1987), p. 695.

electronic materials; advanced materials; semiconductor manufacturing equipment and materials; electronic materials; marine systems, robotics, and avionics; computer hardware; computers; lasers; telecommunications equipment; computer systems; and electronics/capital goods.[30]

Several foreign availability studies have led to the decontrol of assorted technologies. Among the thirteen foreign availability studies conducted between May and November 1986, one indicated that automatic wafering saws for cutting computer chip blanks out of silicon stock were available from firms in Switzerland. As a result, the White House ordered decontrol of the wafering saws. In other cases, OFA studies have resulted in decisions not to control a technology. Included in this category are step-and-repeat mask alignment systems, Winchester disk drives, aerial film, and a digitally controlled office switching system.[31] Table 6-1 gives some indications of OFA activities and their impact. Still other studies have helped the OFA to determine that certain items hasten the process of proliferation and thus warrant export restrictions. In these cases, the OFA does not recommend decontrol. Rather, the information may be used by U.S. negotiators in talks with foreign suppliers representing countries that do not impose restrictions on export of the item.[32]

DRUG ENFORCEMENT ADMINISTRATION INTELLIGENCE

The Drug Enforcement Administration (DEA), which, like the Federal Bureau of Investigation (FBI), is part of the Department of Justice, operates in the United States and abroad. DEA intelligence operations are the responsibility of the Assistant Administrator for Intelligence, who heads the Office of Intelligence of the DEA Operations Division. The office is responsible for:

- providing technical and operational intelligence products and services that identify the structure and members of international and domestic drug trafficking organizations and exploitable areas for enforcement operations;

- preparing strategic intelligence assessments, estimates, and probes focusing on trafficking patterns, source country production, and domestic production and consumption trends;
- developing intelligence that focuses on the financial aspects of drug investigations such as money-laundering techniques, drug-related asset discovery and forfeiture, and macroeconomic impact assessments of the illegal drug trade; and
- providing interagency intelligence support to other federal, state, and local law enforcement organizations and a variety of state and foreign drug intelligence clearinghouses, and participating in the National Narcotics Interdiction System.[33]

As Figure 6-4 illustrates, the DEA's Office of Intelligence consists of four sections: Investigative Intelligence, Collection and Publications, Financial and Special Intelligence, and Strategic Intelligence. The functions of the Investigative Intelligence Section include initiating DEA intelligence criteria and requirements for operational intelligence programs targeted against international and domestic drug traffickers, conducting liaison with intelligence community and foreign counterpart organizations, and analyzing intelligence data related to specific cases to identify major drug organizations and their personnel.[34]

The Collection and Publications Section publishes intelligence assessments, studies, and reports; manages a Collection Management Coordination Facility for the tasking of collection systems and operations; identifies and evaluates intelligence gaps; and assesses field drug intelligence collection. The Financial and Special Intelligence Section develops financial investigative and strategic intelligence collection requirements; analyzes intelligence to identify the financial apparatus of major drug organizations; and identifies money-laundering techniques. The Strategic Intelligence Section produces strategic intelligence assessments, studies, reports, and estimates; analyzes strategic intelligence requirements; and conducts liaison with law enforcement and intelligence agencies.[35]

In 1985 DEA established the U.S. Southwest Border Intelligence Task Force, which supports DEA intelligence operations along the U.S.-Mexican border. The task force provides strategic assessments of all aspects of drug trafficking from Mexico to the United States and, in conjunction with DEA field offices, collates, analyzes, and disseminates intelligence on major Mexican drug traffickers and their organizations.[36]

The office's Special Field Intelligence Program provides funding "to exploit highly specialized or unique collection opportunities against a wide variety of intelligence problems in foreign areas." The objective is to collect data on the entire narcotics raw material production process as well as on smuggling routes and methods, trafficking, and terrorist or financial matters relating to narcotics activities.[37]

138

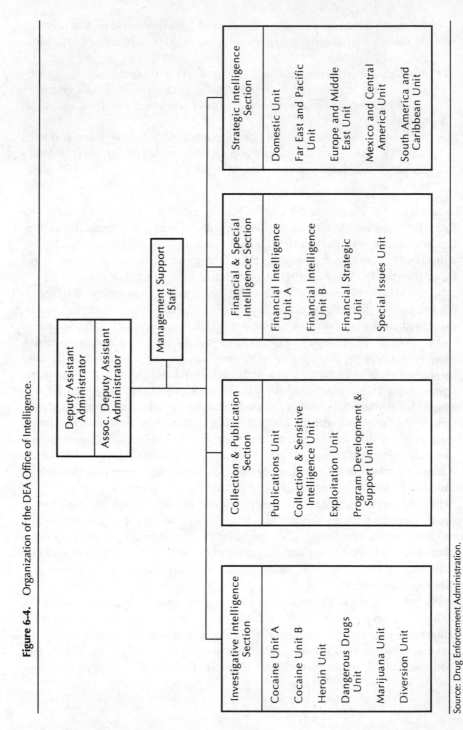

Figure 6-4. Organization of the DEA Office of Intelligence.

Deputy Assistant Administrator

Assoc. Deputy Assistant Administrator

Management Support Staff

Investigative Intelligence Section

Cocaine Unit A

Cocaine Unit B

Heroin Unit

Dangerous Drugs Unit

Marijuana Unit

Diversion Unit

Collection & Publication Section

Publications Unit

Collection & Sensitive Intelligence Unit

Exploitation Unit

Program Development & Support Unit

Financial & Special Intelligence Section

Financial Intelligence Unit A

Financial Intelligence Unit B

Financial Strategic Unit

Special Issues Unit

Strategic Intelligence Section

Domestic Unit

Far East and Pacific Unit

Europe and Middle East Unit

Mexico and Central America Unit

South America and Caribbean Unit

Source: Drug Enforcement Administration.

According to DEA's 1984 congressional budget submission, its major intelligence activities and accomplishments included:

- development of sources of information knowledgeable of illicit cultivation, production, and transportation activities;
- undercover penetration of trafficking organizations in support of host country operations;
- surveillance assistance and development of evidence against major traffickers of drugs destined for the United States; and
- intelligence support to governments in Mexico and Central America in eradicating marijuana and poppy fields.[38]

Additionally, the DEA reported that intelligence probes in West Germany identified a sizable number of Turkish and Pakistani traffickers transporting Southwest Asian heroin into Western Europe. Likewise, DEA personnel conducting intelligence probes in Pakistan, Turkey, and Mexico were reported to have pinpointed illicit laboratory locations, identified the operators, and assessed the potential output of a number of sophisticated morphine, heroin, and opium production operations.[39]

Among the DEA's seventy-three overseas offices (fifty country offices and twenty-three resident offices) is one at the U.S. Embassy in Cyprus. The office collects intelligence on Lebanon's Bekaa Valley, one of the world's fastest-growing heroin and hashish production centers. Apparently, some of Lebanon's most prominent families, as well as Palestinian guerrillas and other militia forces that control illegal ports, are deeply involved in the drug trade and use its revenues to finance their organizations.[40]

In the course of its activities the DEA interacts with several major intelligence agencies. Detection of drug trafficking operations can involve human agents, both DEA and CIA, as well as a variety of technical collection systems. Hence, the DEA has contacts with the CIA, the NSA, the NRO, and Naval Intelligence. The Administrator of the DEA stated in 1981 congressional testimony that he "met with Deputy Director of CIA, Admiral Inman for quite some time at their headquarters and discussed our narcotics problem. I've worked with him in the past, both at NSA and on other matters, and we are expecting increased attention from that agency, and we need it desperately. Because without intelligence, the enforcement effort is immediately limited."[41] The CIA has provided the DEA with international narcotics intelligence derived from both human and electronic surveillance operations overseas.[42]

FEDERAL BUREAU OF INVESTIGATION

The responsibilities of the Federal Bureau of Investigation (FBI) are predominantly in the criminal law enforcement, domestic counterterrorism, and domestic counterintelligence areas, with the last of these responsibilities being performed by the bureau's National Security Division. The division also assumes some responsibility with regard to collection of foreign intelligence in the United States.

Over the years the FBI has tried to expand its role in foreign intelligence collection. In 1939, President Roosevelt gave the FBI responsibility for the collection of intelligence in the Western Hemisphere and created a Special Intelligence Service (SIS) for this function. The SIS had approximately 360 agents, mostly in Mexico, Argentina, and Brazil. Although it was stripped of this function after the war, the bureau maintained representatives as Legal Attachés in ten embassies as of 1970. The attachés' official function was to be a liaison with national police forces on matters of common concern and to deal with Americans who found themselves in trouble with the law. In 1970 the bureau increased from ten to twenty the number of embassies with FBI representation and instructed agents to collect foreign intelligence, particularly interesting intelligence being slugged with the designation HILEV (High Level) by overseas agents. Some such material was distributed to high officials—for example, Henry Kissinger—outside normal channels. In the aftermath of J. Edgar Hoover's death and FBI revelations, the program was terminated and FBI representation abroad was reduced to fifteen embassies.[43]

At least two instances of FBI attempts to engage in foreign clandestine collection have come to light. During the investigation of the murder of former Chilean Defense Minister Orlando Letelier, the FBI operated an undercover agent in Chile. The agent told the FBI that the right-wing Partia y Libertad had contracted with Chilean narcotics traffickers to murder Letelier. The FBI's agent, however, turned out to be a DEA informant who had been terminated and blacklisted years earlier for double dealing, misinterpretation, and moral turpitude. A more successful operation involved the FBI placement of a young woman informant in one of the first groups of U.S. leftists to visit China in the early 1970s.[44]

Despite its failure to acquire a significant *overseas* role in the collection of foreign intelligence, the FBI is involved in domestic activities to generate such intelligence. Thus, Executive Order 12333 allows the FBI to "conduct within the United States, when requested by the officials of the intelligence community designated by the President, activities undertaken to collect foreign intelligence or support foreign intelligence collection requirements of other agencies within the intelligence community."[45]

Thus, in September 1980 two FBI officials were briefed by the Joint Staff on intelligence requirements in support of possible operations in Iran. One of the officials was the Deputy Assistant Director for Intelligence, who was responsible for coordinating the use of non-U.S. persons in the United States for intelligence purposes.[46] The Joint Staff asked the FBI officials for their assistance in developing information pertaining to a Defense Department hostage rescue operation against Iran, instructing them to "seek any potential Iranian leads that they may spot for exploitation in the conduct of their programs."[47]

In the past, FBI foreign intelligence–related activities have also included wiretapping and break-ins. The FBI has operated wiretaps against numerous foreign embassies in Washington. FBI agents regularly monitored the phones in the offices of all Communist governments represented in Washington. Additionally, the phones in the offices of non-Communist governments were also tapped, especially when those nations were engaged in negotiations with the United States or when significant developments were taking place in those countries. At one point, the FBI tapped the phones of an ally's Trade Mission in San Francisco. In addition, the FBI has conducted break-ins at foreign embassies to obtain cryptanalytical and other foreign intelligence.[48]

In August 1993 the FBI opened a National Drug Intelligence Center, headquartered in Jonestown, Pennsylvania. The 130-person staff, which is expected to grow to 211, includes 60 new employees and about 70 agents and analysts on leave from the CIA, the Defense Department, the DEA, and the IRS.[49]

DEPARTMENT OF TRANSPORTATION INTELLIGENCE

The Transportation Department's Office of Intelligence and Security was established in 1990 based on a recommendation of the presidential Commission on Aviation Security and Terrorism, which was set up after the Pan Am 103 bombing. The office, with Intelligence, Plans and Policy, and Security Divisions, is responsible for all strategic planning, coordination, and oversight of transportation intelligence and security.[50]

NOTES

1. U.S. Congress, Senate Select Committee to Study Governmental Operations with Respect to Intelligence Activities, *Final Report, Book 6, Supplementary Reports on Intelligence Activities* (Washington, D.C.: U.S. Government Printing Office, 1976), pp. 271–76.

2. U.S. Congress, House Committee on Foreign Affairs, *The Role of Intelligence in the Foreign Policy Process* (Washington, D.C.: U.S. Government Printing Office, 1980), p. 57.

3. *INR* (Washington, D.C.: Department of State, n.d.), pp. 2, 4.

4. Ibid., pp. 9, 10; *United States Department of State Telephone Directory* (Washington, D.C.: U.S. Government Printing Office, Fall 1992), p. 12.

5. *INR,* p. 10; *United States Department of State Telephone Directory,* p. 13; U.S. Congress, House Committee on Appropriations, *Departments of Commerce, Justice, and State, the Judiciary and Related Agencies Appropriations for FY 1986, Part 6* (Washington, D.C.: U.S. Government Printing Office, 1985), pp. 370, 374; U.S. Congress, House Committee on Appropriations, *Departments of Commerce, Justice, and State, the Judiciary and Related Agencies Appropriations for FY 1987, Part 6* (Washington, D.C.: U.S. Government Printing Office, 1986), p. 351.

6. *INR,* p. 10.

7. *INR* (Washington, D.C.: Department of State, 1983), pp. 12–13; *United States Department of State Telephone Directory,* pp. 12–13; U.S. Congress, House Committee on Appro-

priations, *Departments of Commerce, Justice, and State, the Judiciary and Related Agencies Appropriations for FY 1987, Part 6*, p. 351.

8. *INR*, p. 4.

9. *INR* (1983), pp. 12–13; *INR*, p. 10.

10. *INR*, p. 8.

11. Ibid., p. 9.

12. U.S. Congress, House Committee on Appropriations, *Departments of Commerce, Justice, and State, the Judiciary, and Related Agencies Appropriations for 1992, Part 3* (Washington, D.C.: U.S. Government Printing Office, 1991), p. 451.

13. Statement of Robert W. Daniel, Jr., Director, Office of Intelligence, Department of Energy, in U.S. Congress, House Committee on Appropriations, *Energy and Water Development Appropriations for 1992, Part 6* (Washington, D.C.: U.S. Government Printing Office, 1991), pp. 819–36 at p. 820.

14. Ibid.; "Watkins Reorganizes DOE's Intelligence Work," *Washington Post*, April 18, 1990, p. A25; U.S. Congress, Senate Committee on Armed Services, *Department of Defense Authorization for Appropriations for Fiscal Years 1992 and 1993, Part 1* (Washington, D.C.: U.S. Government Printing Office, 1991), p. 657; Department of Energy, *National Telephone Directory* (Washington, D.C.: Government Printing Office, 1994), p. 46.

15. U.S. Congress, Senate Committee on Armed Services, *Department of Defense Authorization for Appropriations for Fiscal Years 1992 and 1993, Part 1*, p. 657; Daniel, in U.S. Congress, House Committee on Appropriations, *Energy and Water Development Appropriations for 1992, Part 6*, p. 823; Department of Energy, *National Telephone Directory*, p. 46; Statement of Robert W. Daniel, Jr., Director, Office of Intelligence, Department of Energy, in U.S. Congress, House Committee on Appropriations, *Energy and Water Development Appropriations for 1993, Part 6* (Washington, D.C.: U.S. Government Printing Office, 1992), p. 2081.

16. Daniel, in U.S. Congress, House Committee on Appropriations, *Energy and Water Development Appropriations for 1992, Part 6*, p. 823; Daniel, in U.S. Congress, House Committee on Appropriations, *Energy and Water Development Appropriations for 1993, Part 6*, p. 2195.

17. Lawrence Livermore National Laboratory, "Nonproliferation, Arms Control, and International Security," n.d.

18. U.S. Congress, House Committee on Armed Services, *Department of Energy: National Security and Military Applications of Nuclear Energy Authorization Act of 1984* (Washington, D.C.: U.S. Government Printing Office, 1983), p. 394.

19. Ronald Reagan, "Executive Order 12333: United States Intelligence Activities," December 4, 1981, in *Federal Register* 46, 235 (December 8, 1981): 59941–54 at 59946; "Foreign Intelligence—It's More than the CIA," *U.S. News and World Report*, May 1, 1981, pp. 35–37; Department of the Treasury Order 100-3, "Functions of the Executive Secretariat," January 13, 1987, p. 2.

20. Department of the Treasury, "OIS Organization Structure," n.d. (circa 1988); Department of the Treasury, "Department of the Treasury Office of Intelligence Support (OIS) Organization Structure," n.d. (circa 1992).

21. National Academy of Sciences, *Scientific Communication and National Security* (Washington, D.C.: National Academy Press, 1982), p. 99.

22. U.S. Congress, House Committee on Government Operations, *Availability of Information from Federal Departments and Agencies, Part 6* (Washington, D.C.: U.S. Government Printing Office, 1956), pp. 1671–72.

23. National Academy of Sciences, *Scientific Communication and National Security,* p. 99.

24. Department of Commerce, "Department Organization Order Series 10-6, Appendix A," June 10, 1981, p. 2.

25. Ibid.

26. Ibid.

27. Department of Commerce, "Organization and Function Order 41-4, Assistant Secretary for Trade Administration," May 8, 1985, pp. 21, 22.

28. Ibid., p. 17; "OEL Insider Interview with Steven C. Goldman, Director, Office of Foreign Availability," *OEL Insider,* July 1991, pp. 1–2.

29. U.S. Congress, House Committee on Appropriations, *Departments of Commerce, Justice and State, the Judiciary and Related Agencies Appropriations for 1988, Part 6* (Washington, D.C.: U.S. Government Printing Office, 1987), p. 695; U.S. Congress, House Committee on Appropriations, *Departments of Commerce, Justice, and State, the Judiciary and Related Agencies Appropriations for 1992, Part 1A* (Washington, D.C.: U.S. Government Printing Office, 1991), p. 1339.

30. "OEL Insider Interview with Steven C. Goldman, Director, Office of Foreign Availability."

31. James K. Gordon, "Commerce Decontrols Technology Because of Foreign Availability," *Aviation Week & Space Technology,* November 24, 1986, p. 63.

32. "OEL Insider Interview with Steven C. Goldman, Director, Office of Foreign Availability."

33. Drug Enforcement Administration, *Annual Report, Fiscal Year 1986* (Washington, D.C.: DEA, 1986), pp. 9–10.

34. Drug Enforcement Administration, *DEA Organization and Function Manual,* Office of Intelligence section, n.d., n.p.

35. Ibid.

36. Drug Enforcement Administration, *Annual Report, Fiscal Year 1986,* p. 6.

37. U.S. Congress, House Committee on Appropriations, *Departments of Commerce, Justice and State, the Judiciary and Related Agencies Appropriations for 1984, Part 6* (Washington, D.C.: U.S. Government Printing Office, 1983), pp. 3, 21.

38. Ibid. p. 22.

39. Ibid., pp. 22–23.

40. Patrick E. Tyler, "Smugglers, Gun Runners, Spies Cross Paths in Cyprus," *Washington Post,* March 12, 1987, pp. A1, A30; Drug Enforcement Administration, *Briefing Book,* September 1992, p. 30.

41. U.S. Congress, Senate Committee on the Judiciary, *Oversight of the Drug Enforcement Administration* (Washington, D.C.: U.S. Government Printing Office, 1981), p. 9.

42. Department of Justice, *Report on Inquiry into CIA-Related Electronic Surveillance Activities* (Washington, D.C.: Department of Justice, 1976), p. 20.

43. Sanford J. Ungar, *The FBI* (Boston: Little, Brown, 1976), pp. 225–26, 242.

44. Taylor Branch and Eugene M. Proper, *Labyrinth* (New York: Viking, 1982), pp. 231, 350, 358; Ungar, *The FBI,* pp. 240–41.

45. Reagan, "Executive Order 12333: United States Intelligence Activities," Section 1.14, provision c, p. 59949.

46. JCS Joint Staff, Memorandum for the Record, Subject: Briefing of FBI Representatives, September 25, 1980.

47. Ibid.

48. Victor Marchetti and John Marks, *The CIA and the Cult of Intelligence* (New York: Knopf, 1974), p. 204; "Mole Tunnels Under a Soviet Consulate," *Newsweek,* August 15, 1983, p. 21; Douglas Watson, "Huston Says NSA Urged Break-Ins," *Washington Post,* March 3, 1975, pp. 1, 6.

49. Michael deCourcy Hinds, "Center for Drug Intelligence Opens, But Some Ask If It Is Really Needed," *New York Times,* November 17, 1993, p. A16.

50. "Who's Who," *Intelligence Newsletter,* September 2, 1993, p. 8.

CIA headquarters, Langley, Virginia. Photo Credit: Central Intelligence Agency.

CIA's ``Blue U'' at 1000 North Glebe Road, Arlington, Virginia. Courses in photography, clandestine letter opening, and lock picking were given at the Blue U. The Blue U is now the Ballston Campus of Marymount University.

National Security Agency headquarters, Ft. George G. Meade, Maryland. Photo Credit: Department of Defense.

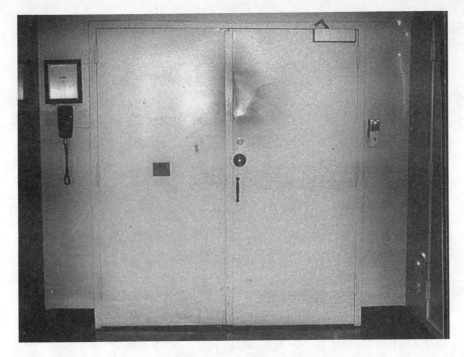

The locked doors to the National Reconnaissance Office Pentagon office.

DIA's Defense Intelligence Analysis Center, Bolling AFB, Washington, D.C. Photo Credit: Department of Defense.

Headquarters, U.S. Army National Ground Intelligence Center (FSTC), Charlottesville, Virginia. FSTC will merge with the Army Intelligence and Threat Analysis Center (ITAC) in 1995 to form the National Ground Intelligence Center. Photo Credit: FSTC.

The National Maritime Intelligence Center (NMIC) in Suitland, Maryland. The NMIC houses the Office of Naval Intelligence (which absorbed the Naval Technical Intelligence Center, Task Force 168, and the Navy Operational Intelligence Center in 1993) along with Coast Guard and Marine Corps intelligence organizations. Photo Credit: U.S. Navy.

7
IMAGERY COLLECTION, PROCESSING, AND DISSEMINATION

The concept of using overhead platforms to observe events on the earth can be traced to the time of the French Revolution, when France organized a company of *aerostiers,* or balloonists, in April 1794. One balloon is said to have been kept in the air for nine hours while the group's commander made continuous observations during the battle of Fleurus in Belgium.[1]

The United States made similar use of balloons during the Civil War, although little valuable intelligence was obtained. By the latter part of the nineteenth century, Britain was conducting experiments using balloons as platforms from which to obtain "overhead photography." In January 1911, the San Diego waterfront became the first subject of airplane-carried cameras. In the same year the U.S. Army Signal Corps put aerial photography into the curriculum at its flight training school. Between 1913 and 1915 visual and photographic reconnaissance missions were flown by the U.S. Army in the Philippines and along the Mexican border.[2]

During World War II the United States made extensive use of airplane photography using remodeled B-17 (Flying Fortress) and B-24 (Liberator) aircraft. The remodeled B-24, known as the F-7, carried six cameras internally—all triggered via remote control by an operator placed over the sealed rear bomb-bay doors. After the war ended and a hostile relationship with the Soviet Union emerged, the United States conducted photographic missions along the Soviet periphery, sending planes to fly outside Soviet territory. The cameras, however, could only capture images of territory within a few miles of the flight path.[3]

Realizing that it was imperative to obtain photographic coverage not just of the periphery but of the Soviet interior, in the early 1950s the United States began exploring new methods. The result was the development, production, and employment of a variety of spacecraft and aircraft that allowed the United States to monitor events in the Soviet Union and other nations by overflight or peripheral missions. In the years since the United States began operating such systems, their capabilities have improved in numerous ways. Satellites now have longer lifetimes, produce more detailed images, and transmit their imagery almost instantly.

In addition, some aircraft and spacecraft are capable of producing high-quality imagery in situations where standard visible-light photography is not feasible.

These alternative means of obtaining imagery rely on equipment sensitive to wavelengths outside of the visible-light portion of the spectrum, which ranges from 0.0004 to 0.00075 mm.[4]

Photographic equipment can be of either the film-based or television type. A conventional camera captures a scene on film by recording the varying light levels reflected from all of the separate objects in that scene. In contrast, an electro-optical camera converts the varying light levels into electrical signals. A numerical value is assigned to each of the signals, which are called picture elements, or pixels. The process transforms a picture (analog) image to a digital image that can be transmitted electronically to distant points. The signal can then be reconstructed from the digital to the analog format. The analog signal can be displayed on a video screen or made into a photograph.[5]

Imagery can be obtained using both visible light and near-infrared portions of the electromagnetic spectrum. Unlike the portion of the spectrum used by visible-light photography, the near-infrared portion is not visible to the human eye. At the same time, infrared, like visible-light photography, depends on the reflective properties of objects rather than on their emission of radiation. As a result, such imagery can only be produced in daylight and in the absence of substantial cloud cover.[6]

Thermal infrared imagery, obtained from the mid- and far-infrared portion of the electromagnetic spectrum, produces imagery purely by detecting the heat produced by objects. Such devices can detect buried structures, such as missile silos or underground construction, by measuring temperature differences between targets and the earth's surface. Since thermal infrared imagery does not require visible light, it can be obtained under conditions of darkness (however, the sky must be free of cloud cover).[7]

A means of producing imagery in the presence of cloud cover is imaging radar (an acronym for *r*adio *d*etection *a*nd *r*anging). Radar imagery is produced by bouncing radio waves off an area or object. The returning waves allow formation of a picture of an object. Since radio waves are not attenuated by the water vapor in the atmosphere, they are able to penetrate cloud cover.[8]

COLLECTION

The most important means of producing imagery is via the use of satellite systems. The United States has relied on a variety of systems since the first satellite was launched in 1960. Some, such as the KH-8 (KEYHOLE-8), took highly detailed pictures of specific targets. Others, such as the KH-9, produced images of broader areas, allowing photo interpreters to examine a large area and select targets for more detailed inspection. In 1976 the KH-8 and KH-9 were joined by the KH-11, which became the sole type of military imaging satellite operated by the United States between October 18, 1984 (when the last KH-9 was deorbited), and December 2, 1988.[9]

The origins of the KH-11 (which has also been known by the BYEMAN codenames KENNAN, and then CRYSTAL) go back, in a sense, to the very origins of the U.S. satellite reconnaissance program. Intelligence and defense officials had always recognized that it would be desirable, particularly for indications and warning purposes, to have imagery data returned in near-real-time. However, they did not feel that such a system was technologically possible until 1969.

In that year, a study conducted by the DCI's Committee on Imagery Requirements and Exploitation (COMIREX) examined the potential utility of a near-real-time system. The study examined how such data could have been used during the Cuban Missile Crisis, the 1967 Six-Day War, and the Soviet invasion of Czechoslovakia. The ultimate result was a presidential decision to authorize development of the near-real-time system proposed by the Central Intelligence Agency.[10]

On December 19, 1976, the first KH-11 was launched on a Titan 3D rocket from Vandenberg AFB into an orbit of 164 by 329 miles. Since that time, an additional seven KH-11s have been orbited, one of which is apparently still operational. The KH-11 spacecraft is 64 feet long and weighs 30,000 pounds.[11] The satellite flies lengthwise, with the axis of the optical system parallel to the earth. In front is a downward-looking mirror that can be rotated from side to side, causing a periscope effect in which the area viewed can change from moment to moment. Two benefits result from this capability: A particular location can be viewed more frequently than it could with a stationary camera, and the satellite can generate a stereoscopic image.

Only a very select set of government officials was permitted to know of the KH-11's existence or even see its product. The KH-11 was treated with an even greater degree of secrecy than is usual in the black world of reconnaissance satellites. The photographs and data derived from those photographs were not incorporated with those of the other operational imaging satellites of the time (the KH-8 and KH-9). The decision to restrict the data to a very small group of individuals was taken at the urging of senior CIA officials but against the recommendations of military officers who wanted information to be more widely distributed throughout the armed forces. It was only after it was discovered that a disgruntled CIA employee, William Kampiles, had sold the KH-11 technical manual to the KGB that the restrictive policy was changed.

The KH-11, in contrast to the KH-8 and KH-9, does not return imagery via film canisters. Instead, to permit instantaneous transmission, its optical system employs an array of light-sensitive silicone diodes and the array's charge is read by an amplifier and converted from analog to digital signals for transmission. The signals then are transmitted to Satellite Data System or other elliptically orbiting relay spacecraft. KH-11 imagery may also be transmitted via the geosynchronous Defense Satellite Communications System (DSCS) spacecraft. The satellites then transmit the imagery to ground stations. The initial and primary KH-11 ground station is the Mission Ground Site at Fort Belvoir, Virginia, about twenty miles

Table 7-1.   KH-11 Lifetimes.

Launch Date	Deorbited	Lifetime (Days)
December 19, 1976	January 28, 1979	770
June 14, 1978	August 23, 1981	1,166
February 7, 1980	October 30, 1982	993
September 3, 1981	November 23, 1984	1,175
November 17, 1982	August 13, 1985	987
December 4, 1984	November 1994	3,625^
October 27, 1987	November 1992*	1,825^
November 6, 1988	Still in Orbit	—

* Inferred from a late 1992 launch.

^ Approximation

south of Washington. The Mission Ground Site is a large, windowless, two-story concrete building officially known as the Defense Communications Electronics Evaluation and Testing Activity. There may also be KH-11 ground stations in Europe (Germany) and in the Pacific (Hawaii).[12]

Partially as a result of its electronic method of transmitting data (and the fact that it cannot run out of film), a KH-11 satellite can stay in orbit for a much longer period than either a KH-8 or KH-9. In addition, the KH-11's higher orbit, approximately 150 by 250 miles, reduces atmospheric drag on the spacecraft. Thus, the lifetime of the first KH-11 was 770 days—almost 500 days longer than that of the longest-lived KH-9. The lifetimes of the subsequent KH-11s, shown in Table 7-1, give it an average lifetime of 1,018 days—almost three years.

Between February 7, 1980, when the third KH-11 was launched, and August 28, 1985, when an attempted launch failed, two operational KH-11s were kept in orbit at all times, except for short breaks to allow for deorbiting and replacement of a satellite. The second KH-11, deorbited on August 23, 1981, was replaced by one put into orbit on September 3, 1981, and the satellite launched on February 7, 1980, and deorbited on October 30, 1982, was replaced by a KH-11 launched on November 17, 1982. Typically, by the time one satellite was ready to be deorbited, both were circling the earth every 90 minutes—a faster speed than usual. Several days after one satellite was removed from orbit, the other would make a major maneuver to increase its orbiting period to 92.5 minutes. The replacement satellite would then be launched and would make a few maneuvers to reach the correct speed and position, and joint operations would begin. As shown in Figure 7-1, the satellite pairs divided up the work of providing late-morning and early-afternoon coverage. The combination of viewing angles helped analysts to interpret the satellite images.[13]

In addition to a longer lifetime, the KH-11 has another, even more significant advantage over the film-return satellites. Its ability to provide data instantaneously allows it to be used in a crisis-monitoring role and an early-warning role. Whereas film-return satellites could take days or even weeks to provide data, the

154

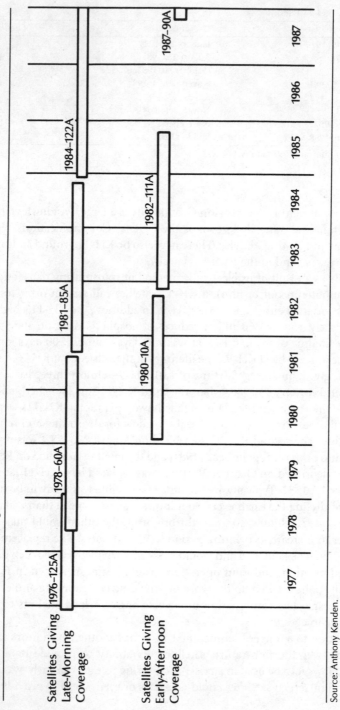

Figure 7-1. KH-11 Coverage, 1977–1987.

Satellites Giving Late-Morning Coverage

1976–125A
1978–60A
1981–85A
1984–122A

Satellites Giving Early-Afternoon Coverage

1980–10A
1982–111A
1987–90A

1977 1978 1979 1980 1981 1982 1983 1984 1985 1986 1987

Source: Anthony Kenden.

KH-11 can return the data instantaneously—and the data can be processed at Mission Ground Site, analyzed at the CIA's National Photographic Interpretation Center, and then put in the hands of decisionmakers in the matter of an hour. According to one person familiar with the system, "You can call up the KH-11 and when it comes up on its geometry to the target area, you can get a photo and have it back down here, printed out, in an hour, and have it over to the White House."[14] In 1985 CIA Deputy Director for Science and Technology Richard Evan Hineman testified that the KH-11 was being used "against active military targets for early-warning purposes."[15]

Several examples of the KH-11's photographic production have been exposed to public view. KH-11 photography was among the data carried to the Desert One site in Iran during the hostage rescue mission—and was left behind when an EC-130 and a helicopter crashed in the process of aborting the mission. Photographs left behind, which later appeared in a book published by Iranian students, included overhead views of a sports stadium and the U.S. Embassy compound. Among other uses, the data were employed to determine the location of the personnel in the compound and to scout the route the rescue team would take.[16]

In December 1981 a KH-11-produced photograph of a future Soviet bomber—the BLACKJACK—appeared in *Aviation Week and Space Technology*. The photograph was taken on November 25, 1981, while the plane sat on the tarmac at Ramenskoye Airfield, a strategic test center. The photograph also showed two TU-144 Charger transports similar to the Concorde. Distinguishable features included the passenger windows on the side of the aircraft. The picture was taken by the KH-11 launched on September 3, 1981, on a southbound pass across the Soviet Union during the late morning, local time. The picture, which was taken at quite a steep slant or oblique angle, indicated a KH-11 capability to obtain a resolution between 5.46 and 17.7 inches, depending on the satellite's distance from the target.[17]

In the summer of 1984, three KH-11 photos, showing a Kiev-class carrier (codenamed BLACK COM II, for Black Sea Combatant II, by the United States and, originally, KREMLIN by the Soviet Navy) under construction, appeared in *Jane's Defence Weekly*. The photos were taken at an oblique angle, although not as oblique as the angle of the BLACKJACK photo. In one case the slant angle was such that the photo must have been taken from 504 miles away.[18]

One computer-enhanced photograph, taken at an oblique angle, shows the general layout of the Nikolaiev 444 yard in the Black Sea, with what would appear to be a foundry in the foreground and assembly shops behind. Buildings housing the technical staff lie alongside the dry dock where the 75,000-ton nuclear carrier is under construction. The photograph also shows the stern section of the KHARKOV, the fourth Kiev-class carrier, in the process of being fitted out. Nearby, an amphibious landing ship, apparently of the 13,000-ton Ivan Roger class, is shown under construction. The photography is distinct enough that objects such as ladders and windows can be identified. A second photo gives a more detailed view of the dry dock. It also indicates the position of vertical silo-launched SAMs forward of the superstructure.[19]

In April and May 1986, a KH-11 monitored the situation at the Chernobyl nuclear power plant, where a disastrous nuclear accident took place on April 26. Before the accident, the KH-11 had last photographed the site on April 16. After the TASS announcement of the accident on April 28, the KH-11 was instructed to take a photograph that very afternoon on its next pass. However, the photography was conducted at a considerable distance and subsequent computer enhancement did not produce a photograph that provided much information. The following morning another photograph was obtained, also from a considerable distance. By that afternoon the satellite was in a good position and obtained the first high-quality photograph of the damaged plant.[20]

At the time of the Chernobyl disaster, the United States was limited to one imaging satellite—the KH-11 launched in December 1984. The KH-8/GAMBIT program had been terminated in 1984. On August 13, 1985, the KH-11 launched on November 17, 1982, had been deorbited after a lifetime of 987 days. The seventh KH-11 was to be placed in orbit on August 28, 1985, using a Titan 34D booster; however, the launch failed when one of the two Aerojet engines of Titan's core vehicle shut down and the booster and payloads splashed into the Pacific.[21]

The only other launch vehicle that could have placed the KH-11, or a soon-to-be-ready advanced version, into orbit was the Space Transportation System. When the space shuttle orbiter *Challenger* exploded on January 28, 1986, the space shuttle program itself suffered a major setback. Then, on April 18, 1986, a Titan 34D booster exploded shortly after launch, 800 feet above the launch pad at Vandenberg AFB. Its payload was the last KH-9. The explosion also delayed the launch of another KH-11 until confidence in the 34D booster could be restored. Finally, on October 26, 1987, a Titan 34D carrying a KH-11 was successfully launched. On November 6, 1988, what has proved to be the final KH-11 was launched.[22]

Since that time two additional imagery programs have become operational. At least two Advanced KH-11/Improved CRYSTAL spacecraft have been placed into orbit (on March 1, 1990, and November 28, 1992). Like the KH-11, the new satellite transmits data in real time—via SDS and possibly DSCS satellites. In addition, like the KH-11, the Advanced KH-11 has a mirror system that makes it possible to produce images of targets in front of or to either side of the spacecraft. Unlike the KH-11, however, the Advanced KH-11 has an infrared/thermal-imaging capability that permits detection of camouflage as well as a limited nighttime imagery capability. Further, the Advanced KH-11 carries the Improved CRYSTAL Metric System (ICMS), which allows imagery to be sent back, when desired, with reseau markings. Such markings are of great value to cartographers in the Defense Mapping Agency.[23]

Additionally, the Advanced KH-11 can carry more fuel than the original model, perhaps 10,000 to 15,000 pounds. This feature will permit a longer lifetime for the new model—possibly up to eight years. A greater fuel supply also allows a greater ability to maneuver. Thus, an Advanced KH-11 can operate at times in higher orbits to produce images covering a larger territory than is possible at lower altitudes—and then maneuver to lower orbits to produce higher-resolution imagery. The maneuvering capability could be employed in attempts to evade ASAT weapons or to defeat denial and deception activities.[24]

The other addition to the U.S. imaging fleet, a radar imagery satellite, was first known as INDIGO, then as LACROSSE. LACROSSE closed a major gap in U.S. satellite imagery capabilities because it is able to penetrate cloud cover.[25]

Cloud cover can be a serious impediment to producing imagery—whether the target is Russia or Iraq. Some areas in Russia are covered by clouds about 70 percent or more of the year. In other cases the cloud cover is such that imaging a particular area or target may take several years. Occasionally, a complete picture can be formed only by constructing a photographic montage of an area made up of pictures taken on a number of orbital passes. During the Persian Gulf War of 1991, Iraq made extensive use of cloud cover in attempting to hide its mobile missile launchers from U.S. electro-optical imaging satellites. Cloud cover also complicated the task of bomb damage assessment.[26]

The first LACROSSE was launched on December 2, 1988, from the space shuttle orbiter *Atlantis*. A second was orbited on March 8, 1991, from Vandenberg AFB on a Titan IV. Built by Martin Marietta at a cost of about $1 billion, LACROSSE was a CIA project. When conceived, its primary target was to be Soviet and Warsaw Pact armor. Orbiting at about 400 miles above the earth, LACROSSE has a resolution in the area of 5–10 feet. Data acquired by LACROSSE is relayed back to a ground station at White Sands, New Mexico, by the Tracking and Data Relay Satellite (TDRS).[27]

In the past several years, the three types of imaging satellites have been used to monitor a large number of activities and facilities around the world. In addition to monitoring traditional targets in the former Soviet Union and successor states, the satellites have conducted extensive reconnaissance of Iraq as well as producing imagery of Iranian, Algerian, and North Korean nuclear facilities, a Libyan chemical warfare plant, Israeli–South African missile development activities, Israeli West Bank settlement construction, and drug production facilities.[28]

Satellite imagery systems may eventually include one designed to provide broad area coverage to tactical/battlefield commanders—nicknamed the 8X, the system is expected to capture images covering eight times as much territory as other U.S. imagery satellites. After the Persian Gulf War of 1991, complaints were heard about the United States's inability to simultaneously monitor significant parts of the battlefield. According to a DIA official, only the enemy's "large static defense strategy allowed us to track his numbers and disposition with acceptable accuracy." The lack of broad, synoptic, or near-simultaneous coverage made it difficult to fix the table of organization of some Iraqi units, led to an overestimation of Iraqi troop numbers, and contributed to the problems NATO countries confronted in trying to completely eliminate the mobile Scuds.[29]

Satellites are the most productive of U.S. imaging collection systems because they are able to overfly without hindrance and can provide imagery almost instantaneously. However, they have limitations. Even if already in orbit, they cannot be dispatched to cover events on short notice. In addition, because they fly on a well-known, predictable path, a nation that seeks to hide its activities from view may be able to take countermeasures. Further, such systems are extraordinarily expensive and priorities must be set; inevitably some areas are neglected.

Aircraft reconnaissance systems can supplement satellite coverage as well as provide a quick reaction capability. With the retirement of the SR-71 in January 1990, the only U.S. strategic reconnaissance aircraft with a worldwide mission that remained in operation was the U-2.[30] More than fifty-five U-2s in various versions are believed to have been built. In 1991 there were seven of them in the U.S. arsenal.[31]

CIA and Lockheed development of the U-2, designated Project AQUATONE, began in 1954 at the urging of the Eisenhower administration's Surprise Attack Panel. The aircraft became operational in 1956 and began overflying the Soviet Union that year. The U-2 proceeded to bring back significant intelligence on airfields, aircraft, missile testing and training, nuclear weapons storage, submarine production, atomic production, and aircraft deployment. The center of U-2 operations against the Soviet Union was Adana, Turkey, where U-2 operations were conducted by the 10-10 Detachment under the cover of the Second Weather Observational Squadron (Provisional). In the late 1950s, the U-2s were used against a variety of other targets, including the Negev desert site (Dimona) where Israel's nuclear weapons production facility was being built.[32]

It was the flight of May 1, 1960, which began in Peshawar, Pakistan, and was to conclude 3,788 miles later in Bodo, Norway, that brought the U-2 to world attention. The plane was shot down, but its pilot, Francis Gary Powers, survived to stand trial. Powers's plane contained a camera with a rotating 944.6-mm lens that peered through seven holes in the belly of the plane. It could take 4,000 paired pictures of a 125-mile-wide, 2,174-mile strip of the Soviet Union.[33]

The U-2R, the version used today, has a wingspan of 103 feet, a height of 16 feet, and a length of 63 feet. It has a range of more than 3,000 miles, a maximum speed of 528 knots at an altitude of 40,000 feet, and an operational ceiling of more than 70,000 feet. Like the SR-71, the U-2R can be equipped with a variety of sensors. The U-2R's H Camera system, with an electro-optical relay capability, can provide 6-inch resolution at its nadir and 12- to 18-inch resolution at a distance of 35–40 nautical miles (nm). The Optical Bar Camera is a thirty-inch focal length panoramic camera capable of providing six-inch resolution. The Advanced Synthetic Aperture Radar System (ASARS) developed for the U-2R is an all-weather, day-night, standoff imaging system designed to detect, locate, classify, and in some cases identify enemy ground targets. The ASARS was developed to collect and process radar imagery in near-real-time at 10-foot resolution. U-2Rs are capable of slant photography—looking into the target area at an angle. Thus, one can be flying along the borders of a region and still get pictures inside those borders.[34]

U-2s have been flown from bases in Cyprus, Turkey, Pakistan, Japan, Formosa, Okinawa, the Philippines, Alaska, West Germany, and England. These flights have provided photographic intelligence not only on the Soviet Union but also on China, North Korea, and the Middle East. In the 1980s, U-2 cameras regularly took pictures of military construction and arms depots in Nicaragua in order to document the buildup of military forces there. U-2s have also been used for overhead reconnaissance directed against other targets in the Caribbean and Central America—for example, Cuba and Grenada. In August 1989, U-2s flew missions over Ethiopia in an attempt to find the missing aircraft of Representative Mickey Leland. During Operations Desert Shield and Desert Storm, they flew more than 800 missions over the Persian Gulf region, enabling U.S. personnel to track Iraqi troop and armor buildups, assess bomb damage, survey Iraq for nuclear, chemical, and biological weapons sites, and monitor a massive Persian Gulf oil spill. On two occasions, U-2s provided warning of incoming Scud missiles. More recently, U-2 missions over Bosnia were conducted three times weekly. At present, U-2s, which are operated by the Air Combat Command, fly from Beale AFB, California, the Middle East (Detachment 3 at RAF Akrotiri on Cyprus), and Asia (Detachment 2 at Osan AB, Korea).[35]

In 1988 a new plane was added to the strategic imaging arsenal. This plane, a modified C-135, is known as the RC-135X or COBRA EYE and has a very limited mission. It is part of the Optical Aircraft Measurement Program, which is jointly managed by the Ballistic Missile Defense Organization and the Army. Equipped with a large optical telescope, it flies BURNING VISION missions to observe Russian ballistic missile tests off Kamchatka. The plane was previously based in Alaska but is now stationed at Offutt AFB, Nebraska.[36]

Several other aircraft are considered tactical reconnaissance planes—although the line between strategic and tactical is not always clear. Just as there is a TENCAP (Tactical Exploitation of National Capabilities) program to provide tactical forces with data from national collection systems, there is a NETCAP (National Exploitation of Tactical Capabilities) program to provide national intelligence using tactical systems.

One "tactical" system is the TR-1A, of which there are presently twenty-five. The TR-1A is a copy of the U-2R and is a single-engine, single-seat, fixed-wing aircraft that has been used to support NATO theater intelligence requirements. It operates at above 60,000 feet and at 430 mph and has a range of more than 3,000 miles. It is in service with the 95th Reconnaissance Squadron at RAF Alconbury, U.K.[37]

In addition, the United States deployed the Tactical Reconnaissance Exploitation Demonstration System (TREDS), which gathered, processed, and disseminated data collected by the TR-1, at METRO TANGO, the codename for an old missile maintenance facility near Hahn Air Base in Germany. TREDS was designed to demonstrate the potential of a large-scale integrated information processing and reporting system in support of battlefield commanders. It was the prototype for TRIGS—the TR-1 Ground Station—a hardened facility that was to be located north of METRO TANGO.[38]

The TR-1 ASARS can transmit intelligence data to the ground in near-real-time. Up to twelve U-2/TR-1 aircraft were deployed to the Persian Gulf during Desert Shield and Desert Storm. Flying from Beale AFB and RAF Alconbury, the aircraft flew seven or eight sorties per day around the clock with an average mission duration of nine hours. A mobile version of the TREDS was deployed in Saudi Arabia to downlink TR-1 data in support of Desert Storm. The mobile station may also have included the TRIGs system, which provides secure, automated processing and dissemination of TR-1 data. Rather than being returned to its original German location, the TRIGs, now known as the Contingency Airborne Reconnaissance System (CARS), is kept in disassembled form, ready to be transported.[39]

Tactical overhead imagery for the Navy is presently obtained by specially equipped F-14s fitted with the Tactical Air Reconnaissance Pod System (TARPS). The TARPS contains two day-only optical imagery sensors (the KS-87B serial frame camera and the KA-99 panoramic camera) and a day-night high-resolution infrared imagery sensor. The KS-87B has high-resolution forward oblique or vertical film, and the KS-99 has high-resolution panoramic film. There is no data link that would allow the real-time transmission of data.[40]

Three TARPS-equipped F-14s are assigned to one of two F-14 squadrons on each carrier air wing. The plane can operate at an altitude of between 500 and 50,000 feet, has a 500-nm range, and can operate for two hours. A total of forty-eight TARPS-equipped F-14s were envisioned in 1983. Targets include land-based installations such as coastal defenses, lines of communications, and foreign ships.[41]

TARPS-equipped F-14s flew 279 missions during Operation Desert Storm. During a period of extremely low tides (January 28 through February 2, 1991) they were used to detect mines, and over land they photographed targets such as Iraqi Scud missile launch sites, storage bunkers, and the Al Qaim superphosphate fertilizer plant.[42] However, according to Admiral Thomas Brooks, Director of Naval Intelligence during Operation Desert Storm, the film-based TARPS "was totally inadequate" in providing satisfactory and timely bomb damage assessment.[43]

During the Persian Gulf War the United States relied on Unmanned Aerial Vehicles (UAVs)/Remotely Piloted Vehicles (RPVs) in addition to manned reconnaissance aircraft. Six units employing Pioneer UAVs were deployed to the Middle East—three with Marine Corps ground units, one attached to the Army's 7th

Corps, and one each on board the battleships *Wisconsin* and *Missouri*. Each unit consisted of about five RPVs that could be controlled from fixed ground stations to a distance of 100 nm and from portable stations to a distance of 40 nm. Equipped with either television or forward-looking infrared sensors, the Pioneers operated day and night, making a total of 307 flights in Operation Desert Storm.[44]

The Navy employed the Pioneers for several purposes—hunting for mines, conducting reconnaissance in support of SEAL missions, and searching for Iraqi Silkworm missile sites, command and control bunkers, and antiaircraft artillery sites. Meanwhile, the Marines employed the RPVs in conjunction with attack aircraft for near-real-time targeting. A Pioneer spotted one of the first Iraqi probes into Saudi Arabia, west of Ras al-Kafki, on January 29, 1991.[45]

A second RPV system employed in the Gulf War was the Pointer. Five Pointer units, each with four air vehicles and two ground stations, operated in the Gulf area with Marine units and the Army's 82nd Airborne Division. Normally operating at an altitude of 500 feet, although it can reach 1,000 feet, the Pointer can fly for about an hour.[46]

While a medium-range UAV program was canceled in 1993, there are several UAV programs in development. The CIA, in conjunction with the Department of Defense, has been pursuing a multitier program to develop new UAVs with a range of capabilities, including varied sensor systems, ranges, degrees of endurance, and stealth capability. Congress, however, may mandate the cancellation or consolidation of various tiers of the UAV program.

Tier I of the program began in February 1994 with the deployment of a CIA unit and two specially modified General Atomics (GNAT) 750 UAVs to an Albanian base on the northern Adriatic coast. Stationing the unit in Albania followed Italy's refusal to serve as host. A primary mission of the UAVs was the monitoring of Serbian artillery emplacements in Bosnia.[47]

Tier II of the program involves the GNAT 750-45, also known as PREDATOR. The enlarged UAV would be fitted with infrared and electro-optical sensors, the latter with a 6-foot resolution. The 500-pound payload will eventually include a synthetic aperture radar and a satellite communications data link. Tier II aircraft would operate at 15,000 to 25,000 feet for twenty-four hours at a time.[48]

The UAV for the Tier II+ program would operate at 65,000 feet. Tier III- will be limited to carrying one imaging sensor at a time and will have less endurance than Tier II+, possibly being able to stay aloft for no more than eight hours. It will, however, have a significant stealth capability.[49] Another large, stealthy, proposed UAV would have been so expensive that a maximum of four could have been built. Called the Advanced Airborne Reconnaissance System, it would have been so heavily classified that if it had crashed "we would have had to bomb it to ensure that it was destroyed," according to a defense official.[50]

PROCESSING AND INTERPRETATION

Imagery can be obtained from the visible-light portion of the electromagnetic spectrum using either film-based or television-type photographic equipment, as described previously. Even imagery obtained via a conventional camera instead of a digital imaging system can be converted into digital signals. The signals can then be computer processed to improve the quantity and quality of information to be extracted. Specifically, computers disassemble a picture into millions of electronic Morse code pulses and then use mathematical formulas to manipulate the color contrast and intensity of each spot. Each image can be reassembled in various ways to highlight special features and objects that were hidden in the original image.[51] Such processing allows:

- building multicolored single images out of several pictures taken in different bands of the spectrum, making the patterns more obvious;
- restoring the shapes of objects by adjusting for the angle of view and lens distortion;
- changing the amount of contrast between objects and backgrounds;
- sharpening out-of-focus images;
- restoring ground details largely obscured by clouds;
- conducting electronic optical subtraction, in which earlier pictures are subtracted from later ones—making unchanged buildings in a scene disappear while new objects, such as missile silos under construction, remain;
- enhancing shadows; and
- suppressing glint.[52]

Such processing plays a crucial role in easing the burden on photogrammetrists and photo interpreters. Photogrammetrists are responsible for determining the size of objects from overhead photographs using, along with other data, the shadows cast by objects. Photo interpreters are trained to provide information about the nature of the objects in photographs—based on information as to what type of crates carry MiG-21s, for instance, or what an IRBM site or fiber optics factory looks like from 150 miles in space. Such information is provided in interpretation keys such as those listed in Table 7-2. Thus, an

> interpreter might see a picture with excavations, mine headframes, derricks, piles of waste, conveyor belts, bulldozers and power shovels, but with just a few buildings. His key would suggest that this is a mine. Special kinds of equipment, the tone or color of the waste piles and the ore piles, as well as knowledge of local geology, might further indicate that this was a uranium mine.[53]

The ultimate utility of any imaging system is a function of several factors—the most prominent being resolution. Resolution can be defined as the minimum size that an object must be in order to be measurable and identifiable by photo analysts. The higher the resolution, the greater the detail that can be extracted from a

Table 7-2.   Joint Imagery Interpretation Keys.

World Tanks and Self-Propelled Artillery	Major Surface Combatants
World Towed Artillery	Minor Surface Combatants
General Transportation Equipment	Mine Warfare Types
World Tactical Vehicles	Amphibious Warfare Types
Combat Engineer Equipment	Naval Auxiliaries
World Mobile Gap and River Crossing Equipment	Intelligence Research Vessels
Coke, Iron, and Steel Industries	Shipborne Electronics
Chemical Industries	Shipborne Weapons
World Electronics	Airfield Installation
World Missiles and Rockets	Petroleum Industries
Military Aircraft of the World	Atomic Energy Facilities
Submarines	

Source: Defense Intelligence Agency Regulation 0-2, "Index of DIA Administrative Publications," December 10, 1982, pp. 35–36.

photo. It should be noted that resolution is a product of several factors—the optical or imaging system, atmospheric conditions, and orbital parameters, for example.[54]

The degree of resolution required depends on the specificity of the intelligence desired. Five different interpretation tasks have been differentiated. *Detection* involves locating a class of units or objects or an activity of military interest. *General identification* involves determining general target type, and *precise identification* involves discrimination within target type of known types. *Description* involves specifying the size-dimension, configuration-layout, components-construction, and number of units. *Technical intelligence* involves determining the specific characteristics and performance capabilities of weapons and equipment.[55] Table 7-3 gives estimates of the resolution required for interpretation tasks.

Factors other than resolution that are considered significant in evaluating the utility of an imaging system include coverage speed, readout speed, analysis speed, reliability, and enhancement capability. Coverage speed is the area that can be surveyed in a given amount of time, readout speed the speed with which the information is processed into a form that is meaningful to photo interpreters, and reliability the fraction of time in which the system produces useful data. Enhancement capability refers to whether the initial images can be enhanced to draw out more useful data.[56]

Digital satellite imagery can also now be employed in some esoteric ways. Satellite imagery, when combined with elevation data, can be used to produce a three-dimensional image of the landscape of an area of interest—whether it be Serbia or south Beirut. The capability, first developed at the Jet Propulsion Laboratory, can be used to familiarize individuals—from national leaders to military personnel to clandestine intelligence personnel—with a particular geographical area.

In the spring of 1994 the CIA acquired an additional capability. Once a three-dimensional view of an area had been created, an individual would be able to use

Table 7-3. Resolution Required for Different Levels of Interpretation.

Target	Detection	General Identification	Precise Identification	Description	Technical Intelligence
Bridge	20 ft.	15 ft.	5 ft.	3 ft.	1 ft.
Communications radar/radio	10 ft./10 ft.	3 ft./5 ft.	1 ft./1 ft.	6 in./6 in.	1.5 in./6 in.
Supply dump	5 ft.	2 ft.	1 ft.	1 in.	1 in.
Troop units (bivouac, road)	20 ft.	7 ft.	4 ft.	1 ft.	3 in.
Airfield facilities	20 ft.	15 ft.	10 ft.	1 ft.	6 in.
Rockets and artillery	3 ft.	2 ft.	6 in.	2 in.	.4 in.
Aircraft	15 ft.	5 ft.	3 ft.	6 in.	1 in.
Command and control hq.	10 ft.	5 ft.	3 ft.	6 in.	1 in.
Missile sites (SSM/SAM)	10 ft.	5 ft.	2 ft.	1 ft.	3 in.
Surface ships	25 ft.	15 ft.	2 ft.	1 ft.	3 in.
Nuclear weapons components	8 ft.	5 ft.	1 ft.	1 in.	.4 in.
Vehicles	5 ft.	2 ft.	1 ft.	2 in.	1 in.
Land minefields	30 ft.	20 ft.	3 ft.	1 in.	–
Ports and harbors	100 ft.	50 ft.	20 ft.	10 ft.	1 ft.
Coasts and landing beaches	100 ft.	15 ft.	10 ft.	5 ft.	3 in.
Railroad yards and shops	100 ft.	50 ft.	20 ft.	5 ft.	2 ft.
Roads	30 ft.	20 ft.	6 ft.	2 ft.	6 in.
Urban area	200 ft.	100 ft.	10 ft.	10 ft.	1 ft.
Terrain	–	300 ft.	15 ft.	5 ft.	6 in.
Surfaced submarines	100 ft.	20 ft.	5 ft.	3 ft.	1 in.

Sources: Adapted from U.S. Congress, Senate Committee on Commerce, Science, and Transportation, *NASA Authorization for Fiscal Year 1978, Part 3* (Washington, D.C.: U.S. Government Printing Office, 1977), pp. 1642–43; and Bhupendra Jasani, ed., *Outer Space—A New Dimension in the Arms Race* (Cambridge, Mass.: Oelgeschlager, Gunn & Hain, 1982), p. 47.

a joystick to wander around the area as well as inside the three-dimensional buildings. Such an orientation experience would be particularly useful to inspectors and intelligence officers—who would benefit from the experience of moving around a building or area before entering it.

DISSEMINATION

Even in crises or war situations far from the United States, a substantial amount of imagery is processed in the United States—since it would be impossible for on-the-scene imagery interpreters to handle the volume of imagery relevant to military operations. Thus, during Desert Storm, the NPIC and other imagery interpretation organizations in Washington served as primary sources of imagery interpretation.

Primary Transmission Systems link Washington (or other locations in the United States) to military command headquarters or facilities in the United States and overseas. Probably the first node in these systems is either the Defense Satellite Communications System (DSCS) or the Fleet Satellite Communications System (FLTSATCOM). One Primary Transmission System is the Digital Imagery

Transmission System (DITS), which links Washington with the U.S. Central Command headquarters at MacDill AFB, Florida.[57]

Another system, consisting of a communications system and a computer link, permitted the transmission of a "relatively high volume" of imagery from the Army Intelligence Agency (AIA) in Washington to the Army component of the U.S. Central Command (ARCENT) in Saudi Arabia during Operation Desert Storm.[58]

Secondary Transmission Systems allow military commands that have received imagery from primary distribution systems or other means to relay such data to subordinate units. One secondary imagery transmission system is the Central Command Imagery Transmission System (CITS). Among its components is the Portable Receive and Transmit System (PORTS). The U.S. Central Command's PORTS reached initial operating capability during 1987.[59]

A Secondary Transmission System also exists within the European Command. The EUCOM Secondary Imagery Transmission System (EUCOMSITS) network consists of five SITS nets composed of Air Force ICON, Fleet Imagery Support Terminals (FISTs), and PORTS Imagery Processing Systems, ancillary devices, and interconnecting communications circuits.[60]

During Operation Desert Shield, at least twelve different secondary imagery dissemination systems were brought into the theater, including the DIA-purchased Digital Video Imagery Transmission System (DVITS) and the Air Force's Tactical Digital Facsimile (TDF). Of the twelve systems deployed, only four were interoperable.[61]

In addition to receiving data via primary and secondary dissemination systems, U.S. forces deployed overseas may also receive data directly from certain collection systems. Among the most prominent systems reported to be involved in the direct readout of data is the CONSTANT SOURCE UHF receipt and exploitation system. The terminals can be used to process the data in ways appropriate for specific missions—airlift, counter-air, interdiction, close air support, and electronic countermeasures/suppression of enemy air defenses.[62]

The Fleet Imagery Support Terminals (FISTs) on U.S. aircraft carriers, which transmit imagery from shore locations to ships, from ship to shore, from ship to ship, or from shore to shore, may receive data directly from the space system. Key Army units also have an imagery reception capability. Included are seven Tactical High-Mobility Terminals that permit the transmission of static photographs down to the location of the terminals.[63]

Eventually, it may be possible to send real-time satellite imagery as well as signals intelligence directly into the cockpits of tactical aircraft. Experiments intended to lead to such an option were under way in early 1993. In addition, real-time information from satellites may be used in the future to cue missiles fired from aircraft at enemy radar systems. Under a program designated TALON SWORD, tests conducted in April 1993 used intelligence data to directly cue missiles fired at simulated enemy radars by F-16 and EA-6B aircraft. Another phase of TALON SWORD involves transmitting satellite intelligence into F-15E cockpits for targeting enemy positions with smart bombs.[64]

Another program, TALON LANCE, would equip aircraft with a computer package that would allow high-speed processing of space intelligence data. TALON LANCE–equipped aircraft would be able to locate and identify an enemy on the ground or in the air. The aircraft crew could then decide whether to attack or avoid contact long before the aircraft's normal on-board sensors could detect the enemy.[65]

A third program, TALON SPECTRUM, involves investigating the feasibility of displaying satellite imagery itself in aircraft *during* combat operations. Air Force technicians already convert imagery into a digital format that can be manipulated on a computer display that pilots and navigators can view to familiarize themselves with their missions prior to takeoff.[66]

NOTES

1. William E. Burrows, *Deep Black: Space Espionage and National Security* (New York: Random House, 1987), p. 28.

2. Ibid., p. 32.

3. See Jeffrey T. Richelson, *American Espionage and the Soviet Target* (New York: William Morrow, 1987), p. 16.

4. Bhupendra Jasani, *Outer Space—Battlefield of the Future?* (New York: Crane, Russak, 1978), p. 12.

5. Farouk el-Baz, "EO Imaging Will Replace Film in Reconnaissance," *Defense Systems Review* (October 1983): 48–52.

6. Richard D. Hudson, Jr., and Jacqueline W. Hudson, "The Military Applications of Remote Sensing by Infrared," *Proceedings of the IEEE* 63, 1 (1975): 104–28.

7. Ibid.; Bruce G. Blair and Garry D. Brewer, "Verifying SALT," in William Potter, ed., *Verification and SALT: The Challenge of Strategic Deception* (Boulder, Colo.: Westview, 1980), pp. 7–48.

8. Homer Jensen, L. C. Graham, Leonard J. Porcello, and Emmet N. Leith, "Side-looking Airborne Radar," *Scientific American,* October 1977, pp. 84–95.

9. For a history of the KEYHOLE program, see Jeffrey T. Richelson, *America's Secret Eyes in Space: The U.S. Keyhole Spy Satellite Program* (New York: Harper & Row, 1990).

10. Richelson, *America's Secret Eyes in Space,* p. 126.

11. D. C. King-Hele, J. A. Pilkington, H. Hiller, and D.M.C. Walker, *The RAE Table of Earth Satellites, 1957–1980* (New York: Facts on File, 1982), p. 474.

12. John Pike, "Reagan Prepares for War in Outer Space," *Counter Spy* 7, 1 (1982): 17–22; James Bamford, "America's Supersecret Eyes in Space," *New York Times Magazine,* January 13, 1985, pp. 39ff.; Paul Stares, *Space and National Security* (Washington, D.C.: Brookings, 1987), p. 18.

13. Letter from Anthony Kenden to author, May 23, 1985.

14. Bamford, "America's Supersecret Eyes in Space."

15. George Lardner, Jr., "Satellite Unchanged from Manual Bought by Soviets, U.S. Official Says," *Washington Post,* October 10, 1985, p. A20.

16. "Inside the Rescue Mission," *Newsweek,* July 12, 1982, p. 19; Richelson, *America's Secret Eyes in Space,* pp. 200–201.

17. "Soviet Strategic Bomber Photographed at Ramenskoye," *Aviation Week & Space Technology,* December 14, 1981, p. 17; Max White, "U.S. Satellite Reconnaissance During the Falklands Conflict," Earth Satellite Research Unit, Department of Mathematics, University of Aston, Birmingham, England, n.d.

18. "Satellite Pictures Show Soviet CVN Towering Above Nikolaiev Shipyard," *Jane's Defence Weekly,* August 11, 1984, pp. 171–73; Lardner, "Satellite Unchanged from Manual Bought by Soviets, U.S. Officials Say."

19. "Satellite Pictures Show Soviet CVN Towering Above Nikolaiev Shipyard."

20. Private information; Nigel Hawkes, Geoffrey Lean, David Leigh, Robin McKie, Peter Pringle, and Andrew Wilson, *Chernobyl: The End of the Nuclear Dream* (New York: Vintage, 1986), pp. 99–103.

21. "Industry Observer," *Aviation Week & Space Technology,* September 9, 1985, p. 150; "Titan 34D Booster Failed Following Premature Shutdown of Aerojet Engine," *Aviation Week & Space Technology,* November 18, 1985, p. 26.

22. "Titan Explosion Cripples U.S. Launch Surveillance Capability," *Aviation Week & Space Technology,* April 28, 1986, pp. 16–19; William J. Broad, "2 Years of Failure End as U.S. Lofts Big Titan Rocket," *New York Times,* October 27, 1987, pp. A1, C4.

23. "KH-11 Overruns Said to Slow Development of Follow-On Spacecraft," *Aerospace Daily,* January 23, 1984, pp. 16–17; "Secret Payload Launched on Titan IV," *Washington Times,* November 30, 1992, p. A2; "Sixth Titan 4 Launched," *Aviation Week & Space Technology,* December 7, 1992, p. 19; Vincent Kiernan, "Titan 4 Launches Spy Satellite from Vandenberg AFB," *Space News,* December 7–13, 1992, p. 26; Richelson, *America's Secret Eyes in Space,* p. 231.

24. Deborah G. Meyer, "DOD Likely to Spend $250 Billion on C³I Through 1990," *Armed Forces Journal International,* February 1985, pp. 72–84; Pat Ohlendorf, "The New Breed of High-Tech Peacekeeper," *Maclean's,* January 23, 1984, pp. 52–53; Walter Pincus, "Hill Conferees Propose Test of Space Arms," *Washington Post,* July 11, 1984, pp. A1, A13; Edward Welles, "The New Right Stuff," *San Jose Mercury News,* January 8, 1984, p. 13.

25. Bob Woodward, *Veil: The Secret Wars of the CIA, 1981–1987* (New York: Simon & Schuster, 1987), p. 221.

26. Paul E. Sherr, Arnold H. Glasser, James C. Barnes, and James H. Williand, *Worldwide Cloud Cover Distributions for Use in Computer Simulations* (Concord, Mass.: Allied Research Associates, 1968), p. 5; William J. Broad, "Iraqis Using Clouds to Cover Scud Firings, Meteorologists Say," *New York Times,* January 25, 1991, p. A10; Gerald F. Seib and Walter S. Mossberg, "Iraqi Missiles Hit Israel as U.S. Presses Air Attacks," *Wall Street Journal,* January 18, 1991, pp. A1, A3.

27. "Space Reconnaissance Dwindles," *Aviation Week & Space Technology,* October 6, 1980, pp. 18–20; "Navy Will Develop All-Weather Ocean Monitor Satellite," *Aviation Week & Space Technology,* August 28, 1978, p. 50; Craig Covault, "USAF, NASA Discuss Shuttle Use for Satellite Maintenance," *Aviation Week & Space Technology,* December 17, 1984, pp. 14–16; "Washington Roundup," *Aviation Week & Space Technology,* June 4, 1979, p. 11; Robert C. Toth, "Anaheim Firm May Have Sought Spy Satellite Data," *Los Angeles Times,*

October 10, 1982, pp. 1, 32; Bill Gertz, "New Spy Satellite, Needed to Monitor Treaty, Sits on Ground," *Washington Times*, October 20, 1987, p. A5; Woodward, *Veil*, p. 221; Bill Gertz, "Senate Panel Asks for Radar Funds," *Washington Times*, April 5, 1988, p. A4; Craig Covault, "Atlantis' Radar Satellite Payload Opens New Reconnaissance Era," *Aviation Week & Space Technology*, December 12, 1988, pp. 26–28.

28. Craig Covault, "Recon Satellites Lead Allied Intelligence Effort," *Aviation Week & Space Technology*, February 4, 1991, pp. 25–26; Bill Gertz, "S. Africa to Test Ballistic Missile," *Washington Times*, May 3, 1991, p. A3; Bill Gertz, "Laotian Military Smuggling Drugs," *Washington Times*, April 25, 1991, p. A11; Bill Gertz, "Soviets Testing Rail-Mobile Rocket," *Washington Times*, April 12, 1991, p. A5; Bill Gertz, "China Helps Algeria Develop Nuclear Weapons," *Washington Times*, April 11, 1991, p. A3; David E. Sanger, "Furor in Seoul over North's Atom Plant," *New York Times*, April 16, 1991, p. A3; Bill Gertz, "Satellites Spot Poison Bomb Plant in Libya," *Washington Post*, March 5, 1991, p. A3; "International," *Military Space*, January 27, 1992, p. 6.

29. R. Jeffrey Smith, "Senators, CIA Fight over $1 Billion," *Washington Post*, July 16, 1993, p. A4; David A. Fulghum, "Key Military Officials Criticize Intelligence Handling in Gulf War," *Aviation Week & Space Technology*, June 24, 1991, p. 83.

30. There have been numerous claims that the United States has developed a Mach 6 successor to the SR-71, codenamed, at one point, AURORA. For example, Bill Sweetman, "Out of the Black: Secret Mach 6 Spy Plane," *Popular Science*, March 1993, pp. 56ff. However, although there appears to have been a program in the early 1980s to develop a Mach 5 successor, and DARPA did experimental work under the codename COPPER CANYON, the program was canceled. A program to develop an unmanned follow-on to the SR-71— the Advanced Airborne Reconnaissance System (AARS)—was canceled in 1993 for budgetary reasons. According to Ben Rich, former head of Lockheed's "Skunk Works," AURORA was the codename for the funding for the competition to develop the B-2. See Malcolm W. Browne, "Rumors of U.S. Superplane Appear Unfounded," *New York Times*, January 19, 1993, p. C8; "Air Force Abandoned SR-71 Follow-on in Mid-1980s," *Aerospace Daily*, January 13, 1993, pp. 55–57; Rich Tuttle, "Airborne Sensors Draw New Interest," *Aviation Week & Space Technology*, January 10, 1994, pp. 61–62; U.S. Congress, Senate Committee on Armed Services, *Department of Defense Authorization for Appropriations for Fiscal Year 1994 and the Future Years Defense Program* (Washington, D.C.: U.S. Government Printing Office, 1993), p. 477; Ben Rich and Leo Janos, *Skunk Works: A Personal Memoir of My Years at Lockheed* (Boston: Little, Brown, 1994), pp. 309–10.

31. "U-2 Facts and Figures," *Air Force Magazine*, January 1976, p. 45; "Reconnaissance and Special Duty Aircraft," *Air Force Magazine*, May 1991, pp. 167–70.

32. David Wise and Thomas B. Ross, *The U-2 Affair* (New York: Random House, 1962), p. 56; Seymour Hersh, *The Samson Option: Israel's Nuclear Arsenal and American Foreign Policy* (New York: Random House, 1991), pp. 52–54.

33. Wise and Ross, *The U-2 Affair*, p. 11.

34. Asa Bates, "National Technical Means of Verification," *Royal United Services Institute Journal* 123, 2 (June 1978): 64–73; Secretary of the Air Force, Office of Public Affairs, United States Air Force Fact Sheet 83-5, "U-2"; Private information.

35. Wise and Ross, *The U-2 Affair*; Howard Silber, "SAC U-2's Provided Nicaraguan Pictures," *Omaha World Herald*, March 10, 1982, p. 2; Brian Bennett, Tony Powell, and John Adams, *The USAF Today* (London: West London Aviation Group, 1981), p. 135; Air Com-

bat Command Regulation 23-1, Volume 15, "Headquarters Air Combat Command Organization and Functions: Summary of Changes," October 23, 1992, p. 4; David A. Fulghum, "U.S. Deploys U-2, TR-1 Spy Aircraft over Gulf in Intelligence Missions," *Aviation Week & Space Technology*, September 3, 1990, pp. 31–32; Office of History, 9th Wing, *History of the 9th Wing* (Beale AFB, Calif.: 9th Wing, 1993), pp. x–xvii, 12; Jerry Gray, "U.N. Using U.S. Spy Planes to Monitor Iraqi Arms," *New York Times*, August 13, 1991, p. A5; U.S. Congress, House Armed Services Committee, *Intelligence Successes and Failures in Operations Desert Shield/Storm* (Washington, D.C.: HASC, 1993), p. 13; Remarks of William F. Lackman, Jr., Director, Central Imagery Office, at National Military Intelligence Symposium, November 15, 1993, Washington, D.C.

36. Craig Covault, "Alaskan Tanker, Reconnaissance Mission Capabilities Expanded," *Aviation Week & Space Technology*, June 6, 1988, pp. 70–72.

37. Office of Legislative Liaison, Secretary of the Air Force, *Systems Information Briefs for Members of Congress* (Washington, D.C.: Department of the Air Force, 1987), p. 45; "Reconnaissance and Special Duty Aircraft"; Office of History, *History of the 9th Wing*, p. 14.

38. John D. Morocco, "Air Force Plans New Engine, Ground Station for TR-1," *Aviation Week & Space Technology*, June 4, 1990, pp. 22–23. With respect to responsibilities for TR-1 operations, see ED (EUCOM Directive) 40-9, TR-1 Tactical Reconnaissance System Operations, June 6, 1989.

39. Bruce D. Nordwall, "U.S. Relies on Combination of Aircraft Satellites, UAV's for Damage Assessment," *Aviation Week & Space Technology*, February 4, 1991, pp. 24–25; Bruce A. Smith, "U-2/TR-1 Provided Critical Data to Theater Commanders," *Aviation Week & Space Technology*, August 19, 1991, pp. 60–61; Remarks of Maj. Gen. Ervin J. Rokke, ACS, I, HQ, USAF, at National Military Intelligence Association Symposium, November 15, 1993, Washington, D.C.

40. Private information.

41. Private information.

42. "'Filtering' Helped Top Military Leaders Get Proper Intelligence Information," *Aviation Week & Space Technology*, April 22, 1991, p. 84; Robert W. Ward et al., *Desert Storm Reconstruction Report, Volume 8, C³/Space and Electronic Warfare* (Alexandria, Va.: Center for Naval Analyses, 1992), pp. 6–10.

43. Barbara Starr, "TARPS Was Weak Link in BDA," *Jane's Defence Weekly*, August 3, 1991, p. 190.

44. "Gulf War Experience Sparks Review of RPV Priorities," *Aviation Week & Space Technology*, April 22, 1991, pp. 86–87.

45. Ibid.

46. Ibid.

47. David A. Fulghum and John D. Morocco, "CIA to Deploy UAVs in Albania," *Aviation Week & Space Technology*, January 31, 1994, pp. 20–22; "Gnats Weathered Out," *Aviation Week & Space Technology*, February 14, 1994, p. 19.

48. Fulghum and Morocco, "CIA to Deploy UAVs in Albania."

49. "Secret Flying Wing Slated for Rollout," *Aviation Week & Space Technology*, September 19, 1994, pp. 27–28.

50. Fulghum and Morocco, "CIA to Deploy UAVs in Albania."

51. Paul Bennett, *Strategic Surveillance* (Cambridge, Mass.: Union of Concerned Scientists, 1979), p. 5.

52. Richard A. Scribner, Theodore J. Ralston, and William D. Mertz, *The Verification Challenge: Problems and Promise of Strategic Nuclear Arms Control Verification* (Boston: Birkhauser, 1985), p. 70; John F. Ebersole and James C. Wyant, "Real-Time Optical Subtraction of Photographic Imagery for Difference Detection," *Applied Optics* 15, 4 (1976): 871–76.

53. Scribner et al., *The Verification Challenge*, p. 69.

54. James Fusca, "Space Surveillance," *Space/Aeronautics* (June 1964): 92–103.

55. U.S. Congress, Senate Committee on Commerce, Science and Transportation, *NASA Authorization for Fiscal Year 1978, Part 3* (Washington, D.C.: U.S. Government Printing Office, 1977), pp. 1642–43.

56. Ibid.; National Photographic Interpretation Center, *Problems of Photographic Imagery Analysis,* February 26, 1968.

57. Central Command, *United States Central Command 1987 Command History,* March 27, 1990, p. II-26.

58. Brig. Gen. John Stewart, Jr., *Operation Desert Storm: The Military Intelligence Story: A View from the G-2 3rd U.S. Army,* April 1991, p. 7.

59. Central Command, *U.S. Central Command 1987 Command History,* p. II-36.

60. Space Applications Corporation, *European Command Secondary Imagery Transmission System (EUCOMSITS)* (Vienna, Va.: Space Applications Corporation, June 1989).

61. U.S. Congress, House Committee on Armed Services, *Intelligence Successes and Failures in Operations Desert Shield/Storm,* p. 20.

62. AFSPACECOM Public Affairs, "AFSPACECOM Assists in Mideast Response," n.d.

63. House Appropriations Committee, *Department of Defense Appropriations for 1992, Part 6* (Washington, D.C.: U.S. Government Printing Office, 1991), p. 470.

64. "AF Would Send Real-time Recce Satellite Images to Tactical Planes," *Aerospace Daily,* January 8, 1993, p. 1; James R. Asker, "F-16, EA-6B to Fire Missiles Cued by Intelligence Satellites," *Aviation Week & Space Technology,* April 19, 1993, p. 25; Ben Iannotta, "Space to Play Bosnian Role," *Space News,* May 10–16, 1993, pp. 1, 2; Tony Capaccio, "Air Force Pushes 'In Your Face from Outer Space,'" *Defense Week,* July 12, 1993, pp. 1, 8.

65. David A. Fulghum, "Talon Lance Gives Aircrews Timely Intelligence from Space," *Aviation Week & Space Technology,* August 23, 1993, p. 71.

66. Ben Iannotta, "USAF Tests Imagery Use in Cockpits," *Space News,* September 20–26, 1993, p. 18.

8
SIGNALS INTELLIGENCE

Signals intelligence (SIGINT) is traditionally considered one of the most important and sensitive forms of intelligence. The interception of foreign signals can provide data on diplomatic, military, scientific, and economic plans or events as well as on the characteristics of radars, spacecraft, and weapons systems.

SIGINT can be broken down into two basic components: communications intelligence (COMINT) and electronics intelligence (ELINT). As its name indicates, COMINT is intelligence obtained through the interception, processing, and analysis of the communications of foreign governments or groups, excluding radio and television broadcasts. The communications may take a variety of forms, such as voice, Morse code, radioteletype, or facsimile, and may be either encrypted or transmitted in the clear.

The targets of COMINT operations are varied. The most traditional COMINT target is diplomatic communications—the communications from each nation's capital to its diplomatic establishments around the world. The United States has intercepted and deciphered the diplomatic communications of a variety of nations—for example, Britain's communications during the 1956 Suez Crisis, Libya's communications to its East Berlin People's Bureau prior to the bombing of a nightclub in West Berlin in 1985, and Iraq's communications to its embassy in Japan in the 1970s.

The United States also targets the communications between different components of a large number of governments—on some occasions both components are located within the country being monitored, but on others at least one is located outside national boundaries. Communications frequently targeted include those between government and/or ministry officials; a ministry or agency and its subordinate units throughout the country and abroad; arms factories and various military or government officials; military units, especially during exercises and operations, or military and government officials; and police and security forces and their headquarters. More specifically, the United States intercepts communications between the Chinese Ministry of Defense and subordinate military units; Russian military units; the Pakistani Atomic Energy Commission and Pakistani nuclear facilities; the President of Egypt and his subordinates (including during the time when Egypt was holding the hijackers of the *Achille Lauro*); and Israeli officials in Tel Aviv and Israeli representatives on the West Bank.

In 1968, intercepted voice communications in the Beijing Military Region indicated a field exercise involving the 4th Armored Division. In 1980, U.S. intercepts of Soviet communications led to a fear that the Soviets were about to invade Iran. Intercepts allowed the United States to piece together the details concerning the sinking of a Soviet submarine in the North Pacific in 1983, and in 1988, Iraqi military communications led U.S. officials to the conclusion that Iraq had used chemical weapons in its war with Iran. In September 1994, the United States intercepted communications from Haitian dictator Raoul Cedras in which he said that he would determine his response to President Clinton's demands based on the reaction of the American public to the president's forthcoming speech on U.S. Haitian policy.[1]

At times, entire sets of targets may be dropped or coverage of others dramatically increased. In the early 1970s, the United States dropped COMINT coverage of the Soviet civil defense network (although later it was resumed). In 1983 it began an all-source intelligence program (that included COMINT) to improve intelligence on the Soviet prison camp system, with the specific intent of issuing a study that would embarrass the Soviets. The intelligence was intended to determine the location of the camps, the conditions, and the number of political prisoners. In recent years, COMINT coverage of targets related to nuclear and ballistic missile proliferation has increased dramatically.

Governmental communications do not exhaust the set of COMINT targets. The communications of political parties and of corporations involved in the sale of technology related to advanced weapons developments may also be targeted. In addition, the communications of terrorist groups are targeted—both to permit understanding of how the group functions and of the personalities of its leaders and to allow prediction of where and how it will strike next.

Another major set of COMINT targets are those associated with economic activity (of both the legal and illegal variety)—the communications of international banking firms and narcotics traffickers, for example. In 1970, the predecessor to the Drug Enforcement Administration informed NSA that it had "a requirement for any and all COMINT information which reflects illicit traffic in narcotics and dangerous drugs." Specific areas of interest included organizations and individuals engaged in such activities, the distribution of narcotics, cultivation and production centers, efforts to control the traffic in narcotics, and all violations of U.S. laws concerning narcotics and dangerous drugs.[2]

Electronic intercept operations are intended to produce electronics intelligence (ELINT) by intercepting the noncommunication signals of military and civilian hardware, excluding those resulting from atomic detonations. Under NSA project KILTING, all ELINT signals are stored in computerized reference files containing the most up-to-date technical information about the signals.

The earliest of ELINT targets were World War II air defense radar systems. The objective was to gather sufficient information to identify the location and operating characteristics of the radars—and then circumvent or neutralize them during bombing raids (through direct attack or electronic countermeasures). The information desired included frequencies, signal strengths, pulse lengths, pulse rates, and other specifications. Since that time, intelligence, space tracking, and ballistic missile early warning radars have joined the list of ELINT targets.

In the early 1950s the primary targets were Soviet bloc (including PRC) radars. Russian radars remain a target, although a less critical one. Monitoring Russian radars also has an arms control verification aspect, since the 1972 Anti-Ballistic Missile (ABM) Treaty restricts the use of radars in an "ABM mode." During the Vietnam War, North Vietnamese radars were also major targets; Libyan and Iranian radars are clearly prime targets of the late 1980s.

A subcategory of ELINT is Foreign Instrumentation Signals Intelligence (FISINT). Foreign instrumentation signals are electromagnetic emissions associated with the testing and operational deployment of aerospace, surface, and subsurface systems that have military or civilian applications. Such signals include, but are not limited to, those from telemetry, beaconing, electronic interrogators, tracking/fusing/aiming/command systems, and video data links.[3]

A subcategory of FISINT is Telemetry Intelligence (TELINT). Telemetry is the set of signals by which a missile, stage of a missile, or missile warhead sends back data about its performance during a test flight. The data relate to structural stress, rocket motor thrust, fuel consumption, guidance system performance, and the physical conditions of the ambient environment. Intercepted telemetry can provide data used to estimate the number of warheads carried by a given missile, its payload and throw-weight, the probable size of its warheads, and the accuracy with which the warheads are guided at the point of release from the missile's post-boost vehicles.[4]

Radar intelligence (RADINT)—the intelligence obtained from the use of nonimaging radar—is similar to ELINT in that no intercepted communications are involved. However, RADINT does not depend on the interception of another object's electronic emanations. Rather, it is the radar that emanates electronic signals—radio waves—and the deflection of those signals that allows for intelligence to be derived. This method allows operators to obtain information on flight paths, velocity, maneuvering, trajectory, and angle of descent. RADINT is not an element of SIGINT but of another variety of technical collection—Measurement and Signature Intelligence (MASINT). The similarity of missions and targets of some ground-based radars, however, makes it appropriate to discuss RADINT and SIGINT together.*

The ease with which signals (electronic or otherwise) can be intercepted and understood depends on three factors: the method of transmission, the frequencies employed, and the encipherment system (or lack thereof) used to conceal signals' meanings from unauthorized personnel.

---

*MASINT will be discussed in more detail in Chapter 9.

The most secure method of transmission is by cable, either via landlines or ocean cables. Communications or other signals transmitted in this manner cannot be snatched out of the air. Interception of cable traffic has involved physically tapping into the cables or the use of "induction" devices placed in the proximity of the cables and maintenance of equipment at the point of access. This option might be impossible in the case of hardened and protected internal landlines— the type that carries much high-priority secret command and control communications.

A tremendous volume of communications is sent via satellite systems—for example, domestic and international telephone messages and military and business communications are regularly transmitted via satellite using ultra, very, super, and extremely high frequencies (UHF, VHF, SHF and EHF). Thus, the United States and other nations have established major programs for the interception of communications transmitted via satellite. By locating satellite dishes at the proper locations, technicians can intercept an enormous volume of traffic. Whereas ground station antennas can direct the signals to a satellite with great accuracy, satellite antennas are smaller and the signals they send back to earth are less narrowly focused—perhaps covering several thousand square miles.[5]

Oftentimes, communications are transmitted partly by satellite and partly via microwave towers. In other cases—particularly in the case of telephone calls within a country, as in Canada—microwave towers serve as the entire means of transmission and reception. As one observer has written with regard to microwave relay towers: "With modern communications, 'target' messages travel not simply over individually tappable wires like those that connect the ordinary telephone, but as part of entire message streams, which can contain up to 970 individual message circuits, and have voice, telegram, telex and high speed data bunched together."[6]

Microwave signals can be intercepted by two means: (1) ground stations near the invisible line connecting the two microwave towers and (2) space collection systems, if the area of transmission is within the footprint of the system.

Radio is the most traditional means for the transmission of signals—including communications, missile telemetry, and foreign instrumentation signals. The accessibility of radio signals to interception often depends on the frequencies upon which the signal is transmitted and the signal's geographic location. Messages transmitted at lower frequencies (ELF, VLF, LF, HF) travel for long distances since they bounce off the atmosphere and will come down in locations far from the transmitting and intended receiving locations. In contrast, data sent at higher frequencies will "leak" through the atmosphere and out into space. To intercept such signals, intercept stations must be within line-of-sight of the radio communications. The curvature of the earth can therefore make monitoring from ground-based sites impossible. Former CIA Deputy Director for Intelligence Sayre Stevens has written of the Soviet ballistic missile defense test center at Sary Shagan: "It lies deeply enough within the USSR to make it difficult to monitor from peripheral intelligence-gathering sites along the border. Because flight test operations at Sary Shagan can be conducted well below the radio-horizon from such external monitoring locations, the Soviet Union has been able to conceal the details of its activities at Sary Shagan for many years."[7] Under such conditions geosynchronous space collection systems may be necessary to collect the signals.

Two additional methods of communication that are targets of interception operations are walkie-talkie and radio-telephone communications. Walkie-talkie communications are employed during military exercises as well as during emergency situations—such as Chernobyl. Radio-telephone communications are used by government officials as they travel in their limousines. Since walkie-talkie traffic, particularly in Russia and China, may occur over areas not accessible to ground stations, satellite interception may be required. Radio-telephone traffic, in contrast, is particularly common in national capital areas, where embassy-based listening posts are often found.

Once intercepted, signals have to be processed. If communications are sent without encipherment or scrambling, then the only processing will be translation. Communications may be sent in the clear either because they are considered to be too low level to justify the time and expense for protection or because the method of transmission (e.g., cable) is believed immune to interception.

Electronic signals sent in the clear still need to be interpreted. Thus, telemetry signals on all channels may be transmitted as numbers. The variables being measured and the units of measurement must be inferred by correlating data on missile maneuvers with the intercepted telemetry. For example, measurement may be made concerning different types of events: one-time events (e.g., the firing of explosive bolts or the separation of RVs from the post-boost bus), discontinuous events (e.g., adjustments to the guidance system during flight), and continuous events (e.g., fuel flow, motor burn, or acceleration of the missile during the boost phase). These events can be expressed in terms of absolute values, arbitrary values (on a one-to-ten scale), relative values (percentages), or inferential values. It will not necessarily be evident what particular characteristic an intercepted reading refers to or the particular values that are being used. A fuel tank reading may be given as "30," which could refer either to a tank that is 30 percent full or 30 percent empty. The temperature in the rocket motor combustion chamber can be measured from the temperature of another part known to have a specific temperature relative to that in the chamber.

Communications or electronic signals may be either encrypted or scrambled, complicating the process of turning the intercepted signals into intelligence. Diplomatic communications are traditionally enciphered. The sophistication of the encipherment and the quality of the operators determine whether such ciphers can be broken. Conversations via radio and radio-telephone are frequently scrambled. Soviet leaders started to have their radio-telephone conversations scrambled after they became aware of a U.S. operation to intercept those conversations. Noncommunications signals may also be encrypted—as were a large portion of Soviet missile telemetry signals.

Interception of signals involves a massive effort employing space and airborne collectors, ground stations, covert listening posts, surface ships, and submarines.

SPACE COLLECTION

The United States operates three basic types of signals intelligence satellite systems. Since 1962 it has been operating low–earth orbiting satellites designed to intercept signals emitted by Soviet, Chinese, and other nations' air defense, ABM, and early-warning radars. Known as *ferrets* in the popular literature, these satellites are actually referred to as *balls* within the U.S. intelligence community.

The first ferret was launched by a Thor-Agena B on May 15, 1962, into an orbit with a 190-mile perigee and a 392-mile apogee. Between the first launch and July 16, 1971, seventeen satellites of the initial type were launched, about one to three satellites each year. The inclination of the earlier ferrets was approximately 82 degrees, whereas the inclination of the later satellites was 75 degrees. Likewise, the orbit changed after the first several launches to a more circular one with about 300 miles separating the satellite from the earth. Switches to new boosters in June 1963 and October 1968 may have been indications of new generations of ferrets coming into operation.[8]

A second class of ferrets was put into operation beginning in August 1963. Whereas each satellite in the first class had been launched as a rocket's sole payload, satellites in the new class served as secondary payloads to imaging satellites. Like the previous models, the new ferrets had elliptical orbits of 180 by 250 miles that gave way to more circular orbits in the vicinity of 300 miles above the earth.[9] By 1972 there were no longer launches solely to place ferret satellites in orbit. From 1972 until 1988 only ferret subsatellites were launched. In general, the satellites were launched as secondary payloads on launches of the KH-9 imaging satellite.

Traditionally, ferrets were arranged in constellations of four to maximize direction-finding capability. On September 5, 1988, the first satellite of what was intended to be a new four-satellite constellation of ferrets was launched. The new-generation ferret was the primary payload on a Titan II launched from Vandenberg AFB. It was placed into an 85-degree inclined, 500-mile circular orbit. This launch was followed by similar Titan II launches on September 5, 1989, and April 25, 1992. The 1989 launch may also have carried an infrared package to test the ability to detect aircraft from space.[10]

It appears that the new constellation may not reach its intended strength. In 1993 three Titan II boosters that had been designated for a "classified user" were reassigned to the Strategic Defense Initiative Organization. In addition, the Joint Chiefs of Staff "Roles and Missions" report indicated that the missions being performed by two existing national satellite systems would be performed by a single new system. The ferret satellite system may be one of the systems referred to in the report.

In addition to ferret satellites, the United States is presently operating three types of geosynchronous satellites. In the early 1970s the United States began employing a set of geosynchronous satellites initially given the codename RHYOLITE. A total of five RHYOLITE spacecraft were placed into orbit, with one launch failure. The orbited RHYOLITEs were launched on June 19, 1970; March 6, 1973; either May 23 or December 11, 1977; and April 7, 1978. All were launched from Cape Canaveral using an Atlas-Agena D booster.[11]

By the time the fourth satellite was in orbit, a two-station arrangement had emerged. Two of the satellites apparently were stationed near the Horn of Africa at 45 degrees east to receive telemetry signals transmitted from liquid-fueled ICBMs launched from Tyuratam in a northeasterly direction toward the Kamchatka Peninsula impact zone. Another two spacecraft were stationed farther east, over Borneo, at 115 degrees east, to monitor Soviet solid-propellant missiles such as the SS-16 ICBM and the SS-20 IRBM, launched from the Soviet Union's northern space launch facility at Plesetsk.[12] Their respective footprints provided coverage of almost all of the USSR, Africa, Europe, Asia, and the Middle East.

In addition to the telemetry signals from Soviet and Chinese missile tests, RHYOLITE satellites collected COMINT. Their COMINT function was dramatically increased on orders from President Nixon and Henry Kissinger once they discovered their capability. The satellites apparently were used to intercept Soviet and Chinese telephone and radio communications across the VHF, UHF, and microwave frequency bands. Robert Lindsey has written that the satellites "could monitor Communist microwave radio and long-distance telephone traffic over much of the European landmass, eavesdropping on a Soviet commissar in Moscow talking to his mistress in Yalta or on a general talking to his lieutenants across the great continent."[13]

Walkie-talkie communications generated by Soviet military exercises, which fall in the VHF/UHF range, also were regularly monitored by RHYOLITE satellites. Beyond the Soviet Union, RHYOLITE satellites intercepted communications from China, Vietnam, Indonesia, Pakistan, and Lebanon.[14]

The RHYOLITE project was described by former CIA official Victor Marchetti as

> a very interesting project, a very much advanced project in terms of technology, and a very desirable project because getting information of the type that we wanted and needed on Soviet ICBM testing, antiballistic missile programs, anti-satellite programs, and the like, much of this activity of course takes place in eastern Siberia and central Asia, getting information on the Chinese ICBM program.[15]

The RHYOLITE program suffered a serious setback in 1975 when a TRW employee, Christopher Boyce, and his boyhood friend Andrew Daulton Lee sold technical details about RHYOLITE to the KGB. In accordance with standard security practice, the NRO changed the codename to AQUACADE.[16]

It is unlikely that any of the RHYOLITE/AQUACADE satellites are operational at this time. The first of a follow-on generation, originally codenamed MAGNUM and subsequently ORION, was launched from the space shuttle Discovery on January 25, 1985. Subsequent ORIONs were launched on November 22, 1989, and November 15, 1990—both by space shuttle orbiters.[17]

The MAGNUM/ORION satellite, which weighs about 6,000 pounds, is reported to have two huge parabolic antennas. One is intended to intercept communications and telemetry signals. The first ORION may have been stationed over Borneo. The three-satellite constellation is probably spaced to cover communications across the Eurasian landmass.[18]

Exactly how much of an improvement ORION is over RHYOLITE/AQUACADE is not known publicly. One possibility is that ORION is able to pick up lower-powered signals than RHYOLITE, such as "turned-down" telemetry. ORION's increased power might come from bigger antennas, and the satellite's potential is suggested by a project that was to be undertaken for NASA by Lockheed's Missile and Space Company. The project involved unfurling an antenna in space from the space shuttle's cargo bay. The umbrella-shaped antenna, nearly twice the size of a football field, is so sensitive to low-powered signals from earth that it can pick up broadcasts from radios the size of a wristwatch.[19]

In addition, ORION may have some stealth or spoofing capabilities that make it harder to find and its signals harder to jam—unlike the AQUACADE, with which the Soviets allegedly interfered in the 1980s. In 1984, Richard Perle, Assistant Secretary of Defense for International Security Policy, charged in testimony before the House Foreign Affairs Committee that the USSR had begun jamming telemetry-monitoring satellites to prevent the collection of even the encrypted data. The jamming was alleged to be electronically precise, to have begun sometime after the Soviets shot down Korean Airlines Flight 007 in 1983, and to occur only during missile testing. The distinctive visual and radar image of ORION ordinarily would allow the Soviets to determine its location and mission.[20] Hence, some sort of stealth technology may have been incorporated to hide it from Soviet detection.

On June 10, 1978, about six and a half years before the first ORION launch, the first launch in another geosynchronous SIGINT satellite program took place. Originally codenamed CHALET, the satellite program was renamed VORTEX after its first codename was revealed in the press.[21]

VORTEX's original mission was strictly COMINT-related. However, after the loss of Iranian ground stations and the discovery of Boyce and Lee's sale of RHYOLITE documents to the KGB, VORTEX was modified to allow it to intercept Soviet telemetry. The first modified VORTEX was launched on October 1, 1979. Subsequent launches occurred on October 31, 1981; January 31, 1984; September 2, 1988; May 10, 1989; and September 4, 1989. In all cases, the spacecraft, which weighed up to 4,200 pounds, were placed into orbit by Titan 3C or Titan 34D boosters. The satellite launched on September 2, 1988, did not initially reach geosynchronous orbit and may never have become operational.[22]

The primary targets of VORTEX, for most of the program's existence, were in the Soviet Union. In particular, they included the communications of Soviet missile and nuclear RDT&E sites, defense-related ministries, and defense industries. At the height of VORTEX operations, there were at least three operating VORTEX satellites—one covering Eastern Europe and the western USSR, another the central USSR, and the third the eastern portion of the Soviet Union. Each also covered non-Soviet targets in its footprint. During the Chernobyl incident, the VORTEX responsible for monitoring the western USSR was employed to intercept all communications within 200 miles of the accident site, including those of the General Staff, KGB, and GRU.[23]

Even before the collapse of the Soviet Union, VORTEX was targeted on the communications of numerous countries outside the Soviet bloc, including Israel, Iran, and other Middle Eastern countries. Thus, the VORTEX ground station at Menwith Hill in the United Kingdom was heavily involved in supporting Desert Shield and Desert Storm operations. In 1989 it received a Joint Meritorious Unit Award from Secretary of Defense Dick Cheney for "meritorious achievement from 1 May 1987 to 1 September 1988"—a period that matches U.S. naval operations in the Persian Gulf.[24]

Although the collapse of the USSR eliminated the need for a significant level of coverage in that region, officials have increased the time and effort devoted to monitoring nations with known or suspected nuclear weapons programs. It appears that the first launch in a new geosynchronous SIGINT satellite program took place on August 27, 1994, from Cape Canaveral. The satellite, which had been in development for more than five years, will apparently combine the VORTEX and ORION missions into a single program. Later versions of the spacecraft, which at one point may have been codenamed MENTOR, may weigh as much as 10,000 pounds.[25]

Unlike AQUACADE, MAGNUM, or VORTEX, a third class of SIGINT satellites did not operate in geosynchronous orbit. Rather, the first generation of this class—known as JUMPSEAT—has been launched into a 63-degree highly inclined elliptical orbit (200 by 24,000 miles) with Titan 3B–Agena D boosters from Vandenberg AFB. Approximately six JUMPSEATs were launched after the initial launch on March 20, 1971. Additional launches included those of August 21, 1973; March 10, 1975; and February 25, 1978. In its highly elliptical orbit, JUMPSEAT "hovered" over the Soviet Union for eight to nine hours at a time. It was developed for only one purpose—the monitoring of Soviet ABM radars.[26]

A far more advanced version of the JUMPSEAT satellite was launched on May 3, 1994. That launch culminated a ten-year effort to orbit the new satellite and a three-year effort from the time it first reached its launchpad at Cape Canaveral. The satellite weighs approximately 10,000 pounds. Like the original JUMPSEAT satellite, it operates in a highly inclined elliptical orbit. However, it appears to have a much more extensive mission, including COMINT. Although the intelligence community wished to leave the satellites in storage, feeling that the cost of operation and maintenance was not worth the benefit in the post–Cold War world, congressional overseers directed otherwise. The program has been cancelled, and no more such spacecraft will be built, but there are still two spacecraft on the ground awaiting launch.[27] There is also under development a SIGINT satellite system, originally codenamed INTRUDER, which is expected to perform the mission of all existing high-altitude SIGINT satellites.[28]

Satellite operations are supported by a worldwide network of ground control stations, which conduct housekeeping operations as well as receive information from the satellites. A key element in the network is the headquarters of the Consolidated Space Test Center (HQ CSTC), formerly the Air Force Satellite Control Facility, at Onizuka AFS (Sunnyvale). The HQ CSTC has ground stations across the globe—Vandenberg AFB; New Boston, New Hampshire; Kaena Point, Hawaii; Thule (AB), Greenland; Mahe, Seychelles; Andersen AFB, Guam; and Oakhanger, England. The stations perform basic housekeeping functions such as communicating commands to the satellites, altering orbits, and checking out the equipment on board. They may also receive ELINT data from the JUMPSEAT and ferret satellites.[29]

In addition to the HQ CSTC, several other specialized stations exist for the control of and reception of signals from SIGINT satellites. Fort Meade (NSA headquarters) is itself able to receive data from the satellites, but three overseas ground stations are the backbone of the network: Pine Gap, Australia; Menwith Hill, United Kingdom; and Bad Aibling, Germany.[30]

RHYOLITE/AQUACADE and MAGNUM satellites have been controlled since the beginning of their respective programs from a facility in Alice Springs, Australia, commonly known as Pine Gap. Officially, the facility is the Joint Defence Space Research Facility and is codenamed MERINO. The facility consists of seven large radomes, a huge computer room, and about twenty other support buildings. The radomes (which resemble gigantic golf balls with one of their ends sliced off) are made of Perspex and mounted on a concrete structure. They were intended to protect the enclosed antennas against dust, wind, and rain and to hide some of the operational elements of the antennas from Soviet imaging satellites.[31]

The first two radomes at Pine Gap were installed in 1968 and remain the facility's largest. The first appears to be about 100 feet in diameter and the second about 70 feet in diameter. They now form the western line of the antenna complex. The third and fourth radomes were fully installed by mid-1969. The third radome is about 55 feet in diameter and some 196 feet east of the largest radome, while the fourth is less than 20 feet in diameter and just north of the second radome. In 1973 the antenna that was originally installed inside the third radome was dismantled and replaced by a 33-foot communications terminal. The fifth radome is less than 40 feet in diameter and was installed in 1971. The sixth is about the same size as the fifth and was installed in 1977. The seventh radome, which was built in 1980, houses a second communications terminal.[32]

Originally, the main computer room was about 210 square feet, but it was expanded twice in the 1970s to its present size—about 60,000 square feet. Its immense size requires that operators at each end of the room communicate with each other using headphones. The room is divided into three principal sections. The Station-Keeping Section is responsible for maintaining the satellites in geosynchronous orbit and for correctly aligning them toward targets of interest. The Signals Processing Office receives the signals transmitted from the satellite and transforms them into a form that can be used by the analysts. The Signals Analysis Section is staffed solely by CIA personnel—no Australian citizens or contractor personnel are included. Many of the individuals in the section are linguists who monitor the voice intercepts.[33]

As of January 1986 there were 557 people employed at Pine Gap—273 Australians and 284 Americans. Although in theory Pine Gap is a joint facility, the fifty-fifty relationship holds only with respect to the gross number of personnel and is achieved by counting Australian housemaids, cooks, and gardeners who work at the base as "equal" to the CIA personnel who conduct the actual operations.[34]

Two other major control stations are located in the United Kingdom and Germany. In 1972–1974 NSA began augmenting its listening posts at Menwith Hill (which it took over from the Army in 1966) and Bad Aibling, West Germany, to permit the planned CHALET system to downlink its intercepted communications to those sites. Information received at either location can be transmitted directly via DSCS satellite to Fort Meade. Menwith Hill will also apparently serve as the primary ground station for the new geosynchronous SIGINT satellite mentioned above. In 1994 the U.S. Army Intelligence and Security Command took over responsibility for operating Menwith Hill and Bad Aibling.[35]

Within the United States, Buckley Air National Ground Base has served as the ground station for the JUMPSEAT program—and apparently performs the same function for the Advanced JUMPSEAT program.

AIRBORNE COLLECTION

At present, the single most important airborne platform involved in the collection of signals intelligence is the RC-135, which is operated by the 55th Strategic Reconnaissance Wing under the Air Combat Command (ACC). There have been twelve versions of the plane. The first RC-135, an RC-135B, entered the SAC reconnaissance inventory in December 1965. This step began the process of replacing thirty obsolescent RB-47Hs and ERB-47Hs that were then "performing the ELINT portion of the Global Peacetime Airborne Reconnaissance Program."[36]

At present there are twenty SIGINT RC-135s in the U.S. inventory. Fifteen are RC-135V/W RIVET JOINT planes, including one trainer. These and the other models of the RC-135 have an overall length of 129 feet, a wingspan of 131 feet, and an overall height of 42 feet. At its operational altitude, 34,990 feet, the plane cruises at 558 miles per hour.[37]

RIVET JOINT planes have flown their missions, known as BURNING WIND missions, from bases in Alaska (Eielson AFB), Nebraska (Offutt AFB), Panama (Howard Air Base), England (RAF Mildenhall), Greece (Hellenikon AB), and Japan (Kadena AB, Okinawa). During Desert Storm a RIVET JOINT began operating from Riyadh, Saudi Arabia.[38]

In the mid-1980s, RIVET JOINT/BURNING WIND missions averaged about seventy flights a month in Western Europe and the Far East and about twelve a month in Central America. As a result of the changed international environment, the frequency of flights targeted on former Soviet bloc states and other factors have led to the termination of RC-135 flights from Eielson AFB and Hellenikon. Flights from Howard AFB, Panama, may also have ceased.[39]

The RC-135V carries a crew of seventeen and flies at 35,000 feet for up to ten hours before it requires refueling. Its COMINT capability can be expanded from a minimum of six positions to thirteen, depending on the requirements of the mission. The RIVET JOINT ELINT system comprises three collection positions—an Automatic ELINT Emitter Location System position supplemented by two manual operator positions. The RIVET JOINT aircraft based at Eielson AFB patrolled along the Kamchatka and Chukotski peninsulas, intercepting short-range tactical signals from Soviet naval and ground forces. The missions proceeded around the southern tip of Kamchatka and into the Sea of Okhotsk, a projected deployment area for Soviet missile submarines. If not assigned to patrol over the Sea of Okhotsk, they slid down the coast toward Sakhalin Island. The missions monitored the alert status of Soviet air squadrons on Sakhalin as well as Soviet Air Force exercises. In the latter case the planes tracked Soviet fighters in flight. The Japanese-based RC-135s patrol along the coasts of Vietnam, China, North Vietnam, and Russia, including over the Sea of Okhotsk.[40]

British-based RIVET JOINT planes flew along the Baltic Sea and over the Barents Sea just off the Kola Peninsula, possibly intercepting signals from the three naval bases in the Murmansk area or the Severodvinsk submarine construction yard. The pilots were traditionally under orders not to get within 40 nm of the Soviet coastline and generally loitered 100 miles or more out over the Barents Sea until they intercepted signals of interest. That policy has probably not changed. The planes based at Hellenikon had among their targets Libya, Egypt, Israel, Syria, and to a lesser extent the USSR. Planes from Hellenikon were also periodically deployed to Saudi Arabia to operate against Iraq and Iran. In the past they have also been deployed to Egypt and the Sudan. RC-135s may now conduct those missions from RAF Akrotiri on Cyprus or Riyadh.[41]

RIVET JOINT/BURNING WIND missions flown from Nebraska and Panama were directed against Spanish- and Russian-language targets in Cuba and Central America. Central American flights were conducted in support of the El Salvador military and the Contra rebels.[42]

The remaining five RC-135 aircraft include two RC-135U and three RC-135S models. The RC-135Us (modified RC-135Cs) bear the nickname COMBAT SENT. COMBAT SENT missions were flown along the periphery of the Soviet Union and other Warsaw Pact countries, with specific routes, tactics, and even aircraft configurations varying with the tasking requirements.[43]

Like the RIVET JOINT planes, COMBAT SENT aircraft fly at 35,000 feet and can fly for ten hours without refueling if necessary. Among their targets have been ODD PAIR, SIDE NET, and TOP STEER radar systems. The primary sensor for COMBAT SENT is the Precision Power Measurement System, which determines the absolute power, power pattern, and polarization of selected target emitters. In addition, there is a high-resolution camera and television and radar sensors in the tail that are used when the occasion permits. One COMBAT SENT plane is equipped with a system known as COMPASS ERA, which contains infrared thermal imaging, interferometer-spectrometer, and spectral radiometer sensors.[44]

The RC-135S planes, which were based at Eielson AFB, Alaska, until late 1991 and operated on occasion from Shemya, are nicknamed COBRA BALL and are the result of a late 1960s modification of two C-135Bs. Their missions, known as BURNING STAR missions, involve monitoring the reentry phase of Russian and Chinese ICBM, SLBM, and IRBM research and development tests. The reentry phase of Russian ICBM tests from Plesetsk and Tyuratam takes place either at Kamchatka Peninsula or in the expanses of the Pacific. For example, in 1974 three Soviet ICBM test reentry phases concluded in the Pacific. In 1987 one test concluded in the vicinity of Hawaii. In late 1991 the COBRA BALL mission was transferred to Offutt AFB, Nebraska.[45]

Because COBRA BALL missions are dictated by foreign government decisions to conduct missile tests, missions cannot be planned on any regular basis. Only some of these tests—specifically, multiple tests or tests that have their reentry phase outside Russian territory—need to be announced in advance. Thus, the COBRA BALL aircraft must be ready to fly on a moment's notice in response to notification by the Defense Special Missile and Astronautics Center (DEFSMAC) that a Russian or Chinese test is about to occur.[46]

The planes operate at 35,000 feet and for up to ten hours unrefueled, and eighteen hours when refueled. Each COBRA BALL carries three sensor systems—one ELINT system and two photographic systems. The ELINT system is the Advanced Telemetry System (ATS), which automatically searches a portion of the frequency band and makes a digital record of all signals present. The operator of the ATS system allocates its collection resources to Soviet reentry vehicle links and records all telemetry detected.[47]

The Ballistic Framing Camera System images all the objects of interest in the reentry phase, and the Medium Resolution Camera (MRC) System photographs individual reentry vehicles.[48] The images produced by the MRC System are used to determine the reentry vehicle size; size estimates, in turn, are used to produce estimates of the explosive yield of the warheads.

During its orbit, the RC-135S records and cross-checks its position coordinates at least every twenty minutes. It is also called on to provide a variety of information—including air speed, altitude, estimated time of arrival, orbit point, adjustments in timing or track, track length in minutes, the status of the equipment, wind direction, and time remaining on the track.[49]

In late 1993, consideration was being given to adapting COBRA BALL aircraft to enable them to locate clandestine testing of ballistic and cruise missiles and possibly stealth aircraft. The aircraft may also be used to determine the precise locations of enemy missiles and aircraft in support of U.S. strikes against such targets. A COBRA BALL aircraft was tested in a Theater Missile Defense Operational Concept Demonstration in January 1993. The aircraft gathered and passed information to the Army's Pathfinder fire control system, which directed missiles and tube artillery.[50]

Also employed for signals intelligence purposes are eight CORONET SOLO EC-130 aircraft, which are flown by the U.S. Air National Guard's 193rd Tactical Electronic Combat Group (headquartered at Harrisburg International Airport, Pennsylvania). The aircraft carried COMFY LEVI SIGINT vans and are equipped with RIVER RIDER blade antennas. The COMFY LEVI vans are being replaced by a system designated SENIOR SCOUT. The planes have flown missions off El Salvador and along the Soviet-Turkish border. Central American missions were codenamed FLOWING PEN.[51]

Also employed for SIGINT collection are the U-2 and the TR-1A. There are three SIGINT collection systems designed for the U-2/TR-1: SENIOR RUBY, SENIOR STRETCH, and SENIOR SPEAR. SENIOR RUBY is a near-real-time ELINT collection, processing, and reporting system that provides information (including type and location) on radar emitters within line-of-sight of the U-2R. It can handle a large number of emitters simultaneously and send its data to a Ground Control Processor colocated with the COMINT Transportable Ground Intercept Facility (TGIF).[52]

SENIOR STRETCH is a near-real-time COMINT collection, processing, and reporting system. The airborne receiver subsystem consists of a multichannel microwave receiver that is remotely controlled via satellite link from the Remote Operations Facility, Airborne (ROFA), at Fort Meade. The data collected is transmitted via DSCS satellite back to the ROFA.[53]

SENIOR SPEAR is also a near-real-time collection, processing, and reporting system that provides a line-of-sight collection capability—out to 300 nm—from the aircraft. Another system, SENIOR SPAN, was under development as of 1983. SENIOR SPAN, to be installed in the U-2R, is a near-real-time SIGINT collection, processing, and reporting system with an airborne receiver subsystem consisting of HF, VHF, UHF, and microwave receivers. The receivers are remotely controlled via a satellite from the ROFA or a TGIF, with the collected data transmitted via satellite back to the control site.[54]

U-2/TR-1 missions have been flown from several bases against a variety of targets. From Patrick AFB, Florida, Detachment 5 of the 9th Strategic Reconnaissance Wing flies SENIOR JUMP U-2Rs in collection missions against Cuba. The main targets are Cuban army, air force, and navy communications, with the intercepts being transmitted to Key West Naval Air Station, Florida.[55]

SENIOR STRETCH U-2Rs fly from RAF Akrotiri (Operating Location OLIVE HARVEST) to intercept signals from Syria, Egypt, and Israel. The data are then uplinked to a DSCS satellite for transmission to the ROFA. From Osan AB, South Korea, SENIOR SPEAR U-2Rs fly OLYMPIC GAME missions against the communications of Chinese and North Korean activities, with the intercepted communications being downlinked to an Air Intelligence Agency unit at Osan.[56]

Two additional airborne SIGINT systems are Army systems: GUARDRAIL V and Improved GUARDRAIL V. GUARDRAIL is a remotely controlled airborne and ground-based intercept and radio-direction finding system, mounted on RU-21H/GUARDRAIL V and RC-12D (Improved Guardrail V) aircraft, designed to exploit HF, VHF, and UHF voice communications. Both aircraft operate at between 10,000 and 20,000 feet, have ranges of 320 km at 20,000 feet, and can spend four hours on station. The RC-12D aircraft produce a wider range of frequencies that can be obtained for intercept or direction-finding purposes. The targets of both sets of aircraft include mobile forces, missile units, aviation elements, air defense units, and artillery regiments. Each system consists of six aircraft—two RU-21Hs and four RC-12Ds.[57]

The RU-21H and RC-12D aircraft will be replaced by RC-12K GUARDRAIL Common Sensor (GRCS) aircraft, sometimes referred to as GUARDLOCK. Plans call for 48 RC-12Ks, several of which may already be in service. The RC-12Ks will combine the functions of RU-21H, RC-12D, and OV-1D Mohawk aircraft. Specifically, they will be able to collect both COMINT and ELINT. The planes will also carry Global Positioning System receivers, which will allow location of data to within 60 feet.[58]

An adjunct to the RC-12K is the Remote Relay System (RRS). Intercepted SIGINT data will be downlinked to the RRS, where it can automatically be relayed by satellite to any location where the appropriate receiving equipment can be set up.[59]

GROUND STATIONS

Beginning in the late 1940s the United States began establishing ground stations from which to monitor the Soviet Union and Eastern Europe. This network changed composition over the years and grew to include stations directed against China, Vietnam, North Korea, the Middle East, Central America, and other areas. Today the network, run by NSA, comprises more than fifty stations in approximately twenty countries. Included are heavily manned stations (employing about 30,000 personnel) and unmanned stations, which relay their "take" to other locations and then Fort Meade. In addition, several radar stations operated by the Air Force Space Command are involved in detecting and tracking Russian missile tests and space launches. The stations collectively conduct intercept operations across the VHF, UHF, and HF bands. Approximately thirty stations collect HF strategic COMINT while others focus on VHF and UHF tactical communications. Other stations target various forms of electronic emanations.

The biggest and most important set of stations are those established during the Cold War to monitor the Soviet Union and Warsaw Pact countries. At Shemya Island, Alaska—which is approximately 400 miles across the Bering Sea from the Russian Eastern Seaboard—is the Anders Facility. Run by the Bendix Field Engineering Corporation for NSA, the facility's Pusher HF antenna monitors Russian communications in the Far East.[60]

Also located on Shemya is the COBRA DANE phased-array radar, run by the Air Force Space Command's 16th Space Surveillance Squadron. The primary purpose of COBRA DANE is "to acquire precise radar metric and signature data on developing [Russian] ballistic missile weapons systems for weapons system characteristics determination. The [Russian] developmental test to Kamchatka and the Pacific Ocean provide[s] the United States with the primary source for collection of these data early in the [Russian] developmental programs."[61]

Its corollary mission, missile warning, is part of the Integrated Tactical Warning and Attack Assessment (ITW/AA) network. COBRA DANE provides warning of all "earth-impacting objects," including ballistic missiles targeted on the United States. Its secondary mission is space object tracking and identification.[62]

The COBRA DANE system consists of an AN/FPS-108 radar facility that measures 87 by 107 feet at its base, rises approximately six stories, or 100 feet, in height, and includes an attached, one-story, 87-square-foot Precision Measurement Equipment Laboratory (PMEL). This facility overlooks the Bering Sea from a 230-foot-high bluff in the northwestern section of Shemya.[63]

The most important characteristic of COBRA DANE is that it is a phased-array radar. To an observer depending only on his eyes or using binoculars, a phased-array radar is simply a dormant structure, sort of an electronic pyramid. This is in sharp contrast to the older, more traditional radar dish "sweeping its beam of microwave radiation along the horizon in search of distant objects." Rather, COBRA DANE consists of 15,360 radiating elements that occupy 95 feet in diameter on the radar's face. Each element emits a signal that travels in all directions. When the signals are emitted at the same time, only targets in the immediate vicinity of the array's perpendicular axis are detectable. By successively delaying the signals by a fraction of a wavelength, however, one can "steer" the beam to detect objects away from the perpendicular axis.[64]

COBRA DANE, which achieved initial operating capability on July 13, 1977, can detect (with a 99 percent probability) and track a basketball-sized object at a range of 2,000 miles with a 120-degree field of view extending from the northern half of Sakhalin Island to just short of the easternmost tip of Russia nearing the

Figure 8-1. Range of COBRA DANE Coverage.

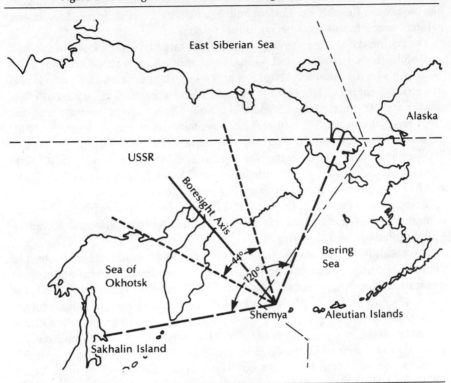

Bering Strait. Its ability to provide information on the size and shape of the object, however, is available only over a 44-degree range centered on the upper portion of Kamchatka, as indicated in Figure 8-1. COBRA DANE can simultaneously track up to 100 warheads when operating in an intelligence collection mode. It can also be employed for early warning and space surveillance; in those modes it can track up to 300 incoming warheads and up to 200 satellites, respectively.[65] The final near-earth trajectory of Soviet reentry vehicles is not visible to COBRA DANE, however, owing to line-of-sight constraints imposed by the curvature of the earth.[66]

Elmendorf AFB, located in Anchorage, is the home of a Naval Security Group Command unit, the 6981st Electronic Security Group of the Air Intelligence Agency, and an AN/FLR-9 "Elephant Cage" antenna. The AN/FLR-9 consists of three circular arrays, each made up of antenna elements around a circular reflecting screen. In the middle of the triple array is a central building containing the electronic equipment used to form directional beams for monitoring and direction-finding. The entire system is about 900 feet in diameter. The AIA contingent has monitored Russian Far Eastern military activity through voice, Morse, and printer intercepts and probably continues to do so.[67]

The equipment at Misawa AB in Japan is also targeted on the Russian Far East and probably North Korea and China. Four miles northwest of Misawa is the "Hill," on which a 100-foot AN/FLR-9 antenna system is situated. The base and its antenna lie at the northern tip of Honshu Island, about 500 miles west of Vladivostok and 400 miles south of Sakhalin Island. Misawa is a major base and employs representatives of all four services' cryptological elements. There is a 900-person detachment from the 6920th Electronic Security Group of the AIA, a 700-person detachment from the Naval Security Group Command (NSGC), 200 representatives from the Army's Intelligence and Security Command (INSCOM), and 80 representatives from Company E, Marine Support Battalion.[68]

Misawa is also the site of Project LADYLOVE, which involves intercepting the communications transmitted via several Russian satellite systems, including Molniya, Raduga, and Gorizont.[69]

Three additional stations, two of which are run by NSA, have been involved in the satellite communications interception project. Rosman Research Station was transferred from NASA to the Department of Defense on February 1, 1981, for use as a "Communications Research Station" and became operational on July 1, 1985, with 250 employees. The station closed in 1994. It had four satellite dishes pointed straight up and four in radomes. Also involved is Menwith Hill station, located 8 miles west of Harrowgate in Yorkshire. The station is located on 562 acres and consists of a large array of satellite-tracking aerials. Under Project MOONPENNY, a variety of Russian satellite communications are intercepted by Menwith Hill's antennas. Finally, the Bad Aibling station in Germany participates in the satellite communications (SATCOM) intercept project.[70]

RAF Chicksands, located in the United Kingdom near Bedford, was heavily involved in the interception of Soviet and West European communications. However, Chicksands is scheduled to close in the spring of 1995.[71]

Outside of Britain, several other important European ground stations, located in Germany, Turkey, and Italy, also monitored Soviet bloc activities. The German and Turkish stations still devote significant attention to Russia and other former Soviet states. A site at San Vito dei Normanni in Italy, with a 700-person Air Force contingent operating an AN/FLR-9 to intercept Russian, East European, and Middle Eastern communications, was abandoned in the summer of 1993.[72]

The single most important U.S. intelligence facility in Turkey is the one at Pirinclik Air Base, a satellite operation of Diyarbakir Air Station, particularly after the closure of Field Station Sinop. Located on a rocky plateau in southeastern Turkey, Pirinclik had its operations suspended from 1974 to 1978. During that time U.S. housekeeping personnel rotated one radar dish to prevent roller bearing damage while the Turks locked up a key piece of radar equipment to make sure the radar was inoperative.[73]

Figure 8-2.   Pirinclik Radar Coverage.

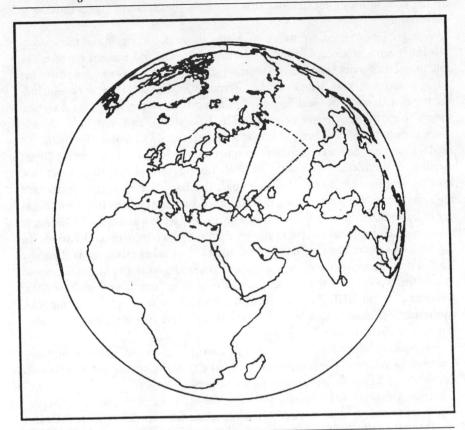

Source: 21st Crew Training Squadron, *Space Operations Orientation Course* (Peterson AFB, Colo.: AFSPACECOM, 1991), p. 36.

The base resumed operations on November 3, 1979, with its two radar antennas fixed permanently toward the northeast, where the CIS border lies 180 miles away. The electronic beams of the radar operate through a natural "duct" in the mountains around the plateau, picking up Russian missiles and space launches as they rise above the horizon. The AN/FPS-17 detection radar can detect an object 1 meter in diameter up to 5,000 miles away. After the AN/FPS-17 indicates that a missile launch or space shot has taken place, the AN/FPS-79 tracking radar "swings its white, round face in a noiseless arc in the same direction, ready to track missiles along their course."[74] The radar's coverage is shown in Figure 8-2.

The radars are operated largely by civilian technicians hired by the contractor, General Electric. In addition to 70 contractor personnel, there are about 145 Air Force personnel, mostly enlisted personnel. Few of the Air Force workers are permitted in the top-secret radar control rooms. Rather, they are more likely to operate the communications facilities that transmit the data via DSCS satellite to Washington.[75]

As might be expected, Germany was home to several strategic and tactical signals intelligence stations targeted on the Soviet Union and Eastern Europe. The collapse of the Soviet Union, East Germany, and other Warsaw Pact countries has brought about several changes in the German-based SIGINT network—including the deactivation of Field Stations Berlin and Augsburg, and several tactical sites. The most important remaining facility is located at Bad Aibling.[76]

As already noted, the Bad Aibling station serves as a downlink for VORTEX SIGINT data and as part of a four-station network involved in intercepting Soviet satellite communications. In addition, Bad Aibling has had two other functions. Employing Rhombic and Pusher antennas, the Bad Aibling station conducted high-frequency direction-finding (HFDF) and communications intercept coverage of Eastern Europe and the southwest portion of what was the Soviet Union. It also serves as the initial reception site for data from two unmanned locations on Cyprus and Oman. The Cyprus station consists of a Pusher HF antenna set up by NSA at the Episkopi Sovereign Base Area to cover targets in the Middle East and the southern portion of the former Soviet Union. The Abut Sovereign Base Area, home to a British SIGINT operation, also serves as a base of operations for NSA equipment designed to monitor military activity in the Near East and the southern former Soviet Union.[77]

A second set of stations are directed primarily against the activities of Asian Communist nations. The major targets are the PRC, Vietnam, and Korea, with Cambodia and Laos being very secondary targets.

Kunia is host to the NSA-run Defense Research Facility, staffed by representatives from INSCOM (703rd Military Intelligence Battalion), the NSGC, and the AIA. The station serves as an NSA Remote Operations Facility, receiving data from two remote facilities, those at Taegu, South Korea, and Khon Kean, Thailand.[78]

The Khon Kean facility was apparently set up in fall 1979 to correct a shortfall of intelligence during the China-Vietnam war earlier that year. The Taegu facility, run for NSA by the Bendix Field Engineering Group, is equipped with a Pusher HF antenna and targeted against communications in China, North Korea, and South Vietnam.[79]

Located at Pyong Taek, Korea, is the 751st Military Intelligence Battalion (formerly the U.S. Army Field Station Korea), a 304-person contingent with three detachments at different operating locations: Detachment J (at Koryo-Son Mountain on the island of Kangwna), Detachment K (at Kanak-San Mountain, six miles from the Demilitarized Zone, or DMZ), and Detachment L (on Yawol-San Mountain, within 1,500 meters of the DMZ). Collectively the installations target a variety of North Korean COMINT and ELINT targets.[80]

Latin America, and particularly Central America, became a target of increased importance during the Reagan administration. Although Central America is no longer a priority, Cuba continues to be a major concern. At Lackland AFB, Medina Annex, San Antonio, is a contingent from INSCOM (the 748th Military Intelligence Battalion) and one from the AIA (the 6948th Electronic Security Squadron). Homestead AFB, Florida, is the headquarters of Naval Security Group Activity Homestead, with its main operations center at Card Sound (known as Site Alpha or Seminole Station), which monitors Cuban HF military communications and all communications involving Cuban and Russian air activity originating in or destined for Cuba. Intercept operations are conducted using an AN/FRD-10 antenna system. Also targeted on Cuba are the antennas of the 749th Military Intelligence Company at Key West.[81]

Two stations on U.S. territory outside of the continental United States contribute to SIGINT operations directed against Latin America. More than 100 members of the Guantanamo Naval Security Group Activity are stationed at Guantanamo Bay, Cuba. Employing an AN/FRD-10 antenna system, the unit intercepts Cuban and Russian military communications in and around Cuba and the Caribbean Basin. A 430-person Naval Security Group Activity at Sabana Seca, Puerto Rico, which also uses an AN/FRD-10, targets international leased carrier and diplomatic communications for all of Central and South America.[82]

Two stations target INTELSAT/COMSAT satellite communications. An NSA facility at Sugar Grove, West Virginia, with 30-, 60-, 105-, and 150-foot satellite antennas, intercepts the signals being sent by the INTELSAT/COMSAT satellite over the Atlantic and intended for the INTELSAT/COMSAT ground station at Etam, West Virginia. A second installation, at the Yakima Research Station in Yakima, Washington, targets the Pacific INTELSAT/COMSAT satellite.[83]

COVERT LISTENING POSTS

In addition to the ground-based listening posts such as those described above, which use large tracts of land, there is a set of posts that are located in and on top of U.S. embassies and consulates. Such listening posts allow the United States to target the internal military, political, police, and economic communications of the nation in which the embassy is located. Such listening posts are joint CIA-NSA operations. Formally known as Special Collection Elements, they exist in approximately forty-five U.S. embassies and consulates.

The best known of the embassy listening posts is the one located in Moscow. In the late 1960s and early 1970s, this post intercepted the radio-telephone conversations of Soviet Politburo members—including General Secretary Leonid Brezhnev, President Nikolai Podgorny, and Premier Alexsei Kosygin—as they drove around Moscow.[84] Traffic from the interception operation was transmitted to a special CIA facility a few miles from the agency's Langley, Virginia, headquarters. Originally, the conversations simply needed to be translated, since no attempt had been made to scramble or encipher the conversations.[85]

After a 1971 disclosure in the press concerning the operation, codenamed GAMMA GUPY, the Soviets began enciphering their limousine telephone calls to plug leaks. Despite that effort, the United States was able to intercept and decode a conversation between General Secretary Brezhnev and Minister of Defense A. A. Grechko that took place shortly before the signing of the SALT I treaty. Grechko assured Brezhnev that the heavy Soviet SS-19 missiles under construction would fit inside the launch tubes of lighter SS-11 missiles, making the missiles permissible under the SALT I treaty.[86]

In general, however, the intelligence obtained was less than earthshaking. According to a former intelligence official involved in GAMMA GUPY, the CIA "didn't find out about, say, the invasion of Czechoslovakia. It was very gossipy—Brezhnev's health and maybe Podgorny's sex life." At the same time the official said that the operation "gave us extremely valuable information on the personalities and health of top Soviet leaders."[87]

Other covert listening posts are located in the U.S. embassies in Tel Aviv, Buenos Aires, and Santiago. The Tel Aviv outpost is targeted on Israeli military and national police communications. Thus, the United States has closely followed police efforts to suppress Palestinian demonstrators. The presence of a U.S. listening post has not gone unnoticed by Israeli officials—a large number of antennas are visible on the roof of the Tel Aviv Embassy.[88]

The Buenos Aires post was used to target the communications of the Argentine General Staff during the Falklands crisis—information that would be quickly passed to the British.[89]

SURFACE SHIPS

At one time the United States placed great reliance on signals intelligence gathered by ship-based sensors and began using combat ships in this role. Destroyers and destroyers' escorts often carried mobile vans packed with antennas as well as special detachments to operate the equipment. The use of destroyers and destroyers' escorts, however, degraded fighting capabilities because combat ships were being assigned to intelligence missions. Further, some Navy officials felt the stationing of a destroyer off a foreign shore, especially that of a hostile nation, to be provocative.[90]

Two alternatives were deployed in 1961 and 1965, respectively—Auxiliary General Technical Research (AGTR) and Auxiliary General Environmental Research (AGER) ships. The AGTRs were converted World War II Liberty ships—each 458 feet long and 10,860 tons. The AGERs were converted World War II–vintage diesel-driven, light-cargo ships approximately 170 feet in length with a maximum speed of 13 knots and a cruising speed of 10 knots. Each had an estimated range of 4,000 nm. AGER collection capability was more restricted than AGTR capability, being concerned with SIGINT and hydrographic information. Elimination of the AGER and AGTR collection ships resulted from events in 1967 and 1969. The AGTR USS *Liberty* was bombed by Israeli aircraft in the midst of the 1967 Six-Day War, resulting in severe damage and the death of thirty-four crew members. The Israeli government said the ship had been mistaken for an Egyptian vessel; others have alleged that the attack was deliberate and intended to prevent the United States from learning of Israeli military gains and pressuring Israel into a "premature" cease-fire.[91]

In 1969 the AGER USS *Pueblo* was captured by the North Koreans and its crew held hostage. Shortly after the *Pueblo* was seized, the USS *Sergeant Joseph P. Muller* almost drifted into Cuban waters. After several attempts the ship was finally towed to safety by its escorting destroyer. Subsequently, the AGERs and AGTRs were decommissioned.[92]

In the 1980s the United States began employing Spruance-class destroyers and frigates to collect intelligence concerning Nicaragua and El Salvador. The 7,800-ton destroyer *Deyo*, as well as its sister ship *Caron*, were stationed in the Gulf of Fonseca. The ships could monitor suspected shipping, intercept communications and encrypted messages, and probe the shore surveillance and defense capabilities of the other nations. With regard to the latter, they can induce nations to turn on shore-to-sea, ship-to-ship, and air-to-sea radar.[93]

In addition to being in the Gulf of Fonseca, the *Caron* has been present in the Baltic, the North Sea, and off the Libyan coast. During the birth of Solidarity in Poland in August 1980, the *Caron* cruised 14 miles off the coast of Gdansk, and in the summer of 1981 the ship was among those that constituted the task force that was on an exercise off the Libyan coast in the Gulf of Sidra. During a North Atlantic cruise, the *Caron* came as close to the Soviet naval base at Murmansk as the Chesapeake Bay Bridge is to the U.S. Naval Base at Norfolk, Virginia.[94]

The *Caron* was again employed in an intelligence-collection mission against the Soviet target in 1986. Along with another warship, the USS *Yorktown*, the *Caron* entered Soviet-claimed territorial waters in the Black Sea on March 10 and remained there a week, coming as close as 6 miles to the Soviet coast. Although a Pentagon official claimed that intelligence collection was not the primary rationale of the exercise—which had been ordered by the Joint Chiefs of Staff in the name of Secretary of Defense Caspar Weinberger—it was at the very least an important secondary mission.[95]

In addition to helicopters to gather information, the *Yorktown* is also outfitted with electronic equipment that can monitor voice communications and radar signals. Such systems were used during the 1986 exercise to determine if new radars had been deployed onshore and to check the readiness of Soviet forces. In a previous expedition, the *Yorktown*'s equipment was used in part to monitor aircraft movements within the Soviet Union.[96]

The Soviets responded to the *Yorktown/Caron* mission both militarily and diplomatically. A destroyer was used to trail both ships while military aircraft overflew them. In addition, a Soviet protest note said the episode "was of a demonstrative, defiant nature and pursued clearly provocative aims."[97]

In February 1988 the *Yorktown* and *Caron* again entered the Black Sea with the same objectives as in 1986—to assert the right to free passage in waters outside the U.S.-recognized three-mile limit and to collect intelligence. When the ships came closer than the twelve-mile limit claimed by the Soviets, destroyers were sent to nudge the ships as a means of indicating Soviet displeasure.[98]

Two Navy frigates stationed in the Pacific were used against targets in Nicaragua, El Salvador, and Honduras in the 1980s. One ship—the 3,990-ton *Blakely*—is a Knox-class frigate commissioned in 1970; the other—the 3,400-ton *Julius A. Furei*—is a Brooke-class guided-missile frigate. The missions involved homing and recording voice and signals communications, locating transmitting stations, logging ships' movements, and studying their waterlines to help determine if they were riding low in the water when entering port and high when exiting—indicating the unloading of cargo.[99]

Frigates have also been used for monitoring Soviet missile telemetry. It was reported in 1979 that "American ships equipped with sensitive listening gear ... patrol the North Atlantic, where they collect telemetry broadcast by the new Soviet submarine-launched missiles tested in the White Sea, northeast of Finland." Likewise, on the night of August 31, 1983, when the United States was expecting the Soviet Union to test an SS-X-24 missile, the frigate *Badger* was stationed in the Sea of Okhotsk.[100]

The most important ship-based system for monitoring Soviet missile tests was a phased-array radar designated COBRA JUDY, which resides on the USNS *Observation Island*. COBRA JUDY was converted for use by the Ballistic Missile Defense Organization after the Air Force ceased funding in October 1993.[101]

UNDERSEAS COLLECTION

The use of submarines for intelligence-gathering purposes had its genesis in the later years of the Eisenhower administration. Known by a variety of codenames, the best known of which is HOLYSTONE, the program has been one of the most sensitive intelligence operations of the United States.[102]

HOLYSTONE, which also has been known as PINNACLE and BOLLARD, and most recently as BARNACLE, began in 1959 and has involved the use of specially equipped electronic submarines to collect electronic communications and photographic intelligence. The primary target through 1991 was the former Soviet Union, but at times countries such as Vietnam and China have been targets of the operations, which occasionally have involved penetration of Soviet, Chinese, and Vietnamese three-mile territorial limits.[103]

It was reported in 1975 that each mission lasted about ninety days. Crew were given cover stories, such as being part of an undersea geodetic survey project that was using sonar to study ocean water temperatures to support data collected by satellites. The crews were forbidden to use any active electronic or sonar gear while on a HOLYSTONE mission so as to avoid detection by Soviet antisubmarine warfare devices. In addition, hatches were tied down to prevent rattling.[104]

Missions conducted through 1975 apparently provided vital information on the Soviet submarine fleet—its configuration, capabilities, noise patterns, missiles, and missile firing capabilities. One mission involved obtaining the "voice autographs" of Soviet submarines. Using detailed tape recordings of noise made by submarine engines and other equipment, analysts of the Naval Scientific and Technical Intelligence Center (now part of the Office of Naval Intelligence) were able to develop a methodology for the identification of individual Soviet submarines, even those tracked at long range under the ocean. The analysts could then follow the submarine from its initial operations to its decommissioning.[105]

HOLYSTONE operations also provided information about theater and strategic sea-based missiles. Some Soviet sea-based missiles were tested against inland targets to reduce U.S. observation. On occasion, HOLYSTONE submarines would penetrate close enough to Soviet territory to observe the missile launchings, providing information on the early stages of the flight. According to one government official, the most significant information provided by the missions was a readout of the computer calculations and signals put into effect by Soviet technicians before launching the missiles. Beyond that, the U.S. submarines also provided intelligence by tracking the flight and eventual landing of the missiles and relaying continuous information on guidance and electronic systems.[106]

In addition to providing acoustic and telemetry intelligence, the HOLYSTONE submarines also tapped into Soviet communications cables on the ocean floor. The tapping operation allowed the United States to intercept higher-level military messages and other communications considered too sensitive to be entrusted to insecure means of communication, such as radio and microwave.[107]

The submarines also were able to bring back valuable photographs, many of which were taken through the submarine's periscope. In the mid-1960s, photographs were taken of the underside of an E-class submarine that appeared to be taken inside Vladivostok harbor.[108]

Like operations during the period when the program was codenamed HOLYSTONE, more recent operations have employed thirty-eight nuclear-powered Sturgeon-class submarines such as the SSN-637. The submarines have dimensions of 292 by 31.7 by 26 feet and carry SUBROC and antisubmarine torpedoes as well as Harpoon and Tomahawk missiles. With their 107-person complement (twelve officers and ninety-five enlisted personnel), the ships can travel at speeds of greater than 20 knots when surfaced and at more than 30 knots underwater and can reach a depth of 1,320 feet. Their standard electronic equipment includes a search radar and both active and passive sonar systems.[109]

The special equipment placed on submarines for HOLYSTONE/BARNACLE missions has included the WLR-6 Waterboy Signals Intelligence System. In the 1980s, the WLR-6 was replaced by a more advanced system known as SEA

NYMPH, described in one document as "an advanced, automatic, modular signals exploitation system designed for continuous acquisition, identification, recording, analysis and exploitation of electromagnetic signals." All the Sturgeon submarines carry a basic skeletal system that can be upgraded to full capacity when authorized.[110]

As late as early 1993 there was evidence that HOLYSTONE/BARNACLE operations continued. In February of that year, the USS *Baton Rouge*, a Los Angeles–class attack submarine, collided with a Russian submarine near the Kola Peninsula. It has been reported that the *Baton Rouge* was on an intelligence-gathering mission targeted on the Russian port of Murmansk.[111]

Another collision occurred on March 20, 1993, when the nuclear-powered attack submarine USS *Grayling* bumped into a Russian Delta III–class ballistic missile submarine in the Barents Sea about 100 miles north of Murmansk. During a summit with Russian President Boris Yeltsin the following month, President Clinton apologized for the incident. He also ordered a review of the submarine reconnaissance operations.[112]

Although such operations may be severely curtailed with respect to Russia, there remain other targets. A new target for such operations is Iran. The USS *Topeka* and the USS *Louisville* arrived in the Persian Gulf in November 1992 and January 1993, respectively. Their mission was to keep watch on Iran's new submarine fleet.[113]

Another reconnaissance project involving submarines that began later than the HOLYSTONE program was codenamed IVY BELLS. The project involved implanting a device to intercept the signals transmitted along a Soviet underwater cable in the Sea of Okhotsk between the Kamchatka Peninsula and the eastern Soviet coastline. A combined Navy-NSA team, operating from a submarine, installed a miniaturized waterproof eavesdropping device—a large tap pod that fit over the Soviet cable, through which key Soviet military and other communications flowed. The pod had a wraparound attachment that intercepted the cable traffic by "induction"—that is, it could intercept the signals being transmitted along the cable without physically tapping into the cable. In addition, if the cable were raised by the Soviets for maintenance, the pod would break away and remain on the ocean floor. Tapes in the pod recorded messages and signals on various channels or communications links for four to six weeks, with the pod being installed for only two recording sessions a year.[114]

IVY BELLS continued until 1981, when former NSA employee Ronald Pelton sold information about the operation to the Soviets.

NOTES

1. Defense Intelligence Agency, *Soviet and People's Republic of China Nuclear Weapons Employment Policy and Strategy*, March 1972, p. II-B-5; George C. Wilson, "Soviet Nuclear

Sub Reported Sunk," *Washington Post,* August 11, 1983, p. A9; David B. Ottaway, "Iraq Said to Have Expelled High-Level US Diplomat," *Washington Post,* November 17, 1988, p. A33; George J. Church, "Destination Haiti," *Time,* September 26, 1994, pp. 21–26.

2. John E. Ingersoll, "Request for COMINT of Interest to Bureau of Narcotics and Dangerous Drugs," in U.S. Congress, Senate Select Committee to Study Governmental Operations with Respect to Intelligence Activities, *The National Security Agency and Fourth Amendment Rights* (Washington, D.C.: U.S. Government Printing Office, 1976), pp. 152–55.

3. U.S. Congress, House Permanent Select Committee on Intelligence, *Annual Report* (Washington, D.C.: U.S. Government Printing Office, 1978), p. 38.

4. John Prados, *The Soviet Estimate: U.S. Intelligence Analysis and Russian Military Strength* (New York: Dial, 1982), p. 203; Farooq Hussain, *The Future of Arms Control, Part 4, The Impact of Weapons Test Restrictions* (London: International Institute for Strategic Studies, 1980), p. 44; Robert Kaiser, "Verification of SALT II: Art and Science," *Washington Post,* June 15, 1979, p. 1.

5. Deborah Shapley, "Who's Listening? How NSA Tunes In on America's Overseas Phone Calls and Messages," *Washington Post,* October 7, 1977, pp. C1, C4.

6. Ibid.

7. Sayre Stevens, "The Soviet BMD Program," in Ashton B. Carter and David N. Schwartz, eds., *Ballistic Missile Defense* (Washington, D.C.: Brookings Institution, 1984), pp. 182–221 at p. 192.

8. Anthony Kenden, "U.S. Reconnaissance Satellite Programs," *Spaceflight* 20, 7 (1978): 243ff.

9. Philip Klass, *Secret Sentries in Space* (New York: Random House, 1971), p. 194.

10. "New Military Satellites," *Aviation Week & Space Technology,* May 25, 1992, p. 13; "Mission Control," *Military Space,* June 15, 1992, p. 1; "Navy Uses Space to Spot Stealth Fighter," *Military Space News,* April 23, 1990, p. 1.

11. Desmond Ball, *Pine Gap: Australia and the US Geostationary Signals Intelligence Satellite Program* (Sydney: Allen & Unwin Australia, 1988), pp. 14–15.

12. Philip Klass, "U.S. Monitoring Capability Impaired," *Aviation Week & Space Technology,* May 14, 1979, p. 18.

13. Robert Lindsey, *The Falcon and the Snowman: A True Story of Friendship and Espionage* (New York: Simon & Schuster, 1979), p. 111.

14. Ball, *Pine Gap,* p. 54.

15. Victor Marchetti, *Allies* (a Grand Bay film directed by Marian Wilkinson and produced by Sylvia Le Clezio, Sydney, 1983).

16. See Lindsey, *Falcon and the Snowman,* for a full-length account; on the renaming of RHYOLITE, see William E. Burrows, *Deep Black: Space Espionage and National Security* (New York: Random House, 1987), p. 192; Glenn Zorpette, "Monitoring the Tests," *IEEE Spectrum* (July 1986): 57–66 at 60.

17. Edward H. Kolcum, "Night Launch of Discovery Boosts Secret Military Satellite into Orbit," *Aviation Week & Space Technology,* November 27, 1989, p. 29; Private information.

18. James Gerstenzang, "Shuttle Lifts Off with Spy Cargo," *Los Angeles Times,* January 25, 1985, pp. 1, 11; "Final Launch Preparations Under Way for Signal Intelligence Satellite Mission," *Aviation Week & Space Technology,* November 6, 1989, p. 24.

19. William J. Broad, "Experts Say Satellite Can Detect Soviet War Steps," *New York Times,* January 25, 1985, p. A12.

20. Walter Andrews, "Defense Aide Confirms U.S. Satellites Jammed," *Washington Times,* June 21, 1984, p. 1.

21. Richard Burt, "U.S. Plans New Way to Check Soviet Missile Tests," *New York Times,* June 29, 1979, p. A3; Burrows, *Deep Black,* p. 192.

22. Hussain, *The Future of Arms Control, Part 4,* p. 42; Ball, *Pine Gap,* pp. 14–15; "U.S. Spy Satellite Falls Short on Orbit and Expectations," *New York Times,* September 4, 1988, p. 22; Edward H. Kolcum, "Titan 34D Upper Stage Failure Sets Back Pentagon Intelligence Strategy," *Aviation Week & Space Technology,* September 12, 1988, p. 26; "Correction," *Aviation Week & Space Technology,* June 5, 1989, p. 32; "Last Titan 3 Rocket Lofts a Secret Military Satellite," *Washington Post,* September 5, 1989, p. A2; Kolcum, "Night Launch of Discovery Boosts Secret Military Satellite into Orbit," p. 29; Edward H. Kolcum, "Last Titan 34D, Transtage Launches Classified Military Spacecraft," *Aviation Week & Space Technology,* September 11, 1989, p. 41.

23. Private information.

24. Dick Cheney, Joint Meritorious Unit Award, June 23, 1989.

25. U.S. Congress, House Committee on Appropriations, *Department of Defense Appropriations for Fiscal Year 1986, Part 2* (Washington, D.C.: U.S. Government Printing Office, 1985), pp. 449–50; Steve Weber, "Third Straight Titan 4 Launch Success Buoys Martin," *Space News,* September 5–11, 1994, pp. 3, 21.

26. Seymour Hersh, *"The Target Is Destroyed": What Really Happened to Flight 007 and What America Knew About It* (New York: Random House, 1986), p. 4; Burrows, *Deep Black,* p. 223; Philip J. Klass, "NSA 'Jumpseat' Program Winds Down as Soviets Shift to Newer Satellites," *Aviation Week & Space Technology,* April 2, 1990, pp. 46–47; Private information.

27. Private information.

28. R. Jeffrey Smith, "As Woolsey Struggles, CIA Suffers," *Washington Post,* May 10, 1994, pp. A1, A7.

29. James B. Schultz, "Inside the Blue Cube," *Defense Electronics,* April 1983, pp. 52–59; *Organization and Functions Chartbook* (Onizuka, AFS, Calif.: Air Force Satellite Control Facility, December 1, 1986), p. 61; Space Division Regulation 23-3, "Air Force Satellite Control Facility," December 16, 1983.

30. Paul Stares, *Space and National Security* (Washington, D.C.: Brookings Institution, 1987), p. 188; James T. McKenna, "Titan 4/Centaur Orbits Classified Payload," *Aviation Week & Space Technology,* May 9, 1994, p. 24; Private information.

31. Desmond Ball, *A Suitable Piece of Real Estate: American Installations in Australia* (Sydney: Hale & Iremonger, 1980), p. 59.

32. Ball, *Pine Gap,* p. 61.

33. Ibid., pp. 67, 80.

34. Ibid., p. 77.

35. Ball, *Pine Gap,* pp. 27–28; Private information; "Bad Aibling—INSCOM's Newest Field Site," *INSCOM Journal,* October 1994, p. 3.

36. ACC Regulation 23-1, Volume 15, "Headquarters Air Combat Command Organization and Functions, Summary of Changes," October 23, 1992, p. 4; Untitled memo, *Declassified Documents Reference System* (*DDRS*) 1982-001583.

37. U.S. Congress, General Accounting Office, *New RC-135 Aircraft Engines Can Reduce Cost and Improve Performance* (Washington, D.C.: GAO, August 1992), p. 384; Martin

Streetly, "U.S. Airborne ELINT Systems, Part 3, The Boeing RC-135 Family," *Jane's Defence Weekly,* March 16, 1985, pp. 460–65.

38. Hersh, *"The Target Is Destroyed,"* p. 9; "How to Be Superpowerful," *The Economist,* August 18, 1990, p. 35.

39. Hersh, *"The Target Is Destroyed,"* p. 9; "6985th ESS Deactivates," *Spokesman,* July 1992, p. 10; "Base Closures Affect US SIGINT Capability in Europe," *Journal of Electronic Defense* (April 1990): 23.

40. George C. Wilson, "U.S. RC-135 Was Assessing Soviet Air Defenses," *Washington Post,* September 7, 1983, p. A-12; Philip Taubman, "U.S. Says Intelligence Plane Was on a Routine Mission," *New York Times,* September 5, 1983, p. 4; Hersh, *"The Target Is Destroyed,"* p. 220; Burrows, *Deep Black,* p. 172; Private information.

41. Hersh, *"The Target Is Destroyed,"* pp. 9–10; Burrows, *Deep Black,* p. 171; Private information.

42. Hersh, *"The Target Is Destroyed,"* p. 9.

43. Private information.

44. Private information; References to the COMBAT SENT missions against the mentioned radars were found in the documents catalog of the Office of Air Force History, Bolling AFB, D.C.

45. Streetly, "U.S. Airborne ELINT Systems, Part 3"; "6985th ESS Deactivates."

46. 6th Strategic Wing Regulation 55-2, "Operations, Aircrew and Staff Procedures," September 30, 1983, pp. 4–11.

47. Private information; Burrows, *Deep Black,* p. 172.

48. Private information; Burrows, *Deep Black,* p. 172.

49. 6th Strategic Wing Regulation 55-2, "Operations, Aircrew and Staff Procedures," pp. 3–5.

50. David A. Fulghum, "Cold War Spy Aircraft Eyed for Tactical Role," *Aviation Week & Space Technology,* October 11, 1993, pp. 53–54.

51. Martin Streetly, "Hercules C-130 Electronic Missions," *Jane's Defence Weekly,* November 16, 1985, pp. 1092–96; "Senior Scout," *Spokesman,* April 1991, p. 9; "Seen at the Show," *Journal of Electronic Defense* (November 1992): 22–23; "Senior Scout Soars," *Insight,* January–March 1990, pp. 2–5; "Just Cause: ESC Units Prove Their Mettle During Action in Panama," *Insight,* January–March 1990, pp. 11–13; Private information.

52. Private information.

53. Private information.

54. Private information; Jim Coulter, "Senior Spear Maintenance Facility," *Spokesman,* January 1992, p. 10.

55. Private information.

56. Private information.

57. Private information.

58. "News in Brief," *Jane's Defence Weekly,* July 22, 1989, p. 110; James W. Rawles, "Guardrail Common Sensor Comes on Line," *Defense Electronics,* October 1990, pp. 33–41.

59. Rawles, "Guardrail Common Sensor Comes on Line."

60. Private information.

61. Dr. Michael E. del Papa, *Meeting the Challenge: ESD and the Cobra Dane Construction Effort on Shemya Island* (Bedford, Mass.: Electronic Systems Division, Air Force Systems Command, 1979), pp. 1–2.

62. AFSPACECOM Regulation 55-123, "Cobra Dane Tactical Requirements and Doctrine (TRD)," December 15, 1992, p. 4.

63. del Papa, *Meeting the Challenge,* pp. 2–3.

64. Eli Brookner, "Phased-Array Radars," *Scientific American,* April 1985, pp. 94–102.

65. Philip J. Klass, "USAF Tracking Radar Details Disclosed," *Aviation Week & Space Technology,* October 25, 1976, pp. 41–46; del Papa, *Meeting the Challenge,* p. 38.

66. Klass, "USAF Tracking Radar Details Disclosed."

67. Duncan Campbell, *The Unsinkable Aircraft Carrier: American Military Power in Britain* (London: Michael Joseph, 1984), p. 155; "British MP Accuses U.S. of Electronic Spying," *New Scientist,* August 5, 1976, p. 268; Department of the Army, Field Manual 34-40-12, *Morse Code Intercept Operations,* August 26, 1991, p. 4-4; "Northern Lights of Freedom," *Insight,* Spring 1991, pp. 16–18; Private information.

68. Hersh, *"The Target Is Destroyed,"* p. 47.

69. U.S. Congress, House Committee on Appropriations, *Military Construction Appropriations for 1981, Part 2* (Washington, D.C.: U.S. Government Printing Office, 1980), p. 875; Hersh, *"The Target Is Destroyed,"* p. 49; David Morison, "Sites Unseen," *National Journal,* June 4, 1988, pp. 1468–72.

70. Duncan Campbell and Linda Melvern, "America's Big Ear on Europe," *New Statesman,* July 18, 1980, pp. 10–14; Stella Trapp, "Rosman Research Center Is a 'Vital Part' of the Security," *Transylvania Times,* August 21, 1986, pp. 1A, 16A; Private information.

71. Gabriel Marshall, "Chicksands—A Rich Legacy," *Spokesman,* July 1994, pp. 24–25.

72. "6917th Bid Dan Vito Arrivederci," *Spokesman,* July 1993, pp. 14–15.

73. Michael K. Burns, "U.S. Reactivating Bases in Turkey," *Baltimore Sun,* October 21, 1978, pp. 1, 23; Ellen Camner, "When Field Station Sinop Closes Its Doors GIs Will Be Missed," *INSCOM Journal,* January–February 1993, pp. 12–17.

74. Michael Getler, "U.S. Intelligence Facilities in Turkey Get New Attention After Iran Turmoil," *Washington Post,* February 9, 1979, p. A15.

75. Ibid.

76. T. K. Gilmore, "Furling of Flag Finalizes Services of Battalion," *INSCOM Journal,* January–February 1993, p. 5; "Two Squadrons Shut Down," *Air Force Times,* May 21, 1991, p. 2.

77. Private information.

78. Private information.

79. Brian Toohey and Marian Wilkinson, *The Book of Leaks: Exposes in Defence of the Public's Right to Know* (North Ryde, Australia: Angus & Robertson, 1987), p. 135; Private information.

80. U.S. Army Field Station Korea, *Fiscal Year 1986, Annual Historical Report,* 1987, p. 2; Private information; History Office, USAINSCOM, *Annual Historical Review: U.S. Army Intelligence and Security Command, Fiscal Year 1988* (Arlington, Va.: INSCOM, 1989), p. 105.

81. Private information; History Office, USAINSCOM, *Annual Historical Review,* p. 105.

82. U.S. Congress, House Committee on Appropriations, *Military Construction Appropriations for 1987, Part 2* (Washington, D.C.: U.S. Government Printing Office, 1986), p. 682; Private information.

83. James Bamford, *The Puzzle Palace: A Report on NSA, America's Most Secret Agency* (Boston: Houghton Mifflin, 1982), pp. 172–73; Private information.

84. Laurence Stern, "U.S. Tapped Top Russians' Car Phones," *Washington Post,* December 5, 1973, pp. A1, A16; Ernest Volkman, "U.S. Spies Lend an Ear to Soviets," *Newsday,* July 12, 1977, p. 7.

85. Stern, "U.S. Tapped Top Russians' Car Phones."

86. Ibid.; Bill Gertz, "CIA Upset Because Perle Detailed Eavesdropping," *Washington Times,* April 15, 1987, p. 2A.

87. Jack Anderson, "CIA Eavesdrops on Kremlin Chiefs," *Washington Post,* September 16, 1971, p. F7.

88. Howard Kurtz, "Pollard: Top Israelis Backed Spy Ring," *Washington Post,* February 28, 1987, p. A8.

89. Arthur Gavshon and Desmond Rice, *The Sinking of the Belgrano* (London: Secker & Warburg, 1984), p. 205, n5.

90. Trevor Armbrister, *A Matter of Accountability* (New York: Coward, McCann, 1970), p. 87.

91. Ibid.; U.S. Congress, House Committee on Armed Services, *Inquiry into the U.S.S. Pueblo and EC-121 Incidents* (Washington, D.C.: U.S. Government Printing Office, 1969), pp. 1632, 1634; James Ennes, *Assault on the Liberty* (New York: Random House, 1980).

92. Paul Backus, "ESM and SIGINT Problems at the Interface," *Journal of Electronic Defense* (July–August 1981): 23ff.

93. Richard Halloran, "U.S. Navy Surveillance Ship Is Stationed Off Central America," *New York Times,* February 25, 1982, pp. 1, 6; Private information.

94. Private information; William M. Arkin, "Spying in the Black Sea," *Bulletin of the Atomic Scientists,* May 1, 1988, p. 5.

95. Richard Halloran, "2 U.S. Ships Enter Soviet Waters Off Crimea to Gather Intelligence," *New York Times,* March 19, 1986, pp. A1, A11; George C. Wilson, "Soviet Ships Shadowed U.S. Vessels' Transit," *Washington Post,* March 20, 1986, p. A33.

96. Halloran, "2 U.S. Ships Enter Soviet Waters Off Crimea to Gather Intelligence"; Private information.

97. Halloran, "2 U.S. Ships Enter Soviet Waters Off Crimea to Gather Intelligence"; Private information.

98. Philip Taubman, "Moscow Blames U.S. for Incident Between Warships," *New York Times,* February 14, 1988, pp. 1, 19; John H. Cushman, Jr., "2 Soviet Warships Reportedly Nudged U.S. Navy Vessels," *New York Times,* February 13, 1988, pp. 1, 6.

99. George C. Wilson, "U.S. Detects Slowdown in Shipments of Weapons to El Salvador," *Washington Post,* April 29, 1983, p. A13.

100. Richard Burt, "Technology Is Essential to Arms Verification," *New York Times,* August 14, 1979, pp. C1, C2; Murray Sayle, "KE 007: A Conspiracy of Circumstance," *New York Review of Books,* April 25, 1985, pp. 44–54.

101. "COBRA JUDY Serving BMDO," *Aviation Week & Space Technology,* February 14, 1994, p. 17.

102. See Chris Drew, Michael L. Millenson, and Robert Becker, "A Risky Game of Cloak-and-Dagger—Under the Sea," *Chicago Tribune,* January 7, 1991, pp. 1, 8–9.

103. Seymour Hersh, "Submarines of U.S. Stage Spy Missions Inside Soviet Waters," *New York Times,* May 25, 1975, pp. 1, 42.

104. Seymour Hersh, "A False Navy Report Alleged in Sub Crash," *New York Times,* July 6, 1975, pp. 1, 26.

105. Hersh, "Submarines of U.S. Stage Spy Missions Inside Soviet Waters."

106. Ibid.

107. Ibid.

108. Ibid.

109. *Jane's Fighting Ships, 1983–1984,* p. 639.

110. Private information.

111. "Pentagon Describes Damage to Sub After Arctic Collision," *New York Times,* February 28, 1992, p. A10; John H. Cushman, Jr., "Two Subs Collide off Russian Port," *New York Times,* Febuary 19, 1992, p. A6; Bill Gertz, "Russian Sub's Sail Damaged in Collision," *Washington Times,* February 27, 1992, p. A4; John Lancaster, "U.S., Russian Subs Collide in Arctic," *Washington Post,* February 19, 1992, pp. A1, A24.

112. Bill Gertz, "Clinton Apologizes for Sub Collision," *Washington Times,* April 5, 1993, p. A7.

113. "Second U.S. Sub Monitors Iran's Fleet," *Washington Times,* February 12, 1993, p. A7.

114. Bob Woodward, *Veil: The Secret Wars of the CIA, 1981–1987* (New York: Simon & Schuster, 1987), pp. 448–49.

9
OCEAN SURVEILLANCE/
SPACE SURVEILLANCE/NUCLEAR
MONITORING/MASINT

Imagery and signals intelligence systems are used to gather information on a wide variety of targets. There are other targets, however, that require the use of a more specialized set of technical collection systems.

Thus, some information about foreign naval activities, particularly in-port activities, is gathered by imaging and signals intelligence systems. U.S. imaging satellites periodically produce imagery of major port areas as well as naval shipyards from Nikolaev to Simonstown. ORION SIGINT satellites may intercept some of the communications from port areas. But a separate set of technical collectors perform the vast majority of the ocean surveillance mission. Likewise, foreign space activities are partially monitored by imagery satellites, and launch areas are monitored by SIGINT systems. However, detecting and tracking satellites in space is the function of a set of radar and optical systems, many designed specifically for the purpose. And, although imagery and SIGINT make important contributions to the monitoring of foreign nuclear activities, the various systems that perform a unique nuclear monitoring mission are at the crux of the U.S. ability to monitor foreign nuclear detonations.

OCEAN SURVEILLANCE

Thirty years ago the Soviet Navy was predominantly concerned with coastal defense and began a process of dramatic expansion to become a well-equipped "blue-water" Navy. In 1987 the Soviet Union possessed 6 aircraft carriers, 283 other major surface combatants (e.g., destroyers), 77 ballistic missile submarines (63 nuclear powered), 269 attack and cruise missile submarines (121 nuclear powered), and a large number of intelligence, oceanographic, and space support ships. Deployment of the Akula-class nuclear-powered submarine (SSN) and the Typhoon nuclear-powered ballistic-missile submarine (SSBN—with six to nine warheads on each of its twenty submarine-launched ballistic missiles, or SLBMs) further increased Soviet naval capabilities.[1] Naturally, the Soviet fleet was a major target of U.S. intelligence collection and its expansion required a similar expansion in the U.S. network for monitoring Soviet surface and underseas naval activity.

However, even during the Cold War the naval activities of numerous other nations, both hostile and friendly, were of interest to the U.S. intelligence community and policymakers. The ability of allied nations to fulfill alliance commitments or contribute to certain operations, such as the protection of ships in the Persian Gulf, was one concern. The naval capabilities and intentions of hostile nations, such as Iran or North Korea, were of even greater concern. The ships of drug smugglers and arms traffickers were also often intelligence targets. Further, any naval activity in a sensitive political, military, or economic area—for example, the Suez Canal, the Sea of Japan, the Panama Canal, the Persian Gulf, or the Hawaiian Islands—was an intelligence target.

Those concerns still remain. Thus, the collapse of the Soviet Union and the huge reduction in Russian fleet activities did not eliminate the requirement for an ocean surveillance capability. This fact was illustrated in February and March 1992, when the United States sought to track a North Korean cargo ship headed for Syria carrying advanced Scud missiles and missile manufacturing equipment. By February 1993, Iran's growing submarine fleet also became a concern. In August 1993, the United States was concerned with a Chinese ship suspected of carrying material for chemical weapons to Iran.[2] Systems employed to monitor such activities operate in space, in the air, on the ground, on the surface of the world's oceans, and underneath those oceans.

Until 1976, the United States Navy did not have a dedicated space-based ocean surveillance capability. Ocean surveillance data were obtained from U.S. imaging satellites, with the Air Force and Navy cooperating on reconnaissance matters. Thus, on April 18, 1975, a high-resolution KH-8 satellite was launched to acquire data on the massive Soviet naval exercise then taking place.[3]

The Navy began to initiate studies on the feasibility of a dedicated ocean surveillance satellite system in 1968 in response to the buildup in Soviet naval forces and capabilities. In 1970, the Chief of Naval Operations ordered a study of overall ocean surveillance requirements. This project resulted in a five-volume publication, *Ocean Surveillance Requirements Study,* by the Naval Research Laboratory (NRL). The study resulted in Program 749, a study that focused on the development of high-resolution, phased-array radars that would allow all-weather ocean surveillance monitoring as well as detection of low-trajectory sea-launched missiles. The possibility of equipping the satellites with an infrared scanner was also explored. Experimental phased-array radars were developed by Hughes Aircraft and Westinghouse Electric.[4]

Despite the emphases of these initial studies, the ocean surveillance satellite system that resulted, CLASSIC WIZARD, lacked radar capability. PARCAE, the spacecraft portion of the system, was a passive interceptor—it was apparently equipped with a passive infrared scanner and millimeter wave radiometers as well as radio-frequency antennas capable of monitoring radio communications and radar emissions from submarines and ships. It used passive interferometry techniques (the use of interference phenomena) to determine the locations of ships—that is, the craft could compute a ship's position from data on radar or radio signals provided by several antennas.[5]

The PARCAE system consisted of a mother ship and three subsatellites. The basic techniques involved in using multiple spacecraft to eavesdrop and direction find on Soviet surface vessels and submarines were first demonstrated using three NRL spacecraft launched on December 14, 1971. The launch vehicle was a McDonnell-Douglas Thorad. A Lockheed Agena was used as the satellite dispenser to place the spacecraft in appropriate orbits.[6]

The subsatellites were relatively small, each measuring approximately 3 by 8 by 1 feet. The largest surface area on one side was covered by solar cells, and four spherical objects deployed on the end of the metal booms were believed to be sensors.[7]

PARCAE satellites were launched with Atlas boosters from the Western Test Range—Vandenberg Air Force Base—into a near-circular 63-degree inclined orbit at an altitude of approximately 700 miles. The three subsatellites were dispersed from the main vehicle into three parallel orbits with latitude separation as well as time/distance separation along their orbital paths. There was a displacement of approximately 1,866 miles between passes. At an altitude of 700 miles, the spacecraft could receive signals from surface vessels more than 2,000 miles away, providing overlapping coverage on successive passes.[8]

In addition to the 1971 test, there was apparently a test of a subsatellite on June 8, 1975, in which the subsatellite was ejected from a payload carrying a KH-9 satellite. Subsequently, there were eight operational clusters placed in orbit: on April 30, 1976; December 8, 1977; March 3, 1980; February 9, 1983; June 9, 1983; February 6, 1984; February 9, 1986; and May 15, 1987. The increased launch rate in the 1980s led the Navy to request and receive funds for antenna upgrades at all CLASSIC WIZARD ground stations.[9]

The ground segment of the CLASSIC WIZARD system consisted of five ground stations managed by the Naval Security Group Command. The stations, which are likely still in use for follow-on systems, are colocated with Navy Regional Reporting Centers at Diego Garcia; Guam; Adak, Alaska; Winter Harbor, Maine; and Edzell, Scotland. Several tracking domes have been built at Edzell to control and receive information from the satellites. Information received at the stations can be quickly transmitted to regional ocean surveillance centers and via satellite to a main downlink at Blossom Point, Maryland.[10]

The first two satellites of an Advanced PARCAE system were apparently deployed in a June 1990 shuttle launch from Cape Canaveral and a November 1991 launch of Titan IV from Vandenberg AFB. In both cases the satellites were deployed in orbits similar to those of PARCAE satellites. However, it appears that the new system does not include a mother ship. An August 1993 launch from

Vandenberg produced an explosion shortly after takeoff that destroyed the booster and the spacecraft.[11]

Shortly after the explosion it was reported that the NRO and the Navy planned to develop a new generation of ocean surveillance spacecraft with improved detection capabilities. The contract for the new spacecraft was signed by the NRO in defiance of congressional instructions. NRO subsequently reopened the bidding on the contract, which was then awarded to Martin Marietta. The new system will apparently operate against both land- and sea-based emitters.[12]

In addition to the satellite systems, the United States employs several aircraft in an ocean surveillance role. Included are the aircraft in the P-3 series, the EP-3E, and the EA-3B. The most important component of the U.S. ocean surveillance program is the P-3C Orion, named after the Greek god of the hunt. The P-3C is the third generation of the P-3 antisubmarine warfare aircraft that succeeded the Neptune P2V in the late 1950s. A typical P-3C mission directed at Soviet submarines could last up to fourteen hours and had three main objectives: selecting the area in which to search for a submarine, finding the submarine, and identifying the submarine.[13]

The first generation of the P-3, the P-3A, was produced by shortening the airframe of an Electra airliner by twelve feet, equipping it with weapons, and giving it an increased fuel capacity. The P-3B version has a fourfold increase in acoustic processing capability over that of the P-3A, and in 1981 infrared detection and HARPOON missile systems were added. Four P-3Bs were reconfigured for multisensor surveillance and codenamed CLIPPER TROOP WEST. Two aircraft were assigned to the Pacific Fleet's Patrol Squadron Special Projects Unit Two (VPU-2) (at Barbers Point NAS in Hawaii) and two to the Atlantic Fleet's Patrol Squadron Special Projects Unit One (VPU-1) (at Brunswick, Maine). All four were then deployed to various areas of Soviet naval activity. The aircraft are equipped with communications intelligence; electronic intelligence; photographic, nuclear, acoustic, and infrared sensors; and their photographic and signals intelligence capabilities were upgraded in 1988. The information collected is forwarded to processing centers. The planes operate at between 200 and 25,000 feet and have a range of 4,000 nm and an endurance of ten hours. In early 1987, a P-3B photographed the Soviet guided-missile destroyer *Osmotritenny* as the vessel crossed the Indian Ocean en route to join the Soviet Pacific Fleet.[14]

The P-3Bs may have been involved in special missions to determine the splashdown point of Soviet Reentry Vehicles from ICBM tests that had their final phase near Hawaii. It was reported that specially modified P-3 aircraft were equipped with an improved version of the Sonobuoy Missile Impact Location System (SMILS). With this system, warheads hitting the water could be detected by small, highly sensitive hydrophones hanging between sonobuoys along the ocean's surface. Using data from Global Positioning System navigational satellites and the hydrophones, analysts could apparently determine the exact point of impact.[15]

In its present configuration, the P-3C stands 33.7 feet high. It is 1,168 feet long and has a 99.7-foot wingspan. Its maximum speed is 410 knots an hour, and it has a service ceiling of 28,300 feet. Its endurance capability—sixteen hours—and maximum speed give it a range of 4,500 nm. It can search up to 95,000 square nm in an hour.[16]

The P-3C can carry up to eighty-four sonobuoys. Forty-eight of them are preset and loaded in external launch chutes prior to takeoff. The remaining thirty-six are carried internally and their operating channels can be chosen during the mission. For many of the sonobuoys, it is possible to select the operating depth and length of transmission time. The acoustic operators on the P-3C can monitor up to sixteen sonobuoys simultaneously. A sonar-type recorder stores all acoustic data for reference to reconstruct the missions in detail.[17]

In addition to the sonobuoys, there are several nonacoustic detection systems on the P-3C. Its Magnetic Anomaly Detector (MAD) is used in concert with the Submarine Anomaly Detector to determine whether known submarine magnetic profiles are present. To get a good MAD reading, the plane must fly 200 to 300 feet above the water. Under the base of the plane are automatic cameras. The Infrared Detection System converts infrared energy into visible light and provides an image of the target. An airborne search radar, designated AN/APS-115, is used to detect radar returns from ships or submarines on the surface and pick out periscopes at the waterline.[18]

The collapse of the Soviet Union, combined with budgetary constraints, has led the United States to reduce the number of P-3s and to cancel some planned upgrades while pursuing others. Pursuant to a 1989 decision by the Secretary of Defense, by February 1991 all P-3A aircraft had been removed from the Navy inventory. The Secretary of Defense also directed that by fiscal year 1994 (beginning in October 1993), the P-3 (P-3B, P-3C) inventory be reduced by 145 planes—of those remaining, eight planes would be assigned to each of eighteen active squadrons and six planes would be assigned to each of nine reserve squadrons. By fiscal year 1996, all P-3B planes are to be removed from the fleet.[19]

The squadrons with P-3 planes have been based at various locations throughout the world, including Misawa and Kadena in Japan; Adak, Alaska; Keflavik, Iceland; Hawaii; Anderson AFB, Guam; Rota, Spain; Italy; Ascension Island; Diego Garcia; Lejes air base on Terciera Island in the Azores; Canada; Bermuda; and Puerto Rico.[20]

Plans to develop a follow-on to the P-3C, the P-7A, were canceled. Likewise, plans for another extensive upgrade to the P-3Cs' antisubmarine warfare capability, converting them to P-3Hs, were also canceled. A program to extend the service life of 193 P-3Cs began in 1993. In addition, the Navy intends to equip at least a portion of the P-3Cs with an improved capability to aid battle groups in detecting, tracking, and targeting small gunboats—specifically, by upgrading the APS-137 Inverse Synthetic Aperture Radar (ISAR), which pinpoints static targets such as gunboats. The upgrade effort will also involve installation of an imaging system to provide a data link for targeting, surveillance, and bomb damage assessment. The upgrade program seeks to maintain and increase the P-3Cs' capability against surface targets such as coastal headquarters and surface-to-air missile sites.[21]

Two modifications of the P-3 are used for intelligence collection. Five P-3C airframes were specifically configured for the collection, analysis, and recording of high-quality acoustic data on Soviet submarines, sonars, and underwater communications equipment. These aircraft, known by the codename BEARTRAP, have a 4,000-nm range, an operational altitude of 200 to 10,000 feet, and an endurance capability of twelve hours. Enhancements of BEARTRAP antisubmarine warfare capabilities during fiscal year 1994 focused on the littoral water/regional conflict environment.[22]

Another modification of the P-3A is the EP-3 ARIES, which has been altered for signals intelligence collection. The plane is distinguished from the Orion by a flat circular radome under the fuselage, and it lacks the long, thin MAD boom at the tail. It is a four-engined land-based aircraft with a 3,400-nm range, an operational altitude of 18,000 to 25,000 feet, and an endurance capability of twelve hours. The targets of the EP-3E may be land-based radars and UHF/VHF communications systems.[23]

Eleven EP-3Es are assigned to the Pacific and Atlantic Fleet Air Reconnaissance Squadrons, VQ-1 and VQ-2, headquartered at Agana, Guam, and Rota, Spain, respectively. The six EP-3Es subordinate to the Guam headquarters operate over all of the Pacific (especially the Sea of Japan and the South China Sea from the Sea of Okhotsk to the west coast of Africa) and Indian Oceans. With the projected closing of NAS Agana on Guam, VQ-1 will probably be relocated to Japan. The SIGINT missions flown in the Far East are designated BEGGAR HAWK, BEGGAR SHADOW, and BEGGAR WATCH. The EC-121 shot down by North Korea in 1969 was on a BEGGAR SHADOW mission.[24]

By the beginning of Operation Desert Storm in January 1991, VQ-1 had established a detachment (E) at Bahrain. During the first three months of 1991, VQ-1 operations were almost exclusively confined to the Arabian Gulf and included 131 direct combat support missions. At the conclusion of Desert Storm the squadron had detachments at NAS Misawa, NAS Atsugi, NAS Cubi Point, Kadena AB, Osan AB, and RMAF Butterworth. According to the unit's 1991 history: "With a changing political climate, VQ-1 has turned its focus to Third World threats and low intensity conflicts and is now flying against a variety of Third World littoral countries."[25]

The Rota-headquartered planes operate over the Mediterranean and Baltic seas and the Atlantic Ocean. Detachments are located at Naval Air Station Sigonella, Italy, and Stuttgart, Germany. Planes also are periodically deployed to RAF Wyton and RAF Akrotiri, Cyprus. From those locations the planes fly missions over the Mediterranean, the Baltic, the Caribbean, the North Atlantic, and the Norwegian

Sea. COMINT missions flown in the West European area are codenamed FLOOR DOOR, while ELINT missions are codenamed FLOOR LEADER.[26]

In the summer of 1990, VQ-2 provided electronic reconnaissance during the evacuation of 2,000 noncombatant personnel from Liberia in Operation SHARP EDGE. From August 1990 to April 1991, the squadron provided combat reconnaissance during Operations Desert Shield, Desert Storm, Proven Force, and Provide Comfort.[27]

Twelve EA-3B Skywarriors are also employed for intelligence purposes, with VQ-2 operating four of them. The EA-3B has also often been employed on aircraft carriers for periods ranging from days to months in order to extend the range of coverage. The EA-3B is primarily targeted against communications and noncommunications emitters in the VHF/UHF frequency range. Its targets may be air, surface, subsurface, or land-based. The aircraft has a recording capability for ground processing of collected signals. Perishable information can be transmitted directly from the aircraft via secure UHF communications. The aircraft flies at 20,000–35,000 feet, has a range of less than 2,000 nm, and can operate for 5.5 hours.[28]

The newest Navy SIGINT aircraft is the ES-3A, which will in a sense replace the EA-3B. The first of sixteen planes was delivered for testing in February 1992. The ES-3A was conceived as part of the Navy's carrier Battle Group Passive Horizon Extension System (BGPHES), which seeks to provide the battle group commander with over-the-horizon (OTH) tactical intelligence without electronic emissions, which would reveal the battle group's existence to an enemy. The ES-3A is able to relay intercepted data to terminals aboard selected vessels. To operate the planes, two new squadrons—Fleet Air Reconnaissance Squadron Five (VQ-5) at Guam and Fleet Air Reconnaissance Squadron Six (VQ-6) at NAS Cecil Field, Florida—were established in 1991.[29]

The future location of those squadrons, as well as that of the Pacific Patrol Squadron Special Projects Unit, is in doubt, as the Defense Base Closure and Realignment Commission ordered Cecil Field NAS, Agana NAS, and Barbers Point NAS closed.[30]

The Naval Security Group Command operates a network of land-based stations directed at HF/DF monitoring of naval activity. The stations generally use the AN/FRD-10 circularly disposed antenna array, which has a nominal range of 3,200 nm. The network, known as CLASSIC BULLSEYE, monitors the Caribbean, Atlantic, Mediterranean, Indian, and Pacific Oceans. A total of twenty-two stations are configured in three operating nodes (Atlantic Fleet, Pacific Fleet, Naval Forces Europe). The individual bearings produced by individual stations are used by a net control station for automated fix production.[31]

A 378-person Naval Security Group Activity headquartered at Homestead, Florida, operating out of Card Sound as part of the North Atlantic–Caribbean–South Atlantic HF/DF net, monitors air and naval activity in the Atlantic and Caribbean employing an AN/FRD-10. Farther up the eastern coast is an NSG Detachment at Sugar Grove, West Virginia, and an NSG Activity at Northwest, Virginia. Both use AN/FRD-10s to monitor naval traffic in the Middle Atlantic. Farther north, the NSG Activity at Winter Harbor, Maine, employs an AN/FRD-10 to monitor naval activity in the North Atlantic.[32]

Two European stations involved in naval monitoring are those located at Edzell, United Kingdom, and Terceira, Portugal. Edzell is home to a 1,000-person NSG Activity, a 79-man Marine Support Battalion, Company B, and an AN/FRD-10 antenna. The 87-person NSG Activity stationed at Terceira, Portugal, conducted intercept operations against Soviet naval and shipping HF communications in the North Atlantic as well as against some diplomatic traffic.[33]

Foreign-based stations in the Pacific and Indian Ocean HF/DF nets are located at Diego Garcia and at Torri Station, Hanza, Okinawa. The Diego Garcia station hosts a 124-man NSG Department that operates a Pusher HF antenna directed at monitoring naval activity in the Indian Ocean area. The NSG Activity at Okinawa employs an AN/FRD-10 to intercept Russian, Chinese, and Vietnamese naval and naval air communications.[34]

Stations in Guam and along the West Coast of the United States also play a substantial role in monitoring naval activity in the Pacific. The NSG Activity at Adak, Alaska, along with Company I, Marine Support Battalion, monitors naval communications in the northern Pacific region. The Naval Security Detachment at Guam, employing an AN/FRD-10, is responsible for high-frequency coverage of Russian, PRC, and Vietnamese naval activity in the western Pacific. At Wahiawa, Hawaii, an NSG unit also employs an AN/FRD-10 antenna to monitor naval traffic around the Hawaiian Islands, as well as collecting international leased carrier and other communications for the Pacific region. At Imperial Beach, California, 60 members of the NSG Activity from San Diego operate an AN/FRD-10.[35]

Ocean surveillance operations are also conducted from surface ship-based platforms. Thirty U.S. Navy surface combatants are outfitted with equipment codenamed CLASSIC OUTBOARD that allows the detection, classification, and location of hostile ships, aircraft, and submarines by exploiting their command and control communications. The data collected are analyzed on board and transmitted to Net Control Centers for correlation.[36]

As of late 1991 the Navy was considering installing the COMBAT DF electronic intercept system as a replacement for CLASSIC OUTBOARD. COMBAT relies on a gigantic antenna built into the hull of a ship to intercept signals and determine the location of long-range high-frequency radios. Only one ship was to be fitted with the system in 1992.[37]

Some surface ships have a portable system known as CLUSTER PACE (Portable Acoustic Collection Equipment). Among the capabilities of the CLUSTER PACE system are a tape-recording capability, which allows postmission retrieval of underwater signals for intelligence exploitation.[38]

As important as intelligence concerning Soviet surface naval activities was during the Cold War, intelligence concerning underseas activities was even more important. Although the Soviet Union placed the preponderance of its strategic nuclear weapons capability on land, it also maintained sixty-two submarines armed with SLBMs and in the late 1980s began to deploy the modern Typhoon SSBN armed with multiwarhead SS-N-20 missiles.

Additionally, Soviet attack submarines represented a threat to the U.S. SSBN fleet. In the midst of the transition from Poseidon to Trident submarines, the United States had only half of the number of SSBNs that the Soviet Union had—although they were qualitatively superior. Since the submarines played a more significant role in U.S. nuclear strategy than Soviet SSBNs played in Soviet strategy, it was imperative to detect and track any possible threats to U.S. SSBNs.

Much of the data gathered about foreign submarines comes under the heading of Acoustic Intelligence (ACOUSTINT, or ACINT)—intelligence derived from the analysis of acoustic waves radiated either intentionally or unintentionally by a submarine into the surrounding ocean. This category of intelligence includes the underwater acoustic waves from submarines, which can be used to determine the "signature" of those vehicles much in the same manner as voice autographs can be developed of individuals. The most important submarine detection and tracking system has been a global network of large, fixed, sea-bottom hydrophones that passively listen for the sounds generated by submarines. These arrays are collectively known as SOSUS (Sound Surveillance System), although only about two-thirds of the arrays were part of the SOSUS network proper. The other third are part of allied systems. The SOSUS system was described by one U.S. admiral in 1979 as the "backbone of our ASW [Antisubmarine Warfare] detection capability."[39]

The system was described by the Stockholm International Peace Research Institute (SIPRI) as follows:

Each SOSUS installation consists of an array of hundreds of hydrophones laid out on the sea floor, or moored at depths most conducive to sound propagation, and connected by submarine cables for transmission of telemetry. In such an array a sound wave arriving from a distant submarine will be successively detected by different hydrophones according to their geometric relationship to the direction from which the wave arrives. This direction can be determined by noting the order in which the wave is detected at the different hydrophones. In practice the sensitivity of the array is enhanced many times by adding the signals from several individual hydrophones after introducing appropriate time delays between them. The result is a listening "beam" that can be "steered" in various sectors of the ocean by varying the pattern of time delays. The distance from the array to the sound source can be calculated by measuring the divergence of the sound rays within the array or by triangulating from adjacent arrays.[40]

Development work on SOSUS began in 1950, at which time the hydrophone arrays were codenamed CAESAR. Installation of the first SOSUS/CAESAR array was completed on the continental shelf off the East Coast of the United States in 1954. Subsequent SOSUS arrays were installed elsewhere off the East Coast, at

Brawdy in Wales, and at other locations. The arrays have been progressively updated and the technology is now in its fifth or sixth generation of development.[41]

The CAESAR arrays proved extremely effective during the Cuban Missile Crisis of October 1962, when every Soviet submarine in the area was detected and closely trailed. As a result, the United States decided to expand and upgrade the network. An array was established to cover the Greenland-Iceland-United Kingdom (GIUK) Gap, that is, the portion of the Atlantic through which Soviet submarines stationed at the Polyarnyy submarine base in the northwestern Soviet Union had to pass in order to head toward the United States. Even earlier warning has been provided by an array strung between Andoya, Norway, and Bear Island.[42]

By the late 1960s, several more arrays had been established. An upgraded variant of CAESAR, COLOSSUS, was deployed along the West Coast of the United States extending from the top of Alaska to the Baja Peninsula. COLOSSUS employed a more advanced form of sonar than CAESAR. Farther out in the Pacific, a 1,300-mile-long circular array codenamed SEA SPIDER surrounds the Hawaiian Islands. Reportedly, it was this array that monitored and localized the breakup of the Soviet submarine that sank north of Hawaii in March 1968. Another Pacific array extended from Alaska and ran parallel to the Aleutian Islands. An array along the western side of the Kuril Islands allowed detection of Russian submarines exiting the naval base at Petropavlovsk or the Sea of Okhotsk.[43]

Construction began on an array known as the Azores Fixed Acoustic Range (AFAR) in September 1968 off the island of Santa Maria, the southernmost of the Azores group. In May 1972 the system was commissioned by NATO with a dual mission—to track Soviet submarines approaching the Strait of Gibraltar or on passage around the Cape of Good Hope. An array in the Bosporus strait between Yugoslavia and Turkey can detect submarines exiting the Black Sea port of Sevastapol. Yet another array was put in place next to the coast of Taiwan and the Philippines, and there is an Indian Ocean array in the vicinity of Diego Garcia. Other arrays were located off Turkey (in addition to the Bosporus array), Japan, Puerto Rico, Barbados, Canada (Argentia, Newfoundland), Italy, Denmark, Gibraltar, Galeta Island (in Panama), and Guam.[44]

The hydrophones are sealed in tanks—approximately twenty-four to a tank—and cables transmit the data to shore facilities. The first step in converting the data collected by the hydrophones to finished intelligence occurs at the Naval Facilities (NAVFACs) and Naval Regional Processing Centers (NRPCs), which are the initial recipients of the data. There has been a repeated reduction in the number of NAVFACs over the years. Among the NAVFACs still operating in 1993 were those at Adak, Alaska; Argentia, Newfoundland; Brawdy, Wales; Centerville Beach, California; Whidbey Island, Washington; and Keflavik, Iceland. The Whidbey Island facility, with a staff of 200, received remote data from unmanned relay centers at Coos Bay and Pacific Beach, provided analysis and processing of underwater signals, and transmitted data to the Pacific Fleet around the clock.

Plans call for a reduction in NAVFACs to four—probably with two on the West Coast and two on the East Coast.[45]

From the NAVFACs and NRPCs, the data has been sent by landline or FLTSATCOM (Fleet Satellite Communications) to Naval Ocean Processing Facilities at Damn Neck, Virginia, and Ford Island, Hawaii. Those facilities have been responsible for centralized reporting, correlation, localization, and tracking of submarine targets. It is intended that much of the data that used to be transmitted to NAVFACs from the arrays will now be transmitted via satellite to a central location—where it would remain unexamined.[46]

The data collected about each submarine detected—its sonar echo and the noises made by its engine, its cooling system, and the movement of its propellers—can be translated into a recognition signal. A distinctive pattern can be determined that indicates not only a particular type of submarine—an Alfa-class attack submarine instead of a Typhoon-class ballistic-missile carrying submarine, for example—but also the individual submarine. Thus the data, when analyzed, operate much like fingerprints or voiceprints do to identify individuals.

Gradually, a fundamental change in Soviet submarine capabilities over the years reduced the value of SOSUS. The first three generations of Soviet sea-based ballistic missile submarines—the SS-N-4 Snark, the SS-N-5 Serb, and the SS-N-6 Sawfly—had ranges of between 350 and 1,600 nm. Beginning in 1973 with the operation of the SS-N-8, with a range of 4,200 nm, Soviet subs did not have to exit Soviet home waters to hit targets in the United States. Soviet capability in this regard grew over the years with the deployment of the SS-N-8 Mod 2, which has a range of 4,900 nm, and of the SS-N-18 and SS-N-20, which have ranges of from 3,500 to 4,500 nm. In recent years, Russian SSBNs have ceased operations off the Atlantic and Pacific coasts, reducing the value of the SOSUS arrays covering those areas.[47]

An advanced version of SOSUS that is under development is the Fixed Distributed Surveillance (FDS) system, which was intended to counter quieter Soviet submarines. FDS would integrate large-scale sea-bottom mounted acoustic sensor arrays on a single fiber-optic cable system. However, in mid-1992 the FDS program was reduced to only one developmental system, with no procurement plans.[48]

Another sonar surveillance system is operated together with SOSUS—the Surface Towed Array Sensor System (SURTASS). Together the two systems form the Integrated Undersea Surveillance System.[49]

The SURTASS was designed to provide a mobile backup to the SOSUS network—to be in areas where SOSUS was unavailable or inoperative and to enhance coverage within SOSUS regions. With the deactivation of numerous SOSUS arrays and a change in the ocean areas and navies that are of prime concern, more reliance will be placed on the mobile SURTASS platforms. SURTASS arrays are deployed from nineteen ships—eighteen monohull and one small waterplane area twin hull (SWATH)—which together make up the T-AGOS

(Auxiliary General Ocean Surveillance) system. Data collected by the 6,000-foot towed array sensor can be processed on board ship and sent via FLTSATCOM and DSCS satellites to the ocean processing facilities at Damn Neck and Ford Island.[50]

In early 1993 the Navy was planning to maintain a fleet of nine new SURTASS ships. In addition, it planned to equip SURTASS with an active acoustic detection capability, Low Frequency Active (LFA). The wisdom of those plans has been questioned, however, on the grounds that the more important threat presently comes not from the former Soviet Union but from regional powers that operate diesel submarines in shallow water—an environment for which SURTASS and its upgrades were not designed.[51]

In 1993 the Navy began allowing civilian researchers to use SOSUS in a six-month experiment to track whales. The arrays are also being used to monitor ocean temperatures and deep-sea eruptions.[52]

SPACE SURVEILLANCE

In addition to being concerned with events on land and sea, the U.S. intelligence community is concerned with events in space. An accurate understanding of the space activities of nations is required for assessing foreign military and intelligence capabilities, determining and implementing necessary operations security measures, warning of actions (whether intended or unintended) that threaten U.S. space systems, warning of space systems or debris that will impact the earth, developing plans for using ground-based equipment for the interception of satellite communications, and preparing and implementing plans to neutralize foreign space systems.

The specific aspects of foreign space activities that are monitored include launch, deployment into orbit, mission, orbital parameters, maneuvering, deployment of subsatellites, breakup of satellites, and reentry of satellites or debris into the earth's atmosphere. Space surveillance systems are also used to determine size and other characteristics of space systems.

During the Cold War, the driving force behind U.S. space surveillance activities was, of course, the Soviet Union. The capabilities of Soviet navigation, communications, meteorological, and other military support satellites had a significant effect on the overall capabilities of Soviet military forces. The capabilities of Soviet reconnaissance satellites had to be factored into plans to provide operational security to U.S. military forces and research and development activities.

In response to the intelligence threat from Soviet imagery satellites, the United States instituted the Satellite Reconnaissance Advance Notice (SATRAN) program, also known by the nickname STRAY CAT, in 1966.[53] The SATRAN program is presently part of the Satellite Reconnaissance Operations Security Program.

By 1987 the Naval Space Surveillance (NAVSPASUR) system was providing satellite vulnerability information in four formats to Navy units:

- Large Area Vulnerability Reports (LAVR) provided satellite vulnerability information to units in established operating areas.
- Satellite Vulnerability Reports (SVR) provided tailored vulnerability information to units in a transit status or operating outside established operating areas.
- Safe Window Intelligence (SWINT) reports provided periods of time when the requesting units were not vulnerable to reconnaissance satellite coverage.
- One-line CHARLIE elements [which enable units to compute their own satellite vulnerability data] are provided to units having the Reconnaissance Satellite Vulnerability Computer (RSVC) program, allowing the units to compute their own satellite vulnerability data.[54]

In 1988 the Naval Space Command instituted the CHAMBERED ROUND program for support to deployed elements of the fleet and the Fleet Marine Force. Under CHAMBERED ROUND, the Naval Space Command provides deployed naval forces with tactical assessments of hostile space capabilities and specific reactions to their operations. The support is tailored to a unit's specific equipment, geographic area of interest, and intentions during the time of its deployment. During Operations Desert Shield and Desert Storm, every battle group received CHAMBERED ROUND support either during their predeployment workups or while in transit to the Middle East theater of operations.[55]

Although the collapse of the Soviet Union has resulted in a reduced Russian military space program, the remaining program is still of interest to the U.S. intelligence community. Operational security measures to prevent Russian imaging satellites from viewing particularly sensitive activities, such as secret airplane developments in Nevada, are still undertaken. Likewise, data concerning Russian communications satellites are still required to support U.S. satellite communications intercept activities.[56]

In addition, other nations have, for many years, made use of space systems. Intelligence on those systems and their operations has been a long-standing requirement of the U.S. intelligence community. In particular, China has orbited spacecraft for photographic reconnaissance, electronic intelligence, meteorology, and communications.[57]

Further, as the Russian space program has decreased, the space activities of other foreign nations have increased and are expected to expand further in the next decade. Israel has launched two experimental satellites that appear to be forerunners to a photographic reconnaissance satellite. France has embarked on an ambitious intelligence satellite program that will involve the deployment of photographic, radar imagery, and signals intelligence satellites. The growing number of foreign military space programs led Congress, in fiscal year 1993, to require the Office of the Secretary of the Defense to produce a report on the proliferation of military satellites.[58]

The focal point of the U.S. space surveillance effort is the U.S. Space Command's Space Surveillance Center located at Cheyenne Mountain Air Force Base. The Space Surveillance Center receives data from two U.S. Space Command orga-

nizations—the 73rd Space Group and the 21st Space Wing. The various field elements of those organizations make up the Space Surveillance Network (SSN).[59]

The Space Surveillance Network consists of three types of sensors: dedicated,
collateral, and contributing. Dedicated sensors are those reserved primarily for
space surveillance. Collateral sensors are used for space surveillance, but they are
meant primarily for other missions. Contributing sensors are those under contract or agreement to provide space surveillance data when requested by U.S.
Space Command headquarters.[60] Sensors can also be differentiated based on
whether they employ radar, electro-optics, or some other means of detection.

Until the mid-1980s, dedicated sensors included a series of Baker-Nunn tele-
scope/cameras at five locations.[61] The central role of the Baker-Nunn cameras in
the U.S. space surveillance system has been taken over by the four detachments of
the 18th Space Surveillance Squadron's Ground-Based Electro-Optical Deep
Space Surveillance System (GEODSS), which consists of electro-optical systems at
Stallion, New Mexico (Detachment 1); Taegu, South Korea (Detachment 2);
Maui, Hawaii (Detachment 3); and Diego Garcia (Detachment 4). A planned fifth
site near Almodovar, in southern Portugal, was never built.[62]

The system provides the capability to optically track objects higher than 3,000
out to 22,000 nm. It is also able to search up to 17,400 square degrees per hour.
Further, GEODSS installations are close enough together to provide overlapping
coverage as a means of overcoming poor weather at any one site.[63]

Like the Baker-Nunn system, GEODSS depends on the collection of light reflected by the objects under investigation and is operational only at night during
clear weather. Additionally, sensitivity and resolution are downgraded by adverse
atmospheric conditions. Unlike the earlier system, however, GEODSS is able to
provide real-time data with a computer-managed instant video display of surveillance data. Further, the computer automatically filters stars from the night sky
backdrop and then uses its memory of known space objects to determine the existence of new or unknown space objects, alerting the user when such objects are
found.[64]

GEODSS consists of three telescopes at each site that work together under
computer control. The Diego Garcia site has three 40-inch telescopes. The other
sites have two 40-inch telescopes and one 15-inch telescope. The larger telescope
is designed primarily for high-altitude object observation and is capable of examining up to 2,400 square degrees of the night sky each hour. The 15-inch telescope
is employed mainly for low-altitude observations and can search up to 15,000
square degrees per hour. Each telescope has a sensitive Ebiscon tube that registers
the image of an object for real-time processing and a radiometer for optical signature characterization and identification.[65]

According to one account, "In a typical operational scenario the small telescope will be conducting a low-altitude, high speed search, one of the large telescopes will be tracking an object at high altitude and the other large telescope will
be tracking an object—at either high or low altitudes and collecting radiometric

data."[66] To locate an object, the system computes an object's position from information on its orbit and points the telescope to the required position. The operator may then pick out the spacecraft by locating a stationary object in a moving star field. The operator may also fix the telescope on the moving star background and collect camera frames that show a satellite streak building up.[67]

The GEODSS telescopes can reach to geosynchronous altitude—as demonstrated in 1985 when a GEODSS site photographed a FLTSATCOM satellite at geosynchronous altitude. At that altitude they can detect a reflective object the size of a soccer ball.[68]

A second set of dedicated sensors are those that constitute the Naval Space Surveillance (NAVSPASUR) system. The NAVSPASUR system, headquartered at Dahlgren, Virginia, detects and tracks satellites that pass through an electronic fence consisting of a fan-shaped radar beam with a 7,500-mile range extending from San Diego, California, to Fort Stewart, Georgia. The beam cannot be steered; detection results when the satellite passing through the beam deflects the beam's energy back to earth, where it is detected by several arrays of dipole antennas—"a form of cheap, unsophisticated antenna not unlike a television receiving aerial."[69]

The central transmitter for the beam is located at Lake Kicapoo, Texas, and there are two smaller transmitting stations at Gila River, Arizona, and Jordan Lake, Alabama. The six receiver stations—at San Diego, California; Elephant Butte, New Mexico; Red River, Arkansas; Silver Lake, Mississippi; Hawkinsville, Georgia; and Tattnall, Georgia—are all located, as are the transmitting stations, across the southern part of the United States along a great circle inclined about 33 degrees to the equator. The data obtained are then transmitted to NAVSPASUR headquarters and the Computation Center at Dahlgren, Virginia.[70]

In June 1991 the Air Force Space Command closed down, for budgetary reasons, a mechanically steered AN/GPS-10 model radar located at San Miguel in the Philippines. The radar had a 60-foot dish and a range of 23,000 miles.[71] In 1992 a similar radar, with a 30-foot dish, became operational at Saipan, Commonwealth of Northern Mariana Islands. The Saipan Space Surveillance Station was intended to be part of the three-site Pacific Radar Barrier (PACBAR), along with San Miguel and the ALTAIR site discussed below.[72]

Two new sets of dedicated sensors were added to the Space Surveillance Network in the 1980s. The 1st Space Surveillance Squadron located at Verona Test Annex, Griffiss Air Force Base, New York, operates a Deep Space Tracking System (DSTS)—a system of passive antennas designed to receive active satellite transmissions, which can be used to locate, identify, and monitor operational spacecraft, including satellites in geosynchronous orbit.[73]

Two additional DSTS systems—one in Europe and one in Asia—are operated by the 5th Space Surveillance Squadron at Feltwell Royal Air Force Base and the 3rd Space Surveillance Squadron at Misawa AB in Japan, respectively. It is expected that the DSTS will provide data on approximately 50 percent of active deep-space satellites.[74]

The second set of new dedicated sensors are those of the 4th Space Surveillance Squadron, headquartered at Lackland Air Force Base, Texas. Subordinate to the 4th Space Surveillance Squadron are three detachments, which conduct actual collection activities. The detachments are located at San Vito dei Normanni (Detachment 1), Royal Air Force Edzell (Detachment 2), and Osan Air Base, Korea (Detachment 3).[75]

All three detachments target satellites in low-earth orbit using one of two Passive Space Surveillance (PASS) systems. Detachment 1 operates the Combined Radio Frequency and Optical Space Surveillance (CROSS) system. The radio frequency dish has a wide-range search capability but produces somewhat inaccurate observations. In contrast, the optical system has limited search capability but provides accurate observations. The systems work together to pinpoint a satellite's location. In addition, Low-Altitude Space Surveillance (LASS) units are operated at San Vito, Edzell, and Osan. The LASS systems are used primarily for gathering space intelligence and tracking space systems in near-earth orbit.[76]

Also among the dedicated sensors is the 20th Space Surveillance Squadron's AN/FPS-85 phased array at Eglin AFB, Florida, constructed in 1967. The radar, thirteen stories high and as long as a city block, has its principal axis aligned due south across the Gulf of Mexico and is capable of receiving and transmitting over an arc extending 60 degrees on either side. Most satellites pass through its beam, which has a range of 2,500 miles, twice a day. The radar provides tracking information on space objects in low-earth orbit and has a limited deep-space capability.[77]

The AN/FPS-85 "consists of several thousand individual transmitters the power outputs of which are added together by controlling their phases to form a single beam which can be electronically swept across the sky in millionths of a second."[78] The radar can search for unknown objects across 120 degrees of azimuth, from horizon to zenith, while simultaneously tracking several already acquired targets. In a typical twenty-four-hour period, it makes 10,000 observations.[79]

Collateral sensors include the mechanically steered Ballistic Missile Early Warning System (BMEWS) radars; the radars at Shemya Island, Alaska, Cavalier, North Dakota, and Pirinclik, Turkey; PAVE PAWS SLBM Early Warning radars; and radars at Ascension Island and Antigua.[80]

The BMEWS is designed primarily to track missiles and determine the number launched and their intended targets. The system is dispersed among three sites—Clear AFS, Alaska; Thule, Greenland; and Fylingdales, Great Britain. The 13th Space Warning Squadron at Clear AFS operates an AN/FPS-92 BMEWS Tracker. The 12th Space Warning Squadron at Thule AB operates an AN/FPS-123V phased-array radar, and the Space Warning Squadron at Fylingdales operates an AN/FPS-126 phased-array radar.[81]

The PAVE PAWS system consists of phased-array radars assigned the primary mission of detecting submarine-launched ballistic missiles. The 6th, 7th, and 8th Space Warning Squadrons at Cape Cod Air Force Station, Beale Air Force Base, California, and Eldorado Air Force Station, Texas, operate AN/FPS-115 large phased-array radars. The fourth component of the PAVE PAWS system is the 9th Space Warning Squadron's AN/FPS-123 (V)3 radar at Robins AFB, Georgia. Each radar has two arrays, providing a total of 240 degrees of coverage out to 3,100 miles.[82]

The phased-array COBRA DANE (AN/FPS-108) and the mechanically steered AN/FPS-79 radar at Pirinclik, Turkey, discussed in Chapter 8 in their strategic verification role, are also used as collateral sensors. The COBRA DANE has a 28,000-mile range, and the AN/FPS-79 has a range of 24,000 miles. With its coverage extending northward over an arc from Kamchatka to the Bering Strait, COBRA DANE can be used for tracking satellites in polar and near-polar orbits.[83]

Also among the collateral sensors are the mechanically steered radars at Antigua Island and Ascension Island. The primary mission of these radars is to provide launch support to the Eastern Test Range. The Antigua site provides data on satellites in low-earth orbit, relying on a high-precision AN/FPQ-14 pulse tracker designed to track missiles and space objects. The AN/FPQ-14 is directly interconnected with other radars of the Eastern Space and Missile Center.[84]

On Ascension Island, located midway between the east coast of Brazil and the west coast of South Africa, are two radars. The primary radar is the AN/FPQ-15, which provides space and missile launch support to the ESMC, near-earth satellite observations to the Space Surveillance Center, and narrow-band space object identification (SOI) data to the Joint Space Intelligence Center.[85]

Contributing sensors are provided by two systems on Kwajalein, two radars in Massachusetts, and three sites in Hawaii.[86] The Advanced Research Projects Agency (ARPA) Lincoln C-Band Observable Radar (ALCOR) on Roi-Namur Island, Kwajalein Atoll, operated by the Army Strategic Defense Command, consists of a 40-foot antenna and provides wideband radar imaging data for space object identification on low-earth orbit satellites. Support to the Space Surveillance Center is on a noninterference basis with Kwajalein Missile Range support.[87]

The second radar located on Roi-Namur Island, the ARPA Long-Range Tracking and Instrumentation Radar (ALTAIR), is also operated by the Army Strategic Defense Command. The ALTAIR is a 150-foot parabloid antenna that provides metric data on spacecraft. The radar operates in a space surveillance mode for 128 hours per week.[88]

The Millstone and Haystack radars, located about half a mile apart at Westford, Massachusetts, are operated by MIT's Lincoln Laboratory. The Millstone is a deep-space, large-dish tracking radar capable of tracking 1-square-meter targets at geosynchronous altitude. The Haystack radar is a high-quality imaging radar that can resolve objects as small as 1 foot in diameter in low-earth orbit. It has been described in congressional hearings as providing "images of orbiting satellites that we can get from no other location. It is a "long range, high altitude capable radar which provides extremely good intelligence data and now has a real-time operational reporting capability."[89]

The final three contributing sensors are those located in Hawaii. The Air Force Maui Optical Station (AMOS) at Mt. Haleakala, Maui, is a Rome Air Development Center photometric and laser facility. Mt. Haleakala's location, 10,000 feet above sea level, places AMOS's equipment above much of the atmosphere and the interference that results. The equipment includes a 5.2-foot Cassegrain telescope, a laser beam director, and an AMOS acquisition system. The space surveillance research and development work at AMOS includes metric tracking, infrared space object identification, and compensated imaging.[90]

AMOS's laser was used to illuminate Soviet spacecraft at night for the purpose of telescope photography. It was also used to determine whether Soviet nuclear-powered radar ocean reconnaissance satellites were operating or properly shut down at the end of their missions. The visible wavelength images of the satellites produced by AMOS were good enough to show a Soviet reactor glowing red hot.[91]

AMOS's telescope has provided high enough resolution to discern objects in the space shuttle's open payload bay. Such a capability could have been used to obtain intelligence on Soviet shuttle missions. Its telescope has allowed identification of objects as small as 3.1 inches in diameter in geosynchronous orbit. Another optical sensor, the AMOS Daylight Near-Infrared Imaging System (ADONIS), underwent testing in 1993.[92]

The mission of the AN/FPQ-14 at Kaena Point, Oahu, Hawaii, is to provide low-earth satellite observation. The AN/FPQ-14 is tasked on a limited basis with supporting the space surveillance mission, primarily for high-priority objects requiring instantaneous observational data. The site is operated by civilians twenty-four hours per day, seven days per week. Kaena Point provides pointing data to the AMOS site.[93]

Colocated with the GEODSS and AMOS systems is the Maui Optical Tracking Identification Facility (MOTIF), codenamed TEAL BLUE. MOTIF consists of two comounted 48-inch Cassegrain telescopes capable of both near-earth and deep-space satellite tracking and object identification using visual light and long-wave infrared imaging. For satellites orbiting at 3,000 miles or less, MOTIF's sensors can measure reflectivity and heat emissions and provide images.[94]

As of 1990, images could be taken for only a few hours after sunset or before dawn, when the telescopes were in darkness and the satellites in the light. Planned improvements would allow one of the telescopes to operate for two hours before sunset or after sunrise by canceling out interference from the sun. As a result, the number of hours that MOTIF could be used daily would expand from six to ten.[95]

Along with the similar telescopes at Malabar, Florida, codenamed TEAL AMBER, the two sites provide computer-enhanced, high-resolution close-up photographs of Soviet and Chinese spacecraft. It has also been reported that the system was used to photograph cosmonauts during one of the extra-vehicular activities conducted from the Soviet SALYUT 6 space laboratory. Such photography implies a resolution of less than 40 inches.[96]

Recently, USSPACECOM has plugged the National Science Foundation UHF radar, developed by MIT's Lincoln Laboratory Electro-Optical Test Site at Socorro, New Mexico, into its network of deep-space sensors.[97]

The Space Surveillance Network makes an average of 45,000 sightings of orbiting objects each day. Twenty percent of the objects and debris cannot be reliably tracked. More than 16,000 objects have been catalogued, and about 7,000 orbiting objects from the size of a baseball on up are tracked on a regular basis.[98]

According to the Commander-in-Chief of the U.S. Space Command, the network is "predictive ... rather than a constant surveillance system." Thus, in 1989 existing sensors at an altitude of 185 kilometers covered less than 20 percent of the earth's surface. Continuity on deep-space objects is sometimes difficult to maintain because the radars are part-time contributors and the optical and electro-optical sensors are restricted to nighttime, clear weather operation.[99]

Figure 9-1 shows the location of U.S. ground-based space surveillance sites.

NUCLEAR MONITORING

As noted in Chapter 1, the nuclear energy programs of foreign nations are of considerable interest to the U.S. intelligence community. Of greatest priority are the nuclear weapons aspects of these programs, particularly when actual nuclear detonations are involved.

It is important that the United States be able to detect such detonations for several reasons. One is that detection allows the United States to monitor compliance with several international agreements and treaties concerning nuclear detonation. The United States is a signatory to the 1963 Partial Test Ban Treaty, which banned atmospheric testing and testing in space; the 1974 Threshold Test Ban Treaty, which barred underground nuclear testing of devices with a yield greater than 150 kilotons; and the Peaceful Nuclear Explosions (PNE) Treaty of 1976, which prohibits peaceful nuclear explosions with a yield greater than 150 kilotons.[100] Of more than 600 Soviet nuclear explosions that have taken place since 1949, more than 400 have taken place under at least one treaty regime.

The same collection systems that can be employed for treaty verification purposes obviously can also be employed to monitor the nuclear detonation activities of nonsignatories. Whether a country is a treaty signatory or not, the United States is concerned with the sophistication and likely future development of its nuclear weapons. Nuclear monitoring can provide at least some clues in this regard. Additionally, nuclear detonation monitoring can provide data on the characteristics of detonated devices that can be employed to develop countermeasures. Thus, it has been noted in congressional testimony that

another aspect [of the U.S. worldwide nuclear test detection system] is devoted to the general area of nuclear weapon diagnostics. As a general rule, the assessment of the sophistication of a foreign weapons development program and the estimation of the probable intent of the developing nation in the application of nuclear weapons require some knowledge of the internal details of the device.

Such questions as yield, nuclear materials employed and the construction characteristics that determine size, weight and output of the device are all-important to determine the type of delivery system that might be required and the vulnerability of U.S. systems to the output of such devices. In other words, in order to determine the response of the U.S. to a foreign nuclear weapons development program, more information than the mere existence of a nuclear explosion is required.[101]

Thus, the Atomic Energy Commission was able to announce a few days after China's first nuclear explosion on October 16, 1964, based on examination of particles from the resulting radioactive cloud, that the bomb used uranium 235 rather than plutonium.[102]

An additional factor appeared in the late 1970s. Revisions in U.S. nuclear strategy—as expressed in President Carter's Presidential Directive (PD) NSC-59 and President Reagan's National Security Decision Directive (NSDD) 13, both titled "Nuclear Weapons Employment Policy"—stipulated that the United States develop the capability to fight a prolonged nuclear war—one that could last up to six months. The strategy for such a war would require intelligence to keep U.S. leaders informed about the precise location of nuclear detonations and the damage that resulted.[103] Such a capability also would allow U.S. officials to obtain precise information on nuclear detonations in other parts of the world, whether in the Middle East, Southwest Asia, or Northeast Asia.

Even before the collapse of the Soviet Union, there was a significant downward trend in Soviet nuclear testing. The twenty-three tests conducted in 1987 were followed by seventeen in 1988 and seven in 1989. In 1990 there was one test. Since then there have been none. Indeed, in 1992 there were only two non-U.S. nuclear tests conducted worldwide—both by China. The single 1993 nuclear test was also conducted by China, and China also conducted the world's only nuclear test in 1994.[104]

At the same time that concern over Soviet and Russian nuclear developments and testing has decreased, the concern over nuclear proliferation has risen dramatically. Postwar information concerning the status of the Iraqi nuclear program indicated significant gaps in U.S. knowledge. In addition, at least four nations (India, Israel, South Africa, and Pakistan) have developed atomic weapons virtually without conducting nuclear tests, and none of these nations has a nuclear testing program of its own.* As a result, less future U.S. nuclear monitoring will need to be directed at monitoring nuclear tests while more emphasis will have

---

*Pakistani generals were present at Chinese nuclear tests and received help in building their bomb. Israel may have received help from France in the 1960s. Israel and South Africa may have conducted a joint test in 1979. Finally, India conducted a single test in 1974.

Figure 9-1. Sites of U.S. Ground-Based Space Surveillance Sensors.

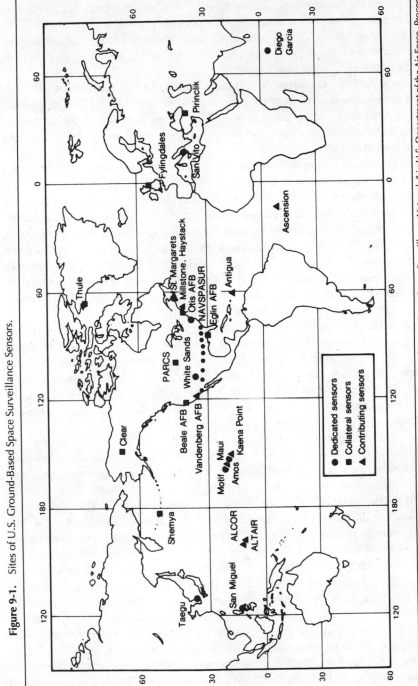

Source: Capt. Dennis K. Harden, "Current Capabilities and Future Requirements of the Air Force Space Surveillance Network," in U.S. Department of the Air Force, *Proceedings of the Tenth Aerospace Power Symposium: The Impact of Space on Aerospace Doctrine* (Maxwell AFB, Ala.: Air War College, 1986), p. 6.

to be placed on monitoring nuclear emissions that might indicate a nuclear program in progress or the number of warheads being produced.

The means that the United States employs to monitor foreign nuclear detonations and emissions include space platforms, airborne platforms, ground sites, and hydroacoustic (underseas) systems.

Detection of nuclear detonations is the secondary function of at least two satellite systems—the Defense Support Program (DSP) satellites and the Global Positioning System (GPS) satellites. The DSP satellites have served the secondary function of detecting nuclear explosions in space or in the atmosphere since their initial launch in 1971.

The principal mission of DSP satellites is to detect the launches of ICBMs and SLBMs. In the 1970s it was observed that DSP satellites could also detect the launches of intermediate-range ballistic missiles such as Scuds. Subsequently, the detection of such launches became an established DSP mission. Hence, the satellites also provide notification of Russian, Chinese, and other nations' missile tests. The satellites are cylindrical and about 33 feet long and 10 feet in diameter, weighing up to 5,300 pounds. The means of detection is a 12-foot-long Schmidt infrared telescope 39 inches in diameter. The telescope has a two-dimensional array of lead sulfide detectors at its focus to sense energy emitted by ballistic missile exhausts during the powered stages of their flights.[105]

DSP satellites are launched into a geosynchronous orbit from the Eastern Test Range (Cape Canaveral). One satellite is maintained on station over the Indian Ocean (70 degrees east) to provide first warning of a Russian or Chinese ICBM launch, and two are maintained on station over the Western Hemisphere (over Brazil, 70 degrees west, and the eastern Central Pacific, 135 degrees west) to monitor SLBM launchings off the East and West Coasts of the United States. An additional two satellites are maintained as spares.[106]

Subsequent to the unsuccessful attempt to launch a DSP in 1970, sixteen DSP satellites have been placed in orbit. Like other satellites, the DSP models have been improved through several modifications. The most recent improvement came about through the installation of the Advanced Atmospheric Burst Locator (AABL). The capability of such a system is multidimensional. The information provided by the AABL allows estimates of yield, location, height of burst, frequency of detonations, and timing. The estimates have a smaller range of uncertainty than the estimates produced by previous sensors, and the improved sensors are able to detect events below the threshold reached by earlier versions.[107]

The ground segment of DSP includes three dedicated ground stations and a main operating base for six Mobile Ground Terminals (MGTs) at Holloman Air Force Base in New Mexico and a DSP multipurpose facility at Lowry AFB, Colorado.[108] The dedicated ground stations include the CONUS Ground Station at Buckley Air National Guard Base, Colorado; the Overseas Ground Station at Woomera Air Station, Australia (also known as Nurrungar); and the European Ground Station at Kapuan, Germany. The Nurrungar facility is codenamed

CASINO and bears the official title of Joint Defense Space Facility. It is operated by the 5th Defense Space Communications Squadron of the 21st Space Wing of the U.S. Space Command. Data from Nurrungar to the United States is transmitted via both submarine cable and the Defense Satellite Communications System (DSCS) satellite stationed over the Western Pacific.[109]

The CONUS Ground Station, formally known as the Aerospace Data Facility and operated by the 2nd Defense Space Communications Squadron, receives data from Nurrungar as well as the DSP West satellites. Buckley is also Operating Location BN (OL-BN) of the Air Force Technical Applications Center (AFTAC). AFTAC personnel stationed at Buckley are responsible for processing any nuclear detonation data provided by the nuclear detonation sensors aboard DSP spacecraft. The Kapuan and Lowry facilities provide backup capabilities to Nurrungar and Buckley, respectively.[110]

The Nuclear Detonation (NUDET) Detection System (NDS) carried on board NAVSTAR Global Positioning System (GPS) satellites was developed to provide trans- and postattack nuclear detonation monitoring. The primary function of the GPS satellites is to provide accurate locational data for targeting and navigational purposes; the NDS represents a major secondary function. The GPS satellite constellation consists of eighteen operational satellites plus three active spares in near-circular 10,900-mile orbits with an inclination of 63 degrees. The eighteen satellites are deployed in three or more planes, with each plane containing no more than six equally spaced satellites. This arrangement guarantees that at least four to six satellites are in view at all times from any point on or near the earth.[111] The GPS constellation is shown in Figure 9-2.

The NDS packages include X-ray and optical sensors, Bhangmeters, EMP sensors, and a data-processing capability that can detect a nuclear weapons detonation "anywhere in the world at any time and get its location down to less than [100 meters]." Data is reported on a real-time basis either directly to ground stations located at Diego Garcia; Kwajalein Atoll; Ascension Island, Kaena Point, Hawaii; Andersen Air Base, Guam; or Adak, Alaska, or first to airborne terminals or other GPS satellites for subsequent downlink transmissions. All principal U.S. command posts, including E-4B and EC-135 aircraft, receive NDS sensor data directly.[112]

At least one other satellite system also appears to be equipped with a NUDET package. This might be the previously discussed Satellite Data System (SDS), which has a classified early warning capability, or the Defense Meteorological Satellite Program. The latter are acknowledged to have "classified sensors" in addition to meteorological sensors.[113] Figure 9-3 shows a sample alert report for atmospheric tests detected by satellites.

On April 25, 1993, a Pegasus booster was used to deploy an experimental 240-pound spacecraft into a 400-nm, 70-degree orbit. The spacecraft, designated ALEXIS (Array of Low-Energy X-Ray Imaging Sensors), carried three pairs of X-ray sensing telescopes. The data collected by the telescopes may be used to de-

Figure 9-2.   The NAVSTAR GPS Operational Constellation.

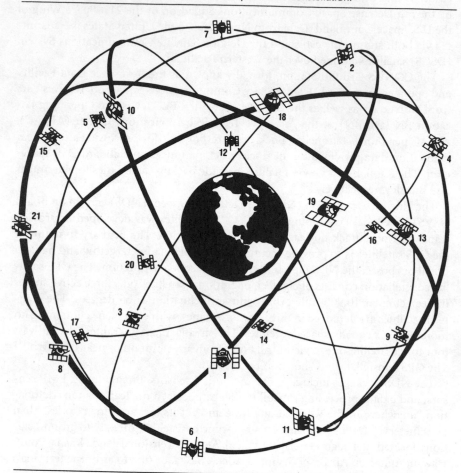

Source: General Accounting Office, *Global Positioning System Acquisition Changes After Challenger's Accident* (Washington, D.C.: GAO, 1987), p. 12.

velop improved systems for detecting clandestine nuclear weapons tests. The successor program to ALEXIS is FORTE (Fast On-Orbit Recording of Transient Events).[114]

In addition to space-based detection systems, aerial sampling is employed to detect the atomic particles that would be emitted by an above-ground nuclear explosion and might be "vented" by an underground test. Aircraft employed in aerial sampling operations include the U-2, the P-3, the WC-135, and the B-52. The WC-135s are equipped with the STARCAST camera system, which is designed to photograph high-speed objects in support of strategic research and development

Figure 9-3. Sample Alert Report Text: Atmospheric.

30		CENR 55-5 Attachment 12 28 May 1992

```
        Figure A12-1.  (U) Sample Alert Report Text:  Atmospheric
                       (This figure is classified SECRET)


SUBJECT:  ALERT _____  (U)

1. (S) DATA RECORDED BY THE US ATOMIC ENERGY DETECTION SYSTEM (USAEDS) INDICATE AN ATMOSPHERIC NUCLEAR

EXPLOSION WITH A YIELD OF ABOUT _____ ( ____ ) KT

OCCURRED AT _____  _____

( ____ ) DEGREES  _____ ( ____ ) MINUTES NORTH,

_____ ( ____ ) DEGREES

_____ ( ____ ) MINUTES EAST, AT _____ COLON

_____ ( _____ ) GMT ON _____(_____) _____ 19 ___ .

2. (S) THE FOLLOWING SATELLITES/LOOK ANGLES (IN DEGREES) RECORDED THE EVENT:

_____/_____

_____/_____

_____/

3. (S) THE LOCATION WAS OBTAINED FROM COMBINED INPUTS FROM ██████████████████████████

4. (S) SEISMIC DATA ARE/ARE NOT AVAILABLE FROM THIS EVENT.

5. (S) THE PRELIMINARY ESTIMATE OF YIELD OF ABOUT _____ ( ___ ) KT, WITH AN UNCERTAINTY RANGE ██████

OF _____ ( ___ ) TO _____ ( ___ ) KT, IS BASED ON ████████████ A YIELD ESTIMATE OF

_____ ( ___ ) KT WAS OBTAINED FROM ██████████████████

6. (S) THE PRELIMINARY ESTIMATE OF HEIGHT OF BURST IS _____ ( ___ ) KILOMETERS.

7. (S) THE EARLIEST THAT ██████████████████████████████████

_____ ( _____ ) _____ 19 ___ .

8. (U) THE INFORMATION CONTAINED IN THIS DOCUMENT WILL BE SAFEGUARDED AS DIRECTED BY NATIONAL SECURITY DECISION

MEMORANDUM NO. 50.

DECL OADR.      OPR: AFTAC/DOB     INITIALS: _____  DATE: _____
========================================================================
```

.b.(1)

Source: AFTAC Regulation 55-5, "Alert Procedures," May 28, 1992.

programs. Aerial sampling operations are conducted over the United States, over the Southern Hemisphere, and over other areas under a variety of codenames, as indicated in Table 9-1. One version of the C-130, the HC-130, is outfitted with a sea water sampler for sorties flown against possible foreign underwater nuclear tests.[115] Some aircraft carrying aerial sampling equipment (filters to absorb nuclear material) are flown under the command of various military units. In these cases, nuclear monitoring is a secondary function.

Aircraft from the 55th Weather Reconnaissance Squadron at McClellan Air Force Base, which operates six WC-135s, were used to monitor fallout from the 1986 Chernobyl accident, designated Special Event 86-05. The planes, which were deployed to RAF Mildenhall, flew missions over Germany, Switzerland, Italy, and the Mediterranean. A May 21, 1992, Chinese nuclear test at Lop Nor produced a

Table 9-1. Varieties of Aerial Sampling Operations.

Codename	Type of Operation
VOLANT CHUCK	Southern Hemisphere Reconnaissance for HQ, USAF
VOLANT CURRY	Special Weather Reconnaissance
VOLANT DOME	Domestic Reconnaissance for HQ, USAF
VOLANT SPECK	Special Reconnaissance for HQ, USAF
VOLANT TRACK	Special Sampling Requirement
COMBAT CATCH	Special USAF Reconnaissance
CONSTANT GLOBE	Worldwide Sampling Operations
CONSTANT DOME	Domestic Reconnaissance for HQ, USAF
CONSTANT FISH	Water Sampling Operations for HQ, USAF
GIANT FISH	Aerial Operations for Atmospheric Sampling
OLYMPIC RACE	Special [U-2] Operations for HQ USAF
PONY EXPRESS	Special Reconnaissance for JCS

Note: Special Operations are sorties flown against foreign nuclear atmospheric and underground tests.

Source: Air Force Technical Applications Center, CENR 55-3, *Aerial Sampling Operations*, Volume 1, December 1, 1991, pp. v, 28.

large cloud of radioactive gas that, by early June, had passed over the Sea of Japan. A WC-135 flew through the cloud to collect nuclear particles. A WC-135 was probably also used to monitor the effects of a plutonium leak from a nuclear plant in Siberia in July 1993.[116]

Given the adherence of the United States and Russia to the Limited Test Ban Treaty and the Chinese restriction of testing to underground sites, monitoring underground explosions is an important part of the U.S. nuclear detonation monitoring program. Detection of underground explosions depends on distinguishing between the seismic waves generated by a nuclear explosion and those created by an earthquake. In most cases, determining the location of seismic events eliminates the large majority of earthquakes from consideration as possible nuclear detonations. In addition, analysts may be able to distinguish earthquakes from detonations by the differing nature of the signals produced by each phenomenon: Detonations emanate from a point source, whereas earthquakes result from two bodies of rock slipping past each other. At distances of less than 625 miles from an event, explosions greater than a few kilotons can easily be distinguished from earthquakes. At greater distances, such distinctions become far more difficult. Moreover, the actual recording of a seismic signal is disturbed by both instrumental and natural background noise, the latter setting a threshold of detectability.[117]

These limitations place a premium on situating monitoring stations or equipment in suitable locations and developing techniques to enhance the signal-to-noise ratio obtained at any location. The simplest form of earth-based monitoring equipment is the seismometer, which basically consists of a magnet fixed to the ground and a spring-suspended mass with an electric coil. According to SIPRI, "When seismic waves move the ground and the magnet attached to it, they leave the mass with the coil relatively unaffected. The relative motion of the magnet and coil generates a current in the coil which is proportional to their relative velocity."[118]

One method of enhancing the signal-to-noise ratio is by means of several seismometers placed in an array. Arrays increase the data set available for analysis in several ways, particularly because they can record the different arrival times of the seismic waves at the different seismometers. The major non-AFTAC arrays are located in Montana, Alaska, and Norway. The largest and most modern is the Large Aperture Seismic Array (LASA) in Montana. It consists of thirteen subarrays, each made up of twenty-five short-period instruments and a three-component set of long-period seismometers. The Alaska Long Period Array (ALPA) originally consisted of nineteen long-period seismometers, but it has been refitted with newly developed long-period borehole seismometers and now consists of seven three-component seismometers with an aperture of 25 miles. The Norwegian Seismic Array (NORSAR) consists of seven subarrays, each with forty-nine short- and seven long-period seismometers, extending over a distance of 32 miles.[119]

The seismic arrays and seismometers operated by the AFTAC are distributed throughout the world. Each detachment possesses broadband seismic detection capabilities and is responsible for detecting, recording, and analyzing all seismic activity that occurs in its area of responsibility, twenty-four hours a day.[120]

In addition to seismic monitoring instruments, some stations are equipped with four types of devices for monitoring the atmosphere for signs of nuclear detonations. One type, the Ground Filter Unit, is an electrically powered, ground-based, air filtering unit. The unit draws free air into a transition cone, which flows through a filter paper and is then emitted back into the atmosphere. The filter paper containing airborne particles from the atmosphere is then removed and forwarded for analysis and classification.[121]

The second type of atmospheric device, the Ground Moisture Unit, is a whole-air sampling device that employs two traps. The first contains a molecular sieve that removes water vapor from free air. The second contains a molecular sieve coated with palladium, which acts as a catalyst to oxidize gaseous hydrogen and form water vapor, which is absorbed. The traps are changed daily and forwarded to AFTAC's McClellan Central Laboratory (MCL) for analysis and classification.[122]

Another unit, the B-20-5, is an automated cryogenic distillation device that employs very low temperatures to isolate rare elements (gases) contained in the atmosphere. The unit is designed to operate continuously over any preset sample run of twenty-four hours (or multiple thereof) for periods of up to seven days. Samples are collected in 800-cc metal containers that are forwarded to the MCL.[123]

The fourth nonseismic system is the Electromagnetic Pulse (EMP) system, which is used to detect, locate, and identify the source of electromagnetic pulse signals in the VLF and HF range. The system is comprised of J Field Sets (JFSs)

Figure 9-4. Sample Alert Report Text: CIS/PRC Underground Test Site Events.

```
CENR 55-5    Attachment 12    28 May 1992                                      31

        Figure A12-2.  (U) Sample Alert Report Text:  CIS/PRC Underground Test Site Events
                       (This figure is classified SECRET)

SUBJECT:  ALERT _____ (U)

1. (S) DATA FROM _____ NORTH AMERICAN AND _____ OVERSEAS SEISMIC STATIONS OF THE US ATOMIC ENERGY DETECTION

SYSTEM (USAEDS) INDICATE AN UNDERGROUND EXPLOSION WITH A YIELD OF ABOUT _____ KT OCCURRED AT THE

_____  _____ TEST SITE, _____ DEGREES _____ MINUTES NORTH

_____DEGREES _____ MINUTES EAST, AT _____ GMT ON _____ 19___. THE ERROR ELLIPSE

ASSOCIATED WITH THE ABOVE LOCATION HAS A ████████████████████████████████████████████████████████

████████████████████████████████████

2. (S) DATA EVALUATED FROM _____ SATELLITES HAVING ████████████████████████████████████████████

█████████████WITH THIS EVENT.

3. (S) THE PRELIMINARY ESTIMATE OF YIELD OF ABOUT _____ KT, WITH AN UNCERTAINTY RANGE ██████████ OF _____

TO _____ KT, IS BASED ON A SEISMIC MAGNITUDE (Mb) OF ABOUT _____ AND AN ASSUMPTION THE DETONATION OCCURRED

AT THE _____ TEST SITE, THE MAGNITUDE-YIELD FORMULA _____ WAS USED IN

DETERMINING THE YIELD.

4. (S) SURFACE WAVE DATA _____

_____.

5. (S) THE EARLIEST THAT ████████████████████████████████████████████████████

19___.   AFTAC PLANS/DOES NOT PLAN TO CONDUCT ████████████████████████████████████████

6. (U) THE INFORMATION CONTAINED IN THIS DOCUMENT WILL BE SAFEGUARDED AS DIRECTED BY NATIONAL SECURITY DECISION

MEMORANDUM NO. 50.


_____


_____


                COORD: _____


                DATE: _____



                    CLASSIFIED BY: AFTAC GSSCG 20 DEC 90
                    DECLASSIFY ON: OADR
================================================================================
```

Source: AFTAC Regulation 55-5, "Alert Procedures," May 28, 1992.

that are linked via dedicated lines to the Central Data Terminal (CDT) located at AFTAC headquarters. Data from EMP signals that satisfy priority criteria at the JFS are transmitted in real time to the CDT via a synchronous communications circuit. The CDT is a continuously operating terminal with the capability of receiving EMP signal data from all JFS sites via dedicated communications lines and of performing real-time data processing of incoming data.[124] The type of alert report that provides notification of a CIS or PRC test is shown as Figure 9-4.

Altogether, AFTAC operates approximately ninety sites capable of detecting nuclear events. Included are eighteen manned detachments in various countries

Table 9-2.   AFTAC Manned Detachments.

Detachment	Location
045	Buckley ANGB, Colorado
046	Falcon AFS, Colorado
057	Lowry AFB, Colorado
301	Belbasi Seismic Research Station, Turkey
313	Sonseca, Spain
315	Iraklion AS, Greece
319	Lindsey AS, Germany
360	Keflavik, Iceland
370	RAF Edzell, United Kingdom
372	Ascension Island
377	Bad Aibling, Germany
407	Yokota AB, Japan
415	Chiang Mai Airport, Thailand
419	Wheeler Army Air Base, Hawaii
421	Alice Springs, Australia
422	Misawa AS, Japan
428	Anderson AFB, Guam
452	Camp Long Wonju, South Korea (Korean Seismological Research Station)
459	Pinedale, Wyoming
460	Eielson AFB, Alaska
471	Elmendorf AFB, Alaska

Source: AFTAC Regulation 4-2, "AFTAC Address Directory," January 9, 1992.

(some of which the United States will not acknowledge) and more than fifty unmanned "equipment locations" and covert stations located within embassies and consulates.[125]

The AFTAC's eighteen detachments are located in the United States, Europe, Australia, and Asia, as indicated in Table 9-2. The installation at Alice Springs, Australia, codenamed OAK TREE, is operated by Detachment 421. An underground seismic array located about 1.5 miles northeast of the detachment consists of nineteen seismometers arranged in a circular pattern over 7.25 miles. Thirteen of the seismometers are buried approximately 200 feet in the ground and designed to pick up the long-period waves that pass through the surface layer of the earth. The remaining six seismometers are buried 1.1 miles deep and tuned to detect the short-period waves that pass through the earth's mantle and core.[126] The seismometers are linked by cables to a central recording station where the signals are processed to provide an indication of the direction and speed at which they are traveling and the amplitude of the ground motion.[127]

Unmanned equipment locations are even more extensive and spread over all continents except Antarctica—as indicated in Table 9-3. These sites are exclusively involved in seismic and electromagnetic pulse detection. Some are located in open territory, but others are covert, embassy-based sites.[128]

One focus of research concerns nonseismic detection—specifically ionospheric and infrasonic monitoring. The shock waves created by nuclear detonations pro-

Table 9-3. AFTAC Equipment Locations.

EL Number	Location
060	Murray Hill, New Jersey
062	[Unknown]
064	[Unknown]
067	[Unknown]
079	Cambridge Bay, NWT, Canada
085	Patrick AFB, Florida
105	Goodfellow AFB, Texas
190	Lajitas, Texas
191	Shafter, Texas
192	Marathon, Texas
206	Pt. Barrow, Alaska
208	NAS Adak, Alaska
223	Juneau, Alaska
244	Flin Flon, Manitoba
300	NAS Bermuda
307	Mahe Island, Seychelles
329	Bremerhaven, West Germany
334	Sinop, Turkey
354	Kinsasha, Zaire
372	Ascension Island
421	Hickam AFB, Hawaii
432	Kadena AB, Japan
461	Shemya AFB, Alaska
462	Kotzebue, Alaska
465	Bangkok, Thailand
466	Naval Ordnance Facility, Sasebo, Japan
468	Anderson AFB, Guam
471	Elmendorf AFB, Alaska
489	Boulder, Wyoming
476	Osan AB, South Korea
	Burnt Mountain Research Site, Alaska
	Attu Research Site, Alaska
	Beaver Creek Research Site, Alaska
	Chena River Research Site, Alaska
	Eielson ALPA Research Site, Alaska
	Indian Mountain Research Site, Alaska

duce perturbations in certain levels of the ionosphere that can be detected by over-the-horizon (OTH) radar. Infrasonic monitoring involves the use of a microphone array for long-range monitoring of very low-frequency sound waves generated by nuclear explosions that propagate in the upper levels of the atmosphere.[129]

The same system employed by the Navy to detect Soviet submarines is also employed for hydroacoustic detection of nuclear detonations. These Equipment Locations (ELs) transmit, in digital form, recorded hydroacoustic data (sound waves in water) to a central analysis terminal located within AFTAC headquarters. Op-

Table 9-4. AFTAC Equipment Locations for Hydroacoustic Detection.

EL Number	Location
69	NAVFAC Whidbey Island
70	NAVFAC Adak, Alaska
72	NAVFAC Bermuda
73	NAVFAC Argentia, Canada
74	NAVFAC Midway
92	NOPF Dam Neck, Virginia
135	NAVFAC Centerville Beach, California
145	NAVFAC St. Nicholas Island, Pt. Mugu, California
360	NAVFAC Keflavik, Iceland
423	NAVFAC Guam

erated twenty-four hours a day, the hydroacoustic data terminal is tasked with identifying the source of each recorded wave.[130]

The Hydroacoustic or Digital "O" System (DOS) is composed of two separate systems that are interrelated—the Acquisition System and the Analysis System. In the former, up to nine "O" Field Sets (OFSs) form a real-time data acquisition system designed to collect raw data and perform frequency filtering, data processing, and data transmissions. The Analysis System is more commonly referred to as the Hydroacoustic Recorder and Processor (HRP). Hydroacoustic Equipment Locations are shown in Table 9-4.[131]

MEASUREMENT AND SIGNATURE INTELLIGENCE (MASINT)

The category of Measurement and Signature Intelligence (MASINT) incorporates a number of nonimagery, non-SIGINT technical collection activities. As indicated in Chapter 8, Radar Intelligence is one of those activities. Other components of MASINT include:

- Acoustical Intelligence (ACINT);
- Optical Intelligence (OPINT);
- Infrared Intelligence (IRINT);
- Laser Intelligence (LASINT);
- Nuclear Intelligence (NUCINT); and
- Unintentional Radiation Intelligence (RINT).[132]

A number of collection systems discussed in this chapter are also MASINT systems—including SOSUS (ACINT) and all the systems used to monitor nuclear detonations.

Some MASINT systems produce information relevant to development of antimissile defenses—such as data on the shapes, sizes, speeds, ranges, trajectories, and thermal signatures of foreign missiles. To help supplement the data provided by DSP satellites, additional sensors, codenamed HERITAGE, have been placed on SDS, and possibly JUMPSEAT, spacecraft. Deployment of an updated set of sensors was being considered in late 1993.[133]

In September 1994 it was reported that the Defense Department was studying a couple of potential large MASINT satellite payloads.[134]

NOTES

1. Warren Strobel and James S. Doresey, "Soviet Navy Now a World Class Power," *Washington Times,* November 2, 1987, p. A6; Department of Defense, *Soviet Military Power, 1987* (Washington, D.C.: U.S. Government Printing Office, 1987), pp. 31–35, 80–86.

2. Elaine Sciolino, "U.S. Tracks a Korean Ship Taking Missiles to Syria," *New York Times,* February 21, 1992, p. A9; Barton Gellman and Ann Devroy, "U.S. to Board N. Korean Ship Carrying Scuds If It Nears Gulf, Officials Say," *Washington Post,* March 8, 1992, p. A32; Bill Gertz and Rowan Scarborough, "U.S. Eyes Syria as Recipient of Scuds," *Washington Times,* March 9, 1992, p. A8; "Second U.S. Sub Monitors Iran's Fleet," *Washington Times,* February 12, 1993, p. A7; Nicholas D. Kristof, "China Says U.S. Is Harassing Ship," *New York Times,* August 9, 1993, p. A6; Daniel Williams, "Pyongyang Rebuffs New Inspections," *Washington Post,* August 17, 1993, p. A15.

3. "U.S. Launches Recon Satellite, Soviet Fleet Maneuvers May Be Target," *Aerospace Daily,* April 22, 1975, pp. 290–91.

4. Anthony Kenden, "U.S. Reconnaissance Satellite Programs," *Spaceflight,* July 20, 1973, pp. 243ff. at p. 257; Janko Jackson, "A Methodology for Ocean Surveillance Analysis," *Naval War College Review* 27, 2 (September/October 1974): 71–89; "Navy Plans Ocean Surveillance Satellite," *Aviation Week & Space Technology,* August 30, 1971, p. 13; "Industry Observer," *Aviation Week & Space Technology,* February 28, 1972, p. 9.

5. "Navy Ocean Surveillance Satellite Depicted," *Aviation Week & Space Technology,* May 24, 1976, p. 22; "Expended Ocean Surveillance Effort Set," *Aviation Week & Space Technology,* June 10, 1978, pp. 22–23; Mark Hewlish, "Satellites Show Their Warlike Face," *New Scientist,* October 1, 1981, pp. 36–40.

6. "Expanded Ocean Surveillance Effort Set"; Hewlish, "Satellites Show Their Warlike Face."

7. "Expanded Ocean Surveillance Effort Set."

8. Ibid.; Hewlish, "Satellites Show Their Warlike Face." For further details on PARCAE, see Maj. A. Andronov, "Kosmicheskaya Sistema Radiotekhnicheskoy Razvedki VMS SShA 'Vayt Klaud,'" *Zarubezhnoye Voyennoye Obozreniyo* [Foreign Military Review] 7 (1993): 57–60.

9. D. C. King-Hele, *The RAE Table of Earth Satellites, 1957–1980* (New York: Facts on File, 1981), pp. 444, 512, 600–601; *The RAE Table of Earth Satellites, 1983–1986* (Farnborough, Hants, England: RAE, 1987), pp. 721, 738, 769–70, 863; "Air Force Launches Secret Satellite for Military," *Washington Post,* May 16, 1987, p. A16.

10. Paul Stares, *Space and National Security* (Washington, D.C.: Brookings Institution, 1987), p. 188; United States Military Communications-Electronics Board, USMCEB Publication No. 6, *Message Address Directory* (Washington, D.C.: U.S. Government Printing Office, July 25, 1986), p. 48.

11. "U.S. Defense and Intelligence Space Programs," *Aviation Week & Space Technology,* March 19, 1990, p. 37; Bruce Van Voorst, "Billion-Dollar Blowup," *Time,* August 16, 1993, p. 41.

12. R. Jeffrey Smith and John Mintz, "Pentagon Plans Multibillion-Dollar Sea Spy Satellite System," *Washington Post,* August 7, 1993, p. A5; John H. Cushman, Jr., "Pentagon Found to Have Ignored Congress in Buying Spy Satellite," *New York Times,* September 24, 1993, p. A14; Theresa Hitchens and Neil Munro, "Pentagon Review Might Terminate Nuclear Spy Plans," *Defense News,* October 18–24, 1993, p. 3.

13. Lori A. McClelland, "Versatile P-3C Orion Meeting Growing ASW Challenge," *Defense Electronics,* April 1985, pp. 132–41.

14. David Miller, *An Illustrated Guide to Modern Sub Hunters* (New York: Arco, 1984), p. 125; George A. Wilmoth, "Lockheed's Antisubmarine Warfare Aircraft; Watching the Threat," *Defense Systems Review* 3, 6 (1985): 18–25; Private information; Brendan M. Greeley, Jr., "Soviets Extend Air, Sea Power with Buildup at Cam Ranh Bay," *Aviation Week & Space Technology,* March 2, 1987, pp. 76–77; "OP-924 Command History, Calendar Year 1988," in *Office of Naval Intelligence (ONI) Annual History, 1987–1988,* April 25, 1990, p. 1; Patrol Squadron Special Project Unit Two, VPU-2INST 5400.1F, *Squadron Organization and Regulations Manual,* June 12, 1991.

15. "Navy Teams with Satellites to Pinpoint Soviet Missile Test Gear," *Defense Week,* January 17, 1988, pp. 1, 19.

16. Miller, *An Illustrated Guide to Modern Sub Hunters,* p. 124; Wilmoth, "Lockheed's Antisubmarine Warfare Aircraft"; U.S. Congress, Senate Committee on Armed Services, *Department of Defense Authorization for Appropriations for Fiscal Year 1986, Part 8* (Washington, D.C.: U.S. Government Printing Office, 1985), p. 4510.

17. McClelland, "Versatile P-3C Orion Meeting Growing ASW Challenge"; Miller, *An Illustrated Guide to Modern Sub Hunters,* p. 124; *P-3C Orion Update Weapon System* (Burbank, Calif.: Lockheed, n.d.), p. 17.

18. *P-3C Orion Update Weapon System,* p. 18; McClelland, "Versatile P-3C Orion Meeting Growing ASW Challenge"; Nicholas M. Horrock, "The Submarine Hunters," *Newsweek,* January 23, 1984, p. 38.

19. U.S. Congress, General Accounting Office, *Issues Concerning the Navy's Maritime Patrol Aircraft* (Washington, D.C.: GAO, September 1991), p. 9.

20. Jeffrey T. Richelson and Desmond Ball, *The Ties That Bind: Intelligence Cooperation Between the UKUSA Countries* (London: George Allen & Unwin, 1985), p. 220; U.S. Congress, House Committee on Appropriations, *Department of Defense Appropriations for 1986, Part 4* (Washington, D.C.: U.S. Government Printing Office, 1985), p. 133; U.S. Congress, Senate Committee on Armed Services, *Department of Defense Authorization for Appropriations for Fiscal Year 1986, Part 8,* pp. 4503, 4510.

21. Bruce A. Smith, "Navy Cancels Lockheed Contract to Develop P-7A," *Aviation Week & Space Technology,* July 30, 1990, pp. 16–17; "USN Proposes P-3C Orion Upgrade," *Jane's Defence Weekly,* November 24, 1990, p. 1011; "U.S. Navy Plans P-3C Plus," *Jane's Defence Weekly,* August 24, 1991, p. 303; "U.S. Navy to Terminate P-3C Update Program," *Aviation Week & Space Technology,* October 19, 1992, p. 26; "P-3C Modernization Program Would Begin in 1994," *Aerospace Daily,* November 18, 1992, pp. 259–60; "U.S. Navy to Upgrade P-3Cs for Coastal Water Missions," *Defense News,* December 21–27, 1992, p. 11; "Navy Has Big Plans for P-3C Orion Upgrade Effort," *Defense Week,* July 12, 1993, p. 13.

22. Private information; U.S. Congress, House Committee on Appropriations, *Department of Defense Appropriations for 1994, Part 1* (Washington, D.C.: U.S. Government Printing Office, 1993), p. 48.

23. Dick Van der Art, *Aerial Espionage: Secret Intelligence Flights by East and West* (New York: Arco/Prentice-Hall, 1986), pp. 53–54; Private information.

24. Private information; Fleet Air Reconnaissance Squadron One, *1991 Command History*, n.d., p. 1.

25. Fleet Air Reconnaissance Squadron One, *1991 Command History*, p. 3.

26. Private information; Fleet Air Reconnaissance Squadron One, *1991 Command History*, p. 4.

27. Fleet Air Reconnaissance Squadron Two, *Fleet Air Reconnaissance Squadron Two History*, n.d.

28. L. T. Peacock, *U.S. Naval Aviation Today* (Uxbridge, England: Cheney Press, 1977), p. 25; Private information. According to Martin Streetly, "ES-3A, US Navy's New Listening Post," *Jane's Defence Weekly*, October 21, 1989, p. 872, the EA-3B was in the process of being phased out. Also see *Fleet Air Reconnaissance Squadron Two*, p. 11.

29. Martin Streetly, "ES-3A, US Navy's New Listening Post," p. 872; "U.S. Navy to Begin Tests on New ES-3A Aircraft," *Defense News*, February 24, 1992, p. 43; "Navy Develops Electronic Intelligence Aircraft for Carrier Battle Groups," *Aviation Week & Space Technology*, September 11, 1989, pp. 62–63; "Fact and Justification Sheet: Fleet Air Reconnaissance Squadron Six (VQ-6), NAS Cecil Field, Florida," 1993; Office of the Chief of Naval Operations, OPNAV Instruction C3501.280, Subject: Required Operational Capability (ROC) and Project Operational Environment (POE) for Fleet Air Reconnaissance Squadrons Five/Six (VQ-5/6), February 10, 1992, Enc. 1–3; Stephen H. Hardy, "Reaping the RF Harvest," *Journal of Electronic Defense* (December 1992): 34ff.

30. "Major Base Closure and Cutback Recommendations," *New York Times*, July 3, 1993, p. 6; "Clinton Proposes to Soften Blow of Base Closings," *New York Times*, July 3, 1993, p. 6.

31. Private information.

32. Private information.

33. U.S. Congress, House Committee on Appropriations, *Military Construction Appropriations for 1981* (Washington, D.C.: U.S. Government Printing Office, 1980), p. 1123; Private information.

34. U.S. Congress, House Committee on Appropriations, *Military Construction Appropriations for 1981*, p. 1123; Private information.

35. Private information; U.S. Congress, House Committee on Appropriations, *Military Construction Appropriations for 1987, Part 2* (Washington, D.C.: U.S. Government Printing Office, 1986), p. 463.

36. Private information.

37. Robert Holzer and Neil Munro, "Navy Eyes Eavesdropping System," *Defense News*, November 25, 1991, p. 12.

38. CINCPACFLT Instruction S3824.1A, "Portable Acoustic Collection Equipment," October 16, 1985, p. 2.

39. Testimony of Admiral Metzel in U.S. Congress, Senate Committee on Armed Services, *Department of Defense Authorization for Appropriations for Fiscal Year 1980, Part 6* (Washington, D.C.: U.S. Government Printing Office, 1979), p. 2925.

40. Owen Wilkes, "Strategic Anti-Submarine Warfare and Its Implications for a Counterforce First Strike," in *World Armaments and Disarmament, SIPRI Yearbook 1979* (London: Taylor & Francis Ltd., 1979), p. 430.

41. U.S. Congress, House Committee on Appropriations, *Department of Defense Appropriations for Fiscal Year 1977, Part 5* (Washington, D.C.: U.S. Government Printing Office, 1976), p. 1255; Drew Middleton, "Expert Predicts a Big U.S. Gain in Sub Warfare," *New York Times*, July 18, 1979, p. A5; Chapman Pincher, "U.S. to Set Up Sub Spy Station," *Daily Express*, January 6, 1973; Harvey B. Silverstein, "Caesar, SOSUS and Submarines: Economic and Institutional Implications of ASW Technologies," *Ocean '78* (Proceedings of the Fourth Annual Combined Conference Sponsored by the Marine Technology Society and the Institute of Electrical and Electronics Engineers, Washington, D.C., September 6–8, 1978), p. 407.

42. U.S. Congress, House Committee on Appropriations, *Department of Defense Appropriations for Fiscal Year 1977, Part 5* (Washington, D.C.: U.S. Government Printing Office, 1976), p. 1255; Middleton, "Expert Predicts a Big U.S. Gain in Sub Warfare."

43. Defense Market Survey, "Sonar-Sub-Surface-Caesar," *DMS Market Intelligence Report* (Greenwich, Conn.: DMS, 1980), p. 1; Clyde W. Burleson, *The Jennifer Project* (Englewood Cliffs, N.J.: Prentice-Hall, 1977), p. 18; Joel S. Wit, "Advances in Antisubmarine Warfare," *Scientific American*, February 1981, pp. 36ff.; Burleson, *The Jennifer Project*, pp. 17–19, 24–25; Silverstein, "CAESAR, SOSUS and Submarines."

44. Howard B. Dratch, "High Stakes in the Azores," *The Nation*, November 8, 1975, pp. 455–56; "NATO Fixed Sonar Range Commissioned," *Armed Forces Journal International*, August 1972, p. 29; "Atlantic Islands: NATO Seeks Wider Facilities," *International Herald Tribune*, June 1981, p. 75; Richard Timsar, "Portugal Bargains for U.S. Military Aid with Strategic Mid-Atlantic Base," *Christian Science Monitor*, March 24, 1981, p. 9; Wit, "Advances in Antisubmarine Warfare."

45. William Arkin and Richard Fieldhouse, *Nuclear Battlefields: Global Links in the Arms Race* (Cambridge, Mass.: Ballinger, 1986), Appendix A; Ed Offley, "Turning the Tide: Soviets Score a Coup with Sub Progress," *Seattle Post-Intelligencer*, April 8, 1987, p. A5; United States Military Communications-Electronics Board, USMCEB Publication No. 6, Issue 25, *Message Address Directory* (Washington, D.C.: U.S. Government Printing Office, January 30, 1993), p. 30; U.S. Congress, House Committee on Appropriations, *Department of Defense Appropriations, Part 1* (Washington, D.C.: U.S. Government Printing Office, 1993), p. 48; William J. Broad, "Scientists Oppose Navy Plan to Shut Undersea Monitor," *New York Times*, June 12, 1994, pp. 1, 18.

46. William E. Burrows, *Deep Black: Space Espionage and National Security* (New York: Random House, 1987), p. 180n.; USN-PLAD, pp. 28, 33 in U.S. Military Communications-Electronics Board, USMCEB Publication No. 6, *Message Address Directory* (Washington, D.C.: U.S. Government Printing Office, July 25, 1986); CINCPACFLT Instruction 5450.76, "Mission and Functions of Naval Ocean Processing Facility, Ford Island, Pearl Harbor, Hawaii," February 22, 1985; Broad, "Scientists Oppose Navy Plan to Shut Undersea Monitor."

47. Robert P. Berman and John C. Baker, *Soviet Strategic Forces: Requirements and Responses* (Washington, D.C.: Brookings Institution, 1982), pp. 106–7.

48. "Stray Voltage," *Armed Forces Journal International*, April 1987, p. 94; Robert Holzer, "U.S. Navy Shifts ASW Priorities to New Technology," *Defense News*, June 8–14, 1992, pp.

6, 18; U.S. Congress, House Committee on Appropriations, *Department of Defense Appropriations for 1993, Part 5* (Washington, D.C.: U.S. Government Printing Office, 1992), p. 342.

49. Office of the Chief of Naval Operations, OPNAV Instruction S3501.132B, Subject: Integrated Undersea Surveillance System (IUSS) Performance Assessment Program, October 21, 1986.

50. Ibid.; James Shultz, "Anti-Sub Warfare Escalates," *Defense Electronics*, June 1983, pp. 76–89; U.S. Congress, Senate Committee on Armed Services, *Department of Defense Authorization for Appropriations for Fiscal Year 1980, Part 6*, pp. 1147–49; Larry L. Booda, "SURTASS, RDSS Augment Ocean Surveillance," *Sea Technology* (November 1981): 19–29; Norman Polmar, "SURTASS and T-AGOS," *U.S. Naval Institute Proceedings* (March 1980): 120–24; U.S. Congress, House Committee on Foreign Affairs and Senate Committee on Foreign Relations, *Fiscal Year 1981 Arms Control Impact Statement* (Washington, D.C.: U.S. Government Printing Office, 1980), p. 342; U.S. General Accounting Office, *Undersea Surveillance: Navy Continues to Build Ships Designed for Soviet Threat* (Washington, D.C.: GAO/NSIAD-93-53, December 1992), pp. 1–2; "U.S. Navy Surveillance Ship Delay Urged," *Jane's Defence Weekly*, January 16, 1993, p. 10.

51. General Accounting Office, *Undersea Surveillance*, pp. 8–9.

52. "ASW Systems Reveal 'Hidden' Whales," *Jane's Defence Weekly*, August 21, 1993, p. 10; Broad, "Scientists Oppose Navy Plan to Shut Undersea Monitor"; William J. Broad, "Long-Secret Navy Devices Allow Monitoring of Ocean Eruption," *New York Times*, August 20, 1993, pp. A1, A6.

53. Aerospace Defense Command, *ADCOM Command & Control*, November 30, 1980, pp. 8–12.

54. Cryptologic Technician Training Series, Module 8 Fleet Operations—Electronic Warfare, NAVEDTRA A 95-08-00-87, 1987.

55. Lt. Frank Murphy, "Chambered Round," *Space Tracks*, March–April 1991, pp. 8–9.

56. "News Breaks," *Aviation Week & Space Technology*, March 15, 1993, p. 23.

57. P. S. Clark, "The Chinese Space Year of 1984," *Journal of the British Interplanetary Society* 39 (1986): 29–34.

58. Peter B. de Selding, "France Steps Up Its Military Space Activity, Spending," *Space News*, November 2–8, 1992, p. 21; Thomas G. Mahnken, "Why Third World Space Systems Matter," *Orbis*, Fall 1991, pp. 563–79; William J. Broad, "Non-Superpowers Are Developing Their Own Spy Satellite Systems," *New York Times*, September 3, 1989, pp. 1, 16.

59. AFSPACECOM Regulation 55-10, "2nd Space Wing (2SWG) Satellite Operations," October 13, 1989, p. 6; Jess Hall, "Command Activates 21st SPW at Peterson," *Space Trace*, June 1992, p. 4.

60. USSPACECOM Regulation 55-12, "Space Surveillance Network," June 1, 1992.

61. USSPACECOM Regulation 55-6, "Space Surveillance Network Data User Support," April 15, 1991, p. 10; AFSPACECOM 002-88, "Statement of Operational Need (SON): Space Surveillance (S2)," August 7, 1989, p. A1-1.

62. Paul Stares, *Space and National Security* (Washington, D.C.: Brookings Institution, 1987), p. 204; AFSPACECOM Regulation 23-42, "Detachment 1, Space Wing," June 30, 1986; "Industry Observer," *Aviation Week & Space Technology*, February 12, 1987, p. 13; U.S. Congress, Senate Committee on Armed Services, *Department of Defense Authorization for Appropriations for Fiscal Year 1980, Part 6*, p. 3022; "U.S. Upgrading Ground-Based Sen-

sors," *Aviation Week & Space Technology,* June 16, 1980, pp. 239–42; David M. Russell, "NORAD Adds Radar, Optics to Increase Space Defense," *Defense Electronics,* July 1982, pp. 82–86; Vincent Kiernan, "Portuguese Balk at U.S. Radar, Leaving Air Force with Blind Spot," *Space News,* October 9, 1989, p. 12; Science Applications International Corporation, *OUSD(A) Defense Space Systems Study, Final Report* (Falls Church, Va.: SAIC, March 1989), p. B-69; AFSPACECOM Regulation 23-58, "18th Surveillance Squadron (18 SURS)," September 10, 1990; AFSPACECOM Regulation 23-42, "Detachment 1, 18th Surveillance Squadron (Det 1, 18 SURS)," September 28, 1990; AFSPACECOM Regulation 23-43, "Detachment 2, 18th Surveillance Squadron (Det 2, 18 SURS)," September 28, 1990; AFSPACECOM Regulation 23-44, "Detachment 3, 18th Surveillance Squadron (Det 3, 18 SURS)," September 28, 1990; AFSPACECOM Regulation 23-19, "Detachment 4, 18th Surveillance Squadron (Det 4, 18 SURS)," September 28, 1990.

63. Russell, "NORAD Adds Radar, Optics to Increase Space Defense"; Lt. Col. William C. Jeas and Robert Anctil, "The Ground-Based Electro-Optical Deep Space Surveillance (GEODSS) System," *Military Electronics/Countermeasures,* November 1981, pp. 47–51.

64. "U.S. Upgrading Ground Based Sensors"; Russell, "NORAD Adds Radar, Optics to Increase Space Defense."

65. "U.S. Upgrading Ground-Based Sensors"; Science Applications International Corporation, *OUSD(A) Defense Space Systems Study, Final Report,* p. B-69.

66. "U.S. Upgrading Ground-Based Sensors," p. 239.

67. "GEODSS Photographs Orbiting Satellite," *Aviation Week & Space Technology,* December 5, 1983, pp. 146–47.

68. Ibid.; *Anti-Satellite Weapons, Countermeasures and Arms Control* (Washington, D.C.: Office of Technology Assessment, 1985), p. 55; USSPACECOM Regulation 55-12, "Space Surveillance Network (SSN)," p. 15.

69. "Spacetrack," *Jane's Weapons Systems, 1982–1983* (London: Jane's Publishing, 1982), pp. 233–34; Russell, "NORAD Adds Radar, Optics to Increase Space Defense"; "The Arms Race in Space," *SIPRI Yearbook 1978: World Armaments and Disarmaments* (New York: Crane, Russak, 1978), pp. 104–30; Brendan M. Greeley, Jr., "Navy Expanding Its Space Command to Bolster Readiness," *Aviation Week & Space Technology,* February 3, 1986, pp. 54–57; Office of the Chief of Naval Operations, OPNAV Instruction 5450.206, Subject: Naval Space Surveillance; Mission and Functions of, June 22, 1991.

70. "Spacetrack"; United States Space Command, "Space Surveillance Network (SSN)," June 1, 1992, p. 15.

71. Kiernan, "Portuguese Balk at U.S. Radar, Leaving Air Force with Blind Spot."

72. USSPACECOM Regulation 55-6, "Space Surveillance Network Data User Support," p. 10; USSPACECOM Regulation 55-12, "Space Surveillance Network (SSN)," pp. 15–17; AFSPACECOM Regulation 23-58, "18th Surveillance Squadron (18 SURS)."

73. AFSPACECOM Regulation 23-56, "1st Surveillance Squadron (1SURS)," January 4, 1991; Jesse Hall, "PASS Systems Enhance Surveillance Network," *Space Trace,* September 1992, p. 3; "73rd Changes Name, Becomes Space Group," *Space Trace,* June 1992, p. 4; USSPACECOM Regulation 55-12, "Space Surveillance Network (SSN)," p. 15; AFSPACECOM 002-88, "Statement of Operational Need (SON): Space Surveillance (S2)," p. 3.

74. AFPSACECOM Regulation 23-61, "5th Space Surveillance Squadron (5SURS)," March 28, 1991; "73rd Changes Name, Becomes Space Group"; USSPACECOM Regulation

55-12, "Space Surveillance Network (SSN)," p. 15; "USAF to Open Facility Monitoring Satellites," *Space News,* May 10–16, 1993, p. 2.

75. AFSPACECOM Regulation 23-65, "4th Surveillance Squadron (4SURS)," June 14, 1991; AFSPACECOM Regulation 23-64, "Detachments 1–3, 4th Surveillance Squadron (4SURS)," June 14, 1991; USSPACECOM Regulation 55-12, "Space Surveillance Network (SSN)," p. 15; "73rd Changes Name, Becomes Space Group"; Hall, "PASS Systems Enhance Surveillance Network."

76. Hall, "PASS Systems Enhance Surveillance Network."

77. "AN/FPS-85," *Jane's Weapons Systems, 1982–1983* (London: Jane's Publishing, 1982), pp. 505–6; "The Arms Race in Space," pp. 114–24 at p. 116; John Hambre et al., *Strategic Command, Control and Communications: Alternate Approaches for Modernization* (Washington, D.C.: Congressional Budget Office, 1981), p. 10; USSPACECOM Regulation 55-12, "Space Surveillance Network (SSN)," p. 15; Science Applications International Corporation," *OUSD(A) Defense Space Systems Study, Final Report,* p. B-68; AFSPACECOM Regulation 23-40, "20th Surveillance Squadron (20 SURS)," June 29, 1990.

78. Owen Wilkes, *Spacetracking and Spacewarfare* (Oslo: International Peace Research Institute, 1978), p. 27.

79. Ibid.

80. Stares, *Space and National Security,* p. 204.

81. "U.S. Upgrading Ground Sensors"; Stares, *Space and National Security,* p. 204; "The Arms Race in Space," p. 116; "Improved U.S. Warning Net Spurred," *Aviation Week & Space Technology,* June 23, 1980, pp. 38ff.; USSPACECOM Regulation 55-12, "Space Surveillance Network (SSN)," p. 16.

82. "Pave Paws Radar," *Jane's Weapons Systems, 1982–1983* (London: Jane's Publishing, 1982), p. 501; "U.S. Upgrading Ground Sensors"; Stares, *Space and National Security,* p. 205; AFSPACECOM Regulation 23-50, "9 Missile Warning Squadron," September 2, 1986; "Space Command Completes Acquisition of Pave Paws Warning Radar Installations," *Aviation Week & Space Technology,* May 18, 1987, pp. 128–29; Office of Legislative Liaison, Office of the Secretary of the Air Force, *Systems Information Briefs for Members of Congress* (Washington, D.C.: Department of the Air Force, 1987), p. 80; AFSPACECOM Regulation 23-36, "6th Missile Warning Squadron (6MWS)," April 27, 1990; AFSPACECOM Regulation 23-37, "7th Missile Warning Squadron (7MWS)," April 27, 1990; AFSPACECOM Regulation 23-49, "8th Missile Warning Squadron (8MWS)," April 27, 1990; AFSPACECOM Regulation 23-50, "9th Missile Warning Squadron (9MWS)," May 21, 1990; USSPACECOM Regulation 55-12, "Space Surveillance Network (SSN)," p. 16; Jesse Hall, "Command Activates 21st SPW at Peterson," *Space Trace,* June 1992, p. 4.

83. AFSPACECOM Regulation 23-33, "16 Surveillance Squadron (16 SURS)," June 30, 1986; AFSPACECOM Regulation 23-35, "19 Surveillance Squadron (19 SURS)," June 30, 1986; U.S. Air Force, "SAC Fact Sheet," August 1981; "The Arms Race in Space"; Stares, *Space and National Security,* p. 205.

84. USSPACECOM Regulation 55-12, "Space Surveillance Network (SSN)," p. 16; Science Applications International Corporation, *OUSD(A) Defense Space Systems Study, Final Report,* p. B-66.

85. Science Applications International Corporation, *OUSD(A) Defense Space Systems Study, Final Report,* p. B-65.

86. USSPACECOM Regulation 55-12, "Space Surveillance Network (SSN)," p. 17.

87. Science Applications International Corporation, *OUSD(A) Defense Space Systems Study, Final Report,* p. B-62.

88. Ibid., p. B-63.

89. U.S. Air Force, "SAC Fact Sheet"; Defense Marketing Survey, *Codename Handbook 1981* (Greenwich, Conn.: DMS, 1981), p. 168; Stares, *Space and National Security,* p. 205; U.S. Congress, House Committee on Appropriations, *Department of Defense Appropriations for 1981, Part 8* (Washington, D.C.: U.S. Government Printing Office, 1980), p. 241; Science Applications International Corporation, *OUSD(A) Defense Space Systems Study, Final Report,* p. B-71.

90. Science Applications International Corporation, *OUSD(A) Defense Space Systems Study, Final Report,* p. B-64; Vincent Kiernan, "Air Force Begins Upgrades to Satellite Scanning Telescope," *Space News,* July 23–29, 1990, p. 8.

91. Craig Covault, "Maui Optical Station Photographs External Tank Reentry Breakup," *Aviation Week & Space Technology,* June 11, 1990, pp. 52–53.

92. Ibid.; Bruce D. Nordwall, "Air Force Uses Optics to Track Space Objects," *Aviation Week & Space Technology,* August 16, 1993, pp. 66–68; Bruce D. Nordwall, "Optics/Laser Research Seeks to Improve Images," *Aviation Week & Space Technology,* August 16, 1993, p. 69.

93. Science Applications International Corporation, *OUSD(A) Defense Space Systems Study, Final Report,* pp. B-64, B-70.

94. Stares, *Space and National Security,* p. 204; John L. Piotrowski, "C^{3}I for Space Control," *Signal,* June 1987, pp. 23–33; AFSPACECOM Regulation 23-44, "Detachment 3, 1 Space Wing," August 18, 1986; Science Applications International Corporation, *OUSD(A) Defense Space Systems Study, Final Report,* p. B-72; Vincent Kiernan, "Air Force Begins Upgrades to Satellite Scanning Telescope," p. 8.

95. Kiernan, "Air Force Begins Upgrades to Satellite Scanning Telescope."

96. Joel W. Powell, "Photography of Orbiting Satellites," *Spaceflight* (February 1983): 82–83; Stares, *Space and National Security,* p. 204.

97. Stares, *Space and National Security,* p. 205; U.S. Air Force, "SAC Fact Sheet."

98. William J. Broad, "New Space Challenge: Monitoring Weapons," *New York Times,* December 8, 1987, pp. C1, C6; AFSPACECOM 002-88, "Statement of Operational Need (SON): Space Surveillance (S2)," p. 3.

99. AFSPACECOM 002-08, "Statement of Operational Need (SON): Space Surveillance (S2)," p. 3.

100. U.S. Arms Control and Disarmament Agency, *Arms Control and Disarmament Agreements: Texts and Histories of Negotiations* (Washington, D.C.: ACDA, 1980), pp. 34–47, 161–89.

101. U.S. Congress, Senate Committee on Appropriations, *Department of Defense Appropriations for Fiscal Year 1972, Part 1* (Washington, D.C.: U.S. Government Printing Office, 1971), p. 672.

102. "Forum: The Explosion of October 16," *Bulletin of the Atomic Scientists,* February 1965.

103. See Jeffrey Richelson, "PD-59, NSDD-13 and the Reagan Strategic Modernization Program," *Journal of Strategic Studies* 6, 2 (1983): 125–46.

104. "Worldwide Nuclear Testing, 1945–1992," *Arms Control Today,* November 1992, p. 37; Lena H. Sun, "Chinese Conduct Atomic Test," *Washington Post,* October 6, 1993, pp.

A1, A23; Patrick E. Tyler, "China Sets Off H-Bomb Test Underground," *New York Times*, June 11, 1994, p. 6.

105. Desmond Ball, *A Suitable Base for Debate: The U.S. Satellite Station at Nurrungar* (Sydney: Allen & Unwin Australia, 1987), pp. 20–21.

106. Ibid., p. 17.

107. U.S. Congress, Senate Committee on Armed Services, *Department Defense Authorization for Appropriations for FY 1981, Part 6* (Washington, D.C.: U.S. Government Printing Office, 1980), p. 3449.

108. Ball, *A Suitable Base for Debate*, p. 4.

109. Ibid., pp. 47–49.

110. Ibid., p. 50; Arkin and Fieldhouse, *Nuclear Battlefields*, p. 181.

111. U.S. Congress, General Accounting Office, *Satellite Acquisition: Global Positioning Acquisition Changes After Challenger's Accident* (Washington, D.C.: GAO, 1987), pp. 8, 29.

112. U.S. Congress, House Committee on Appropriations, *Department of Defense Appropriations for 1983, Part 5* (Washington, D.C.: U.S. Government Printing Office, 1982), p. 16; U.S. Congress, House Committee on Appropriations, *Department of Defense Appropriations for 1984, Part 8* (Washington, D.C.: U.S. Government Printing Office, 1983), p. 337; U.S. Congress, House Committee on Armed Services, *Department of Energy National Security and Military Applications of Nuclear Energy Authorization Act of 1984* (Washington, D.C.: U.S. Government Printing Office, 1983), pp. 383–84; Stares, *Space and National Security*, p. 29; Charles A. Zraket, "Strategic Command, Control, Communications and Intelligence," *Science*, June 22, 1984, p. 1309; "Navstar Bloc 2 Satellites to Have Crosslinks, Radiation Hardening," *Defense Electronics*, July 1983, p. 16; Department of the Air Force, *Supporting Data for Fiscal Year 1985* (Washington, D.C.: Department of the Air Force, 1984), pp. 394–95; AFSPACECOM Regulation 55-29, "Global Positioning System and Nuclear Detonation (NUDET) Detection System (GPS/NDS) Mission Requirements and Doctrine (MRD)," September 1, 1989, pp. 4, 6, 9.

113. U.S. Congress, House Committee on Armed Services, *Department of Energy National Security and Military Applications*, pp. 383–84, 392; RCA Astro-Electronics Briefing Slides, "Defense Meteorological Satellite Program," n.d.

114. Ben Iannotta, "Alexis X-Ray Sensor Begins Functioning," *Space News*, August 2–8, 1993, p. 8; James R. Asker, "Science Experiments Begin on Ailing ALEXIS Satellite," *Aviation Week & Space Technology*, July 19, 1993, p. 68; Ben Iannotta, "Labs vs. Industry Debate Revived by Legislation," *Space News*, May 2–8, 1994, pp. 1, 29.

115. Air Technical Applications Center, CENR 55-3, "Aerial Sampling Operations," October 22, 1982, p. 2-7; Scott Weathers, Steve Greene, Greg Barge, Paul Schultz, and Chris Clements, *History of the 55th Weather Reconnaissance Squadron, July–December 1989* (McClellan AFB, Calif.: 55th WRS, December 31, 1989), p. 1.

116. Jerry King, Chris Lucey, Mike Lyons, Grant Phifer, and Leslie Yokoyama-Peralta, *History of the 55th Weather Reconnaissance Squadron, 1 Jan to 30 June 1986* (McClellan AFB, Calif.: 55th WRS, n.d.), p. 11; Bill Gertz, "Chinese Nuke Test Releases Gas Cloud," *Washington Post*, June 11, 1992, p. A5; James Rupert, "Plutonium Leak Reported at Russian Nuclear Plant," *Washington Post*, July 20, 1993, p. A14.

117. Henry R. Myers, "Extending the Nuclear Test Ban," *Scientific American*, January 1972, pp. 13–23; Lynn R. Sykes and Jack F. Evernden, "The Verification of a Comprehensive Nuclear Test Ban," *Scientific American*, October 1982, pp. 47–55; "The Comprehensive

Test Ban," in *SIPRI Yearbook 1978: World Armaments and Disarmament* (New York: Crane, Russak, 1978), pp. 317–359 at p. 335.

118. "The Comprehensive Test Ban," p. 335.

119. Ibid., p. 340.

120. 3400 Technical Training Wing, *Introduction to Detection Systems* (Lowry Air Force Base, Colo.: 3400 TTW, October 18, 1984), p. 17.

121. Ibid., p. 17.

122. Ibid.

123. Ibid.

124. Ibid., p. 18.

125. "Secret Test Monitors," *Bulletin of the Atomic Scientists,* July/August 1987, p. 63; Private information.

126. Desmond Ball, *A Suitable Piece of Real Estate: American Installations in Australia* (Sydney, Australia: Hale & Iremonger, 1980), pp. 84–85.

127. Ibid.

128. Private information.

129. U.S. Congress, Senate Committee on Appropriations, *Energy and Water Development Appropriations FY 1986, Part 2* (Washington, D.C.: U.S. Government Printing Office, 1985), pp. 1360–61.

130. 3400 Technical Training Wing, *Introduction to Detection Systems,* p. 18.

131. Ibid., p. 18; AFTAC CENR 55-8, "Management of Digital O Stations," July 27, 1990; AFTAC CENR 55-1, "O Technique Signal Analysis Handbook," November 5, 1991, p. 1-1.

132. Joint Chiefs of Staff, JCS Pub 2-0, *Doctrine for Intelligence Support to Joint Operations,* June 30, 1991, p. IV-3.

133. Neil Munro, "DoD Eyes New Black Satellite Sensor," *Defense News,* November 15–21, 1993, pp. 1, 28.

134. "Already Smarting, TRW Space Operations Face Combined Lockheed Martin," *Aerospace Daily,* September 8, 1994, pp. 378–80.

10
HUMAN SOURCES

The increasing capability to collect intelligence via technical means has reduced reliance on human sources; however, human sources are not inconsequential. Much valuable information, particularly documents, is accessible only through human sources. Such sources can be used to fill gaps—in some cases important gaps—left by technical collection systems.

Sometimes gaps will result because of the inherent limitations of technical systems; with proper security, many discussions will be immune to interception. Also, technical systems cannot photograph planning or policy documents locked in a vault. Nor can technical systems physically acquire weapons systems or weapons system components.

Additionally, technical systems are expensive and can be employed against a limited number of targets. Thus, information on lower-priority targets may be desired, but only if it can be acquired without the introduction of a new or enhanced technical collection system or the diversion of an operating system away from higher-priority targets. Human sources can also serve to determine targets for technical collection systems.

A high priority for U.S. intelligence is to understand the decision processes involved in foreign, military, and economic policymaking in both hostile and friendly nations. An understanding of both the processes and people can lead to a more accurate estimation of the likely course of action in a given circumstance. Some data on such matters may be obtained by technical means, but there will be gaps that may be filled only by other sources.

A further objective of human intelligence activities is the acquisition of planning documents, technical manuals, contingency plans, and weapons systems blueprints. As Amrom Katz has noted, "The analysts ... want the designer's plan, notebooks, tests on components, tests of materials, conversation between designer and the customer."[1] Although in most cases the analyst must settle for images and electronic data concerning test activities, it is often the designer's documentation that constitutes the "best evidence."

Certain stages of military R&D are simply not available for technical monitoring. Once plans have reached the testing stage, a variety of U.S. technical collection systems can be employed. But when the weapon is being designed, and its characteristics debated, technical collection can be of very limited utility—particularly if communications security is stringent. It is desirable to know about the characteristics of weapons systems when they have reached the testing stage, but it is also important to know whatever possible about activity in the design bureaus. Even nations that purchase weapons abroad may develop their own modified versions of those systems. Thus, Iraq developed modified versions of the Scuds that it purchased from the Soviet Union.

In the case of terrorist groups, drug cartels, underground political parties, and dictators, intelligence about intentions may be obtainable only through infiltration of an agent. Such an agent might be able to cast light on a situation discovered by overhead photography—for example, the massing of Libyan troops near Chad's border.

Statistics derived from twelve 1994 intelligence reviews provide some measure of the value of HUMINT. Of 376 specific intelligence issues, HUMINT was judged as making a "critical contribution" toward 205. In regard to terrorism, HUMINT items represented 75 percent of the critical items. The figures for other areas were: narcotics, over 50 percent; nonproliferation, over 40 percent; and international economics, over 33 percent.[2]

OFFICERS

Human sources include officers, their agents, and attachés as well as defectors, émigrés, and travelers. The core of U.S. human intelligence operations is composed of the intelligence officers of the CIA's Directorate of Operations. These officers are U.S. citizens who almost always operate under cover of U.S. embassies and consulates. Although business or other forms of deep cover may be used on occasion, only official diplomatic establishments provide the CIA officer abroad with secure communications (within the embassy and to other locations), protected files, and diplomatic immunity.

CIA stations in foreign countries are headed by the Chief of Station (COS) and vary substantially in size, from just a few officers to more than 150, as was the case in the Philippines in the late 1980s. The COS and his officers operate under a variety of cover positions that vary from embassy to embassy, including political counselor, second secretary, and economic attaché. They also operate under the cover of a variety of offices in the embassy. Thus, in the late 1970s, the CIA station in London, the agency's largest liaison station, was staffed by some forty CIA officers who worked out of five cover offices—the Political Liaison Section; the Area Telecommunications Office, with a staff of between nine and thirteen at any one time; the Joint Reports and Research Unit, with a staff of about thirty; the Foreign Broadcast Information Service; and the Office of the Special U.S. Liaison Officer, with mostly NSA but some CIA officers. The station is generally headed by a very senior CIA officer.[3]

In France, the Regional Reports Office, the Regional Administrative Support, and the American Liaison Section served as cover offices in the late 1970s. In Italy, the Embassy Political Section and the United States Army Europe Southern Projects Unit served as covers, and in West Germany the Office of the Coordinator and Adviser, the Research Office, the Records Office, and the Liaison Office performed that function. The CIA has also made great use in Germany of the United States Army Europe (USAREUR) for cover. Among the units it has used for cover are the U.S. Army Field Systems Office, the U.S. Army General Research Detachment, the U.S. Army Scientific and Technical Programming Detachment (Provisional), the U.S. Army Scientific Projects Group, the U.S. Army Security Evaluation Group, and the U.S. Army Technical Analysis Unit.[4]

The attachés who operate as part of the Defense Attaché system also constitute a second group of intelligence officers. The functions of Defense Attachés include:

- identifying and gaining cooperation of human sources believed to possess the ability to furnish intelligence information;
- identifying and capturing collection opportunities presented by trade fairs, military demonstrations, parades, symposia, convocations, conferences, meetings, and the like;
- traveling to identified geographic target areas to observe, photograph, and report information specifically needed by consumers/users;
- identifying, establishing contact, and maintaining liaison with foreign military officers who, by virtue of rank, position, or assignment, can furnish potential intelligence information or are considered to be future leaders;
- gaining and maintaining area reality to observe and report political, sociological, psychological, and economic developments of potential value in gauging the military plans, capabilities, and intentions of foreign governments and their military forces and their stability; and
- identifying and gaining access to assist in the acquisition and exploitation of foreign military equipment and materiel.[5]

In addition to cultivating sources and collecting open source material, CIA Defense Attachés may also engage in clandestine collection on their own. In 1985 the Polish government claimed to have stopped a car in a restricted military zone near the town of Makow Mazowiecki, 65 miles north of Warsaw. According to the Polish story, the passengers, U.S. Defense Attaché Colonel Frederick Myer, Jr., and his wife, covered themselves with blankets and exposed six roles of film. Police were said to have found two cameras with telephoto lenses and detailed maps of the area that had been produced by the Defense Mapping Agency. Subsequently, Albert Mueller, then Second Secretary in the U.S. Embassy's Political Section, was arrested for allegedly attempting to photograph a Polish Army radar and Soviet helicopters. In addition, he was accused of passing espionage equipment, orders, ciphers, and money to a Polish citizen. The Polish government supported its charges with videotape.[6]

In May 1986, the Nicaraguan government charged that two military officers, including the U.S. Embassy's military attaché, were discovered traveling without permits in a restricted war zone and suggested they were involved in espionage activity. The two were found traveling near the town of Siuna, a remote area in north Central Nicaragua that had been a focus of combat between the Sandinista Army and guerrilla forces.[7]

In early 1987, Colonel Marc B. Powe, the attaché at the U.S. Embassy in Baghdad, was declared persona non grata and given two weeks to leave Iraq after he was accused of spying on and photographing truckloads of tanks and other military equipment in Kuwait in early December. Powe, who also served as attaché to Kuwait, had discovered a convoy of Soviet military equipment in Kuwait en route to Baghdad, and Kuwaiti authorities spotted him photographing the convoy and taking notes.[8]

In early 1989, two U.S. attachés, Colonel Clifford Robert Ward and Major Robert Siegel, were apprehended on the perimeter of a Palestinian commando base 25 miles from Damascus. Taken into custody by armed guerrillas of the Popular Front for the Liberation of Palestine–General Command (PFLP-GC), Ward and Siegel were reported to have been carrying cameras, maps, binoculars, and telephoto lenses.[9]

As noted in Chapter 3, the HUMINT operations formerly carried out by the DIA and various military intelligence service components will now be conducted by the Defense HUMINT Service. Those operations include activities carried out by INSCOM's Foreign Intelligence Activity, INSCOM units deployed to various military theaters, the Collection Operations Department of ONI's Collection Directorate, and the AIA's 696th Intelligence Group.

Other Army groups involved in HUMINT activities have included the 470th Military Intelligence Group (Fort Clayton, Panama), the 501st Military Intelligence Group (Seoul, Korea), the 500th Military Intelligence Group (Camp Zama, Japan), the 66th Military Intelligence Group (Munich), and the 513th Military Intelligence Brigade (headquartered at Ft. Gordon, Georgia, but operating in the Central Command theater).[10]

Specific responsibilities of U.S. Army HUMINT units included:

- debriefing of émigrés, defectors, detainees, and internees;
- tasking and/or debriefing of Army personnel whose placement or travel provided access to information of Army interest;
- acquisition and exploitation of foreign documents;
- acquisition of foreign materiel;
- strategic clandestine human source collection;
- liaison with foreign human intelligence agencies;
- participation in joint HUMINT activities with allied forces;
- participation in joint collection activities with other U.S. government intelligence agencies;
- debriefing of Army personnel who evaded capture, escaped, or were released from enemy control.[11]

The 513th Military Intelligence Brigade reported on Saudi control of the CSS-2 ballistic missile system and the Pakistani use of Chinese nuclear weapons facilities. In the latter report, the 513th noted that Pakistani generals were present to observe Chinese nuclear tests. The 500th Military Intelligence Group at Camp Zama, Japan, reported on Chinese arms exports to Iran. The Army Operational Group (later the INSCOM Foreign Intelligence Activity) reported, in 1986, on Chinese-Iraqi discussions for construction of a nuclear power plant in Iraq. In 1987 the same unit reported on Iranian Navy modifications to Silkworm missiles.[12]

As was noted in Chapter 4, ONI's Collection Operations Department is responsible for a variety of intelligence collection activities, including identifying Soviet ships carrying nuclear weapons. It has also conducted overt human intelligence operations, including interviewing businesspeople and travelers. During the Persian Gulf War, its predecessor, Task Force 168, interviewed individuals who worked on Saddam Hussein's communications bunker.[13]

In the 1980s, the 696th Intelligence Group (then known as the Air Force Special Activities Center) produced intelligence reports on the delivery of Super Etendard aircraft to Iraq; the Royal Saudi Air Force Peace Shield, Peace Sentinel, and Hush House programs; and the Royal Saudi C^3 system.[14]

AGENTS

Agents are foreign nationals recruited by U.S. intelligence officers to collect information either in their home country or in a third nation. Obviously, the identities of present U.S. agents are not known publicly. However, revelations of recent years indicate the types of recruits, many of whom were operating until quite recently, and the types of information acquired in this manner.

During the Cold War, the primary target was, of course, the Soviet Union. Despite the closed nature of Soviet society and the size of the KGB's counterintelligence operation, the United States had some notable successes in recruiting Soviet citizens to provide valuable information. The most significant success remains GRU Colonel Oleg Penkovskiy. In 1961 and 1962, Penkovskiy passed great quantities of material to the CIA and the British Secret Intelligence Service, including information on Soviet strategic capabilities and nuclear targeting policy. Additionally, he provided a copy of the official Soviet MRBM (Medium-Range Ballistic Missile) manual—which was of crucial importance at the time of the Cuban Missile Crisis.[15]

GRU Colonel Anatoli Nikolaevich Filatov and Alexsandr Dmitrevich Ogorodnik were recruited in the 1970s. During the mid-1970s, Filatov, then based in Algiers, approached the CIA with a proposal to pass information to the United States. Over the next fourteen months, Filatov provided the United States with a variety of Soviet intelligence and military secrets, including details of Soviet links with national liberation movements. After being reassigned to GRU headquarters in Moscow, Filatov continued to provide the CIA with information. This arrangement continued for about a year—at which time he was detected filing a dead drop, which the KGB had probably located from routine surveillance on known CIA agents.[16]

Filatov's was only one of two penetrations that shook the Soviet establishment in the 1970s. The second also began abroad—this time in Bogota, Colombia, where Ogorodnik was serving as a Secretary in the Soviet Embassy. According to one account, Ogorodnik was an official "who changed from an idealistic Communist to a passionate anti-Communist"; another account described him as the victim of a sexual blackmail operation.[17]

Whatever his motivation, Ogorodnik became a CIA agent in 1974 and was assigned the codename TRIGON. By the time his tour ended in 1975, he had been thoroughly trained in espionage tradecraft. Upon his return to Moscow he managed to get a position in the Foreign Ministry's Global Affairs Department, "one of the few MFA [Ministry of Foreign Affairs] sections the KGB trusts with sensitive intelligence" and "the repository of other exceedingly secret and revealing data."[18]

The department would receive the year-end comprehensive report of each Soviet ambassador—analyzing the political situation, likely developments, and Soviet standing in the country where he was stationed. The KGB residency was required to assist by contributing information and judgments based on the reports of its agents. In cases where the chief resident and ambassador were on good terms, the chief resident often would make available virtually all the information obtained from his agent network. Examination of such reports could reveal Soviet views of the world and Soviet strengths and weaknesses in specific countries, allow inferences about Soviet intentions, and in some cases permit an estimation of the nature and extent of KGB penetrations.[19]

Exactly how long TRIGON escaped Soviet detection has been the subject of dispute. According to John Barron's account, over the twenty months following his transfer back to Moscow Ogorodnik provided the CIA with microfilm of hundreds of secret Soviet documents, including ambassadorial reports. Soviet defector Arkady Shevchenko's account states that the KGB had begun to suspect the loyalty of a Secretary in a Soviet embassy in Latin America and thus arranged what appeared to be a routine transfer back to Moscow. Whatever the case, it is clear that before fall 1977 Ogorodnik had been detected by the KGB, apparently as a result of a tip from a Czech agent in the CIA. Ogorodnik apparently committed suicide shortly after his arrest by swallowing a cyanide pill.[20]

Another U.S. recruit—a Colonel attached to the General Staff—provided information in the mid-1970s on the Soviet Five-Year Defense Plan. The Colonel reported that the Soviets were planning to build five SS-20 (PIONEER) IRBMs for each SS-20 launcher—a piece of information that was relied upon in U.S. intelligence estimates for many subsequent years.[21]

Another, and more recent, penetration of the Soviet national security establishment involved a civilian employee of the Moscow Aviation Institute. *Pravda* reported on September 22, 1985: "The USSR State Security Committee has uncovered and arrested an agent of the U.S. secret service—A. G. Tolkachev, a staff member of one of Moscow's research institutes. The spy was caught in the act during an attempt to pass on secret defense materials to Paul M. Stombaugh, an officer of the U.S. CIA, who acted under the cover of the second secretary of the U.S. Embassy in Moscow."[22]

An electronics expert at the Moscow Aviation Institute, Tolkachev was, according to a U.S. official, "one of our most lucrative agents"; he "saved us billions of dollars in development costs" by telling the United States about the nature of Soviet military aviation efforts. The information made it significantly easier for the United States to develop systems to counter Soviet advances.[23]

Over a period of years, Tolkachev passed on information concerning Soviet research efforts in electronic guidance and countermeasures, advanced radar, and "stealth," or radar-avoidance, technologies. In addition, Tolkachev may have been the key to the U.S. discovery of a large phased-array radar being built at Krasnoyarsk in violation of the ABM Treaty. U.S. satellite photography of the area was obtained, according to one expert, only after "we were told where to look."[24]

Tolkachev was arrested in June 1985 (and subsequently executed), but announcement of his arrest was withheld until after CIA officer Edward Lee Howard, who apparently told the KGB of Tolkachev's role as a spy, had been exposed and had fled the United States. Howard had been trained to become Tolkachev's case officer but had been discharged by the agency when a routine polygraph indicated drug use and petty theft.[25]

Tolkachev was only one of about a dozen Soviet officials providing information to the United States in the mid-1980s before Howard and CIA officer Aldrich Ames betrayed them to the KGB. Agents who were compromised by Ames before his arrest in 1994 included General Dimitri Polyakov of the GRU (whose codename was GTACCORD), a Soviet intelligence officer stationed in Moscow (GTCOWL), an East European security officer (GTMOTORBOAT), a lieutenant colonel in the GRU (GTMILLION), a KGB officer (GTFITNESS), as well as others who were codenamed GTBLIZZARD, GTGENTILE, GTPROLOGUE, GTPYRRHIC, and GTWEIGH. Polyakov, GTFITNESS, and GTMILLION were all executed.[26]

HUMINT activities in the Soviet Union and Eastern Europe were a particular priority during William Casey's tenure as DCI. By the time he had held the position for three years, the CIA had more than twenty-five regularly reporting sources within the Soviet Union and Eastern Europe, nearly all of whom had been developed since 1981.[27]

Among the sources in Eastern Europe was Colonel Wladyslaw Kuklinski, a longtime CIA asset in Poland. Between 1971 and 1981, Kuklinski provided a massive amount of Soviet documents and information to the CIA—including Warsaw Pact strategic five-year plans, critical documents on the T-72 battle tank and more than 200 other Soviet weapons systems, contingency plans for war in Europe, and details about Project ALBATROSS, the construction of three concealed command and control bunkers in Eastern Europe that would serve as Soviet C^2 headquarters in wartime. In addition, he provided details about hundreds of advanced Soviet weapons systems, electronic warfare and cryptography, and wartime intelligence plans.[28]

Kuklinski was a senior staff officer involved in planning the martial law crackdown conducted by General Wojciech Jaruzelski. By the time Jaruzelski sent his tanks and troops into the streets, the CIA had a complete copy of his operations plan for a full month. Kuklinski was not, however, able to provide the date of the crackdown.[29]

In fall 1980, when labor unrest in Poland first aroused fear of a Soviet invasion, Kuklinski reported that the Polish Army had no intention of initiating or joining an operation that might end in violence and bloodshed. According to one account, a U.S. official observed, "It was precisely because of this guy that we knew the Poles weren't going to act in December." Without Polish help, the Soviets would have needed forty divisions to invade. Having only twenty-seven divisions ready for action, the Soviets could not seriously consider invasion as an option. Another account states that in December 1980 Kuklinski warned that fifteen Soviet divisions, along with East German and Czech troops, were planning to invade Poland. According to that account, based on Kuklinski's information President Carter warned Brezhnev not to invade.[30]

Subsequently, in late March and early April 1981 Kuklinski reported that the KGB had instigated disturbances in the Polish industrial city of Bydgoszcz. He had reported further that Jaruzelski had refused the KGB's gambit and declined to ask for Soviet aid, deciding instead to wait for the guidance of the Polish Communist Party Congress in July. The Colonel also reported Jaruzelski's hardening attitude and growing confidence among both the Polish and Soviet military establishments that Polish security forces could handle the situation on their own.[31]

U.S. HUMINT operations in East Germany met with far less success than those in Poland. It was discovered after the fall of East Germany that most East Germans recruited by the CIA since the early 1950s had been double agents operating under the direction of the East German Ministry for State Security (MfS). In addition to allowing the identification of CIA officers, the operation also passed misleading intelligence to the CIA.[32]

HUMINT operations in Latin America have involved Cuba, El Salvador, Nicaragua, and Argentina. The operations in Cuba highlighted the potential dangers of HUMINT operations. During 1987, Cuban television showed films of apparent CIA officers operating in Cuba picking up and leaving material at dead drops. The programs claimed that since September 1977, thirty-eight of sixty-nine diplomats permanently accredited to the U.S. diplomatic mission in Havana had been CIA officers. Apparently a significant number of Cubans had been operating as double agents, feeding information to CIA officers under the supervision of Cuban security officers. The Cubans decided to reveal the operation as a result of the defection of a senior intelligence officer.[33]

In Central America the head of El Salvador's Treasury Police, Nicolas Carranza, was an informant of the CIA in the late 1970s, having received more than $90,000 a year from the CIA for at least six years. In Nicaragua, General Reynaldo Perez Vega, a second-ranking officer in the National Guard under Somoza, was a CIA asset.[34]

Another high Central American official who was on the CIA payroll is Manuel Antonio Noriega, formerly of Panama. Noriega is alleged to have worked for the CIA while at military college in Peru, supplying information on suspected leftists among his fellow cadets. When he became head of the intelligence (G-2) section of the National Guard, he worked for both the CIA and the DIA, being paid for particular deals. Subsequently, he received a regular stipend from the CIA in exchange for providing information on Cuban activities and Panamanian politics.[35]

Allegations of CIA clandestine collection activities in Nicaragua came with the arrest, in March 1986, of three Nicaraguans accused of working to infiltrate the Interior Ministry. One of the three was Jose Edwards Trejas Silva, a sublieutenant in the Interior Ministry who was allegedly recruited by the CIA while he was outside of Nicaragua in November 1983. He had been tasked to provide information on connections between the Sandinistas and leftist guerrillas in Colombia and El Salvador.[36]

Among those Haitians serving as paid agents of the CIA in the 1990s was Emmanuel (Toto) Constant. Constant is head of the Front for the Advancement and Progress of Haiti, better known by the acronym derived from the initials of its name in French—FRAPH. Despite its title, FRAPH is a paramilitary "gang of thugs unusually vicious even by Haitian standards."[37]

Although refusing to specifically confirm reports that Constant had been paid by the CIA, Undersecretary of Defense for Policy Walter Slocombe observed that the United States often buys information from shadowy figures. Slocombe told the House Armed Services Committee, "We don't do it because they are nice people, but because they are good intelligence sources."[38]

Evidence of U.S. operations in the Middle East and Africa have emerged with respect to Israel, Egypt, the PLO, Iraq, Ethiopia, Ghana, and Iran.

An Israeli Army officer, Major Yosef Amit, apparently began providing the CIA with information in 1982. In 1987 he was secretly sentenced to twelve years' imprisonment for espionage. The Egyptian government has apparently been penetrated extensively by the CIA. The CIA also has had a variety of sources in the PLO that have provided operational details of PLO attacks in Israel.[39]

In Ethiopia the CIA has had a senior official on its payroll; in Ghana, several individuals were convicted of spying for the CIA in 1985. Felix Peasah, a security officer at the U.S. Embassy in Accra, and Theodore Atiedu, a police inspector with Ghana's Bureau of National Investigation, pleaded guilty. Also convicted were

Stephen Balfour Ofusu, a former Chief Superintendent of Police, who gave government secrets to the CIA and arranged taps on the telephones of diplomatic missions and high-level government officials, and Robert Yaw Appiah, a technician with the Post and Telecommunications Corporation, who gave a CIA officer copies of keys to utility hole covers.[40]

In April 1989, a number of Iranian military officers were arrested and charged with spying for the United States. Before the network, which was coordinated from Frankfurt, was detected, it apparently produced valuable military intelligence about Iranian operations in the Persian Gulf at a time when U.S. naval forces were confronting Iranian forces.[41]

The CIA's targets in Asia have included India, China, and the Philippines. In India six individuals were arrested for spying for the United States in 1977. The kingpin of the operation was P. E. Mehta, who apparently confessed to selling information to U.S. Embassy officials between 1962 and 1977. Also arrested were K. K. Sareen, a former Director at the Planning Commission who had also worked for the Soviet Union; E. L. Choudhuri of the State Trading Corporation; R. P. Varshney of the Planning Commission; Mahabir Prasid, personal secretary to Y. B. Chaven when he was External Affairs Minister; and C. S. Balakrishanan, a clerk in the office of the Minister for Defense Production. Mehta received secret reports of the external affairs, chemicals, and petroleum ministries as well as information about India's main aircraft design and production center, plus drawings of Soviet-made guns, missiles, and radar.[42]

At least one CIA penetration of the Chinese establishment has involved someone with access to information concerning Chinese nuclear relations with Pakistan. That source reported on:

- China's nuclear exports to Argentina and South Africa;
- Chinese technicians helping at a suspected Pakistani bomb development site;
- Chinese scientific delegations who were spending a substantial amount of time at a centrifuge plant in Kahuta where Pakistani scientists were attempting to produce enriched uranium, which can be used to trigger a nuclear detonation;
- Pakistani scientists from a secret facility at Wah showing a nuclear weapon design to some Chinese physicists in late 1982 or early 1983, seeking Chinese evaluation of whether the design would yield a nuclear blast; and
- the triggering mechanism for the Pakistani bomb design, which appeared to be very similar to one used by China in its fourth nuclear test.[43]

Information about the Taiwanese nuclear program was also provided by an informant. The informant, Colonel Chang Hsien-Yi, worked in a Taiwanese research institute. The information he provided indicated that the Taiwanese were in the process of building a secret installation that could be used to obtain plutonium. Construction of the installation would have violated Taiwanese commitments to the United States not to undertake nuclear weapons research. U.S. pressure forced the Taiwanese to stop work on the secret installation, as well as to shut down its largest civilian reactor, which the United States felt had military potential.[44]

CIA assets in the Philippines have provided important information at crucial times. On September 17, 1972, a CIA asset in the Philippines informed the CIA station that Ferdinand Marcos was planning to proclaim martial law. Another asset provided a list of the individuals whom Marcos planned to arrest and imprison. In 1982, a CIA officer was able to locate a Philippine immigration official who was willing to provide the names of two doctors who visited the Philippines to treat Marcos, giving the agency a clue to the nature of Marcos's health problems.[45]

At any given time the United States may have developed a wide array of agents in a particular society. Table 10-1 lists some of the agents the United States had in Iran before the fall of the Shah.

DEFECTORS AND ÉMIGRÉS

Defectors and émigrés also sometimes serve as human intelligence sources. The United States attaches major importance to the intelligence information that can be obtained via defectors. Thus, it has a coordinated Defector Program managed by the CIA-led Interagency Defector Committee (IDC).[46]

In the past, the prime defectors were Soviet bloc officials such as scientists, diplomats, or intelligence officers. In the aftermath of the declaration of martial law in Poland, several Polish ambassadors defected to the West, bringing with them their knowledge of personalities, procedures, policies, and relations with the Soviet Union.

A defector may be able to settle disputes concerning matters of data acquired via technical collections systems. Thus, one defector was asked to

> look at an elaborate analysis of something our cameras detected by chance when there was an abnormal opening in clouds that normally covered a particular region. Learned men had spent vast amounts of time trying to figure out what it was and concluded that it was something quite sinister, an Air Force officer said. "Viktor took one look at it and convincingly explained why what we thought was so ominous was in fact comically innocuous."[47]

During the 1980s, CIA informants included defectors from Cuba and Nicaragua, such as Rafael Del Pino Diaz and Roger Miranda Bengoechea. Diaz apparently had held important aviation posts in the 1960s, including head of Cubana Airlines and the Cuban Aviation Agency. He claimed to be the Cuban Air Forces Deputy Chief of Staff; the Cuban government, however, claimed he had been relegated to organizing a museum about the history of the Cuban Air Force.[48]

Table 10-1. CIA Iranian Assets Circa 1979.

Codename	Comments
SD/BEEP-1	———
SD/BETTLE	———
SD/BLADE	———
SD/CARAWAY	———
SD/DAZE	———
SD/ENORMOUS-1	———
SD/FACE-1	Iranian informant in London
SD/FICKLE	Member of Democratic Party of Kurdistan of Iran. Contacted the CIA in 1976 and passed on information to the CIA, for which was paid monthly fee. In May-June 1979 was meeting with Soviets as CIA double agent.
SD/FORWARD-1	———
SD/FORGIVE-1	———
SD/JANUS-13	SAVAK employee
SD/JANUS-20	SAVAK employee
SD/JANUS-38	SAVAK employee
SD/JULEP-1	Journalist
SD/MARKET	———
SD/PECAN	———
SD/PEPPER-11	Iranian exile living in Washington, former Chief of Iranian Embassy Secretariat in Washington.
SD/PLOD	———
SD/PRAWN	———
SD/PRETEXT	———
SD/PROB	———
SD/PUTTY	———
SD/RAP	Iranian exile living in New Jersey, wanted to lead exile movement.
SD/RIGHT	———
SD/ROOF-1	Close friend and relative of Lt. General Siavouch Behzradi
SD/ROTTER-4	———
SD/SLIPPERY	Lebanese businessman in Paris
SD/STAY	Liaison with Khomeini during Bakhtiar premiership.
SD/THROB-1	Worked for SAVAK as Kurdish expert before the revolution.
SD/TRAMP-1	Provided complete list of PLO delegation to Iran, October 1979.
SD/ULTIMATE	———
SD/UPBEAT-1	Iranian military attaché in Paris, broke with government around September 1979.
SD/URN-1	———
SD/VALID	———

Source: Volumes published by Students Following the Line of the Iman.

Roger Miranda Bengoechea, a senior military officer, was chief contact for all military advisers in Nicaragua—which probably gave him knowledge concerning the Cuban presence in that country. He had toured all Sandinista military bases the week prior to his defection. Miranda, who made frequent trips to Mexico for medical reasons, may have been passing information to the CIA before his defection. According to the Nicaraguan Defense Minister, Miranda had made copies of Air Force plans as well as documents concerning artillery brigades and other Managua installations.[49]

Today, the most desirable defectors would be those from Iraq, Iran, and North Korea. In the aftermath of the 1991 Persian Gulf War, Iraqi defectors provided valuable information about the Iraqi nuclear weapons program. Emigrés—those legally allowed to leave a country—may also provide useful information, particularly if they are coming from a relatively closed society.

Neither defectors nor émigrés need be high-level officials to provide valuable strategic or tactical information. A workman at a military base may be able to provide information concerning the functions of structures identified by satellite photography—and whether a structure is a command and control bunker or a repair facility will have important implications for targeting. Thus,

> although a comparatively low-level Soviet defector ... would seem to have a small potential for providing useful intelligence, the CIA ... had so little success in penetrating the Soviet military that the [defector] underwent months of questioning. Through him, agency analysts were able to learn much about how Soviet armor units, and the ground forces in general, are organized, their training and tactical procedures, and the mechanics of their participation in the build-up that preceded the invasion of Czechoslovakia.[50]

Emigrés who were ordinary citizens in their country of origin can provide information concerning local events of international interest. Initial reports of the 1979 Soviet anthrax incident circulated internally among dissidents and were carried abroad by émigrés.[51]

TRAVELERS

Travelers who are not necessarily intelligence officers may often be able to provide useful intelligence information. At one time, before the United States developed satellites to penetrate the Soviet interior, travelers played a more significant role in intelligence activities than they do today.[52]

Among present traveler collection programs is CREEK GRAB, a USAFE program. USAFE Regulation 200-6 states that:

> During peacetime, USAFE military and DAF [Department of the Air Force] civilian personnel, other US employees, and contractors may occasionally have opportunities to acquire information of intelligence value either while performing their normal duties or by pure chance. ... USAFE intelligence personnel must be able to respond ef-

fectively to unexpected opportunities for foreign intelligence collection in peacetime as well as wartime.[53]

Among those considered potential intelligence contributors are not just travelers but also amateur radio operators, persons in contact with foreign friends and relatives, and persons living adjacent to sites where foreign military aircraft have landed or crashed. Regulation 200-6 also specifies procedures for photographing aircraft, specifying that photographs should be obtained of the following items:

a. Cockpit interior
b. Weapons system controls, panel instruments
c. Seat(s)
d. Weaponry
e. Electronics gear (avionics, radar, black boxes, etc.)
f. Propulsion system (air intake, variable geometry, fuel parts and fuel tankage)
g. Documents, maintenance records.[54]

The CIA's Domestic Resources Division, through its National Collection Branch (NCB), seeks to interview businesspeople, tourists, and professionals, either because of specific contacts they may have had during their foreign travels or because of the sites of their travel—for example, Cuba or North Korea. The information sought may include the health and attitudes of a national leader or the military activities in a particular region. In some instances, the NCB, upon hearing that a particular person plans to visit a particular location, will get in touch in advance and ask the traveler to seek out information on certain targets. However, the NCB has been reluctant to assign specific missions. Since the travelers are not professional agents, they may wind up being arrested as a result of taking their espionage roles too seriously.[55]

HUMINT AND THE PERSIAN GULF WAR

During the Persian Gulf War of 1991, U.S. Army HUMINT units, particularly the 66th and 513th Military Intelligence Brigades, collected valuable overt HUMINT, according to an Army intelligence history. That HUMINT may have come from diplomats, businesspeople or other travelers, émigrés, or defectors. According to the history, the overt HUMINT was employed, in real time, "to nominate, target, and destroy key Iraqi command, control, communications, and other military targets."[56]

HUMINT was used, in combination with imagery, both to destroy targets and to avoid others. The information that identified mosques and hospitals allowed U.S. war planners to take account of political and religious sensitivities and avoid targeting such facilities.[57]

One source provided information that, according to the history, "significantly contributed to the impact of the air campaign and thereby shortened the ground campaign, which undoubtedly saved many American and coalition lives."[58]

NOTES

1. Amrom Katz, "Technical Collection Requirements for the 1980s," in Roy Godson, ed., *Intelligence Requirements for the 1980s: Clandestine Collection* (New Brunswick, N.J.: Transaction, 1982), pp. 101–17 at pp. 106–7.

2. John I. Millis, "Our Spying Success Is No Secret," *Wall Street Journal*, October 12, 1994, p. A15.

3. Philip Agee and Louis Wolf, eds., *Dirty Work: The CIA in Western Europe* (Secaucus, N.J.: Lyle Stuart, 1978), pp. 131–32.

4. Ibid., pp. 721–22, 726; Private information.

5. Defense Intelligence Agency, *Capabilities Handbook, Annex A, to the Department of Defense Plan for Intelligence Support to Operational Commanders (U)* (Washington, D.C.: DIA, 1983), p. 352.

6. "Poland Expelling Army Attaché," *New York Times*, February 26, 1985, p. A3; Bradley Graham, "Poland Expelling U.S. Attaché as Spy," *Washington Post*, February 26, 1985, pp. A1, A10; "A Colonel with a Camera," *Newsweek*, March 11, 1985, p. 47; "Poland Claims U.S. Envoy Snared While Spying," *Washington Times*, April 23, 1987, p. 8A; Michael T. Kaufman, "Warsaw Accuses U.S. Aide of Spying," *New York Times*, April 23, 1987, p. A9.

7. Nancy Nusser, "U.S. Officials Cited as Spies by Managua," *Washington Post*, May 10, 1986, p. A14.

8. Richard Mackenzie, "A Gulf War Intrigue: The Tale of the Colonel's Camera," *Washington Times*, April 20, 1987, p. 9A.

9. Nora Boustany and Patrick E. Tyler, "Syria Suspects U.S. Attachés Meant to Aid Israel," *Washington Post*, March 13, 1989, p. A28.

10. Defense Intelligence Agency, *Capabilities Handbook, Annex A, to the Department of Defense Plan for Intelligence Support to Operational Commanders*, p. 344.

11. Ibid.

12. IIR 2-340-0229-92, from CDR 513th MIBDE, to JCS, Subject: Saudi Control of CSS-2 Ballistic Missile System; IIR 2-72-0085-91, from CDR 513th MIBDE, to JCS, Subject: Pakistani Use of Chinese Nuclear Weapons Facilities, June 19, 1991; U.S. Army Operational Group, "Nuclear Power Plant Development Plans," May 12, 1986; IIR 2-721-0179-87, "CH Arms Exports to IR," July 7, 1987; IIR 2-764-0037-88, "IR Navy Modifications to HY-2 Silkworm Missile," December 21, 1987; Private information.

13. Private information.

14. IIR 1-517-83, "French Postpone Delivery of Super Etendard Aircraft to Iraq [Excised]," September 9, 1983; IIR 1-517-0329-83, "French Delivery of Super Etendard Aircraft to Iraq [Excised]," November 23, 1983; IIR 1-517-0127-87, "Royal Saudi Air Force Peace Shield Program [Excised]," February 6, 1987; IIR 1-517-0220-87, "Royal Saudi Peace Shield, Peace Sentinel, and Hush House Program [Excised]," April 4, 1987; IIR 1-517-0062-87, "Royal Saudi Air Force C^3 System [Excised]," December 21, 1987.

15. See Jerrold L. Schecter and Peter S. Deriabin, *The Spy Who Saved the World: How a Soviet Colonel Changed the Course of the Cold War* (New York: Scribner's, 1992).

16. John Barron, *The KGB Today: The Hidden Hand* (New York: Reader's Digest Press, 1983), p. 428.

17. Ibid.; Ernest Volkman, *Warriors of the Night: Spies, Soldiers and American Intelligence* (New York: Morrow, 1985), p. 224.

18. Barron, *The KGB Today*, p. 428.

19. Ibid., pp. 428–29.

20. Barron, *The KGB Today*, p. 429; Arkady Shevchenko, *Breaking with Moscow* (New York: Knopf, 1985), p. 314; Volkman, *Warriors of the Night*, pp. 224–25; David Martin, "A CIA Spy in the Kremlin," *Newsweek*, July 21, 1980, pp. 69–70; Ronald Kessler, "Moscow's Mole in the CIA," *Washington Post*, April 17, 1988, pp. C1, C4.

21. Peter Samuel, "1977 Spy Data on SS-20's Cast Shadow Over INF Talks," *New York City Tribune*, November 17, 1987, p. 1; Walter Pincus, "U.S. May Have Miscounted Some Soviet Missiles," *Washington Post*, December 16, 1987, p. A6.

22. Foreign Broadcast Information Service, "Pravda: KGB Arrests CIA-Controlled Moscow Spy," *Daily Report: Soviet Union*, September 24, 1985, p. A1.

23. William Kucewicz, "KGB Defector Confirms Intelligence Fiasco," *Wall Street Journal*, October 17, 1985, p. 28.

24. Ibid.; Private information.

25. Patrick E. Tyler, "Soviet Seized as U.S. Spy Exposed by Howard," *Washington Post*, October 18, 1985, p. A10; Stephen Engelberg, "U.S. Indicates Ex-CIA Officer Helped Soviet Capture a Russian," *New York Times*, October 18, 1985, p. A18.

26. Bill Miller and Walter Pincus, "Ames Pleads Guilty to Spying, Gets Life Term," *Washington Post*, April 29, 1994, pp. A1, A18; "Statement of Facts, *United States of America v Aldrich Hazen Ames*," Criminal Case No. 94-64-A, United States Court for the Eastern District of Virginia, April 28, 1994, p. 10.

27. Bob Woodward, *Veil: The Secret Wars of the CIA, 1981–1987* (New York: Simon & Schuster, 1987), p. 306.

28. Benjamin Weiser, "A Question of Loyalty," *Washington Post Magazine*, December 13, 1992, pp. 9ff.; Benjamin Weiser, "Polish Officer Was U.S.'s Window on Soviet War Plans," *Washington Post*, September 29, 1992, pp. A1, A38.

29. Bob Woodward and Michael Dobbs, "CIA Had Secret Agent on Polish General Staff," *Washington Post*, June 4, 1986, pp. A1, A31; "A Polish Agent in Place," *Newsweek*, December 20, 1982, p. 49.

30. "A Polish Agent in Place"; Weiser, "Polish Officer Was U.S.'s Window on Soviet War Plans."

31. Ibid.

32. Bill Gertz, "Stasi Files Reveal CIA Two-Timers," *Washington Times*, September 12, 1991, pp. A1, A11.

33. "Cuban TV Purports to Show U.S. Spies," *Washington Times*, July 8, 1987, p. A8; Lewis H. Diuguid, "Spy Charges Strain U.S.-Cuban Ties," *Washington Post*, July 25, 1987, p. A17; Michael Wines and Ronald J. Ostrow, "U.S. Duped by Cuban Agents, Defector Says," *Los Angeles Times*, August 12, 1987, pp. 1, 14.

34. Philip Taubman, "Top Salvador Police Official Said to Be CIA Informant," *New York Times*, March 22, 1984, pp. A1, A4; Stephen Kinzer, "Sandinistas Tap Heroine as Envoy, But Some in U.S. Oppose Her," *New York Times*, March 22, 1984, pp. A1, A4.

35. "Drugs, Money, and Death," *Newsweek*, February 15, 1988, pp. 32–38.

36. Stephen Kinzer, "Nicaragua Says It Has Cracked CIA Spy Ring," *New York Times*, March 15, 1986, p. 3.

37. George J. Church, "Lying Down with Dogs," *Time*, October 17, 1994, pp. 26–29.

38. Stephen Engelberg, "A Haitian Leader of Paramilitaries Was Paid by C.I.A.," *New York Times*, October 8, 1994, pp. 1, 4.

39. Wolf Blitzer, "U.S. Changed Rules of the Spy Game," *Jerusalem Post International Edition,* March 28, 1987, pp. 1, 2; Woodward, *Veil,* pp. 87, 161; David Hoffman, "Israel Army Major Was a Spy," *Washington Post,* June 3, 1993, p. A18.

40. Philip Smith, "Events Spark Speculation That Spy Swap Is Imminent," *Washington Post,* November 21, 1985, p. A16; "2 More Convicted in Ghana of Spying for CIA," *Washington Post,* November 23, 1985, p. A8; Woodward, *Veil,* p. 167.

41. Youssef M. Ibrahim, "Teheran Is Said to Arrest Officers on Charges of Spying for U.S.," *New York Times,* April 22, 1989, p. 5; Stephen Engelberg and Bernard E. Trainor, "Iran Broke C.I.A. Spy Ring, U.S. Says," *New York Times,* August 8, 1989, p. A6.

42. Sanjoy Hazarika, "In Secret Trial, India Sentences 6 for Spying for U.S.," *New York Times,* October 30, 1986, p. A5.

43. Jack Anderson and Dale Van Atta, "Nuclear Exports to China?" *Washington Post,* November 3, 1985, p. C7; Patrick E. Tyler and Joanne Omang, "China-Iran Nuclear Link Is Reported," *Washington Post,* October 23, 1985, pp. A1, A19; Joanne Omang, "Nuclear Pact with China Wins Senate Approval," *Washington Post,* November 22, 1985, p. A3; Patrick E. Tyler, "A Few Spoken Words Sealed China Atom Pact," *Washington Post,* January 12, 1986, pp. A1, A20–A21.

44. Stephen Engelberg and Michael R. Gordon, "Taipei Halts Work on Secret Plant to Make Nuclear Bomb Ingredient," *New York Times,* March 23, 1988, pp. A1, A15.

45. Raymond Bonner, *Waltzing with a Dictator* (New York: Times Books, 1987), pp. 3, 5, 340.

46. E. Howard Hunt, *Undercover: Memoirs of an American Secret Agent* (New York: Berkley, 1974), p. 80.

47. John Barron, *MIG Pilot* (New York: Avon, 1981), p. 186.

48. John M. Goshko and Julia Preston, "Defector Arrives for Debriefing; Cuba Plays Down Military Role," *Washington Post,* May 30, 1987, p. A3.

49. Glenn Garvin and John McCaslin, "Key Nicaraguan Aide Dubs Military Defector U.S. Spy," *Washington Times,* November 4, 1987, p. A10.

50. Victor Marchetti and John Marks, *The CIA and the Cult of Intelligence* (New York: Dell, 1980), p. 185.

51. Roy Godson, "Collection Against the Soviet Union and Denied Areas," in Roy Godson, ed., *Intelligence Requirements for the 1980s: Clandestine Collection,* p. 28.

52. See Jeffrey T. Richelson, *American Espionage and the Soviet Target* (New York: William Morrow, 1987), pp. 52–55.

53. USAFE Regulation 200-6, "CREEK GRAB," May 31, 1986, p. 2.

54. Ibid., p. 15.

55. Marchetti and Marks, *The CIA and the Cult of Intelligence,* pp. 236–37.

56. Office of the Deputy Chief of Staff for Intelligence, *Annual Historical Review, 1 October 1990 to 30 September 1991* (Washington, D.C.: ODCSI, 1993), pp. 4-10 to 4-11.

57. Ibid., p. 4-11.

58. Ibid., p. 4-12.

11
OPEN SOURCES, TECHNICAL SURVEILLANCE AND EMPLACED SENSORS, AND MATERIEL EXPLOITATION

Significant intelligence concerning the political, military, and economic affairs of other nations can be obtained through means other than remote technical and human source collection. Included in this category are open sources, technical surveillance and emplaced sensors, and materiel exploitation.

Open source collection includes the acquisition of any verbal, written, or electronically transmitted material that can be legally acquired. Thus, it includes the acquisition of newspapers, magazines, and unclassified journals as well as the monitoring of public radio and television.

A large portion of the intelligence gathered by the CIA and other intelligence units is acquired by means of electronic surveillance or emplaced sensors. The electronic surveillance usually takes the form of bugging or phone tapping. Although strictly a "technical collection" activity, bugging and phone tapping are so different from satellite, aircraft, or ground station interception as to merit separate consideration. Further, such operations are often conducted as an adjunct to CIA and military HUMINT activities.

Another significant aspect of intelligence collection revolves around "materiel exploitation"—the acquisition and analysis of foreign weapons, communications, and other systems. Such acquisition and analysis yield information that cannot be acquired by overhead photography, such as information on firearms and more detailed information on systems such as tanks, which can then be used to design countermeasures. Although the weapons designed for the Soviet armed forces are now far less threatening in the hands of the Russian armed forces, the Soviet export of such weapons to Iraq, Libya, and a variety of other nations makes intelligence on them of continuing relevance.

OPEN SOURCES

Open source collection involves three separate activities: collection of legally available documents, open observation of foreign political, military, and eco-

261

nomic activity; and the monitoring and recording of public radio and television broadcasts. In open societies, a variety of data concerning political, military, and economic affairs is available through newspapers, magazines, trade journals, academic journals, and government publications. These published sources may yield intelligence concerning the internal disputes plaguing a European political party, French nuclear strategy, Japanese willingness to restrict exports, or advances in computer or laser technologies.

The statement of Roscoe Hillenkoeter, the Director of Central Intelligence in 1948, that "80 percent of intelligence is derived from such prosaic sources as foreign books, magazines, technical and scientific surveys, photographs, commercial analysis, newspapers and radio broadcasts, and general information from people with a knowledge of affairs abroad" remains approximately true today.[1]

Of course, in a closed society much less information will be available. Most particularly, direct reporting on internal political and military affairs will be absent. Further, all reporting will be conducted under the direction of government propaganda guidelines. Even in a closed society, however, there is a significant amount of intelligence that can be gleaned from legally obtainable documents—including newspapers, magazines, collected speeches, academic journals, and even official documents on military affairs.

For many years the prime focus of U.S. open source collection was the Soviet Union. From August 1947 through April 1951, all articles in Soviet scientific and technical journals were abstracted, and some were translated in full. As of 1952, there were 87 Soviet journals available. In 1954 there were 165 available. A joint CIA–Air Force program selected 58 journals of prime intelligence interest for cover-to-cover abstracting.[2]

By April of 1956 the number of available Soviet scientific and technical journals had virtually doubled again, to 328. Those journals contained information on Soviet research and development in, or related to, atomic energy, missiles, electronics, and atomic, biological, and chemical warfare. Upon close examination, it was determined that there were far more than 58 journals of prime interest.[3]

The large volume of these publications led to two approaches. The Air Force conducted a cover-to-cover abstracting program for more than 100 journals. For other consumers, the CIA began issuing the twice-monthly *Scientific Information Report,* which sought to cover the entire range of Soviet bloc scientific literature. In addition to journals there were about 3,000 books and monographs per year that were surveyed for scientific and technical intelligence, along with two Soviet newspapers that regularly covered the subject.[4]

Similarly, the U.S. intelligence community examined other aspects of Soviet open source literature for information of political and military intelligence value. In addition to general circulation organs such as *Pravda* and *Izvestia,* the CIA and other agencies would examine the eleven major Soviet military journals and approximately 500 books on military affairs published in the Soviet Union each year.[5]

The introduction of *glasnost* in the Soviet Union, and then the transformation of the Soviet Union into Russia, has dramatically increased the value of open source intelligence. Whereas political maneuvering was concealed within a small and secretive elite before Mikhail Gorbachev's rise to power, domestic politics in Russia are now conducted in public view, including the view of television cameras. Thus, even before the collapse of the Soviet Union, a senior governmental official observed, "It used to be that you'd go through reams of stuff, and just come up with dross. Now there's so much gold that they could work around the clock."[6]

The type of military intelligence that can now be obtained from Russian open sources is qualitatively different from that which could be acquired under the Soviet regime. Thus, an August 1993 broadcast from Moscow reported on the threat that a lack of funding posed to the MiG-29M program. That same month *Rossiyskaya Gazeta* reported on an air defense missile demonstration at Kapustin Yar.[7]

Chinese open sources can also be exploited to produce intelligence. The journal *Knowledge of Ships,* which is considered to generally provide low-quality and unreliable naval information, occasionally contains useful data. One article, "The Role of the Guided Missile Speedboat in Engagement," stated that "planners" were considering assigning an antiaircraft mission to one or two of the six boats in a typical OSA or KOMAR squadron.[8]

The Journal of Shipbuilding in China focuses on research topics in marine engineering in considerable detail and demonstrates that the Chinese are actively exploiting U.S., British, Soviet, Japanese, and German work in the field. Examination of this journal also reveals that the instruments being employed by China for test purposes are of German, Japanese, and Chinese manufacture and that the Chinese experiments generally pick up where the exploited source stopped—either advancing the testing process a step further or seeking empirical verification of a theory propounded by the source.[9]

According to one analyst: "From the technical intelligence perspective the publication can be valuable in providing new information about the marine engineering topics of interest to China, an appreciation of the foreign sources being exploited by the Chinese and the results of their experiments in the field." This information, when combined with other intelligence, "offers a reasonably accurate assessment of where China stands in this area of technology."[10]

Also of interest to intelligence analysts is a publication entitled *Contemporary Military Affairs,* in which the Pacific and Indian Ocean theaters of operation receive good coverage.[11]

Today, the volume of open source material around the world dwarfs what was available only twenty years ago. The number of worldwide periodicals has grown from 7,000 in 1972 to 116,000 in 1991. As of December 1992, there were 1,700 newspapers published in Russia and the other former Soviet states that did not exist in 1989. At that time, the CIA's Foreign Broadcast Information Service (FBIS) monitored more than 3,500 publications in 55 foreign languages.[12]

FBIS monitoring leads to a variety of publications, including five-times-a-week compilations for Eurasia, Africa, Latin America, Western Europe, Eastern Europe, the Middle East, the Near East, and Asia. The reports include fully translated texts of articles. Similarly, the CIA's Joint Publications Research Service (JPRS) produces weekday compilations concerning subjects such as "Science and Technology—Europe," and "Nuclear Proliferation." In addition, both the FBIS and the JPRS prepare special products for use by intelligence community analysts.[13]

The DIA and military service intelligence organizations acquire foreign S&T publications and materials, publications concerning foreign weapons systems, training and doctrine manuals, military organization and planning documents, and map and town plans. A database of foreign scientific and technical information references and abstracts contains about 10 million records, of which approximately 6 million are unclassified. Included in one of those databases, for example, are the transactions of the Third International Conference on Nuclear Technology Transfer. Papers presented at the conference included "Issues and Experiences in the Transfer of Nuclear Technology," "Advanced Reactor Concepts," and "The Nuclear Fuel Cycle."[14]

The massive volume of open source material that is available has also been affected by the information technology revolution, which has led to the creation of databases. As of late 1992, the CIA had identified 8,000 commercial databases worldwide.[15]

To coordinate open source collection, DCI Robert Gates established an Intelligence Community Open Source Coordinator. Within the Defense Department, a General Defense Intelligence Program (GDIP) Open Source Program Manager now chairs the GDIP Open Source Steering Group.[16]

The monitoring of radio and television broadcasts can also be valuable. Through the FBIS and its partner, the BBC Monitoring Service, the United States obtains a vast amount of information concerning political, military, and economic events throughout the world. In 1988 the Air Force Intelligence Service observed that:

> broadcasts can provide information on development of new weapons systems, deployment and modifications of existing systems, military operations, daily life in the armed forces of foreign countries. High level personalities can be identified—the West can better understand a country's foreign and internal policies by viewing the broadcasts and analyzing statements by leadership.[17]

According to Deputy DCI Admiral William O. Studeman, "Each week FBIS monitors 790 hours of television from over 50 countries in 29 languages. Foreign TV programs, such as news programs and documentaries—give analysts a multi-dimensional feel for a country or material that other open source media cannot provide. TV allows us to broaden our knowledge of more restrictive societies."[18]

During May 1989, U.S. monitoring of Chinese radio broadcasts provided important information on the support for the student protesters in Beijing. The reports indicated that 40,000 students, teachers, and writers in Chengdu marched in support of democracy in mid-May. Guangdong provincial radio reported a march of 30,000 students. Altogether, radio reports indicated that there had been demonstrations of more than 10,000 people in at least nine other provinces.[19]

During Operation Desert Shield, the CIA and other intelligence agencies found that the television appearances of Saddam Hussein and other Iraqi officials provided useful information. CIA doctors and psychologists examined interviews with Iraqi leaders to look for signs of stress and worry. DIA analysts studied TV reports, particularly those from Baghdad, that might show scenes with military vehicles in the background. DIA analysts would freeze the frames and try to compare a vehicle's unit designation with the lists of Iraqi equipment in DIA computers in order to determine whether anything new had been added to the force.[20]

U.S. intelligence analysts have also studied transcripts of radio broadcasts "by both sides [in the Yugoslav crisis] to gain insights into the intensity of the conflict."[21]

FBIS monitoring stations are located at: Abidjan, Ivory Coast; Amman, Jordan; Asuncion, Paraguay; Athens, Greece; Bangkok, Thailand; Chiva Chiva, Panama; Hong Kong; Key West, Florida; London; Nicosia, Cyprus; Okinawa; Seoul; Tel Aviv; Vienna; and Washington, D.C.[22] The station in Key West targets Cuban radio and television. Of particular interest is any information on Cuban military exercises.

TECHNICAL SURVEILLANCE AND EMPLACED SENSORS

The technical surveillance and emplaced sensor operations conducted by the CIA and other intelligence units constitute another important aspect of intelligence gathering. These methods supplement human intelligence activities and can provide detailed information not available by other means. Technical penetration of a presidential residence offers twenty-four-hour coverage and captures the exact conversations that occur. Such operations in foreign embassies can provide information on the plans, policies, and activities of diplomats and intelligence agents.

Two prominent forms of technical surveillance are "bugs" and telephone taps. A bug, or audio device, which will transmit all conversations in a room to a monitoring site, is planted by experts from the Office of Technical Services of the Directorate of Science and Technology. Planting such a device is a complex operation involving surveillance of the site, acquisition of building and floor plans, and determination of the color of the interior furnishings and the color and texture of the walls. Activity in the room as well as the movements of security patrols are noted. When the information is acquired and processed, it will be employed to determine the time of surreptitious entry and the materials needed to install the device in such a way as to minimize the probability of a discovery.[23]

During the early 1970s one target of CIA audio devices was Nguyen Van Thieu, President of South Vietnam. Presents given to Thieu by the CIA—television sets and furniture—came equipped with audio devices, allowing the agency to monitor his personal conversations. The CIA also attempted to install devices in the office and living quarters of the South Vietnamese observer at the Paris Peace Talks.[24]

Another Asian ally that has been subject to CIA and NSA technical penetration is South Korea. A substantial part of the evidence against Tongsun Park concerning his alleged attempt to bribe U.S. Congressmen came from tape recordings of incriminating conversations inside the South Korean presidential mansion.[25]

Audio devices and telephone taps have, at least in the past, produced much of the CIA's intelligence on Latin America. A report on clandestine collection activities in Latin America during the 1960s revealed that the CIA had managed to place audio devices in the homes of many key personnel, including cabinet ministers.[26]

During E. Howard Hunt's tenure in Mexico City, the CIA bugged or tapped several Iron Curtain embassies. During his tenure in Uruguay, the CIA station conducted technical penetrations of embassies and the living quarters of key personnel. During Philip Agee's time in Uruguay, seven telephone lines were being monitored. Included were phones of the Soviet and Cuban embassies, consulates, and commercial offices.[27]

In 1982 or 1983, a unit of INSCOM, then known as the Quick Reaction Team (QRT), and subsequently as the Technical Analysis Unit, placed an electronic listening device in a Panamanian apartment belonging to General Manuel Antonio Noriega. Paying bribes to the maids who cleaned the apartment, and to the guards who protected it, a QRT agent was able to place a listening device in Noriega's conference room. The six ninety-minute tapes that resulted did not produce any substantial intelligence information.[28]

QRT agents also bugged the apartment of a Cuban diplomat in Panama. When the diplomat was away, agents slipped into his apartment and wired it with microtransmitters; again the take was of little value.[29]

In 1983, the QRT targeted Soviet representatives on several occasions during their visit to the United States. Soviet officials who traveled to Livermore, California, home of the Lawrence Livermore National Laboratory, had their rooms bugged by QRT agents. The bugging was repeated when the Soviets moved on to Denver. This time the results were more useful—sensitive discussions were recorded and leads obtained on possible Soviet agents in the United States.[30]

Technical surveillance operations may also employ lasers. A laser beam can be directed at a closed window from outside and used to detect the vibrations of the sound waves resulting from a conversation inside the room. The vibrations can be transformed back into the words spoken. Such a device was successfully tested in

West Africa but never seemed to function properly elsewhere except in the United States.[31]

Whereas technical surveillance devices are used to monitor communications, emplaced sensors are often designed to monitor noncommunications signals or emissions. Emplaced sensors may have the same purpose as sensors placed on spacecraft, aircraft, ships, or other mobile platforms. However, placing them covertly in a single location rather than on mobile platforms can offer two advantages. First, their proximity to the target may increase the value of the intelligence they produce. In many cases, no mobile platform operating from a distance could produce the necessary intelligence. Second, an emplaced sensor can monitor a facility or activity continuously.

Such operations are as sensitive as certain HUMINT operations, since if the target is aware of the operation it can be easily neutralized. There can also be significant risks for those involved in installing the sensors. Former DCI Stansfield Turner recalled "the very risky planting of a sensing device to monitor a secret activity in a hostile country. The case officer had to do the placement himself, escaping surveillance and proceeding undetected to a location so unusual that had he been found, he undoubtedly would have paid with his life."[32]

In 1965 the CIA planted a nuclear monitoring device on the summit of Nanda Devi in Garhwal, India. The device was intended to monitor Chinese nuclear tests being conducted at China's Lop Nor nuclear test site, approximately 900 miles away. After it was swept away in an avalanche, a second device was placed, in 1967, on the summit of the neighboring 22,400-foot Nanda Kot. That device remained in place for a year before being removed.[33]

In 1974 and 1975, and possibly subsequently, the U.S. Navy and Israeli Defense Forces conducted a joint operation designated CLUSTER LOBSTER. The operation involved planting an acoustic and magnetic sensor/recorder package in the Strait of Gubal. The tapes yielded valuable information on Soviet mine-sweeping operations.[34]

East Germany was also the target of emplaced sensor operations. In one operation, nuclear detection equipment was installed in a series of road posts on an East German road. The equipment transmitted its data back to an antenna on a pile of rubble in West Berlin.* In another instance, seismic monitoring devices were placed underground near a road. The data they transmitted (to a satellite) allowed intelligence analysts to differentiate between seven different weight classes (e.g., jeep, passenger car, truck, tank).[35]

Some of the most exotic emplaced sensors were those used in an attempt to monitor various Soviet weapons programs. One was a round device that could be

---

*On one occasion the equipment stopped transmitting. KH-11 photography indicated that the East Germans had pulled all the posts out for road repairs. After they were done, the East Germans obligingly replaced the posts, which resumed transmitting.

hidden in a tree stump, which sent data to satellites.[36] Another appeared to be a tree branch. It could be fitted around the stump of a tree and contained a sensor at one end to detect signals from a nearby Soviet laser test facility.

The Defense Intelligence Agency is developing Unattended Ground Sensors (UGS), employing imagery and acoustic sensors to covertly monitor activity around critical targets such as North Korean nuclear facilities. UGS may eventually be used to monitor nuclear power plants, deeply buried bunkers, mobile missile launch sites, and weapons manufacturing facilities. A high-speed digital signal processor board inside the UGS would handle both the processing for the acoustic sensor and the image compression for the imager.[37]

MATERIEL EXPLOITATION

An important source of information comes from the acquisition of new or used foreign weapons systems, communications equipment, and other devices of military significance. In many cases information on small systems cannot be obtained by overhead reconnaissance or signals intelligence. In any case, possession of the actual system adds significant new information to whatever is already known. The acquisition and analysis—materiel exploitation—of such systems, a function of all military scientific and technical intelligence units, allows scientists to determine not only the capabilities of the system but how such capabilities are achieved. Such knowledge can then be exploited to improve U.S. systems as well as to develop countermeasures.

According to Army Regulation 381-26, materiel exploitation allows:

- production of scientific and technical intelligence in support of force, combat, and materiel development;
- assessment of foreign technology, design features, and scientific developments for infusion into U.S. developmental efforts;
- support of U.S. systems and developmental testing/operational testing by providing adversary systems for use in evaluating U.S. systems capabilities; and
- development of simulator systems in support of simulation of foreign systems.[38]

During the course of the Cold War, U.S. materiel acquisition activities focused primarily on Soviet and Chinese systems. In Indonesia in the 1960s, the CIA conducted an operation known as HABRINK. In one phase of the operation, CIA operatives entered a warehouse holding SAM-2 missiles, removed the guidance system from one of them, and took it with them. The acquisition allowed U.S. Air Force scientists to equip B-52s with appropriate countermeasures. HABRINK also obtained the designs and workings of numerous Soviet weapons—the surface-to-surface Styx naval missile, the W-class submarine, the Komar guided-missile patrol boat, a RIGA-class destroyer, a Sverdlov cruiser TU-16 (BADGER) bomber, and a KENNEL air-to-surface missile.[39]

In a more recent version of HABRINK, the CIA purchased, from retired officers of the Indian Army and Air Force, details on weapons furnished to India by the Soviet Union. The Indian officers involved included an Army Major General, an Army Lieutenant Colonel, and an Air Vice Marshal.[40]

In 1979 the CIA and DIA planned Operation GRAY PAN, which was to involve the theft of a Soviet-made antiaircraft gun and an armored personnel carrier that the Soviets had sold to the Iranian Army in 1978.[41]

The most significant ground forces equipment the CIA obtained during the Cold War was a T-72 tank; only the T-80 is newer. In 1981 the Intelligence Support Activity (ISA), in an operation codenamed GREAT FALCON, attempted to obtain a T-72 and other equipment (including a MiG-25) from Iraq in exchange for U.S. 175-mm cannons. Ultimately, Iraqi officials vetoed the deal. A CIA attempt to acquire a T-72 from Romania also failed in 1981. Another ISA attempt to acquire a T-72, at the behest of Lieutenant Colonel Oliver North, involved the attempted delivery of U.S.-made machine guns to Iran in October 1986 in exchange for a T-72 captured from Iraq. By March 1987 the CIA had acquired several T-72 tanks.[42]

The United States acquired advanced Soviet aircraft from pilots who defected or purchased the aircraft from third parties. Once obtained, the planes were examined thoroughly by Foreign Technology Division (FTD) officers and scientists. Thus, when a MiG-25 pilot defected from the Soviet Union in 1976 with his plane, landing in Japan, examination of the airplane was a high priority. Before being returned to the Soviet Union, the entire MiG-25 was disassembled at Hyakuri Air Base in Japan. The engines, radar, computer, electronic countermeasures, automatic pilot, and communications equipment were placed on blocks and stands for mechanical, metallurgical, and photographic analysis.[43]

This examination, as well as the pilot's debriefing, sharply altered Western understanding of the plane and its missions. Among the discoveries was a radar more powerful than that ever installed in any other interceptor or fighter. In addition, the Soviet designers had used vacuum tubes rather than transistors.[44] (Although vacuum tubes represent a more primitive technology than transistors, they are resistant to the electromagnetic pulse (EMP) created by nuclear detonations.)

The MiG-25 was far from the first MiG obtained for purposes of exploitation. In early 1951 the Allied Air Force Commander in Korea was asked to make every effort to obtain a complete MiG-15 for analysis. As a result, a MiG that was shot down off Korea was retrieved within a short time. Portions of another MiG were recovered by helicopter. The FTD (then the Air Technical Intelligence Center) personnel landed, ran up to the crashed plane, threw grenades into it to separate assemblies small enough to carry, and left under hostile fire. In 1953, a defecting North Korean pilot flew an intact MiG-15 to South Korea.[45]

In some instances, Soviet equipment was sold to the United States by nominal Soviet allies—particularly Romania. During the final ten years of the Ceausescu regime, the CIA was able to buy advanced Soviet military technology through Ceausescu's two brothers, one of whom was the Deputy Defense Minister. The equipment acquired from Romania included:

- the latest version of the Shilka, one of the more effective Soviet antiaircraft systems;
- mobile rocket launchers that had been modified and improved by the Romanian military; and
- radar systems used in identifying targets and directing the firing of various Soviet AA weapons.[46]

In other cases materiel exploitation follows from the completion of a recovery operation in which a crashed plane or sunken ship is retrieved. In 1970 the United States recovered a nuclear weapon from a Soviet aircraft that crashed into the Sea of Japan; in 1971 the Navy recovered electronic eavesdropping equipment from a sunken trawler; and in 1972 a joint U.S.-British operation recovered electronic gear from a Soviet plane that had crashed earlier that year into the North Sea. In 1975, in Project JENNIFER, the CIA recovered half of a Golf-II submarine that had sunk northwest of Hawaii.[47]

In the aftermath of the 1973 Yom Kippur War, the United States received from Israel a variety of Soviet materiel. In addition to a Soviet AMD-500 mine, the Israelis provided SA-2, SA-3, SA-6, and SA-7 missiles.[48]

In 1983, during Operation BRIGHT STAR, personnel from INSCOM's 513th Military Intelligence Group were able to examine and evaluate Soviet and other foreign communications equipment that had been left behind in Somalia. The INSCOM personnel examined and repaired eighty-one pieces of Soviet and other foreign communications equipment.[49]

In the 1980s the CIA acquired several advanced Soviet military helicopter gunships, specifically Mi-24 Hinds, from both Pakistan and Chad. The helicopters were obtained by Pakistan and Chad as a result of the defection of a Soviet pilot from Afghanistan and Chad's victory over Libya in their border war. It has been reported that as a result of acquiring the helicopters, the United States determined how to penetrate the Mi-24's electronic defense systems with Stinger surface-to-air missiles.[50]

A repeated recovery operation was Operation SAND DOLLAR. SAND DOLLAR involved the recovery of Soviet test warheads that landed in the ocean. By international agreement, the Soviet Union was required to specify the impact areas for such tests. U.S. radars tracked the warheads to determine the precise points of impact. What appeared to be civilian drilling ships were sent to the Pacific test range after the tests had been completed to recover nosecones that had not self-destructed. Ships were guided to the proper locations by computers coordinated with U.S. satellites, and the objects were located by sonar and magnetom-

Figure 11-1. Navy FMEP Proposal.

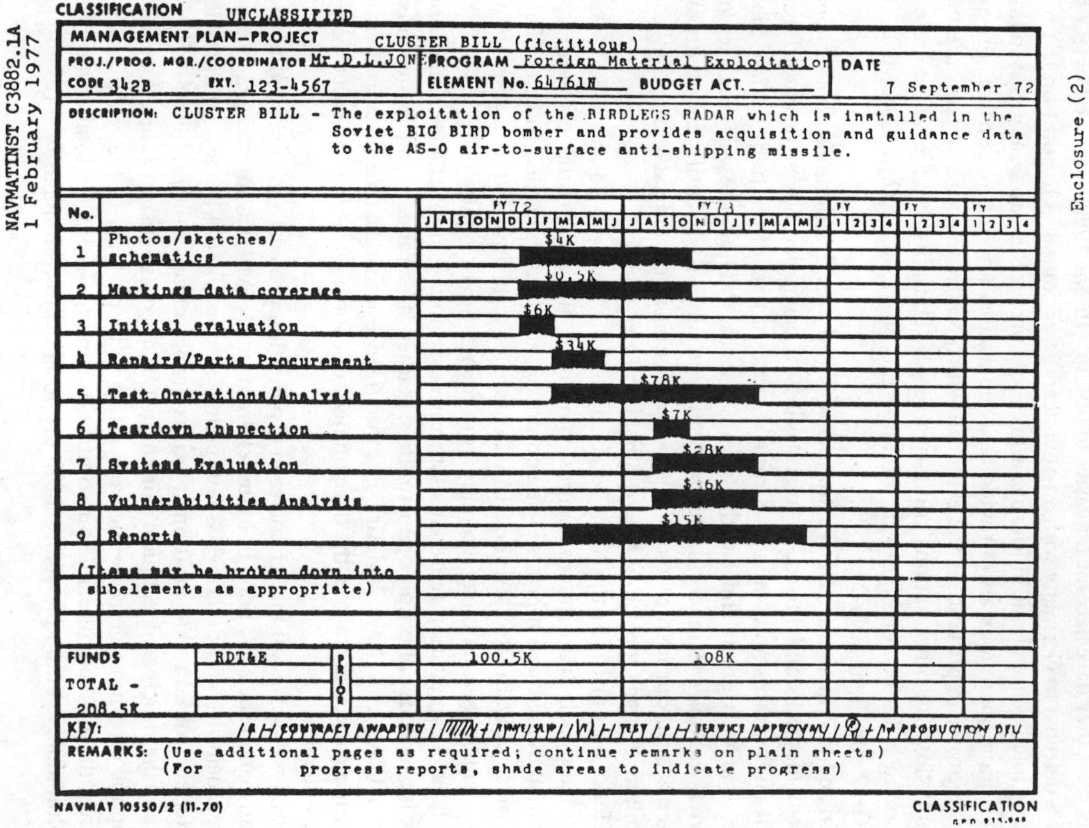

CLASSIFICATION   UNCLASSIFIED

MANAGEMENT PLAN—PROJECT   CLUSTER BILL (fictitious)

PROJ./PROG. MGR./COORDINATOR Mr. D. L. JONES PROGRAM Foreign Material Exploitation DATE

CODE 342B   EXT. 123-4567   ELEMENT No. 6476LN   BUDGET ACT. ____   7 September 72

DESCRIPTION: CLUSTER BILL - The exploitation of the BIRDLEGS RADAR which is installed in the Soviet BIG BIRD bomber and provides acquisition and guidance data to the AS-0 air-to-surface anti-shipping missile.

No.		FY72	FY73	FY	FY	FY	FY
1	Photos/sketches/schematics	$4K					
2	Markings data coverage	$0.5K					
3	Initial evaluation	$6K					
4	Repairs/Parts Procurement	$34K					
5	Test Operations/Analysis	$78K					
6	Teardown Inspection	$7K					
7	Systems Evaluation	$28K					
8	Vulnerabilities Analysis	$6K					
9	Reports	$15K					
	(Items may be broken down into subelements as appropriate)						

FUNDS

RDT&E

TOTAL - 208.5K   100.5K   .08K

KEY: ▆ FORMAL ENTRY ▓ HOST OPS/SAF ▒ HOST TEST ░ HOST MOD/EVAL ▤ LTM PRODUCTION PRV

REMARKS: (Use additional pages as required; continue remarks on plain sheets)
(For progress reports, shade areas to indicate progress)

NAVMAT 10550/2 (11.70)

CLASSIFICATION

NAVMATINST C3882.1A
1 February 1977

Enclosure (2)

Source: Naval Material Command Instruction C3882.1A, "Prosecution of the Navy Foreign Materiel Program (NFMP) in the NMC (U)," February 1, 1977.

eter devices. Scientists at the FTD then analyzed the design and construction of the captured nosecones.[51]

The end of the Cold War and collapse of the Soviet Union did not in any way decrease the emphasis on acquiring Soviet-produced weapons systems, particularly since they have become far easier to obtain. (In one 1990 case, two Soviet officers defected to Germany with an advanced Soviet missile.) In addition to providing intelligence about innovative aspects of current Russian weapons systems, acquisition operations also provide a hedge against any future conflict. But of much greater importance is the extent to which Soviet weapons systems are the foundations for other nations' military arsenals. Thus, in 1990 the Soviet Union exported a variety of high-tech aircraft—the Su-7, Su-24, MiG-21, MiG-23, MiG-29, Mi-17, and Mi-24.[52]

In addition to aircraft, a large number of Third World nations also possess Soviet-made tanks and surface-to-air missiles. In particular, Soviet-produced aircraft and surface-to-air missiles form a significant part of the Iraqi, Syrian, Libyan, Iranian, Cuban, and North Korean arsenals.[53] Thus, the vast analyses of Soviet weapons systems conducted by Army and Air Force scientific and technical organizations during the Cold War served as the basis for understanding Iraqi capabilities during Operations Desert Shield and Desert Storm.

Hence, in April 1991 the Army received, from Germany, T-55 and T-72 tanks, assorted signals and communications equipment, and small battlefield weapons, automatic rifles, and mortars. The equipment had been inherited from the East German Army. In late 1992 the CIA was reported to be involved in a program of buying up high-technology weapons from former Soviet republics.[54]

Materiel exploitation represents far more than the result of chance defections and intelligence collection opportunities. Rather, it is a major and coordinated part of CIA, Army, Navy, and Air Force intelligence activities, the military services having a particular stake in the development of countermeasures to Soviet weapons systems.

Proposals for naval foreign materiel exploitation projects are submitted to the Chairman of the Navy Foreign Materiel Program (NFMP) Committee. Each proposal identifies and describes as completely as possible the foreign equipment/materiel involved and its location as well as the objectives of the exploitation project and the anticipated technical gain to the U.S. Navy as a result of the effort. The proposal then must describe the work effort to be performed, the resources required, the planned timetable for completion, and the estimated total cost of the exploitation. An example of an NFMP proposal is shown in Figure 11-1.

NOTES

1. Roscoe H. Hillenkoeter, "Using the World's Information Sources," *Army Information Digest*, November 1948, pp. 3–6.

2. J. J. Bagnall, "The Exploitation of Russian Scientific Literature for Intelligence Purposes," *Studies in Intelligence* 2, 3 (Summer 1958): 45–49.

3. Ibid.

4. Ibid.

5. Andrew Cockburn, *The Threat: Inside the Soviet Military Machine* (New York: Random House, 1983), p. 22; Jonathan Samuel Lockwood, *The Soviet View of U.S. Strategic Doctrine* (New Brunswick, N.J.: Transaction, 1983), p. 5.

6. Michael Wines, "Kremlin Watchers Cope with Data Glut," *New York Times*, January 14, 1990, p. 14.

7. "Lack of Funding Threatens 'MiG-29M' Development Program," *FBIS-SOV-93-164*, August 26, 1993, pp. 32–33; "Air Defense Missile Demonstration Observed," *FBIS-SOV-93-164*, August 26, 1993, pp. 33–34.

8. Carl B. Crawley, "On the Intelligence Exploitation of Open Source Chinese Documents," *Naval Intelligence Quarterly* 2, 4 (1981): 7–9.

9. Ibid.

10. Ibid.

11. Ibid.

12. Remarks by Admiral William O. Studeman, Deputy Director of Central Intelligence, to the First International Symposium on National Security and National Competitiveness: Open Source Solutions, December 1, 1992, McLean, Virginia, pp. 12, 20.

13. Herman L. Croom, "The Exploitation of Foreign Open Sources," *Studies in Intelligence* (Summer 1969): 129–36.

14. Remarks by A. Denis Clift, Chief of Staff, Defense Intelligence Agency, to the First International Symposium on National Security and National Competitiveness: Open Source Solutions, December 1, 1992, McLean, Virginia, pp. 5, 6; *Transactions*, Third International Conference on Nuclear Technology Transfer, Madrid, Spain, October 14–18, 1985, p. III.

15. Remarks by Admiral William O. Studeman, p. 12.

16. Remarks by A. Denis Clift, pp. 8, 10.

17. Air Force Intelligence Service, "Video Intelligence (VIDINT)," 1988.

18. Remarks by Admiral William O. Studeman, p. 15.

19. Robert Pear, "Radio Broadcasts Report Protests Erupting All over China," *New York Times*, May 23, 1989, p. A14.

20. "Live, from Baghdad," *Newsweek*, September 24, 1990, p. 4.

21. Remarks by Admiral William O. Studeman, p. 5.

22. United States Military Communications-Electronics Board, *Joint Department of Defense Plain Language Address Directory* (Washington, D.C.: Department of Defense, August 9, 1982), p. II-15.

23. Victor Marchetti and John Marks, *The CIA and the Cult of Intelligence* (New York: Knopf, 1974), p. 189.

24. John Stockwell, *In Search of Enemies: A CIA Story* (New York: Norton, 1978), p. 107; Thomas Powers, *The Man Who Kept the Secrets: Richard Helms and the CIA* (New York: Knopf, 1979), p. 198.

25. Steve Weissman and Herbert Krosney, *The Islamic Bomb* (New York: Times Books, 1981), p. 151.

26. Marchetti and Marks, *The CIA and the Cult of Intelligence*, p. 189.

27. E. Howard Hunt, *Undercover: Memoirs of an American Secret Agent* (New York: Berkley, 1974), pp. 80, 126; Philip Agee, *Inside the Company: A CIA Diary* (New York: Stonehill, 1975), pp. 346–47.

28. Steve Emerson, *Secret Warriors: Inside the Covert Military Operations of the Reagan Era* (New York: Putnam's, 1988), p. 111.

29. Ibid., p. 112.

30. Ibid., p. 116.

31. Marchetti and Marks, *The CIA and the Cult of Intelligence,* pp. 190–91.

32. Stansfield Turner, *Secrecy and Democracy: The CIA in Transition* (Boston: Houghton Mifflin, 1985), pp. 59–60.

33. "The Indian Connection," *India Today,* December 31, 1983, p. 10; "$ Diplomacy," *India Today,* May 1–15, 1979, p. 107.

34. Naval Intelligence Command, *Naval Intelligence Command (NAVINTCOM) History for CY-1975, Basic Narrative,* 1976, p. 18.

35. Interview; "Seismic Sensors," *Intelligence Newsletter,* January 17, 1990, p. 2.

36. NBC, *Inside the KGB: Narration and Shooting Script,* May 1993, p. 39.

37. Barbara Starr, "Super Sensors Will Eye the New Proliferation Frontier," *Jane's Defence Weekly,* June 4, 1994, p. 19.

38. AR 381-26, "Army Foreign Materiel Exploitation Program," March 6, 1987, p. 3.

39. John Barron, *The KGB Today: The Hidden Hand* (New York: Reader's Digest, 1983), pp. 233–34; Statement of Facts, *United States of America v David Henry Barnett,* K 80-0390, United States District Court, Maryland, 1980.

40. William J. Eaton, "CIA Reportedly Caught Buying Indian Military Secrets," *Los Angeles Times,* December 15, 1983, p. 4.

41. "What the U.S. Lost in Iran," *Newsweek,* December 28, 1981, pp. 33–34.

42. Emerson, *Secret Warriors,* p. 185; Michael Wines and Richard E. Meyer, "North Apparently Tried a Swap for Soviet Tank," *Washington Post,* January 22, 1987, p. A37; Richard Halloran, "U.S. Has Acquired Soviet T-72 Tanks," *New York Times,* March 13, 1987, p. A12; Benjamin Weiser, "One That Got Away: Romanians Were Ready to Sell Soviet Tank," *Washington Post,* May 6, 1990, p. A30.

43. John Barron, *MIG Pilot* (New York: Avon, 1981), pp. 172–73.

44. Ibid.

45. Foreign Technology Division, *FTD 1917–1967* (Dayton, Ohio: FTD, 1967), p. 24.

46. Benjamin Weiser, "Ceaucescu Family Sold Soviet Military Secrets to U.S.," *Washington Post,* May 6, 1990, pp. A1, A30.

47. Clyde W. Burleson, *The Jennifer Project* (Englewood Cliffs, N.J.: Prentice-Hall, 1977), p. 47; "The Great Submarine Snatch," *Time,* March 31, 1975, pp. 20–27; William J. Broad, "Russia Says U.S. Got Sub's Atom Arms," *New York Times,* June 30, 1993, p. 4; "CIA Raising USSR Sub Raises Questions," *FBIS-SOV-92-145,* July 28, 1992, pp. 15–16.

48. Naval Intelligence Command, *Naval Intelligence Command History for CY-1973,* April 29, 1974, p. 50.

49. U.S. Army Intelligence and Security Command, *Annual Historical Review FY 1983,* September 1984, p. 72.

50. James Bruce, "CIA Acquires Soviet MI-24 and T-72," *Jane's Defence Weekly,* March 28, 1987, p. 535; James Brooke, "Chad, with Victories, Is Awash in War Booty," *New York Times,* August 17, 1987, p. A4.

51. Roy Varner and Wayne Collier, *A Matter of Risk* (New York: Random House, 1977), p. 26.

52. Statement of Rear Admiral Thomas A. Brooks, USN, Director of Naval Intelligence, before the Seapower, Strategic, and Critical Materials Subcommittee of the House Armed Services Committee on Intelligence Issues, March 7, 1991, p. 36; Paul Quinn-Judge, "CIA Buys Ex-Soviet Arms, US Aide Says," *Boston Globe*, November 15, 1992, pp. 1, 14; Bill Gertz, "Soviets Flee with Secrets," *Washington Times*, January 1, 1991, pp. A1, A6.

53. Quinn-Judge, "CIA Buys Ex-Soviet Arms, US Aide Says."

54. Richard H.P. Sia, "U.S. Army Gets Soviet Weapons from Germany," *Philadelphia Inquirer*, May 5, 1991, p. 14-E.

12
EXCHANGE AND LIAISON ARRANGEMENTS

Despite its huge investment in technical and human intelligence activities, the United States relies on exchange and liaison arrangements with a variety of foreign nations for a significant portion of its intelligence. As then Defense Secretary Caspar Weinberger explained in 1985: "The United States has neither the opportunity nor the resources to unilaterally collect all the intelligence information we require. We compensate with a variety of intelligence sharing arrangements with other nations of the world."[1]

Some arrangements are long-standing, highly formalized, and involve the most sensitive forms of intelligence collection. Others are less wide-ranging and reflect limited common interests between the United States and particular nations. Thus, the United States has shared satellite intelligence concerning drug production with Mexico.[2] In addition, exchange arrangements may involve different components of the intelligence communities in the United States and other nations. Whereas some arrangements may involve links between the CIA and a nation's counterpart agency, for example, others may involve cooperation between the Office of Naval Intelligence and one or more foreign naval intelligence organizations.

The most important arrangements are multilateral agreements between the United States and the United Kingdom, Australia, Canada, and New Zealand concerning the collection and distribution of signals intelligence and ocean surveillance data. The United States also maintains bilateral arrangements with each of those nations. Also of major importance are the arrangements with Israel, Norway, the People's Republic of China, Japan, Russia, and the United Nations.

UKUSA

The U.S.-British military alliance in World War II necessitated a high degree of cooperation with respect to intelligence activities. It was imperative that the United States and Britain, as the main allied combatants in the European and Pacific theaters, establish a coordinated effort in the acquisition of worldwide intelligence and its evaluation and distribution.

276

The most important aspect of that cooperation was in the area of signals intelligence. An apparently limited agreement on SIGINT cooperation was reached in December 1940. That was followed by the visit to the British Government Code and Cipher School of four U.S. officers, including two members of the Army Signal Intelligence Service, in January 1941. In June of that year the United States and Britain agreed to exchange signals intelligence concerning Japan. But it was not until October 2, 1942, that the United States and Britain signed an agreement for extensive cooperation in the area of naval SIGINT. That was followed by a May 17, 1943, agreement, generally known as the British-U.S. Communications Intelligence Agreement (BRUSA), that provided for extensive cooperation between the U.S. Army's SIGINT agency and the British Government Code and Cipher School. SIGINT cooperation also included Canada, Australia, and New Zealand.[3]

The intelligence relationships among Australia, Britain, Canada, New Zealand, and the United States that were forged during World War II did not end with the war. Rather, they became formalized and grew stronger. In 1946 William Friedman, America's premier cryptographer, visited British cryptographers to work out methods of postwar consultation and cooperation. A U.S. Liaison Office was set up in London, and schemes were derived for avoiding the duplication of effort. It was agreed that solved material was to be exchanged between the two agencies. In addition, an exchange program was started under which personnel from each agency would work for two or three years at the other site.[4]

An event that occurred in 1948 set the stage for post–World War II signals intelligence cooperation: the formulation and acceptance of the UKUSA Agreement, also known as the UK-USA Security Agreement or "Secret Treaty." The primary emphasis of the agreement was to provide for a division of SIGINT collection responsibilities between the First Party (the United States) and the Second Parties (Australia, Britain, Canada, and New Zealand).* The specific agencies now involved are the U.S. National Security Agency (NSA), the Australian Defence Signals Directorate (DSD), the British Government Communications Headquarters (GCHQ), the Canadian Communications Security Establishment (CSE), and the New Zealand Government Communications Security Bureau (GCSB).[5]

Under the present division of responsibilities, the United States is responsible for SIGINT in Latin America, most of Asia, Asiatic Russia, and northern China. Australia's area of responsibility includes its neighbors (such as Indonesia), southern China, and the nations of Indochina. Britain is responsible for the former Soviet Union west of the Urals and Africa. The polar regions of Russia are the responsibility of Canada, and New Zealand's area of responsibility is the western Pacific. Specific tasking assignments are specified in the SIGINT Combined Operating List (SCOL).[6]

---

*There are also ten Third Parties to the treaty: Austria, Thailand, Japan, South Korea, Norway, Denmark, Germany, Italy, Greece, and Turkey.

Britain's geographical position gives it a significant capability for long-range SIGINT collection against certain targets in Russia and former Soviet states such as the Ukraine. Britain's historical role in Africa led to its assumption of SIGINT responsibility for that area. Canada's responsibility for northern Russia stems from its geographical position, which gives it "unique access to communications in ... northern [Russia]." The areas of responsibility for Australia and New Zealand clearly result from their geographical location.[7]

The UKUSA relationship (and its SIGINT aspect) is more than an agreement to coordinate separately conducted intelligence activities and share the intelligence collected. Rather, it is cemented by the presence of U.S. facilities on British, Canadian, and Australian territory; by joint operations (U.S.-U.K., Australian-U.S., U.K.-Australian) within and outside UKUSA territory, and, in the case of Australia, of U.K. and U.S. staff at all DSD facilities.[8]

In addition to specifying SIGINT collection responsibilities, the agreement addresses access to the collected intelligence and security arrangements for the handling of data. Standardized codewords (e.g., UMBRA for signals intelligence), security agreements that all employees of the respective SIGINT agencies must sign, and procedures for storing and disseminating codeword material are all implemented under terms of the agreement.[9]

Similarly, in 1967, the "COMINT Indoctrination" declaration, which all British-cleared personnel had to sign, included in the first paragraph the statement, "I declare that I fully understand the information relating to the manner and extent of the interception of communications of foreign powers by H.M. Government and *other cooperating Governments,* and intelligence produced by such interception known as Communications Intelligence (COMINT) is information covered by Section 2 of the Official Secrets Act 1911 (as amended)" (emphasis added).[10] These requirements for standardized codewords (see Chapter 18), security arrangements, and procedures for the handling and dissemination of SIGINT material are detailed in a series of *International Regulations on SIGINT* (IRSIG), which was in its third edition as of 1967.

Despite numerous references to the agreements in print, officials of some of the participating countries have refused to confirm not only the details of the agreement but even its existence. Thus, on March 9, 1977, the Australian Opposition Defence Spokesman asked the Prime Minister:

1. Is Australia a signatory to the UKUSA Agreement?
2. Is it a fact that under this agreement, NSA operates electronic intercept stations in Australia?
3. Does any other form of station operate in Australia under the agreement? If so, is it operated by an Australian or overseas authority or is it operated under some sort of joint authority?
4. Will the [Prime Minister] identify the participating country or countries in any such agreement?

The Prime Minister refused to answer and referred to a previous response wherein he said the government would not confirm or deny speculation in that area. And the Australian D Notice, "Ciphering and Monitoring Activities," requests the media to refrain from publishing material on Australian collaboration with other countries in monitoring activities.[11]

Similarly, in the United States a 1982 Freedom of Information Act request to the NSA asking for "all documents from 1947 outlining United States-United Kingdom-Australian-Canadian-New Zealand cooperation in Signals Intelligence" brought the response that: "We have determined that the fact of the existence or non-existence of the materials you request is in itself a currently and properly classified matter." [12]

Cooperation exists on a similar level in the area of ocean surveillance, with British and Australian stations feeding into the U.S. Ocean Surveillance Information System (OSIS). A station at Hong Kong jointly operated by the United Kingdom and Australia was, until the mid-1970s, directed almost entirely against the People's Republic of China. Subsequently, it was involved in monitoring Soviet naval movements down the coast of Asia from major Soviet naval bases at Vladivostok and Petropavlovsk-Kamchatka to Cam Ranh Bay in Vietnam. Likewise, an Australian–New Zealand unit, the Australia–New Zealand Military Intelligence Service (ANZMIS), located in Singapore, monitored Soviet naval activities in the region. The information collected, including intercepts and photographs, was distributed to the United States, Britain, Singapore, and Malaysia.[13]

Several Australian-operated stations also contribute significantly to the OSIS. These stations are located at Pearce, Western Australia; Cabarlah, Queensland; and Shoal Bay, New Territories. The Pearce station has as its primary purpose the monitoring of naval and air traffic over the Indian Ocean. In the early 1980s a Pusher antenna was installed for the purpose of intercepting, monitoring, direction finding, and analyzing radio signals in a portion of the HF band.[14]

The Cabarlah station on the east coast of Australia is operated by the DSD. Its main purpose is monitoring radio transmissions throughout the Southwest Pacific. Thus, the Cabarlah system was used to monitor Soviet intelligence-gathering trawlers that were watching the Kangaroo II naval exercise of October 1976.[15]

The most important station for monitoring the Southeast Asian area is the DSD station at Darwin (Shoal Bay), which originally had a very limited direction-finding capability. However, contracts signed in 1981 provided for the procurement of modern DF equipment to enable the station to "participate fully in the OSIS." Canadian stations at Halifax and a joint U.S.-British station on Ascension Island (which monitors naval traffic in the South Atlantic) contribute to monitoring naval movements in the Atlantic Ocean.[16]

Overhead maritime surveillance is the subject of a 1977 agreement between Australia, New Zealand, and the United States, the Agreement for the Coordination of Maritime Surveillance and Reconnaissance in the South/Southwest Pacific and Eastern Indian Oceans.[17]

In addition to cooperating on collection activities, the UKUSA nations are also involved in cooperative arrangements concerning defense intelligence analysis, holding periodic conferences dealing with a wide range of scientific and defense intelligence matters. Thus, in 1974 the United States participated in the Annual Land Warfare Intelligence Conference, the International Scientific Intelligence Exchange, the Quadripartite Intelligence Working Party on Chinese Guided Missiles, and the Tripartite Defense Intelligence Estimates Conference. Held in London in May 1974, the Annual Land Warfare Intelligence Conference involved members of U.S., British, Canadian, and Australian defense intelligence organizations in discussions about the armaments used by Communist armies.[18]

The Third International Scientific Intelligence Exchange, involving U.S., British, New Zealand, and Australian defense intelligence organizations, was held in Canberra from June 18 to June 27, 1974. Initially established to discuss Chinese scientific developments, particularly with respect to nuclear weapons, the 1974 meeting also focused on technical developments in India and Japan, nuclear proliferation in Asia, development and military applications of lasers, and application of peaceful nuclear explosives.[19]

The Quadripartite Intelligence Working Party on Chinese Guided Missiles met in London in 1974. The panel, consisting of representatives from the U.S., British, Australian, and Canadian defense intelligence organizations, focused on Chinese guided missiles and satellite launch vehicles. The United States, New Zealand, and Australia constituted the participants in the Tripartite Defense Intelligence Estimates Conference. This 1974 conference, held in Wellington, New Zealand, involved "the exchange of military estimates and assessments among the countries."[20]

U.S., Canadian, and U.K. representatives regularly attend the Annual CANUKUS Maritime Intelligence Conference. Air force intelligence representatives from each nation have also met to examine topics such as Soviet surface-to-air missiles.[21] U.S. and U.K. military intelligence representatives have also participated in the US/UK Chemical Warfare Intelligence Conference and the US/UK Armor Conference (held at the CIA).[22]

The U.S. Armed Forces Medical Intelligence Center (AFMIC) has also been involved in medical intelligence exchanges with Australia, Canada, and the United Kingdom. AFMIC is a member of the Quadripartite Medical Intelligence Committee. Other members include the Canadian and U.K. medical liaison offices and the Australian scientific attaché.[23]

In addition to positive intelligence links, the UKUSA nations also cooperate in matters of counterintelligence. Since the 1950s, representatives of Canada, Australia, New Zealand, Canada, and the United Kingdom would meet every eighteen months for a week-long conference on counterintelligence matters of common interest. Subjects have included joint operations, research of old cases, investigations of penetrations, assessments of defectors, and technical and communications advances.[24]

As a result of New Zealand's policy, adopted in 1985, of prohibiting nuclear vessels, the United States decreased New Zealand's access to intelligence gathered by U.S. sources—although the extent of the reduction was the subject of controversy. According to an internal New Zealand document, the United States stopped providing intelligence on the military situation in Southeast Asia, the overall strategic balance, actual or potential crisis situations worldwide, and technological developments in the Soviet Union. The United States also halted intelligence briefings for New Zealand liaison officers and excluded New Zealand from intelligence conferences in which both nations had previously participated. The United States did agree to continue providing New Zealand with intelligence relating to threats to New Zealand and counterespionage matters.[25]

According to the New Zealand Ministry of Defense (MOD),

> It is of particular concern that Maritime Defence Commander (NZ) now has an incomplete picture of movements of ships within his area of responsibility. NZ has also lost access to communication/electronic information. ... Although NZ Defence has continued to provide intelligence to the United States without change since 15 Feb 85, intelligence information from US Defense Intelligence Agencies has virtually ceased, except for selected maritime information. Exchange officers have been withdrawn and New Zealand participation in all intelligence conferences attended by US agencies has been denied. However, NZ Defence (DDI) continued to receive some unprocessed intelligence from US sources but the continued flow is less than 20% of that received before the last election.[26]

The Prime Minister, David Lange, called the MOD claim of a greater than 80 percent cutoff "totally and absolutely wrong."[27] Additionally, the Chairman of the New Zealand Intelligence Committee said the loss of U.S. intelligence had not had a significant effect on New Zealand's knowledge of events in the South Pacific. Defense officials disputed the Chairman's statement, suggesting that information on military movements and changes, and assessments of the implications, had been reduced and that the Chairman had been referring to mainly economic and political intelligence.[28]

A March 26, 1985, CONFIDENTIAL NEW ZEALAND EYES ONLY document of the Cabinet's External Relations and Security Committee supported the MOD claim. It noted:

> It is estimated that at least 80% of New Zealand's Defence Intelligence has come directly or indirectly from American sources. ... The embargo on release of United States-sourced material by third country recipients will thus restrict intelligence exchange between New Zealand and such countries as Australia, Canada and Britain.
>
> In practical terms United States restrictions on the intelligence flow will make it extremely difficult to formulate policy advice on the basis of up to date and authenticated information. A principal concern is to maintain our ability to monitor developments in the wider Pacific area: Cam Ranh Bay, Kampuchea, the Philippines, Timor, PNG border etc as well as in the South Pacific. In the absence of US satellite in-

formation increased maritime surveillance, particularly in the northern portion of New Zealand's area of maritime interest is necessary.[29]

In 1991, improvements in U.S.–New Zealand relations led to renewed access to some U.S. intelligence. The United States agreed to keep New Zealand up-to-date on Middle East developments. After the Gulf War, Foreign Minister Don McKinnon characterized New Zealand as receiving "a level of intelligence which we consider quite satisfactory."[30] In February 1994 President Clinton signed a directive that restored high-level contacts.[31]

AUSTRALIA

Although there are formal arrangements among the UKUSA countries with respect to signals intelligence, ocean surveillance, and radio monitoring, no such agreement exists with respect to human intelligence activities. There has been significant cooperation, however, between the United States and Australia in this area.[32]

Both the British Secret Intelligence Service (SIS) and the U.S. CIA have sought Australian cooperation in areas where it has been easier for the Australian Secret Intelligence Service (ASIS) to operate. The ASIS has provided significant assistance in Chile, Thailand, Indonesia, and Cambodia. Thus, in 1975, William Colby, then the Director of the CIA, stated that

> ASIS reporting has naturally been of most value in areas where our own coverage is limited, including the following:
>
>   (a) reporting on Portuguese Timor and North Vietnam
>   (b) reporting from Indonesian sources
>   (c) operations and reporting on Chile; and
>   (d) unique operations and reporting on Cambodia
>
> … During the period we were not present in Chile the service was of great help in assisting us to maintain coverage of that country's internal developments. For example, two of our Santiago Station assets were turned over to ASIS for handling and produced 58 disseminated reports during the period January, 1972 through July 1973. The effective and professional handling of these assets by ASIS made possible continued receipt of this very useful information. The same basic comments apply to the case of Cambodia.[33]

An ASIS station in Phnom Penh was approved by the Department of Foreign Affairs on February 5, 1965, and opened later in the year with one officer and one operational assistant. A second officer slot was added in 1970 but eliminated in 1972. The opening of the second station coincided, approximately, with the withdrawal of the United States Mission in Cambodia.[34]

The CIA had strongly supported the ASIS proposal to open a new station and, upon U.S. withdrawal, turned over to the ASIS a network of agents, some of whom were still operating when Australia withdrew from Cambodia in 1974 following the fall of the Cambodian government. Information collected by the ASIS-CIA network was made available to the CIA.[35]

The presence of the Australian Secret Intelligence Service in Chile can be traced back to a CIA request for ASIS support in early November 1970. It appeared to the U.S. government that the Allende government might sever diplomatic relations with the United States. The CIA, in anticipation of such a move, sought the opening of at least a limited ASIS network. The proposal was supported by Australia's Secretary of the Department of Foreign Affairs and approved by the Foreign Affairs Minister. The justification was not in terms of the ability of a Santiago station to produce intelligence important to Australia but rather in terms of reciprocation for the large amount of intelligence made available to Australia by the United States.[36]

Actual agent-running operations did not begin until early 1972, after a five-month period dedicated to establishing embassy cover, assessing the operational climate, and insuring sufficient language fluency. Details concerning three agents were passed to the ASIS by the CIA for approval. After ASIS was satisfied that the agents were trustworthy, approval was given to begin operations. In March 1973, the Minister requested a review of the Chilean station, and in April he decided that it should be closed down. This decision was communicated to the CIA, active operations were halted on May 1, 1973, and the agents were returned to CIA control. For cover purposes, the ASIS officer remained in Santiago until July, and the operational assistant remained until October 1973.[37]

According to the findings of an Australian Royal Commission report, ASIS activities in support of the CIA in Cambodia and Chile were strictly confined to intelligence gathering and did not involve covert action (destabilization) activities. Thus, according to the report, "At no time was ASIS approached by CIA, nor made aware of any plans that may have been prepared to affect the internal political situation in Chile. The ASIS station in Santiago was concerned only with intelligence gathering via the agents handed over to it."[38]

In return for such help, the ASIS has received CIA human intelligence reports concerning areas of the world where ASIS is represented, although little or nothing concerning areas without ASIS representation. These reports, codenamed REMARKABLE, were described in one official study of ASIS as being large in quantity and high in quality. In 1974 and 1975, they numbered 588 and 794, respectively, and focused mainly on China and Southeast Asia, ranging "from high-grade political and scientific intelligence to relatively humdrum, but intensely detailed, reporting on insurgency in Southeast Asia and sociological conditions within China."[39]

The ASIS presence does not, apparently, guarantee access to CIA reporting. It has been reported that, in 1986, the CIA failed to provide ASIS with intelligence on developments in the Philippines, where ASIS had opened a station.[40]

CANADA

Canada and the United States have signed a variety of bilateral intelligence agreements and have worked together on a number of projects. U.S.-Canadian joint estimates produced in the late 1950s focused on Soviet capabilities and likely actions in the event of a major Soviet attack on North America. Thus, the document *Soviet Capabilities and Probable Courses of Action Against North America in a Major War During the Period 1 January 1958 to 31 December 1958*, as well as a similarly titled document prepared by the Canadian-U.S. Joint Intelligence Committee, assessed the Soviet threat to North America. These documents considered factors such as Communist bloc political stability and economic support; the internal threat to North America; Soviet nuclear, radiological, biological, and chemical weapons; aircraft, including bombers, transport aircraft, and tanker aircraft; guided missiles; naval weapons; electronics; ground, naval, and surface strength and combat effectiveness; Soviet worldwide strategy; and Soviet capabilities to conduct air and airborne missile, naval, amphibious, and internal operations against North America. Preparation of such estimates continued on a yearly basis under the title *Canadian–United States Intelligence Estimate of the Military Threat to North America*.[41]

Canada's SIGINT relationship to the United States is defined by the CANUS Agreement (as well as the UKUSA Agreement). On September 15, 1950, Canada and the United States exchanged letters giving formal recognition to the Security Agreement Between Canada and the United States of America (which was followed exactly two months later by the Arrangement for Exchange of Information between the U.S., U.K. and Canada).[42]

Negotiations for the CANUS Agreement had been taking place since at least 1948. There was some concern on the part of U.S. intelligence officials that original drafts of the agreement provided for too much exchange. Thus, a 1948 memorandum by the Acting Director of Intelligence of the U.S. Air Force noted that paragraph 6a of the proposed agreement was

> not sufficiently restrictive. In effect, it provides for the complete exchange of information. Not only is it considered that the Canadians will reap all the benefits of complete exchange but wider dissemination of the information would jeopardize the security of the information. It is believed that the exchange should be related to mutually agreed COMINT activities on a "need to know" basis.[43]

A more recent agreement is the Canadian–United States Communications Instructions for Reporting Vital Intelligence Sightings (CIRVIS/MERINT), signed in March 1966. This agreement specifies the type of information to be reported by airborne or land-based observers—that is, information concerning:

- hostile or unidentified single aircraft or formations of aircraft that appear to be directed against the United States or Canada or their forces;
- missiles;

- unidentified flying objects;
- hostile or unidentified submarines;
- hostile or unidentified groups of military vessels;
- individual surface vessels, submarines, or aircraft of unconventional design, or engaged in suspicious activity or observed in a location or on a course that may be interpreted as constituting a threat to the United States, Canada, or their forces;
- any unexplained or unusual activity that may indicate a possible attack against or through Canada or the United States, including the presence of any unidentified or other suspicious ground parties in the Polar Region or other remote or sparsely populated areas.[44]

The agreement also specifies eleven types of information that should be provided in any MERINT report, including a description of the object sighted (covering each of nine different aspects of the object), a description of the course of the object and the manner of observation, and information on weather and wind conditions.[45]

The agreement, which will need updating in light of world events, further specifies that seaborne vessels are to submit MERINT reports concerning:

- the movement of Warsaw Pact or unidentified aircraft (single or in formation);
- missile firings;
- the movement of Warsaw Pact or unidentified submarines;
- the movement of Warsaw Pact or unidentified groups of surface combatants;
- any airborne, seaborne, ballistic, or orbiting object that the observer feels may constitute a military threat against the United States or Canada or may be of interest to military and civilian government officials;
- individual surface ships, submarines, or aircraft of unconventional design or engaged in suspicious activities or observed in unusual locations;
- any unexplained or unusual activity that may indicate possible attack against or through the United States or Canada, including the presence of any unidentified or suspicious ground parties in the Polar Region or other remote or sparsely populated areas.[46]

UNITED KINGDOM

Bilateral intelligence relations between the United States and the United Kingdom include human intelligence, signals intelligence, and radio and television broadcast monitoring. The British–United States (BRUSA) Communications Intelligence Agreement of 1943 is still in force and regulates the bilateral part of the British-U.S. SIGINT relationship.

A second highly formalized arrangement consists of an agreement to divide up, on a geographic basis, the responsibility for monitoring public radio and television broadcasts—mainly news and public affairs broadcasts. The specific organizations involved are the British Broadcasting Corporation (BBC) Monitoring Service and the CIA's Foreign Broadcast Information Service (FBIS). Together, these two organizations monitor most of the world's most significant news reports and other broadcasts. Both the BBC Monitoring Service and the FBIS have a network of overseas stations that operate with varying degrees of secrecy to gather raw material.[47]

Cooperation between the BBC Monitoring Service and the FBIS began in 1948 as an openly acknowledged arrangement. Thus, the BBC Annual Report for 1948–1949 noted: "There [is] close cooperation between the BBC's Monitoring Service and its American counterpart, the Foreign Broadcast Information Branch of the United States Central Intelligence Agency, and each of the two services maintained liaison units at each other's stations for the purpose of a full exchange of information."[48]

The area of responsibility for the Monitoring Service is roughly equivalent to GCHQ's area of responsibility for SIGINT collection—Europe, Africa, and western Russia. Thus, the Monitoring Service maintains a remotely controlled listening post on the rooftop of the British Embassy in Vienna to monitor VHF radio and television broadcasts originating in Hungary and Czechoslovakia. It also maintains listening posts in Accra, Ghana, and Abidjan, Ivory Coast. In 1976–1977 the Monitoring Service turned over responsibility for monitoring Far East broadcasts to the FBIS. To compensate, it stepped up its reporting of events in Portugal and Spain to meet CIA requirements.[49]

ISRAEL

One of the strongest Western intelligence links is that between the United States and Israel. These arrangements involve the Mossad (the Israeli Central Institute for Intelligence and Special Tasks), AMAN (the Israeli Defense Forces Intelligence Branch), and a variety of U.S. intelligence agencies—the CIA, the FBI, the DIA, the NSA, the Foreign Aerospace Science and Technology Center, and the National Ground Intelligence Center.

The intelligence liaison between the United States and Israel dates back to 1951, when Prime Minister David Ben-Gurion arrived in the United States for a fund-raising drive. Ben-Gurion also paid an unpublicized visit to DCI Walter Bedell Smith and his Deputy, Allen Dulles. At that meeting Ben-Gurion offered, and the CIA accepted, the concept of a liaison relationship between the U.S. and Israeli intelligence communities. In October 1951, James Jesus Angleton, then director of the CIA's Staff A (Foreign Intelligence), arrived in Israel to establish a cooperative arrangement. Angleton would direct the liaison relationship with Israel until his forced retirement in 1975.[50]

Angleton had developed extensive contacts with future Israeli intelligence officials during his World War II activities in Europe with the Office of Strategic Services. In 1957, he set up a liaison unit to deal with the Mossad. This unit was made responsible for producing Middle East intelligence for both services. In addition, the CIA received intelligence from Mossad networks in the Soviet Union.[51]

By the early 1970s the United States and Israel established a joint debriefing operation to interview émigrés from the Soviet Union. The joint operation was located in Tel Aviv under Mossad auspices, with CIA officers participating.[52]

After Angleton's dismissal as counterintelligence chief in 1975, the liaison unit was abolished and the Israeli account was moved to the appropriate Directorate of Operations regional division of the CIA. The CIA also began to operate more independently of the Mossad. In the late 1970s the agency began operating on the West Bank.[53]

Through this liaison relationship, the U.S. intelligence community gained access to Soviet weapons systems and data on their wartime performance. Such exchanges took place after the 1967 and 1973 Arab-Israeli wars. Israel furnished the United States with captured Soviet air-to-ground and ground-to-air missiles and antitank weapons. Also furnished were Soviet 122- and 130-mm artillery pieces, along with ammunition for evaluation and testing. Additionally, extensive joint analyses conducted after the 1973 war produced eight 200- to 300-page volumes of intelligence. These analyses influenced subsequent developments in U.S. weapons tactics and military budgets.[54]

In early 1983 the Israeli government offered to share military intelligence gained during the war in Lebanon. The offer included details of an "Israeli invention" that was alleged by Prime Minister Menachem Begin to be the key to Israel's ability to destroy Syria's Soviet-made surface-to-air missiles during the war. However, Secretary of Defense Caspar Weinberger rejected a proposed agreement for sharing that information, feeling that it would have trapped the United States into undesirable long-range commitments to Israel. Administration officials argued that the information had already been learned through normal military contacts.[55]

As a condition for sharing the information, Israel insisted on sending Israeli experts to the United States with captured weapons for U.S. analysis, stipulating that the United States share the results of the analysis. Israel also insisted on the right to veto the transfer of information and analysis to third-party countries, including members of NATO, and on measures to ensure that sensitive data remained secret. According to diplomats, the Israelis expressed fears that Soviet intelligence agents who had penetrated Western European governments would find out what Israel had learned and would then pass that information along to the Soviet Union's Arab allies. Subsequently, an agreement was reached that continued the flow of information.[56]

In late 1983, as the situation in Lebanon deteriorated and Syrian intransigence continued, the United States conducted a reassessment of U.S. policy in the Middle East. This project resulted in the Top Secret National Security Decision Directive 111, "Next Steps Toward Progress in Lebanon and the Middle East." The directive reportedly specified a "tilt" toward Israel and expanded U.S.-Israeli strategic cooperation.[57]

The expanded cooperation reportedly involved greater sharing of reconnaissance satellite data, including data on Saudi Arabia and Jordan. William J. Casey, in his first three years as CIA Director (1981–1984), provided the Israelis with access to sensitive photographs and other reconnaissance information that they had been denied under the Carter administration. The head of AMAN from 1979 to 1983, Major General Yehoshua Saguy, said in early 1984 that the CIA was providing Israel with access to data from reconnaissance satellites, and "not only the information but the photos themselves." Under the Carter administration, DCI Stansfield Turner had refused to provide the satellite imagery that had been collected during George Bush's tenure as DCI in 1976 and 1977.[58]

After 1981, inside the Israeli intelligence community the satellite photos were often referred to as "Casey's gift," and they were considered invaluable. After Israel used some of the photos to aid in targeting the Osirak reactor, Deputy DCI Bobby Ray Inman restricted Israeli access to photographs of targets within 250 miles of the Israeli border.[59]

Another aspect of the expanded cooperation was reported to be greater Israeli access to the "take" of Cyprus-based SR-71 flights. The United States had been sharing such data with Israel, Egypt, and Syria on a "highly selective basis" as a result of an agreement signed in 1974 after the October War of 1973. The information previously transmitted to Israel primarily concerned Egyptian or Syrian military developments but was now to be expanded to cover a "broader range."[60]

Israel did not, however, receive everything it wanted. Among the items it did not receive were a dedicated satellite and a system of ground stations that would "directly access" the KH-11 as it passed over the Middle East.[61]

In return for intelligence from the United States, Israel has supplied the United States with intelligence on the Middle East—including both reports from agents and finished intelligence analyses. Some U.S. officials have not been impressed by the political intelligence, however. One CIA official said that he was "appalled at the lack of quality, of the political intelligence on the Arab world. ... Their tactical military intelligence was first rate. But they didn't know their enemy. I saw this political intelligence and it was lousy, laughably bad. ... It was gossip stuff mostly."[62]

The United States and Israel have also exchanged intelligence during crises situations. During the 1973 war, Israel received data obtained by the RHYOLITE satellite. In 1976 the United States supplied Israel with both aerial and satellite reconnaissance photographs of Entebbe airport to supplement the information obtained by Israeli agents in preparation for the Israeli hostage rescue mission. During the 1985 hijacking of the *Achille Lauro,* Israel provided the United States with the location of the ship on several occasions, the location of the ship's hijackers when they were in Egypt, and the identification number and call sign of the plane carrying the hijackers seconds after it took off from Egypt.[63]

The United States and Israel also exchanged intelligence during Operations Desert Shield and Desert Storm. Israel provided the United States with data on Iraqi air defenses, and the United States granted Israel increased access to U.S. satellite imagery. Once again, Israel pressed for establishment of a receiving station to allow real-time access.[64]

NORWAY

Intelligence cooperation between the United States and Norway dates back to the 1950s, when Norway served as the launching site for the GENETRIX reconnaissance balloons and as a base for U-2 operations.[65] By early 1963, Norway was the site of Project SOUTH SEA. SOUTH SEA was "an integrated technical collection system intended for operation in northern Norway to monitor Soviet submarine-launched missiles." The system consisted of electronic intelligence, infrared, and photographic equipment connected to a missile tracking system.[66]

The project was first approved in November 1961, and development continued throughout 1962. By February 1963 SOUTH SEA was undergoing testing and checkout.[67] It is not clear whether the system ever became fully operational or, if so, how long it continued in operation.

Norway not only provided a desirable location from which to monitor Soviet naval activities in the Barents Sea but was also well located to monitor the Soviet missile test and space launch center at Plesetsk as well as Soviet nuclear testing activities at Novaya Zemlaya and Semipalatinsk. The SIGINT stations are still in operation, monitoring Russian and other former member states of the Soviet Union. They are operated by Norwegian Military Intelligence but were erected by NSA and operated for them. Further, according to a former U.S. intelligence official, Victor Marchetti, CIA and NSA personnel were regularly on assignment at those stations in the 1960s. Although U.S. personnel are no longer assigned there, Norway does pass the information it acquires on to the United States.[68]

One of the stations is at Vadso, a small fjord town in Norway's Arctic region close to the former Soviet border. Somewhere between several hundred and 1,500 of the town's 5,000 residents are said to work at the intercept station. There are four interception locations at Vadso. The station conducts high-frequency (HF) listening primarily by means of an array of monopole antennas, within which is a further array of monopoles. The large array is 492 feet in diameter. About 2 miles to the southeast is a smaller circular antenna array with an outer ring that is 82 feet in diameter and consists of twelve dipoles. An inner ring consists of six dipoles, and there is a hut in the center of the array. The array's location apart from the main HF site suggests that it is used for transmission rather than reception. The location of the antenna arrays on the northern shore of Varangerfjord gives them uninterrupted overseas propagation paths all the way to the Soviet Union.[69]

In addition to the circular arrays, there are two VHF-UHF interception sites in the Vadso area. The main site is at the summit of a 397-foot hill. The site is the home of a variety of VHF-UHF antennas known as Yagis, log-periodic arrays (LPAs), vertical wire dipoles, and broadband dipoles. Four of the antennas are pointed in the direction of Murmansk and the associated complex of naval and air facilities—one toward Wickel; two to the coast; and one northeast, toward the Barents Sea. The antennas at the smaller site also point toward Russia. It has been reported that Vadso has the capability of intercepting voice communications from Russian pilots down to their ground controllers.[70]

Also in the very north of Norway are Viksjofell and Vardo. At Viksjofell, on a 1,476-foot-high hill only 3 miles from the former Soviet border, is a concrete tower with a geodesic radome. On the side of the tower facing toward the border is a semi-cylindrical extension apparently made of the same material as the radome and surmounted by a VHF log-periodic antenna. The dome itself is surmounted by a VHF Adcock direction-finding antenna. The Viksjofell facility appears to be a very sophisticated VHF installation, and it might be presumed that the dome contains a movable dish antenna that can be constantly rotated in either a scanning mode or a tracking mode. Installations of this type are capable of monitoring all VHF-SHF frequencies, including ground-based and air-based radars, communications, and missile command and control links.[71]

At Vardo there is a tower identical to the one at Viksjofell except that the external direction-finding and log-periodic antennas are absent. Vardo can intercept signals from Plesetsk. Another likely target in the past was telemetry from Soviet SLBM tests in the Barents Sea. The Soviet Union tested the SS-N-18 missile as well as the Typhoon-based SS-N-20 missile from the White Sea and the Barents Sea. The Viksjofell station apparently was established in 1972 and the Vardo one in 1971, at the same time that an earlier submarine-launched missile, the SS-N-8, became operational.[72]

At Skage (in Namdalen) and Randaberg (near Stavanger, on Norway's western coast), there are arrays similar to the smaller of the Vadso arrays. These arrays probably are used mainly to intercept HF communications from Russian ships, submarines, and long-range marine reconnaissance aircraft in the Norwegian Sea. The two stations are probably operated as pairwise units to allow triangulation of emitter locations.[73]

In addition to SIGINT operations, naval intelligence matters have long been a focus of U.S.-Norway cooperation. In 1973 such cooperation was designated CLUSTER SUN. At that time Norway was providing substantial amounts of intelligence on Soviet naval activities—for instance, Norway acquired and shared the first nonsatellite images and acoustic recordings of new Soviet Delta SSBN and Victor SSN submarines. That same year Norway also provided a Soviet BM-2 sonobuoy (designated CLUSTER SHELL II) and a second Soviet submarine-towed VLF antenna (designated CLUSTER CORAL II). The Naval Intelligence Command's Foreign Operations Division was also working to provide Norway with advanced intelligence collection equipment—the BEARTRAP sonobuoy system and a CLUSTER CARVE nuclear detection system.[74]

PEOPLE'S REPUBLIC OF CHINA

The PRC's intelligence relationship with the United States had its origins in the April 1970 visit to Beijing of National Security Adviser Henry Kissinger. Kissinger presented his hosts with communications intelligence and high-resolution satellite imagery concerning Soviet forces on China's border.[75]

In May 1978, Morton Abramowitz, Deputy Assistant Secretary of Defense for International Security Affairs, accompanied National Security Adviser Zbigniew Brzezinski to Beijing. In a meeting with a senior Chinese defense official, Abramowitz conducted a highly classified briefing on the deployment of Soviet forces along the Chinese border and pulled out of his briefcase satellite photographs of Soviet military installations and armor facing China. China continued to receive such photography. In 1984, a U.S. official stated that the Chinese reconnaissance satellite's footprint was "very small, and they want mapping support, especially of the Soviet Union" in addition to photographs of Soviet forces deployed along their border.[76]

The Abramowitz meeting led to the most important element of U.S.-PRC intelligence cooperation—the two SIGINT stations in western China, located at Qitai and Korla in the Xinjiang Uighur Autonomous Region. The United States initially suggested setting up such posts in 1978, prior to the establishment of diplomatic relations. At first, the Chinese, apparently concerned about cooperating too closely with the United States, were reluctant to agree. The issue was raised again after the overthrow of the Shah of Iran in January 1979. In an April 1979 meeting with a visiting U.S. Senate delegation, PRC Vice Premier Deng Xiaoping indicated that China was willing to use U.S. equipment "to monitor Soviet compliance with a proposed new arms limitation treaty." Deng also indicated that the monitoring stations would have to be run by the Chinese and that the data would have to be shared with the PRC.[77]

The United States and the PRC reached a basic agreement in January 1980 during a secret visit to Beijing by DCI Stansfield Turner. Actual collection operations began in the fall of 1980. The stations were constructed by the CIA's Office of SIGINT Operations, which sent personnel to train the Chinese technicians, and which still periodically sends advisers and service technicians as required.[78] The initial set of equipment allowed for the interception of telemetry from Soviet missile test and space shots conducted from two major Soviet launch sites—at Tyuratam near the Aral Sea and at Sary Shagan near Lake Balkash. Although they are somewhat farther from Tyuratam than the Iranian sites were, the Chinese sites are closer to the Sary Shagan ABM test site.

JAPAN

Japan has an extensive intelligence exchange relationship with the United States. One aspect of that relationship is the sharing of signals intelligence, as indicated by the Japanese sharing of Soviet communications intercepted by a unit on Wakkania on the night the Soviets shot down Korean Air Lines Flight 007. The United States maintains SIGINT facilities on Japanese territory and in return shares SIGINT information of mutual interest.[79] The Japan-U.S. SIGINT relationship is a formal one, with Japan being one of ten Third Parties to the UKUSA Agreement.

Japan has also received satellite photographs from U.S. authorities. In 1982, Secretary of Defense Caspar Weinberger presented the chief of the Japanese Defense Agency with satellite photographs "showing a Japanese-made floating dock being used in the repair of the Soviet aircraft carrier *Minsk*."[80] That revelation was made to convince the Japanese that technology made available to the Soviets for nonmilitary purposes was being misused.

In addition, it is likely that the Japanese Defense Agency receives, on a regular basis, satellite photographs or at least satellite photograph–derived information. Such information would concern naval movements in the vicinity of Japan as well as North Korean military and nuclear research activity.

A substantial amount of U.S.-Japanese intelligence cooperation has focused on SIGINT concerning naval activities. In 1972 the U.S. Naval Intelligence Command began discussions with the CIA, the NSA, and the DIA that led to the expansion of SIGINT exchange with the Japanese Maritime Self-Defense Forces (JMSDF) regarding Soviet and Chinese naval activities. In addition, under the terms of Project COMET, Japan provided the United States with foreign materiel recovered from the Sea of Japan.[81]

One vehicle for such cooperation is the CINCPACFLT-JMSDF (U.S. Commander-in-Chief Pacific Fleet–Japanese Maritime Self-Defense Forces) Intelligence Exchange Conference. Likewise, the Intelligence Liaison and Production Section of the Intelligence Division, U.S. Naval Forces, Japan, is responsible for coordinating the Commander-in-Chief, U.S. Pacific Fleet, and Commander, U.S. Naval Forces, Japan intelligence exchange, with the Chief of the Intelligence Division, Maritime Staff Office, and the Intelligence Officer, CINCSDFLT (Commander-in-Chief Self Defense Fleet).[82]

Information derived from U.S. worldwide ocean surveillance assets—especially from ocean surveillance satellites and the SOSUS network—can substantially increase the effectiveness of Japan's surface ship and submarine detection efforts. Information likely to be passed on to Japan includes much of that coming into the fleet ocean surveillance information center at Kamiseya, Japan. At the same time, the Japanese share information obtained by their sonar arrays and P-3Cs.

RUSSIA

Even before the collapse of the Soviet Union the subject of intelligence cooperation between Gorbachev's KGB and the U.S. intelligence community was raised by Soviet and U.S. intelligence officials. Such discussions apparently resulted, by late 1988, in an agreement that both nations would exchange intelligence on narcotics shipments headed for each other's territory as well as information on the methods used by traffickers to conceal illicit drugs.[83]

The next year, DCI William Webster announced that the U.S. and Soviet governments had discussed exchanging information concerning international terrorism. In 1990, following the Iraqi invasion of Kuwait, the Soviet Union began to provide the United States with data about Iraqi weapons capabilities, Iraqi air defenses, and Iraqi communications networks. The Soviets may also have provided information on Iraqi military officials.[84] Later that year, in October, the acting DCI, Richard Kerr, noted that the CIA was "quite willing to talk and discuss with the KGB those areas where we have a common interest, whether they are terrorism or narcotics or issues of proliferation."[85]

In October 1992, DCI Robert Gates journeyed to Moscow to discuss intelligence sharing. In addition to meeting with President Yeltsin, Gates met Yevgeniy Primakov and General Fyodor Ladygin—the heads of the Foreign Intelligence Service (SVR) and the Chief Intelligence Directorate of the General Staff (GRU), respectively. Intelligence sharing was probably discussed with respect to terrorism, narcotics, Islamic fundamentalism, and proliferation of ballistic missiles and weapons of mass destruction.[86] Gates may have also met with officials of the Ministry of Security. Even before his trip, agreements had been reached with that organization to share certain intelligence information.[87]

The U.S. Embassy noted of the visit that "the possibility of contact and joint activity between the Russian and American intelligence services was discussed." During the visit, SVR chief Primakov observed, "The exchange of intelligence is crucial. If an intelligence service has information about terrorist acts planned against the citizens of other countries, it must give its partners this information. We will do this."[88]

The discussions may have produced specific agreements for intelligence sharing, possibly formalizing already existing exchanges on subjects such as the advanced weaponry of former Soviet client states. Further discussions concerning sharing information on terrorism, proliferation, and drug trafficking took place during DCI James Woolsey's August 1993 visit to Moscow.[89]

Moreover, the United States has been reported to have established intelligence-sharing arrangements with several former Soviet republics, including Lithuania, Latvia, and Kazakhstan.[90]

THE UNITED NATIONS AND THE INTERNATIONAL ATOMIC ENERGY AUTHORITY

Inasmuch as the United Nations has no organic intelligence capability, any U.S. intelligence exchange relationship must be one-sided. But, in recent years, the United States has found it desirable to provide information to U.N. bodies for at least two purposes.

The United States has shown satellite imagery to the U.N. Security Council as evidence of Iraqi violations of the cease-fire agreement. At a private briefing on June 26, 1991, U.S. intelligence officials showed the council's members satellite images of uranium-enrichment machinery being moved around on trucks or being buried to avoid detection by U.N. inspectors.[91]

The photographs showed uncrated calutrons, which are used in electromagnetic isotope separation, being moved onto trucks just before U.N. inspectors arrived at the sites. The satellite images also showed that sometimes the Iraqis buried equipment at the sites. When they were dug up, the holes would be filled with fresh earth so there would be no radioactive traces left in the soil.[92]

More important, U.S. intelligence, including imagery as well as SIGINT, has been used to guide the movements of U.N. inspectors. Thus, the inspectors' trip that ended in standoff in September 1991, as well as other trips, was guided largely by tips from U.S. intelligence. David A. Kay, who headed the U.N. inspection effort, told the Senate Foreign Relations Committee that "without that data, we would not have been able to operate" against Iraqi deception efforts. He also observed that "the lesson of Iraq, where you combine that information-gathering capacity at the national level with an international inspectorate, is one that I find encouraging."[93]

In November 1993 a team of inspectors from the International Atomic Energy Authority (IAEA) conducted an examination of previously unchecked buildings at Iranian nuclear sites, looking for evidence of a clandestine nuclear weapons program. The targets of the unannounced inspection included sites that the U.S. intelligence community suspected might be involved in nuclear-related work. The buildings are isolated, camouflaged, and surrounded by tall wire fencing and tight security.[94]

NOTES

1. Declaration of the Secretary of Defense, *United States of America v Jonathan Jay Pollard*, defendant, United States District Court for the District of Columbia, Criminal No. 86-, p. 22.

2. American Embassy, Mexico, to State Department, Subject: Weekly Narcotics Roundup: August 13–17, August 22, 1990, p. 1.

3. On the British-U.S. World War II SIGINT alliance, see Bradley F. Smith, *The Ultra-Magic Deals* (Novato, Calif.: Presidio, 1993). On Canadian participation, see John Bryden, *Best Kept Secret: Canadian Secret Intelligence in the Second World War* (Toronto: Lester, 1993). On Australian–New Zealand involvement, see Jeffrey T. Richelson and Desmond Ball, *The Ties That Bind: Intelligence Cooperation Among the UKUSA Countries* (Boston: Allen & Unwin, 1985), pp. 3–4.

4. Ronald Clark, *The Man Who Broke Purple* (Boston: Little, Brown, 1977), p. 208.

5. Desmond Ball, "Allied Intelligence Cooperation Involving Australia During World War II," *Australian Outlook* 32, 4 (1978): 299–309; Duncan Campbell, "The Threat of the

Electronic Spies," *New Statesman*, February 2, 1979, pp. 140–44; John Sawatsky, *Men in the Shadows: The RCMP Security Service* (New York: Doubleday, 1980), p. 9n; Transcript of "The Fifth Estate—The Espionage Establishment," broadcast by the Canadian Broadcasting Company, 1974.

6. Private information; Seymour Hersh, *"The Target Is Destroyed": What Really Happened to Flight 007 and What America Knew About It* (New York: Random House, 1986), p. 48n.

7. Chapman Pincher, *Inside Story: A Documentary of the Pursuit of Power* (New York: Stein & Day, 1979), p. 157; Sawatsky, *Men in the Shadows*, p. 9n.

8. Desmond Ball, *A Suitable Piece of Real Estate: American Installations in Australia* (Sydney: Hale & Iremonger, 1980), p. 40.

9. Campbell, "Threat of the Electronic Spies."

10. See Richelson and Ball, *The Ties That Bind*, pp. 148–49.

11. Paul Kelly, "NSA, the Biggest Secret Spy Network in Australia," *The National Times*, May 23–28, 1977.

12. Letter, Eugene Y. Yeates, Director of Policy, National Security Agency, to the author, December 7, 1982.

13. Desmond Ball, "The U.S. Naval Ocean Surveillance Information System (NOSIS)—Australia's Role," *Pacific Defence Reporter*, June 1982, pp. 40–49; Michael Richardson, "Australia and NZ Use Singapore Base to Spy on Soviet Ships for CIA," *The Age*, April 12, 1984, p. 1.

14. Ball, "The U.S. Naval Ocean Surveillance Information System."

15. Ibid.

16. "Britania Scorns to Yield," *Newsweek*, April 19, 1982, pp. 41–46.

17. Centre for Peace Studies, The University of Auckland, "New Zealand's International Military Connections: Agreements and Arrangements," 1986.

18. Joint Intelligence Organization, *Fourth Annual Report, 1974* (Canberra: JIO, 1974), pp. F1–F2.

19. Ibid., pp. 36, F1–F2.

20. Ibid., p. F2.

21. Navy Field Operational Intelligence Office, *Command History for CY 1981*, April 15, 1982, p. 5; Assistant Chief of Staff for Intelligence, Air Force, *History of the Assistant Chief of Staff, Intelligence Hq., United States Air Force, 1 July 1974–31 December 1974*, n.d., p. 9.

22. Department of the Army, Office of the Assistant Chief of Staff for Intelligence, *Annual Historical Review, 1 October 1985–30 September 1986*, n.d., p. 4-5.

23. Armed Forces Medical Intelligence Center, *Organization and Functions of the Armed Forces Medical Intelligence Center* (Ft. Detrick, Md.: AFMIC, April 1986), p. vii.

24. Tom Mangold, *Cold Warrior, James Jesus Angleton: The CIA's Master Spy Hunter* (New York: Simon & Schuster, 1991), p. 292.

25. "Impact of the ANZUS Rift," portion of Government of New Zealand document, c. 1985.

26. New Zealand Ministry of Defense, Answer to a Parliamentary Question.

27. Kevin O'Connor, "Defence Heads Shy from PM Clashes," *Dominion*, October 8, 1986.

28. Ibid.

29. New Zealand, Cabinet External Relations and Security Committee, "1985 Preliminary Defence Review," March 26, 1985, p. 7.

30. "USA Relaxes Ban on Intelligence," *Jane's Defence Weekly*, January 26, 1991, p. 110; Colin James, "Bolger's Balm," *Far Eastern Economic Review*, March 28, 1991, p. 18.

31. Christine A. Kohn, "Patching Up a Strained Relationship," *National Journal*, August 6, 1994, p. 1861.

32. Justice Hope, *The Fifth Report of the Royal Commission on Intelligence and Security* (Canberra: Australian Government Printer, 1977), Appendix 5-E, para. 19.

33. Ibid., n5-38.

34. Ibid., para. 142–144.

35. Ibid., para. 143.

36. Ibid., para. 179–180.

37. Ibid., para. 181.

38. Ibid., para. 184. Some of the intelligence collected may have been of use to the Pinochet dictatorship, if it was provided. See Brian Toohey and William Pinwill, *Oyster: The Story of the Australian Secret Intelligence Service* (Port Melbourne, Victoria: William Heinemann Australia, 1989), pp. 142–43.

39. Hope, *The Fifth Report of the Royal Commission on Intelligence and Security*, para. 236, 239; Appendix 5-E, para. 21.

40. Toohey and Pinwill, *Oyster*, pp. 256–57.

41. Canadian–U.S. Joint Intelligence Committee, *Soviet Capabilities and Probable Course of Action Against North America in a Major War Commencing During the Period 1 January 1958 to 31 December 1958* (Washington, D.C.: CIA, March 1, 1957), *Declassified Documents Reference System (DDRS)* 1981-169A; U.S. Congress, Senate Committee on Armed Services, *Department of Defense Authorization for Appropriations for Fiscal Year 1984, Part 5* (Washington, D.C.: U.S. Government Printing Office, 1983), p. 2708.

42. *Canada–U.S. Arrangements in Regard to Defence, Defence Production, Defence Sharing* (Washington, D.C.: Institute for Policy Studies, 1985), p. 31.

43. Walter Agee, Acting Deputy Director of Intelligence, "Memorandum for the Coordinator of Joint Operations: Proposed U.S.–Canadian Agreement," Modern Military Branch, National Archives, RG 341, Entry 214, File Nos. 2-1900 through 2-1999.

44. Joint Chiefs of Staff, *Canadian–United States Communications Instructions for Reporting Vital Intelligence Sightings (CERVIS/MERINT)* (Washington, D.C.: JCS, March 1966), p. 2-1.

45. Ibid., pp. 2-4 to 2-6.

46. Ibid., p. 3-1.

47. Duncan Campbell and Clive Thomas, "BBC's Trade Secrets," *New Statesman*, July 4, 1980, pp. 13–14.

48. Ibid., p. 14.

49. Ibid., pp. 13–14.

50. Andrew Cockburn and Leslie Cockburn, *Dangerous Liaison: The Inside Story of the U.S.-Israeli Covert Relationship* (New York: HarperCollins, 1991), p. 41.

51. Judith Perera, "Cracks in the Special Relationship," *The Middle East* (March 1983): 12–18.

52. Cockburn and Cockburn, *Dangerous Liaison*, p. 187.

53. Ibid.

54. Richard Halloran, "U.S. Offers Israel Plan on War Data," *New York Times,* March 13, 1983, pp. 1, 13.

55. Edmund Walsh, "Begin Offers to Give War Intelligence to U.S." *Washington Post,* October 15, 1982, p. A18; Richard Halloran, "U.S. Said to Bar Deal with Israel," *New York Times,* February 10, 1983, pp. A1, A7.

56. Halloran, "U.S. Said to Bar Deal with Israel"; Bernard Gwertzman, "Israelis to Share Lessons of War with Pentagon," *New York Times,* March 22, 1983, pp. 1, 12.

57. National Security Decision Directive 111, "Next Steps Toward Progress in Lebanon and the Middle East," October 28, 1983. The directive has been released in heavily sanitized form. The tilt toward Israel is reported in Bernard Gwertzman, "Reagan Turns to Israel," *New York Times Magazine,* November 27, 1983, pp. 62ff.

58. Bob Woodward, "CIA Sought 3rd Country Contra Aid," *Washington Post,* May 19, 1984, pp. A1, A13.

59. "Statement of Bobby Ray Inman on Withdrawing His Nomination," *New York Times,* January 19, 1994, p. A14.

60. "U.S. to Share More Recon Data, Tighten Air Links with Israel," *Aerospace Daily,* December 8, 1983, pp. 193–94.

61. Ibid.

62. Charles Babcock, "Israel Uses Special Relationship to Get Secrets," *Washington Post,* June 15, 1986, p. A1.

63. "How the Israelis Pulled It Off," *Newsweek,* July 19, 1976, pp. 42–47; David Halevy and Neil C. Livingstone, "The Ollie We Knew," *The Washingtonian,* July 1987, pp. 77ff.

64. Theodore Stanger, "The Israelis: A Not Very Hidden Agenda," *Newsweek,* September 10, 1990, p. 20; Gerald F. Seib and Bob Davis, "Fighting Flares Again at Saudi Town; Allied Planes Attack Big Iraqi Column," *Wall Street Journal,* February 1, 1991, p. A12; Martin Sieff, "Israelis Press U.S. for Direct Access to Intelligence Data," *Washington Times,* November 28, 1992, p. A7.

65. Curtis Peebles, *The Moby Dick Project: Reconnaissance Balloons over Russia* (Washington, D.C.: Smithsonian, 1991), p. 169; Rolf Tamnes, *The United States and the Cold War in the High North* (Oslo: Ad Notam, 1991), pp. 126–27.

66. Assistant Chief of Staff for Intelligence, *History: Directorate of Collection Office, ACS, Intelligence, 1 January–30 June 1963,* n.d., p. 2.

67. Ibid.

68. F. G. Samia, "The Norwegian Connection: Norway (Un)willing Spy for the U.S.," *Covert Action Information Bulletin,* June 1980, pp. 4–9.

69. Ibid.; R. W. Apple, Jr., "Norwegians, Ardent Neutralists, Also Want Their Defense Strong," *New York Times,* August 5, 1978, p. 2; Owen Wilkes and Nils Petter Gleditsch, *Intelligence Installations in Norway: Their Number, Location, Function and Legality* (Oslo, Norway: Peace Research Institute Oslo, 1979), pp. 17–20.

70. Wilkes and Gleditsch, *Intelligence Installations in Norway,* pp. 24–26; Hersh, *"The Target Is Destroyed,"* p. 4.

71. Wilkes and Gleditsch, *Intelligence Installations in Norway,* p. 32.

72. Ibid., p. 35; Hersh, *"The Target Is Destroyed,"* p. 42.

73. Wilkes and Gleditsch, *Intelligence Installations in Norway,* p. 20.

74. Naval Intelligence Command, *Command History for CY-1973,* April 29, 1974, pp. 48–49.

75. John Newhouse, *War and Peace in the Nuclear Age* (New York: Knopf, 1989), p. 224.

76. Nayan Chandra, *Brother Enemy: The War After War* (New York: Harcourt, Brace, Jovanovich, 1983), p. 280; "Washington Round-Up," *Aviation Week & Space Technology,* March 19, 1984, p. 15; Daniel Southerland, "U.S. Navy Call at Chinese Port Symbolizes Growing Military Relationship," *Washington Post,* November 5, 1986, pp. A23, A29.

77. Philip Taubman, "U.S. and Peking Jointly Monitor Russian Missiles," *New York Times,* June 18, 1971, pp. 1, 14; Murrey Marder, "Monitoring Not So-Secret-Secret," *Washington Post,* June 19, 1981, p. 10.

78. Robert C. Toth, "U.S., China Jointly Track Firings of Soviet Missiles," *Los Angeles Times,* June 18, 1981, pp. 1, 9; David Bonavia, "Radar Post Leak May Be Warning to Soviet Union," *London Times,* June 19, 1981, p. 5; Taubman, "U.S. and Peking Jointly Monitor Russian Missiles"; George Lardner, Jr., and R. Jeffrey Smith, "Intelligence Ties Endure Despite U.S.-China Strain," *Washington Post,* June 25, 1989, pp. A1, A24.

79. Hersh, *"The Target Is Destroyed,"* pp. 63–72.

80. "U.S. Warns Japan Not to Increase Soviet Military Power," Xinhau General Overseas News Service, March 30, 1982.

81. Naval Intelligence Command, *Naval Intelligence Command (NAVINTCOM) History for CY-1972,* August 1, 1973, p. 35; Naval Intelligence Command, *Naval Intelligence Command History for CY-1973,* p. 48.

82. U.S. Naval Forces Japan, COMNAVFORJAPAN Staff Instruction 5450.1G, *Staff Organization Manual,* May 13, 1983, p. V-5.

83. "Glasnost for Drugs," *U.S. News and World Report,* November 28, 1988, p. 18.

84. Bill Gertz, "Joint CIA-KGB Targeting of Terrorism Talked About," *Washington Times,* April 7, 1989, p. A4; Tim Weiner and Mark Thompson, "Soviets Give U.S. Significant Intelligence Help," *Philadelphia Inquirer,* January 26, 1991, pp. 1A, 6A.

85. Gerald F. Sieb, "CIA's Acting Chief Says U.S. Is Ready to Cooperate with Soviet Spy Agency," *Wall Street Journal,* October 4, 1991, p. A4.

86. Margaret Shapiro, "Ex-KGB, CIA Talk of Sharing," *Washington Post,* October 19, 1992, pp. A14, A22; Bill Gertz, "Gates Plans Moscow Talks on CIA-KGB Cooperation," *Washington Times,* September 10, 1992, p. A9.

87. Private information.

88. Shapiro, "Ex-KGB, CIA Talk of Sharing"; Janet Guttsman, "CIA Director Seeks Russia's Assistance on Terrorism, Drugs," *Washington Times,* October 19, 1992, p. A8.

89. "CIA Takes on a Client," *Los Angeles Times,* August 12, 1993, p. A10.

90. Paul Quinn-Judge, "CIA Buys Ex-Soviet Arms, US Aide Says," *Boston Globe,* November 15, 1992, pp. 1, 14.

91. Paul Lewis, "U.S. Shows Photos to Argue Iraqi Hides Nuclear Material," *New York Times,* June 27, 1991, p. A12.

92. Ibid.

93. Melissa Healy, "U.N. Sleuth Credits Allied Data on Iraq," *Los Angeles Times,* October 18, 1991, p. A12.

94. Steve Coll, "Nuclear Inspectors Check Sites in Iran," *Washington Post,* November 20, 1993, pp. A13, A16.

13
PRODUCTION

The immediate rationale for the vast effort the United States makes to collect information is the production of finished intelligence. That finished intelligence is used by a variety of government officials at different levels. Finished intelligence comes in a variety of forms, some of which overlap.

The categories of national intelligence produced for the use of national decisionmakers include current intelligence, estimates, analysis, and other reports. Current intelligence focuses on a situation of immediate concern. Estimates both summarize a present state of affairs and project those affairs into the future. Some reports analyze a political, military, or economic situation, and other reports may be concerned solely with summarizing a particular situation.

This chapter examines the intelligence product of the intelligence community as a whole (i.e., national intelligence) as well as of a variety of significant analytical units—the Central Intelligence Agency, the Defense Intelligence Agency, the Bureau of Intelligence and Research, the Drug Enforcement Administration, the military service intelligence units, and selected unified commands.

NATIONAL INTELLIGENCE

National intelligence produced by the U.S. intelligence community comes in the form of several types of publications. These include the *President's Daily Brief,* the *National Intelligence Daily,* the *National Intelligence Situation Report,* National Intelligence Estimates, Special National Intelligence Estimates, Interagency Intelligence Memoranda, Special Interagency Intelligence Memoranda, National Intelligence Analytical Memoranda, and at least seven other products.

The *President's Daily Brief* (*PDB*) is delivered to the President six days a week. This brief, which used to have a print run of under ten but now has a daily run of thirty-two, contains information from the most sensitive U.S. sources. Designed to be read in ten to fifteen minutes at the beginning of the day, it provides whatever significant information has been acquired during the previous day and commentary as to its significance.[1] According to Cord Meyer, a former CIA official, in the hands of the CIA Director the *PDB* "is a powerful tool for focusing the attention of the President on potential crisis areas and for alerting him to situations that may require rapid policy adjustment. Occasionally, when fresh intelligence sheds new light on a complex problem an annex is attached to the PDB to give the President more extensive background for the decisions he has to make."[2]

The size and structure of the *PDB* may change from President to President. Under Gerald Ford the brief was rather lengthy, but it was reduced to a maximum of about fifteen pages under Jimmy Carter, although DCI Stansfield Turner occasionally appended longer "trend pieces" at the end. Carter would often write in the margins of the *PDB* to request more information.[3]

The second daily national current intelligence publication is the *National Intelligence Daily (NID)*. The *NID* was the idea of former CIA Director William Colby, who had repeatedly recommended during the mid-1960s that the CIA's daily intelligence report, then known as the *National Intelligence Digest*, be issued in newspaper format to emphasize the more important items and to offer its readers a choice between a headline summary and in-depth reports. Colby's interest was sufficient to lead him to join, on every evening possible, the editorial conference that determined subjects to be carried in the next day's edition. Subsequently, the newspaper format was judged to be too inflexible and the publication reverted to a magazine format.[4]

The *NID* is somewhat longer than the *PDB* and serves a larger audience—several hundred top-level foreign policy officials in Washington plus a limited number of U.S. Ambassadors and CIA Station Chiefs. A total of 900 copies of the *NID* are printed each day. For security reasons, it does not contain some of the more sensitive items contained in the *PDB*.[5]

Despite deletion of such items, the *NID* may be classified TOP SECRET RUFF UMBRA, indicating the presence of intelligence derived from satellite photography as well as signals intelligence. The issue of November 12, 1975, for example, contained the following front-page headlines: "Motion to Impeach President Gaining Support in Argentina," "Disorders Seen in Aftermath of Whitlam Firing," "Military Leader Warns Turkey on Violence," "Morocco, Spain Discuss Sahara," and "Israel Is Exaggerating Gravity of Deteriorating Trade Situation."[6] The article on the Whitlam firing stated, "Australia may be entering a period of unprecedented disorder in the wake of Governor General Kerr's sacking of former Prime Minister Whitlam. Inflammatory remarks by Whitlam could turn scattered demonstrations and work stoppages supporting him to a nationwide general strike, despite calls for restraint by some trade union leaders."[7]

A more recent *NID*, that of May 9, 1985, contained a review of Libya on the first anniversary of the May 8, 1984, attempted coup, in which Qaddafi's barracks had been attacked. According to the *NID*, Libyan dissident and exile groups led by the National Front for the Salvation of Libya were planning to blow up a military installation in Libya to demonstrate their ability to attack Qaddafi on Libyan soil.[8]

The *Midday Intelligence Report* is a collection of brief current intelligence items prepared for early-afternoon delivery to a very limited number of key officials. Coordinated only within the CIA, it updates and supplements the *NID* with "quick-reaction analytical judgements on new developments."[9]

The best-known national intelligence products are the National Intelligence Estimates (NIEs) and Special National Intelligence Estimates (SNIEs). As their names imply, these documents attempt to project existing military, political, and economic trends into the future and to estimate for policymakers the likely implications of these trends. According to the House Committee on Foreign Affairs, an NIE is "a thorough assessment of a situation in the foreign environment which is relevant to the formulation of foreign, economic, and national security policy, and which projects probable future courses of action and developments."[10]

Many NIEs have been issued on an annual or biannual basis, particularly, in the past, those that concerned the Soviet Union. Others—for example, *The Prospects for Burma*—are issued less frequently. As of the mid-1970s, the NIE-11 series, which concerned the Soviet Union, consisted of twelve estimates—including ones on Soviet general purpose forces, military R&D, the economy, political-military operations outside the Soviet Union and the Warsaw Pact, Soviet space programs, and Soviet foreign policy.[11]

The single most important Soviet estimate was the yearly NIE 11-3/8. The most recent partially declassified version is the 1982 *Soviet Capabilities for Strategic Nuclear Conflict, 1982–1992*. The estimate consisted of three volumes. Volume 1 contained "key judgements about and a summary of Soviet programs and capabilities believed to be of greatest interest to policymakers and defense planners." The forty-one pages included chapters on recent developments, Soviet strategic policies and doctrine, future strategic forces and programs, operations of Soviet strategic forces in conflict, trends in Soviet capabilities to perform strategic missions, and concluding observations.[12] Volume 2 contained more detailed discussions of the topics covered in Volume 1, and Volume 3 contained annexes and detailed force projections and weapons characteristics.[13]

Other Soviet NIEs over the past decade have included 11-1 (*Space Operations*), 11-3/8-89 (*Soviet Forces and Capabilities for Strategic Nuclear Conflict Through the 1990s*), 11-4-82 (*The Soviet Challenge to US Security Interests*), 11-7-89 (*Soviet Aerodynamic Counterstealth and Stealth Capabilities*), 11-10 (*Soviet Policy in the Third World*), 11-11 (*Intelligence Denial and Deception in Soviet Strategic Military Programs: Implications for U.S. Security*), 11-13-82 (*Soviet Ballistic Missile Defense*), 11-15 (*Soviet Naval Strategy*), 11-17 (*Chemical Warfare*), 11-18-85 (*Domestic Stresses on the Soviet System*), 11-18-89 (*The Soviet System in Crisis: Prospects for the Next Two Years*), 11-30-86 (*Gorbachev's Policy Toward the Middle East*), and 11-34-89 (*Trends and Developments in Warsaw Pact Theater and Forces Doctrine Through the 1990s*).[14]

In late December 1991, in the aftermath of the failed coup in the Soviet Union, the intelligence community was commissioned to produce at least ten new NIEs concerning subjects in the Soviet Union such as food, fuel, the consumer distribution system, economic stagnation and the potential for civil disorder, ethnic strife, military conditions, control over nuclear weapons and technology, and nuclear forces.[15]

Table 13-1.   Special National Intelligence Estimates, 1982.

SNIE	Title
2-20-82	The Peace Movement in Western Europe
3/11-82	Western Alternatives to Soviet Natural Gas: Prospects and Implications
11/30-82	Soviet Short-Term Options in South Asia
11/50/37-82	Use of Toxins and Other Lethal Chemicals in Southeast Asia and Afghanistan
11/80/90-92	Soviet Policies in Latin America and the Caribbean
12/6-82	Poland's Prospects over the Next 12 to 18 Months
21/91-82	The Falklands Crisis
31-82	India: Trends in Domestic and International Politics
32-82	Pakistan—The Next Year
34/36.2-82	Implications of Iran's Victory over Iraq
36.1-82	Egypt: Prospects for Domestic Stability
36.1-2-82	Prospects for US-Egyptian Relations
36.4-82	Lebanon, Prospects for Hostilities
N.A.	Likelihood of Attempted Acquisition of Nuclear Weapons or Materials by Foreign Terrorist Groups
36.11-82	PLO Dispersal: Regional Impact and Implications
41-82	Japan's View of the US Relationship
55-82	Indonesia: Prospects into the Mid-1980s
57-82	Conflict in Kampuchea: Prospects for the Resistance and Selected Implications for the US
78-82	The Outlook for Sudan
81-82	Implications of Mexico's Financial Crisis
82/83-82	Short-Term Prospects for Central America
90/91-3-82	Implications of the Falklands Conflict for Territorial Disputes in Latin America

Source: Department of the Army, Office of the Assistant Chief of Staff for Intelligence, *Annual Historical Review, 1 October 1981–30 September 1982,* n.d., pp. 4-8 to 4-9.

There are of course a large number of NIEs that were prepared each year on non-Soviet topics. NIEs from 1982, for example, included 13-10-82 (*Political Succession in China*), 30-82 (*Key Military Issues in the Middle East*), 56-82 (*The Philippines Under Marcos: His Prospective Legacy and US Interests*), and 4-82 (*Nuclear Proliferation Trends Through 1987*).[16]

Subsequent non-Soviet/Russian NIEs have included *Nicaragua: Prospects for Sandinista Consolidation* (February 1985), *Nicaragua: Prospects for the Insurgency* (March 1986), *State-Sponsored Terrorism, Terrorist Use of Chemical and Biological Warfare, The International Narcotics Trade: Implications for U.S. Security* (November 1985), and *The Global Energy Environment into the Next Century* (1990).[17]

In addition to the regularly scheduled NIEs, the President and members of the National Security Council may call for production of SNIEs when some unforeseen development occurs. As with NIEs, in any one year there may be a large, diverse number of SNIEs produced. SNIEs produced in 1982 covered the Soviet Union, Eastern Europe, the Middle East, the Falklands, Asia, and Latin America. Table 13-1 lists some of the 1982 SNIEs.

More recent SNIEs include the 1983 SNIE on *Implications of Soviet Use of Chemical and Toxin Weapons for U.S. Security Interests,* SNIE 34-84 on *Iran: The Post Khomeini Era,* the 1985 SNIEs titled *Libya's Qaddafi: The Challenge to the United States and Western Interests,* and *Iran: Prospects for Near Term Instability,* and SNIE 36-2-90 on *Iraq's Saddam Husayn.*[18]

An Interagency Intelligence Memorandum (IIM), is coordinated like an NIE, but is more detailed and generally more descriptive. The IIM was promoted while James Schlesinger was DCI to deal in-depth with highly technical issues, such as Soviet civil defense and defense spending. IIMs from 1981 and 1982 included "INF Support: Theater Nuclear Forces" (December 1981), "SALT Support: European Theater Nuclear Forces" (March 1981), "Prospects for Anti-US Terrorism" (1981), "Deng Xiaoping and the FX Aircraft Issue" (1981), "Zimbabwe: Trends and Prospects" (1982), and "Prospects for Iran" (1982). IIMs from 1989 include "On Site Inspection—Intelligence Gains and Issues" and "The Outlook for Terrorism in Western Europe."[19]

Special Interagency Intelligence Memoranda are short estimates that are "produced very quickly when a more detailed or leisurely study is inappropriate."[20]

A fifth type of noncurrent national intelligence product is the National Intelligence Analytical Memorandum (NIAM). One NIAM, 11-20-1-75, considered "Soviet Policy Toward Selected Countries of Southern Europe."[21] NIAMs include more detailed analyses of political, military, or economic situations than are possible with the other formats.

The importance and frequency of the NIEs and other national intelligence products have varied from administration to administration. In 1961 there were more than twenty-five NIEs issued. The yearly total rose to fifty in the late 1960s before falling to eleven or twelve a year during the final years of the Carter administration. The decline was largely due to CIA Director Stansfield Turner's view that "national intelligence estimates are [not] a very efficient way of preparing finished intelligence." Under the Reagan administration and then CIA Director William Casey, the number of NIEs rose to thirty-eight in 1981 and sixty in 1982.[22]

However, the 1989 Office of Naval Intelligence history indicates the existence of two products that some officials considered more useful than NIEs and SNIEs. According to the history, "The less formal, more quickly coordinated Executive Briefs and Sense of the Community Memoranda have in many cases replaced the more lengthy NIEs and SNIEs, particularly for fast-breaking issues where timeliness and policy-relevance are paramount."[23]

Additional national intelligence products include the NIE President's Summary, the NIE Update Memorandum, the Intelligence Community Assessment, the National Intelligence Council Memorandum, the Warning Memorandum, the Warning Committee Report, the Regional Forecast Memorandum, and the Monthly Global Warning Report.[24]

An NIE President's Summary is a shorter version of an NIE, usually three to four pages long, that is distributed only to the President, members of the Cabinet, and other top U.S. policymakers. An NIE Update Memorandum is a three- to four-page-long follow-up to an NIE that presents new information. It is coordinated within the intelligence community but does not require approval by the DCI or the National Foreign Intelligence Board (NFIB). An Intelligence Community Assessment addresses important subjects but not ones requiring presidential attention. It also does not require approval by the NFIB.[25]

A National Intelligence Council Memorandum is a three- to four-page-long memorandum issued by the NIC and coordinated within the intelligence community. It does not require DCI or NFIB approval. A Warning Memorandum is published weekly and is eight to ten pages long. Prepared for senior U.S. policymakers, it concerns a possible crisis situation and requires DCI and NFIB approval. The three- to four-page Regional Forecast Memorandum is published every month or two. It is coordinated within the intelligence community but does not require DCI or NFIB approval. The Monthly Global Warning Report, also three to four pages in length, focuses on critical hotspots throughout the world. It requires neither coordination nor approval.[26]

CENTRAL INTELLIGENCE AGENCY

In addition to providing much of the analytical capability for the production of national intelligence products, the CIA also produces a wide variety of studies on political, economic, social, and military matters.

The primary focus of CIA analyses and reports for many years was, of course, the Soviet Union. It was particularly with regard to the Soviet Union that CIA reports touched all aspects of a nation's activities. CIA reports on the Soviet Union show particular concern about both civilian and military decisionmaking. Thus, the CIA's Directorate of Intelligence produced codeword-level reports entitled *The Soviet Defense Council and Military Policy Making* (April 1972), *The Soviet Decision Making Process for the Selection of Weapons Systems* (June 1973), and *The Politburo and Soviet Decisionmaking* (April 1972).

The CIA was also concerned with the key individuals in the Soviet Union who made and implemented decisions as well as with many lesser individuals. Thus, the April 1977 *Biographic Handbook, USSR, Supplement IV*, included profiles on twenty-one officials, including the Chief Editor of *Pravda*, the Chairman of the State Committee for Prices, the Minister of Construction, and the Chairman of the Board for the State Bank. The biography of Eduard Shevardnadze, then a Georgia party official and later Foreign Minister, is shown as Figure 13-1. With regard to Soviet military activities, one area of CIA concern was the amount of money spent on defense. This concern resulted in *Soviet and US Defense Activities: A Dollar Cost Comparison, 1971–80* (1980), *Estimated Soviet Defense Spending*

Figure 13-1. Biography of Eduard Shevardnadze.

USSR **Eduard Amvrosiyevich SHEVARDNADZE**
First Secretary, Central Committee, Communist Party of Georgia

One of the youngest regional Party leaders in the Soviet Union, Eduard Shevardnadze (pronounced shevardNAHDzeh) became first secretary of the Georgian Communist Party in September 1972, at the age of 43. He was a newcomer to the Georgian Party hierarchy, having served in the government for the previous 7 years as republic minister of internal affairs, charged with the preservation of law and order. The chief factor in Shevardnadze's promotion was his experience as a police administrator.

In the Soviet Union, Georgia has long been known as an enclave of high living and fast runners. Its most important economic activity, wine production, is one of the oldest and the best loved branches of Georgian agriculture. Georgians are freedom loving and individualistic; they have always lived by looser rules than other Soviet nationalities, first because former Premier Josif Stalin (himself a Georgian by birth) indulged them, and later, apparently, because the pattern had been established.

Disciplinarian in a Loose Republic

Former police official Shevardnadze, who has nurtured an image as a firm, austere disciplinarian (the Georgians refer to him as the "boss"), has tried since 1972 to overturn the habits of generations regarding easy virtue, political corruption, underground capitalism and heavy drinking. The Georgians are not giving in easily. Shevardnadze's cleanup campaign met with early and continued foot dragging, and during his first years as Georgian Party leader he encountered considerable bureaucratic opposition. Speakers at an August 1973 Party Plenum hinted at disorders among the public at large, and rumors of anonymous threats against Shevardnadze and his family were prevalent throughout 1973.

Several recent developments indicate that Shevardnadze's cleanup campaign in Georgia has been intense, broad and continuous. An underground Soviet publication that appeared in 1975 claimed that nearly 25,000 persons had been arrested in Georgia in the past 2 years. (A Soviet who visited Georgia in late 1974 reported that 13,000 Party and Komsomol members had been arrested.) In addition, the republic's second secretary, Al'bert Churkin, was dismissed in April 1975 for gross errors and shortcomings.

During 1976 there was a series of bomb and arson attacks in the republic as Shevardnadze continued his all-out campaign against corruption, nationalism and ideological deviation in Georgia. The attacks may have been intended to blacken Shevardnadze's reputation by showing his inability to control the Georgian situation; there were rumors that the first secretary was on the way out because of the disorders. A long hard-hitting report delivered by Shevardnadze in July 1976 seemed to indicate that despite the disturbances he was still in control. His repeated allusions to approval of his campaign by the central authorities in Moscow, however, betrayed a certain unease about his authority in the republic.

Views on Agriculture

In 1975, when Georgia was suffering from the Soviet Union's general harvest failure, Shevardnadze set forth several new ideas on agriculture. In a report delivered to a local Party meeting, he attacked the existing program for construction of large mechanized livestock facilities—a pet project of top Soviet agricultural officials—and proposed instead to divert a part of the material and money to help expand the feed base. Shevardnadze also made several proposals designed to strengthen the position of individual farmers. For example,

Figure 13-1. continued

he asked that the feed allotment be ensured for livestock owned by individuals; that unwanted land (swamp lands or rocky areas) be turned over to the population, with technical assistance and fertilizer provided by the state; and that individual farmers form cooperative associations. Little has been heard of these proposals since 1975, but they are indicative of Shevardnadze's surprisingly pragmatic leadership style, which may serve him well in the face of continuing political problems in his republic.

Early Life and Career

A native Georgian, Eduard Amvrosiyevich Shevardnadze was born on 25 January 1928. He was the son of a teacher and was educated as a historian at a pedagogical intitute, but he began his career as a Komsomol functionary in 1946. He rose through the ranks to become first secretary of the Georgian Komsomol Central Committee in December 1957. Shevardnadze was elected a nonvoting member of the Bureau of the Georgian Party Central Committee, his first Party post, in 1958; and 3 years later he advanced from nonvoting to voting membership on the Bureau of the All-Union Komsomol Central Committee.

Political Eclipse and Recovery

In 1961 Shevardnadze was released without explanation as Komsomol chief and removed from his position on the Party Bureau. His career in eclipse, he served for 3 years in minor Party posts in Tbilisi, the Georgian capital. He began his political comeback in 1965, when he was appointed Georgian minister for the protection of public order, a title later changed to minister of internal affairs. His career may have benefited at this stage from an association with Aleksandr Shelepin, at that time a member of the Communist Party of the Soviet Union (CPSU) Politburo: When Shevardnadze became Georgian Komsomol chief, Shelepin was first secretary of the All-Union Komsomol, and when he was named minister, Shelepin's influence in Moscow was at its peak.

In July 1972 Shevardnadze was elected a voting member of the republic's Party Bureau and first secretary of the Tbilisi City Party Committee. Shevardnadze did not serve as first secretary for long—2 months later he became Georgian Party chief. He has been a Deputy to the USSR Supreme Soviet since 1974.

Travel

While he was Komsomol first secretary, Shevardnadze made several trips abroad to attend youth conferences, visiting Belgium, Tunisia and France. Since becoming republic first secretary, he has increased his contacts with foreign officials through travel and attendance at official functions. During 1974 he headed a CPSU delegation to the Austrian Communist Party Congress, attended a dinner in Moscow given by CPSU General Secretary Leonid Brezhnev for the President of France, met with Senator Edward Kennedy in Georgia, and traveled with Politburo member Nikolay Podgorny to Sofia. He accompanied Brezhnev to the Hungarian Party Congress in March 1975.

Shevardnadze has a brother, Ippokrat, who has been active in the Georgian Party apparatus. No further personal information on Shevardnadze is currently available.

CIA/DDI/OCR
JZebatto

1 April 1977

Source: Central Intelligence Agency, *Biographic Handbook USSR, Supplement 4* (Washington, D.C.: CIA, April 1977).

in Rubles, 1970–1975 (May 1976), *Soviet and U.S. Investment in Intercontinental Attack Forces, 1960–1980*, and *Outlook for the Future* (August 1981).[27]

Other reports on Soviet military matters focused on personnel issues (*Soviet Military Manpower Issues in the Eighties*, May 1980), political issues (*Political Control of the Soviet Armed Forces*, July 1980), the uses of Soviet attack submarines (*The Soviet Attack Submarine Force and Western Lines of Communications*, April 1979), and topics that would be more suited to DIA or service intelligence units—for example, *Soviet Military Aircraft Maintenance* (October 1979) and *Soviet Naval Mine Counter-Countermeasures* (June 1980).[28]

Scientific intelligence reports on the Soviet Union included *Soviet Research on Excimer Lasers* (1979), *Soviet and East European Parapsychology Research* (April 1977), and *New Soviet Large-Scale Scientific Computer* (April 1979). Both broad trends in the Soviet economy and the situation in particular industries were the subjects of Intelligence Directorate studies such as *The Soviet Economy in 1976–1977 and Outlook for 1978* (1978), *Soviet Long Range Energy Forecasts* (1978), *Outlook for Soviet Oil and Gas* (1976), and *The Soviet Tin Industry: Recent Developments and Prospects Through 1980* (1977).[29]

Soviet grain production, with its impact on Soviet internal and external developments, was also the subject of numerous reports. Included among them were *Biological and Environmental Factors Affecting Soviet Grain Quality* (1978), *USSR: The Long Term Outlook for Grain Imports*, and *USSR: The Impact of Recent Climate Change on Grain Production* (1976).[30]

The collapse of the Soviet Union has produced a dramatic decrease in the number of individuals within the CIA studying Soviet military affairs, from 125 to 9. Yet the political, economic, social, and ethnic issues that plague Russia and other former Soviet republics, and the importance to the West of a democratic free-market society taking hold, provide the basis for continued production of a large number of studies concerning the former Soviet republics.

Like CIA research on the Soviet Union, which covered virtually all aspects of Soviet life, research on the People's Republic of China is quite detailed. CIA reports on the PRC have included *Defense Modernization in China* (October 1980), *China's First Nuclear Powered Ballistic Missile Submarine* (April 1981), *China: Agricultural Performance* (1975), *China: International Trade, 1976–1977* (1978), and *China: Gross Value of Industrial Output, 1965–1977* (1978).[31]

Even before the collapse of the Soviet Union, a substantial portion of the CIA's analytical resources were devoted to non-Soviet subjects. Reports on allied, Third World, and other countries have include *Haiti: The Emigration Issue* (1981); *Guatemala: The Climate for Insurgency* (1981); *France: Nuclear Non-Proliferation Policy* (1982), *French Nuclear Reactor Fuel Reprocessing Program* (1984), *Korea: The Economic Race Between the North and South, Kampuchea: A Demographic Catastrophe, The Refugee Resettlement Problem in Thailand, Pakistan: The Ethnic Equation*, and *Elites and the Distribution of Power in Iran* (1976), *Canadian Gas Out-*

look: A US Supply Issue (1985), and *Cuba: Economic Performance, Policy, and Proposals* (1986).[32]

Other analyses focus not on individual nations or regions but on regional or international issues or problems such as international energy levels, markets, narcotics trafficking, terrorism, or nuclear proliferation. Reports produced since 1977 in these areas include *World Shipbuilding: Facing Up to Oversupply, World Steel Market: Continued Trouble Ahead, The International Energy Situation: Outlook to 1985, External Debt Positions and Prospects of the Non-OPEC LDCs* (September 1981), *Political Stability: The Narcotics Connection* (March 1987), and *The Abu Nidal Terror Network: Organization, State Sponsors, and Commercial Enterprises* (July 1987).[33]

Moreover, the CIA reported on key officials in other nations besides the Soviet Union. Its nine-page 1974 *Biographic Report* on Yitzhak Rabin, then and presently the Israeli Prime Minister, contained seven subheadings: "Prime Minister," "The Sons of Founding Generation," "Military Hawk/Political Dove," "The General as Ambassador," "'Exodus' Hero," "Strong Belief and Extreme Caution," and "A Fighting Family."[34]

The CIA also publishes a current intelligence product, the *Central Intelligence Bulletin*, on a daily basis. This publication is, in effect, the CIA's version of the *NID*.[35]

In addition, CIA offices produce a variety of periodic intelligence reviews containing articles on a variety of subjects. Included among these reviews is the monthly *Terrorism Review*. Articles that appeared in the *Review* when it was published on a weekly basis included "Italian Leftist Terrorism: Defeated but Not Destroyed" (November 23, 1983), "The Shia Urge Toward Martyrdom" (January 24, 1985), "Iran: Spreading Islam and Terrorism" (March 1, 1984), "Islamic Jihad: Increasing Threat to US Interests in Western Europe" (February 2, 1984), and "The Surprising Absence of the Red Brigades" (March 25, 1985).[36]

Other weekly reviews include the *Economic Intelligence Weekly* as well as reviews published by the Office of Leadership Analysis and the Office of Scientific and Weapons Research. The Directorate of Intelligence's regional offices also publish weekly and monthly reviews.[37]

DEFENSE INTELLIGENCE AGENCY

Like the CIA, the DIA produces a wide variety of intelligence products, including current intelligence briefings, estimates, general intelligence reports, and scientific and technical intelligence reports. The DIA also coordinates the counterintelligence products of the military departments.

One of the DIA's reports is intended specifically for the President—the weekly *Defense Intelligence Supplement* to the *PDB*.[38]

For many years, the DIA produced a DOD version of NIEs and SNIEs—the Defense Intelligence Estimates (DIEs) and Special Defense Intelligence Estimates

(SDIEs). DIEs and SDIEs were originated in late 1969 or early 1970 as a means of expressing independent DIA judgments on estimative issues prior to U.S. Intelligence Board meetings. The estimates often covered topics similar to those covered by NIEs and SNIEs; however, they also tended to deal in depth with military issues that were treated only briefly in NIEs and SNIEs. Being departmental estimates, they were produced without interdepartmental coordination.[39]

DIEs produced in the 1970s included *Military Significance of Soviet Developed Facilities in Somalia* (1976), *Prospects for Soviet Naval Aviation* (1976), and *PRC Strategic Nuclear Forces: How Much Is Enough?* (1977). More recent DIEs have included *The U.S. Central Command Area of Operations: Challenge for US Security Interests Abroad* (March 1986) and *The Eastern Caribbean: Prospects for the Regional Security System* (April 1986). SDIEs have included *Vietnam's China Problem* (May 1986), *IndoChina: Embers of Resistance Through 1990* (February 1986), and *Future Soviet Threat to US Airbreathing Reconnaissance Platforms* (April 1986).[40]

The DIEs and SDIEs were replaced by Defense Intelligence Assessments in the late 1980s. Assessments have included *Implications of Directed Energy Weapons in a Ground Combat Environment over the Next Twenty Years* (1990), *Soviet Ballistic Missile Defense Options for the 1990s* (1990), *South Africa: Defense Forces Transition to Majority Rule* (1991), *East Africa in the 1990s: The Evolving Challenge to United States Security* (1990), and *Balkan Instability—Europe's Vulnerable Underbelly* (1991).[41]

The DIA also produces Defense Estimative Briefs (DEBs) and Defense Intelligence Estimative Memoranda (DIEMs). DEBs, which are coordinated within the military intelligence community, are mini-estimates a page or two in length that "tackle priority, contentious or heretical issues on a quick-reaction basis." DIEMs usually cover important topics that require an immediate response. They are coordinated within the DIA but not with the military service intelligence organizations.[42]

DEBs have included *New Zealand: Security Implications of the Labor Victory* (July 27, 1984), *Australia: Political and Defense Prospects* (1986), *China: Implications of Retirement of Senior Military Leaders* (1985), *Cuba and the SA-5: Prospects and Implications* (1984), and *Prospects for Iraq* (1985). DIEMs have included *New Zealand's Anti-Nuclear Policies: Problems and Prospects* (March 1985), *Cuban Intervention in Angola: Impact on Latin America* (March 1976), and *Latin America: Security Implications Through 1986* (1986).[43]

In addition, the DIA produces Defense Research Assessments, Defense Intelligence Appraisals, and Defense Research Commentaries. Defense Research Assessments have included such titles as *South Pacific Island Countries: Security Implications and Defense Force Status* (January 1987) and *The North Korean Arms Connection* (May 1987). Examples of Defense Intelligence Appraisals have been *Iran: Renewal of Civil Disturbances* (August 16, 1978), *Iran: Economic Problems* (December 30, 1978), and *Iran: Dissent in the Air Force* (January 27, 1979). Finally, Defense Research Commentaries have included *China-India: Probing for a Border Settlement* (1988), *The Sino-Soviet Summit: Regional Security Implications* (1989), and *OHX: Japan's New Military Observation Helicopter* (1989).[44]

Along with NSA and the military services, the DIA publishes the daily *Defense Intelligence Digest* (*DID*). Other current intelligence products produced by the DIA include the *Daily Intelligence Summary* (*DINSUM*) and the daily *Defense Intelligence Terrorist Summary* (*DITSUM*).[45]

The *DID* provides current intelligence on military and military-related topics—including significant political, scientific and technical, and economic developments. Among the items contained in the September 25, 1990, *Daily Intelligence Digest* were "USSR–Eastern Europe: SRBM Situation" and "USSR-Poland: Air Army Exercises."[46]

The *DINSUM* provides the JCS, the National Military Intelligence Center, the unified and specified commands, the military services, and selected agencies with a daily analysis of an actual or simulated crisis situation and a summary of related intelligence of significance produced during the preceding twenty-four-hour period. Each *DINSUM* is expected to include, at a minimum, information in four areas: general hostile situations, hostile operations during the period, other intelligence factors, and the counterintelligence situation.[47]

The DIA also publishes the *Weekly Intelligence Summary* (*WIS*), which contains items on foreign defense personnel as well as military hardware and activities. The July 4, 1975, *WIS*, for example, contained a SECRET NOFORN item entitled "New Australian Defense Minister Is Whitlam's Man," which called Minister William L. Morrison "an articulate, if sometimes blustery, opposition spokesman on foreign affairs" and noted that he had "routine access to sensitive U.S. and Australian intelligence, including information on U.S. military facilities." It also noted, "Morrison may have an unsettling impact on the top management of the Defense Department in view of his long-standing enmity with Defense Permanent Secretary Sir Arthur Tange."[48]

The July 23, 1982, issue of the *WIS* included articles entitled "New Philippine Defense Attaché Team Is Assigned" and "Tracked Multiple Rocket Launchers Noted in Beijing Military Region." The first article, classified SECRET NOFORN, noted that the attachés would undoubtedly report on, and possibly operate against, anti-Marcos Philippine activists in the United States. The second reported that "eighteen tracked MRL's [Multiple Rocket Launchers] were sighted with the 359th Artillery Regiment of the 79th Infantry Division, 27th Army, at Xingtai, Hebei on 18 May. This is the second infantry division noted with tracked MRLs." A third article concerned the testing of a possible Soviet chemical weapon launcher and included satellite photography of the test area.[49]

Altogether the July 23, 1982, issue contained twenty-one articles on five different regions of the world: the Soviet Union/Eastern Europe, Asia, Western Europe, Africa, and Latin America. The table of contents for the issue is shown in Table 13-2. Other *WIS* articles have included "Soviet Space and Missile Wrapup" (De-

Table 13-2. Table of Contents for Defense Intelligence Agency, *Weekly Intelligence Summary,* July 23, 1982.

cember 15, 1978), "Flexibility of Soviet Air Defense Forces Increased" (March 5, 1982), and "Chinese IRBM Training Activity" (January 18, 1980).[50]

Other DIA intelligence products include the *Defense Intelligence Notice* (*DIN*), the *Spot Intelligence Report* (*SPIREP*), and the *Periodic Intelligence Summary.* Normally, each *DIN* addresses a single development, situation, event, or activity that is felt to have a possible impact on future planning and operations. The primary objectives are to report the event, to explain why it occurred, and to assess its impact on the United States.[51]

The *Spot Intelligence Report* is intended to inform the Joint Chiefs of Staff, the unified and specified commands, the military services, and selected agencies of particular events of importance. The events that are the subject of a *SPIREP*, however, are required to have an immediate and significant effect on current planning and operations. The report is intended to answer four questions: (1) What is the nature of the event? (2) When did the event occur? (3) Where did the event occur? (4) What is the source of the information?[52]

The *Periodic Intelligence Summary* provides the JCS, the military services, and military commanders worldwide with periodic intelligence concerning actual or training exercises that could have an immediate actual (or simulated) effect on U.S. plans and operations. Information, if applicable, is included in the following format:

1. Situation summary/highlights
2. Military activity
   a. Air
   b. Ground
   c. Navy
   d. Missile
   e. Space
   f. Other
3. Political issues
4. Collection posture
5. Outlook[53]

The DIA has also produced Defense Intelligence Projections for Planning (DIPPs), Joint Intelligence Estimates for Planning (JIEP), and the Joint Long-Range Estimative Intelligence Document (JLREID). The DIPPs summarized the state of the Soviet and Chinese armed forces and projected future trends and force levels. Each set consisted of seven volumes. Volume 1 examined ballistic missile forces. Volume 2 of the PRC DIPP concerned strategic bomber forces while Volume 2 of the Soviet DIPP focused on long-range aviation. In both DIPPs, Volume 3 was devoted to aerospace defense forces. This volume contained at least four sections, with the third and fourth being concerned with surface-to-air missile forces and ballistic missile defenses, respectively. Volume 4, on general-purpose forces, had at least five sections, including sections on ground forces, general-purpose naval forces, military transport aviation, and military helicopter aviation. Volume 5 was entitled *Space Systems for the Support of Military Operations,* and Volume 7 bore the title *Military Manpower Implications.*[54]

Other projections may be done on either a regular or occasional basis. Some have been entitled *Projected Space Programs—USSR* (1982), *ASW Weapons and Decoys (Current and Projected)—ECC* (1976), and *Combat Vehicle Systems (Current and Projected)—European Communist Countries* (1976).[55]

Within the general intelligence category the DIA publishes a variety of products. These include Area Handbooks, Order of Battle Studies, Military Intelligence Summaries, Defense Intelligence Studies, Targeting/Installation Documents, Lines of Communication Studies, and Tactical Commanders Terrain

Analysis Studies. Examples of such products include *Soviet Strategic Surface-to-Surface Missile Order of Battle* (September 1978), *Defense Intelligence Electronic Order of Battle,* Volume 1: *USSR and Mongolia* (March 1982), *Ground Order of Battle: PRC* (January 1980), *Military Intelligence Summary,* Volume 7: *People's Republic of China and Eastern Asia* (January 1980), *Naval Forces Intelligence Study: People's Republic of China* (March 1981), *Handbook on the Chinese Armed Forces* (July 1976), and *Soviet Kola Peninsula Missile Submarine Base: Two Decades in the Making* (August 1978).[56]

All such studies are intended to form an extensive database relevant to assessing foreign military capabilities in general or with regard to specific matters (e.g., seizure of the Falklands or the Iran-Iraq War) and for use in U.S. military operations. Order of Battle Studies specify in as much detail as possible the organization and armaments of a nation's military establishment or a component of that establishment. Targeting/Installation Documents are used by operations planners in assessing the requirements for destroying or damaging an airfield, a port facility, or a missile base. Lines of Communications Studies describe the means by which military forces are supported and supplied and thus are used in designing plans to sever those lines.

In addition, the DIA produces thousands of reports on military and military-related scientific and technical matters that are not part of the series mentioned above. The subjects of these reports include strategy, politico-military relations, scientific and technical matters, weapons systems, C^3, and R&D.

DIA reports on strategy have included *Luring Deep: China's Land Defense Strategy* (September 1980), *Detente in Soviet Strategy* (September 1975), *China's Evolving Nuclear Strategies* (May 1985), and *Japan's Evolving Maritime Strategy: Time for an Aircraft Carrier* (1989). Political-military subjects were the focus of *China's Urban Militia: Military Arm or Political Tool?* (June 1974) and *USSR: The Unity and Integration of Soviet Political, Military and Defense Industry Leadership* (March 1977).[57]

Scientific and technical reports concern general assessments, computer technology, microelectronics, and medical activities. Included among such reports have been titles such as *Long Range Scientific and Technical Assessment: The People's Republic of China* (October 1973) and *Psychopharmacological Enhancement of Human Performance—USSR*.[58]

As might be expected, reports on specific weapons systems constitute the bulk of DIA reports. The reports vary from overviews of entire classes of weapons to analyses of individual weapons systems. Such reports have included *Antisatellite System—USSR* (November 1979), *Over the Horizon Radars for Air Defense* (December 1979), *Soviet ALFA Class SSN Study* (December 1979), *Backfire Weapon System* (July 1980), *SS-17 ICBM System* (March 1982), *China: Land-Based Strategic Missile Forces—Tables of Organization and Equipment* (1985), *KFIR Weapon System* (1987), and *Pakistan: Chemical Warfare Capabilities* (1989).[59]

Additional reports have focused on C³ capabilities as a whole as well as on the command structures for particular military regions. Titles have included *Warsaw Pact Forces Command, Control and Communications* (August 1980), *New Military Command Structure of Soviet Forces Opposite China* (1980), *Soviet Command, Control and Communications Capabilities* (1979), *China: National Command, Control, and Communications—Beijing* (1984), and *Lines of Communication: Israel* (1988).[60]

Another major area of DIA analysis concerns R&D weapons acquisition, particularly the decisionmaking and acquisition process, the role of design bureaus, and design and testing philosophy. DIA studies dealing with these subjects have included a 1972 study entitled *Soviet Military Research and Development—An Overview,* a five-volume 1980 study on *U.S. and Soviet Weapon System Design Practice,* and *Chinese Aerospace Research, Development, and Test Facilities* (1984).[61]

Other DIA reports have focused on political, economic, social, and international issues. Included among these reports have been the following: *East Asia and Pacific: 1984 Economic Performance and Prospects for 1985* (1985), *China and Israel: An Update of the Military Relationship* (May 1985), *China and the Iranian Arms Connection: The Significance for US-Chinese Security Relations* (1988), *The Cuban Nickel Industry* (1984), *Latin American Military Involvement in the Illicit Drug Trade* (1984), and *Turkey: Attempts to Counter Islamic Fundamentalism* (1987).[62]

The DIA is responsible for preparing biographic sketches of foreign military officers—even junior officers. The agency prepared its first sketch of Andres Rodriguez, for example, no later than April 1966, at which time he was Commander of the 1st Cavalry Division of the Paraguayan Army. In February 1989, he led the coup that deposed Paraguay's longtime dictator, Alfredo Stroessner.[63]

Each sketch usually runs several single-spaced pages and provides information on the subject's position, significance, politics, personality, personal life, and professional career. A November 1987 sketch of Philippino General Fidel V. Ramos, then Army Chief of Staff and now President of the Republic of the Philippines, describes him as "staunchly anti-communist" and one who "does not question the US military presence in the Philippines." The Personal Data section notes his age, educational record (as well as that of his wife), and fluency in English. It also notes that "while Ramos has been described as conscientious, highly principled, cooperative, and congenial, he can, at times, be quite arrogant." The final section traces his career from his days as a cadet at West Point to his promotion to Armed Forces Chief of Staff.[64] The sketch is reproduced in Figure 13-2.

More recently, sketches have been prepared on USSR General of the Army Anatoliy Ivanovich Gribkov (February 1988), the First Deputy Chief of the General Staff at the time when the sketch was compiled; Iraqi Lieutenant General Husayn Rashid Mohammad Hasan (December 18, 1990), Chief of the General

Figure 13-2. DIA Biographic Sketch of Gen. Fidel V. Ramos.

BIOGRAPHIC SKETCH

PHILIPPINES
GEN Fidel V. <u>RAMOS</u>
November 1987

(U) <u>NAME</u>: General (GEN) Fidel Valdes <u>Ramos</u>,
Philippine Army (PA). Pronounced (RAHmos).
Nickname: "Eddie."

(U) <u>POSITION</u>: Chief of Staff, Armed Forces of the
Philippines (AFP) since February 1986. Ramos
succeeded Gen Fabian Ver.

(U)   UNK

███ SIGNIFICANCE: Since his appointment as Chief
of Staff, AFP, Ramos has been the linchpin
sustaining military support for the Aquino
Government. However, there are still those within
the military who are dissatisfied with the
Administration. Some military factions perceive the
Government as being penetrated by leftists who have diminished the status of
the armed forces. The rebellions initiated by discontented military officers
have, in part, been frustrated by the support Ramos has mustered for the new
Government.

███ Ramos has been criticized by antagonists on both sides of the civil-
military dispute. ██
██
██ Rumors indicated that
the strain from his role would force Ramos to retire in advance of February
1989. There were numerous reports during the month of June 1987 speculating
that Ramos would retire along with Vice Chief of Staff, LTG Salvador Mison and
CG, PA Rudolfo Canieso. Reports also indicated Ramos has Presidential
aspirations.

███ Ramos has defused much of this speculation. He has appointed chiefs of
service with whom he is comfortable and whose political persuasions compliment
his own. The possibility remains that Ramos will retire to permit Vice Chief
of Staff, LTG Renato DeVilla to succeed him. However, one-third of the current
crop of general officers are mandated to retire in April 1988. Ramos may
believe his guidance will be necessary to select replacements, who, due to
changes in AFP retirements procedures, will serve longer and have greater
impact than the retiring year group 1957.

███ POLITICS: General Ramos is staunchly anti-Communist and is favorably
disposed towards the United States. According to officials, Ramos does not
question the US military presence in the Philippines. He is a 1950 graduate of
the US Military Academy at West Point; fought with US forces in Korea; and was
the Chief of Staff of the Philippines Civic Action Group in Vietnam. He has
also received US training at Ft. Benning and Ft. Bragg. Since 1972, Ramos has

Figure 13-2. continued

served as a member of the Mutual Defense Board, tasked with the implementation of the US–Philippine Mutual Defense Treaty. He was awarded the US Legion of Merit in 1975. There is no doubt, however, that General Ramos is a Filipino first and foremost. Despite his gratitude for US aid to the Philippines, he has emphasized that his country must learn not to rely on Washington for support.

PERSONAL DATA: General Ramos was born on 18 March 1928 in Lingayan, Pangasinan Province. He is the son of the former Foreign Affairs Secretary, Narciso Ramos. Ramos is married to the former Amelita "Ming" Martinez and has five daughters. Mrs. Ramos holds a degree from Boston University and an M.S. degree from UCLA. General Ramos has a quick wit and an excellent memory and is at ease in social situations. While Ramos has been described as conscientious, highly principled, cooperative, and congenial, he can, at times, be quite arrogant.

Ramos smokes cigars, and drinks Scotch sparingly. He enjoys golf, chess and photography. His favorite pastime is scuba diving, and he is apparently quite proficient in underwater photography. Following his graduation from West Point, Ramos attended the University of Illinois at Urbana, where he earned a M.S. degree in Civil Engineering. He also holds an M.B.A. degree from the Ateneo de Manila, and another Master's degree in National Security Administration from the National Defense College of the Philippines. Ramos speaks excellent English.

(U) CAREER: Ramos was a Cadet at West Point from 1946 thru 1950 and graduated in the top ten percent of his class. In 1951 he was commissioned into the Armed Forces of the Philippines by the military attache in Washington, D.C. with the rank of second lieutenant. His first encounter with war took place in Korea in 1952 (the History of the United Nations Forces in the Korean War, published by the Ministry of Defense, Republic of Korea, devotes one section of a chapter to the successful attack of Hill Eerie by young Second Lieutenant Ramos). From 1955 to 1956 Captain Ramos attended the Infantry Officers Course, Ft. Benning, GA. In 1960 Ramos attended the Special Forces and Airborne courses at Ft. Bragg, NC. He was promoted to major in 1964; served as Acting Officer in Charge, Office of Military Assistance to the President in 1966; and served as Chief of Staff, 1st Philippine Civic Action Group, RVN. He was promoted to lieutenant colonel while in Vietnam. Ramos served as Special Military Assistant to the President in 1968–69; and concurrently as Assistant Chief of Staff, Intelligence, and Chief, Intelligence Service of the Armed Forces in 1969–70. He was promoted to colonel during this assignment; to brigadier general in 1971 when he was chief of the Philippine Constabulary; and to major general in December, 1973. In 1975, he assumed the position of Director General of the Integrated National Police. He was promoted to lieutenant general and became Vice Chief of Staff of the Armed Forces in 1981.

Following the implication of General Ver in 1984, by the board investigating the assassination of former Senator Benigno Aquino, President Marcos selected General Ramos to his first appointment as Acting Chief of Staff. In February 1986, President Aquino selected Ramos to be the new military chief and promoted him to the rank of general.

Staff at the time; and Lieutenant General Ayyad Futayih Khalifa Al Rawi (October 18, 1990), the Commander of the Iraqi Republican Guard Forces.[65]

In addition to its printed reports the DIA also distributes finished intelligence via television through the Defense Intelligence Network (DIN), known formally as the Joint Worldwide Intelligence Communications System. For approximately twelve hours a day, five days a week, the DIN broadcasts Top Secret reports to about 1,000 defense intelligence and operations officers at the Pentagon and nineteen other military commands in the United States. Early 1992 plans called for an expansion to seventy-three additional sites, including U.S. commands abroad.[66]

In addition to having anchors who report finished intelligence, the DIN also shows satellite reconnaissance photos, reports communications intercepts, and carries reports from defense attachés overseas. Reporting begins at 6:15 A.M. with a 30-minute "Global Update." At 6:45 the head of the DIA Directorate for Intelligence (J-2) conducts a 45-minute interview show that features visiting briefers who give classified reports on developing events. "Global Update" resumes at 8:00 A.M. and continues at the top of each hour, updated as required and interspersed with special features. In addition, there are regular features such as "Regional Intelligence Review," and "Military Trends and Capabilities."[67]

BUREAU OF INTELLIGENCE AND RESEARCH

As noted in Chapter 6, the State Department's INR contributes to national intelligence production and provides the Secretary of State, and the rest of the State Department, with intelligence support. In the latter role it provides both current and long-term intelligence.

Daily current intelligence is contained in the *Morning Summary*, which is published seven days a week. It contains about a dozen brief reports with commentary and three or four longer policy-sensitive articles. A supplementary weekend edition covers particular issues in detail. The publications are intended to inform the Secretary and principal Deputies of current events and intelligence and provide concise commentaries concerning their significance. The first part of the summary consists of short "gist and comment" reports based on newly available information. The second part usually consists of three one-page essays drafted by INR analysts.[68]

INR's offices, like those of the CIA's Directorate of Intelligence, publish a series of regional functional magazines. Some are published on a weekly basis; others on a biweekly, monthly, or quarterly basis. Shortly before the attempted coup in the Soviet Union, the journals included *African Trends, East-Asia Pacific Dynamics, Economic Commentary, Inter-American Highlights, Soviet–East European Review, Strategic Forces Analysis Biweekly, War Watch Weekly,* and *Western Europe and Canada—Issues and Trends.* Each issue consists of short essays, brief analyses of intelligence reporting, and selected chronologies.[69]

Single subject reports were for many years published under three titles: *Current Analyses, Assessments and Research,* and *Policy Assessments. Current Analyses* papers analyzed recent or ongoing events and assessed prospects and implications for the following six months. *Assessment and Research* (AR) papers either assessed past trends or projected the course of events more than six months into the future. The analysts who prepared these reports conducted substantial background or in-depth research. *Policy Assessments* analyzed the context or results of past policies or assessed comparative policies or policy options. Those distinct series have been merged into a single *Intelligence Research Report* series.[70]

INR reports produced over the past decade have included *Canada: Quebec Separatists to Try Again* (1983), *Iraqi Foreign Policy: The Impact of the Iran-Iraq War* (1984), *China: Will the Army Cut 1 Million Men?* (1985), *The Southern Arabia Peninsula: Boundary Issues* (1985), *China: Recent Developments in Arms Control Policies* (1986), and *Soviet-Cuban Relations Smolder over Perestroyka and Rectification* (1988).[71]

INR also publishes the *Spot Intelligence Report.* An October 15, 1987, issue consisted of a five-paragraph SECRET/NOFORN report entitled "Persian Gulf: Fourth Time Lucky for Iranian Silkworm at Kuwait." The document reported on an Iranian attack against a U.S.-managed flag tanker.[72]

DRUG ENFORCEMENT ADMINISTRATION

In addition to participating in the production of an annual NIE on narcotics trafficking, the DEA produces a variety of intelligence reports. Its primary recurring reports are the *Monthly Digest of Drug Intelligence* and *Quarterly Intelligence Trends.* It also publishes the annual *Narcotics Intelligence Estimate* and a compendium of worldwide production, smuggling, and trafficking trends and projections. In 1985 it also produced the 135-page *Worldwide Narcotics Threat Assessment* to provide specifics on quantities and types of narcotics as well as conveyances and routes used by international narcotics traffickers to introduce narcotics into the United States. Another report dealt with the illicit drug traffic from the Mideast to and through Bulgaria.[73]

MILITARY SERVICE INTELLIGENCE

As noted in Chapter 4, each military service has at least one organization that produces general military as well as scientific and technical (S&T) intelligence. These organizations produce a substantial number of recurring publications.

The Air Force publishes the *Air Force Intelligence Weekly,* which contains a synopsis of current events and developments from a political-military perspective. Two current intelligence publications are the *Air Force Intelligence Daily* and the *Air Force Intelligence Morning Highlights.*[74]

The Army's National Ground Intelligence Center (NGIC) publishes several current intelligence products—the *Biweekly Scientific and Technical Intelligence Summary* (*BSTIS*), the *Army Scientific and Technical Intelligence Bulletin* (*ASTIB*), the *Scientific and Technical Analysis Bulletin*, and the *Weekly Wire*. Among the articles in the September 1981 *ASTIB* was "Recent Developments in Soviet Artillery."[75]

Studies by the NGIC have focused on subjects directly and indirectly related to the Army mission. These studies have included: *Microelectronics Technology and Applications—Eurasian Communist Countries and Japan* (December 1974), *Chinese Land Defense Forces* (June 1973), *Soviet Twin 57-mm Self Propelled Antiaircraft Gun ZSU-522-2* (June 1976), *Soviet Large Helicopter Mil Mi-12* (June 1972), *USSR Ground Forces R&D Overview, 1975* (June 1975), *An Outstanding Weapons System for Soviet Air Defense Troops* (1972), *Chemical Warfare Capabilities—Warsaw Pact* (October 1979), and *Recent Developments in Chinese and North Korean Artillery* (1986).[76]

The Army's Intelligence and Threat Analysis Center (ITAC) has produced studies such as the *Soviet Tactical Nuclear Study (U)* (July 1, 1977) and the six-volume *Army Intelligence Surveys*. The titles of the six volumes of the *Survey* are: *Country Resume, Military Geography, Handbook of Ground Forces/Ground Forces Order of Battle Book, Counterintelligence* (or *Intelligence and Security*), *Medical Intelligence* (prepared by the Armed Forces Medical Intelligence Center, AFMIC), and *Psychological Operations*.[77] The surveys were produced "in order to aid and support tactical commanders and/or contingency planners at corps/division level in responding to crisis events and international situations requiring US involvement."[78]

ITAC also produces short "ITAC Intelligence Notes" (IINs), "ITAC Intelligence Briefs," and "Foreign Forces Capabilities." The IINs include IIN 83-04, "Activities at Iranian Embassy Beirut."[79]

Other ITAC studies include: *Iran-Iraq: The Gulf War* (1984), *Biological Weapons: The Terrorist Threat* (1985), *Army Regional Threat—Southwest Asia* (1987), *Army Regional Threat: Northeast Asia* (1989), *Eastern Europe: Potential for Instability* (1989), and *Analysis of the Area of Operation: Saudi Arabia* (1990).[80]

Foreign Aerospace Science and Technology Center (FASTC) studies included *Chinese Ballistic Missile Development Activity* (1990).[81]

UNIFIED COMMANDS

Among the major functions of the intelligence components of the unified commands is the preparation of current intelligence and other reports specifically geared to the needs of the command and its Commander-in-Chief. In many cases the publications are derived from already existing CIA and DIA publications.

The U.S. Space Command produces two daily publications—the *USSPACECOM Space Intelligence Notes* (*SPIN*) and the *USSPACECOM Strategic*

Posture Aerospace Threat Summary (SPATS). The *SPIN* provides a summary of foreign space activity, whereas the *SPATS* provides information on the status of strategic posture indicators. On a weekly basis, the Space Command produces *USSPACECOM Defense Intelligence Space Order of Battle (DISOB)*, which summarizes the status of Russian, PRC, and Indian satellites. An event-generated report is the *USSPACECOM Intelligence Report*, which contains data on the deorbiting of foreign satellites, launch notification messages, and preliminary launch assessments.[82]

NOTES

1. Cord Meyer, *Facing Reality: From World Federalism to the CIA* (New York: Harper & Row, 1980), p. 352; Zbigniew Brzezinski, *Power and Principle: Memoirs of the National Security Adviser, 1977–1981* (New York: Farrar, Straus & Giroux, 1983), p. 224; Central Intelligence Agency, *A Consumer's Guide to Intelligence* (Washington, D.C.: CIA, 1993), p. 21; Private information.

2. Meyer, *Facing Reality,* p. 352.

3. Loch K. Johnson, "Making the Intelligence 'Cycle' Work," *International Journal of Intelligence and Counterintelligence* 1, 4 (1987): 1–23.

4. William Colby with Peter Forbath, *Honorable Men: My Life in the CIA* (New York: Simon & Schuster, 1978), p. 354; Letter, Arthur S. Hulnick, CIA Office of Public Affairs, to author, April 7, 1988.

5. Meyer, *Facing Reality,* pp. 352–54; Private information.

6. Brian Toohey and Dale Van Atta, "How the CIA Saw the 1975 Crisis," *National Times,* March 28–April 3, 1982, pp. 16ff.

7. Ibid.

8. Bob Woodward, *Veil: The Secret Wars of the CIA, 1981–1987* (New York: Simon & Schuster, 1987), pp. 410–11.

9. Central Intelligence Agency, *A Consumer's Guide to Intelligence,* pp. 22.

10. U.S. Congress, House Committee on Foreign Affairs, *The Role of Intelligence in the Foreign Policy Process* (Washington, D.C.: U.S. Government Printing Office, 1980), p. 235.

11. Bruce Berkowitz, "Intelligence in the Organizational Context," *Orbis,* Fall 1985, pp. 571–76; Victoria S. Price, *The DCI's Role in Producing Strategic Intelligence Estimates* (Newport, R.I.: Naval War College, 1980), p. 37.

12. Director of Central Intelligence, *Soviet Capabilities for Strategic Nuclear Conflict, 1982–1992, Volume 1, Key Judgements and Summary,* NIE 11-3/8-82, February 15, 1983, pp. iii, 3.

13. Ibid., p. 4.

14. Navy Operational Intelligence Center, *Navy Operational Intelligence Center Command History, 1986* (Washington, D.C.: NOIC, 1987), p. 8; Diane T. Putney, *History of the Air Force Intelligence Service, 1 January–31 December 1984, Volume 1, Narrative and Appendices* (Ft. Belvoir, Va.: AFIS, n.d.), p. 349; Office of Naval Intelligence, *Office of Naval Intelligence 1989 Command History,* n.d., Intelligence Analysis Division section, pp. 1–2; Deputy Director of Central Intelligence, Note to Fritz Ermath, Subject: NIE 11/30-86: Gorbachev's

Policy Toward the Middle East, May 5, 1986; U.S. Congress, Senate Select Committee on Intelligence, *Nomination of Robert M. Gates to Be Director of Central Intelligence* (Washington, D.C.: U.S. Government Printing Office, 1991), p. 131; Department of the Army, Office of the Assistant Chief of Staff for Intelligence, *Annual Historical Review, 1 October 1981–30 September 1982,* n.d., p. 4-7.

15. John M. Broder, "CIA Scrambles to Evaluate Breakaway Soviet Republics," *Los Angeles Times,* December 12, 1991, p. A14; Sam Vincent Meddis, "Soviet Disunion Keeps U.S. Spymasters Busy," *USA Today,* December 11, 1991, p. 6A.

16. Department of the Army, Office of the Assistant Chief of Staff for Intelligence, *Annual Historical Review, 1 October 1981–30 September 1982,* p. 4-7.

17. U.S. Congress, Senate Select Committee on Intelligence, *Nomination of Robert M. Gates to Be Director of Central Intelligence,* pp. 121, 123; Private information; Peter Kornbluh, *Nicaragua: The Price of Intervention* (Washington, D.C.: Institute for Policy Studies, 1987), p. 243, n22; Bob Woodward, *Veil,* p. 400; Brian Barger and Robert Parry, "Nicaraguan Rebels Linked to Drug Trafficking," *Washington Post,* December 27, 1985, p. A22; Office of Naval Intelligence, *Office of Naval Intelligence (ONI) Annual History 1985, Annex C,* September 1986, p. 4; U.S. Congress, House Committee on Appropriations, *Department of Energy and Water and Water Development Appropriations for 1992, Part 6* (Washington, D.C.: U.S. Government Printing Office, 1991), p. 828.

18. Woodward, *Veil,* pp. 94, 409; *The Tower Commission Report* (New York: Times Books, 1987), pp. 114–15; Bob Woodward and Dan Morgan, "Soviet Threat Toward Iran Overstated, Casey Concluded," *Washington Post,* January 13, 1987, pp. A1, A8; U.S. Congress, House Permanent Select Committee on Intelligence, *U.S. Intelligence Performance on Central America: Achievements and Selected Instances of Concern* (Washington, D.C.: U.S. Government Printing Office, 1982), p. 7; Office of Naval Intelligence, *Office of Naval Intelligence (OP-092) Command History 1990,* n.d., Intelligence Division (OP-922) submission, p. 6.

19. U.S. Congress, Senate Committee on Armed Services, *Department of Defense Authorization for Appropriations FY 1983, Part 7* (Washington, D.C.: U.S. Government Printing Office, 1982), p. 4393; Price, *The DCI's Role in Producing Strategic Intelligence Estimates,* p. 44; Harold P. Ford, *Estimative Intelligence: The Purposes and Problems of National Intelligence Estimating* (Washington, D.C.: Defense Intelligence College, 1989), p. 121; Office of Naval Intelligence, *Office of Naval Intelligence 1989 Command History,* Intelligence Analysis Division input, p. 2; Department of the Army, Office of the Deputy Chief of Staff for Intelligence, *Annual Historical Review, 1 October 1989–30 September 1990,* n.d., p. 5-20; Department of the Army, Office of the Assistant Chief of Staff for Intelligence, *Annual Historical Review, 1 October 1981–30 September 1982,* pp. 4-9 to 4-10.

20. Ford, *Estimative Intelligence,* p. 121.

21. AR 381-19, "Military Intelligence: Intelligence Support," July 19, 1981, p. 2-5; *History of the Assistant Chief of Staff, Intelligence, United States, 1 January–30 January 1975,* 1975, p. 7.

22. Philip Taubman, "Casey and His CIA on the Rebound," *New York Times Magazine,* January 16, 1983, pp. 20ff.

23. Office of Naval Intelligence, *Office of Naval Intelligence 1989 Command History,* Intelligence Analysis Division input, p. 2.

24. National Intelligence Council, *A Guide to the National Intelligence Council,* 1994, p. 4.

25. Ibid., p. 42.

26. Ibid.

27. Air University Special Bibliography No. 205, *Soviet Military Capabilities* (Maxwell AFB, Ala: Air University, February 1977), p. 9; Air University Special Bibliography No. 205, Supplement 2, *Soviet Military Capabilities, Part 1* (Maxwell AFB, Ala: Air University, March 1982), p. 7.

28. Air University Special Bibliography No. 205, Supplement 2, *Soviet Military Capabilities, Part 1*, pp. 11, 33, 38.

29. Ibid., pp. 70, 72, 86.

30. Myron Smith, ed., *The Secret War: Intelligence, Espionage and Covert Operations* (Santa Barbara, Calif.: ABC-Clio, 1980), p. 122; *Documents for the U.S. Espionage Den 50: U.S.S.R., The Aggressive East, Section 2* (Tehran: Muslim Students Following the Line of the Iman, n.d.), p. 3.

31. Air University Special Bibliography No. 207, Supplement 1, *Communist China: Military Capabilities* (Maxwell AFB, Ala: Air University, August 1981), p. 9.

32. Air University Library, *Canada* (Maxwell AFB, Ala.: Air University Library, May 1989), p. 7; Air University Library, *Cuba* (Maxwell AFB, Ala.: Air University Library, March 1990), p. 5.

33. Smith, *The Secret War*, p. 122.

34. Central Intelligence Agency, *Biographic Report: Yitzhak RABIN, Prime Minister of Israel*, June 1974.

35. Armed Forces Staff College, *AFSC Pub 5: Intelligence for Joint Forces* (Hampton, Va.: AFSC, July 1990), p. L-1.

36. Central Intelligence Agency, *A Consumer's Guide to Intelligence*, p. 14; issues of *Terrorism Review* partially released under the FOIA.

37. Central Intelligence Agency, *A Consumer's Guide to Intelligence*, p. 23.

38. Ibid., p. 21.

39. Ford, *Estimative Intelligence*, p. 136.

40. Air University Special Bibliography No. 205, *Soviet Military Capabilities*, p. 43; Air University Special Bibliography No. 207, *Communist China: Military Capabilities* (Maxwell AFB, Ala.: Air University, September 1977), p. 28; Title pages of recent DIEs and SDIEs obtained under FOIA.

41. Title pages obtained under FOIA.

42. Ford, *Estimative Intelligence*, p. 137.

43. Air University Library, *Australia and the Pacific Islands* (Maxwell AFB, Ala.: Air University Library, June 1989), p. 22; Air University Library, *China: Military Capabilities* (Maxwell AFB, Ala.: Air University Library, February 1988), p. 16; Air University Library, *Cuba*, pp. 12, 47; Air University Library, *Iraq-Iran Conflict* (Maxwell AFB, Ala: Air University Library, March 1986), p. 7; Air University Library, *Latin America* (Maxwell AFB, Ala.: Air University Library, December 1989), p. 61.

44. Air University Library, *China: Military Capabilities* (Maxwell AFB, Ala.: Air University Library, August 1990), pp. 22, 25; Air University Library, *Japan: Military Capabilities* (Maxwell AFB, Ala.: Air University Library, October 1990), p. 21.

45. Barbara Starr, "DIA Plans Global Data Network," *Jane's Defence Weekly*, June 8, 1991, p. 956; Loch K. Johnson, *America's Secret Power: The CIA in a Democratic Society* (New York: Oxford University Press, 1989), p. 91.

46. Central Intelligence Agency, *A Consumer's Guide to Intelligence*, p. 22; *Daily Intelligence Digest*, September 25, 1990.

47. Joint Chiefs of Staff, *Joint Reporting Structure (JRS), Volume 2, Joint Reports, Part 10—Intelligence* (Washington, D.C.: March 15, 1985), pp. 10-3-1 to 10-3-3.

48. "New Defense Minister Is Whitlam's Man," *Weekly Intelligence Summary*, July 4, 1975, pp. 10–11.

49. *Weekly Intelligence Summary* 29-82, July 23, 1982.

50. Ibid.

51. Joint Chiefs of Staff, *Joint Reporting Structure (JRS), Volume 2, Joint Reports, Part 10—Intelligence*, pp. 10-1-1 to 10-1-2.

52. Ibid., pp. 10-2-1 to 10-2-2.

53. Ibid., pp. 10-4-1 to 10-4-3.

54. Air University Special Bibliography No. 205, *Soviet Military Capabilities*, pp. 19, 33, 62; Air University Special Bibliography No. 207, *Communist China: Military Capabilities*, pp. 17, 22, 24, 28, 33; Air University Special Bibliography No. 205, Supplement 1, *Soviet Military Capabilities* (Maxwell AFB, Ala.: Air University, July 1979), pp. 23, 34, 43, 68; Air University Special Bibliography No. 205, Supplement 2, *Soviet Military Capabilities, Part 1*, pp. 18, 26, 28, 31; Air University Special Bibliography No. 207, Supplement 1, *Communist China: Military Capabilities*, pp. 5, 13; Air University Special Bibliography No. 204, Supplement 6, *Strategic Triad* (Maxwell AFB, Ala.: January 1983), p. 57; Armed Forces Staff College, *AFSC Pub 5 Intelligence for Joint Forces* (Hampton, Va.: AFSC, 1990), p. L-1.

55. Air University Special Bibliography No. 205, Supplement 2, *Soviet Military Capabilities*, p. 88; Air University Special Bibliography No. 205, *Soviet Military Capabilities*, p. 42.

56. Air University Special Bibliography No. 207, *Communist China: Military Capabilities*, pp. 5, 12; Air University Special Bibliography No. 205, Supplement 1, *Soviet Military Capabilities*, p. 35; Air University Special Bibliography No. 204, Supplement 2, *Strategic Triad* (Maxwell AFB, Ala.: Air University, March 1978), p. 52; Air University Special Bibliography No. 205, Supplement 2, *Soviet Military Capabilities, Part 1*, p. 13; Air University Special Bibliography No. 207, Supplement 1, *Communist China: Military Capabilities*, p. 5.

57. Air University Special Bibliography No. 207, Supplement 1, *Communist China: Military Capabilities*, pp. 9, 11; Air University Special Bibliography No. 205, Supplement 1, *Soviet Military Capabilities*, p. 7; Air University Special Bibliography No. 207, *Communist China: Military Capabilities*, p. 12; Air University Library, *China: Military Capabilities* (February 1988), p. 17; Air University Library, *Japan: Military Capabilities*, p. 23.

58. Air University Special Bibliography No. 207, *Communist China: Military Capabilities*, p. 12; Air University Special Bibliography No. 205, Supplement 2, *Soviet Military Capabilities, Part 1*, p. 72.

59. Air University Special Bibliography No. 205, Supplement 2, *Soviet Military Capabilities, Part 1*, pp. 16, 26, 38, 52, 55; Air University Special Bibliography No. 204, Supplement 6, *Strategic Triad*, p. 53; Air University Library, *China: Military Capabilities* (February 1988), p. 16; Air University Library, *The Middle East* (Maxwell AFB, Ala.: Air University Library, May 1989), p. 170; Air University Library, *NCB: Nuclear, Chemical, Biological Warfare* (Maxwell AFB, Ala.: Air University Library, February 1990), p. 35.

60. Air University Special Bibliography No. 205, Supplement 1, *Soviet Military Capabilities*, p. 41; Air University Special Bibliography No. 205, Supplement 2, *Soviet Military Capabilities, Part 1*, p. 74; Air University Library, *China: Military Capabilities* (February 1988), p. 16; Air University Library, *The Middle East*, p. 187.

61. Air University Special Bibliography No. 205, Supplement 2, *Soviet Military Capabilities, Part 1*, p. 55; Air University Library, *China: Military Capabilities* (February 1988), p. 17.

62. Air University Library, *Australia and the Pacific Islands*, p. 7; Air University Library, *China: Military Capabilities* (February 1988), p. 32; Air University Library, *China: Military Capabilities* (August 1990), p. 1; Air University Library, *Cuba*, p. 5; Air University Library, *Latin America*, p. 47; Air University Library, *The Middle East*, p. 76.

63. Defense Intelligence Agency, "Biographic Sketch: Andres Rodriguez," April 1966.

64. Defense Intelligence Agency, "Biographic Sketch: General Fidel V. RAMOS," November 1987.

65. Sketches obtained under the Freedom of Information Act.

66. George Lardner, Jr., and Walter Pincus, "On This Network, All the News Is Top Secret," *Washington Post*, March 3, 1992, pp. A1, A9.

67. Ibid.

68. *INR: Intelligence and Research in the Department of State* (Washington, D.C.: Department of State, n.d.), p. 4; Central Intelligence Agency, *A Consumer's Guide to Intelligence*, p. 22.

69. Central Intelligence Agency, *A Consumer's Guide to Intelligence*, p. 22.

70. Ibid., p. 4.

71. Air University Library, *Canada*, p. 16; Air University Library, *China: Military Capabilities* (February 1988), p. 24; Air University Library, *Cuba*, p. 24; Air University Library, *The Future, Part 2: Warfare, Military Forces and Technology* (Maxwell AFB, Calif.: Air University Library, March 1989), p. 7; Air University Library, *The Middle East*, p. 233; Bureau of Intelligence and Research, 1251-AR, *China: Recent Developments in Arms Control Policies*, March 25, 1986.

72. Bureau of Intelligence and Research, "Persian Gulf: Fourth Time Lucky for Iranian Silkworms at Kuwait," October 15, 1987.

73. U.S. Congress, House Committee on Appropriations, *Departments of Commerce, Justice and State, the Judiciary and Related Agencies Appropriations for FY 1986, Part 7* (Washington, D.C.: U.S. Government Printing Office, 1985), p. 492.

74. AFSPACECOM Regulation 200-1, "Air Force Space Command Unit Intelligence Program," February 17, 1989, p. 7; Air Force Intelligence Agency, AFIAR 23-1, "Organizations and Functions, Air Force Intelligence Agency (AFIA)," June 7, 1990, p. F-6.

75. *U.S. Army Foreign Science and Technology Center* (Charlottesville, Va.: FSTC, n.d.), p. 19.

76. Air University Special Bibliography No. 207, *Communist China: Military Capabilities*, pp. 11, 14; Air University Special Bibliography No. 205, *Soviet Military Capabilities*, pp. 30, 61; Air University Library, *China: Military Capabilities* (February 1988), p. 13.

77. INSCOM, *ITAC Intelligence Production Program*, February 1983, pp. 133–36.

78. Intelligence and Threat Analysis Center, *1984 ITAC Historical Report*, Appendix N, p. 1.

79. Ibid., p. 4; CDRUSAITAC, Subject: "USAITAC Production Activities Highlights," Rpt. 05-83, 1983, p. 12.

80. Air University Library, *China: Military Capabilities* (August 1990), p. 15; Air University Library, *Eastern Europe* (Maxwell AFB, Ala.: Air University Library, November 1990), p. 20; Air University Library, *Iraq-Iran Conflict*, p. 6; Air University Library, *Iraq-Kuwait*

Crisis, August 2, 1990–January 15, 1991 (Maxwell AFB, Ala.: Air University Library, n.d.), p. 6; Air University Library, *Persian Gulf Area* (Maxwell AFB, Ala.: Air University Library, April 1988), p. 8; Air University Library, *Terrorism* (Maxwell AFB, Ala.: Air University Library, January 1987), p. 40.

81. Air University Library, *China: Military Capabilities* (August 1990), p. 18.

82. AFSPACECOM Regulation 200-1, "Air Force Space Command Unit Intelligence Program," p. 7.

14
COUNTERINTELLIGENCE

Counterintelligence is often associated with the catching of spies. However, it is necessary to distinguish between *counterintelligence* and *counterespionage*. Counterespionage is a narrower activity than counterintelligence and is concerned simply with preventing a foreign government's illicit acquisition of government secrets. Counterintelligence is concerned with understanding, and possibly neutralizing, the entire intelligence operations of foreign nations.

Counterintelligence was defined by President Reagan's Executive Order 12333 as both "information gathered" and "activities conducted" in order "to protect against espionage, other intelligence activities, sabotage or assassination conducted on behalf of foreign powers, organizations or persons, or international terrorist activities but not including personnel, physical documents or communications security."[1] Thus, as defined in Executive Order 12333, counterintelligence incorporates a wide range of activities not strictly in the counterintelligence tradition. The definition stresses the *counter* aspect and lets the term *intelligence* represent activities below the conventional military level, including terrorist attacks and sabotage. Some would also consider counterdeception and counter–illicit technology transfer to be part of the list of counterintelligence subcategories.[2] Such a view essentially mixes traditional counterintelligence with positive intelligence designed to counter any form of hostile activity, with a framework (counterdeception) for the analysis of positive intelligence.

The traditional notion of counterintelligence, the one that will be used here, focuses on information gathered and activities conducted with the purpose of understanding and possibly neutralizing the activities of foreign intelligence services. In this view there are four basic functions of counterintelligence activity:

- collection of information on foreign intelligence and security services through open and clandestine sources;
- the evaluation of defectors;
- research and analysis concerning the structure, personnel, and operations of foreign intelligence and security services;
- operations for the purpose of disrupting and neutralizing intelligence and security services engaging in activities hostile to the United States.

Some nations are allies of the United States on one level but also employ their intelligence services to engage in activities—such as industrial espionage—inimical to U.S. interests. Most prominently, the French Directorate General of External Security (DGSE) has penetrated several U.S. companies, including IBM, Texas Instruments, and Bell Textron. A French government document apparently obtained by the CIA indicated a broad effort to obtain information about the work of U.S. aerospace companies. Thus, the United States may seek to penetrate such services in an attempt to neutralize that aspect of their activities.[3]

COLLECTION

Information concerning the activities of foreign intelligence and security services comes from a variety of sources. Open sources concerning both friendly and hostile services may include official government documents (e.g., telephone directories, yearly reports, parliamentary hearings, reports of commissions of inquiry), books, and articles in magazines and newspapers. In the case of closed societies, open source material is limited; nevertheless, even in these countries analysts may get some useful insights into high-ranking personnel or some aspects of internal operations from the occasional government-approved account of intelligence and security service actions.

Information about friendly services may also come from liaison and training arrangements. Thus, Dominic Perrone of the U.S. Military Liaison Office, U.S. Embassy, Rome, was able, in 1978, to gather inside information on the effectiveness of the newly established Italian intelligence and security services (the SISMI, or Military Security and Information Service, and the SISDE, or Democratic Security and Information Service) from several sources inside the Italian government. As a result, Perrone was able to prepare a 4,000-word report for the DIA that indicated that the resources devoted to SISDE's antiterrorist activities were making effective counterespionage impossible, that the Commander of SISDE was not qualified for the job, and that both SISDE and SISMI were performing poorly.

Liaison with allied services also provides information about the activities of hostile services—such as when the French Directorate for Territorial Surveillance (DST) provided the CIA with information about its agent, Vladimir Vetrov, codenamed FAREWELL, in Directorate T of the KGB. Beginning in 1981, FAREWELL provided the DST with more than 4,000 documents on Soviet scientific and technical espionage, including information on the Soviet Union's plans to steal Western technological secrets and internal assessments of its covert technology acquisitions activities. Specifically, FAREWELL provided: (1) a complete, detailed list of all Soviet organizations involved in scientific and technical intelligence; (2) reports on Soviet plans, accomplishments, and annual savings in all branches of the military industry due to the illegal acquisition of foreign technology; (3) a list of all KGB officers throughout the world involved in scientific and technical espionage; and (4) the identities of the principal agents recruited by the officers of "line X" in ten Western nations, including the United States, West Germany, and France. French President François Mitterrand informed President Reagan about FAREWELL in 1981 and gave him a sample of the intelligence material the agent had transmitted. Several weeks later, the head of the DST at the time, Marcel Chalet, visited Vice President Bush in Washington to discuss FAREWELL.[4]

Two types of human sources may provide useful information. The first type is an agent who holds an official position within a hostile service. This type is either a mole (someone recruited prior to their entry into the service—for example, Kim Philby) or a "defector in place" (someone who agrees to provide information after having attained an intelligence or security position—for example, FAREWELL). An individual may agree to provide information for ideological or financial reasons or as the result of coercion or blackmail, which might be based on evidence of misbehavior (sexual or financial).

The United States had some significant successes in penetrating the Soviet military intelligence organization, the Chief Intelligence Directorate of the General Staff (GRU). In the late 1950s and early 1960s, Peter Popov and Oleg Penkovsky, both Colonels in the GRU, volunteered their services to the CIA. In addition to providing detailed information concerning the structure of the GRU, they supplied information on the physical layout of the GRU's headquarters and identified GRU agents and described their personalities. The CIA also began receiving information in the early 1960s from GRU officer Dimitri Polyakov, who was codenamed BOURBON by the CIA and TOP HAT by the FBI. Polyakov, who reached the rank of Major General, was eventually betrayed, and he was executed in 1988.[5] In addition, as noted in Chapter 11, GRU Colonel Anatoli Filatov and several other Soviet intelligence officers provided the CIA with information in the 1970s and 1980s.

The CIA also apparently penetrated the Indian Research and Analysis Wing (RAW). In 1987 a senior RAW man, K. V. Unnikrishnan, was arrested and charged with spying for the CIA. Unnikrishnan was reported to have been stationed in Madras where he was responsible for coordinating Tamil insurgency activities. Unnikrishnan was reportedly blackmailed with compromising photographs of himself and a "stewardess."[6]

The second type of human source is the defector. Defectors provide information concerning various aspects of an intelligence or security service's structure, operations, and leadership. The CIA certainly reaped an intelligence bonanza when Major Bolanos Hunter of the Nicaraguan Directorate General of State Security (Direccion General de Seguridad del Estado, DGSE) defected in 1983. For almost all of the period between January 1980 and May 7, 1983, Hunter had special responsibility for surveillance of the U.S. Embassy and CIA activities in Nicaragua. He provided information on the structure of the DGSE, the numbers of Nicaraguans in the DGSE (2,800–3,000), the presence of foreign advisers to the

DGSE (70 Soviets, 400 Cubans, 40 to 50 East Germans, 20 to 25 Bulgarians), and the Soviet provision of sophisticated bugging devices.[7]

Similarly, senior intelligence officers who have defected from Cuba and China have provided the United States with new information on intelligence and counterintelligence operations in those nations. In June 1987, Major Florentino Apillaga Lombard defected to the United States from the Cuban DGI (General Directorate of Intelligence) and proceeded to inform CIA officials that the great majority of CIA "assets" in Cuba were actually double agents working for the Cuban government. In 1986, Yu Zhensan, the former head of the Foreign Affairs Bureau of the PRC's Ministry of State Security, defected and provided the United States with extensive information about Chinese intelligence operations abroad, including the names of Chinese agents and suspected agents from other nations working in China. Before defecting, he apparently provided the United States with information leading to the arrest of Larry Wu-Tai Chin, an employee of the CIA's Foreign Broadcast Information Service, as a long-term Chinese mole.[8]

During the course of the Cold War the United States benefited from information provided by a substantial number of KGB and GRU defectors. As a result, the CIA was able to develop a comprehensive picture of the structures and activities of those organizations.

Before his redefection, KGB official Vitaly Yurchenko provided the CIA with information concerning several Soviet penetrations of the U.S. intelligence community—revealing that former CIA officer Edward Lee Howard and former NSA employee Ronald Pelton had been providing intelligence to the Soviet Union. He also stated that Pelton and naval spy John Walker were the KGB's most prized assets in the United States.[9]

In January 1986 it was reported that another KGB officer may have been the most valuable defector from the Soviet bloc in recent years—providing far more information than that provided by Yurchenko. The defector allegedly defected in spring 1985 by escaping from East Germany via helicopter. His reported expertise was in the area of KGB organization and procedures rather than ongoing operations. The existence of the alleged defector, however, was adamantly denied by the White House and the CIA.[10]

In June 1986, it was reported that the head of KGB operations in North Africa and KGB liaison to the Palestine Liberation Organization, Oleg Agraniants, had defected to the United States. Agraniants, who may have been working for the CIA for the three years prior to his defection, apparently supplied the names of KGB agents in Tunisia, Algeria, Morocco, and Libya.[11]

The changing domestic situation in the Soviet Union during the Gorbachev era, as well as the collapse of the Soviet Union, led to the defection of numerous KGB officers. Thus, in 1990, Igor Cherpinski, reportedly the KGB station chief in Belgium, defected. In 1991, Sergei Illarionov, a KGB Colonel based in Genoa, defected and helped Western security services identify KGB espionage networks in Europe.[12]

Recent non-Soviet defectors have included Majid Giaka, a Libyan intelligence officer who provided information on the 1988 bombing of Pan Am Flight 103.[13]

EVALUATION OF DEFECTORS

The evaluation and debriefing of defectors are another important aspect of counterintelligence operations. The United States has provided political asylum to officials from the Soviet Union and Russia, China, Nicaragua, Cuba, and a number of East European countries. When the defector is not an intelligence officer, the debriefers seek information on the policies and leaders of whatever government component employed the defector. In addition to eliciting information, the debriefers seek to determine the reliability of the information offered.

When the defector has been employed by a foreign intelligence service, the debriefers attempt to extract the maximum information possible on the structure, functions, agents, operations, procedures, and leaders of the defector's intelligence community as well as to determine the defector's reliability. They try to obtain the information as soon as possible so that if a response is necessary, action can be taken before the hostile intelligence service realizes its officer or agent has defected. When dealing with defectors from hostile intelligence services, the debriefers must determine where the officer's knowledge ends and where exaggeration or fabrication in the face of depleted information begins. Complicating the debriefers' task is the fact that many defectors hold back information as insurance for continued protection.[14]

The inability of the CIA's Counterintelligence Staff to determine conclusively the bona fides of several important defectors was a vital factor in much of the conflict that divided the U.S. intelligence community and hindered collection operations against the Soviet Union for many years. In addition to the problems of defector exaggeration and fabrication, there is the possibility that the defector is a plant—a hostile counterintelligence operation directed at the CIA. A false defector might allege, for example, the existence of a highly placed mole. Thus, a high official of the British Security Service and subsequent Director-General was at one point the subject of a KGB disinformation campaign alleging that he was a Soviet agent. Such an allegation can lead to huge expenditures of resources chasing false leads, damage the careers and reputations of effective intelligence officers, and cause a decline in the morale of the allegedly penetrated service.[15]

This was the case in the controversy that stemmed from the defection in 1962 of Anatoli Golitsin. When Golitsin defected to the CIA from Helsinki, Finland, he identified himself as a Major in the First Chief Directorate of the KGB and said he had worked primarily against targets in the NATO alliance. Given the codename AE/LADLE and the cover name John Stone by the United States (he was KAGO to the British and MARTEL to the French), Golitsin caused a sensation. According to Golitsin, the KGB had planted an agent within the highest echelons of U.S. intelligence. The penetration agent, he said, was assisted by "outside" men—other

Soviet-controlled agents masking themselves as defectors or double agents—who supplied pieces of disinformation designed to bolster the "inside" man's credibility. The inside agent in turn helped to confirm the authenticity of the outside agents.[16]

During his debriefing sessions with James Angleton in 1962, Golitsin called particular attention to a trip that V. M. Kovshuk had made to the United States in 1957 under diplomatic cover. Golitsin identified Kovshuk, who had used the alias Komarov, as the then-reigning head of the all-important American Embassy section of the KGB and stressed that only an extremely important mission would account for his leaving his post in Moscow to come to the United States. He suggested that Kovshuk's mission might have involved contacting or activating a high-level Soviet penetration agent within the CIA who had been recruited years before in Moscow.[17]

Golitsin further cautioned that the KGB, realizing that he knew about Kovshuk's mission, would almost certainly attempt to discredit or deflect the CIA from the information he was providing. He warned Angleton that Soviet disinformation agents could be expected to make contact with the CIA for this purpose. When Yuri Nosenko defected to the CIA in 1964, he supplied information that ran counter to that of Golitsin in many instances. Nosenko tended to downplay the possibility of a Soviet penetration of the CIA and stressed Soviet security measures in response to the detection of Peter Popov. There were, however, several problems with Nosenko's story and bona fides that made him and his explanations suspect to some. Indeed, the extent of doubt about Nosenko led to his being incarcerated by the CIA for a period of three years until he was finally released by Director Richard Helms. After Nosenko's release he became a paid consultant to the CIA. No subsequent Soviet defector cast doubt on Nosenko being a true defector. Those who had specific information backed his legitimacy. The suspicions that Golitsin generated seriously impeded the CIA's HUMINT collection operations in the Soviet Union throughout the 1960s and damaged the careers of several CIA officers.[18]

In the case of Vitaly Yurchenko, the CIA Counterintelligence Staff was faced with assessing whether he was a legitimate defector who changed his mind or a plant who intended to redefect from the beginning. Yurchenko, a KGB staff officer with twenty-five years of service, requested political asylum in the United States at the U.S. Embassy in Rome on August 1, 1985.[19]

In 1960, Yurchenko had been transferred from the Soviet Navy to the KGB's Third Chief Directorate; from 1961 to 1965 and from August 1967 until December 1968 he worked as an operations officer and the Deputy Chief of the KGB Special Department for the Black Sea Fleet. From December 1968 until May 1972, he was assigned to the KGB residency in Egypt as a Soviet adviser to the staff of the Egyptian fleet in Alexandria. From May 1972 to May 1975 he was Deputy Chief of the Third (Intelligence) Department of the Third Chief Directorate, responsible—among other things—for the recruitment of foreigners using the resources of Soviet military counterintelligence as well as the insertion of agents into Western intelligence services.[20]

From August 1975 until August 1980, Yurchenko was the security officer at the Soviet Embassy in Washington. There, he was responsible for ensuring the security of Soviet establishments and citizens in Washington, for protecting classified information, and for handling foreign visitors. In September 1980, he was transferred to the First Chief Directorate. From that date until March 1985 he was chief of the Fifth Department of Directorate K, where he was responsible for investigating suspected espionage incidents involving KGB staff personnel and information leaks concerning the First Chief Directorate, among other security functions. From April to July 1985, he was Deputy Chief of the First Department, which carried out operations against the United States and Canada.[21]

Three months after his defection, Yurchenko appeared at a press conference at the Soviet Embassy in Washington claiming to have been kidnapped, drugged, and kept in isolation at a CIA safehouse in Fredricksburg, Virginia. His "escape" was due, according to Yurchenko, to a "momentary lapse" by his captors. (In fact, he walked out of a Georgetown restaurant without opposition from his CIA escort.) Two days later, Yurchenko, after a visit by U.S. officials to determine he was acting of his own free will, flew back to Moscow. In Moscow, he held a two-hour press conference at which he and other Soviet officials accused the United States of "state terrorism." Subsequent reports that he had been executed were proved incorrect when he was discovered walking on a Moscow street.[22]

Following Yurchenko's redefection, U.S. officials speculated on the reasons for his actions. If Yurchenko was a plant who had planned to redefect from the beginning, KGB motives could have been to gather information on CIA treatment and debriefing of defectors or to embarrass the CIA and discourage CIA acceptance of defectors. Among those suggesting that Yurchenko was a plant were President Reagan, Senator Patrick Leahy (then Vice Chairman of the Senate Select Committee on Intelligence), and other officials who considered Yurchenko's information to be largely "historical."[23]

Others suggested that Yurchenko had been a legitimate defector who had changed his mind. Reasons given for an actual change included his rejection by the wife of a Soviet official stationed in Canada with whom Yurchenko had had a relationship and visited almost immediately after his arrival in the United States, the great publicity generated by his defection, a general homesickness for "Mother Russia" often experienced by Soviet defectors, and a specific longing to be reunited with his family—especially his sixteen-year-old son. Among those doubting a staged defection was then FBI chief William H. Webster, who said that Yurchenko had provided the United States with valuable information concerning Soviet espionage activities—including information on the roles of Edward Lee Howard and Ronald Pelton.[24]

In early 1993, DCI Robert Gates stated that the CIA had concluded that Yurchenko was a bona fide defector. According to Gates: "My view, and I think the view of virtually everybody in this building, is that Yurchenko was genuine. He provided too much specific information, including in the counterintelligence arena, that has been useful, for him, in my judgement to have been a plant."[25]

RESEARCH AND ANALYSIS

It is fundamental to both intelligence and counterintelligence missions that there exists a store of knowledge concerning the personalities, past operations, structure, and activities of other nations' intelligence and security services. Only with such knowledge can positive intelligence collection operations be planned and conducted effectively. Likewise, only with such knowledge can effective penetration and disruption and neutralization activities be conducted.

The most significant research and analysis on foreign intelligence services conducted within the U.S. intelligence community are those reports prepared by the CIA's Counterintelligence Center (CIC), which is the successor to the Counterintelligence Staff. The CIC prepares reports ranging from 50 to 100 pages on all intelligence communities of interest, both hostile and friendly. Many of those reports bear the title "Foreign Intelligence and Security Services" along with the name of the country that is the subject of the report. The reports detail the origins of the intelligence services, their structure, function, and mode of operation, and the arrangements for control by higher authority.

Thus, the forty-seven-page study *Israel: Foreign Intelligence and Security Services,* published in March 1977, focused in its first section on the background and development of the Israeli services, objectives, and structure; the relationship between the government and the services; and professional standards. The second, third, and fourth sections focused on the three major Israeli intelligence and security units—the Mossad, Shin Bet, and AMAN, respectively. In each case, the report examined the service's function, organization, administrative practice (including training), and methods of operation. Additionally, liaison with other Israeli and foreign services was considered. The three penultimate sections examined the Foreign Ministry's Research and Political Planning Center, the National Police, and key officials, and the final section commented on principal sources.[26]

A 1984 study entitled *Soviet Intelligence: KGB and GRU* discussed the background and development of the Soviet services, national intelligence objectives and structure, the relationship between the Communist party/government and the services, the internal security and counterintelligence operations of the KGB, and the foreign operations of the KGB and the GRU. The study's Table of Contents is shown in Table 14-1.

Counterintelligence studies are also prepared by the Defense Intelligence Agency and the INSCOM's Intelligence and Threat Analysis Center. DIA prepared a November 15, 1978, Intelligence Appraisal entitled *Italy: Reorganization of Intelligence and Security Services,* which discussed the background and structure of the intelligence and security services, key intelligence and security service personali-

334

Table 14-1. Table of Contents for Central Intelligence Agency, *Soviet Intelligence: KGB and GRU* (Washington, D.C.: CIA, 1984).

Table of Contents

Table 14-1. Table of Contents for Central Intelligence Agency, *Soviet Intelligence: KGB and GRU* (Washington, D.C.: CIA, 1984). (*continued*)

Table 14-1. Table of Contents for Central Intelligence Agency, *Soviet Intelligence: KGB and GRU* (Washington, D.C.: CIA, 1984). (*continued*)

FIGURES

ties, intelligence reforms, and the outlook for the future. The studies prepared by ITAC include: *Italy: A Counterintelligence Assessment* (April 1984), which reviewed the various intelligence and security services of the Italian government and various threats, including terrorism, wartime sabotage, and espionage; *The DST: An Organization in Flux* (September 1986); *France: A Counterintelligence Assessment* (June 1981); *GRU Activity in the Washington, D.C., Area* (April 1983); and *The Cuban Intelligence Threat in Panama* (May 1978).[27] Shorter "ITAC Intelligence Notes" have included *Israel's Shin Bet Scandal* (June 1986) and *Greenpeace: Repercussions in the French I&SS*.[28]

NEUTRALIZATION

The neutralization of the activities of hostile intelligence services can be accomplished by various means. Penetrations of a hostile service can be used not only to gather information but also to damage the service's operations. In 1980 the Polish civilian intelligence and security service, the SB, began receiving classified information from James D. Harper, a Silicon Valley engineer. Harper, via his wife, who worked for a southern California defense contractor, obtained copies of well over 100 pounds of classified reports—which he sold to the SB for more than $250,000. Most of the documents pertained to the U.S. Minuteman missile and ballistic missile defense programs and were classified Confidential or Secret. Documents sold to the SB included the 1978 *Minuteman Defense Study (Final Report)*, the 1981 *Report on the Task Force on U.S. Ballistic Missile Defense*, and a 1978 Martin Marietta Corporation study entitled *Endoatmospheric Nonnuclear Kill Technology Requirements and Definition Study*. Harper was detected by a CIA penetration of the SB. When arrested he was preparing to deliver an additional 150 to 200 pounds of documents.[29]

A second way to neutralize a hostile intelligence service is by means of passing information to a third country that will lead that country to take action against the officers and agents of the hostile service. In many cases the CIA passes such information on as a natural result of its liaison with a friendly security service—such as when it provided the British Security Service with information on East German intelligence operations in the United Kingdom. When GRU officer Sergei Bokhane, who had been stationed in Greece, defected, he provided information on at least three Greeks involved in spying for the Soviet Union. Included was Michael Megalokonomos, who, when apprehended, was in possession of a codebook, a microfilm reading device, a radio for picking up special frequencies, and instructions on how to work a radio transmitter. Also named by Bokhane was Nikos Pipitsoulis, who sold an electrical device to Soviet officials for $43,000. In addition, a Lieutenant Commander working in the data processing unit at Greece's defense headquarters was involved in passing information to the Soviet Union. The information provided to the CIA by Bokhane was passed on to Greek security authorities, leading to the arrest of the three agents.[30]

On other occasions the recipient of the information may itself be a hostile nation. In the spring of 1983, when the Iranian Communist (Tudeh) party had been closed down, the CIA provided a list of Soviet agents and collaborators operating in Iran to the Khomeini regime and its security service (SAVAMA). As a result, 18 Soviet diplomats were expelled, 200 suspects executed, and Tudeh party leaders imprisoned.[31]

Another method of neutralization entails running double agents. One CIA double agent operation that came to light is one that backfired. In 1959, Captain Nikolai Federovich Artamanov, the youngest commanding officer of a destroyer in Soviet naval history, defected to Sweden. Information about Artamanov was transferred to the United States by the CIA Station Chief in Sweden.[32]

Artamanov was subsequently recruited by the Office of Naval Intelligence (ONI) to come to the United States. In his debriefing, he provided the ONI with information on the Soviet use of travelers for intelligence collection, Soviet nuclear strategy, and Soviet destroyer tactics against submarines. Subsequently, he was given a new name, Nicholas Shadrin, and a position as a translator in the Naval Scientific and Technical Intelligence Center. In 1966 two events of importance occurred. Shadrin went to work for the Defense Intelligence Agency and was also approached by a Soviet intelligence officer who tried to recruit him. Shadrin did not close the door on the officer but reported it to the FBI. After initial hesitation, Shadrin was persuaded to become a double agent, to "accept" the Soviet offer and feed the KGB CIA-doctored disinformation.[33]

Among the reasons for U.S. pressure on Shadrin to accept the double agent role was that his recruiter, "Igor," was believed to be a Soviet defector-in-place who had been assigned the task of recruiting Shadrin. Successful completion of his mission, said Igor, would help propel him to a new position—Chief of the KGB's American Department.[34]

After several years of pretending to work for the KGB, Shadrin began to make trips abroad to meet his controller. He never returned from a December 20, 1975, meeting in Vienna. According to temporary defector Vitaly Yurchenko, Shadrin was, by accident, fatally chloroformed while struggling in the backseat of a sedan with Soviet agents trying to spirit him out of Austria.[35]

The military, particularly the Army, also runs double agent operations. According to U.S. Army Regulation 381-47, offensive counterintelligence operations, such as double agent operations, "may require engagement in unorthodox operations and activities. These unorthodox activities may be at variance with recognized standards or methods normally associated with the military Service. They will be undertaken only when authorized by the commander of a counterintelligence unit or higher authority."[36]

Double agent operations often are initiated after a member of the U.S. armed forces reports an approach made by a foreign intelligence officer. In 1984 there were 481 incidents of soldiers being approached by people suspected of being Soviet bloc intelligence officers or sympathizers.[37]

Under the direction of counterintelligence authorities, the service personnel maintain contact with the foreign intelligence officers, providing a combination of factual low-level and false high-level information supplied by INSCOM, the Naval Investigative and Security Command, or the Air Force Office of Special Investigations. Such operations yield information on the intelligence targets of hostile services; allow identification of the intelligence officers and agents of hostile services; tie up hostile service resources; and permit the transmission of disinformation concerning the plans and capabilities of U.S. military forces. The INSCOM agents involved in such operations bear codenames such as ROYAL MITER, LANCER FLAG, HOLE PUNCH, LARIAT TOSS, CANARY DANE, and LANDSCAPE BREEZE.[38]

One operation involved Chief Warrant Officer Janos Szmolka, who had left Hungary to become a U.S. citizen. Szmolka eventually joined the U.S. Army and was stationed in West Germany. From there, he went on authorized leaves to Budapest to visit his mother in 1978 and 1979. On his third trip he was approached by a man described as a Hungarian intelligence officer who offered to insure better living conditions for Szmolka's family in exchange for information.

Szmolka returned to West Germany and reported the offer to his superiors. For the next four years, under the direction of Army counterintelligence officers, he was in contact with Hungarian agents in Europe and the United States. In 1980, under normal rotation procedures, he was transferred to the States, and in 1982, when the Army desired to uncover the Hungarian intelligence network in the United States, Szmolka was instructed to inform the Hungarians, through coded letters, that he had valuable information to turn over. On April 17, 1982, he went to the Confederate monument in August, Georgia, near his post at Fort Gordon, to meet a Hungarian agent. Federal agents arrested Otto A. Gilbert, an expatriate Hungarian and naturalized U.S. citizen, and charged him with espionage. Gilbert received a reduced sentence in exchange for information about Hungarian intelligence.[39]

NOTES

1. Ronald Reagan, "Executive Order 12333: United States Intelligence Activities," December 4, 1981, in *Federal Register* 46, 235 (December 8, 1981): 59941–55 at 59953.

2. For example, William Harris, "Counterintelligence Jurisdiction and the Double Cross System by National Technical Means," in Roy Godson, ed., *Intelligence Requirements for the 1980s: Counterintelligence* (New Brunswick, N.J.: Transaction, 1980), pp. 53–82.

3. Jay Peterzell, "When 'Friends' Become Moles," *Time*, May 28, 1990, p. 50; "Parlez-Vous Espionage?" *Newsweek*, September 23, 1991, p. 40; Douglas Jehl, "U.S. Expanding Its Effort to Halt Spying by Allies," *New York Times*, April 30, 1993, pp. A1, A10; R. Jeffrey Smith, "U.S. to Protest Industrial Spying by Allies," *Washington Post*, April 30, 1993, p. A39; ABC, "World News Tonight," April 29, 1993.

4. Thierry Wolton, *Le KGB en France* (Paris: Bernard Grasset, 1986), pp. 248–49.

5. Tom Mangold, *Cold Warrior, James Jesus Angleton: The CIA's Master Spy Hunter* (New York: Simon & Schuster, 1991), pp. 227–36; David Wise, *Molehunt: The Secret Search for Traitors That Shattered the CIA* (New York: Random House, 1991), pp. 153–54.

6. Inderjit Badhwar, "Spy-Catching," *India Today*, September 20, 1987, p. 33.

7. Don Oberdorfer and Joanne Omang, "Nicaraguan Bares Plan to Discredit Foes," *Washington Post*, June 19, 1983, pp. 1, 4.

8. Jack Anderson and Dale Van Atta, "Cuban Defector Impeaches CIA Spies," *Washington Post,* March 21, 1988, p. B15; Jack Anderson and Dale Van Atta, "CIA Recruits Were Castro's Agents," *Washington Post,* March 23, 1988, p. D11; Jack Anderson and Dale Van Atta, "CIA, Cubans in Looking-Glass War," *Washington Post,* March 25, 1988, p. E5; "Chinese Official Said Exposer of CIA Turncoat," *Washington Post,* September 5, 1986, p. A18; Michael Wines, "Spy Reportedly Unmasked by China Defector," *Los Angeles Times,* September 5, 1986, pp. 1, 12; Daniel Southerland, "China Silent on Reported Defection of Intelligence Official," *Washington Post,* September 4, 1986, p. A30.

9. "Did Yurchenko Fool the CIA?" *Newsweek,* November 18, 1985, pp. 34–39.

10. Philip Shenon, "High K.G.B. Officer Is Said to Defect," *New York Times,* January 26, 1986, pp. A1, A18; Lou Cannon and Patrick Tyler, "KGB Defector Report Flatly Denied," *Washington Post,* January 28, 1986, p. A10.

11. "High-Ranking KGB Agent Defects," *Washington Post,* June 20, 1986, p. A5.

12. "Defection of KGB Agent Causes Stir," *Washington Times,* June 6, 1990, p. A11; Bill Gertz, "CIA Learning from KGB Defector," *Washington Times,* March 5, 1992, p. A3.

13. George Lardner, Jr., "Libyan Named as Informer in Bombing," *Washington Post,* September 18, 1992, p. A30.

14. Ralph Blumenthal, "Moscow Moves Rapidly in Defections to the U.S.," *New York Times,* November 7, 1985, p. A12.

15. For details of the Soviet campaign against Michael Hanley, see Nigel West, *Molehunt: The Full Story of the Soviet Spy in MI5* (London: Weidenfeld and Nicolson, 1987), p. 45.

16. Edward Jay Epstein, *Legend: The Secret World of Lee Harvey Oswald* (New York: McGraw-Hill, 1978), p. 27.

17. Ibid., pp. 46–47, 264–65; David C. Martin, *Wilderness of Mirrors* (New York: Harper & Row, 1980), p. 110.

18. Thomas Powers, *The Man Who Kept the Secrets: Richard Helms and the CIA* (New York: Knopf, 1979), p. 284; Mangold, *Cold Warrior,* pp. 244–65; Wise, *Molehunt.*

19. Central Intelligence Agency, "Vitaly Sergeyevich Yurchenko," November 8, 1985, p. 1.

20. Ibid. pp. 1–2.

21. Ibid., pp. 2–3.

22. "Did Yurchenko Fool the CIA?"; Celestine Bohlen, "Yurchenko Regales Moscow Audience," *Washington Post,* November 15, 1985, p. A33; "How Yurchenko Bade C.I.A. Adieu," *New York Times,* November 7, 1985, p. A12; Stephen Engelberg, "U.S. Is Convinced that K.G.B. Agent Wants to Go Home," *New York Times,* November 6, 1985, pp. A1, A12.

23. "Did Yurchenko Fool the CIA?"; Stephen Engelberg, "President Sees a Soviet 'Ploy' in 3 Defections," *New York Times,* November 7, 1985, pp. A1, A12; Stephen Engelberg, "Washington Ponders Yurchenko: A Troubled Spy or Actor?" *New York Times,* November 10, 1985, p. 20; Bob Woodward, "CIA Takes Serious Look at Theory That Yurchenko Was Double Agent," *Washington Post,* November 20, 1985, p. A35; Stephen Engelberg, "U.S. Aides Split on Yurchenko's Authenticity," *New York Times,* November 8, 1985, p. A10.

24. John Mintz, "FBI Chief Doubts Defection of Yurchenko Was Staged," *Washington Post,* December 2, 1985, pp. A1, A14; Joel Brinkley, "Publicity Said to Have Upset Defector," *New York Times,* November 14, 1985, p. A12; Christopher S. Wren, "K.G.B. Man Reportedly Met with Envoy's Wife," *New York Times,* November 9, 1985, p. 4; Arkady N. Shevchenko, "A Lesson of the Yurchenko Affair," *New York Times,* November 12, 1985, p.

35; Dale Russakof, "In Yurchenko Case, Truth Remains a Covert Factor," *Washington Post,* November 10, 1985, pp. A1, A40–41.

25. "Gates Calls '85 Defector Bona Fide," *Washington Post,* January 16, 1993, p. A7.

26. Central Intelligence Agency, *Israel: Foreign Intelligence and Security Services* (Washington, D.C.: CIA, March 1977).

27. Documents obtained under the Freedom of Information Act.

28. Documents obtained under the Freedom of Information Act.

29. "Partners in Espionage," *Security Awareness Bulletin,* August 1984, pp. 1–8; Linda Melvern, David Hebditch, and Nick Anning, *Techno-Bandits: How the Soviets Are Stealing America's High Tech Future* (Boston: Houghton Mifflin, 1984), p. 242; Affidavit of Allen M. Power, Federal Bureau of Investigation, submitted to State and Northern District of California, City and County of San Francisco, October 16, 1983, pp. 1–2; "For Love of Money and Adventure," *Time,* October 31, 1983, pp. 39–40; Howard Kurtz, "California Man Charged with Spying," *Washington Post,* October 18, 1983, pp. A1, A4; David Wise, "How Our Spy Spied Their Spy," *Los Angeles Times,* October 23, 1983, pp. 1–6.

30. "Greece Charges Three as Spies After U.S. Tip," *Washington Post,* September 17, 1985, p. A29.

31. Bob Woodward and Dan Morgan, "Soviet Threat Toward Iran Overstated, Casey Concluded," *Washington Post,* January 13, 1987, pp. A1, A8.

32. Henry Hurt, *Shadrin: The Spy Who Never Came Back* (New York: McGraw-Hill, 1981), p. 52.

33. Ibid., pp. 52–82; 140–51.

34. Ibid., pp. 120–51.

35. Ibid., p. 206; Patrick E. Tyler, "Missing U.S. Agent Dead," *Washington Post,* October 30, 1985, p. A9.

36. AR 381-47, "U.S. Army Offensive Counterintelligence Operations," May 15, 1982, p. 7.

37. Richard Halloran, "Overtures to Soldiers to Spy for Soviet Bloc Said to Rise," *New York Times,* June 29, 1985, pp. A1, B5.

38. "Former Counterspy for Army Is Indicted on Subversion Charges," *New York Times,* April 10, 1984, p. A20.

39. Ibid.

15
COVERT ACTION

Traditionally, covert action, which has often been the most visible aspect of U.S. intelligence activity, involves activities designed to influence foreign governments, events, organizations, or persons in support of U.S. foreign policy in such a way that the involvement of the U.S. government is not apparent. During the Reagan and Bush administrations, the notion of the "overt covert operation" emerged—the clearest example being U.S. attempts to overthrow the Sandinista government in Nicaragua.

U.S. covert actions have taken place in all major (and many minor) areas of the world: Europe and the Soviet Union, Africa, the Middle East, Asia, and Latin America. The operations have included: (1) political advice and counsel; (2) subsidies to an individual; (3) financial support and technical assistance to political parties; (4) support to private organizations, including labor unions and business firms; (5) covert propaganda; (6) training of individuals; (7) economic operations; (8) paramilitary or political action operations designed to overthrow or support a regime; and (9) attempted assassination.[1]

Many of these activities, such as paramilitary or political action operations, have had high visibility and have been designed to achieve a specific objective—for example, the overthrow of a regime or the defeat of an insurgent force. Many behind-the-scenes political support and propaganda activities have also been designed to achieve a specific objective, such as the electoral defeat or victory of a political candidate or party. Such low-visibility operations were conducted for an extended period of time in Italy in the late 1940s. Other low-visibility operations involving propaganda or aid to individuals or organizations have been less directed toward achieving a specific objective than toward enhancement of long-term U.S. objectives and the provision of a counter to similar Soviet activities. A high-visibility operation might also be conducted without expectation of "success." When the United States began aiding the Afghan rebels, for example, there was no expectation of actually inducing Soviet withdrawal, only of draining Soviet resources and keeping international attention on the Soviet role in Afghanistan.

HISTORY

The initial U.S. covert action undertaken in Europe was a low-visibility operation with a specific goal: prevention of a Communist victory in Italy. On December 20, 1947, a special procedures group was set up to organize propaganda in Italy. This group continued to initiate projects until its functions were taken over by the Office of Policy Coordination (OPC). Some $10 million were secretly taken from the economic stabilization fund and used to pay for local election campaigns, anti-Communist propaganda, and bribes. The covert operation was coupled with Italian-American lobbying and dire threats by President Truman about reductions in aid if the Communists won. In the 1948 election the Christian Democrats gained an overall majority of forty seats.[2]

In France, also in the late 1940s, CIA covert action had two objectives: to reduce the influence of the Communist party, especially in the unions, and to sway French public opinion in support of the European Defense Community. The CIA helped the moderate Force Ouvriere to split away from the Communist-dominated CGT labor union. Aid was also given to the Catholic CFTC labor union and several other non-Communist groups.[3]

In Eastern Europe and the Soviet Union, CIA-supported resistance groups engaged in sabotage and assisted in developing escape and evasion networks. The earliest operation involved the establishment of guerrilla networks in countries surrounding the Soviet Union in case of a Soviet invasion. Additionally, the OPC supported Polish resistance groups operating south of Warsaw and pumped money and arms into Lithuania and the Ukraine to assist local resistance groups. These operations ended by the mid-1950s. The Polish resistance organization turned out to have been under the control of Polish security forces, and Soviet forces had demolished the Ukrainian resistance by 1953.[4]

The CIA has been involved in numerous covert actions in Latin America, frequently of the high-visibility variety and with a specific objective in mind—a change in government or the death of a leader. The earliest major operation was targeted against the leftist government of Guatemala. The United States created, trained, funded, and directed a paramilitary force that succeeded, in 1954, in overthrowing the leftist government of Jacobo Arbenz. The regime was alleged to be Communist-dominated and had alienated the powerful United Fruit Company with its social welfare legislation, including minimum wage rates, strict tax laws, and land redistribution.[5]

Cuba was the target of an intense covert action campaign beginning shortly after Castro's rise to power in 1959. Before the Eisenhower administration had left office it had trained Cuban exiles and developed plans for an invasion of Cuba. Those efforts culminated in the Kennedy administration's first foreign policy disaster, the Bay of Pigs landing of April 17, 1961.[6]

The assassination of Castro was timed to coincide with the Bay of Pigs landing. At the behest of the CIA, Robert Maheu, an official of Howard Hughes's Summa

Corporation, had recruited mobster Johnny Rosselli to kill Castro. Several other attempts followed. A former employee of the Cuban Treasury Ministry was brought to Florida, trained to make the hit, and then infiltrated back into Cuba. On September 24, 1961, the Cuban government announced that it had discovered the plot. Then, in September 1963, Major Roland Cubela, a Castro official, offered to kill Castro for the CIA.[7]

After the Bay of Pigs, a new set of operations was undertaken in Cuba. On November 30, 1961, a memorandum instructed that the program "use our available assets ... to help overthrow the Communist regime." The actions were to be part of Operation MONGOOSE. The first planned mission, the demolition of a railroad yard and a bridge on Cuba's north coast, was aborted when the boat carrying the saboteurs was spotted. Other missions involved pressuring European shippers to turn down Cuban consignments, persuading a German ball bearing manufacturer to send off-center bearings to Cuba, and sabotaging Leyland buses on order by Cuba on the London docks.[8]

Operation MONGOOSE was terminated in January 1963, only to be followed by a new set of operations. On June 19, 1963, President Kennedy authorized an escalated program of sabotage in Cuba. Targets included facilities connected to the petroleum industry, railroad and highway transportation, electric power, and communications. The anti-Castro Movement for the Recovery of the Revolution (MRR) was revived and soon received $250,000 a month to launch a campaign known as Second Naval Guerilla. The purpose of this operation was to attack Cuban shipping and mount commando raids on shore installations. The CIA would supply the funding, logistical support, intelligence data, and guidance. The MRR would function "independently" of the CIA but submit each operation to the CIA for approval.[9]

In addition to the high-visibility operations, the CIA conducted low-visibility operations such as forgeries of various kinds. One such operation began with the unexpected resignation of the Cuban Consul in Buenos Aires, who had held his post through several previous Cuban administrations. Arriving in Miami, he presented the Cuban Revolutionary Council (CRC) with eighty-two documents that he said he had taken from the Cuban Embassy safe. The documents detailed a master plan, allegedly devised in Cuba, for the overthrow of Argentina's Frondizi government via infiltrations of business and politics and guerrilla training.[10]

The CRC held onto the documents so as to use them to maximum advantage during the Argentine President's state visit to the United States. The week before the Argentine chief of state left, however, La Nacion of Buenos Aires ran a long article accompanied by photocopies of the documents. This publicity resulted in a clamorous protest against Cuba. The Cubans claimed that the documents had been forged by Cuban exiles working in collusion with the CIA, which was true. The forgery was the beginning of a campaign aimed at "documenting" the idea that Castro was exporting revolution by subverting Organization of American States (OAS) nations, the goal being to get Cuba ousted from the OAS.[11]

Another dramatic instance of CIA covert action in Latin America occurred in Chile. The 1973 coup against Salvador Allende followed a long series of covert action operations that sought to prevent Allende from coming to power and to remove him once he did. The CIA worked secretly in 1958 and 1964 to block Allende's election to the presidency. In 1964, the CIA spent more than $2.6 million in support of Chile's Christian Democratic party. The candidate, Eduardo Frei, was victorious, with 56 percent of the total vote.[12]

In the next presidential election, in 1970, Allende was again a candidate, competing with a Christian Democrat and a right-wing candidate, and the CIA was again involved in attempting to prevent his election. Despite a variety of media and propaganda operations as well as continued support for the Christian Democratic candidate, Allende emerged as the plurality winner with 36 percent of the vote. Since Allende failed to obtain an absolute majority, the final choice had to be determined by a joint vote of the 50 Senators and 100 members of the Chamber of Deputies. Traditionally, Congress confirmed the plurality winner as President.

In the wake of Allende's victory, the U.S. government explored a variety of options to block his accession to power. On September 15, 1970, President Nixon informed CIA Director Richard Helms that an Allende regime was unacceptable to the United States and instructed the CIA to play a role in organizing a military coup to prevent Allende from ever taking office. A Chilean Task Force was assembled and began operations on September 18. Four CIA officers were inserted into Chile, and the U.S. Army Attaché in Santiago was placed under operational direction of the CIA Chief of Station.[13]

The subsequent campaign proceeded on two tracks. Under Track I (which was approved by the interagency 40 Committee responsible for supervising covert operations), the CIA employed a variety of covert political, economic, and propaganda tactics to manipulate the political scene. This track included the allocation of $25,000 to bribe members of the Chilean Congress—money that was never spent. Other CIA funds were spent on a propaganda campaign designed to convince three key elements in Chile—Frei, the Chilean political elite, and the Chilean military—of the need to remove Allende. Under the propaganda campaign, the CIA subsidized the radio programs, political advertisements, and political rallies of an anti-Allende group, placed articles in newspapers, and financed a small newspaper. In addition, foreign news articles were mailed directly to President Frei, Mrs. Frei, selected military leaders, and the Chilean domestic press. U.S. journalists were also enlisted, unwittingly, through special intelligence and inside briefings. According to the CIA, a *Time* magazine cover story "owed a great deal to written materials and briefings provided by CIA." At least 726 articles, broadcasts, editorials, and similar items were a direct result of agent activity.[14]

In addition, the CIA attempted to create financial and political panic sufficient to produce a military coup. Helms's instructions from Nixon had been to "make the economy scream," and multinationals were approached to take such actions as cutting off aid to Chile, stopping the shipments of spare parts, and causing runs on financial institutions.[15]

Track II involved direct efforts to produce a military coup, but neither the State Department nor the 40 Committee was informed about such activities. Helms was told that at least $10 million would be available to do the job. The CIA proceeded to make twenty-one contacts in two weeks with key Chilean military personnel to assure them that the United States would support a coup d'état. The main obstacle to such a coup was Army Chief of Staff General Rene Schneider, a strong supporter of the Chilean military's tradition of nonintervention in political affairs. Fearing the weight that Schneider's dissent would carry, the CIA passed three submachine guns and ammunition to Chilean officers planning to abduct the General. In the third kidnap attempt, on October 22, 1970, General Schneider was mortally wounded. The Church committee later found that the guns used in the abortive kidnapping were probably not those supplied by the CIA.[16]

Allende was confirmed as President on October 24, 1970. Track II, however, continued. The CIA was instructed to "stay alert and to do what we could to contribute to the objectives and purposes of Track II." In the aftermath of Allende's inauguration, the CIA operated in several key areas. It spent an additional $1.5 million in support of the opposition newspaper El Mercurio. It gave financial support to labor unions and trade associations with the intention of encouraging economic, and thus political, disorder. It has been suggested that the economically crippling truckers' strikes of 1972 and 1973, which preceded the September 1973 coup that ousted Allende and resulted in his death, were CIA supported.[17]

Probably the most successful CIA covert action, in the short term, was Operation AJAX. AJAX was the U.S.-British response to the 1951 nationalization of the Anglo-Iranian Oil Company by Iranian Prime Minister Mohammad Mossadegh. AJAX—the plan for toppling Mossadegh—was first proposed to the British government by the Anglo-Iranian Oil Company nine months after the nationalization had occurred.[18]

The British Secret Intelligence Service (SIS) approached the CIA with the plan in November 1952. The plan ultimately involved the organization of pro-Shah gangs with clubs, knives, and occasionally rifles or pistols. CIA representative Kermit Roosevelt was approached by the Anglo-Iranian Oil Company and met the SIS spokesman for AJAX, Deputy Director General John Sinclair. It was explained to Roosevelt that AJAX involved the overthrow of Mossadegh and that the British desired to begin the operation immediately.[19]

SIS officials traveled to Washington in December 1952 and February 1953. The first meeting involved purely operational discussions. The February 1953 delegation attended a series of formal planning meetings at which CIA Director Allen Dulles was also present. At these meetings the British briefed the CIA on the capabilities of their principal agents and gave their assessment of the Iranian Army and the loyalty of the population. Dulles gave his support to AJAX, and plans were developed to attain the AJAX objective with the British government and SIS as the "driving force."[20]

Although the SIS was the driving force, Kermit Roosevelt was selected as overall commander of the operation, at British suggestion, and in conducting the operation Roosevelt relied on both U.S. and British agents. At Roosevelt's instruction, the Shah attempted to fire Mossadegh and name General Fazollah Zahedi as the new premier. But the Shah's representative, who carried his order discharging Mossadegh, was arrested, Mossadegh announced that a foreign-backed coup had been attempted, and his supporters took to the streets. But, up to 6,000 pro-Shah rioters were turned out by the CIA, and full-scale rioting broke out on August 18 and 19, 1953. The rioting was followed by an attack against Mossadegh's residence by pro-Shah tank units. With his allies in control, the Shah returned from Italy, where he had fled after the rioting started, and assumed control.[21]

Two African nations that have been the subject of intensive covert action operations are Zaire and Angola. Covert action in Zaire resulted from the June 30, 1960, grant of independence to the Belgian Congo under a democratic coalition government headed by "militant nationalist" Patrice Lumumba. Shortly after independence, the Congolese Army mutinied; Belgian troops reoccupied part of the country and helped to organize the secession of Katanga province. The Prime Minister, Lumumba, and Chief of State Joseph Kasavubu called in U.N. forces to help reorganize the Army and remove the Belgians. The United Nations, with U.S. approval, delayed, and secessionist pressures against the Lumumba government began to mount.[22]

U.S. policymakers viewed Lumumba's threats to expel the U.N. force (except for African left-nationalist contingents) and invade Katanga with Afro-Asian and Soviet military assistance with alarm. On August 18 the Station Chief in the Congo cabled CIA headquarters that: "Embassy and Station believe Congo experiencing classic Communist takeover government. ... Whether or not Lumumba is actually Commie or just playing Commie games to assist in his solidifying power, anti-west forces rapidly increasing power Congo and there may little time left in which to take action to avoid another Cuba."[23]

In light of those reports, President Eisenhower approved an agenda of covert action measures, possibly including assassination. The CIA station began covert operations through labor groups and attempted to arrange a vote of no confidence in Lumumba in the Congolese Senate. On August 25, the Special Group (then in charge of supervising covert action) decided that "planning for the Congo would not necessarily rule out consideration of any particular kind of activity which might contribute to getting rid of Lumumba," and a series of assassination plots were encouraged and developed. Ultimately, Lumumba was captured by troops loyal to opponent Joseph Mobutu and transferred to Katanga province, where he was murdered.[24]

Subsequently, the CIA became heavily involved in the Angolan Civil War. In January 1975, Portugal set up a transitional tripartite coalition in Angola. The parties were Holden Roberto's National Front for the Liberation of Angola (FNLA) (backed by the People's Republic of China and Zaire), the Soviet-backed Popular Movement for the Liberation of Angola (MPLA), and Joseph Savimbi's National Union for the Total Independence of Angola (UNITA). In late January a CIA proposal to bolster the FNLA with $300,000 in political action funds was approved by the 40 Committee and President Ford.[25]

On July 17, 1975, the 40 Committee approved a $14 million, two-stage program of sending arms, communications gear, and other aid to Roberto and Savimbi, with an additional $10.7 million being approved in early September. The covert action program apparently had three objectives: to avoid a precedent of "Soviet expansion," to work with the "moderate" anti-Communist leaders of Zaire and Zambia, and to prevent Soviet- and MPLA-assisted black extremists from making gains in Namibia, Rhodesia, and the rest of southern Africa.[26]

Among the CIA's lower-visibility operations are propaganda and media activities. At its peak, the CIA's Propaganda Assets Inventory contained more than 800 news and public information organizations and individuals. Among these propaganda assets were the well-known "Radio Free Europe" and "Radio Liberty" as well as the lesser-known "Radio Free Asia," which began broadcasting to mainland China from Manila in 1951. Radio Free Asia went off the air in 1965. "Free Cuba Radio" did not have its own station but purchased airtime on Florida and Louisiana stations.[27]

CIA propaganda operations have also included the subsidization of anti-Castro publications in the United States. These included *Advance, El Mundo, El Prensa, Libre, Bohemia,* and *El Diario de las Americas.* In addition, AIP, a radio news agency in Miami, produced programs that were sent free to more than 100 small stations in Central and Latin America.[28]

In addition, the CIA subsidized numerous social democratic magazines in Europe and elsewhere to project the center-left alternative. Thus, CIA conduits provided support to *Prevves* (France), *Der Monat* (West Germany), *El Mundo Nuevo* (Latin America), *Quiet* and *Thought* (India), and *Argumenten* (Sweden).[29]

The CIA was also active in book publishing. Nearly a dozen publishing houses printed at least twenty of the more than 200 English-language books financed or produced by the CIA since the early 1950s. Altogether, more than 1,000 volumes were produced or subsidized in some way by the CIA by the late 1970s. Some publishers were unaware of any CIA connection with the books they published; others knew some books to be CIA produced or subsidized. Some, like Allied Pacific Printing of Bombay and the Asia Research Center in Hong Kong, were simply CIA proprietaries.[30]

THE CARTER YEARS

At the beginning of the Carter administration, in the wake of the Church committee, covert action represented a smaller than usual proportion of U.S. intelli-

gence activities. Over the course of time this proportion grew steadily. By 1981 the CIA was conducting a substantial number of propaganda operations.[31]

Most of the covert operations undertaken were in the form of propaganda and media support. One program, strongly advocated by National Security Adviser Zbigniew Brzezinski, involved smuggling thousands of books and other written materials into Eastern Europe and the Soviet Union. Another operation took place in Western Europe and concerned the intended deployment of the neutron bomb. In the face of unfavorable reactions in the West European press and from the West European population, and a massive Soviet propaganda campaign to block deployment of the enhanced radiation weapon, a covert action campaign was initiated to place articles in the West European press comparing the neutron bomb to the newly deployed Soviet SS-20. The articles began to appear frequently in February and March 1978. Newspapers such as the *Dusseldorf Rheinische Post, Die Welt, Bonn General Anzeiger, Freiburg Badische Zeitung, Suddeutsche Zeitung, Koblenz Rhein-Zeitung,* the *London Times,* the *London Daily Telegraph,* and *The Economist* began either to highlight the dangers of the SS-20 in comparison to the neutron bomb or to ridicule the Soviet propaganda campaign against the bomb.[32]

Additionally, within six months of the Sandinista takeover in Nicaragua, President Carter had signed a top-secret finding authorizing the CIA to provide political support to opponents of the Sandinista regime. The support would take the form of money and backing to encourage and embolden the opposition, pay for newsprint, and help to keep the newspaper *La Prensa* alive.[33]

At least two paramilitary operations were initiated during the Carter administration. One involved limited paramilitary support to undermine the Soviet-supported state of South Yemen. In this operation, several small teams of Yemenis were trained to blow up bridges and sabotage other targets. Second, prior to the Soviet invasion of Aghanistan, the United States supplied medical supplies, communications equipment, and technical advice to those opposing the Marxist regime. In the hours after the Soviets crossed the border, President Carter told an NSC meeting that the United States had a moral obligation to help arm the resistance. According to then Egyptian President Anwar Sadat: "The first moment that the Afghan incident took place, the U.S. contacted me … and the transport of armaments to the Afghan rebels started from Cairo on U.S. planes." The United States did not expect, however, that the rebels would be able to drive the Soviets out. Rather, the program was intended to help the rebels in conducting "harassment" of the Soviet occupying forces.[34]

THE REAGAN-BUSH YEARS

The Reagan administration considerably expanded the scope of covert activities. During the 1980s, covert action was considered a fundamental part of foreign policy and a means of overthrowing Marxist regimes outside of the Warsaw Pact. While continuing the general propaganda and media operations of the Carter administration, the Reagan administration undertook new covert actions directed against the governments of Afghanistan, Angola, Cambodia, Ethiopia, Iran, Libya, and Nicaragua. It also undertook covert actions in support of the governments of El Salvador and the Philippines.

During the Bush administration several Reagan administration programs were continued and others reduced or terminated in response to new international conditions, and some new programs were initiated.

Afghanistan

Reagan administration covert action in support of the Afghan resistance (which revolved around six major political groups and a variety of tribal bands, with 90,000–100,000 active insurgents at any one time) continued and expanded the program begun by the Carter administration. By fall 1981 the United States was involved with China, Pakistan, Egypt, and Saudi Arabia in a covert aid program. Saudi Arabia provided money, Egypt provided training, China provided weapons, and the United States provided Kalishnikov rifles, antitank missiles, and other weapons from U.S. and Egyptian stocks. Copies of Soviet weapons were produced by CIA-controlled factories in Egypt and the United States. In addition, some weapons, such as SA-7 antiaircraft missiles, were upgraded.[35]

Weapons would arrive by air in Pakistan aboard planes that were constantly being repainted with new markings. Under agreement with Pakistani ruler Zia-ul Huq, the arms were then placed under the jurisdiction of Pakistan's Inter-Services Intelligence Directorate (ISID) and, under ISID's supervision, transferred by a Pakistani Army unit, the National Logistics Cell, to mujahideen leaders. Among the arms were surface-to-air missiles, which were responsible for shooting down at least sixty Soviet helicopters in the first year.[36]

In December 1982, Ronald Reagan instructed the CIA to again increase the quality and quantity of weapons being sent to the resistance. The CIA began to supply heavier weapons, including bazookas, mortars, grenade launchers, mines, and recoilless rifles, for the first time, and by late January 1983 these weapons were reportedly entering Afghanistan in increasing numbers. Also sighted were U.S.-supplied communications equipment, range-finders for rocket launchers, silencers, and other equipment.[37]

A large increase in funding began in the fall of 1983 with a secret amendment to the defense appropriations bill authored by Representative Charles Wilson. The amendment rechanneled $40 million of DOD money to the CIA for the Afghan operation. Part of the money was for Oerlikon heavy antiaircraft cannons. At Wilson's initiative, Congress authorized another $50 million for more supplies and weapons in July 1984.[38]

By fiscal year 1985, expenditures for support of the resistance reached $250 million per year. The money was used mainly to purchase Soviet-made arms and ammunition from countries such as China, Egypt, and Israel. The arms would then be delivered to Pakistani ports and airfields, at which point the ISID would take control and deliver the weapons (or at least a portion of them) to the mujahideen leaders who lived in Peshawar. In addition to weapons, U.S. dollars bought medical supplies, food, and clothing for an estimated 200,000–300,000 full- or part-time insurgents.[39]

In March 1985 Ronald Reagan signed National Security Decision Directive 166, which authorized increased military aid to the mujahideen and made it clear that the goal of the effort was to drive the Soviets from Afghanistan. The directive was, at least in part, a product of intelligence concerning changes in Soviet strategy and tactics. As a result of the new policy, CIA and military officers supplied communications equipment and trained Pakistani instructors on how to use it. The Pakistanis, in turn, trained the mujahideen. The CIA also supplied delayed timing devices for tons of C-4 explosives to be used for urban sabotage and guerrilla attacks, long-range sniper rifles, a targeting device for mortars, and wire-guided antitank missiles. Of critical importance, the CIA also provided satellite reconnaissance data of Soviet targets on the Afghan battlefield, plans for military operations based on the satellite data, and communications intelligence.[40]

Support was further increased in the last part of 1985. In October 1985 Congress secretly appropriated $470 million for operations in Afghanistan during fiscal year 1986. Part of the funding was used for ammunition and small weapons. More significantly, part of those millions went for the purchase of advanced Stinger missiles. The decision to provide Stingers was made in March 1986. By summer the initial shipment of 150 was being distributed to some of the insurgents.[41]

U.S. instructors trained rebels in a camp in Pakistan after the guerrillas had initial difficulties in handling the weapon. Once the Afghan resistance began effectively employing the Stingers, Soviet pilots were forced to fly higher, reducing the effectiveness of air power against the guerrillas. The first day the Stingers were used in Afghanistan, the missiles were responsible for three Soviet helicopters being shot down. Several hundred additional aircraft succumbed to the Stingers in the following two years.[42]

The success of the initial shipment led to a more widespread program. By March 1987, more than 300 missiles had been delivered, with hundreds (maybe 600) more in the pipeline. In addition, the Stingers, including some of a more accurate later model, were being widely distributed among the resistance groups. When the program had begun in 1986, each four-man rebel unit had been given just one launcher and one missile at a time after undergoing a six- to eight-week course of training. Before receiving another missile, the unit had to show that it still had the launcher. By mid-1987, each unit was receiving more than one missile at a time.[43]

The initial proposal to supply Stingers was opposed by the CIA, at least partially on the grounds that the missiles were too easy to trace. It was only in March 1986 that the decision was made to send the missiles. Previously, when the resistance was using outdated SA-7 Strela SAMs, the Soviets were "able to operate with virtual impunity in the air, which given the fact that perhaps 80 percent of Soviet combat and logistics operations depend on air, virtually preclude[d] any significant and lasting mujahideen military gains."[44]

Some 40 to 80 percent of the missiles fired hit their targets. Moreover, the Stingers clearly had an effect beyond the simple destruction of Soviet planes. Because Soviet and Afghan warplanes were forced to drop bombs from an altitude of 10,000 feet rather than from 2,000 to 4,000 feet, their accuracy was greatly reduced. A U.S. Army study concluded that the Stingers "changed the nature of combat" in the civil war and constituted the "war's decisive weapon."[45]

In the latter half of 1987 the Reagan administration decided to provide the guerrillas with long-range 120-mm mortars and mine-clearing equipment to help them attack Soviet and Afghan military bases. The insurgents had been pressing for such materiel so as to be able to more effectively attack eight major Soviet airbases and approximately thirty smaller Soviet or Afghan garrisons with airstrips scattered around Afghanistan. The long-range mortars allowed attacks from a greater distance, and the mine-clearing equipment allowed insurgents to penetrate isolated bases.[46]

In addition to supplying the resistance with weapons, the CIA also provided at least $2 billion in counterfeit Afghan currency. The counterfeit currency allowed the resistance to pay the exorbitant fees that Afghan mule drivers and truckers charged to haul supplies and to offer bribes.[47]

The Soviet and Afghan governments took countermeasures against these resistance operations, however, and moreover, the resistance was hampered by a persistent leakage problem. According to one report, at least $340 million worth of weapons—and perhaps more—intended for the insurgents never reached them. In January 1985 the CIA withdrew $50 million from a Swiss bank account to buy forty Oerlikon antiaircraft guns, but only eleven guns made it to the guerrillas. The reasons for disappearing weapons ranged from expediency to personal profit. Those siphoning off the weapons included Pakistani forces, Afghan political parties in Pakistan, rebel commanders (who stole AA guns, rocket-propelled grenades, AK-47 rifles, and other weapons for personal use or for sale on the black market), and individual guerrillas. Islamic fundamentalists in the resistance stockpiled weapons in preparation for a power struggle after the Soviet withdrawal. Others who acquired the weapons included Iranian revolutionaries (who bought or stole twelve Stingers from Afghan rebels in the summer of 1987) and drug traffickers in Afghanistan and Pakistan.[48]

Six weeks before the Soviet Union was to begin its withdrawal on May 15, 1988, weapons were pouring into Afghanistan for the resistance fighters. Included were TOW antitank missiles, 120-mm Spanish mortars, and advanced antitank cannons. Giant U.S. C-5A transports were being met by scores of trucks belonging to Pakistan's government-run trucking line. Despite the Soviet withdrawal, the United States continued, at first, to supply the mujahideen. After initial opposition, the Soviet Union accepted the U.S. position that the United States would reserve the right to provide aid to the resistance as long as the Soviets continued to aid the Afghan government. The U.S. program effectively ended on January 1, 1992, in response to a fall 1991 U.S.-Soviet agreement to cut off all arms to the factions. By that time the alliance that had driven the Soviets from Afghanistan had fragmented.[49]

Angola

The Reagan administration's military aid to the rebels fighting the Marxist government of Angola did not begin until the latter half of 1985. It was in June 1985 that the U.S. Senate, by a 63 to 34 vote, approved an amendment to the State Department authorization bill that reversed the 1976 Hughes-Ryan Amendment, which prohibited military assistance. Although the Senate had taken similar action in 1981, that amendment died in a conference committee with a strongly opposed House of Representatives. In 1985, however, the House concurred.[50]

Both the Department of Defense and the CIA urged the White House to approve a large covert military operation to aid the Joseph Savimbi–led UNITA forces, estimated to number between 200,000 and 300,000. In early 1986 the Reagan administration informed Congress that it had decided to provide UNITA forces with antiaircraft and antitank missiles at a cost of approximately $15 million.[51]

Weapons were apparently first shipped to Kinshasa, Zaire, and then to a small abandoned former Belgian airbase at Kamina in Zaire. On three occasions in 1986, C-141 aircraft flown by "Santa Lucia Airways" arrived at Kamina from Kinshasa loaded with arms. From there a light blue C-130 cargo plane shuttled the weapons to areas in Angola. In 1987, a new $15 million package was sent to the UNITA forces. In addition to Stingers, the UNITA forces were to receive antitank missiles to counter a new shipment of Soviet tanks to the Angolan government.[52]

In 1989 President Mobuto Sese Seko of Zaire halted U.S. arms shipments through Zaire as a means of pressuring UNITA leader Savimbi to accept an African cease-fire plan. In late fall of that year he permitted a resumption. Shortly afterward, a CIA plane carrying arms for UNITA crashed in Africa.[53]

In the spring of 1990, the Bush administration requested an additional $10 million to $15 million in extra covert aid for UNITA (above the already budgeted $50 million). Subsequently, the administration requested a delay, in view of negotiations that promised to bring a halt to the civil war.[54]

Following the early June 1991 agreement to end the civil war, the House voted to continue covert aid. The aid was to be at a reduced level and to be employed to sustain UNITA, aid the transition to civilian life, and provide civil services for the part of Angola under rebel control. The agreement subsequently collapsed. Talks were opened in January 1993 concerning restoration of the cease-fire.[55]

Cambodia

Beginning in 1982 the Reagan administration began providing millions of dollars for nonmilitary purposes to non-Communist Cambodian resistance groups. The CIA aid was funneled through Thailand, with the objective of strengthening the position of those resistance groups in their loose coalition with the Communist Khmer Rouge. Apparently, CIA officers in Thailand worked closely with the Thai military to advise the insurgents and to insure that none of the covert aid wound up in the hands of the Khmer Rouge.[56]

In June 1990 the Senate Select Committee on Intelligence voted to cut off funds to the Cambodian rebels. Some funds were restored as a result of a fall compromise with the House intelligence oversight committee. The compromise plan, however, apparently did not include funds for weapons.[57]

In June 1993, Cambodian Prince Norodom Sihanouk announced the formation of a coalition government to run the country until the election of a National Assembly.[58]

El Salvador

Under the Reagan administration, the CIA undertook a number of operations to support the government of Christian Democratic leader Jose Napoleon Duarte. One operation, phased out in 1985, involved organizing special Salvadoran Army antiguerrilla units to track leftist rebels attempting to overthrow the government.[59]

In 1982, the CIA supplied invisible ink to stamp the wrists of Salvadoran voters as well as ultraviolet light devices to illuminate the ink. The ink allowed polling officials to determine whether a prospective voter had already voted but prevented rebels from detecting the ink and retaliating against those who voted.[60]

Another operation was directed toward preventing the election of right-wing Arena (National Republican Alliance) party leader Roberto D'Aubuisson. Between 1982 and 1984, the CIA gave $960,000 to Duarte's Christian Democratic Party and $437,000 to the National Conciliation Party to aid its candidate, Francisco Jose Guerrero, with advertising and media assistance. The agency spent an additional $700,000 to bolster the electoral process and discredit D'Aubuisson. The CIA covertly subsidized visits to El Salvador by unwitting European and Latin journalists and provided them with derogatory information about D'Aubuisson. The first group of journalists visited in early October 1983; a group of European television journalists then visited on December 6–9, 1983, and the final group, several Venezuelans and a Colombian journalist, visited during the last weekend of February 1984.[61]

Another part of the operation involved a "nonpartisan" effort to streamline election logistics and provide media advice and technical assistance throughout the election to ease the financial burden on interest groups such as trade unions and peasant cooperatives. In addition, the CIA helped in computerizing voting lists.[62]

Ethiopia

In 1981 President Reagan signed a Presidential Finding authorizing the CIA to conduct a "nonlethal campaign" to support the resistance to the Marxist regime.

As a result, the CIA set aside $500,000 to help the Ethiopian People's Democratic Alliance conduct a small propaganda campaign. The campaign included a CIA contract with a Washington consultant, who wrote material criticizing the regime's internal policies. The written material, along with audio and video tapes of anti-Mengistu speeches by leading exiles in the United States and Europe, was shipped to Addis Ababa in diplomatic pouches then given to dissident "cells" for distribution throughout the country.[63]

The CIA rejected a request for $546,000 from an Alliance splinter group, which in October 1982 presented the CIA with a twenty-eight-page memorandum spelling out how the funds would be spent. The group planned to train an initial group of 350 Ethiopian guerrillas who would enter western Ethiopia to organize and spread the resistance already under way.[64]

Iran

The NSC-directed covert operation that ended in the Iran-Contra affair was highly publicized, but other covert operations—directed by the CIA—were not. CIA operations during the Reagan and Bush years were designed to aid Iranian paramilitary and political exile groups, counter Soviet influence in Iran, and give the United States a role of its own in the event that the Khomeini regime fell. The initial goal was to knit together a coalition of exile groups and their supporters still in Iran so that if the opportunity arose they could become a significant factor in shaping the future of Iran.[65]

The covert action included providing several million dollars to units composed largely of Iranian exiles in eastern Turkey. The larger of the paramilitary groups had 6,000 to 8,000 men under the command of former Rear Admiral Ahmad Madani, the Commander of the Iranian Navy under the Shah who was court-martialed for "being against the government." Madani was the first Defense Minister in the Khomeini regime. The second unit, which consisted of less than 2,000 men, was commanded by General Bahram Aryana, Chief of Staff of the Iranian Army under the Shah. The paramilitary groups were intended to perform two functions. In the event of a Soviet invasion of Iran they could harass the flanks of the Soviet armed forces, and in the event of a civil war or domestic upheaval they would be able to enter Iran to protect and bolster any centrist forces.[66]

The CIA was also reported to be financing Iranian exile groups said to be situated principally in France and Egypt. Support was made available to groups both on the Left (up to but not including Bani-Sadr) and the Right (up to but not including the monarchist factions).[67]

The CIA established and financed a radio station in Egypt to broadcast anti-Khomeini information. In 1987, regular features included reports on long food lines, pockets of opposition and small uprisings against the clergy and revolutionary guards, torture and killings by the government, and gains made by Iranian Communists and agents of the Soviet Union. In September 1986 the agency provided a miniaturized television transmitter for an eleven-minute clandestine broadcast to Iran by the Shah's son. The CIA provided technical assistance and a miniaturized suitcase transmitter. The broadcast disrupted two channels of Iranian television for eleven minutes at 9 P.M. on September 5.[68]

In addition, the CIA supplied information to Iraq to aid the country in its war with Iran. The CIA secretly supplied Iraq with detailed intelligence to assist with Iraqi bombing raids on Iran's oil terminals and power plants. In 1984, when some feared that Iran might overrun Iraq, the United States began supplying Iraq with intelligence that reportedly enabled Iraq to calibrate mustard gas attacks on Iranian ground troops.[69]

In early 1985, Iraq began receiving regular satellite information from Washington, particularly after Iraqi bombing raids. It is not clear whether the Iraqis were receiving actual photos or information derived from the photos at that point.[70]

In any case, in August 1986 the CIA established a direct top secret Washington-Baghdad link to provide the Iraqis with better and more timely satellite information. The Iraqis thus would receive information from satellite photos "several hours" after a bombing raid in order to assess damage and plan the next attack. By December 1986 the Iraqis were receiving selected portions of the actual photos taken by KH-11 and SR-71 overhead platforms. According to one account, some of the information or images provided were incomplete or doctored—inflating the size of the Soviet troop strength on the Iranian border—in order to further the Reagan administration's goals.[71]

Iraq

The August 2, 1990, Iraqi invasion of Kuwait brought to an unsuccessful conclusion attempts by the Reagan and Bush administrations to transform the nature of Saddam Hussein's regime. Before, during, and after Operation Desert Storm, the United States sought to partially fulfill its goals in Iraq through covert action.

Shortly after the Iraqi invasion, the CIA began training Kuwaitis in Saudi Arabia with the objective of increasing the scope and effectiveness of resistance attacks on Iraqi forces, including attacks on military convoys and killings of sentries at key installations.[72]

It was reported that George Bush signed three Presidential Findings in January 1991 with respect to Iraq. One authorized CIA-sponsored propaganda and deception operations. A second allowed the CIA to work with Army Special Forces to resupply and support resistance forces in Kuwait. The third gave the CIA authority to aid rebel factions inside Iraq in an attempt to destabilize Hussein's government.[73]

According to some Kurdish nationalists, the *Voice of Free Iraq*, which began broadcasting in January 1991, was sponsored by the CIA. (Other sources indicated that the radio station operated under the authority of Saudi intelligence.) The station, located on the outskirts of Jedda, was managed by forty Iraqi expatriates and protected by armed Saudi guards. Broadcasting on four frequencies, it called for the withdrawal of Iraqi forces from Kuwait, the overthrow of Hussein, and the creation of a democratic Iraqi state.[74]

The station continued to operate after the conclusion of Desert Storm. During late March 1991 it called on Iraqi Army officers to "champion your people's uprising" and counseled rebels to form a unified military command "to swoop in on the regime of the Saddam Hussein gang and destroy it."[75]

In late 1991 a Presidential Finding authorized CIA contacts with Iraqi military leaders and opposition groups in an attempt to organize a successful coup that would unseat Hussein. The finding also provided for increased funding for propaganda broadcasts into Iraq and authorized $30 million for this purpose from a special contingency fund.[76]

By March 1992 the CIA had launched an operation to undermine the Iraqi economy by flooding Iraq with counterfeit money. The CIA systematically dumped large amounts of forged dinars, of two relatively low denominations that circulated extensively. The forged currency was apparently smuggled into Iraq from Jordan, Iran, and Turkey by agents and unwitting merchants. The fake currency further contributed to Iraq's severe inflation problem.[77]

In late May or early June 1992, the House Permanent Select Committee approved $40 million to help overthrow Hussein. The money was intended to expand and strengthen a number of opposition groups and individuals inside Iraq. The money also was intended to finance opposition groups outside Iraq, increase an anti-Hussein propaganda program carried out through clandestine radio stations, allow publication of leaflets and other printed propaganda, and finance the spreading of disinformation inside Iraq.[78]

A late June coup attempt against Hussein collapsed after a clash with forces loyal to Hussein.[79]

Libya

In addition to authorizing an NSC disinformation operation, Ronald Reagan authorized a CIA covert operation to undermine the Libyan regime. The plan involved CIA assistance to other countries in North Africa and the Middle East that opposed Qaddafi. Authorized in a fall 1985 Presidential Finding, the program's first objective was to disrupt, preempt, and frustrate Qaddafi's subversive and terrorist plans. Beyond that, the CIA hoped to lure him into some foreign adventure or terrorist exploit that would give a growing number of Qaddafi opponents in the Libyan military a chance to seize power or justify a military response by Algeria or Egypt.[80]

Another CIA operation, codenamed TULIP, involved support for anti-Qaddafi exile movements, including the National Front for the Salvation of Libya, and the efforts of other countries, such as Egypt.[81]

In 1988 the CIA began an operation to destabilize Qaddafi's regime via U.S.-trained Libyan commandos. The program, which began in the final months of the Reagan administration, provided military aid and training to 600 former Libyan soldiers at a base outside the Chadian capital of Ndjamena. The Libyan force consisted of soldiers who had been captured in 1988 during border fighting between Libya and Chad.[82]

The commandos never actually launched a serious military operation. After the Chad government fell in December 1990, the force was moved to Zaire and then to Kenya. The commandos were disarmed before leaving Chad and subsequently permanently disbanded.[83]

Nicaragua

In March of 1981 President Reagan transmitted his first "Presidential Finding on Central America" to Congress. The finding authorized CIA operations in Nicaragua—specifically, continued funding to "moderate" opponents of the Sandinistas and a covert "arms interdiction program" with the stated aim of halting any flow of weapons from Nicaragua to guerrillas in El Salvador, Honduras, and Guatemala. The CIA then proceeded to funnel money indirectly to Miami-based exiles and to 300 former National Guardsmen (the 15th of September Legion).[84]

The main guerrilla force took shape in August 1981 when the 15th of September Legion and the Nicaragua Democratic Union joined with other anti-Sandinista forces to form the Nicaraguan Democratic Force, with 4,000 to 5,000 soldiers. Subsequently, the National Liberation Army joined the Force.[85]

On January 4, 1982, President Reagan signed National Security Decision Directive 17, "National Security Decision Directive on Cuba and Central America." The directive noted that it was U.S. policy "to assist in defeating the insurgency in El Salvador, and to oppose actions by Cuba, Nicaragua, or others to introduce into Central America heavy weapons, troops from outside the region, trained subversives, or arms and military supplies for insurgents."[86]

That statement of policy and the measures to implement it were the product of a November 16, 1981, National Security Council meeting. The CIA was given responsibility for creating a paramilitary squad of exiles and authorized to work with foreign governments (i.e., Honduras and Argentina) as "appropriate." Envisioned was a 500-man U.S.-trained paramilitary force to supplement a 1,000-man force being trained by Argentina. On December 1, DCI William Casey presented the second Presidential Finding to Congress and depicted the program as being limited to attacks against the Cuban presence and the Cuban/Sandinista support infrastructure in Nicaragua. The cost was estimated at $19.9 million.[87]

Shortly after Casey's appearance before Congress, new U.S. intelligence operatives began to arrive in Honduras. The CIA station in Tegucigalpa doubled in size. After the initial phase of CIA training in weapon uses, tactics, and communications, which was conducted in Honduras, the Contras began, in January and February 1982, raiding small outputs in villages in northern Nicaragua. On March 14, CIA-equipped saboteurs blew up two major bridges in the Chinandega and Nueva Segovia provinces. According to the July 16, 1982, DIA-produced *Weekly Intelligence Summary,* between March 14 and June 21, 106 insurgent incidents occurred. The incidents included sabotage of highway bridges, attempted destruction of fuel tanks, sniper fire and attacks against small military patrols, attacks by small guerrilla units against individual Sandinista soldiers, and several incidents of arson. The targets were a customs warehouse, buildings belonging to the Ministry of Construction, and crops. The Contras also targeted civilian personnel involved in Nicaraguan social service programs.[88]

In July 1983 the CIA began aiding another anti-Sandinista group, Eden Pastora's Democratic Revolutionary Alliance (ARDE). The agency supplied ARDE with 500 Soviet AK-47 assault rifles, transporting them from Israel to Venezuela and finally to Tortuguero, a Costa Rican fishing lodge near the Nicaraguan border.[89]

In addition to supporting the Contras, the CIA initiated its own campaign against the Sandinistas. To supplement the activities of its own agents, it recruited a group of specially trained "unilaterally controlled Latino assets" (UCLAs)—Spanish-speaking operatives recruited from El Salvador, Honduras, Chile, Argentina, Ecuador, and Bolivia. Between September 1983 and April 1984, the agency carried out twenty-two or more attacks against vital Nicaraguan installations, particularly industrial and transportation targets, apparently in an effort to deliver quicker and more effective strikes against the Sandinistas than had been provided by previous efforts. The first U.S. attack occurred on September 8, 1983. Speedboats manned by UCLAs, and launched from a mother ship anchored 12 miles offshore, hit Puerto Sandino. Five weeks later they returned to sabotage an underwater oil pipeline. On October 10, the port of Corinto, Nicaragua's largest commercial port, was hit. The CIA's Latin commandos positioned their speedboats behind a South Korean ship and then fired mortars and grenades at five large oil and gasoline storage tanks, igniting 3.4 million gallons of fuel. According to the Nicaraguan government, more than 100 people were injured in the attack and 25,000 inhabitants of the city had to be evacuated while a fire raged out of control for two days.[90]

Beginning in January 1984, the CIA's assets and Contra guerrillas, operating from a mother ship, used speedboats to begin depositing mines in the shipping channels of Nicaragua's major Atlantic and Pacific coast ports—Corinto, Puerto Sandino, and El Bluff. The mines were large metal cylinders stuffed with 300 pounds of C-4 plastic explosives, sufficient to sink small boats and damage larger vessels. They were placed 2 to 3 feet below the surface of the water, anchored into the bottom, in all channels of the three ports. The mine casings were produced by the CIA Weapons Group from sewer pipes, and the fuses were apparently provided by the Mines Division of the Naval Surface Weapons Center in Maryland.[91]

By the first week of April 1984, ten commercial vessels had hit the CIA mines—four Nicaraguan and six non-Nicaraguan (registered to Japan, the Netherlands, Liberia, Panama, and the Soviet Union). At least eight merchant marine vessels turned back from Nicaraguan ports to find safer waters, including a Mexican oil tanker carrying 75,000 barrels of much-needed fuel. The mining operation cost the Nicaraguans more than $10 million—cotton and coffee piled up on the docks, and imports and exports had to be trucked to and from ports in neighboring Central American countries.[92]

Two further CIA operations involved the production of two manuals. One was a comic book–style manual produced by the CIA urging Nicaraguans to call in sick to work, pour sand into engines, hurl firebombs, and engage in various acts of sabotage. The introduction to the sixteen-page *Freedom Fighters Manual* called the booklet "a practical guide to liberate Nicaragua from oppression and misery by paralyzing the military-industrial complex of the traitorous Marxist state without having to use special tools and with minimal risk for the combatant." Its captioned drawings illustrated thirty-eight ways to sabotage or undermine the Nicaraguan government. The booklet urged Nicaraguans to report late to work and take it easy on the job, leave the lights and water on, damage books and office equipment, smash windows, clog up toilets, cut telephone lines, call in false alarms, slash tires, spread rumors, make false hotel and plane reservations, short-circuit electrical systems, paint antigovernment slogans, damage truck engines, fell trees, release farm animals, steal government food supplies, set fires, and throw firebombs at police officers and fuel depots.[93]

The second manual, *Psychological Operations in Guerilla Warfare,* was prepared by a CIA contract employee, allegedly in response to his learning of corruption and abuses in Contra operations. The manual, of which 2,000 copies were printed, covered various aspects of the guerrilla operation. It suggested that in order to conduct "armed propaganda" in an effective manner, the rebels, when occupying a town, should

- destroy the military or police installations and remove the survivors to a "public place";
- cut all the outside lines of communication, including cables, radio, and messengers;
- set up ambushes in order to delay the reinforcements in all the possible entry routes; and
- kidnap all officials or agents of the Sandinista government and replace them in "public places" with military or civilian persons of trust.[94]

The manual also suggested that if it were necessary for one of the advanced posts to fire on an individual attempting to leave the town or city in which the guerrillas were carrying out armed propaganda or political proselytism, the rebels should

- explain that if that citizen had managed to escape he would have alerted the enemy near the town or city, who would carry out acts of reprisal such as rapes, pillage, and destruction;

- make the town see that the individual was an enemy of the people and was shot because the guerrillas recognized as their first duty the protection of their citizens.[95]

Several controversial recommendations led to a public outcry in the United States, resulting in internal inquiry and disciplinary action at the CIA. At one point the manual suggested that "it is possible to *neutralize* carefully selected and planned targets, such as court judges, *mesta* judges, police and State Security officials, CDS [Committee for Defense of Sandinismo] chiefs, etc." (emphasis added). It also suggested that "the notification of the police, denouncing a target who does not want to join the guerrillas, can be carried out easily, when it becomes necessary, through a letter with false statements of citizens who are not implicated in the movement." The manual also instructed readers in how to create martyrs by "taking the demonstrators to a confrontation with the authorities in order to bring about uprisings or shootings, which will cause the death of one or more persons, who would become the martyrs, a situation that should be made use of immediately ... in order to create greater conflicts."[96]

A limited number of manuals (fewer than 100) were distributed by attaching them to balloons and floating them from Honduras into Nicaragua. In disseminating the booklet, the CIA was apparently attempting to create the perception that the U.S.-backed insurgency was more serious than it was. A shortage of funds curtailed the program.[97]

The CIA's direct entry into the conflict added to the actions being taken by the Contras. In early September 1984, the Contras used three rocket-equipped Cessna 02A observation planes to conduct a raid on a Nicaraguan military school near the Honduran border. Two Americans were killed when the accompanying helicopter they were flying in was shot down. The planes had been obtained from the CIA.[98]

Another CIA-funded Contra operation involved bribing journalists. Rebel leaders, under CIA instruction and using CIA funds, bribed nearly two dozen Honduran and Costa Rican journalists to write favorable stories about rebel activities, paying each of them $50 to $100 a month.[99]

Between October 1984, when Congress adopted the second Boland amendment, and October 1986, no funds were authorized by Congress for lethal assistance (although NSC/"private" supply efforts took up some of the slack). In October 1986 Congress voted to appropriate $70 million for lethal aid. As a result, Nicaraguan rebels, estimated by that time to number 11,000, began receiving military training in Florida. By January 1987 they had returned to Central America and a second group was in training.[100]

The CIA resumed providing the Contras with precise information on dams, bridges, electrical substations, port facilities, and other targets inside Nicaragua. Many of those installations had been built by the Army Corps of Engineers and other U.S. agencies in the 1960s and 1970s. The CIA found and turned over to the Contras detailed maps, blueprints, and floor plans.[101]

On February 16, 1987, a new wave of Contra sabotage attacks began when Contra commandos blasted a power station near the town of La Trinidad, blacking out three northern provinces for four days. On March 16, commando groups hit a high-tension tower on the outskirts of Managua, but it did not fall. Altogether, in the last weeks of March Contra saboteurs struck ten times along Nicaragua's Pacific coast, toppling electric towers and putting out lights in towns on Nicaragua's northern and southern borders. The destruction of undefended telephone-relay stations, electrical switching stations, and bridges disrupted the daily lives of many Nicaraguans and presumably demonstrated that the Sandinistas could not maintain control over the areas involved.[102]

The CIA supplied the Contras with more weapons than Congress had mandated by retaining legal title to some of the materials it turned over to them. The material included new planes, hundreds of .50 caliber machine guns, Redeye surface-to-air missiles, LAW antiarmor rockets, and C-4 plastic explosives.[103]

In late 1987, the CIA followed up the defection of a top aide to Nicaraguan Defense Minister Humberto Ortega by producing a videotape for distribution throughout Central America. In a forty-five-minute statement, broadcast on San Salvador television and circulated in Honduras and Nicaragua, Major Roger Miranda Bengoechea embraced the "heroic struggle" of the Contras and painted the Sandinistas as a privileged class that betrayed the goals of the revolution. He also claimed that Humberto Ortega had maintained sexual relationships with the wives of at least three leading Sandinistas.[104]

U.S. lethal aid to the Contras was not continued by Congress in the aftermath of the 1987 cease-fire between the Contras and the Sandinistas and their agreement to hold open elections. However, the United States did provide funds for a variety of programs. In the summer of 1989, the CIA established the Nicaraguan Emergency Relocation Program (NERP). Between July 1989 and February 1990, up to $600,000 was dispensed to thirty Contra leaders in Miami. They were, in turn, responsible for redistribution of the money to subordinates for the purpose of supporting political action in Nicaragua in preparation for the February 25, 1990, elections. Several million additional dollars were provided through the National Endowment for Democracy to supply the opponents of the Sandinistas (United Nicaraguan Opposition, UNO) with cars, offices, computers, and other equipment. The elections resulted in the choice of Sandinista opponent Violeta Chamorro as President.[105]

The Bush administration had considered conducting a major covert operation to influence the outcome of those elections. However, as a result of congressional pressure, it was decided that aid would only be provided openly. The CIA spent about $6 million to continue support of the Contras and maintain the international spotlight on the Sandinistas. The agency provided travel funds for European journalists to observe the elections firsthand and funded radio broadcasts to Nicaragua from Costa Rica.[106]

Panama

Before adopting a direct approach to the removal of General Manuel Antonio Noriega from power, the United States contemplated and/or employed a variety of covert action programs to achieve that objective. In 1987 the Reagan administration considered supporting a plan by a former Panamanian Army Colonel living in Florida that called for establishment of a beachhead in Panama that would trigger the internal overthrow of General Noriega. The Colonel, Eduardo Herrera Hassan, had been assisting the CIA in psychological operations directed against Noriega. His plan, however, met with a hostile reception in the Senate Select Committee on Intelligence, and the Reagan administration ceased contact with the Colonel.[107]

In February 1988 Noriega was indicted by federal grand juries in Miami and Tampa, Florida, on drug-trafficking charges.

In July 1988 it was reported that President Reagan had authorized additional measures to bring about Noriega's ouster. The measures were intended to damage the Panamanian economy, funnel assistance to the civilian opposition, and aid dissident military officers who might eventually unseat Noriega.[108]

However, a proposed operation designated Panama-3, which called for CIA support for a group of about two dozen officers plotting Noriega's overthrow, produced objections from the Senate Select Committee on Intelligence. Committee members considered the plan poorly organized and unlikely to achieve its goal. In addition, the Senators warned against assisting plotters whose plans were likely to lead to Noriega's death.[109]

One of the first Bush administration operations directed against Noriega was a $10 million initiative that relied heavily on clandestine radio broadcasts. However, the program, apparently run in Panama by a CIA cover organization, the Program Development Group, may not have had wholehearted CIA support. In any case, few Panamanians appeared to pay much attention. On April 5, 1989, Panamanian authorities seized approximately $350,000 worth of radio and communications equipment from eight apartments in Panama City. The operation also provided funds for printing, advertising, transportation, and communications equipment for Noriega's opposition.[110]

In November 1989, the month before the United States launched Operation Just Cause, President Bush approved another plan directed at toppling Noriega. The plan, designated Panama-5, called for spending up to $3 million in its first stages to recruit Panamanian Defense Force officers and exiled opposition figures to stage a coup. Although there was a prohibition against assassination, the White House, with congressional approval, was willing to accept the possibility that Noriega might die as a by-product of violence generated by the coup.[111]

Philippines

In attempting to bring about the ouster of Ferdinand Marcos, the CIA secretly funded a group of Philippine military officers who formed, in March 1985, the Reform the Armed Forces Now Movement (RAM). RAM leaders were brought to the United States to meet with members of Congress and other opinion makers as proof of the possibility of reform in the Philippines.[112]

Subsequent to the fall of Marcos and the collapse of negotiations between the Aquino government and Communist insurgents, the CIA launched a $10 million operation against the insurgents. The plan called for the CIA to gather intelligence—including by airborne reconnaissance—to map areas controlled by insurgents, train soldiers, and launch undercover political activities.[113]

South Yemen

In March 1982 a thirteen-man team of Yemenis sponsored by the CIA and Saudi intelligence was sent into South Yemen to conduct sabotage. The team was captured, and a second team already inserted in South Yemen had to be withdrawn.[114]

THE CLINTON ADMINISTRATION

Many of the areas of concern during the Reagan-Bush years have ceased to be significant concerns. One concern that does remain is Iraq. The Clinton administration apparently decided on a scaled-down program, which might cost half the $40 million spent under the Bush program. The new administration concluded that much of the aid provided under previous administrations had been given to groups with no popular backing. In addition, it was judged that too much money had been spent on leaflets and other propaganda devices that had little impact.[115]

NOTES

1. "The Bissell Philosophy," Appendix to Victor Marchetti and John Marks, *The CIA and the Cult of Intelligence* (New York: Knopf, 1974), p. 387; U.S. Congress, Senate Select Committee to Study Governmental Operations with Respect to Intelligence Activities, *Alleged Assassination Plots Involving Foreign Leaders* (Washington, D.C.: U.S. Government Printing Office, 1976).

2. Trevor Barnes, "The Secret Cold War: The CIA and American Foreign Policy in Europe, 1946–1956, Part 2," *Historical Journal* 25, 3 (1982): 399–415.

3. Ibid.

4. John Prados, *President's Secret Wars: CIA and Pentagon Covert Operations from World War II Through Iranscam* (New York: Quill, 1988), pp. 30–44.

5. See Stephen Schlesinger and Stephen Kinzer, *Bitter Fruit* (Garden City, N.Y.: Doubleday, 1982); Richard H. Immerman, *CIA in Guatemala: The Foreign Policy of Intervention* (Austin: University of Texas Press, 1982).

6. For an account of the Bay of Pigs episode see Peter Wyden, *Bay of Pigs: The Untold Story* (New York: Simon & Schuster, 1979).

7. Warren Hinckle and William Turner, *The Fish Is Red: The Story of the Secret War Against Castro* (New York: Harper & Row, 1981), pp. 101, 108, 191, 219.

8. Ibid., pp. 121, 122, 143.

9. Ibid., p. 148.

10. Ibid., pp. 129–30.

11. Ibid.

12. U.S. Congress, Senate Select Committee to Study Governmental Operations with Respect to Intelligence Activities, *Covert Action in Chile* (Washington, D.C.: U.S. Government Printing Office, 1976), pp. 1, 9.

13. Ibid.; Central Intelligence Agency, "Report on CIA Chilean Task Force Activities, 15 September to 18 November 1970," p. 3.

14. Central Intelligence Agency, "Report on CIA Chilean Task Force Activities, 15 September to 18 November 1970," pp. 5, 9, 10.

15. U.S. Congress, Senate Select Committee to Study Governmental Operations with Respect to Intelligence Activities, *Covert Action in Chile*, pp. 23–25.

16. Ibid., pp. 25–26; U.S. Congress, Senate Select Committee to Study Governmental Operations with Respect to Intelligence Activities, *Alleged Assassination Plots Involving Foreign Leaders*, p. 226.

17. U.S. Congress, Senate Select Committee to Study Governmental Operations with Respect to Intelligence Activities, *Alleged Assassination Plots Involving Foreign Leaders*, p. 254; U.S. Congress, Senate Select Committee to Study Governmental Operations with Respect to Intelligence Activities, *Covert Action in Chile*, pp. 29–31.

18. M. Richard Shaw, "British Intelligence and Iran," *Counter Spy* (May–June 1982): 31–33.

19. Ibid.; Kermit Roosevelt, *Countercoup: The Struggle for Control of Iran* (New York: McGraw-Hill, 1979), pp. 3, 107, 119.

20. Shaw, "British Intelligence and Iran"; Roosevelt, *Countercoup*, pp. 119, 121.

21. Prados, *President's Secret Wars*, pp. 96–97.

22. Stephen R. Weissman, "CIA Covert Action in Zaire and Angola: Patterns and Consequences," *Political Science Quarterly* 94, 2 (1979): 263–86.

23. Ibid., p. 266.

24. Ibid., pp. 267, 269.

25. Ibid., p. 282.

26. Ibid., pp. 282–83.

27. John Crewdson, "Worldwide Propaganda Network Built by the CIA," *New York Times*, December 26, 1977, pp. 1, 37.

28. Ibid.

29. Ibid.

30. Ibid.

31. Stansfield Turner, *Secrecy and Democracy: The CIA in Transition* (Boston: Houghton Mifflin, 1985), pp. 88–89.

32. David Whitman, *The Press and the Neutron Bomb* (Cambridge, Mass.: Kennedy School of Government, 1984), pp. 96–97; Bob Woodward, *Veil: The Secret Wars of the CIA, 1981–1987* (New York: Simon & Schuster, 1987), p. 78.

33. Woodward, *Veil*, p. 113; Jay Peterzell, *Reagan's Secret Wars* (Washington, D.C.: Center for National Security Studies, 1984), p. 9.

34. Woodward, *Veil*, p. 78; Steve Coll, "Anatomy of a Victory: CIA's Covert Afghan War," *Washington Post*, July 17, 1992, pp. A1, A24.

35. Carl Bernstein, "CIA's Secret Arms Aid to Afghanistan," *Chicago Sun-Times*, September 6, 1981, p. 1; Tim Weiner, "The CIA's Leaking Pipeline," *Philadelphia Inquirer*, February 28, 1988, pp. 1-A, 12-A; Peterzell, *Reagan's Secret Wars*, pp. 9, 10, 13; Prados, *President's Secret Wars*, p. 359; Coll, "Anatomy of a Victory: CIA's Covert Afghan War."

36. Bernstein, "CIA's Secret Arms Aid to Afghanistan."

37. Peterzell, *Reagan's Secret Wars*, p. 11.

38. Mohammad Youssaf, *The Bear Trap: Afghanistan's Untold Story* (London: Leo Cooper, 1992), p. 87; Robert Pear, "Arming the Afghan Guerillas: A Huge Effort Led by U.S.," *New York Times*, April 18, 1988, pp. A1, A11; Bob Woodward and Charles R. Babcock, "U.S. Covert Aid to Afghans on the Rise," *Washington Post*, January 13, 1985, pp. A1, A30.

39. Leslie H. Gelb, "U.S. Aides Put '85 Arms Supplies to Afghan Rebels at $280 Million," *New York Times*, November 28, 1984, pp. A1, A9; Woodward and Babcock, "U.S. Covert Aid to Afghans on the Rise"; Youssaf, *The Bear Trap*, p. 85.

40. Coll, "Anatomy of a Victory: CIA's Covert Afghan War."

41. Joanne Omang, "Secret Votes Give Afghans $300 Million," *Washington Post*, October 10, 1985, p. A16; "Leaks in the Pipeline," *Time*, December 9, 1985, pp. 50–51; David B. Ottaway, "Afghan Rebels to Get More Missiles," *Washington Post*, February 8, 1987, pp. A1, A28.

42. Bernard Gwertzman, "Stingers Aiding Afghans' Fight, U.S. Aides Say," *New York Times*, December 13, 1986, pp. 1, 9; Ottaway, "Afghan Rebels to Get More Missiles"; "Afghan Transport Plane Downed by Guerilla Force with a Missile," *New York Times*, February 10, 1987, pp. A1, A5; Pear, "Arming the Afghan Guerillas: A Huge Effort Led by U.S."

43. David B. Ottaway, "Afghanistan Rebels Due More Arms," *Washington Post*, April 5, 1987, pp. A1, A19; James M. Dorsey, "Afghan Rebels Receive Hundreds of Stingers," *Washington Times*, March 25, 1987, p. 9A.

44. Gelb, "U.S. Aides Put '85 Arms Supplies to Afghan Rebels at $280 Million"; Woodward and Babcock, "U.S. Covert Aid to Afghans on the Rise."

45. David B. Ottaway, "U.S. Missiles Alter War in Afghanistan," *Washington Post*, July 19, 1987, p. A16; David B. Ottaway, "Stingers Were Key Weapon in Afghan War, Army Finds," *Washington Post*, July 5, 1989, p. A2.

46. David B. Ottaway, "U.S. Widens Arms Shipments to Bolster Afghan Guerillas," *Washington Post*, September 21, 1987, pp. A1, A7.

47. Tim Weiner, "U.S. Used Secret Global Network to Arm Afghans," *Philadelphia Inquirer*, February 29, 1988, pp. 1-A, 8-A.

48. Weiner, "The CIA's Leaking Pipeline."

49. Richard M. Weintraub, "New Arms Reaching Afghans," *Washington Post*, April 5, 1988, pp. A1, A19; Steve Coll, "In CIA's Covert Afghan War, Where to Draw the Line Was Key," *Washington Post*, July 20, 1992, pp. A1, A2.

50. David B. Ottaway, "Senate Votes to End Ban on Aiding Angola Rebels," *Washington Post*, June 12, 1985, p. A6.

51. David B. Ottaway, "Angola Rebel Aid Is Pushed," *Washington Post*, November 1, 1985, pp. A1, A14; Bernard Gwertzman, "Reagan Decides to Send Weapons to Angola Rebels," *New York Times*, February 19, 1986, pp. A1, A3; David B. Ottaway and Patrick E. Tyler, "Superpowers Raise Ante as Fighting Intensifies," *Washington Post*, July 27, 1986, pp. A1, A21.

52. James Brooke, "CIA Said to Send Rebels in Angola Weapons via Zaire," *New York Times*, February 1, 1987, pp. 1, 2; Neil A. Lewis, "Administration Decides That Aid to Angola Rebels Will Continue," *New York Times*, June 11, 1987, pp. A1, A9; James Brooke, "U.S. Arms Airlift to Angola Rebels Is Said to Go On," *New York Times*, July 27, 1987, pp. A1, A2.

53. David B. Ottaway, "Zaire Is Said to Cut CIA Arms Flow to Angolan Rebels," *Washington Post*, October 4, 1989, p. A8; David B. Ottaway, "CIA Plane Carrying Arms to Angolan Rebels Crashes," *Washington Post*, November 30, 1989, pp. A1, A50; Robert Pear, "CIA Plane Crash Hurting Peace Drive in Angola, U.S. Says," *New York Times*, December 1, 1989, p. A9.

54. David B. Ottaway, "U.S. Seeking More Aid for Angolan Rebels," *Washington Post*, June 18, 1990, p. A17; Al Kamen and George Lardner, Jr., "Covert Action Budget Deferred," *Washington Post*, July 21, 1990, p. A14.

55. "House Votes for Plan for More Covert Aid to Angolan Rebels," *New York Times*, June 12, 1991, p. A8; Jennifer Parmelee, "Angola, UNITA Open Talks on Restoring Cease-Fire," *Washington Post*, January 29, 1993, p. A24.

56. Charles R. Babcock and Bob Woodward, "CIA Covertly Aiding Pro-West Cambodians," *Washington Post*, July 8, 1985, pp. A1, A18.

57. Al Kamen and George Lardner, Jr., "Senate Panel Votes to Cut Off Covert Aid to Cambodian Rebels," *Washington Post*, June 30, 1990, p. A27; George Lardner, Jr., "Afghan, Cambodia Covert Aid Cut," *Washington Post*, October 24, 1990, p. A7.

58. Philip Shenon, "Sihanouk Forms a Government, Regaining Power After 23 Years," *New York Times*, June 4, 1993, pp. A1, A8.

59. Doyle McManus, "Inquiry Discloses CIA Officers' Aid to Salvador Army," *Los Angeles Times*, July 9, 1987, pp. 1, 22.

60. Philip Taubman, "C.I.A. Chief Tells of Attempt to Aid Salvador Vote," *New York Times*, July 30, 1982, p. 2.

61. Philip Taubman, "C.I.A. Said to Have Given Money to 2 Salvador Parties," *New York Times*, May, 12, 1984, p. 6.

62. Joanne Omang, "CIA Channeled $2 Million into Salvador Voting," *Washington Post*, May 11, 1984, p. A24.

63. Patrick E. Tyler and David B. Ottaway, "Ethiopian Security Police Seized, Tortured CIA Agent," *Washington Post*, April 25, 1986, pp. A1, A16.

64. Ibid.; James Brooke, "In Ethiopia, Rulers Seem to Be Widely Resented," *New York Times*, March 15, 1987, p. 14; David B. Ottaway and Joanne Omang, "U.S. Course Uncharted on Aid to Insurgencies," *Washington Post*, May 21, 1985, pp. A1, A23.

65. Leslie H. Gelb, "U.S. Said to Aid Iranian Exiles in Combat and Political Units," *New York Times*, March 7, 1982, pp. 1, 12.

66. Ibid.

67. Ibid.

68. Ibid.; Bob Woodward, "CIA Curried Favor with Khomeini Exiles," *Washington Post*, November 19, 1986, pp. A1, A28.

69. Bob Woodward, "CIA Aiding Iraq in Gulf War," *Washington Post*, December 15, 1986, pp. A1, A18–A19.

70. Ibid.

71. Ibid.; Stephen Engelberg, "Iran and Iraq Got 'Doctored' Data, U.S. Officials Say," *New York Times*, January 12, 1987, pp. A1, A16.

72. Nick B. Williams, Jr., and Robin Wright, "CIA Training Kuwait to Harass Iraqis," *Los Angeles Times,* August 31, 1990, pp. A1, A8.

73. Paul Bedard and Warren Strobel, "Bush Again Urges Ouster of Saddam," *Washington Times,* April 4, 1991, pp. A1, A10; Michael Wines, "C.I.A. Joins Military Move to Sap Iraqi Confidence," *New York Times,* January 19, 1991, p. 7.

74. Wines, "C.I.A. Joins Military Move to Sap Iraqi Confidence," p. 7; Barton Gellman, "Kurds Contend U.S. Encouraged Rebellion Via 'Voice of Free Iraq,'" *Washington Post,* April 9, 1991, p. A17; Michael Wines, "Kurd Gives Account of Broadcasts to Iraq Linked to the C.I.A.," *New York Times,* April 6, 1991, pp. 1, 5; Elaine Sciolino, "Radio Linked to C.I.A. Urges Iraqis to Overthrow Hussein," *New York Times,* April 16, 1991, p. A9.

75. Gellman, "Kurds Contend U.S. Encouraged Rebellion Via 'Voice of Free Iraq.'"

76. Patrick E. Tyler, "Saudis Press U.S. for Help in Ouster for Iraq's Leader," *New York Times,* January 19, 1992, pp. 1, 10; Patrick E. Tyler, "Plan on Iraq Coup Told to Congress," *New York Times,* February 9, 1992, pp. 1, 16; John M. Broder and Robin Wright, "CIA Authorized to Target Hussein," *Los Angeles Times,* February 8, 1992, pp. A1, A11.

77. Christy Campbell and Adrian Porter, "U.S. Carrier Moves Toward Iraq Targets," *Washington Times,* March 16, 1992, pp. A1, A6; Youssef M. Ibrahim, "Fake-Money Flood Is Aimed at Crippling Iraq's Economy," *New York Times,* May 27, 1992, pp. A1, A6.

78. Elaine Sciolino, "Greater U.S. Effort Backed to Oust Iraqi," *New York Times,* June 2, 1992, p. A3.

79. Don Oberdorfer, "U.S. Had Covert Plan to Oust Iraq's Saddam," *Washington Post,* January 20, 1993, p. A4.

80. Bob Woodward, "CIA Anti-Qaddafi Plan Backed," *Washington Post,* November 3, 1985, pp. A1, A19.

81. Woodward, *Veil,* p. 411.

82. Clifford Krauss, "Failed Anti-Qaddafi Effort Leaves U.S. Picking Up the Pieces," *New York Times,* March 12, 1991, p. A15; "Have Rebels, Will Travel, *Newsweek,* March 26, 1991, p. 43.

83. Krauss, "Failed Anti-Qaddafi Effort Leaves U.S. Picking up the Pieces"; "Have Rebels, Will Travel."

84. Peter Kornbluh, *Nicaragua: The Price of Intervention, Reagan's War Against the Sandinistas* (Washington, D.C.: Institute for Policy Studies, 1987), pp. 18–20.

85. James LeMoyne, "The Secret War Boils Over," *Newsweek,* April 11, 1983, pp. 46–50; Joanne Omang, "A Historical Background to the CIA's Nicaraguan Manual," *Psychological Operations in Guerilla Warfare* (New York: Vintage, 1985), pp. 15, 22.

86. National Security Decision Directive 17, "National Security Directive on Cuba and Central America," January 4, 1982, TOP SECRET (Sanitized).

87. "A Secret War for Nicaragua," *Newsweek,* November 8, 1982, pp. 42–53; Kornbluh, *Nicaragua,* pp. 22–23; Robert C. Toth, "CIA Covert Action Punishes Nicaragua for Salvador Aid," *Los Angeles Times,* December 20, 1982, p. 11.

88. LeMoyne, "The Secret War Boils Over"; Kornbluh, *Nicaragua,* pp. 23, 24, 40.

89. "The CIA Blows an Asset," *Newsweek,* September 3, 1984, pp. 48–49.

90. Kornbluh, *Nicaragua,* p. 48; Philip Taubman, "U.S. Officials Say C.I.A. Helped Nicaraguan Rebels Plan Attacks," *New York Times,* October 16, 1984, pp. 1, 22; "Oct. 10 Assault on Nicaraguans Is Laid to C.I.A.," *New York Times,* April 18, 1984, pp. A1, A12.

91. Kornbluh, *Nicaragua,* pp. 48–50; Hedrick Smith, "Britain Criticizes Mining of Harbors Around Nicaragua," *New York Times,* April 7, 1984, pp. 1, 4; Fred Hiatt and Joanne

Omang, "CIA Helped to Mine Ports in Nicaragua," *Washington Post,* April 7, 1984, p. 1; Philip Taubman, "Americans on Ship Said to Supervise Nicaragua Mining," *New York Times,* April 8, 1984, pp. 1, 12; Leslie H. Gelb, "Officials Say CIA Made Mines with Navy Help," *New York Times,* June 1, 1984, p. A4.

92. Kornbluh, *Nicaragua,* pp. 48–50; Smith, "Britain Criticizes Mining of Harbors Around Nicaragua"; Hiatt and Omang, "CIA Helped to Mine Ports in Nicaragua"; Taubman, "Americans on Ship Said to Supervise Nicaragua Mining."

93. "CIA-Produced Comics Inspire Revolutionaries with Rebellious Antics," *Toronto Globe and Mail,* June 30, 1984, p. 11.

94. *Psychological Operations in Guerilla Warfare* (New York: Vintage, 1985), p. 52.

95. Ibid., p. 56.

96. Ibid., pp. 57, 74, 85.

97. "Balloons Took CIA Manuals to Nicaragua," *Washington Post,* December 7, 1984, p. A44.

98. Blaine Harden and Joe Pichirallo, "CIA Is Said to Supply Planes to Nicaraguan Rebels," *Washington Post,* September 15, 1984, pp. A1, A24–A25.

99. Joel Brinkley, "Nicaraguan Rebel Tells of Killings as Devices for Forced Recruitment," *New York Times,* September 12, 1985, p. A10.

100. Joe Pichirallo and Molly Moore, "70 Contras Said to Be Training in U.S.," *Washington Post,* November 20, 1986, pp. A1, A34; James LeMoyne, "First Group of the Contras Completes Florida Training," *New York Times,* January 9, 1987, p. A10; "Turning Points in the Contra War," *Newsweek,* March 28, 1988, p. 38.

101. Joel Brinkley, "C.I.A. Gives Contras Detailed Profiles of Civil Targets," *New York Times,* March 19, 1987, pp. A1, A10.

102. Julia Preston, "Nicaraguan Rebels Increase Pace of Sabotage Attacks," *Washington Post,* April 3, 1987, pp. A29–A30.

103. Kornbluh, *Nicaragua,* p. 211.

104. Douglas Farah, "Videotape of Defector Circulated," *Washington Post,* December 17, 1987, pp. A41, A43.

105. "The CIA on the Stump," *Newsweek,* October 21, 1991, pp. 46–47; "Bush: Intervention Aboveground," *Newsweek,* March 12, 1990, p. 36.

106. "Bush: Intervention Aboveground."

107. Stephen Engelberg, "Panamanian's Tale: '87 Plan for a Coup," *New York Times,* October 29, 1988, p. 18.

108. Stephen Engelberg, "President Is Said to Order C.I.A. to Press Action to Oust Noriega," *New York Times,* July 28, 1988, p. A12; Lou Cannon and Joe Pichirallo, "U.S. Covert Action Seeks to Discredit Noriega," *Washington Post,* July 27, 1988, pp. A1, A29.

109. Stephen Engelberg, "Reagan Agreed to Shun Killing Noriega," *New York Times,* October 23, 1989, p. A10; Stephen Engelberg, "White House Supports C.I.A. Call for Greater Leeway During Coups," *New York Times,* October 18, 1989, pp. A1, A12.

110. William Branigan, "U.S. Move in Panama Called Inept," *Washington Post,* April 30, 1989, pp. A1, A22; "Taking Aim at Noriega," *U.S. News and World Report,* May 1, 1989, pp. 40–41.

111. Robin Wright, "U.S. in New Bid to Oust Noriega," *Los Angeles Times,* November 16, 1989, p. 1; Engelberg, "White House Supports C.I.A. Call for Greater Leeway During Coups," pp. A1, A12; Bill Gertz, "CIA Working to Oust Noriega in Operation with Blessing

of Hill," *Washington Times,* November 17, 1989, p. A4; Michael Wines, "U.S. Plans New Effort to Oust Noriega," *New York Times,* November 17, 1989, p. A3; Tom Kenworthy and Joe Pichirallo, "Bush Clears Plan to Topple Noriega," *Washington Times,* November 17, 1989, pp. A1, A58.

112. Raymond Bonner, *Waltzing with a Dictator: The Marcoses and the Making of American Policy* (New York: Times Books, 1987), p. 368.

113. "Covert Help for Cory Aquino," *Newsweek,* March 23, 1987, p. 7; Nayan Chanda, "Here Come the Spies," *Far Eastern Economic Review,* April 9, 1987, p. 19.

114. Woodward, *Veil,* p. 215.

115. Elaine Sciolino, "Clinton to Scale Down Program to Oust Iraqi Leader," *New York Times,* April 11, 1993, p. 3.

ELEMENTS OF A REPUBLICAN GUARD DIVISION
AN NASIRIYAH RAIL TRANSHIPMENT POINT

VICINITY OF 3101N/04614E

13 OCT 94

SUPPLY/TRANSPORT TRKS

SUPPLY/TRANSPORTATION

SA-8 RESUPPLY/TEL

BRDM

T-72

MTLB APC

T-72

TYPE 63

T-72

An overhead photo of an Iraqi Republican Guard Division, October 1994. Photo Credit: Department of Defense.

Defense Communications Electronics Evaluation and Testing Activity at Fort Belvoir, Virginia, the U.S. receiving station for KH-11 and Advanced KH-11 imagery. Photo Credit: Robert Windrem.

The SR-71 reconnaissance aircraft. The SR-71 fleet was retired in 1991. A planned successor, the unmanned Advanced Airborne Reconnaissance System, was subsequently canceled because of its projected cost. Photo Credit: Lockheed.

The U-2 reconnaissance aircraft. U-2s first began operating in 1956 and are still in service, performing both imagery and SIGINT missions.

An overhead view of the Al Qaim superphosphate fertilizer plant, showing some of the damage caused by Allied bombing attacks during Operation Desert Storm. The photograph was taken by an F-14A using the Tactical Air Reconnaissance Pod System (TARPS). Photo Credit: U.S. Navy.

P-3C ocean surveillance/antisubmarine warfare aircraft. Photo Credit: Lockheed.

COBRA DANE phased-array radar, Shemya Island. COBRA DANE is used to track Russian missile warheads as they descend to earth during tests. Photo Credit: Raytheon.

Ground station for the VORTEX SIGINT satellite in Menwith Hill, England. Menwith Hill is also the site of the MOONPENNY satellite communications intercept project. Photo Credit: Duncan Campbell.

Joint Defense Space Research Facility at Alice Springs, Australia (Pine Gap), the ground control station for RHYOLITE and ORION satellites. Photo Credit: Desmond Ball.

Kiev communications tower, a target of NSA's intercept operations. Photo Credit: Bob Windrem.

The Teal Blue space surveillance site in Hawaii. Photo Credit: Bob Windrem.

A USS Sturgeon (SSN-637) submarine. Sturgeon submarines are used on submarine reconnaissance programs. Photo Credit: U.S. Navy.

Soviet T-72 tanks. After several attempts, U.S. intelligence acquired one for analysis. Photo Credit: Department of Defense.

16
MANAGEMENT AND DIRECTION

Given the number of intelligence agencies, services, and offices, the conflicting and diverse supervisory executive departments, and the wide range of intelligence activities, it is clear that the U.S. intelligence community requires coordination and control to guide its work. Furthermore, the highly sensitive nature of some of these activities requires approval by high-level officials. Thus it is not surprising that over the past thirty years an elaborate system of directives, committees, offices, plans, and programs has been established.

This system can be divided into three basic categories. Executive Orders, presidential directives, and agency or departmental regulations establish the basic missions and structure of the intelligence community. Individuals, committees, and offices implement and formulate directives, seek to resolve conflicts, provide advice and counsel, and establish collection and analysis priorities. Finally, there are the plans, programs, and requirements documents that establish objectives or specify resource allocation for the attainment of specific collection or analysis tasks.

ORDERS, DIRECTIVES, AND REGULATIONS

The orders, directives, and regulations that guide the activities of the intelligence community all stem from documents issued by the President's office. These documents represent the apex of the system and come in two varieties—unclassified Executive Orders and (often classified) presidential directives. The title of the second type of document changes with presidential administrations. Thus, Bill Clinton's Presidential Decision Directives (PDDs) were National Security Directives (NSDs) in the Bush administration, National Security Decision Directives (NSDDs) in the Reagan administration, Presidential Directives (PDs) in the Carter administration, National Security Decision Memoranda (NSDM) in the Nixon and Ford administrations, and National Security Action Memoranda (NSAMs) in the Kennedy and Johnson administrations.

Each administration generally issues a new Executive Order governing the intelligence community. Although the orders reflect different concerns, they often overlap in content with previous orders. However, there was no Executive Order on intelligence during the Bush administration, nor has there been one during the Clinton administration (as of 1994). Thus, at present, Reagan Executive Order 12333, "United States Intelligence Activities" of December 4, 1981, is still operative. It is divided into three parts: Goals, Direction, Duties, and Responsibilities with Respect to the National Intelligence Effort; The Conduct of Intelligence Activities; and General Provisions.[1] Part 1 authorizes the establishment of National Foreign Intelligence Advisory Groups, specifies the agencies and offices that constitute the intelligence community, defines their general functions, and lists the duties and responsibilities of the senior officials of the community.

Part 2, on the conduct of intelligence activities, establishes procedures and restrictions concerning the collection of information abroad and in the United States concerning U.S. persons. It also establishes (or continues) procedures concerning assistance to law enforcement authorities and human experimentation and prohibits assassinations. Part 3 deals with congressional oversight, implementation, and definitions.

Changes in the content of the Executive Orders have been the product of three factors: different modes of National Security Council (NSC) organization, revelations concerning abuses by the intelligence community, and differing attitudes concerning domestic intelligence activities. Thus, Gerald Ford's Executive Order, "United States Foreign Intelligence Activities" of February 18, 1976, imposed restrictions on physical and electronic surveillance activities, experimentation, and assistance to law enforcement authorities in response to the 1974–1975 revelations concerning various CIA, FBI, and NSA activities. It also specified for the first time that "no employee of the United States Government shall engage in, or conspire to engage in, political assassination."[2]

The Carter Executive Order was primarily concerned with restrictions and oversight.[3] The Reagan Executive Order loosened some of those restrictions, allowing the collection of "significant foreign intelligence" within the United States by the CIA so long as the collection effort was not undertaken for the purpose of acquiring information concerning the domestic activities of U.S. persons.

In addition to an Executive Order governing the intelligence community, each President has generally also issued an order concerning national security information. These orders deal with classification levels and authority, downgrading and declassification, safeguards for classified information, and implementation of their provisions. The most recent of these orders is Executive Order 12356 of April 2, 1982, which reversed trends that began during the Nixon administration favoring the lowering of classification levels and reductions in the absolute quantity of classified material. The 1982 order does not require a balancing of national security considerations with the public interest in access to information and allows "reclassification" of previously declassified material if such material is considered "reasonably recoverable."[4]

The usually classified presidential directives on intelligence matters tend to deal with specific areas of intelligence operations—intelligence community organization and procedures, covert operations, and space reconnaissance, for example. Carter administration PDs concerning intelligence included PD-9 of March 30, 1977, "Army Special Operations Field Office Berlin"; PD-17 of August 4, 1977, "Reorganization of the Intelligence Community"; PD-19 of August 25, 1977, "Intelligence Structure and Mission (Electronic Surveillance Abroad and Physical Searches for Foreign Intelligence Purposes)"; and PD-55 of January 10, 1980, "Intelligence Special Access Programs: Establishment of the APEX Program."[5]

At least seven Reagan NSDDs concerned intelligence matters. NSDD-17 of January 4, 1982, "National Security Directive on Cuba and Central America," dealt with covert operations in that region. NSDD-19 of January 12, 1982, is entitled "Protection of Classified National Security Council and Intelligence Information," and NSDD-22 of January 29, 1982, concerned the "Designation of Intelligence Officials Authorized to Request FBI Collection of Foreign Intelligence." NSDD-42 of July 4, 1982, "National Space Policy," dealt, in part, with space reconnaissance. NSDD-84 of March 11, 1983, "Safeguarding National Security Information," specified new security requirements for individuals permitted access to codeword information. NSDD-159 of January 18, 1985, specified "Covert Action Policy Approval and Coordination Procedures"; NSDD-196 of November 1, 1985, concerned the "Counterintelligence/Countermeasure Implementation Task Force"; NSDD-202 concerned the impact of a new methodology for assessing the yields of Soviet nuclear weapons tests; NSDD-204 concerned "Transfer of National Intelligence Collection Tasking Authority"; and NSDD-286 dealt with covert action procedures.[6]

Bush administration National Security Directives concerning intelligence organization or operations included a February 1989 NSD on support to the Afghan rebels; NSD 30 of November 2, 1989, on "National Space Policy"; an August 1990 NSD on covert action directed against Iraq; the October 1990 NSD 47 on counterintelligence; NSD 63 on "Single Scope Background Investigations"; and NSD 67 on intelligence priorities. The only known Clinton Presidential Decision Directive to deal directly with intelligence matters is PDD-24 on "U.S. Counterintelligence Effectiveness." The directive was the product of the interagency review mandated by Presidential Review Directive 44 (PRD-44).[7]

Both Executive Orders and presidential directives deal with subjects in fairly general terms. Implementation requires more detailed directives. Two basic types of implementation directives are: (1) National Security Council Intelligence Directives (NSCIDs) and their descendants and (2) departmental directives and their descendants.

NSCIDs offer guidance to the entire intelligence community, and the Director of Central Intelligence (DCI) in particular, concerning specific aspects of U.S. intelligence operations. The NSCID numbering system is unlike that for Presidential Decision Directives or their predecessors, which are numbered according to the sequence in which they are issued. In general, an NSCID number is assigned to a particular topic and subsequent revisions of the NSCID bear the same num-

Table 16-1. NSCIDs Issued on February 17, 1972.

Number	Title
1	Basic Duties and Responsibilities
2	Coordination of Overt Activities
3	Coordination of Intelligence Production
4	The Defector Program
5	U.S. Espionage and Counterintelligence Activities Abroad
6	Signals Intelligence
7	Critical Intelligence Communications
8	Photographic Interpretation

ber. The topic assigned to a particular number may change over time, or one topic may be subsumed under another.

NSCIDs were first issued in 1947 and have been updated numerous times since then. Sometimes revisions have been of selected documents; other times an entire group has been revised. As of 1987 the last major revision appears to have been completed on February 17, 1972, when updated versions of all eight NSCIDs were issued. The numbers and names of those NSCIDs are listed in Table 16-1. A 1970s project to establish a single omnibus NSCID was never completed.

NSCID No. 1, "Basic Duties and Responsibilities," was first issued in 1947 and subsequently updated in 1952, 1958, 1961, 1964, and 1972. The NSCID No. 1 of February 17, 1972, assigned four major responsibilities to the DCI:

1. planning, reviewing, and evaluating all intelligence activities and the allocation of all intelligence resources;
2. producing national intelligence required by the President and national consumers;
3. chairing and staffing all intelligence advisory boards; and
4. establishing and reconciling intelligence requirements and priorities with budgetary constraints.[8]

NSCID No. 1 also (1) instructs the DCI to prepare and submit to the Office of Management and Budget (OMB) a consolidated budget, (2) authorizes the issuance of Director of Central Intelligence Directives as a means of implementing the NSCIDs, and (3) instructs the DCI to protect sources and methods.[9]

NSCID No. 2 of February 17, 1972, makes the DCI responsible for planning how the collection and reporting capabilities of the various government departments will be utilized and makes the CIA responsible for conducting, as a service of common concern, radio broadcast monitoring. The Department of State is charged with overt collection of political, sociological, economic, scientific, and technical information; military-pertinent scientific and technical intelligence; and economic intelligence.[10]

The 1972 version of NSCID No. 3 makes the Department of State responsible for the production of political and sociological intelligence on all countries and economic intelligence on countries of the "Free World." It makes the Department of Defense (DOD) responsible for the production of military intelligence and scientific and technical intelligence pertinent to the missions of DOD components. The CIA is given responsibility for economic and scientific and technical intelligence plus "any other intelligence required by the DCI."[11] In practice, this clause has meant that the CIA is heavily involved in the production of political and military intelligence, especially strategic intelligence. In addition, atomic energy intelligence is decreed, by NSCID No. 3, to be the responsibility of all National Foreign Intelligence Board (NFIB) agencies.[12]

Originally, NSCID No. 4 concerned Priority National Intelligence Objectives (PNIOs)—a system for prioritizing collection efforts. The PNIO system has been eliminated; hence, NSCID No. 4 now bears the title "The Defector Program" and presumably concerns the inducement of defections and the responsibilities of the CIA and other agencies in the program.[13]

NSCID No. 5 of February 17, 1972, "U.S. Espionage and Counterintelligence Activities Abroad" is the successor to versions issued in 1947, 1951, 1958, and 1961. The directive authorizes the DCI to "establish the procedures necessary to achieve such direction and coordination, including the assessment of risk incident upon such operations as compared to the value of the activity, and to ensure that sensitive operations are reviewed pursuant to applicable direction."[14]

NSCID No. 6, "Signals Intelligence," serves as the charter for the NSA. The February 17, 1972, version was still effective as of 1987. It defines the nature of SIGINT activities and directs the Director of NSA (DIRNSA) to produce intelligence "in accordance with objectives, requirements and priorities established by the Director of Central Intelligence and the United States Intelligence Board." It further authorizes the DIRNSA "to issue direct to any operating elements engaged in SIGINT operations such instructions and assignments as are required. All instructions issued by the Director under the authority provided in this paragraph shall be mandatory, subject only to appeal to the Secretary of Defense."[15]

NSCID No. 7 establishes the Critical Intelligence Communications (CRITICOMM) System. This system governs procedures and criteria for the transmission of particularly important intelligence to top officials, including the President, within the shortest possible period of time. The information may concern an imminent coup, the assassination of a world leader, or, as in September 1983, the shooting down of a civilian airliner. The information may be acquired by HUMINT, SIGINT, or PHOTINT. It has been NSA's goal to have a CRITIC message on the President's desk within ten minutes of the event.[16]

The original NSCID No. 8 was issued on May 25, 1948, and was entitled "Biographical Data on Foreign Scientific and Technological Personalities." By 1961 the NSCID dealt, instead, with "Photographic Interpretation." NSCID No. 8 of February 17, 1972, continues the National Photographic Interpretation Center (NPIC) as a service of common concern to be provided by the DCI. Additionally, it specifies that the Director of the NPIC is to be selected by the DCI with the concurrence of the Secretary of Defense.[17]

The NSCIDs state, in general terms, the responsibilities of the DCI and other components of the intelligence community. One provision of NSCID No. 1 authorizes the DCI to issue more detailed directives—the Director of Central Intelligence Directives (DCIDs)—in pursuit of the implementation of the various NSCIDs. DCIDs are keyed to the NSCIDs from which they follow according to the NSCID numbering system. Thus, DCID 1/3 is the third DCID issued pursuant to NSCID No. 1.

DCIDs in the DCID 1/ series include 1/2, 1/3, 1/5, 1/7, 1/8, 1/10, 1/11, 1/13, 1/14, 1/15, 1/16, 1/17, 1/18, 1/19, 1/20, 1/21, and 1/22. DCID 1/2 of January 21, 1972, "U.S. Intelligence Requirements Categories and Priorities" provided guidance for planning and programming for the subsequent five years. It identified intelligence targets in terms of the information needed "to enable the U.S. intelligence community to provide effective support for decision-making, planning and operational activities of the United States government."[18] DCID 1/3 of May 18, 1976, entitled "Committees of the Director of Central Intelligence," outlined the basic composition and organization of the committees and authorized the DCI to designate their Chairmen. DCID 1/5 of May 1976 dealt with "Data Standardization for the Intelligence Community." DCID 1/7 of May 4, 1981, "Security Controls on the Dissemination of Intelligence Information," imposed restrictions on the dissemination of intelligence to immigrant aliens and foreign governments. DCID 1/8 of May 6, 1976, "The National Foreign Intelligence Board," established the board as the successor to the United States Intelligence Board. A more recent version of DCID 1/8 was issued on January 28, 1982.[19]

DCID 1/10 of January 18, 1982, is entitled "Security Policy Guidance on Liaison Relationships with Foreign Intelligence Organizations and Foreign Security Services." DCID 1/11 of July 15, 1982, spelled out the mission, functions, and composition of the now defunct Security Committee, and DCID 1/17 of May 18, 1976, did the same for the Human Resources Committee. Another NFIB committee, the Committee on Imagery Requirements and Exploitation (COMIREX), was the main subject of DCID 1/13, "Coordination of the Collection and Exploitation of Imagery Intelligence." DCID 1/15 of May 18, 1976, concerned "Data Standardization for the Intelligence Community."[20]

Security standards are the subject of DCIDs 1/14, 1/16, 1/19, 1/20, and 1/21. DCIDs 1/14 and 1/19 are concerned with the protection of Sensitive Compartmented Information (SCI). DCID 1/14 of April 14, 1986, is entitled "Minimum Personnel Security Standards and Procedures Governing Eligibility for Access to Sensitive Compartmented Information." The directive focuses on personnel security standards, investigative requirements, the implications of various outside activities on security, the determination of access eligibility, continuing security programs, and security violations. DCID 1/16 deals with "Guidance on SCI Automated Systems." DCID 1/19, "SCI Administrative Guidance," focuses on the handling and accountability of SCI, and DCID 1/20 concerns "Security Policy Concerning Travel and Assignment of Personnel with Access to Sensitive Compartmented Information." DCID 1/21 is titled "SCI Physical Security Guidance," and DCID 1/22 is concerned with "Technical Surveillance Countermeasures."[21]

DCID 1/18 of May 18, 1976, "Recognition of Exceptional Service to the U.S. Intelligence Community," established criteria for the National Intelligence Distinguished Service Medal, the National Intelligence Medal of Achievement, and the Intelligence Community Certificate of Distinction.

DCID 2/1 of March 8, 1960, concerned the "Coordination of Overt Collection Abroad." Today's version of 2/1 apparently deals with the same subject and would thus cover the procurement of foreign publications and the acquisition of intelligence information from nongovernment organizations and individuals (such as businesses and travelers). DCID 2/9 of June 1, 1992, bears the title "Management of National Imagery Intelligence" and defines the functions and responsibilities of the Central Imagery Office.[22]

DCIDs in the 3/ series have involved implementation of NSCID No. 3, "Coordination of Intelligence Production." These directives have dealt with the production of National Intelligence Estimates as well as the establishment of numerous NFIB committees to facilitate production of intelligence in specific areas. Early versions of DCID 3/1 (July 8, 1948), 3/2 (September 13, 1948), and 3/5 (September 1, 1953) were entitled, respectively, "Standard Operating Procedures for Departmental Participation in the Production and Coordination of National Intelligence"; "Policy Governing Departmental Concurrences in National Intelligence Reports and Estimates"; and "Production of National Intelligence Estimates."[23]

Later DCIDs in the 3/ series defined the mission and functions of the Economic Intelligence Committee (3/1), the Joint Atomic Energy Intelligence Committee (3/3), the Intelligence Producers Council (3/3 of March 30, 1983), the Guided Missile and Astronautics Intelligence Committee (3/4), the Scientific and Technical Intelligence Committee (3/5), the Human Resources Committee (3/7 of October 12, 1982), the Critical Intelligence Problems Committee (3/8 of April 6, 1983), the Technology Transfer Intelligence Committee (3/13 of December 3, 1981), the Information Handling Committee (3/14 of May 4, 1982), the Foreign Language Committee (3/15 of March 5, 1982), and the Community Personnel Coordination Committee (1989). The most recent versions of DCIDs 3/1 (January 28, 1982), 3/2 (January 18, 1982), and 3/3 (June 1, 1992) established the National Foreign Intelligence Board, the National Foreign Intelligence Council, and the Community Management Staff, respectively.[24]

DCIDs 4/1 and 4/2 of May 1976 concerned the "Interagency Defector Committee" and "The Defector Program Abroad." DCIDs in the 5/ series include 5/1 of May 1976, "Coordination of U.S. Clandestine Foreign Intelligence Activities Abroad," and 5/2, also of May 1976, "U.S. Clandestine Foreign Intelligence and Counterintelligence Liaison." DCID 6/1 of May 12, 1982, focuses on the functions, composition, and mission of the SIGINT Committee. DCID 7/1 of August 1976 dealt with "Handling of Critical Information."[25]

DCIDs for which numbers are not available include the April 30, 1983, DCID, which established the now defunct Intelligence Producers Council, and the DCID of May 25, 1983, on "Intelligence Disclosure Policy."[26]

Both the DCI and the Director of NSA are authorized to issue directives concerning aspects of the signals intelligence effort. The DCI issues Communications Intelligence Supplementary Regulations, whereas the Director of NSA issues U.S. Signals Intelligence Directives.[27]

The most important departmental regulations and directives on intelligence matters are DOD Directives, which concern both intelligence policies and the operations of specific units. Hence, DOD Directive 3310.1, "International Intelligence Agreements," included the following specifications:

1. The Deputy Under Secretary of Defense (Policy) ... is the principal within the Department of Defense responsible for oversight, coordination, and policy review of intelligence matters relating to agreements with foreign parties.
2. The Director, Defense Intelligence Agency (DIA), shall exercise, for the Department of Defense, approval authority (which may not be further delegated) to negotiate and conclude non-SIGINT intelligence agreements.[28]

A related DOD Directive, C-5230.23 of November 18, 1983, on "Intelligence Disclosure Policy," specifies the functions of various DOD officials in the disclosure process. Thus, the Director of the DIA is to "coordinate within and for the Department of Defense, proposed disclosures of classified U.S. intelligence to senior foreign officials" and the Deputy Undersecretary for Policy is to "resolve conflicts among DOD components relating to disclosure of classified U.S. intelligence to senior foreign officials."[29]

Other DOD Directives concerning intelligence policy include "Signals Intelligence" (S-3115.7, January 25, 1983); "Implementation of National Security Council Intelligence Directive No. 7" (S-5100.19, March 19, 1959); "Human Resources Intelligence Activities" (S-5105.29, July 9, 1987); "The Security, Use and Dissemination of Communications Intelligence (COMINT)" (S-5200.17, January 26, 1965); "Coordination and Reporting of Foreign Intelligence Related Contacts and Arrangements" (S-3315.1, March 23, 1984); "Foreign Materiel Program" (S-3325.1, September 18, 1986); "Transfer of National Intelligence Collection Authority" (S-3325.2, June 18, 1987); "Protection of Classified National Security Council and Intelligence Information" (5230.21, March 15, 1982); and "Support to Department of Defense Offensive Counterintelligence Operations" (S-5240.9, November 28, 1989).[30]

These directives may represent initial DOD implementation of an NSCID, DCID, or presidential directive. Thus, S-5100.19 represents initial implementation of NSCID No. 7; 3310.1 represents implementation of DCID 1/10; and 5230.21 represents implementation of NSDD-19.

Table 16-2.   Selected Air Force Regulations (AFRs) Concerning Intelligence Activities.

AFR	Title	Date
200-1	Air Force Intelligence Mission and Responsibilities	June 1984
200-5	Air Force Intelligence Support of the Defense Attaché System	July 1985
200-7	Sensitive Compartmented Information (SCI) Security System	April 1987
200-11	Air Force Space Intelligence Mission and Responsibilities	Nov. 1983
200-12	Foreign Materiel Program	Jan. 1983
200-19	Conduct of Intelligence Activities	Oct. 1983
200-25	International Intelligence Agreements	Jan. 1984
200-26	USAF Participation in the Defector Program	Oct. 1985

Source: Air Force Regulation 0-2, "Numerical Index of Standard and Recurring Air Force Publications," July 1, 1992, p. 75.

Other DOD Directives specify the mission and functions of the National Reconnaissance Office (TS-5105.23, March 27, 1964); the National Security Agency and Central Security Service (S-5100.20, December 23, 1971); the Defense Intelligence Agency (5105.21, May 19, 1977); the Defense Special Missile and Astronautics Center (S-5100.43, April 27, 1964); the Central Imagery Office (5105.56, May 6, 1992); the Defense Mapping Agency (5125.40, April 23, 1986); and the Armed Forces Medical Intelligence Center (6240.1, December 9, 1982; 6240.1-R, April 1986).[31]

Military service and command regulations also state intelligence policies as well as define the mission and functions of service intelligence units. Among Air Force Regulations (AFRs) governing intelligence policy are those listed in Table 16-2. AFRs governing the activities of specific intelligence units include AFR 23-30 of October 1987, "Electronic Security Command," as well as those dealing with the Air Force Technical Applications Center (AFR 23-44, March 1986) and the Air Force Intelligence Support Agency (AFR 23-45, March 1992).[32]

Army Regulations (ARs) governing intelligence units and activities are listed in Table 16-3. The most detailed regulations and directives are those issued by the intelligence units themselves. These directives seek to implement the broader DOD and military service directives by adopting the guidelines, restrictions, and procedures mandated by those broader directives and by specifying the internal structure and organization of the unit and the functions of its components.

Among the eighty-one INSCOM Regulations is INSCOM Regulation 10-2, "Organization and Functions, United States Army Intelligence and Security Command," of June 25, 1989, which is 119 pages long and enumerates the functions of each of the Deputy Chiefs of Staff and the divisions, branches, and offices that make up the organization. Likewise, the Air Force Technical Application Center (AFTAC) publications index lists hundreds of regulations covering administrative practices, organization and mission, personnel operations, equipment maintenance, R&D, security, and supply. Among the regulations are R55-3, "Aerial Sampling Operations," and numerous regulations specifying require-

Table 16-3.   Selected Army Regulations (ARs) Concerning Intelligence Activities.

AR	Title	Date
10-53	U.S. Army Intelligence and Security Command	June 15, 1978
10-61	U.S. Army Intelligence Operations Detachment	March 1, 1983
10-86	U.S. Army Intelligence Agency	Feb. 27, 1986
381-1	Control of Dissemination of Intelligence Information	Feb. 12, 1990
381-3	Signals Intelligence	Jan. 15, 1982
381-10	U.S. Army Intelligence Activities	July 1, 1984
381-19	Intelligence Dissemination and Production Support	July 15, 1981
381-20	U.S. Army Counterintelligence Activities	Sept. 26, 1986
381-26	Army Foreign Materiel Exploitation Program	May 27, 1991
381-47	U.S. Army Offensive Counter-espionage Operations	July 30, 1990
381-100	Army Human Intelligence Collection Programs	May 15, 1988
381-171	International Intelligence Agreements	Oct. 21, 1986

Source: Department of the Army, Information Management Pamphlet 25-30, *Consolidated Index of Army Publications and Blank Forms,* October 1992, pp. K1, L3, M3.

ments for specific AFTAC detachments. Similarly, the 1982 DIA Index of Administrative Publications covers thirty-eight categories in thirty-four pages, listing administrative, intelligence collection and production, and counterintelligence regulations.[33]

INDIVIDUALS, COMMITTEES, AND OFFICES

No matter how thorough the documents and directives described above or the plans described below are in stating the responsibilities and subjects for collection and analysis, they will, for several reasons, be insufficient as complete guides. First, every document leaves some room for interpretation. Second, attainment of the objectives specified will require coordination and cooperation on a regular basis. Hence, it is necessary to maintain a structure that facilitates such coordination and cooperation. Third, it is necessary to see that the components of the intelligence community are performing their activities within the restrictions imposed on them—that is, that the activities planned to attain specified objectives must be acceptable to a higher authority. Fourth, some management structure is needed to generate the directives, plans, and programs under which the intelligence community operates. Finally, changing circumstances will require an alteration in preconceived plans and priorities.

At the top of the management system, which includes individuals, committees, and offices, are the President and the National Security Council committees. Under the Carter administration, there were two such committees: the Special Coordination Committee (SCC) and the Policy Review Committee (PRC). The SCC had jurisdiction over covert operations and counterintelligence matters, whereas two components of the PRC were concerned with positive intelligence. PRC-Intelligence (PRC-I) was concerned with the preparation of a consolidated national intelligence budget and with resource allocation for the entire intelligence community. PRC-Space probably had some role in space reconnaissance decisions.[34]

The SCC and the PRC were two more in a long line of NSC committees responsible for supervising intelligence activities. Until the Nixon administration, such committees were exclusively concerned with covert operations. The first of these committees was established in 1948 by NSC 10/2 and known as the 10/2 Panel. In subsequent years, as the panel was re-created and its membership and functions altered or maintained, it was renamed the 10/5 Panel (NSC 10/5, October 23, 1951), the Operations Coordinating Board (NSC 5412, NSC 5412/1 of March 12–15, 1954), the 5412 Group or Special Group (NSC 5412/2, December 28, 1955), and the 303 Committee (NSAM 303, June 2, 1964). In 1959 the Special Group became responsible for the approval of sensitive air and naval reconnaissance missions conducted on the Soviet periphery.[35]

With the signing of National Security Decision Memorandum 40, "Responsibility for the Conduct, Supervision and Coordination of Covert Action Operations," on February 17, 1970, the Director of Central Intelligence was required to "obtain policy approval for all major and/or politically sensitive covert action operations through the 40 Committee." The memorandum also called for an annual review of all covert action programs previously approved.[36]

In addition to the 40 Committee, the Nixon administration created the National Security Council Intelligence Committee (NSCIC), which was responsible for supervising the intelligence activities not under the purview of the 40 Committee. By creating the NSCIC, Nixon acknowledged that there were intelligence issues of importance in addition to covert action and sensitive reconnaissance operations. These issues included the need to make the intelligence community more responsive to policymakers, the establishment of intelligence priorities, and the allocation of resources.[37]

The basic two-committee system was continued by the Ford administration and, as already noted, the Carter administration. With Executive Order 11905, President Ford established the Committee on Foreign Intelligence (CFI) and the Operations Advisory Group (OAG). The CFI was chaired by the DCI, with the Deputy Secretary of Defense for Intelligence and the Deputy Assistant to the President for National Security Affairs as members. The CFI was given control over budget preparation and resource allocation for the National Foreign Intelligence Program (NFIP). Supervision of covert operations was the responsibility of the OAG, which consisted of the Assistant to the President for National Security Affairs, the Secretary of State, the Secretary of Defense, the Chairman of the Joint Chiefs of Staff, and the DCI—with the Chairman being determined by the President.[38] The membership of the OAG represented an upgrading in the status of the covert action supervision mechanism. Previously, membership on such committees involved officials at the Undersecretary and Deputy Secretary levels.

The upgrading was maintained under Carter Executive Order 12036 and extended to both committees. The SCC consisted of the Assistant to the President for National Security Affairs as Chairman, the Secretary of State, the Secretary of Defense, the DCI, the Chairman of the JCS, the Attorney General, and the Director of OMB. The PRC consisted of the same group except that the Vice-President and Secretary of the Treasury were members instead of the Attorney General and Director of the OMB.[39]

Ronald Reagan established Senior Interagency Groups (SIGs), including the Senior Interagency Group—Intelligence (SIG-I). SIG-I was given the responsibility of advising and assisting the NSC with respect to intelligence policy and intelligence matters. It was chaired by the DCI, and its members included the Assistant to the President for National Security Affairs, the Deputy Secretary of State, the Deputy Secretary of Defense, and the Chairman of the JCS. In addition to the statutory members, provision was made for attendance by the heads of organizations with a direct interest in the activities under consideration. When meeting to consider counterintelligence activities, the membership of the group was augmented by the Director of the FBI and the Director of the National Security Agency. When meeting to consider sensitive intelligence collection activities, the SIG-I's membership was augmented as required by the head of each organization within the intelligence community directly involved in the activity in question.[40]

Under the Bush administration a series of Policy Coordinating Committees were established within the NSC to handle substantive areas, including intelligence. The provisions of President Clinton's Presidential Decision Directive 2 (PDD 2), "Organization of the National Security Council," established three levels of committees under the NSC. In descending order of seniority, they are the Principals Committee (which includes the DCI as a member), the Deputies Committee, and Interagency Working Groups. No specific intelligence committees were established by PDD 2.[41]

Responsibility for management of the intelligence community emanates in two different but not totally distinct directions from the President and the NSC. One direction is toward the DCI, the other toward the Secretary of Defense.

The DCI is the statutory head of the intelligence community. Executive Order 12333 instructs him to:

1. act as the primary adviser to the President and the NSC on national foreign intelligence;
2. develop such objectives and guidance for the intelligence community as will enhance capabilities for responding to expected future needs for national foreign intelligence;
3. promote the development and maintenance of service of common concern by designated intelligence organizations on behalf of the intelligence community;
4. ensure implementation of special activities;
5. coordinate foreign intelligence and counterintelligence relationships between agencies of the intelligence community and the intelligence or internal security services of foreign governments;

6. ensure the establishment by the intelligence community of common security and access standards for managing and handling foreign intelligence systems, information, and products;

7. ensure that programs are developed which protect intelligence sources, methods, and analytical procedures;

8. establish uniform criteria for the determination of relative priorities for the transmission of critical national foreign intelligence and advise the Secretary of Defense concerning the communications requirements of the intelligence community for the transmission of such intelligence;

9. establish appropriate staffs, committees, or other advisory groups to assist in the execution of the Director's responsibilities;

10. have full responsibility for production and dissemination of national foreign intelligence, and authority to levy analytical tasks on departmental intelligence production organizations, in consultation with those organizations' policymakers;

11. ensure the timely exploitation and dissemination of data gathered by national foreign intelligence collection means;

12. establish mechanisms that translate national foreign intelligence objectives and priorities approved by the NSC into specific guidance for the intelligence community, resolve conflicts in tasking priority, and provide for the development of plans and arrangements for transfer of required collection tasking authority to the Secretary of Defense when directed by the President;

13. develop, with the advice of the program managers and departments and agencies concerned, the consolidated National Foreign Intelligence Program budget;

14. monitor National Foreign Intelligence Program implementation, and, as necessary, conduct program and performance audits and evaluation; and

15. together with the Secretary of Defense, ensure that there is no unnecessary overlap between national foreign intelligence programs and Department of Defense intelligence programs consistent with the requirement to develop competitive analysis, and provide to and obtain from the Secretary of Defense all information necessary for this purpose.[42]

The responsibilities of the DCI, as stated in Executive Order 12333, previous Executive Orders, and the National Security Act of 1947, have not been matched by the power to fulfill these responsibilities. As Richard Helms noted in 1969, although the DCI was theoretically responsible for 100 percent of U.S. intelligence activities, he controlled less than 15 percent of the intelligence community's assets, while almost 85 percent were controlled by the Secretary of Defense and the JCS. And, until the signing of PD-17 during the Carter administration, the DCI had neither budgetary nor day-to-day management control. Management control of the National Reconnaissance Office and the National Security Agency remained with the Secretary of Defense. The DCI did receive full and exclusive authority to approve the National Foreign Intelligence Program budget—which includes the Department of Defense portion, made up of the General Defense Intelligence Program, the National Reconnaissance Program (Air Force Special Reconnaissance Activities), Navy Special Reconnaissance Activities, the Consolidated Cryptologic Program, and the Defense Foreign Counterintelligence Program.[43]

Seven organizations help the DCI fulfill his responsibilities: the Community Management Staff (CMS), the National Intelligence Collection Board (NICB), the National Intelligence Council (NIC), the National Intelligence Production Board (NIPB), the National Counterintelligence Policy Board (NCIPB), the National Foreign Intelligence Board (NFIB), and the Intelligence Community Executive Committee (IC/EXCOM).

The CMS was created in June 1992 by DCID 3/3 to replace the Intelligence Community Staff, which was a descendant of the National Intelligence Programs Evaluation Staff (created in 1963) as well as the more recent Resource Management Staff. According to the directive, the CMS is responsible for "developing, coordinating, and implementing DCI policy and exercising DCI responsibilities" with respect to:

a. intelligence policy and planning;
b. National Foreign Intelligence Program and budget development, evaluation, justification, and monitoring;
c. intelligence requirements management and evaluation; and
d. performance of such other functions and duties as determined by the DCI.[44]

The CMS operates under the direction of the Executive Director for Intelligence Community Affairs. As of July 1992, it had a staff of 70—although 161 personnel were authorized by Congress—compared to the 230 for its predecessor, the Intelligence Community Staff. The CMS is divided into three offices—Resource Management, Systems and Architecture, and Requirements and Evaluation.[45]

The Resource Management Office is charged with budget development, evaluation, justification, and monitoring for the National Foreign Intelligence Program. The Systems and Architecture Office conducts strategic planning to define long-range objectives and priorities for the intelligence community as well as methods for evaluating progress toward the objectives. The Requirements and Evaluations Office is responsible for "translating the needs of customers of the [intelligence community] products and services into national intelligence needs, for integrating the efforts of the collection disciplines to address these needs, and for evaluating the Community's performance in satisfying them."[46]

In addition, the CMS is supported by a National Intelligence Collection Board (NICB). The board, which is composed of senior officials "representing the intelligence collection disciplines and the principal Intelligence Community production offices," was established to "act as a forum for integrating the efforts of the separate collection disciplines and issuing guidance to collectors."[47]

The CMS is also responsible for coordinating the activities of four other entities. It oversees the Open Source Program, which is managed by the Community Open-Source Program Office; the Advanced Technology Office, the entity responsible for coordination of scientific and technical matters related to the NFIP Advanced Research & Development (AR&D) Program; the Community Counterintelligence and Security Measures Office, concerned with the development, coordination, and implementation of counterintelligence, security countermeasures, Sensitive Compartmented Information (SCI), and intelligence sources and methods protection policies; and the Foreign Language Coordinator, the person responsible for coordination of foreign language issues—including the recruitment and training of linguists, technologies, and development of an annual strategic plan.[48]

The National Intelligence Council (NIC) is the DCI's principal means of producing National Intelligence Estimates, Special National Intelligence Estimates, and Interagency Intelligence Memoranda. The council consists of a Chairman, twelve National Intelligence Officers responsible for specific geographic or substantive areas, and an Analytic Group consisting of approximately fifteen analysts.[49]

The National Intelligence Production Board operates under the NIC. In addition to advising the DCI on all production matters, it "oversees several Community programs that focus on minimizing unnecessary duplication of effort and maximizing efforts to meet consumer needs."[50]

The National Counterintelligence Policy Board was established in May 1994 by PDD-24 and consists of senior executive representatives from the DCI/CIA, the FBI, the Defense Department, the State Department, and the Justice Department plus a military service counterintelligence component and the NSC staff. The board will consider, develop, and recommend counterintelligence policy and planning directives to the President's national security adviser.[51]

Subordinate to the policy board is the National Counterintelligence Operations Board. The operations board consists of representatives from the CIA; the FBI; the Defense, State, and Justice Departments; and the military service counterintelligence components and the Chief of the National Counterintelligence Center.[52]

While the CMS and the NIC are subordinate to the DCI, the National Foreign Intelligence Board (NFIB) and the Intelligence Community Executive Committee (IC/EXCOM) provide advice and counsel to the DCI and serve as his principal means of coordinating intelligence community activities and attaining consensus on major issues.

The NFIB is the successor to the United States Intelligence Board (USIB), which was formed in 1958 by the merger of the Intelligence Advisory Committee and the Communications Intelligence Board. The functions of the NFIB, as defined in DCID 1/8 of May 6, 1976, consist of:

a. review and coordination of national intelligence products;
b. maintenance of effective interface between intelligence producers and consumers and the development of procedures for continuing identification of consumer needs for intelligence;
c. the establishment of appropriate objectives, requirements and priorities for substantive intelligence;
d. the review of requirements coordination and operational guidance for intelligence collection systems;
e. the protection of sensitive intelligence sources and methods and sensitive intelligence information;
f. the development as appropriate, of policies regarding arrangements with foreign governments on intelligence matters; and
g. such other matters as the Director of Central Intelligence may refer to the Board for advice.[53]

The DCI serves as Chairman of the NFIB. The board's other members include the Directors of the NSA, the DIA, and the Bureau of Intelligence Research as well as representatives of FBI, Department of Energy, and Department of the Treasury intelligence components and the Deputy Director of the CIA. The Directors of the NRO and the CIO attend as necessary. The Deputy Chief of Staff for Intelligence, Army; the Director of Naval Intelligence; the Assistant Chief of Staff, Intelligence, Air Force; and the Director of Intelligence for the Marine Corps sit on the board as observers.[54]

The NFIB's predecessor, the USIB, operated through an elaborate committee structure. It was observed in 1974, before the NFIB replaced the USIB, that through the committee structure the USIB

lists the targets for American intelligence and the priority attached to each one, coordinates within the intelligence community the estimates of future events and enemy strengths, controls the classification and security systems for most of the U.S. government, directs research in the various fields of technical intelligence, and decides what classified information will be passed on to foreign friends and allies.[55]

The committees also served as a means of informing the members of the intelligence community on particular matters (e.g., weapons and space systems) and providing support to agencies outside the intelligence community.

In 1976, in the interval between the abolition of the USIB and the creation of the NFIB, the committees were redesignated as DCI committees. Present DCI committees include the National SIGINT Committee, the Technology Transfer Intelligence Committee (TTIC), the Economic Intelligence Committee (EIC), the Human Resources Committee (HRC), the Foreign Intelligence Priorities Committee (FIPC), the Critical Intelligence Problems Committee (CIPC), the Scientific and Technical Intelligence Committee (STIC), the Information Handling

Committee (IHC), the Joint Atomic Energy Intelligence Committee (JAEIC), the Weapons and Space Systems Intelligence Committee (WSSIC), the Foreign Language Committee, the Narcotics Intelligence Issues Committee (NIIC), the Interagency Intelligence Committee on Terrorism (IICT), the Interagency Defector Committee (IDC), the Measurement and Signature Intelligence (MASINT) Committee, the Warning Committee, the Community Nonproliferation Committee (CNC), the Open Source Committee (OSC), the Community Counterintelligence and Security Countermeasures Committee (CCSCC), and the Advanced Research and Development Program Committee.[56]

In 1992, three of the committees, the JAEIC, WSSIC, and STIC, were made directly responsible to the National Intelligence Council. In addition, several other committees now operate within the agencies they supervise. Thus, the National SIGINT Committee is now "within NSA," the Committee on Imagery Requirements and Exploitation (COMIREX) became part of the Central Imagery Office, and the MASINT Committee operates under the DIA's Central MASINT Office.[57]

The SIGINT Committee was formed in 1962 by the merger of the COMINT and ELINT Committees. It reviews and validates all proposed requirements before they are levied on the NSA. The Technology Transfer Intelligence Committee (TTIC) was created in 1981 to deal with what was perceived to be a growing hemorrhage of critical technology to the Soviet Union. The TTIC, which operates through two subcommittees (the Subcommittee on Exchanges and the Subcommittee on Export Control), draws on scientific and technical analysts throughout the military technical intelligence centers and elsewhere in the intelligence community.[58]

The TTIC's functions are to:

a. advise the DCI on the effectiveness of the Intelligence Community's role in support of U.S. Government policy on technology transfer issues;
b. as directed, prepare coordinated intelligence assessments on the significance of technology transfer and, as appropriate, their implications for national security;
c. advise appropriate U.S. government departments and agencies of the technology transfer implications and foreign intelligence equities involved in exchange programs and commercial contacts with nationals from designated foreign countries and recommend changes as appropriate;
d. provide foreign intelligence support on export control issues to appropriate U.S. Government agencies;
e. monitor all technology transfer intelligence concerning foreign efforts to acquire U.S. and Western technology and provide appropriate analyses to U.S. Government organizations concerned with protection and countermeasures, including counterintelligence organizations;
f. provide priority guidance to collection systems on technology transfer issues; and
g. establish an exchange of information with all departments and agencies concerned with the technology transfer program to ensure that utility of the Intelligence Community's activities is maintained.[59]

The TTIC's products have included "Soviet Requirements for Western Technology: A Forecasting Methodology" (May 1987), "National Security and Export Controls: A Decision Aid" (September 1988), and "Israel: Marketing U.S. Strategic Technology" (September 1990).[60]

The Economic Intelligence Committee (EIC) was established in 1948 as a subsidiary of the Intelligence Advisory Committee and has continued as a subsidiary of the USIB and as a DCI committee. The Subcommittee on Requirements and Coordination of the EIC produces the Economic Alert List (EAL), which highlights the current economic information needs of all agencies participating in the Combined Economic Reporting Program (CERP).[61]

The Joint Atomic Energy Intelligence Committee (JAEIC) was created to "foster, develop and maintain a coordinated community approach to the problems in the field of atomic energy intelligence, to promote interagency liaison, and to give added impetus and community support to the efforts of individual agencies."[62]

The JAEIC meets twice a month to discuss items related to nuclear intelligence. Its focus ranges from the nuclear weapons programs of states that already possess nuclear weapons to questions of nuclear proliferation and the methodology used for assessing the yield of nuclear detonations. Its products have included a 1976 assessment of "The Soviet Atomic Energy Program" and a 1989 assessment of Iraq's ability to build an atomic weapon. Its components include a Nuclear Weapons Logistics Working Group.[63]

The Critical Intelligence Problems Committee (CIPC) was created in 1958—as was the Critical Collection Problems Committee (CCPC)—to examine, as its name suggests, particularly difficult collection problems regardless of the technique involved. In 1971, one subject considered by the CCPC was narcotics intelligence, and it has a permanent Narcotics Working Group.[64]

According to DCID 3/8 of April 6, 1983, the committee is to identify:

a. the specific intelligence requirements and shortfalls associated with the critical intelligence problem under review;

b. current and programmed collection, processing, and production resources directed against the critical intelligence problem;

c. options for adjustments in collection, processing and production efforts which could be accomplished within existing resources, and the associated impact such adjustments would have on the Intelligence Community's ability to respond to other priority intelligence needs; and

d. recommendations for new initiatives which could increase collection, processing, and production efforts against the critical intelligence problem, noting which options would require reprogramming of supplemental funding actions.[65]

In 1975 the CIPC prepared the "Study on Intelligence Activities Against International Terrorism." In 1985 it sponsored a conference on Combat Intelligence Analysis and produced at least three studies—on combat intelligence analysis, cruise missile collection, and Strategic Defense Initiative intelligence. Two years later it prepared a study on "Soviet Enigma Satellites."[66]

The Foreign Intelligence Priorities Committee (FIPC) is the executive agent for managing the DCI's statement of "Foreign Intelligence Categories and Priorities" in DCID 1/2. An October 20, 1986, order by the FIPC raised the collection of intelligence related to American MIAs to "Priority One." Although that priority level is formally reserved for information considered "vital to U.S. survival," the order waived the definition for the POW-MIA issue.[67]

The Scientific and Technical Intelligence Committee (STIC) serves as the supervisory committee for all civilian and military scientific and technical intelligence production and acquisition. STIC subcommittees, working groups, and panels have included the Collection Subcommittee, the Open Sources Subcommittee, the Technology Forecasting Working Group, the Computer Working Group, the Electro-Optics Working Group, the Directed Energy Weapons Working Group, the Signal Processing Working Group, the Technology Processing Working Group, the Electronics Working Group, the Electro-Optics and Technology Working Group, the Life Sciences Working Group, the Radar and Optical Steering Group, the Radar Subcommittee, the Multispectral High Energy Laser Panel, the Scientific and Technical Information Support Program Committee, the Scientific and Technical Thermal Applications Group, and the Multispectral/Laser Applications Group.[68]

STIC products have included "Soviet R&D Related to Particle Beam Weapons" (October 1976), "Collection Guide: Chinese Students and Visitors from Important Institutes Seeking Critical Technologies" (1986), and "A Preliminary Assessment of Soviet Kinetic Energy Weapons Technology" (June 1986).[69]

The Information Handling Committee (IHC) is responsible for all aspects of information handling—supervising research and development of information-handling systems, developing rules and procedures for the exchange of information between agencies, and establishing education and training programs in information science. Its subcommittees include the Geographic Information Systems Subcommittee and the Access Control Subcommittee.[70]

The Weapons and Space Systems Intelligence Committee (WSSIC), chaired by the head of the Office of Scientific and Weapons Research (OSWR), was originally called the Guided Missile Intelligence Committee, which was created in 1956. In addition to producing analyses of the technical characteristics of foreign missile systems, it assigns designators and codenames for such systems. It also disseminates weapons and space system intelligence to the rest of the intelligence community and promotes liaison among intelligence units on weapons and space system matters.[71]

Table 16-4 lists subcommittees, panels, and working groups of the WSSIC. The Biological and Chemical Warfare Working Group, the predecessor to the Chemical and Biological Warfare Intelligence Subcommittee, reviewed all available intelligence concerning the suspected biological warfare incident at Sverdlovsk in 1979. It concluded that there was a high probability that the Soviets still had some anthrax for biological warfare purposes and that they maintained an active bio-

Table 16-4. Subcommittees and Panels of the Weapons and Space Systems Intelligence Committee.

Subcommittee	Last Reference
Ballistic Missile Systems Subcommittee	1990
Naval Weapons Systems Subcommittee	1990
Ground Weapons Subcommittee	1990
Electronic Warfare Subcommittee	1990
Aviation Subcommittee	1990
Air Defense Subcommittee	1990
Space Systems Subcommittee	1991
GLONASS Panel	1991
Chemical and Biological Warfare Intelligence Subcommittee	1990
CBWIS Chemical Agent Panel	1991
Command, Control, and Communications Subcommittee	1991
Rest of World C3 Panel	1991
Sub-HF Panel	1991
CROSSBOW C^{3}SS Data Base Subcommittee	1991

Sources: U.S. Army, Deputy Chief of Staff for Intelligence, *Annual Historical Review, 1 October 1989–30 September 1990*, n.d., pp. 6–25; Naval Maritime Intelligence Center, *Naval Maritime Intelligence Center Command History 1991*, 1992, pp. 11, 14, 34; Air Force Intelligence Agency, *History of the Air Force Intelligence Agency, 18 April 1987–31 December 1989, Volume 1, Narrative and Appendices*, 1990, p. 79.

logical warfare program at the Sverdlovsk facility. Previous committee products included "Soviet Medium Tank Developments" (1976), "Low Altitude Air Defense Capabilities of Soviet Nuclear Equipped SAMs" (August 1976), and "Soviet ICBM Silo Hardness Estimates" (November 1976).[72]

The Foreign Language Committee has three basic responsibilities, to:

a. appraise the effectiveness of programs to recruit, train, and retain personnel with adequate foreign language competence for elements of the Intelligence Community;

b. recommend to the DCI new initiatives to be undertaken to ensure the continuing availability within the Intelligence Community of requisite foreign language competence;

c. coordinate replies to all queries from Congressional committees concerning the Community's overall foreign language competence.[73]

The Warning Committee is chaired by the National Intelligence Officer for Warning. Its members include the Directors of DIA and NSA, the CIA Deputy Director for Intelligence, and the Assistant Secretary of State for Intelligence and Research. The committee's *Warning Committee Report* summarizes the results of the Warning Committee's weekly meetings. The report focuses on near-term potential threats for a period of up to about two months in the future and is distributed to those who receive the *PDB* as well as a few other senior officials.[74]

The National Foreign Intelligence Council (NFIC), now the Intelligence Community Executive Committee (IC/EXCOM), was created under the Reagan administration. The council evolved out of the NFIB and dealt with priorities and budgets. As with the NFIB, the DCI is designated as Chairman and the Deputy DCI as Vice Chairman representing the CIA. Other members include the Vice Chairman, JCS; Director, NSA; Director, DIA; Assistant Secretary of State, INR; Director, NRO; Director, CIO; Chairman, NIC; Assistant Secretary of Defense for Command, Control, Communications, and Intelligence (C^3I); and Executive Director for Intelligence Community Affairs.[75]

The functions of the IC/EXCOM involve intelligence policy and planning; National Foreign Intelligence Program budget development, evaluation, justification, and monitoring; and intelligence requirements management and evaluation.[76]

The CMS, NIC, NFIB, and IC/EXCOM are all entities designed to facilitate the DCI's functions. The Secretary of Defense also exerts control over intelligence matters through several channels: These consist of two executive committees, his Undersecretaries and Assistant Secretaries, and the JCS.

The executive committees responsible to the Secretary are both concerned with reconnaissance matters. The National Reconnaissance Executive Committee (NREC) makes basic decisions concerning the operation of the NRO, including overall budgeting and allocation of funds to different projects. It is chaired by the DCI, and its members include the Assistant to the President for National Security Affairs and a DOD representative. A second executive committee, probably called the National Executive Committee for Special Navy Activities, supervises sensitive underseas intelligence programs. Like the NREC, it is chaired by the DCI and reports to the Secretary of Defense.[77]

Decisions made by the NREC go to the Secretary of Defense for approval. If the DCI disagrees with the decision of the Secretary of Defense, he may appeal to the President. In 1975, the committee, with the concurrence of DCI William Colby, approved development and deployment of a SIGINT satellite codenamed ARGUS. ARGUS was intended as a follow-on to the RHYOLITE signals intelligence satellite. Secretary of Defense James Schlesinger ruled the system unnecessary, apparently preferring to maintain a peak level of photo reconnaissance coverage. Colby appealed to President Ford, who ordered the National Security Council to examine the issue. On the basis of that review, Ford sided with Colby. However, funding for the satellite was deleted by the congressional supervisory committee.[78]

Subordinate to the Deputy Undersecretary of Defense for Security Policy is the Special Advisory Staff.[79] The Director of the advisory staff is:

responsible for serving as the principal assistant to the DUSD [Deputy Undersecretary of Defense] (Policy) for all matters relating to the conduct of sensitive intelligence, intelligence-related and reconnaissance activities. In this regard, the Director, Special Advisory Staff, will formulate policy positions that will strongly influence the deployment of U.S. reconnaissance assets, the movement of personnel in

support of special operations, and the allocations of DOD fiscal and physical resources to operations within and outside DOD.[80]

On November 6, 1993, Secretary of Defense William Perry established a new
office under the "authority, direction, and control" of the Deputy Undersecretary
of Defense (DUSD) (Advanced Technology). The Defense Airborne Reconnaissance Office (DARO) was established to manage the development and acquisition
of aerial reconnaissance platforms (manned and unmanned) as well as their "sensors, data links, data relays, and ground stations." DARO also is responsible for
"modifications to Service and Agency unique ground stations to achieve and
maintain interoperability with Defense-wide airborne reconnaissance collectors."
DARO, however, has no operational control over reconnaissance platforms.[81]

Subordinate to the Director of DARO (D/DARO) are five Project Managers for:
Architecture and Integration, Reconnaissance Infrastructure, Advanced Development, Manned Reconnaissance, and Unmanned Aerial Vehicles. Specific platforms that are the responsibility of DARO include the U-2, the RC-135, the EP-3,
and Tier II, Tier II+, and Tier III- unmanned aerial vehicles. Among the documents produced by DARO in performance of its mission are the *Airborne Reconnaissance Technical Architecture Plan,* which describes how U.S. aerial reconnaissance assets will interface with each other and with international standards,
ground stations, and other relevant equipment, and the *National Reconnaissance
Program Integration Plan.*[82]

Supervising DARO is the Defense Airborne Reconnaissance Steering Commit-
tee (DARSC), chaired by the DUSD (Advanced Technology), with the Vice Chair-
man of the JCS also serving as Vice Chairman of the DARSC. Also serving on the
DARSC are the DCI and representatives from several components of the Office of
the Secretary of Defense, ARPA, the military services, the Defense Information
Systems Agency, and several intelligence organizations (CIA, NSA, DIA, DSPO,
CIO, and the Joint Staff J-2). Advising the Director of DARO is the User Advisory
Committee.[83]

The Assistant Secretary of Defense responsible for all other aspects of Defense
Department intelligence is the ASD (C³I). Subordinate to the ASD (C³I) is a Deputy Assistant Secretary of Defense (Intelligence) and the Intelligence Program
Support Group, which is responsible for program evaluation, product evaluation,
customer support, and architecture development.[84]

Also subordinate to the ASD (C³I) is the Defense Support Project Office
(DSPO), which was established in response to a November 1981 memorandum
from Deputy Defense Secretary Frank Carlucci. The DSPO provides central management for the Defense Reconnaissance Support Program (DRSP)—a program
directed at providing space reconnaissance data in support of operational military forces. Subordinate to the Director and Deputy Director of the DSPO is the
DSPO Staff Director, who supervises a small staff of Army, Navy, and Air Force
personnel divided into divisions for Resource Management, Systems, and Inte-

gration. The DSPO also funds studies concerning systems to provide tactical intelligence as well as the systems themselves. Thus, the DSPO provided funding for the LANDSAT 7 earth-resources satellite program in its budget for fiscal year 1994.* The Director of the NRO is also Director of the DSPO.[85]

Another mechanism for the coordination of military intelligence is the Military Intelligence Board (MIB), chaired by the Director of the DIA. The MIB is composed of the Director and Deputy Director of the DIA, the Directors of NSA and the CIO, and service intelligence chiefs. In addition, the Deputy Assistant Secretary of Defense (Intelligence), the Associate Deputy Director for Operations (Military Affairs), the CIA, and the intelligence director for the JCS participate in the MIB. There are three groups associated with the MIB (although they are not subordinate to it). They are the Council of Defense Intelligence Producers, the Military Target Intelligence Committee, and the Council on Functional Management.[86]

PROGRAMS, PLANS, AND REQUIREMENTS DOCUMENTS

In any given year there must be a specific allocation of resources (collection systems) to targets in order to produce the intelligence required by decisionmakers and other government officials. Two programs govern the allocation of resources: the National Foreign Intelligence Program (NFIP) and the Tactical Intelligence and Related Activities (TIARA) program.

The NFIP encompasses all national foreign intelligence activity. The nonmilitary components of the NFIP are the Central Intelligence Agency Program, the State Department Intelligence Program, the Community Management Staff, and the Intelligence Elements of the FBI, Department of Energy, and Department of the Treasury. There are five DOD components: the Consolidated Cryptographic Program (CCP), the General Defense Intelligence Program (GDIP), Navy Special Reconnaissance Activities, the National Reconnaissance Program (NRP), and the Defense Foreign Counterintelligence Program.[87]

The CCP is managed by NSA and includes all SIGINT resources in the NFIP. The GDIP includes all non-SIGINT, nonreconnaissance programs. Specifically, the GDIP includes eight activities:

1. general military production;
2. imagery collection and processing;
3. HUMINT;

---

*In keeping with the tradition of excessive secrecy on reconnaissance matters, DSPO funding for the unclassified LANDSAT system was funded under the "Major Equipment, DSPO" budget line. (U.S. Congress, House Committee on Appropriations, *Department of Defense Appropriations Bill, 1994* [Washington, D.C.: U.S. Government Printing Office, 1993], p. 179.)

4. nuclear monitoring;
5. R&D and procurement;
6. field support;
7. general support; and
8. scientific and technical intelligence production.

The CCP and the GDIP, when combined, form the Consolidated Defense Intelligence Program.

The Navy Special Reconnaissance Activities Program allocates attack submarines (SSNs) and other craft for sensitive reconnaissance missions. As noted in Chapter 8, these missions took U.S. submarines into Soviet territorial waters. The National Reconnaissance Program specifies the spending, procurement, and operational activities of the NRO.

The TIARA program is composed of three elements: Tactical Intelligence, Reconnaissance, Surveillance, and Target Acquisition; the DRSP; and the Tactical Cryptologic Program.[88] The number of individual programs that constitute a military service's portion of TIARA may be quite large. In 1983 the Navy's portion of TIARA consisted of the following thirty-three programs: AN/SKR-7, Battle Group Passive Horizon System, BEARTRAP, Classic Wizard, Combat Direction Finding, Combat Underwater Exploitation System, Crpytologic Direct Support, Cryptologic Training, Defense Meteorological Satellite Program (DMSP), Fleet Intelligence Support Center (Western Pacific), Guardian Bear, Integrated Tactical Surveillance System (ITSS), Intelligence Engineering, Intelligence Staff Support, Joint Tactical Fusion Program, Naval Intelligence Processing System, Naval Space Surveillance System, Ocean Surveillance Information System, Outboard, Over the Horizon Targeting, Photo Reconnaissance Squadrons–Tactical Air Reconnaissance Pod System, Prairie Wagon Augmentation, Rapidly Deployable Surveillance System (RDSS), Reserve Intelligence Program, Tactical Air Reconnaissance System (RF/A-18), Shore-Based Electronic Warfare Squadrons (VQ), Fixed Underseas Surveillance System (SOSUS), Surface Towed Array Sensor System (SURTASS), Tactical Intelligence Support, Tactical Cryptologic Shore Support, Tactical Cryptologic Technical Development, Training, and Tactical Exploitation of National Capabilities (TENCAP).[89]

There is also a National Consolidated Imagery Program and a Tactical Imagery Program, which presumably mirror the CCP and the TCP. In addition, there is a National Tasking Plan for the National IMINT Program and a Defense Wide Intelligence Plan.[90]

Based on such plans devised at the national level, plans are established at lower levels to specify the allocation of resources to target activities and objectives. Thus, the Air Force established the Air Force Intelligence Plan with three subsidiary plans: the Signals Intelligence Baseline Plan, the Imagery Architecture Plan, and the Air Force Intelligence Communication Plan. In addition, there is an Army HUMINT Plan and a Navy HUMINT Plan.[91]

Prior to the allocation of resources to collection tasks, there needs to be (at least in theory) appropriate guidance telling intelligence officials which items or subjects are of greatest priority to their customers. Guidance documents are of varying levels of specificity, and several guidance documents might emerge from the same source. One document used to guide SIGINT collection is the "Intelligence Guidance for COMINT Production."[92]

During the Ford administration, the DCI had a *Directive* (a matrix of 120 countries against 83 topics, with numerical priorities assigned from one to seven for each country); *Perspectives*, defining the major problems that policymakers would face over the next five years; *Objectives*, detailing resources management, and Key Intelligence Questions (KIQs) identifying topics of particular interest to national policymakers.[93]

The KIQs were introduced by William Colby during his tenure as DCI. They were designed to help all intelligence agencies to respond to policymakers' needs rather than just their own operational requirements. They also were designed "to replace an enormous paper exercise called the requirements process with a simple set of general questions about the key problems we should concentrate on."[94]

As the process was described by Colby, "once each KIQ was formulated, the various agencies discussed what each would do to answer the question. This was followed by a statement of the resources that each agency would apply, so that an initial judgement would be made as to whether too many or too few were involved in the resolution of each KIQ."[95]

In fiscal year 1975 there were sixty-nine KIQs covering military, political, and economic topics. KIQ 57 asked: "What are the principal objectives of the major economic powers (especially France, West Germany, Japan, the U.K., Italy, Canada and Brazil) in forthcoming multi-lateral trade (GATT) and financial negotiations (IMF)?" KIQ 59 asked: "What are the policies, negotiating positions and vulnerabilities of the major petroleum exporters with respect to the production and marketing of oil, and how are their policies affected by the prospects for development of non-OPEC energy sources?"[96]

The KIQs apparently never had the desired effect of directing the intelligence collection units toward addressing the concerns of national leaders. Thus, the Church committee concluded that the "DIA and DDO [Deputy Director for Operations, CIA] invoked the KIQs to justify their operations and budgets, however they did not appear to be shaping the programs to meet KIQ objectives."[97]

The KIQs were replaced by the National Intelligence Topics (NITs). The NITs were first issued by the NSC Policy Review Committee and were intended to "articulate National level policymakers' intelligence requirements which are reflective of current national policy." The NITs were intended to "provide all elements of the intelligence community with guidance for the conduct of collection, analysis, and production management activities."[98] They have apparently been replaced by the National Intelligence Needs Process.

NOTES

1. Ronald Reagan, "Executive Order 12333: United States Intelligence Activities," December 4, 1981, in *Federal Register* 46, 235 (December 8, 1981): 59941–54.

2. Gerald Ford, "Executive Order 11905: United States Intelligence Activities," February 18, 1976, in *Weekly Compilation of Presidential Documents* 12, 8 (1976): 234–43.

3. Jimmy Carter, "Executive Order 12036: United States Intelligence Activities," *Federal Register* 43, 18 (January 24, 1978): 3675–98.

4. Ronald Reagan, "Executive Order 12356: National Security Information," April 2, 1982, in *Federal Register* 47, 66 (April 6, 1982): 14874–84.

5. Lawrence J. Korb, "National Security Organization and Process in the Carter Administration," in Sam C. Sarkesian, ed., *Defense Policy and the Presidency: Carter's First Years* (Boulder, Colo.: Westview, 1979), pp. 111–37; Presidential Directives 37 and 55 were obtained from the National Archives and under the Freedom of Information Act, respectively.

6. On NSDD-17 see Raymond Bonner, "President Approved Policy of Preventing 'Cuba-Model' States," *New York Times*, April 7, 1983, pp. 1, 16. On NSDD-42 see U.S. Congress, House Committee on Science and Technology, *National Space Policy* (Washington, D.C.: U.S. Government Printing Office, 1982), p. 13; NSDDs 17, 19, 22, 42, 84, 196, and 204 were obtained, in whole or in part, under the Freedom of Information Act. NSDD-159 was released during the Iran-Contra hearings.

7. National Security Council, Fact Sheet, "U.S. Counterintelligence Effectiveness," May 1994; Elaine Sciolino, "Pakistan Keeping Afghan Aid Role," *New York Times*, February 26, 1989, p. 15; "Saudi Help for the CIA," *Newsweek*, September 10, 1990, p. 6; Bill Gertz, "Despite Thaw in Cold War, Bush Heats Up Counterspy Operations," *Washington Times*, October 24, 1990, pp. A1, A6; Edward D. Sheafer, Jr., *Strategic Planning for the Office of Naval Intelligence: Vision and Direction for the Future* (Washington, D.C.: Office of Naval Intelligence, 1992), p. 10.

8. NSCID No. 1, "Basic Duties and Responsibilities," February 17, 1972, *Declassified Documents Reference Service (DDRS)* 1976-167G.

9. Ibid.

10. NSCID No. 2, "Coordination of Overt Collection Activities," February 17, 1972, *DDRS* 1976-253D.

11. NSCID No. 3, "Coordination of Intelligence Production," February 17, 1972, *DDRS* 1976-253E.

12. Ibid.

13. U.S. Congress, House Permanent Select Committee on Intelligence, *Annual Report* (Washington, D.C.: U.S. Government Printing Office, 1978), p. 70.

14. NSCID No. 5, "U.S. Espionage and Counterintelligence Activities Abroad," February 17, 1972, *DDRS* 1976-253F.

15. Department of Justice, *Report on Inquiry into CIA-Related Electronic Surveillance Activities* (Washington, D.C.: Department of Justice, 1976), pp. 77–78.

16. National Security Agency/Central Security Service, *NSA/CSS Manual 22-1* (Ft. Meade, Md.: NSA, 1986, p. 1; Department of Defense Directive S-5100.9, "Implementation of National Security Council Directive No. 7," March 19, 1960; James Bamford, *The Puzzle Palace: A Report on NSA, America's Most Secret Agency* (Boston: Houghton Mifflin, 1982), p. 104; Seymour M. Hersh, *"The Target Is Destroyed": What Really Happened to Flight 007 and What America Really Knew About It* (New York: Random House, 1986), p. 53.

17. NSCID No. 8, "Photographic Interpretation," February 17, 1972, *DDRS* 1976-253G.

18. Department of Justice, *Report on Inquiry into CIA-Related Electronic Surveillance Activities*, p. 100.

19. DCID 1/3, "Committees of the Director of Central Intelligence," May 18, 1976; DCID 1/4, "Intelligence Information Handling Committee," May 18, 1976; U.S. Congress, House Permanent Select Committee on Intelligence, *Annual Report*, p. 70; Enclosure 1 of DOD Instruction 5230.22, "Control of Dissemination of Intelligence Information," April 1, 1982; DCID 1/8, "The National Foreign Intelligence Board," May 6, 1976; HQ USAF, ACS, I, INOI 11-3, "Intelligence Community Boards, Councils and Committees," December 30, 1983.

20. Reference (d) to Department of Defense Directive 3310.1, "International Intelligence Agreements," October 22, 1982; DCID 1/11, "Security Committee," July 15, 1982; DCID 1/17, "Human Resources Committee," May 18, 1976; DCID 1/13, Coordination of the Collection and Exploitation of Imagery Intelligence," February 2, 1973, *DDRS* 1980-132D; DCID 1/15, "Data Standardization for the Intelligence Community," May 18, 1976.

21. U.S. Congress, House Permanent Select Committee on Intelligence, *Security Clearance Procedures in the Intelligence Agencies* (Washington, D.C.: U.S. Government Printing Office, 1979), pp. 25–29; U.S. Congress, House Permanent Select Committee on Intelligence, *Espionage Laws and Leaks* (Washington, D.C.: U.S. Government Printing Office, 1979), p. 276; Working Group on Computer Security, *Computer and Telecommunications Policy* (Washington, D.C.: National Communications Security Committee, July 1981), p. 158; DCID 1/14, "Minimum Personnel Security Standards and Procedures Governing Eligibility for Access to Sensitive Compartmented Information," April 14, 1986; Department of Energy Order 5636.2, "Security Requirements for Classified Automatic Data Processing Systems," January 10, 1980; USSPACECOM Regulation 200-1, "The Security, Use and Dissemination of Sensitive Compartmented Information (SCI)," April 15, 1992, p. 2; AFSPACECOM Regulation 200-2, "The Security, Use and Dissemination of Sensitive Compartmented Information (SCI)," August 31, 1990; Naval Intelligence Activity, *Calendar Year 1991 History, Naval Intelligence Activity (NIA), 1 January–30 September 1991*, 1992, p. 4; "Changes Ahead for Security," *INSCOM Journal*, September 1993, pp. 38–39.

22. DCID 2/1, "Coordination of Overt Collection Abroad," March 8, 1960, *DDRS* 1980-131B; DCID 2/9, "Management of National Imagery Intelligence," June 1, 1992.

23. John Prados, *The Soviet Estimate: U.S. Intelligence Analysis and Russian Military Strength* (New York: Dial, 1982), pp. 306–7.

24. DCID 3/1, "Production and Coordination of Foreign Economic Intelligence," May 18, 1976; U.S. Congress, House Permanent Select Committee on Intelligence, *Annual Report*, pp. 35, 49; DCID 3/3, "Production of Atomic Energy Intelligence," April 23, 1965, *DDRS* 1980-131G; DCID 3/4, "Production of Guided Missile and Astronautics Intelligence," April 23, 1965, *DDRS* 1980-132A; DCID 3/3, "Community Management Staff," June 1, 1992; USAF, Air Force Assistant Chief of Staff, Intelligence, "Intelligence Community Boards, Councils, and Groups," January 9, 1989; Department of the Army, Office of the Deputy Chief of Staff for Intelligence, *Annual Historical Review, 1 October 1989–30 September 1990*, n.d., p. 11-11.

25. U.S. Congress, House Permanent Select Committee on Intelligence, *Annual Report*, pp. 42, 70–71; DCID 6/1, "SIGINT Committee," May 12, 1982.

26. HQ USAF, ACS, I, INOI 11-3, "Intelligence Community Boards, Councils and Committees."

27. U.S. Congress, House Permanent Select Committee on Intelligence, *Security Clearance Procedures*, p. 29.

28. Department of Defense Directive 3310.1, "International Intelligence Agreements," October 22, 1982.

29. Department of Defense Directive C-5230.23, "Intelligence Disclosure Policy," November 18, 1983.

30. Department of Defense 5025.1-I, *DOD Directives System Annual Index* (Washington, D.C.: DOD/NTIS, January 1993), pp. 2-34, 2-56, 2-71 to 2-72.

31. Ibid., pp. 2-52 to 2-59; Department of Defense Directive TS-5105.23, "National Reconnaissance Office," March 27, 1964.

32. Air Force Regulation 0-2, "Numerical Index of Standard and Recurring Air Force Publications," July 1, 1992, p. 75.

33. INSCOM Pamphlet 25-30, "Index of Administrative Publications and Command Forms," June 25, 1991; AFTAC Center Regulation 0-2, "Numerical Index of Center Publications," November 1986; DIA Regulation 0-2, "Index of DIA Administrative Publications," December 10, 1982.

34. Korb, "National Security Organization and Process in the Carter Administration."

35. Emmanuel Adler, "Executive Command and Control in Foreign Policy: The CIA's Covert Activities," *Orbis* 23 (1979): 671–96; U.S. Congress, Senate Select Committee to Study Governmental Operations with Respect to Intelligence Activities, *Final Report, Book 1, Foreign and Military Intelligence* (Washington, D.C.: U.S. Government Printing Office, 1976), p. 53.

36. National Security Decision Memorandum 40, "Responsibility for the Conduct, Supervision and Coordination of Covert Action Operations," *DDRS* 1976-297A.

37. U.S. Congress, Senate Select Committee to Study Governmental Operations with Respect to Intelligence Activities, *Final Report, Book 1, Foreign and Military Intelligence*, p. 61.

38. Ford, "Executive Order 11905: United States Intelligence Activities."

39. Carter, "Executive Order 12036: United States Intelligence Activities."

40. NSDD-2, "National Security Council Structure," January 12, 1982; National Defense University, *Publication 5—Intelligence for Joint Forces* (Norfolk, Va.: Armed Forces Staff College, August 1985), pp. 2-1 to 2-2.

41. Unclassified Summary of NSD 1, "National Security Council Organization," January 30, 1989; William J. Clinton, Presidential Directive 2, "Organization of the National Security Council," January 20, 1993.

42. Reagan, "Executive Order 12333: United States Intelligence Activities," pp. 59943–44.

43. Victor Marchetti and John Marks, *The CIA and the Cult of Intelligence* (New York: Knopf, 1974), pp. 98–99; Caspar Weinberger, *FY 1983 Report of Secretary of Defense Caspar Weinberger* (Washington, D.C.: U.S. Government Printing Office, 1982), p. III-88.

44. DCID 3/3, "Community Management Staff," June 1, 1992.

45. DCID 3/3, "Community Management Staff"; Central Intelligence Agency, *A Consumer's Guide to Intelligence* (Washington, D.C.: CIA, 1993), p. 29; Central Intelligence Agency, "What's News at CIA," July 16, 1992; U.S. Congress, PL-102-496, *Intelligence Au-*

thorization Act for Fiscal Year 1993 (Washington, D.C.: U.S. Government Printing Office, 1992), p. 106, STAT. 3182.

46. Central Intelligence Agency, *A Consumer's Guide to Intelligence*, p. 29.

47. DCID 3/3, "Community Management Staff."

48. Central Intelligence Agency, *A Consumer's Guide to Intelligence*, p. 29; House Permanent Select Committee on Intelligence, *Intelligence Authorization Act for Fiscal Year 1995* (Washington, D.C.: U.S. Government Printing Office, 1994), p. 42.

49. Vice Admiral E. A. Burkhalter, Jr., "The Role of the Intelligence Community Staff," *Signal*, September 1984, pp. 33–35; U.S. Congress, House Committee on Foreign Affairs, *The Role of Intelligence in the Foreign Policy Process* (Washington, D.C.: U.S. Government Printing Office, 1980), pp. 73, 135.

50. National Intelligence Council, *A Guide to the National Intelligence Council,* 1994, p. 41.

51. National Security Council, Fact Sheet, "U.S. Counterintelligence Effectiveness," p. 2.

52. Ibid.

53. DCID 1/8, "National Foreign Intelligence Board," May 6, 1976.

54. DIA Regulation 50-17, "Release of Classified DOD Intelligence to Non-NFIB U.S. Government Agencies," July 26, 1978; Central Intelligence Agency, *A Consumer's Guide to Intelligence*, p. 41.

55. Marchetti and Marks, *The CIA and the Cult of Intelligence*, pp. 81, 84.

56. Letter, Lee S. Strickland, CIA Information and Privacy Coordinator, to the author, June 5, 1987; Naval Intelligence Command, *Naval Intelligence Command Historical Review, 1976,* 1977, p. 3; Office of Naval Intelligence, *Office of Naval Intelligence (OP-92) Command History 1990,* n.d., p. 2, Assistant for Counternarcotics Section; Department of the Army, Office of the Deputy Chief of Staff for Intelligence, *Annual Historical Review, 1 October 1987–30 September 1988,* n.d., p. 2-37; Eagle Research Group, *ERG Support to OTA* (Arlington, Va.: ERG, December 14, 1990), p. 11; Central Intelligence Agency, *A Consumer's Guide to Intelligence*, p. 29.

57. Central Intelligence Agency, *A Consumer's Guide to Intelligence*, p. 2; Telephone conversation between a representative of the CIA Office of Public and Agency Information and the author, December 10, 1993.

58. National Academy of Sciences, *Scientific Communication and National Security* (Washington, D.C.: National Academy Press, 1983), pp. 72, 141–42.

59. DCID 3/13, "Technology Transfer Intelligence Committee," December 3, 1981.

60. Edward T. Pound, "U.S. Sees New Signs Israel Resells Its Arms to China, South Africa," *Wall Street Journal,* March 13, 1992, pp. A1, A6.

61. Konrad Ege, "CIA Targets African Economies," *Counter Spy* (July–August 1982): 30–38.

62. DCID 3/3, "Production of Atomic Energy Intelligence."

63. U.S. Congress, House Committee on Energy and Commerce, *Nuclear Nonproliferation: Failed Efforts to Curtail Iraq's Nuclear Weapons Program* (Washington, D.C.: U.S. Government Printing Office, 1992), p. 20; William J. Broad, "Warning on Iraq and Bomb Bid Silenced in '89," *New York Times,* April 20, 1992, pp. A1, A5; NIE 11-3/8-76, *Soviet Forces for International Conflict Through the Mid-1980s, Volume 1, Key Judgements and Summary,* 1976, p. iii; Air Force Intelligence Agency, *History of the Air Force Intelligence Agency, 18 April 1987–31 December 1989, Volume 1, Narrative and Appendices,* 1990.

64. Department of Justice, *Report on Inquiry into CIA-Related Electronic Surveillance Activities*, pp. 72–73; Office of Naval Intelligence, *Office of Naval Intelligence (ONI) Annual History 1985*, 1986, pp. 5, 9.

65. DCID 3/8, "Critical Intelligence Problems Committee," April 6, 1983.

66. Office of Naval Intelligence, *Office of Naval Intelligence (ONI) Annual History 1985*, p. 9; Edward C. Mishler, *History of the Air Force Office of Special Investigations, 1 July 1975–31 December 1976, Volume 1, Narrative* (Washington, D.C.: AFOSI, 1978), p. 23.

67. Central Intelligence Agency, *A Consumer's Guide to Intelligence*, p. 40; Bob Woodward and John Mintz, "Despite Vast U.S. Hunt, Perot Says POWs Held," *Washington Post*, June 21, 1992, p. A18.

68. Diane T. Putney, *History of the Air Force Intelligence Service, 1 January–31 December 1984* (Ft. Belvoir, Va.: AFIS, n.d.), pp. 335–36; Department of the Air Force, *Headquarters Publication 21-1: Department of the Air Force Organization and Functions (Chartbook)*, March 1986, p. 6-23; Diane T. Putney, *History of the Air Force Intelligence Service, 1 January–31 December 1983, Volume 1, Narrative and Appendices* (Ft. Belvoir, Va.: AFIS, n.d.), p. 340; Naval Intelligence Support Center, *Naval Intelligence Support Center Command History, 1983*, 1984, p. 24; Naval Intelligence Support Center, *Naval Intelligence Support Center Command History, 1982*, p. VII-III; Department of the Army, Office of the Deputy Chief of Staff for Intelligence, *Annual Historical Review, 1 October 1989–30 September 1990*, Glossary 11; Naval Intelligence Support Center, *Naval Intelligence Support Center Command History, 1981*, n.d., p. VIII-6.

69. NIE 11-3/8-76, *Soviet Forces for Intercontinental Conflict Through the Mid-1980s, Volume 1, Key Judgements and Summary*, p. iii.

70. DCID 3/14, "Information Handling Committee," May 4, 1982; Naval Intelligence Activity, *Calendar Year 1991 History, Naval Intelligence Activity (NIA) 1 January–30 September 1991*, 1992, p. 6; Putney, *History of the Air Force Intelligence Service, 1 January–31 December 1983, Volume 1, Narrative and Appendices*, p. 95.

71. Prados, *The Soviet Estimate*, pp. 59–61; U.S. Congress, House Committee on Appropriations, *Department of Defense Appropriations for 1978, Part 1* (Washington, D.C.: U.S. Government Printing Office, 1977), p. 224.

72. Department of the Army, Office of the Assistant Chief of Staff for Intelligence, *Annual Historical Review, 1 July 1975–30 September 1976*, n.d., pp. 39–40; NIE 11-3/8-76, *Soviet Strategic Forces for International Conflict Through the Mid-1980s, Volume 1, Key Judgements and Summary*, p. iii.

73. DCID 3/15, "Foreign Language Committee," March 5, 1982.

74. Central Intelligence Agency, *A Consumer's Guide to Intelligence*, p. 25.

75. Ibid., p. 27.

76. Defense Intelligence Agency, *DIA Transition Book* (Washington, D.C.: DIA, 1992).

77. U.S. Congress, Senate Select Committee to Study Governmental Operations with Respect to Intelligence Activities, *Final Report, Book 4, Supplementary Detailed Staff Reports* (Washington, D.C.: U.S. Government Printing Office, 1976), p. 75; U.S. Congress, Senate Select Committee to Study Governmental Operations with Respect to Intelligence Activities, *Final Report, Book 1, Foreign and Military Intelligence*, p. 335.

78. Philip Klass, "U.S. Monitoring Capability Impaired," *Aviation Week & Space Technology*, May 14, 1979, p. 18; Robert Lindsey, *The Falcon and the Snowman: A True Story of Friendship and Espionage* (New York: Simon & Schuster, 1979), p. 347.

79. *Department of Defense Telephone Directory* (Washington, D.C.: U.S. Government Printing Office, August 1994), p. 0-7.

80. Senior Executive Service Vacancy Announcement No. SES 3-83, 1983.

81. William J. Perry, Memorandum for Secretaries of the Military Departments, Subject: Establishment of the Defense Airborne Reconnaissance Office (DARO), November 6, 1993.

82. Ibid.; Neil Munro, "Taking Off: A New Airborne Reconnaissance Office Hits the Pentagon," *Armed Forces Journal International*, June 1994, pp. 46–47; "DARO to Release Airborne Recce Technology Roadmap," *Aerospace Daily*, September 19, 1994, pp. 436–37.

83. Perry, Establishment of the Defense Airborne Reconnaissance Office.

84. *Department of Defense Telephone Directory, April 1994* (Washington, D.C.: U.S. Government Printing Office, 1994), p. 0-7.

85. "DSPO Organization Chart," n.d.; Frank Carlucci, Memorandum for the Secretary of the Air Force, Subject: Defense Reconnaissance Support Program (DRSP), November 13, 1981; U.S. Congress, House Committee on Appropriations, *Department of Defense Appropriations Bill, 1994* (Washington, D.C.: U.S. Government Printing Office, 1993), p. 179.

86. U.S. Congress, House Committee on Appropriations, *Department of Defense Appropriations for 1994, Part 1* (Washington, D.C.: U.S. Government Printing Office, 1993), p. 40.

87. Weinberger, *FY 1983 Report of Secretary of Defense*, p. III-88; Department of Defense Inspector General, *Defense Intelligence Agency Inspection Report 91-INS-06*, 1991, p. 14.

88. Ibid.

89. "Navy's Portion of TIARA Consists of 23 [*sic*] Programs," *Aerospace Daily*, April 8, 1983, p. 231.

90. Department of Defense Directive 5105.56, "Central Imagery Office," May 6, 1992, p. 4; Central Imagery Office, *CIO Briefing Slides*, n.d., p. 5; Department of the Army, Office of the Assistant Chief of Staff for Intelligence, *Annual Historical Review, 1 October 1985–30 September 1986*, n.d., p. 3-25; Office of Naval Intelligence, *Office of Naval Intelligence 1989 Command History*, n.d., OP-921 Section, p. 7.

91. William E. Parson, "Improving Intelligence Communications Programming," *Signal*, January 1983, pp. 74–75; Department of the Army, Intelligence and Security Command, *Annual Historical Review, Fiscal Year 1985*, 1986, p. 51.

92. DIA, DIAM 56-3, *Defense Intelligence Organization: Operations and Management* (Washington, D.C.: DIA, 1979), p. 54.

93. Richard Betts, "American Strategic Intelligence: Politics, Priorities and Direction," in Robert L. Pfaltzgraff, Jr., Uri Ra'anan, and Warren Milberg, eds., *Intelligence Policy and National Security* (Hamden, Conn.: Archon, 1981), pp. 245–67 at p. 251.

94. Ibid.; William Colby and Peter Forbath, *Honorable Men: My Life in the CIA* (New York: Simon & Schuster, 1978), p. 361.

95. Colby and Forbath, *Honorable Men*, p. 361.

96. Philip Agee, "What Uncle Sam Wants to Know About You: The KIQ's," in Philip Agee and Louis Wolf, eds., *Dirty Work: The CIA in Western Europe* (Secaucus, N.J.: Lyle Stuart, 1978), pp. 111–26.

97. U.S. Congress, Senate Select Committee to Study Governmental Operations with Respect to Intelligence Activities, *Final Report, Book 1, Foreign and Military Intelligence*, p. 91.

98. U.S. Congress, House Committee on Foreign Affairs, *The Role of Intelligence in the Foreign Policy Process*, p. 112; Michael F. Munson, "Defense Intelligence Resource Activities 1994–1995" (Washington, D.C.: Intelligence Program Support Group, 1994); Stephen J. Flanagan, "The Coordination of National Intelligence," in Duncan Clarke, ed., *Public Policy and Political Institutions: United States Defense and Foreign Policy—Policy Coordination and Integration* (Greenwich, Conn.: JAI Press, 1987), p. 163.

17
MANAGING INTELLIGENCE COLLECTION AND COVERT ACTION

Management of the three different types of collection—imagery, SIGINT, and HUMINT—reflects the commonality and diversity of the operations and collection systems the intelligence community employs. Both imagery and SIGINT are collected by satellites as well as by aircraft—which can be involved in international incidents. At the same time, SIGINT is collected by land stations, ships, and submarines—which are not employed, to a significant extent, for the acquisition of imagery. And, of course, human collection is a quite different method of collection.

Managing covert action is yet another aspect of the management task. Inadequate management can result not only in an inefficient use of resources but in political disaster.

MANAGING SATELLITE IMAGING

Basic decisions concerning satellite imaging activities have been the responsibility of the National Foreign Intelligence Board (NFIB), two DCI committees, and the National Reconnaissance Executive Committee (NREC). The board and its committees are concerned with collection priorities and their implementation, whereas the NREC focuses on the budget, structure, and R&D program of the National Reconnaissance Office (NRO).

As noted in Chapter 16, the NREC is chaired by the Director of Central Intelligence and reports to the Secretary of Defense. If the DCI objects to a decision made by the Secretary, he may appeal directly to the President. When initially formed, the committee consisted of the President's Science Adviser and an Assistant Secretary of Defense in addition to the DCI. Subsequently, the Assistant to the President for National Security Affairs replaced the Science Adviser.[1] The position of the DOD representative has changed as the upper echelons of the department have been reorganized. Presently, the DOD representative is probably the Deputy Assistant Secretary of Defense (Intelligence).

The concept of the NREC emerged from the conflicting views of the reconnaissance program held by NRO and CIA officials in the early 1960s. Undersecretary of the Air Force and NRO Director Brockway MacMillan believed that the Air Force should run the reconnaissance program without CIA "interference." The CIA's chief reconnaissance officials, Pete Scoville, Jr., and Albert Wheelon, disagreed with this view.[2]

The NREC was created through an agreement that was reached in 1965. The committee would be chaired by the DCI but would report to the Secretary of Defense, who had final authority subject only to the DCI's appeal to the President. The agreement also specified the committee's role in overseeing the operations of the NRO.[3]

The budgeting and oversight responsibilities give the NREC, in conjunction with the Secretary of Defense, considerable say over the types of equipment the NRO will use. The choice of one satellite system over another obviously has significant implications with regard to the types of targets chosen and the amount of detail possible for the information that is acquired. Clearly, the choice of a SIGINT system over a photo reconnaissance system, or of a high-resolution system over a low-resolution area surveillance system, automatically constrains coverage in one direction and enhances it in another.

Overall responsibility for approval of imaging and SIGINT satellite collection requirements has been assigned to the National Foreign Intelligence Board and two DCI committees. Thus, in 1970 the Air Force requested permission from the board—then the United States Intelligence Board—to alter the targeting of a "very sophisticated satellite." The alteration apparently involved maneuvering the satellite, and the board, citing the great cost of the satellite and the possibility that maneuvering might lead to malfunction, denied the request. Ten years later, a KH-11 that was maneuvered to increase coverage of the Iran-Iraq War malfunctioned.[4]

Until recently, the actual job of translating general imagery collection priorities into the targeting of systems against installations has been the responsibility of the Committee on Imagery Requirements and Exploitation (COMIREX). COMIREX was established on July 1, 1967, by Director of Central Intelligence Directive 1/13 as the successor to the Committee on Overhead Reconnaissance (COMOR). COMOR's responsibilities included coordination of collection requirements for the development and operation of all imaging satellites. As these programs grew, the number of photographs substantially increased, resulting in serious duplication of imagery exploitation activities. One solution to this problem involved replacing COMOR with COMIREX. COMIREX's membership consisted of representatives from all NFIB agencies plus the Assistant Chief of Staff for Intelligence for the Army; the Director of Naval Intelligence; and the Assistant Chief of Staff for Intelligence of the Air Force. The committee has been staffed by personnel from the CIA and the DIA.[5]

The functions of COMIREX have been summarized by former COMIREX Chairman Roland S. Inlow:

> COMIREX performs the interagency coordination and management functions needed to direct photographic satellite reconnaissance, including the process of deciding what targets should be photographed and what agencies should get which photos to analyze. It also evaluates the needs for, and the results from, photographic reconnaissance, and oversees security controls that are designed to protect photography and information derived from photography from unauthorized disclosure.[6]

COMIREX dealt with three basic questions with regard to the establishment of targets and priorities:

1. What installations/areas were to be imaged?
2. What systems were to be targeted on specific installations/areas?
3. What was to be the frequency of coverage?

When the United States operated a single type of satellite imaging system (the KH-11), COMIREX's decision problem with regard to the second question was simple, but as Advanced KH-11s and LACROSSE satellites joined the U.S. imagery constellation, the decision became more complicated. In any case, there are always significant areas of contention among consumers over priorities and targeting.

Conflicts over satellite imagery targeting and priorities occur primarily between those consumers with national intelligence responsibilities (e.g., the CIA) and the military services, which are more concerned with tactical intelligence. The military, with its mission of being able to fight a war, wants as much warning as possible as well as up-to-date and detailed coverage concerning the capabilities of potential enemies. Day-to-day coverage is thus seen as valuable on the tactical level—in revealing movements of troops or weapons and small changes in capabilities; at the national level, in the absence of a crisis, such information is of little interest. The COMIREX served to prioritize the claims of the CIA, the DIA military services, and other consumers with the objective of distributing a strictly limited resource in such a way as to at least minimally satisfy the legitimate requests of several competitive bureaucracies.

In the area of imagery exploitation, COMIREX allocated interpretation tasks among the National Photographic Interpretation Center, the CIA's Office of Imagery Analysis, and the imagery exploitation components of the DIA and the DIA Missile and Space Intelligence Center, ITAC, ONI, FSTC, and AFIC's FASTC. The basic division of labor was spelled out in COMIREX's National Tasking Plan for Imagery Processing and Exploitation.[7]

In carrying out these responsibilities COMIREX functioned through a network of subcommittees and working groups. The 1982 structure of COMIREX is shown in Table 17-1. Following the creation of the Central Imagery Office, the COMIREX was colocated with the CIO. According to Director of Central Intelli-

Table 17-1.   COMIREX Structure, 1982.

Imagery Planning Subcommittee (IPS)
    Exploitation Programs Working Group (EPWG)
    Advanced Systems Working Group (ASWG)
    Radiometrics Capabilities Working Group
    National Tasking Plan Review Group
    CAMS II Task Force
    Exploitation Softcopy Systems Working Group (ESSWG)

Operations Subcommittee (OPSCOM)
    Current Requirements Working Group (CRWG)
    Standing Requirements Working Group (SRWG)
    Data Base Administration Working Group (DBAWG)

Exploitation Research and Development Subcommittee (EXRAND)
    Procurement and Coordination Team (PCT)
    Technical Task Team (TTT)

Mapping, Charting and Geodesy Working Group (MC&CWG)
TK Modification Working Group (TKMWG)
Sanitization and Decontrol Working Group

Source: Naval Intelligence Support Center, *Command History 1982*, March 4, 1983, p. IX-1.

gence Directive 2/9 of June 1, 1992, "Management of National Imagery Intelligence," the CIO was to "perform those Intelligence Community responsibilities previously vested in COMIREX." Tasking was to be done by a Central Imagery Tasking Authority "in accordance with intelligence requirements established by the DCI in peacetime and the Secretary of Defense in wartime." The CIO was also to produce the *National Tasking Policy for Imagery Exploitation* to allocate interpretation tasks among different agencies.[8]

MANAGING SIGINT

Management of the United States SIGINT System (USSS) is vested in the Director of the NSA by National Security Council Intelligence Directive No. 6. The most recently available version of NSCID No. 6, that of February 17, 1972, was still operative as of 1987.[9] In addition to defining the components of SIGINT—COMINT and ELINT—the directive states:

> The Secretary of Defense is designated as Executive Agent of the Government for the conduct of SIGINT activities in accordance with the provisions of this directive and for the direction, supervision, funding, maintenance and operation of the National Security Agency. The Director of the National Security Agency shall report to the Secretary of Defense, the Director of Central Intelligence, and the Joint Chiefs of Staff. The Secretary of Defense may delegate in whole or part authority over the Director of the National Security Agency within the Office of the Secretary of Defense.
> ...

It shall be the duty of the Director of the National Security Agency to provide for the SIGINT mission of the United States, to establish an effective unified organization and control of all SIGINT collection and processing activities of the United States, and to produce SIGINT in accordance with the objectives, requirements and priorities established by the Director of Central Intelligence Board. No other organization shall engage in SIGINT activities except as provided for in this directive.

Except as provided in paragraphs 5 and 6 of this directive (re unique responsibilities of CIA and FBI) the Director of the National Security Agency shall exercise full control over all SIGINT collection and processing activities. ... The Director of the National Security Agency is authorized to issue direct to any operating elements engaged in SIGINT operations such instructions and assignments as are required. All instructions issued by the Director under the authority provided in this paragraph shall be mandatory, subject only to appeal to the Secretary of Defense. ...

The Armed Forces and other departments and agencies often require timely and effective SIGINT. The Director of the National Security Agency shall provide such SIGINT. ...

The intelligence components of the individual departments and agencies may continue to conduct direct liaison with the National Security Agency in the interpretation and amplification of requirements and priorities within the framework of objectives, requirements and priorities established by the Director of Central Intelligence. (Emphasis in original.)[10]

One means of managing the SIGINT system is via the U.S. Signals Intelligence Directives (USSIDs) issued by the Director of NSA. USSIDs include USSID 3, "SIGINT Security" (August 1972); USSID 4, "SIGINT Support to Military Commanders" (July 1, 1974); USSID 18, "Limitations and Procedures in Signals Intelligence Operations of the U.S.S.S." (May 18, 1976); USSID 40, "ELINT Operating Policy" (October 1970); USSID 52, "SIGINT Support to Electronic Warfare Operations"; USSID 56, "Exercise SIGINT"; USSID 58, "SIGINT Support to MIJI"; USSID 101, "COMINT Collection Instructions" (December 1, 1989); USSID 110, "Collection Management Procedures" (December 18, 1987); USSID 150, "SIGINT Numerical Tasking Register" (February 1, 1985); USSID 240, "ELINT Processing, Analysis and Reporting"; USSID 300, "SIGINT Reporting"; USSID 301, "Handling of Critical (CRITIC) Information" (November 25, 1987); USSID 302, "SIGINT Alert Systems"; USSID 316, "Non-Codeword Reporting System" (June 19, 1987); USSID 319, "Tactical Reporting"; USSID 325, "AIRBOAT Procedures"; USSID 326, "Electronic Warfare Mutual Support Procedures"; USSID 341, "Technical ELINT Product Reporting"; USSID 369, "Time-Sensitive SIGINT Reporting"; USSID 402, "Equipment and Manning Standards for SIGINT Positions" (September 8, 1986); USSID 404TM, "Technical Extracts from Traffic Analysis (TEXTA)" (December 14, 1988); USSID 505, "Directory of SIGINT Organizations"; USSID 550, "Technical SIGINT Support Policies, Procedures, and Responsibilities"; USSID 601, "Technical Support for Cryptologic Training"; USSID 602, "Specialized Operational Training"; USSID 701, "Sanitizing and Declassifying ADP Storage Devices" (September 30, 1976); USSID 702, "Automatic Data Processing Systems Security" (September 1980); USSID 1045, "SIGINT Tasking for USM-45, Misawa" (January 16, 1980); and USSID 1600, "SIGINT Tasking for US Army Tactical SIGINT Units" (June 7, 1989). Of particular importance are USSIDs 404, 4000, and 4001. USSID 404 is the basic UKUSA requirements document—the SIGINT Combined Operating List (SCOL). USSID 4000 provides tasking for the NSA station at Menwith Hill, and USSID 4001 governs the operations of the National SIGINT Operations Center at Fort Meade.[11]

As indicated in the extract from NSCID No. 6 above, although the Secretary of Defense is the executive agent and the Director of NSA is the program manager of the USSS, requirements and priorities are to be established by the NFIB and the National SIGINT Committee. The committee is the successor to a series of predecessors. As of 1950, prior to the creation of the NSA, the work was divided between the Armed Forces Security Agency Council's Intelligence Requirements Committee (AFSAC/IRC) and the U.S. Communications Intelligence Board's Intelligence Committee (USCIB/IC). The AFSAC/IRC consisted of representatives from the Office of Naval Intelligence, Army Intelligence, Air Force Intelligence, and the AFSA and was responsible primarily for targeting and setting priorities for military traffic intercepts. The USCIB/IC was primarily concerned with nonmilitary traffic.[12]

Following the creation of the NSA, NSCID No. 9 of December 9, 1952, reconstituted the USCIB to operate under the Special Committee of the NSC for COMINT, which consisted of the Secretary of State, the Secretary of Defense, and the Attorney General and was assisted by the DCI. In 1958, when the USCIB and the Intelligence Advisory Committee were merged into the USIB, two committees were created: the COMINT Committee and the ELINT Committee (by means of DCID 6/1 and DCID 6/2, respectively, both issued on October 21, 1958). The ELINT and COMINT Committees were merged to form the SIGINT Committee by DCID 6/1 of May 31, 1962.[13]

The responsibilities of the SIGINT Committee are extensive, as indicated by DCID 6/1 of May 12, 1982, reprinted as Figure 17-1. They include developing specifications for SIGINT collection requirements, monitoring the responsiveness of U.S. and cooperating foreign SIGINT agencies, and developing policies for the conduct of SIGINT liaison and the security of SIGINT-obtained information.

Prior to the Middle East war in 1973, the USIB SIGINT Committee recommended that the Middle East be a priority target for intelligence collection if hostilities erupted. The NSA was asked to evaluate the intelligence collected and to determine appropriate targets. Upon the outbreak of war, the NSA implemented these policies under the SIGINT Committee's guidance. The committee discussed and approved the DIA's recommendation to change the primary target of one collector.[14]

The SIGINT Committee operates with two permanent subcommittees: the SIGINT Requirements Validation and Evaluation Subcommittee (SIRVES) and the SIGINT Overhead Reconnaissance Subcommittee (SORS). It also employs

Figure 17-1. DCID 6/1, The SIGINT Committee.

SECRET
NOFORN

DIRECTOR OF CENTRAL INTELLIGENCE DIRECTIVE[1]
SIGINT Committee
(Effective 12 May 1982)

Pursuant to the provisions of Section 102, the National Security Act of 1947, and Executive Order 12333, there is established a Signals Intelligence (SIGINT) Committee.

1. Mission

The mission of the SIGINT Committee is to advise and assist the Director of Central Intelligence (DCI) and the Director, National Security Agency (DIRNSA) in the discharge of their duties and responsibilities with respect to Signals Intelligence as specified in Executive Order 12333, to monitor and assist in coordinating within the Intelligence Community the accomplishment of objectives established by the DCI, and to promote the effective use of Intelligence Community SIGINT resources.

2. Functions:

Under the general guidance of the Deputy Director of Central Intelligence, the SIGINT Committee shall:

a. advise the DCI on the establishment of SIGINT requirements, priorities, and objectives;

b. develop statements, based on the DCI's objectives and priorities, of collection and exploitation requirements for COMINT, ELINT, foreign instrumentation signals, nonimagery infrared, coherent light, and nonnuclear electromagnetic pulse (EMP) sources. (These statements will provide guidance for resource programming, mission planning, and reporting. Each statement should take into account practical limitations, costs, and risk factors.)

c. monitor and evaluate the responsiveness of present and programmed United States and cooperating foreign SIGINT resources to United States needs for intelligence information;

d. monitor the impact on SIGINT programs of information needs levied by intelligence comsumers;

e. advise and make recommendations on the dissemination and sanitization of SIGINT or information derived therefrom and the release of disclosure of SIGINT or derived information to foreign governments or international organizations in which the United States Government participates;

f. develop and recommend to the DCI policies, directives, and guidance for the conduct of SIGINT arrangements with foreign governments;

g. assess and report to the DCI on the potential impact on current and future United States SIGINT capabilities of providing cryptographic assistance to foreign governments; and

---

[1]This directive supersedes DCID No. 6/1, 18 May 1976.

SECRET

Classified by: DCI
Declassify on: OADR

Figure 17-1. continued

h. review, develop, and recommend to the DCI policies for the protection, through classification and compartmentation, of COMINT, ELINT, and other SIGINT or of information about them or derived from them and procedures enabling United States Government entities outside of the Intelligence Community to receive and use SIGINT.

3. Intelligence Community Responsibilities

Upon request of the Committee Chairman, Intelligence Community elements shall provide information pertinent to the Committee's mission and functions within DCI-approved security safeguards.

4. Composition and Organization

The Committee Chairman will be appointed by the Director of Central Intelligence.

The members of the committee will be representatives designated by Intelligence Community principals.

The Chairman will establish subcommittees or task forces as required.

With the approval of the DCI, the Committee Chairman may invite representatives of relevant United States Government entities to participate as appropriate.

The Committee will be supported by an Executive Secretariat.

William J. Casey
Director of Central Intelligence

working groups and task forces on a short-term basis—such as the Third Party Ad Hoc Working Group of 1972.[15]

SIRVES validates and evaluates general SIGINT requirements. It has restructured the key SIGINT requirements covering the former USSR and Eastern Europe. SORS is "responsible for receipt, approval, and subsequent generation of intelligence guidance in response to tasks to be levied on national resources [a standard euphemism for space systems]" and "continually monitors requirements and provides collection and processing guidance for both long and short terms needs."[16]

In addition to validating requirements and tasking collection assets, the SIGINT Committee examines the relationships between U.S. SIGINT agencies and foreign SIGINT agencies. Thus, in 1972 the committee developed a new set of objectives regarding SIGINT relations with Japan.[17]

A second DCI committee that might on occasion have input on the subject of SIGINT requirements is the Critical Intelligence Problems Committee (CIPC). Thus, on January 31, 1972, the DCI requested the Critical Collection Problems Committee (CCPC), the CIPC's predecessor, to conduct a review of intelligence efforts against narcotics. The CCPC report of October 1972 noted in a section entitled "SIGINT Information on Narcotics and Dangerous Drugs" that

1. No SIGINT resources are dedicated solely to the intercept of narcotics information. The SIGINT which is now being produced on the international narcotics problem is a by-product of SIGINT reporting on other national requirements. ...
5. The effective use of SIGINT information in support of ongoing operations while at the same time protecting the source has been a problem.
6. Successful usage of the SIGINT product is largely contingent upon close collaboration between the SIGINT producers and the appropriate customer agencies.

The CCPC therefore recommended that the "NSA, in conjunction with the interested customers, particularly BNDD and Customs, make appropriate determination of what COMINT support is required on the narcotics problem and that the requisite priorities be established through the SIGINT Committee."[18]

During 1975 the USIB approved a new National SIGINT Requirements System. Under this system, the NFIB must conduct formal community review and approval procedures for each requirement before it can be validated and placed on the National SIGINT Requirements List (NSRL). The NSRL is today the basic guidance document for the NSA and specifies SIGINT targets according to well-defined priorities, including cross-references to the DCI and other national requirements documents. The system does not, however, prevent the Director of NSA from determining which specific signals to intercept in fulfillment of requirements. Nor does it prevent the Secretaries of State and Defense or military commanders from directly tasking the NSA in a crisis, informing the DCI and SIGINT Committee afterward.[19]

The yearly statements of objectives, requirements, and priorities are given in the yearly Consolidated Cryptologic Program (CCP) and Tactical Cryptologic Program (TCP), as noted in Chapter 16. The majority of U.S. signals intelligence activities are funded through the CCP. The TCP "was established in 1979 to correct the problem of disparate requirements competing for limited available funding within the NFIP which resulted in inadequate treatment of Service tactical support needs."[20]

MANAGING SENSITIVE RECONNAISSANCE MISSIONS

Reconnaissance conducted by satellite is relatively nonintrusive because it does not require actual violation of a target nation's airspace. Further, with the exception of Russia, no nation possesses means of destroying U.S. satellites. And, even during the Cold War, the likely costs to the Soviet Union of interfering in an obvious way with such satellites was likely to be far greater than the potential benefits.

When airborne overflights or air, sea, or submarine missions close to a nation's borders are involved, the potential for an international incident is much greater. The early U.S. aircraft reconnaissance missions directed at the Soviet Union involved this risk because they approached or penetrated the margins of Soviet and East European territory to collect a variety of intelligence, including the signatures and operating frequencies of air defense systems.[21]

Over the years incidents occurred involving air and sea missions, some of which have been mentioned earlier. In 1962, during the Cuban Missile Crisis, one U-2 strayed into Soviet territory and another was shot down during a flight over Cuba. In 1967 the Israeli Air Force bombed the USS *Liberty* while it was collecting signals intelligence in the midst of the Six Day War. In 1968 the USS *Pueblo* was seized by North Korea during a SIGINT mission off the North Korean coast, and in 1969 an EC-121 SIGINT aircraft was shot down by North Korean forces while it patrolled off the same coast. The North Koreans also made hundreds of attempts to shoot down overflying SR-71s. In addition, there have been several incidents involving U.S. submarines conducting HOLYSTONE-type missions, including collisions with Soviet submarines.[22]

The U.S. system for management of these missions reflects many considerations. Many of the missions are conducted in support of and proposed by the unified and specified commands. Others are clearly designed to provide national intelligence. In either case, such missions could cause an international incident and thus require national-level approval.

As noted in Chapter 16, the special Navy reconnaissance programs are the initial responsibility of the National Executive Committee for Special Navy Activities, chaired by the DCI and reporting to the Secretary of Defense. Missions originating from the Commanders-in-Chief of the unified commands go through a chain of supervisory offices and divisions beginning with the Joint Reconnaissance Center (JRC), which is subordinate to the J-3 (Operations) Directorate of the Joint Chiefs of Staff and colocated with the National Joint Military Intelligence Center.[23]

The JRC was established in 1960 after the loss of an RB-47 over the Barents Sea. In the aftermath, President Eisenhower assigned General Nathan Twining the task of avoiding a repetition. The Air Force proposed that it become executive agent, a proposal strongly resisted by the Navy. Finally, the JRC was established as part of the J-3 on October 24, 1960.[24]

The JRC acts as an initial approval authority for reconnaissance plans developed by unified, specified, and theater commands; develops a Joint Reconnaissance Schedule (JRS), which is "always several inches thick and filled with hundreds of pages of highly technical data and maps"; monitors the progress of the missions; and provides the National Military Command Center with real-time information regarding the status and disposition of forces, mission activity, and other reconnaissance related information.[25] Figure 17-2 shows a 1980 request related to planning for a possible second mission to rescue U.S. hostages in Iran.

The JRC operates through three branches: the Reconnaissance Programs Branch, the Reconnaissance Plans Branch, and the Reconnaissance Operations Branch. The Reconnaissance Programs Branch receives, reviews, evaluates, and submits for approval to the JCS the reconnaissance plans, programs, and schedules originated by the commanders of the unified and specified commands, the military services, and other governmental agencies. It also prepares the planning guidance for the execution of reconnaissance operations of special significance or sensitivity.[26]

The Reconnaissance Plans Branch participates in the review of intelligence support plans and prepares policy guidance, planning, analysis, and review of reconnaissance related activities that support trans- and post-SIOP nuclear operations.[27]

The Reconnaissance Operations Branch is responsible for monitoring the missions approved by the JRC and insuring that all incidents and significant activities are promptly brought to the attention of appropriate authorities. It is also responsible for displaying on a current basis all peacetime military reconnaissance and some other sensitive operations.[28] Thus, on any given day the branch may be monitoring on a real-time basis the flights of all RC-135 and U-2 aircraft, the journeys of a variety of surface ships, and the exploits of submarines performing reconnaissance missions.

MANAGING HUMAN COLLECTION

Human source collection requires a diverse set of management arrangements to deal with a variety of sources, including foreign service officers, clandestine agents, and defectors as well as nongovernment individuals.

Figure 17-2.   SR 71 Mission Request.

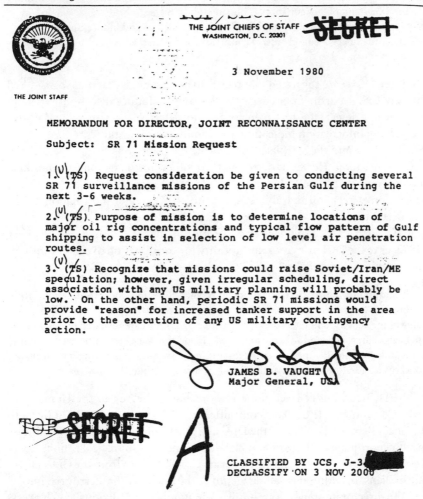

THE JOINT CHIEFS OF STAFF   ~~SECRET~~
WASHINGTON, D.C. 20301

3 November 1980

THE JOINT STAFF

MEMORANDUM FOR DIRECTOR, JOINT RECONNAISSANCE CENTER

Subject: SR 71 Mission Request

1. (U)(TS) Request consideration be given to conducting several
SR 71 surveillance missions of the Persian Gulf during the
next 3-6 weeks.

2. (U)(TS) Purpose of mission is to determine locations of
major oil rig concentrations and typical flow pattern of Gulf
shipping to assist in selection of low level air penetration
routes.

3. (U)(TS) Recognize that missions could raise Soviet/Iran/ME
speculation; however, given irregular scheduling, direct
association with any US military planning will probably be
low. On the other hand, periodic SR 71 missions would
provide "reason" for increased tanker support in the area
prior to the execution of any US military contingency
action.

JAMES B. VAUGHT
Major General, USA

~~TOP SECRET~~

CLASSIFIED BY JCS, J-3
DECLASSIFY ON 3 NOV 2000

The titles of NSCID No. 4 of February 4, 1972, "The Defector Program," and
two DCIDs—4/1, "The Interagency Defector Committee," and 4/2, "Defector
Program Abroad"—suggest the importance with which defectors were viewed
during the Cold War. In addition to defining a variety of terms (defectors, inducement, potential defector, disaffected person, walk-in, refugee, and escapee), the
directive also stated that "defection, particularly from the USSR, should be encouraged and induced, employing both conventional and unconventional means,
whenever there is a net advantage to U.S. interests" and that the United States
should:

(1) Encourage and induce the defection of the maximum number of persons from the USSR and of Soviet nationals outside the USSR

(2) Continue, and if possible expand, efforts to encourage and induce the defection of key members of elite groups of countries other than the USSR who may qualify as defectors.

In addition, DCID 4/2 suggested that recruitment in place be carefully considered before any U.S. department or agency took action to induce defection. When an individual did defect, the first priority was to determine whether the defector possessed any information indicating the imminence of hostilities.[29]

NSCID No. 4 and the associated DCIDs were written long before the collapse of the Soviet Union. However, defectors from other hostile nations, Communist and non-Communist, are still considered of importance. Thus, in the aftermath of Operation Desert Storm, Iraqi defectors provided valuable information on the Iraqi nuclear program.

NSCID No. 5, "U.S. Espionage and Counterintelligence Abroad," of February 17, 1972, gave the DCI primary responsibility for coordination of clandestine collection activities. Paragraphs 2a and 2b authorized the DCI to

establish the procedures necessary to achieve such direction and coordination, including the assessment of risk incident upon such operations as compared to the value of the activity, and to ensure that sensitive operations are reviewed pursuant to applicable directives [and to] coordinate all clandestine activities authorized herein and conducted outside the United States and its possessions, including liaison that concerns clandestine activities or that involves foreign clandestine services.[30]

At the DCI committee level, these responsibilities belong to the Human Resources Committee (HRC). This committee was first proposed in 1970 by General Donald Bennett, Director of the DIA, as a means of providing a national-level forum to coordinate both overt and clandestine human source collection. It was not established immediately, however, because of objections from the CIA's Directorate of Plans. In addition to falling victim to the bureaucratic "territorial imperative," the directorate sought to minimize the number of individuals with access to information concerning clandestine sources. As a result, DCI Richard Helms established an ad hoc task force to study the problem of human source collection. After a year of study, the task force recommended the establishment of a USIB committee on a one-year trial basis—a suggestion endorsed by the President's Foreign Intelligence Advisory Board (PFIAB) in a separate study. In June 1974, the committee attained permanent status as the Human Sources Committee, and in 1975 its name was changed to the Human Resources Committee.[31]

The committee's functions, specified by DCID 3/7 of October 12, 1982, are

a. to examine problems and consider possible improvements in collection and procedures for dissemination of intelligence obtained by human resources and to provide recommendations to the DCI related thereto; and

b. to encourage and promote collection activities and coordination among human resources collection agencies concerning the allocation of effort and responsibility for the satisfaction of foreign intelligence needs.[32]

Through its Assessments Subcommittee, the HRC has conducted community-wide assessments of human source reporting in individual countries. In 1976 and 1977 the subcommittees of the HRC included those for Collection Program Evaluation; Research and Development; Organization, Training, and Advisory; Planning and Programming; and Guidance and Requirements.[33]

The guidelines establishing the committee specifically avoided giving it responsibility for reviewing the operational details or internal management of the individual departments or agencies. Departments and agencies were authorized to withhold "sensitive" information from the committee and to report directly to the DCI.[34]

As of 1975, the HRC had "only just begun to expand community influence over human collection," issuing a general guidance document called the Current Intelligence Reporting List (CIRL). The military made some use of the document, but the CIA's Directorate of Operations instructed CIA stations that the list was provided only for reference and did not constitute collection requirements for CIA operations.[35]

During 1977 the committee provided the U.S. Ambassador in Iran, William Sullivan, with a short prioritized list of items of national intelligence interest. The list was developed by the HRC with the advice of the National Intelligence Officer for the Near East and South Asia. The Chairman of the Human Resources Committee, in his cover letter, expressed his hope that the list would "be of some use … as a coordinated interagency expression of the most important information Washington needs."[36]

In addition to the HRC, the now-defunct Intelligence Community Staff played a role in HUMINT Tasking. During the 1970s it began to issue the National Human Intelligence Collection Plan. The plan included an advisory for HUMINT collectors, such as foreign service officers, who are outside the National Foreign Intelligence Program (NFIP). Apparently, it included a variety of subplans for specific subject areas. Thus, in 1988 there were National HUMINT Collection Plans on Space, Soviet Naval Forces, Soviet Strategic Forces, and Soviet S&T. The plan's effect was limited by being only one of several guidance documents levied on human source collectors.[37]

More recently several initiatives have been launched to improve coordination of clandestine collection. In 1992 a HUMINT Requirements Tasking Center was established within the CIA's Directorate of Operations to allocate collection tasks between all HUMINT agencies. Then DCI Robert Gates described the center as "an integrated interagency mechanism for tasking human intelligence requirements to that part of the community that has the best chance of acquiring the information at least cost and risk." There is also a National HUMINT Collection Directive (NHCD).[38]

430

Figure 17-3. Presidential Finding on Iran.

Finding Pursuant to Section 662 of
The Foreign Assistance Act of 1961
As Amended, Concerning Operations
Undertaken by the Central Intelligence
Agency in Foreign Countries, Other Than
Those Intended Solely for the Purpose
of Intelligence Collection

I hereby find that the following operation in a foreign country (including all support necessary to such operation) is important to the national security of the United States, and due to its extreme sensitivity and security risks, I determine it is essential to limit prior notice, and direct the Director of Central Intelligence to refrain from reporting this Finding to the Congress as provided in Section 501 of the National Security Act of 1947, as amended, until I otherwise direct.

SCOPE   DESCRIPTION

Iran   Assist selected friendly foreign liaison services, third countries and third
                parties which have established relationships with Iranian elements,
                groups, and individuals sympathetic to U.S. Government interests and
                which do not conduct or support terrorist actions directed against U.S.
                persons, property or interests, for the purpose of: (1) establishing a
                more moderate government in Iran, (2) obtaining from them significant
                intelligence not otherwise obtainable, to determine the current Iranian
                Government's intentions with respect to its neighbors and with respect
                to terrorist acts, and (3) furthering the release of the American hostages
                held in Beirut and preventing additional terrorist acts by these groups.
                Provide funds, intelligence, counter-intelligence, training, guidance and
                communications and other necessary assistance to these elements,
                groups, individuals, liaison services and third countries in support of
                these activities.

                The USG will act to facilitate efforts by third parties and third countries
                to establish contact with moderate elements within and outside the
                Government of Iran by providing these elements with arms, equipment
                and related materiel in order to enhance the credibility of these
                elements in their effort to achieve a more pro-U.S. government in Iran
                by demonstrating their ability to obtain requisite resources to defend
                their country against Iraq and intervention by the Soviet Union. This
                support will be discontinued if the U.S. Government learns that these
                elements have abandoned their goals of moderating their government
                and appropriated the material for purposes other than that provided by
                this finding.

The White House
Washington, D.C.
Date January 17, 1986

Also of note is DCID 2/3 of July 25, 1963, entitled "Domestic Exploitation of Nongovernmental Organizations and Individuals," which vests in the CIA responsibility for managing the domestic exploitation program. The CIA is instructed to determine the foreign intelligence potential of nongovernmental organizations and individuals, to serve as coordinator for other government agencies, and to disseminate to intelligence departments and agencies all foreign intelligence information obtained through the program.[39]

MANAGING COVERT ACTION

Management of U.S. covert action programs involves procedures and review groups within the CIA and NSC. To initiate a covert action, a Presidential Finding is required by the Hughes-Ryan Amendment to the Foreign Assistance Act of 1961. The finding must state that the President has determined that the "operation in a foreign country ... is important to the national security of the United States" and then go on to describe the scope (the country or countries that are the target) and a description of what the operation involves. Present findings also specify whether significant foreseeable DOD support will be required.[40] Figure 17-3 shows one of the findings signed in pursuit of the attempt to establish contact with Iranian "moderates."

Findings are initially prepared within the CIA's Directorate of Operations, either as a result of a directorate initiative or in response to requests from the DCI, who in turn may be responding to a presidential request.[41] Before a proposed finding leaves the Directorate of Operations it is reviewed by the Covert Action Planning Group (CAPG), composed of the Associate Deputy Director for Operations, senior staff chiefs, and those individuals who have a substantive responsibility for the finding and its eventual implementation. If approved by the CAPG, the finding is sent on to the top echelon of CIA management for review and recommendations and then to the DCI.[42]

Under the Reagan administration, if the proposed finding was approved by the DCI it would go to the Planning and Coordination Group (PCG) of the NSC, which consists of senior representatives of the State Department, the Defense Department, and NSC. If the PCG supported the finding, it sent a favorable recommendation to the National Security Planning Group (NSPG). Approval of the NSPG then resulted in a Presidential Finding. NSDD 159, of January 18, 1985, "Covert Action Policy Approval and Coordination Procedures," specified that all intelligence findings be written and circulated among the eight senior members of the NSPG before being put into effect.[43]

NOTES

1. U.S. Congress, Senate Select Committee to Study Governmental Operations with Respect to Intelligence Activities, *Final Report, Book 1, Foreign and Military Intelligence*

(Washington, D.C.: U.S. Government Printing Office, 1976), p. 75; Victor Marchetti and John Marks, *The CIA and the Cult of Intelligence* (New York: Dell/Laurel, 1983), p. 206.

2. See Jeffrey T. Richelson, *America's Secret Eyes in Space: The U.S. Keyhole Spy Satellite Program* (New York: Harper & Row, 1990), pp. 79–82.

3. U.S. Congress, Senate Select Committee to Study Governmental Operations with Respect to Intelligence Activities, *Final Report, Book 4, Supplementary Detailed Staff Reports on Foreign and Military Intelligence* (Washington, D.C.: U.S. Government Printing Office, 1976), pp. 74–75; James Bamford, *The Puzzle Palace: A Report on NSA, America's Most Secret Agency* (Boston: Houghton Mifflin, 1982), p. 189.

4. Marchetti and Marks, *The CIA and the Cult of Intelligence*, pp. 85–86; Philip Taubman, "Gulf War Said to Reveal U.S. Intelligence Lapses," *New York Times*, September 27, 1980, p. 3.

5. DCID 1/13, "Coordination of the Collection and Exploitation of Imagery Intelligence," February 2, 1973, *Declassified Documents Reference System* (*DDRS*) 1980-132D; DCID 1/13, "Committee on Imagery Requirements and Exploitation," July 1, 1967, *DDRS* 1980-132B; U.S. Congress, Senate Select Committee to Study Governmental Operations with Respect to Intelligence Activities, *Final Report, Book 1, Foreign and Military Intelligence*, p. 85.

6. Roland S. Inlow, "An Appraisal of the Morison Espionage Trial," *First Principles* 11, 4 (May 1986): 1, 2–5.

7. CINCPACFLT Instruction S3822.1E, "PACOM Imagery Reconnaissance Procedures and Responsibilities," July 5, 1983, p. 1; HQ EUCOM Directive No. 40-4, "Exploitation and Dissemination of Time Sensitive Imagery," November 4, 1983, p. 1.

8. DCID 2/9, "Management of National Imagery Intelligence," June 1, 1992.

9. National Security Agency, *NSA Transition Briefing Book* (Ft. Meade, Md.: NSA, 1980), n.p.; National Security Agency/Central Security Service, *NSA/CSS Manual 22-1* (Ft. Meade, Md.: NSA, 1986).

10. Department of Justice, *Report on CIA-Related Electronic Surveillance Activities* (Washington, D.C.: Department of Justice, 1976), pp. 77–79.

11. U.S. Congress, House Permanent Select Committee on Intelligence, *Annual Report* (Washington, D.C.: U.S. Government Printing Office, 1978), pp. 70, 72; Working Group on Computer Security, *Computer and Telecommunications Security* (Washington, D.C.: National Communications Security Committee, July 1981), pp. 110, 157; Defense Intelligence College, *Instructional Management Plan: Advanced Methods of Intelligence Collection*, March 1984; Department of the Army, AR 350-3, "Tactical Intelligence Readiness Training (REDTRAIN)," November 20, 1984, p. 7; Department of the Army, *FM 34-1, Intelligence and Electronic Warfare Operations*, July 1987, Ref. 2; Department of the Army, *FM 34-40-12, Morse Code Intercept Operations (U)*, August 26, 1991, Ref. 3; ED (EUCOM Directive) 40-6, "Operation and Administration of JIC," April 25, 1989; Private information.

12. George A. Brownell, *The Origins and Development of the National Security Agency* (Laguna Hills, Calif.: Aegean Park Press, 1981), p. 3.

13. Bamford, *The Puzzle Palace*, p. 50; Department of Justice, *Report on CIA-Related Electronic Surveillance Activities*, p. 91; DCID 6/1, "Communications Intelligence Committee," October 21, 1958, *DDRS* 1980-130C; DCID 6/2, "Electronics Intelligence Committee," October 21, 1958, *DDRS* 1980-130D; DCID 6/1, "SIGINT Committee," May 1, 1962, *DDRS* 1980-131D.

14. U.S. Congress, Senate Select Committee to Study Governmental Operations with Respect to Intelligence Activities, *Final Report, Book 1, Foreign and Military Intelligence,* p. 85.

15. Naval Intelligence Command, *Naval Intelligence Command (NAVINTCOM) History for CY-1972,* August 1, 1973, p. 20.

16. Department of the Army, Office of the Assistant Chief of Staff for Intelligence, *Annual Historical Review, 1 October 1984–30 September 1985,* p. 2-30; Office of the Deputy Chief of Staff for Intelligence, *Annual Historical Review, 1 October 1990–30 September 1991,* 1993, p. 4-34.

17. Naval Intelligence Command, *Naval Intelligence Command (NAVINTCOM) History for CY-1972,* p. 19.

18. Department of Justice, *Report on CIA-Related Electronic Surveillance Activities,* pp. 101–3.

19. U.S. Congress, Senate Select Committee to Study Governmental Operations with Respect to Intelligence Activities, *Final Report, Book 1, Foreign and Military Intelligence,* pp. 85–86; U.S. Congress, House Permanent Select Committee on Intelligence, *Annual Report,* p. 55; Stephen J. Flanagan, "The Coordination of National Intelligence," in Duncan Clarke, ed., *Public Policy and Political Institutions: United States Defense and Foreign Policy—Policy Coordination and Integration* (Greenwich, Conn.: JAI, 1985), p. 177.

20. National Security Agency, *NSA Transition Briefing Book,* n.p.

21. See Jeffrey Richelson, *American Espionage and the Soviet Target* (New York: Morrow, 1987), pp. 120–26.

22. Bamford, *The Puzzle Palace,* pp. 184–85, 216–31; U.S. Congress, House Committee on Armed Services, *Inquiry into the U.S.S. Pueblo and EC-121 Plane Incidents* (Washington, D.C.: U.S. Government Printing Office, 1969); "Radar Detector Aboard SR-71 Alerted Plane Missile Attack," *New York Times,* August 29, 1983, p. 3.

23. U.S. Congress, House Appropriations Committee, *Department of Defense Appropriations for 1994, Part 1* (Washington, D.C.: U.S. Government Printing Office, 1993), p. 37.

24. Col. Thomas G. Shepherd, Chief, Reconnaissance Programs Division J-3, Memorandum for the Record: "Conversation between Colonel Earnest R. Harden (USAF Ret.) and Colonel Thomas G. Shepherd, OJCS/JRC, 11 August 1977," August 12, 1977.

25. Joint Chiefs of Staff, JCS Publication 4, *Organization and Functions of the Joint Chiefs of Staff* (Washington, D.C.: JCS, 1985), p. III-3-73; Marchetti and Marks, *The CIA and the Cult of Intelligence,* p. 332.

26. Joint Chiefs of Staff, JCS Publication 4, *Organization and Functions of the Joint Chiefs of Staff,* p. III-3-28; *Department of Defense Telephone Directory* (Washington, D.C.: U.S. Government Printing Office, December 1987), p. O-12.

27. Joint Chiefs of Staff, JCS Publication 4, *Organization and Functions of the Joint Chiefs of Staff,* p. III-3-28.

28. Ibid., p. III-3-29.

29. DCID 4/2, "The Defector Program Abroad," June 26, 1959, *Documents from the Espionage Den (53): U.S.S.R., The Aggressive East, Section 4* (Tehran: Muslim Students Following the Line of the Imam, n.d.), pp. 4–11; U.S. Congress, House Permanent Select Committee on Intelligence, *Annual Report,* p. 70.

30. NSCID No. 5, "U.S. Espionage and Counterintelligence Activities Abroad," February 17, 1972, *DDRS 1976-253F.*

31. U.S. Congress, Senate Select Committee to Study Governmental Operations with Respect to Intelligence Activities, *Final Report, Book 1, Foreign and Military Intelligence,* p. 85, n42.

32. DCID 3/7, "Human Resources Committee," October 12, 1982.

33. U.S. Congress, Senate Select Committee to Study Governmental Operations with Respect to Intelligence Activities, *Final Report, Book 1, Foreign and Military Intelligence,* pp. 86–87; Department of the Army, Office of the Assistant Chief of Staff for Intelligence, *Annual Historical Review, 1 October 1976–30 September 1977,* n.d., pp. 28–34.

34. U.S. Congress, Senate Select Committee to Study Governmental Operations with Respect to Intelligence Activities, *Final Report, Book 1, Foreign and Military Intelligence,* p. 86.

35. Ibid.

36. Scott Armstrong, "Intelligence Experts Had Early Doubts About Shah's Stability," *Washington Post,* February 2, 1982, pp. 1, 9.

37. Flanagan, "The Coordination of National Intelligence," p. 177; Navy Operational Intelligence Center, *Command History for CY 1987,* May 20, 1988, p. 7.

38. Remarks by Robert M. Gates, Director of Central Intelligence, to Association of Former Intelligence Officers, November 14, 1992, Boston, p. 5.

39. DCID 2/3, "Domestic Exploitation of Nongovernmental Organizations and Individuals," July 25, 1963, *DDRS* 1980-131E.

40. U.S. Congress, House Select Committee to Investigate Covert Arms Transactions with Iran and Senate Select Committee on Secret Military Assistance to Iran and the Nicaraguan Opposition, *Report of the Congressional Committees Investigating the Iran-Contra Affair with Supplemental, Minority, and Additional Views* (Washington, D.C.: U.S. Government Printing Office, 1987), pp. 376–77; Caspar Weinberger, Memorandum to the Secretary of the Army, Subject: DOD Support [to CIA Special] Activities, June 13, 1983, p. 1.

41. Wilhelm G. Hinsleigh, "Covert Action: An Update," *Studies in Intelligence* (Spring 1986).

42. Ibid.

43. Ibid., NSDD 159, "Covert Action Policy Approval and Coordination Procedures," January 18, 1985; NSDD 266, "Implementation of the Recommendations of the President's Special Review Board," March 31, 1987, p. 7.

18
MANAGING INFORMATION ACCESS AND ANALYSIS

The U.S. intelligence collection effort produces an enormous volume of information, particularly from its numerous technical collection systems. The National Security Agency alone generates several tons of paper on a daily basis.

Collection, however, is only an intermediary step in the intelligence process between the statement of requirements and the production of finished intelligence. Thus, the information collected must be channeled to those who are responsible for processing and analysis—the National Photographic Interpretation Center, the Defense Intelligence Agency, the State Department's Bureau of Intelligence and Research, the Central Intelligence Agency's Directorate of Intelligence, and the intelligence analysis components of the military services. The same information, either in its raw or processed and analyzed form, must also be made available to a wide variety of individuals—policymakers, policy implementers, strategists, contractors, and consultants—who need it in order to perform their jobs. Information is also made available to U.S. allies under treaty or other arrangements for intelligence sharing. At the same time, much of the information needs to be protected, since its disclosure might reveal nonobvious targets of collection and/or collection capabilities—disclosures that could lead to effective countermeasures and precautions and the denial of such information in the future. Hence, it is necessary to establish guidelines for the classification and distribution of intelligence information as well as for access to that information by both U.S. citizens and foreign governments.

Although the numerous analytical intelligence units have distinct functions, it is still necessary to manage the analytical process on a community-wide basis. Aside from the avoidance of undesired duplication where the potential for such duplication exists, officials must ensure that intelligence production is responsive to the requirements of national and departmental leaders. The intelligence community must have mechanisms to deal with analytical problems, and agencies working on similar problems must maintain an adequate degree of cooperation on a day-to-day basis. Further, coordinating the production of national estimates is a delicate process involving several agencies with differing perspectives.

MANAGING THE ACCESS TO INFORMATION

The basic means of managing or controlling access to intelligence information are delineated in the classification system, which defines different levels of sensitivity and restricts access to those who have been cleared at that level and have a "need to know." The best-known classifications are those used to restrict access to a wide range of national security information: Confidential, Secret, and Top Secret.

Confidential information is defined as information "the unauthorized disclosure of which reasonably could be expected to cause damage to the national security." Secret information differs from Confidential information in that the expected damage would be "serious." In the case of Top Secret information, the damage would be "exceptionally grave."[1]

In theory, at least, access for an individual with clearance at a certain level is further restricted to the information the individual needs to know in order to perform his or her job. In some cases the need-to-know principle is implemented by compartmentalizing certain sets of data—such as that concerning specific types of operations or individuals. Thus, the Army Intelligence and Security Command's offensive counterintelligence operations are designated by a special codeword used to restrict access to information about those operations. Similar operations conducted by the Air Force Office of Special Investigations have had the designation SEVEN DOORS. Information about sensitive or clandestine attaché collection activities involving non-U.S. sources or foreign materiel acquisition projects is sent via the DOD RODCA channel.[2]

The CIA's Directorate of Operations maintains several dozen compartments for the transmission of human source reports. The compartments are informally designated "blue border" or "blue stripe" material for the blue stripes on the border of the cover sheet to any document containing such material. The CIA's Soviet Bloc Division used compartments such as REDWOOD, REDCOAT, and RYBAT. Among the documents classified SECRET RYBAT was a January 9, 1973, message from the Chief of the Soviet Bloc Division to Chiefs of Station and Base on "Turning Around REDTOP [Soviet Bloc] Walk-ins."[3]

In addition to the traditional Confidential, Secret, and Top Secret classifications, the intelligence community employs classifications for information that falls into the Sensitive Compartmented Information (SCI) category. According to a 1984 report by the NFIB Security Committee,

Sensitive Compartmented Information is data about sophisticated technical systems for collecting intelligence and information collected by those systems. The characteristics of the systems that necessitated the development of SCI programs are (a) that compared to conventional intelligence activities employing human sources, many more people normally must know sensitive information in order to develop, build and operate the systems and to analyze the material they collect; (b) that they generally produce large quantities of accurate, detailed intelligence, which is needed and relied upon by senior planners and policymakers, and which, by its nature, is extremely fragile, in that it reveals the characteristics of the systems that collect it; and (c) that they are extremely vulnerable to adversary countermeasures, i.e. denial or deception.[4]

The systems that generate SCI are imaging and signals intelligence satellites; aircraft such as the U-2 and RC-135; submarines involved in Special Navy reconnaissance missions; and ground stations involved in the interception of foreign signals. Information about imaging and signals intelligence satellites also falls into the SCI category.

Traditionally, a more stringent background investigation was required to gain access to SCI than was required to gain access to Top Secret information. The logic was that whereas denial of a Top Secret clearance required the presence of a well-defined character or personality defect that posed a threat to national security, "no risk is tolerable where SCI is involved, and individuals who have been granted Top Secret clearances may be denied approval for access to SCI." National Security Directive 63, of October 21, 1991, established the practice of single scope background investigations, which allow the same minimum standards for Top Secret and SCI background investigations.[5] The directive does not prohibit more stringent requirements for access to SCI, however. Thus, an SCI screening interview might delve into an individual's family, financial, sexual, drug, criminal, political, travel, mental health, and physical histories.[6] Moreover, it is still the case that the physical security measures used to protect SCI are more extensive than those used to protect Top Secret information—particularly the holding of SCI in vault areas from which it is not permitted to be removed.[7]

The first public hint of the existence of such a category occurred during the Senate hearing on the Gulf of Tonkin Resolution in 1964, when Senate Foreign Relations Committee Chairman William Fulbright inquired into the source of a report that North Vietnamese patrol boats were about to attack the *Turner Joy* on the night of August 4, 1964. Defense Secretary Robert McNamara, Fulbright, and Senators Frank Lausche and Albert Gore engaged in the following colloquy:

McNamara: We have some problems because the [committee] staff has not been cleared for certain intelligence.

Lausche: I do not understand that. The members of our staff are not cleared?

Fulbright: All of those who have worked on this matter, but he is talking of a special classification of intelligence communications. ...

Gore: Mr. Chairman, could we know what particular classification that is? I had not heard of this particular super classification.

McNamara: ... Clearance is *above* Top Secret for the particular information on the situation. (Emphasis added.)[8]

The "above Top Secret" category dealt with communications or signals intelligence (rather than intelligence communications), and McNamara revealed that it was called Special Intelligence (SI).[9] SI is one of several categories of SCI.

The institutionalization of such categories and clearances, particularly SI, can be traced to the successful interception and decryption of Japanese, German, and Italian signals during World War II by the United States and Great Britain. The machine by which the United States was able to decode Japanese diplomatic messages was known as PURPLE, and the intelligence provided by the decryption activity was known as MAGIC. Distribution of MAGIC material was sharply restricted by George Marshall, who drew up a "Top List" of those authorized to have access. The list was restricted to President Roosevelt; the Secretaries of State, War, and the Navy; and the Directors of Military and Naval Intelligence. Among those not on the list was the Commander of U.S. Naval Forces at Pearl Harbor, Admiral Husband Kimmel.[10]

The British also instituted a codeword system to guard the fact that they were able to decrypt German and Italian military and intelligence communications. The most sensitive military material was originally designated PEARL, ZYMOTIC, SWELL, and SIDAR. Later, the British settled on three codewords—ULTRA, PEARL, and THUMB—to indicate material of special sensitivity. Eventually, PEARL and THUMB were combined into a single codeword—PINUP. Intercepts of German intelligence communications by the British Radio Security Service were given the labels ISOS and ISK depending on whether they were intercepts of ENIGMA-generated or hand-generated cipher systems. This information, when passed to the United States, became ICE and PAIR.[11]

In addition to intercepting Japanese diplomatic communications, the United States also spent considerable effort in intercepting and trying to decipher Japanese military communications. The United States employed several codenames to represent the product of such activity. DEXTER was the codeword used for intercepts of the highest-level traffic—for example, Admiral Yamomoto's travel plans. CORRAL indicated less sensitive intercepts. RABID was used to indicate Traffic Analysis intelligence. With the signing of the BRUSA Communications Intelligence Agreement in May 1943, which standardized signals intelligence procedures between the United States and Britain, ULTRA was made a prefix to each classification so that the codewords became ULTRA DEXTER, ULTRA CORRAL, and ULTRA RABID.[12]

Although the outbreak of World War II required a significant expansion of those with a need to know ULTRA information, extraordinary security procedures were maintained and distribution was restricted as much as possible. Thus, the British maintained a system of Special Liaison Units to facilitate the transmission of ULTRA from the Government Code and Cypher School in Bletchley to military commanders. It was required that those with knowledge of ULTRA remain outside of battle areas to avoid any chance of capture. On occasions where exceptions were made and ULTRA-cleared personnel did risk capture, they carried cyanide pills to allow them to commit suicide to avoid interrogation.[13]

The degree of restriction placed on ULTRA information by the United States is indicated by the fact that in 1943 there were only sixty-one individuals in the China-Burma-India theater, outside of the personnel in the Signals Intelligence Service and Radio Intelligence Units, who were ULTRA cleared. It was required that "requests for ... additions [to the list] ... be kept by each headquarters to the absolute minimum necessary for the efficient handling of the material."[14]

The restricted nature of the material was clearly indicated by the same directive, which stated:

The Assistant Chief of Staff, G-2, War Department, requires that all ULTRA DEXTER material be classified TOP SECRET and so marked in addition to the prescribed codewords. This classification will in no way be interpreted as releasing ULTRA DEXTER from the requirements defined herein or authorizing TOP SECRET control officers or other personnel to handle, see, or discuss ULTRA DEXTER in any form, unless they are also on the list of authorized ULTRA DEXTER recipients.[15]

Within the SCI category are several sets of clearances—the most common being Special Intelligence (SI), GAMMA (G), TALENT-KEYHOLE (TK), and BYEMAN (B).

As McNamara indicated, the SI category concerns signals intelligence. Just as there were different ULTRA levels (for the United States), there are different compartments of the SI category corresponding to different levels of sensitivity. UMBRA is the successor to DINAR and TRINE as the compartment for the most sensitive SI material. Less sensitive is the SPOKE compartment, which might contain information from intercepts of PLO communications. Least sensitive is the information in the MORAY compartment.[16]

To express these differing levels of sensitivity, a page containing only UMBRA SCI will be stamped TOP SECRET UMBRA; a page containing only SPOKE SCI will be stamped SECRET SPOKE; and a page containing only MORAY SCI will be stamped SECRET MORAY. While the use of the Top Secret and Secret prefixes may appear to imply that UMBRA, SPOKE, and MORAY are simply "need-to-know" compartments of those conventional classifications, such a conclusion is inconsistent with, among other things, the fact that greater physical security measures are taken to protect a SECRET MORAY or SECRET SPOKE document than are taken for a plain Top Secret document.[17]

Further designators are employed by the NSA for especially sensitive UMBRA information. GAMMA is a designator that was reserved exclusively for intercepts of Soviet communications until 1969, when the NSA received orders to use the same methods and procedures to monitor the communications of U.S. antiwar leaders. At one point, there were at least twenty GAMMA designations, including GILT, GOAT, GULT, GANT, GUPY, GABE, GYRO, and GOUT, each of which referred to a specific operation or method. GAMMA GUPY referred to the interception of radio-telephone conversations being conducted by Soviet leaders as they were driven around Moscow in their limousines, for example, and GAMMA GOUT referred to the material obtained by interception of South Vietnamese government communications.[18] Thus, a document might bear the classification TOP SECRET UMBRA GAMMA GYRO.

At one time, there was a DELTA compartment of UMBRA for intercepts relating to Soviet military operations, such as the location of Soviet submarines or aircraft operations. DELTA categories included DACE, DICE, and DENT.[19]

SI documents might also bear a codeword indicating that the SIGINT was obtained from a Third Party to the UKUSA Agreement. DRUID designates a Third-Party intercept. Other designations indicate the specific nations involved: JAEGER (Austria), ISHTAR (Japan), SETEE (Korea), DYNAMO (Denmark), RICHTER (Germany), and DIKTER (Norway).[20]

The TK, or TALENT-KEYHOLE, clearance restricts access to information concerning the product of certain overhead collection systems—specifically, imaging and signals intelligence satellites and the U-2. Compartments within the TK system include RUFF, ZARF, and CHESS. RUFF pertains to information produced by imaging (KEYHOLE) satellites; ZARF indicates ELINT obtained by satellite; and CHESS designates certain U-2 photography. Thus, the December 1986 final report of the DCI Mobile Missile Task Force Intelligence Requirements and Analysis Working Group is classified TOP SECRET RUFF ZARF UMBRA.[21]

On some occasions, it is felt that certain codeword information needs to or should be made available to a larger audience than the codeword system permits. In such cases, the Secret or Top Secret documents containing the information bear the additional designator WNINTEL: Warning Notice—Intelligence Sources and Methods Involved.

In practice, SI and TK clearances, which both permit access to the product of technical collection systems, are almost always awarded jointly. Hence, the term "SI-TK clearance" is more common than the terms "SI clearance" or "TK clearance." Although the SI-TK clearance gives individuals access to the product of sensitive intelligence systems, it does not grant access to information concerning the systems themselves. Information about the type of system, its location, name, orbit, or capabilities is not accessible to an individual simply on the basis of an SI-TK clearance. Clearances for such information are granted on a system-by-system basis, with each system having a specific codeword. These codewords represent the compartments of the BYEMAN system. CANYON, RHYOLITE, AQUACADE, CHALET, VORTEX, JUMPSEAT, MAGNUM, and ORION represent the BYEMAN compartments pertaining to past and present SIGINT satellites, while CORONA, ARGON, LANYARD, GAMBIT, HEXAGON, KENNAN, CRYSTAL, INDIGO, and LACROSSE represent the BYEMAN compartments of past and present imaging satellites. PARCAE was the BYEMAN codename for the first generation of ocean surveillance satellites, while VEGA is a more recent codename for a space reconnaissance system.[22]

In recent years two new clearances appear to be widely held in the SCI world. One of these is SPECTRE,* which is concerned with intelligence relating to terrorist activities. The other, the subject matter of which is not known, is LOMA.[23]

Additional CIA, NSA, and Navy SCI compartments included, as of 1985, CS, PM, VER, SNCP, and M.[24] One of the CS or PM systems may concern emplaced sensors. VER probably refers to NSA's "Very Restricted Knowledge" SCI system. Different levels of that system involve access to varying types of SCI—for example, satellite imagery. SNCP referred to the Special Navy Control Program, which employed submarines to collect intelligence in or near the territorial waters of the Soviet Union, as discussed in Chapter 8. M also represented a Navy SCI system— MEDITATE—which concerned information about IVY BELLS–type operations. In recent years the terms Naval Activities Support Program (NASP) and DNI's Special Access Program (DSAP) may have replaced SNCP and MEDITATE, respectively.[25]

The classification system described above, as well as personnel and security standards for access to and handling of intelligence information, is defined in a series of Executive Orders, National Security Decision Directives (NSDDs), National Security Council Intelligence Directives (NSCIDs), Director of Central Intelligence Directives (DCIDs), and DOD Directives. Additionally, several NSC committees are concerned with the security of the information acquired as well as that of sources and methods.

As noted in Chapter 16, since the Eisenhower years most administrations have issued an Executive Order on National Security Information, the latest three being Executive Order 11652 of March 10, 1972, "Classification and Declassification of National Security Information and Material," with amendments during the Ford administration; Executive Order 12065 of June 28, 1978, "National Security Information"; and Executive Order 12356 of April 2, 1982, "National Security Information." In April 1993 President Clinton signed Presidential Review Directive 29 on "National Security Information," which set forth a review process to be completed prior to the issuance of new Executive Orders. As of January 1995 that order had not been issued.[26]

Part 1 of Executive Order 12356 defines classification levels (Top Secret, Secret, and Confidential) and specifies the officials (by position) who can classify information or delegate the authority to do so. This section also specifies the identifications and markings that are to be shown on the face of all classified documents and basic rules concerning the duration of the classifications.

---

*Those familiar with the James Bond novels will recognize SPECTRE as the acronym for the Special Executive for Counterintelligence, Terrorism, Revenge, and Extortion. It is reasonable to assume that the codeword was not chosen by U.S. intelligence officials by coincidence.

In addition, Part 1 defines the types of information that shall be considered for classification and establishes limitations on classification. Information may be considered for classification if it concerns

1. military plans, weapons, or operations;
2. the vulnerabilities or capabilities of systems, installations, projects, or plans relating to the national security;
3. foreign government information;
4. intelligence activities (including special activities), or intelligence sources or methods;
5. foreign relations or foreign activities of the United States;
6. scientific, technological, or economic matters relating to the national security;
7. United States Government programs for safeguarding nuclear materials or facilities;
8. cryptology;
9. a confidential source; or
10. other categories of information that are related to national security and that require protection against unauthorized disclosure as determined by the President or by agency heads or other officials who have been delegated original classification authority by the President.[27]

Section 1.6, which deals with limitations on classification, forbids classification meant to conceal violations of law, inefficiency, or administrative error or to prevent embarrassment to a person, organization, or agency. It also prohibits classification of basic scientific research information "not clearly related to national security." However, in a sharp reversal from past orders, Part 1 of Executive Order 12356 contains the provision that

The President or an agency head or official designated under Section 1.2(a) (1), 1.2(b) (1) or 1.2(c) (1) may reclassify information previously declassified and disclosed if it is determined in writing that (1) the information requires protection in the interest of national security; and (2) the information may reasonably be recovered.[28]*

The remaining parts of the order deal with derivative classification, declassification and downgrading, safeguarding, implementation, and review. Part 4, "Safeguarding," includes Section 4.2, "Special Access Programs," which states that

agency heads designated pursuant to Section 1.2(a) may create special access programs to control access, distribution and protection of particularly sensitive informa-

---

*In 1982 the Justice Department attempted to recover from author James Bamford the sanitized version of the department's study on *CIA Related Electronic Surveillance*, which it had provided to him in response to an FOIA request. Bamford had already provided a copy to another journalist, however, and refused to comply with the department's "request," which was supplemented by threats of prosecution.

tion classified pursuant to this order or predecessor orders. Such programs may be created or continued only at the written direction of these agency heads. For special access programs pertaining to intelligence activities (including special activities but not including military operational, strategic and tactical programs), or intelligence sources or methods, this function will be exercised by the Director of Central Intelligence.[29]

The Reagan administration issued two NSDDs concerning the control of intelligence information: NSDD-19 of January 12, 1982, "Protection of Classified National Security Council and Intelligence Information," and NSDD-84 of March 11, 1983, "Safeguarding National Security Information."[30]

NSDD-19 required advance senior-level approval for all contacts with the news media that would involve discussions about classified National Security Council (NSC) or classified intelligence information. It also specified that the number of officials with access to documents relating to NSC matters be kept to a minimum and that, in the event of unauthorized disclosure of such information, government employees with access to the information would be subject to investigation. The investigations could employ all legal methods.[31]

Because of NSDD-19, those granted access to classified NSC information were required to sign a cover sheet acknowledging access and agreeing to "cooperate fully with any lawful investigation by the United States Government into any unauthorized disclosure of classified information contained therein."[32]

NSDD-84 specified that all government officials and employees with access to SCI sign a nondisclosure agreement providing for prepublication review of any of their writings or speeches dealing with subjects relating to SCI—for example, START verification. Beginning in 1981, individuals with access to SCI had been required to sign Form 4193 (shown in Figure 18-1), which provided for lifetime prepublication review of all writings, "including works of fiction, which contain or purport to contain SCI or that I have reason to believe are derived from SCI." After the promulgation of NSDD-84, Form 4193 was revised (see Figure 18-2). The prepublication review provision of the new form was suspended by President Reagan in response to congressional criticism. However, employees were still required to sign the prior version of Form 4193 before being granted access to SCI.[33]

The present SCI form is shown as Figure 18-3.

NSCID No. 1 of February 17, 1972, "Basic Duties and Responsibilities," authorized the Director of Central Intelligence to

disseminate national intelligence and interdepartmental intelligence on a strictly controlled basis to foreign governments and international bodies upon his determination after consultation with the United States [now National Foreign] Intelligence Board, that such action would substantially promote the security of the United States, provided that such dissemination is consistent with existing statutes and Presidential policy, including that reflected in international agreements.[34]

444

Figure 18-1. Form 4193.

FORM 4193

SENSITIVE COMPARTMENTED INFORMATION NONDISCLOSURE AGREEMENT

An Agreement Between _____ and the United States
(Name - Printed or Typed)

1. Intending to be legally bound, I hereby accept the obligations contained in this Agreement in consideration of my being granted access to information protected within Special Access Programs, hereinafter referred to in this Agreement as Sensitive Compartmented Information (SCI). I have been advised that SCI involves or derives from intelligence sources or methods and is classified or classifiable under the standards of Executive Order 12065 or other Executive order or statute. I understand and accept that by being granted access to SCI, special confidence and trust shall be placed in me by the United States Government.

2. I hereby acknowledge that I have received a security indoctrination concerning the nature and protection of SCI, including the procedures to be followed in ascertaining whether other persons to whom I contemplate disclosing this information have been approved for access to it, and I understand these procedures. I understand that I may be required to sign subsequent agreements upon being granted access to different categories of SCI. I further understand that all my obligations under this Agreement continue to exist whether or not I am required to sign such subsequent agreements.

3. I have been advised that direct or indirect unauthorized disclosure, unauthorized retention, or negligent handling of SCI by me could cause irreparable injury to the United States or be used to advantage by a foreign nation. I hereby agree that I will never divulge such information to anyone who is not authorized to receive it without prior written authorization from the United States Government department or agency (hereinafter Department or Agency) that last authorized my access to SCI. I further understand that I am obligated by law and regulation not to disclose any classified information in an unauthorized fashion.

4. In consideration of being granted access to SCI and of being assigned or retained in a position of special confidence and trust requiring access to SCI, I hereby agree to submit for security review by the Department or Agency that last authorized my access to such information, all information or materials, including works of fiction, which contain or purport to contain any SCI or description of activities that produce or relate to SCI or that I have reason to believe are derived from SCI, that I contemplate disclosing to any person not authorized to have access to SCI or that I have prepared for public disclosure. I understand and agree that my obligation to submit such information and materials for review applies during the course of my access to SCI and thereafter, and I agree to make any required submissions prior to discussing the information or materials with, or showing them to, anyone who is not authorized to have access to SCI. I further agree that I will not disclose such information or materials to any person not authorized to have access to SCI until I have received written authorization from the Department or Agency that last authorized my access to SCI that such disclosure is permitted.

5. I understand that the purpose of the review described in paragraph 4 is to give the United States a reasonable opportunity to determine whether the information or materials submitted pursuant to paragraph 4 set forth any SCI. I further understand that the Department or Agency to which I have submitted materials will act upon them, coordinating within the Intelligence Community when appropriate, and make a response to me within a reasonable time, not to exceed 30 working days from date of receipt.

6. I have been advised that any breach of this Agreement may result in the termination of my access to SCI and retention in a position of special confidence and trust requiring such access, as well as the termination of my employment or other relationships with any Department or Agency that provides me with access to SCI. In addition, I have been advised that any unauthorized disclosure of SCI by me may constitute violations of United States criminal laws, including the provisions of Sections 793, 794, 798, and 952, Title 18, United States Code, and of Section 783(b), Title 50, United States Code. Nothing in this Agreement constitutes a waiver by the United States of the right to prosecute me for any statutory violation.

7. I understand that the United States Government may seek any remedy available to it to enforce this Agreement including, but not limited to, application for a court order prohibiting disclosure of information in breach of this Agreement. I have been advised that the action can be brought against me in any of the several appropriate United States District Courts where the United States Government may elect to file the action. Court costs and reasonable attorneys fees incurred by the United States Government may be assessed against me if I lose such action.

8. I understand that all information to which I may obtain access by signing this Agreement is now and will forever remain the property of the United States Government. I do not now, nor will I ever, possess any right, interest, title, or claim whatsoever to such information. I agree that I shall return all materials, which may have come into my possession or for which I am responsible because of such access, upon demand by an authorized representative of the United States Government or upon the conclusion of my employment or other relationship with the United States Government entity providing me access to such materials. If I do not return such materials upon request, I understand this may be a violation of Section 793, Title 18, United States Code, a United States criminal law.

9. Unless and until I am released in writing by an authorized representative of the Department or Agency that last provided me with access to SCI, I understand that all conditions and obligations imposed upon me by this Agreement apply during the time I am granted access to SCI, and at all times thereafter.

10. Each provision of this Agreement is severable. If a court should find any provision of this Agreement to be unenforceable, all other provisions of this Agreement shall remain in full force and effect. This Agreement concerns SCI and does not set forth such other conditions and obligations not related to SCI as may now or hereafter pertain to my employment by or assignment or relationship with the Department or Agency.

11. I have read this Agreement carefully and my questions, if any, have been answered to my satisfaction. I acknowledge that the briefing officer has made available Sections 793, 794, 798, and 952 of Title 18, United States Code, and Section 783(b) of Title 50, United States Code, and Executive Order 12065, as amended, so that I may read them at this time, if I so choose.

12. I hereby assign to the United States Government all rights, title and interest, and all royalties, remunerations, and emoluments that have resulted, will result, or may result from any disclosure, publication, or revelation not consistent with the terms of this Agreement.

FORM 4193 OBSOLETE PREVIOUS (Replaces Form 4066, 3968, 4193a and 4193b
12 81 EDITION which are obsolete and will not be used.)

(12)

Figure 18-1. continued

13. I make this Agreement without any mental reservation or purpose of evasion.

_____   _____
SIGNATURE   DATE

The execution of this Agreement was witnessed by the undersigned who accepted it on behalf of the United States Government as a prior condition of access to Sensitive Compartmented Information.

WITNESS and ACCEPTANCE: _____   _____
                        SIGNATURE   DATE

SECURITY BRIEFING ACKNOWLEDGMENT

I hereby acknowledge that I was briefed on the following SCI Special Access Program(s):

_____

(Special Access Programs by Initials Only)

Signature of Individual Briefed   Date Briefed

Printed or Typed Name

Social Security Number (See Notice Below)   Organization (Name and Address)

I certify that the above SCI access(es) were approved in accordance with relevant SCI procedures and that the briefing presented by me on the above date was also in accordance therewith.

Signature of Briefing Officer

Printed or Typed Name   Organization (Name and Address)

Social Security Number (See Notice Below)

* * * * *

SECURITY DEBRIEFING ACKNOWLEDGMENT

Having been reminded of my continuing obligation to comply with the terms of this Agreement, I hereby acknowledge that I was debriefed on the following SCI Special Access Program(s):

_____

(Special Access Programs by Initials Only)

Signature of Individual Debriefed   Date Debriefed

Printed or Typed Name

Social Security Number (See Notice Below)   Organization (Name and Address)

I certify that the debriefing presented by me on the above date was in accordance with relevant SCI procedures.

Signature of Debriefing Officer

Printed or Typed Name   Organization (Name and Address)

Social Security Number (See Notice Below)

NOTICE: The Privacy Act, 5 U.S.C. 522a, requires that federal agencies inform individuals, at the time information is solicited from them, whether the disclosure is mandatory or voluntary, by what authority such information is solicited, and what uses will be made of the information. You are hereby advised that authority for soliciting your Social Security Account Number (SSN) is Executive Order 9397. Your SSN will be used to identify you precisely when it is necessary to 1) certify that you have access to the information indicated above, 2) determine that your access to the information indicated has terminated, or 3) certify that you have witnessed a briefing or debriefing. Although disclosure of your SSN is not mandatory, your failure to do so may impede such certifications or determinations.

Figure 18-2.   Revised Form 4193.

Revised Form 4193

AUG 2 4 1983

SENSITIVE COMPARTMENTED INFORMATION NONDISCLOSURE AGREEMENT

An Agreement Between _____ and the United States
                        (Name-Printed or Typed)

1. Intending to be legally bound, I hereby accept the obligations
contained in this Agreement in consideration of my being granted
access to information known as Sensitive Compartmented Information
(SCI). I have been advised and am aware that SCI involves or
derives from intelligence sources or methods and is classified or
classifiable under the standards of Executive Order 12356 or under
other Executive order or statute. I understand and accept that by
being granted access to SCI, special confidence and trust shall be
placed in me by the United States Government.

2. I hereby acknowledge that I have received a security indoctrination
concerning the nature and protection of SCI, including the procedures
to be followed in ascertaining whether other persons to whom I
contemplate disclosing this information have been approved for
access to it, and that I understand these procedures. I understand that
I may be required to sign subsequent agreements as a condition of
being granted access to different categories of SCI. I further
understand that all my obligations under this Agreement continue to
exist whether or not I am required to sign such subsequent agreements.

3. I have been advised and am aware that direct or indirect unauthorized
disclosure, unauthorized retention, or negligent handling of SCI by
me could cause irreparable injury to the United States or could be
used to advantage by a foreign nation. I hereby agree that I will
never divulge such information unless I have officially verified
that the recipient has been properly authorized by the United States
Government to receive it or I have been given prior written notice of
authorization from the United States Government Department or Agency
(hereinafter Department or Agency) last granting me either a security
clearance or an SCI access approval that such disclosure is permitted.

4. I further understand that I am obligated to comply with laws and
regulations that prohibit the unauthorized disclosure of classified
information. As used in this Agreement, classified information is
information that is classified under the standards of E.O. 12356, or
under any other Executive order or statute that prohibits the
unauthorized disclosure of information in the interest of national
security.

5. In consideration of being granted access to SCI and of being
assigned or retained in a position of special confidence and trust
requiring access to SCI and other classified information, I hereby
agree to submit for security review by the Department or Agency
last granting me either a security clearance or an SCI access
approval all materials, including works of fiction, that I contemplate
disclosing to any person not authorized to have such information,

Figure 18-2. continued

8 or that I have prepared for public disclosure, which contain or
9 purport to contain:

10   (a) any SCI, any description of activities that produce or
11   relate to SCI, or any information derived from SCI;
12   (b) any classified information from intelligence reports
13   or estimates; or
14   (c) any information concerning intelligence activities,
15   sources or methods.

16 I understand and agree that my obligation to submit such information
17 and materials for review applies during the course of my access to
18 SCI and at all times thereafter. However, I am not required to
19 submit for review any such materials that exclusively contain
20 information lawfully obtained by me at a time when I have no employment,
21 contract or other relationship with the United States Government,
22 and which are to be published at such time.

1   6. I agree to make the submissions described in paragraph 5 prior
2   to discussing the information or materials with, or showing them to
3   anyone who is not authorized to have access to such information. I
4   further agree that I will not disclose such information or materials
5   unless I have officially verified that the recipient has been
6   properly authorized by the United States Government to receive it or
7   I have been given written authorization from the Department or
8   Agency last granting me either a security clearance or an SCI
9   access approval that such disclosure is permitted.

1   7. I understand that the purpose of the review described in paragraph 5
2   is to give the United States a reasonable opportunity to determine
3   whether the information or materials submitted pursuant to paragraph 5
4   set forth any SCI or other information that is subject to classification
5   under E.O. 12356 or under any other Executive order or statute that
6   prohibits the unauthorized disclosure of information in the interest
7   of national security. I further understand that the Department or
8   Agency to which I have submitted materials will act upon them,
9   coordinating with the Intelligence Community or other agencies when
10 appropriate, and substantively respond to me within 30 working days
11 from date of receipt.

1   8. I have been advised and am aware that any breach of this Agreement
2   may result in the termination of any security clearances and SCI
3   access approvals that I may hold; removal from any position of
4   special confidence and trust requiring such clearances or access
5   approvals; and the termination of my employment or other relationships
6   with the Departments or Agencies that granted my security clearances
7   or SCI access approvals. In addition, I have been advised and am
8   aware that any unauthorized disclosure of SCI or other classified
9   information by me may constitute a violation or violations of United
10 States criminal laws, including the provisions of Sections 641, 793,
11 794, 798, and 952, Title 18, United States Code, the provisions

Figure 18-2. continued

12 of Section 783(b), Title 50, United States Code, and the provisions
13 of the Intelligence Identities Protection Act of 1982. I recognize
14 that nothing in this Agreement constitutes a waiver by the United
15 States of the right to prosecute me for any statutory violation.

1 9. I hereby assign to the United States Government all royalties,
2 remunerations, and emoluments that have resulted, will result, or
3 may result from any disclosure, publication, or revelation not
4 consistent with the terms of this Agreement.

1 10. I understand that the United States Government may seek any
2 remedy available to it to enforce this Agreement including, but not
3 limited to, application for a court order prohibiting disclosure of
4 information in breach of this Agreement.

1 11. I understand that all information to which I may obtain access
2 by signing this Agreement is now and will forever remain the property
3 of the United States Government. I do not now, nor will I ever,
4 possess any right, interest, title, or claim whatsoever to such
5 information. I agree that I shall return all materials which have
6 or may come into my possession or for which I am responsible
7 because of such access, upon demand by an authorized representative
8 of the United States Government or upon the conclusion of my employment
9 or other relationship with the Department or Agency that last
10 granted me either a security clearance or an SCI access approval.
11 If I do not return such materials upon request, I understand that
12 this may be a violation of Section 793, Title 18, United States
13 Code, a United States criminal law.

1 12. Unless and until I am released in writing by an authorized
2 representative of the United States Government, I understand that
3 all conditions and obligations imposed upon me by this Agreement
4 apply during the time I am granted access to SCI and at all times
5 thereafter.

1 13. Each provision of this Agreement is severable. If a court should
2 find any provision of this Agreement to be unenforceable, all other
3 provisions of this Agreement shall remain in full force and effect.

1 14. I have read this Agreement carefully and my questions, if any,
2 have been answered to my satisfaction. I acknowledge that the
3 briefing officer has made available to me Sections 641, 793, 794,
4 798, and 952 of Title 18, United States Code, Section 783(b) of
5 Title 50, United States Code, the Intelligence Identities Protection
6 Act of 1982, and Executive Order 12356 so that I may read them at
7 this time, if I so choose.

1 15. I make this Agreement without mental reservation or purpose of
2 evasion.

Figure 18-2. continued

_____   _____
SIGNATURE   DATE

_____   _____
SOCIAL SECURITY NUMBER   ORGANIZATION
(SEE NOTICE BELOW)

1   The execution of this Agreement was witnessed by the undersigned,
2   who, on behalf of the United States Government, agreed to its terms
3   and accepted it as a prior condition of authorizing access to
4   Sensitive Compartmented Information.

WITNESS and ACCEPTANCE:

_____   _____
SIGNATURE   DATE

_____
ORGANIZATION

SECURITY BRIEFING ACKNOWLEDGEMENT

I hereby acknowledge that I was briefed on the following SCI Special
Access Program(s):

_____
(Special Access Programs by Initials Only)

_____   _____
Signature of Individual Briefed   Date Briefed

_____   _____
Printed or Typed Name

_____   _____
Social Security Number (See Notice   Organization (Name and Address)
Below)

I certify that the above SCI access(es) were approved in accordance
with relevant SCI procedures and that the briefing presented by me on the
above date was also in accordance therewith.

_____   _____
Signature of Briefing Officer

_____   _____
Printed or Typed Name   Organization (Name and Address)

_____   _____
Social Security Number (See Notice
Below)

450

Figure 18-2. continued

SECURITY DEBRIEFING ACKNOWLEDGEMENT

Having been reminded of my continuing obligation to comply with the terms of this Agreement, I hereby acknowledge that I was debriefed on the following SCI Special Access Program(s):

_____
(Special Access Programs by Initials Only)

_____   _____
Signature of Individual Debriefed   Date Debriefed

_____   _____
Printed or Typed Name

_____   _____
Social Security Number (See Notice   Organization (Name and Address)
Below)

I certify that the debriefing presented by me on the above date was in accordance with relevant SCI procedures.

_____   _____
Signature of Debriefing Officer

_____   _____
Printed or Typed Name   Organization (Name and Address)

_____   _____
Social Security Number (See Notice
Below)

1 NOTICE: The Privacy Act, 5 U.S.C. 552a, requires that federal
2 agencies inform individuals, at the time information is solicited
3 from them, whether the disclosure is mandatory or voluntary, by
4 what authority such information is solicited, and what uses will
5 be made of the information. You are hereby advised that authority
6 for soliciting your Social Security Account Number (SSN) is Executive
7 Order 9397. Your SSN will be used to identify you precisely when
8 it is necessary to 1) certify that you have access to the information
9 indicated above, 2) determine that your access to the information
10 indicated has terminated, or 3) certify that you have witnessed
11 a briefing or debriefing. Although disclosure of your SSN is not
12 mandatory, your failure to do so may impede the processing of such
13 certifications or determinations.

(391557)

Figure 18-3. Current DOD SCI Agreement.

SENSITIVE COMPARTMENTED INFORMATION
NONDISCLOSURE AGREEMENT

An Agreement Between _____ and the United States

(Name—Printed or Typed) (Last, First, Middle Initial)

1. Intending to be legally bound, I hereby accept the obligations contained in this Agreement in consideration of my being granted access to information protected within Special Access Programs, hereinafter referred to in this Agreement as Sensitive Compartmented Information. I have been advised that Sensitive Compartmented Information involves or derives from intelligence sources or methods and is classified or classifiable under the standards of Executive Order 12356 or other Executive order or statute. I understand and accept that by being granted access to Sensitive Compartmented Information special confidence and trust shall be placed in me by the United States Government.

2. I hereby acknowledge that I have received a security indoctrination concerning the nature and protection of Sensitive Compartmented Information, including the procedures to be followed in ascertaining whether other persons to whom I contemplate disclosing this information have been approved for access to it, and I understand these procedures. I understand that I may be required to sign an appropriate acknowledgment upon being granted access to each category of Sensitive Compartmented Information. I further understand that all my obligations under this Agreement continue to exist with respect to such categories whether or not I am required to sign such an acknowledgment.

3. I have been advised that direct or indirect unauthorized disclosure, unauthorized retention, or negligent handling of Sensitive Compartmented Information by me could cause irreparable injury to the United States or be used to advantage by a foreign nation. I hereby agree that I will never divulge such information to anyone who is not authorized to receive it without prior written authorization from the United States Government department or agency (hereinafter Department or Agency) that last authorized my access to Sensitive Compartmented Information. I further understand that I am obligated by law and regulation not to disclose any classified information in an unauthorized fashion.

4. In consideration of being granted access to Sensitive Compartmented Information and of being assigned or retained in a position of special confidence and trust requiring access to Sensitive Compartmented Information, I hereby agree to submit for security review by the Department or Agency that last authorized my access to such information, all information or materials, including works of fiction, which contain or purport to contain any Sensitive Compartmented Information or description of activities that produce or relate to Sensitive Compartmented Information or that I have reason to believe are derived from Sensitive Compartmented Information, that I contemplate disclosing to any person not authorized to have access to Sensitive Compartmented Information or that I have prepared for public disclosure. I understand and agree that my obligation to submit such information and materials for review applies during the course of my access to Sensitive Compartmented Information and thereafter, and I agree to make any required submissions prior to discussing the information or materials with, or showing them to anyone who is not authorized to have access to Sensitive Compartmented Information. I further agree that I will not disclose such information or materials to any person not authorized to have access to Sensitive Compartmented Information until I

have received written authorization from the Department or Agency that last authorized my access to Sensitive Compartmented Information that such disclosure is permitted.

5. I understand that the purpose of the review described in paragraph 4 is to give the United States a reasonable opportunity to determine whether the information or materials submitted pursuant to paragraph 4 set forth any Sensitive Compartmented Information. I further understand that the Department or Agency to which I have submitted materials will act upon them, coordinating within the Intelligence Community when appropriate, and make a response to me within a reasonable time, not to exceed 30 working days from date of receipt.

6. I have been advised that any breach of this Agreement may result in the termination of my access to Sensitive Compartmented Information and retention in a position of special confidence and trust requiring such access, as well as the termination of my employment or other relationships with any Department or Agency that provides me with access to Sensitive Compartmented Information. In addition, I have been advised that any unauthorized disclosure of Sensitive Compartmented Information by me may constitute violations of United States criminal laws, including the provisions of Sections 793, 794, 798, and 952, Title 18, United States Code, and of Section 783(b), Title 50, United States Code. Nothing in this Agreement constitutes a waiver by the United States of the right to prosecute me for any statutory violation.

7. I understand that the United States Government may seek any remedy available to it to enforce this Agreement including, but not limited to, application for a court order prohibiting disclosure of information in breach of this Agreement. I have been advised that the action can be brought against me in any of the several appropriate United States District Courts where the United States Government may elect to file the action. Court costs and reasonable attorneys fees incurred by the United States Government may be assessed against me if I lose such action.

8. I understand that all information to which I may obtain access by signing this Agreement is now and will forever remain the property of the United States Government. I do not now, now will I ever, possess any right, interest, title, or claim whatsoever to such information. I agree that I shall return all materials, which may have come into my possession or for which I am responsible because of such access, upon demand by an authorized representative of the United States Government or upon the conclusion of my employment or other relationship with the United States Government entity providing me access to such materials. If I do not return such materials upon request, I understand this may be a violation of Section 793, Title 18, United States Code, a United States criminal law.

9. Unless and until I am released in writing by an authorized representative of the Department or Agency that last provided me with access to Sensitive Compartmented Information, I understand that all the conditions and obligations imposed upon me by this Agreement apply during the time I am granted access to Sensitive Compartmented Information, and at all times thereafter.

DD FORM 1847-1
83 JAN

Page 1

S/N 0102-LF-001-8475

Figure 18-3. continued

10. Each provision of this Agreement is severable. If a court should find any provision of this Agreement to be unenforceable, all other provisions of this Agreement shall remain in full force and effect. This Agreement concerns Sensitive Compartmented Information and does not set forth such other conditions and obligations not related to Sensitive Compartmented Information as may now or hereafter pertain to my employment by or assignment or relationship with the Department or Agency.

11. I have read this Agreement carefully and my questions, if any, have been answered to my satisfaction. I acknowledge that the briefing officer has made available Sections 793, 794, 798,

and 952 of Title 18, United States Code, and Section 783(b) of Title 50, United States Code, and Executive Order 12356, as amended, so that I may read them at this time, if I so choose.

12. I hereby assign to the United States Government all rights, title and interest, and all royalties, remunerations, and emoluments that have resulted, will result, or may result from any disclosure, publication, or revelation not consistent with the terms of this Agreement.

13. I make this Agreement without any mental reservation or purpose of evasion.

Signature _____   Organization _____

Printed/Typed Name (Last, First, Middle Initial) _____   SSN (See Notice Below) _____

Rank/Grade _____ Date (YY, MM, DD) _____   Billet Number (Optional) _____

FOR USE BY MILITARY AND GOVERNMENT CIVILIAN PERSONNEL

Witness and Acceptance:

The execution of this Agreement was witnessed by the undersigned who accepted it on behalf of the United States Government as a prior condition of access to Sensitive Compartmented Information.

Signature _____   Organization _____

Printed/Typed Name (Last, First, Middle Initial) _____   Date (YY, MM, DD) _____

FOR USE BY CONTRACTORS/CONSULTANTS/NON-GOVERNMENT PERSONNEL

Witness:

The execution of this Agreement was witnessed by the undersigned.

Signature _____   Organization _____

Printed/Typed Name (Last, First, Middle Initial) _____   Date (YY, MM, DD) _____

Acceptance:

This Agreement was accepted by the undersigned on behalf of the United States Government as a prior condition of access to Sensitive Compartmented Information.

Signature _____   Organization _____

Printed/Typed Name (Last, First, Middle Initial) _____   Date (YY, MM, DD) _____

Notice: The Privacy Act, 5 U.S.C. 552a, requires that federal agencies inform individuals, at the time information is solicited from them, whether the disclosure is mandatory or voluntary, by what authority such information is solicited, and what uses will be made of the information. You are hereby advised that authority for soliciting your Social Security Account Number (SSN) is Executive Order 9397. Your SSN will be used to identify you precisely when it is necessary to certify that you have access to the information indicated above. While your disclosure of SSN is not mandatory, your failure to do so may delay the processing of such certification.

NSCID No. 1 also makes the DCI responsible for developing policies and procedures for the protection of intelligence, intelligence sources, and methods from unauthorized disclosure. In carrying out these responsibilities, the DCI has issued several DCIDs concerning the dissemination of intelligence information to foreign governments, personnel matters, and physical security.

DCID 1/7, "Control of Dissemination of Intelligence Information," contains several provisions concerning the release of intelligence information to foreign governments. Such releases always require originator approval if the documents are to be released *in original form*. In addition, the information contained in classified intelligence documents originated by another component may be released if it bears no restrictive markings prohibiting such transfer and

1. no reference is made to the source documents upon which the released product is based;
2. the information is extracted or paraphrased to ensure that the source or manner of acquisition of the intelligence cannot be deduced or revealed in any manner; and
3. foreign release is made through established foreign disclosure channels and procedures.[35]

The directive also authorizes control markings in addition to the classification levels. ORCON, for example, is the abbreviation used to indicate that dissemination and extraction of information is controlled by the originator. This marking is employed "when unique source sensitivity factors, known to the originator, require strict compliance with third agency rule procedures, in addition to continuing knowledge and supervision on the part of the originator as to the extent to which the original document and information therein is disseminated." NOCONTRACT indicates that the document is not available to contractors or consultants, *regardless of their level of clearance*. PROPIN is short for "CAUTION—PROPRIETARY INFORMATION INVOLVED." It is used for foreign intelligence obtained from various sources in the U.S. private business sector and indicates that a source has a proprietary interest in the information or that the information could be used to the source's detriment.[36]

The most significant control marking with respect to foreign release is the NOFORN marking, which is short for "SPECIAL HANDLING REQUIRED— NOT RELEASABLE TO FOREIGN NATIONALS." According to DCID 1/7, this control marking may be used when the document could compromise "the status of relations with collaborating foreign governments or officials or jeopardize "the continuing viability of vital technical collection programs."[37]

One document labeled SECRET NOFORN ORCON PROPIN is the 1977 CIA study entitled *Israel: Foreign Intelligence and Security Services*. Its NOFORN control marking was assigned for a variety of reasons, including its likely impact on U.S.-Israeli relations. When the study was made public in 1979 after its seizure by Iranian militants from the U.S. Embassy in Tehran, it caused acute embarrassment to both the Israeli and the U.S. governments because it alleged that Israeli intelligence agencies had blackmailed, bugged, wiretapped, and offered bribes to U.S. government employees in an effort to gain sensitive information. An Israeli spokesman denounced the allegations as "ridiculous."[38]

As its title indicates, DCID 1/10 of January 18, 1982, "Security Policy Guidelines on Liaison Relationships with Foreign Intelligence Organizations and Foreign Security Services," establishes procedures concerning liaison relationships with foreign organizations, including the exchange of information.

Personnel and physical security have been the subject of several DCIDs, including DCID 1/14 of April 14, 1986, "Minimum Personnel Security Standards and Procedures Governing Eligibility for Access to Sensitive Compartmented Information"; DCID 1/19, "Uniform Procedures for Administrative Handling and Accountability of Sensitive Compartmented Information"; DCID 1/20, "Security Policy Concerning Travel and Assignment of Personnel with Access to Sensitive Compartmented Information"; and DCID 1/21, "Physical Security Standards for Sensitive Compartmented Information Facilities."

DCID 1/14 specifies that the "granting of access to SCI shall be controlled under the strictest application of the 'need-to-know' principle and all individuals who are given access are required, as a condition of gaining access, to sign an agreement that they will not disclose that information to persons not authorized to receive it."[39]

The directive also stipulates that, except under special circumstances (which include liaison arrangements), individuals to be given SCI access and their families must be U.S. citizens. It requires that intended recipients undergo a Special Background Investigation (SBI) before being awarded SCI access—an investigation that, until National Security Directive 63 was signed, was certain to be more extensive, in theory, than the Background Investigation required for a Top Secret clearance. After the initial investigation, a periodic reinvestigation is conducted at least every five years. Additionally, the directive requires all departments employing personnel with SCI access to institute security programs that involve security education, security supervision, and security review.[40] As of 1979, 115,000 individuals had SCI clearances, including 13,000 contractor employees.

According to DCID 1/14, items to be considered in determining eligibility for access to SCI include: loyalty, close relatives and associates, sexual considerations, cohabitation, undesirable character traits, financial irresponsibility, alcohol abuse, use of illegal drugs and drug abuse, emotional and mental disorders, law violations, security violations, and involvement in outside activities.[41]

DCID 1/19 concerns physical security issues such as the establishment of vault facilities for holding SCI; intrusion detection, communications, computer, and data-processing security systems relating to the transmission of SCI; and other physical security systems. It also regulates the location of vault facilities in exposed or combat areas. Thus, the directive requires that "all electronic equipment which is used to process or transmit Sensitive Compartmented Information (SCI) shall meet national standards for TEMPEST."[42]

DCID 1/20 specifies that "no person with access to SCI will be assigned or directed to participate in a hazardous activity, as defined herein, until he or she has been afforded a defensive security briefing and/or risk of capture briefing."[43] The directive also requires that all individuals with access to SCI who plan unofficial travel through hazardous countries must give prior notification of all planned travel, receive a defensive security briefing, immediately contact certain U.S. authorities if detained or subject to harassment, and report any unusual incidents to the appropriate security official upon return.[44]

On the basis of the Executive Orders, presidential directives, NSCIDs, and DCIDs, the Departments of Defense, State, Treasury, and others produce implementation directives and manuals. Some of these include DOD Instruction 5230.22, "Control of Dissemination of Foreign Intelligence"; DIA Regulation 50-10, "Control of Dissemination of Foreign Intelligence"; and DIA Manual 50-3, *Physical Security Standards for Construction of Sensitive Compartmented Information Facilities.*[45]

Since the abolition of the DCI Security Committee in 1981, two DCI committees have been concerned, in part, with security issues. The Committee on Imagery Requirements and Exploitation (COMIREX) dealt with the security of information about and derived from satellite imaging systems. The Information Handling Committee, established by DCID 1/4 of May 18, 1976, but now governed by DCID 3/14 of May 4, 1982, is responsible, in coordination with the DCI SCI Forum, for ensuring that the "security aspects of information handling systems are given appropriate consideration."[46]

MANAGING THE ANALYTIC PROCESS

Management of the analytic process takes two basic forms. Management of the production of national intelligence reports—including the National Intelligence Estimates (NIEs) and the Special National Intelligence Estimates (SNIEs)—is the most visible of these. But in addition to the national reports, the U.S. intelligence community, as is clear from Chapter 13, produces a vast amount of finished intelligence on military, economic, political, and scientific and technical topics. Although much of this intelligence is not "national" in the sense of being produced for national policymakers, it is important to the attainment of national security objectives.

Extensive intelligence production on atomic energy problems, space and weapons systems, and economic, social, and political matters provides input to national estimates as well as supplying the detailed information needed by officials in various departments. Thus, it is necessary to ensure that departmental intelligence production is consistent with national priorities.

As with other types of intelligence activities, management of the analytical process is handled through NSCIDs, DCIDs, various committees, and requirements documents. NSCIDs No. 1 and No. 3 are the general guidance documents for all aspects of intelligence production.

Section 6 of NSCID No. 1 defines national intelligence as intelligence required for the formulation of national security policy, concerning more than one department or agency, and transcending the exclusive competence of a single department or agency. It authorizes the DCI to produce national intelligence and disseminate it to the President, the NSC, and other appropriate U.S. government components. In addition, this section stipulates that national intelligence must carry a statement of abstention or dissent of any NFIB member or intelligence chief of a military department who disagrees with the intelligence findings.[47]

NSCID No. 3 of February 17, 1972, "Coordination of Intelligence Production," distinguishes between different types of intelligence—basic intelligence, current intelligence, departmental intelligence, interdepartmental intelligence, and national intelligence—and assigns responsibilities for the production of basic and current intelligence to the CIA and a variety of other agencies.

The directive also specifies the following requirements:

a. The Department of State shall produce political and sociological intelligence on all countries and economic intelligence on countries of the Free World.
b. The Department of Defense shall produce military intelligence. This production shall include scientific, technical and economic intelligence directly pertinent to the mission of the various components of the Department of Defense.
c. The Central Intelligence Agency shall produce economic, scientific and technical intelligence. Further, the Central Intelligence Agency may produce such other intelligence as may be necessary to discharge the statutory responsibilities of the Director of Central Intelligence.

The directive assigns to all NFIB members charged with the production of finished intelligence the responsibility of producing atomic energy intelligence. In addition, when an intelligence requirement is established for which there is no existing production capability, the DCI, in consultation with the NFIB, is responsible for determining which departments or agencies of the intelligence community can "best undertake the primary responsibility as a service of common concern."[48]

On the basis of NSCIDs No. 1 and No. 3, the DCI issues DCIDs in the 1/ and 3/ series to further implement the NSCIDs. The original DCIDs governing the national intelligence process were issued in July and September 1948. DCID 3/1 of July 8, 1948, "Standard Operating Procedures for Departmental Participation in the Production and Coordination of National Intelligence," required, except under exceptional circumstances, that, upon initiation of a report or estimate, the CIA inform departmental intelligence organizations of

1. the problem under consideration;
2. the nature and scope of the report or estimate involved;
3. the scheduled date of issuance of the first draft;
4. the requirements for departmental contributions ... ; and
5. the date upon which such departmental action should be completed.[49]

Under normal procedures the CIA was to prepare an initial draft and then furnish copies to departmental intelligence organizations with a request for review and preparation. If the comments received indicated differences of opinion, the CIA was instructed to arrange for an informal discussion with departmental personnel. The CIA was then to prepare a final draft and distribute it to departmental intelligence organizations for concurrence or statements of substantial dissent, which would be incorporated in the final paper.

DCID 3/2 of September 13, 1948, complemented 3/1. Entitled "Policy Governing Departmental Concurrences in National Intelligence Reports and Estimates," the directive specified three options for departmental intelligence organizations: concur, concur with comment, or dissent. It further stated the considerations that should be involved in choosing among the options.[50]

Subsequently, DCIDs 3/1 and 3/2 were superseded by DCID 3/5 of September 1, 1953, entitled "Production of National Intelligence Estimates." The directive reflected the changes that had occurred in the intervening years—particularly the establishment of the Board of National Estimates (BNE) and the Intelligence Advisory Committee (IAC)—and required the BNE to present a production program for NIEs and SNIEs to the IAC every year by January 1.[51]

In 1950 an Office of National Estimates (ONE) was established within the CIA's Directorate of Intelligence. This office, tasked with drafting national and special national estimates, consisted of the Board of National Estimates and its staff. The board consisted of between seven and twelve senior officials with expertise in particular areas who were initially drawn from academia and subsequently from the CIA.[52]

The board was serviced initially by fifty professional analysts, subsequently by thirty. In theory, the board reacted to specific requests from the NSC, and in emergencies this was often the case. Thus, several SNIEs were commissioned during the Cuban Missile Crisis. However, the subject of NIEs became routine on the basis of the board's judgment as to the requirements of policymakers.[53]

The process for drafting NIEs was established by DCID 3/1. It included initial drafting by BNE/ONE, interagency review, revision, and submission to the USIB with dissenting footnotes, if any. During the process, the BNE operated in collegial fashion, taking collective responsibility for the estimates produced and exercising collective judgment in approving them.[54]

The ONE suffered a decline of prestige and influence during the Nixon administration for a variety of reasons, including Henry Kissinger's unhappiness with its product. In June 1973, John Huizenga, the BNE Chairman, was forced to retire. DCI William Colby decided not to replace him and abolished the ONE.[55] Colby gave two reasons for his decision:

> One, I had some concern with the tendency to compromise differences and put out a document which was less sharp than perhaps was needed in certain situations. Second, I believed that I needed the advantage of some individuals who could specialize in some of the major problems not just as estimative problems but as broad intelligence problems. They could sit in my chair, so to speak, and look at the full range of an intelligence problem: Are we collecting enough? Are we processing the raw data properly? Are we spending too much money on it? Are we organized right to do the jobs?[56]

Colby created the National Intelligence Officer (NIO) system whereby specific individuals were held solely responsible for producing a particular estimate. In a 1987 memo on "The Integrity and Objectivity of National Foreign Intelligence Estimates," Richard J. Kerr, then Deputy Director for Intelligence, observed:

> The role of the *National Intelligence Officer*, in our judgement, is critical. An impartial estimative process requires the full expression of views by participating agencies and the clear identification for our consumers of areas of agreement and, often most importantly, disagreement. In order to fight what is often an unhealthy desire to reach consensus, the NIO must, above all, see himself as a manager of the process, the one who ensures that the tough questions are addressed, that consensus views represent real agreement, and not papered-over differences, and that minority views are fully expressed. It has been our experience that when the NIO subordinates this responsibility to the advocacy of a particular analytic line that the integrity of the estimative process suffers.[57]

NIOs are recruited mainly, but not exclusively, from the CIA and are specialists in a specific functional or geographic area. The number of NIOs, originally thirteen, went to eight, then seventeen, then the present twelve.

In the mid-1980s, in addition to three at-large NIOs, there were NIOs for Africa, East Asia, Europe, the Near East and South Asia, Latin America, the USSR, Counter-Terrorism, Science and Technology, Economics, General Purpose Forces, Strategic Programs, Warning, Foreign Denial and Intelligence Activities, and Narcotics.

The responsibilities of the NIO for Foreign Denial were summarized by one former holder of that position:

> The responsibilities for the National Intelligence Officer for Foreign Denial and Intelligence Activities focuses on the question and issue of what are foreign governments doing to deny us the capabilities of collecting certain intelligence, to analyze the degree to which that has been done, to make recommendations as to how that might be alleviated. The intelligence activities aspect of it is related to that, but also includes such items as foreign disinformation programs, what are people doing to make it difficult for us to get at the truth.[58]

Today, there are NIOs for Europe; Russia and Eurasia; the Near East and South Asia; Africa; East Asia; Latin America; Strategic Programs; General Purpose Forces; Warning; Economics; Science and Technology; and Global and Multilateral Issues.[59]

The NIOs with regional responsibilities focus on issues such as: emerging relationships among the states of the former Soviet Union; the Arab-Israeli peace process; Cuba and Haiti; Central European reform; emerging economies in Southeast Asia; and the transition to democracy in South Africa.[60]

The NIO for Strategic Programs is responsible for producing studies on the current and future strategic forces of the former Soviet states and China; C^3 and the safety of nuclear weapons; chemical, biological, and strategic missile programs throughout the world; treaty monitoring; and space programs. The portfolio of the NIO for General Purpose Forces includes worldwide conventional ground, air, and naval forces; regional military relationships; current and future advanced conventional weapons balances; and monitoring of assessments of conventional and chemical weapons arms control.[61]

The responsibilities of the NIO for Warning include producing analytical reports on regional conflicts triggered by ethnic, religious, or national differences; proliferation threats involving weapons of mass destruction; and transnational threats such as terrorism, narcotics, and technology transfer. The NIO for Economics is concerned with bilateral and regional economic developments; world economic trends; and economic reform and transition to market economies.[62]

The NIO for Science and Technology focuses on future technologies for weapons and military systems; nuclear materials disposition and disposal; information infrastructure issues; and technology sales and exports. The NIO for Global and Multilateral Issues reports on population and other demographic issues as well as environmental issues.[63]

Initially, NIOs were purposely not given a staff but were expected to draw on the resources of the CIA, the DIA, the INR, and other analytical units to produce the required estimates. On January 1, 1980, with the establishment of the National Intelligence Council (NIC), the NIOs were given not only a collective existence but also a staff.[64] The NIOs are specifically tasked with

1. becoming knowledgeable of what substantive intelligence questions policymakers want addressed;
2. drawing up the concept papers and terms of references for the NIE;
3. participating in the drafting and draft review of the NIE;
4. chairing coordinating sessions and making judgements on substantive questions in debate; and
5. ensuring that the final text accurately reflects the substantive judgement of the DCI.[65]

In addition to the NIEs, the NIOs are responsible for the SNIEs, Interagency Intelligence Memoranda (IIMs), and Special IIMs.

When created, the BNE/ONE was firmly a part of the CIA. Under DCI John McCone the BNE was attached to the DCI's office and made responsible to him alone. During the Carter administration, the NIOs became part of the National Foreign Assessment Center (NFAC) and hence placed under the direct control of the CIA's Deputy Director for National Foreign Assessment.[66]

One of the Reagan administration's earliest actions concerning intelligence was the downgrading of the NFAC to its previous identity—that is, the Directorate of Intelligence. With that change, the NIOs were once again placed under the control of the DCI. According to the Director of NFAC at the time, John McMahon, that was a decision that

the Director and I debated long and hard because at the time that happened I was in charge of national foreign assessments, and I did not want it to happen out of the symmetry of management. The Director wanted to have it because he felt that intelligence was so vital, so important that it should not be left to one person to manage and control. And so by having the NIOs separate and under himself, he could insure that he could get a balanced view coming out of the agency on one hand and the rest of [the] intelligence community and [the] NIOs on the other. And it was just his way of assuring that all alternative views bubbled to the top.[67]

Subsequently, the NIC was moved back within the Directorate of Intelligence. In 1992, however, DCI Robert Gates announced plans to move the NIC out of the CIA and into an independent facility. In addition, a post of Vice Chairman for Evaluation and a Subordinate Evaluation Group were established to conduct postmortems on previous estimates to assess the quality and accuracy of the work and to work with the NIOs to determine critical intelligence gaps. The estimates production program is managed by a Vice Chairman for Estimates, who is responsible for ensuring that all draft estimates encompass dissents and alternative scenarios to take into account potential dramatic unanticipated developments.[68]

Subordinate to the Vice Chairman for Estimates is the Analytic Group. The group is responsible for supervising the production of NIEs, the President's NIE Summary, NIE Update Memoranda, Intelligence Community Assessments, and NIC Memoranda. Its staff redrafts, edits, and monitors production of estimates from the initial outline through community coordination.[69]

Gates also transferred three intelligence community production committees— the Joint Atomic Energy Intelligence Committee (JAEIC), the Weapons and Space Systems Intelligence Committee (WSSIC), and the Scientific and Technical Intelligence Committee (STIC)—to the NIC.[70]

In 1965, DCID 3/3, "Production of Atomic Energy Intelligence," spelled out the responsibilities of the JAEIC. The directive, pursuant to NSCID No. 3, notes that atomic energy intelligence is the responsibility of all NFIB committees and further declares that "the mission of the Joint Atomic Energy Intelligence Committee (JAEIC) shall be to foster, develop and maintain a coordinated community approach to the problems in the field of atomic energy intelligence, to promote interagency liaison and to give impetus and community support to the efforts of individual agencies."[71]

The JAEIC's specific responsibilities are classified but certainly must include assessing the adequacy of the U.S. nuclear monitoring program, evaluating the methodology used in estimating the yield of foreign nuclear detonations, assessing major developments in the nuclear weapons programs of the nuclear powers, considering the possible impact of atomic power programs on proliferation in countries not yet possessing nuclear weapons, providing national decisionmakers with advice on the possible authorization of U.S. foreign sales in the nuclear energy area, providing warning of a country "going nuclear," and assessing the regional impact of such an event.

The WSSIC was created in 1956 as the Guided Missile Intelligence Committee and subsequently became the Guided Missile and Astronautics Intelligence Committee (GMAIC). According to DCID 3/4, "Production of Guided Missiles and Astronautics Intelligence," the committee's membership consists of representatives of all NFIB agencies plus Army, Navy, and Air Force representatives. Its Chairman is named by the DCI with approval of the NFIB, and the CIA provides secretarial support. In addition to coordinating the guided missile and astronautics intelligence activities of the intelligence community, during the Cold War the WSSIC performed technical studies on Soviet missiles as *inputs* to the NIEs. These papers were coordinated in the same manner as NIEs but were directed at informing the intelligence community.[72]

Also involved in directing production is the Economic Intelligence Committee (EIC). At one time, the functions of the EIC were governed by DCID 15/1, "Production and Coordination of Foreign Economic Intelligence." The directive allocated primary production responsibilities for economic intelligence to the Department of State's INR and the CIA. The former was responsible for economic intelligence for all non-Soviet bloc countries, the latter for Soviet bloc economic intelligence. The EIC conducted periodic review of the allocations and interpreted the provisions of the directive in areas of common or overlapping interest.[73]

The present committee plays a significant role in establishing economic reporting requirements. It also probably plays a role in coordinating the production of economic intelligence, especially since the relative importance of such intelligence relative to military and political intelligence has increased in recent years.

Similar to the NIO system is the Defense Intelligence Officer (DIO) system. There are DIOs for Africa; East Asia and the Pacific; Latin America; the Middle East, South Asia, and Terrorism; Europe; Russia and Eurasia; Military Forces; Acquisition Support; Counterproliferation; and Arms Control. DIOs serve as senior advisers to the Director and Deputy Director of the DIA and prepare specialized intelligence reports on issues that cut across the assigned responsibilities of more than one element of the DIA. [74]

Management of intelligence production is also partially carried out by means of the requirements documents discussed in Chapter 16.

NOTES

1. Ronald Reagan, "Executive Order 12356: National Security Information," April 2, 1982, in *Federal Register* 47, 66 (April 6, 1982): 14874–84 at 14874–75.

2. *Documents from the U.S. Espionage Den (52): U.S.S.R., The Aggressive East, Section 3-2* (Tehran: Muslim Students Following the Line of the Imam, n.d.), pp. 46–94; Army Regulation 381-47, "U.S. Army Offensive Counterintelligence Operations," May 15, 1982, p. B-1.

3. Philip Agee, *Inside the Company: CIA Diary* (New York: Stonehill, 1975), p. 68; *Documents from the U.S. Espionage Den (52): U.S.S.R., The Aggressive East, Section 4*, p. 28.

4. NFIB Security Committee, "Sensitive Compartmented Information: Characteristics and Security Requirements," June 1984, p. 1.

5. Ibid., p. 3; National Security Directive 63, "Single Scope Background Investigations," October 21, 1991.

6. U.S. Strategic Command, USSTRATCOM Administrative Instruction 321-28, "Sensitive Compartmented Information (SCI) Personnel Security Operating Policy and Procedures," June 30, 1992, pp. 25–27.

7. NFIB Security Committee, "Sensitive Compartmented Information: Characteristics and Security Requirements," p. 3; Defense Intelligence Agency, *Physical Security Standards for Construction of Sensitive Compartmented Information Facilities* (DIAM 50-3) (Washington, D.C.: DIA, February 1990).

8. Quoted in David Wise, *The Politics of Lying: Government Deception, Secrecy and Power* (New York: Vintage, 1973), p. 86.

9. Ibid.

10. Ronald Lewin, *The American Magic: Codes, Ciphers and the Defeat of Japan* (New York: Farrar, Straus & Giroux, 1982), p. 17; Anthony Cave-Brown, *The Last Hero* (New York: Times Books, 1982), p. 193.

11. James Bamford, *The Puzzle Palace: A Report on NSA, America's Most Secret Agency* (Boston: Houghton Mifflin, 1982), p. 314; Nigel West, *MI6: British Secret Intelligence Service Operations, 1909–1945* (London: Weidenfeld & Nicolson, 1983), p. 163; Cave-Brown, *The Last Hero*, p. 182; David Martin, *Wilderness of Mirrors* (New York: Harper & Row, 1980), p. 15.

12. Bamford, *The Puzzle Palace*, p. 314.

13. F. W. Winterbotham, *The Ultra Secret* (New York: Harper & Row, 1974), pp. 88–89.

14. *Procedures for Handling ULTRA DEXTER Intelligence in the CBI* (Rear Echelon, HQ U.S. Army Forces, China, Burma, India Theater, March 22, 1944), SRH-046, RG 457, Military Reference Branch, U.S. National Archives.

15. Ibid.

16. Wise, *The Politics of Lying*, p. 83; Jack Anderson, "Syrians Strive to Oust Arafat as PLO Chief," *Washington Post*, November 10, 1982, p. D-22; Bob Woodward, "ACDA Aide Faulted on Security," *Washington Post*, November 4, 1986, pp. A1, A16; National Intelligence Council, *National Intelligence Daily (Cable)*, December 13, 1983.

17. Bamford, *The Puzzle Palace*, p. 120.

18. Bob Woodward, "Messages of Activists Intercepted," *Washington Post*, October 13, 1975, pp. 1, 14; Seymour Hersh, *The Price of Power: Kissinger in the Nixon White House* (New York: Summit, 1983), p. 183.

19. Woodward, "Messages of Activists Intercepted."

20. Seymour Hersh, *"The Target Is Destroyed": What Really Happened to Flight 007 and What America Knew About It* (New York: Random House, 1986), p. 4; Private information.

21. James Ott, "Espionage Trial Highlights CIA Problems," *Aviation Week & Space Technology*, November 27, 1978, pp. 21–22; Gregory A. Fossedal, "U.S. Said to Be Unable to Verify Missile Ban," *Washington Times*, November 18, 1987, p. A6; Dale Van Atta, "The Death of the State Secret," *New Republic*, February 18, 1985, pp. 20–23.

22. William Burrows, *Deep Black: Space Espionage and National Security* (New York: Random House, 1987), p. 23; Bob Woodward, *Veil: The Secret Wars of the CIA, 1981–1987* (New York: Simon & Schuster, 1987), pp. 221–24, 402–3; Private information.

23. U.S. Strategic Command, *Organization and Functions Manual*, August 17, 1992, p. 61; Private information.

24. HQ USAF, ACS, I, INOI 205-4, "Designation of Special Security Officer (SSO), TK Control Officer (TCO), Gamma Control Officer (GCO), and Bravo Control Officer (BCO)," March 15, 1985, p. 2.

25. Naval Technical Intelligence Center, NAVTECHINTCEN C 3120.1C, *NAVTECHINTCEN Organization and Regulations Manual*, May 1990, p. 2-71.

26. Richard Nixon, "Executive Order 11652, Classification and Declassification of National Security Information and Material," *Federal Register* 57, 48 (March 10, 1972): 5209–18; Jimmy Carter, "Executive Order 12065, National Security Information," *Federal Register* 43, 128 (July 3, 1978): 28950–61; Reagan, "Executive Order 12356, National Security Information."

27. Reagan, "Executive Order 12356, National Security Information," p. 14876.

28. Ibid., pp. 14877–78.

29. Ibid., p. 14881.

30. Department of Defense Instruction 5230.21, "Protection of Classified National Security Council and Intelligence Information," March 15, 1982; NSDD-84, "Safeguarding National Security Information," March 11, 1983.

31. NSDD-19, "Protection of Classified National Security Council and Intelligence Information," January 12, 1982.

32. Ibid.; William Clark, "Implementation of NSDD-19 on Protection of Classified National Security Council and Intelligence Information" (Washington, D.C.: Office of the Assistant to the President for National Security Affairs, February 2, 1982).

33. U.S. Comptroller General, General Accounting Office, *Information and Personnel Security: Data on Employees Affected by Federal Security Programs* (Washington, D.C.: GAO, 1986), p. 2.

34. NSCID No. 1, "Basic Duties and Responsibilities," February 17, 1972, *Declassified Documents Reference System (DDRS)* 1976-167G.

35. DCID 1/7, "Control of Dissemination of Intelligence Information," May 4, 1981, enclosure to Department of Defense Directive 5230.22, "Control of Dissemination of Intelligence Information," April 1, 1982, pp. 2–3.

36. Ibid., pp. 3–4.

37. Ibid., p. 4.

38. Scott Armstrong, "Israelis Have Spied on U.S., Secret Papers Show," *Washington Post,* February 1, 1982, pp. A1, A18; "Israel Calls Report of CIA Findings Ridiculous," *Washington Post,* February 3, 1982, p. 10.

39. DCID 1/14, "Minimum Personnel Security Standards and Procedures Governing Eligibility for Access to Sensitive Compartmented Information," April 4, 1986, Annex A.

40. Ibid.

41. Ibid., p. 7.

42. Defense Intelligence Agency, *Physical Security Standards for Sensitive Compartmented Information Facilities* (DIAM 50-3) (Washington, D.C.: DIA, 1980), p. i; Defense Intelligence Agency, *Physical Security Standards for Construction of Sensitive Compartmented Information Facilities* (DIAM 50-3) (Washington, D.C.: DIA, 1990); USAF AFR 200-7, "Sensitive Compartmented Information (SCI) Security System," October 16, 1992.

43. DCID 1/20, "Security Policy Concerning Travel and Assignment of Personnel with Access to Sensitive Compartmented Information (SCI)," July 20, 1987, p. 2.

44. Ibid.

45. Ibid., entire text; Department of Defense Instruction 5230.22, "Control of Dissemination of Intelligence Information"; Defense Intelligence Agency Regulation 50-10, "Control of Dissemination of Foreign Intelligence," May 11, 1977.

46. DCID 1/4, "Intelligence Information Handling Committee," May 18, 1976; DCID 3/14, "Intelligence Information Handling Committee," May 14, 1982, updated January 1987.

47. NSCID No. 1, "Basic Duties and Responsibilities."

48. NSCID No. 3, "Coordination of Intelligence Production," February 17, 1972, *DDRS* 1976-253E.

49. DCID 3/1, "Standard Operating Procedures for Departmental Participation in the Production and Coordination of National Intelligence," July 8, 1948.

50. DCID 3/2, "Policy Governing Departmental Concurrences in National Intelligence Reports and Estimates," September 13, 1948.

51. DCID 3/5, "Production of National Intelligence Estimates," September 1, 1953.

52. Lawrence Freedman, *U.S. Intelligence and the Soviet Strategic Threat* (Princeton, N.J.: Princeton University Press, 1986), p. 31.

53. Ibid.

54. DCID 3/1, "Standard Operating Procedures for Departmental Participation in the Production and Coordination of National Intelligence."

55. Freedman, *U.S. Intelligence and the Soviet Strategic Threat,* p. 54.

56. Ibid.

57. Richard J. Kerr, Deputy Director for Intelligence, Memorandum for Chairman, National Intelligence Council, Subject: The Integrity and Objectivity of National Foreign Intelligence Estimates, May 12, 1987, p. 1. The memo is reprinted in U.S. Congress, Senate Select Committee on Intelligence, *Nomination of Robert M. Gates, Volume 2* (Washington, D.C.: U.S. Government Printing Office, 1992), pp. 106–8.

58. *United States of America v Samuel L. Morrison,* U.S. District Court, Baltimore, Case Y-84-00455, October 8–16, 1985, p. 1025.

59. National Intelligence Council, *A Guide to the National Intelligence Council,* 1994, p. 4.

60. Ibid., pp. 16–27.

61. Ibid., pp. 28–31.

62. Ibid., pp. 32–35.

63. Ibid., pp. 36–39.

64. U.S. Congress, House Select Committee on Intelligence, *U.S. Intelligence Agencies and Activities: Fiscal Costs and Procedures, Part 1* (Washington, D.C.: U.S. Government Printing Office, 1975), p. 389; U.S. Congress, House Committee on Foreign Affairs, *The Role of Intelligence in the Foreign Policy Process* (Washington, D.C.: U.S. Government Printing Office, 1980), p. 135.

65. U.S. Congress, House Committee on Foreign Affairs, *The Role of Intelligence in the Foreign Policy Process,* p. 230.

66. Freedman, *U.S. Intelligence and the Soviet Strategic Threat,* p. 31.

67. U.S. Congress, Senate Select Committee on Intelligence, *Nomination of John N. McMahon* (Washington, D.C.: U.S. Government Printing Office, 1982), pp. 48–49.

68. Robert M. Gates, Director of Central Intelligence, "Statement on Change in CIA and the Intelligence Community," April 1, 1989, pp. 21, 22.

69. National Intelligence Council, *A Guide to the National Intelligence Council,* pp. 39, 44.

70. Gates, "Statement on Change in CIA and the Intelligence Community," p. 21.

71. DCID 3/3, "Production of Atomic Energy Intelligence," April 23, 1965, *DDRS* 1980-131G.

72. DCID 3/4, "Production of Guided Missile and Astronautics Intelligence," April 23, 1965, *DDRS* 1980-132A; John Prados, *The Soviet Estimate: U.S. Intelligence Analysis and Russian Military Strength* (New York: Dial, 1982), p. 202.

73. DCID 15/1, "Production and Coordination of Foreign Economic Intelligence," September 14, 1954, *DDRS* 1980-129E.

74. *Department of Defense Telephone Directory, August 1994* (Washington, D.C.: U.S. Government Printing Office, 1994), p. 0-24.

19
ISSUES

The dramatic changes in the international environment since 1988—the collapse of the Soviet Union, the coming of democracy to Eastern Europe, the increased threat of advanced weapons proliferation, and the heightened concern with economic issues—have refocused attention on some long-standing issues concerning intelligence, as well as raising new ones. Issues facing the U.S. intelligence community as a new century approaches include organization and structure, the role of human intelligence, economic espionage, support to military operations, requirements and budgets, and secrecy.

ORGANIZATION AND STRUCTURE

Over the years there have been numerous suggestions for reorganization of various parts of the intelligence community. Suggestions have included creating a Director of National Intelligence (DNI) separate from the head of the CIA with an office in the White House, separating the analytical and clandestine operations sides of the CIA, creating a separate covert action agency, establishing a central collection agency (to handle both technical and human collection), establishing national HUMINT and imagery agencies parallel to the National Security Agency, and having the DIA absorb the military service intelligence units. Many of these ideas were examined during the Carter administration's PRM-11 review of "Intelligence Structure and Mission," incorporated in proposed 1980 legislation, suggested during hearings on intelligence reorganization in 1991 and 1992, or written into proposed 1992 legislation produced by the House Permanent Select Committee on Intelligence and the Senate Select Committee on Intelligence.[1]

The notion of separating the head of the intelligence community from direct control of the CIA has been advocated by numerous observers and professional intelligence officers and was included as a provision of the National Intelligence Act of 1980. It also was a key aspect of the ultimately unsuccessful 1992 intelligence reorganization legislation proposed by Representative David McCurdy and Senator David Boren, Chairmen of the congressional intelligence oversight committees. Advocates have viewed such a separation as a means of placing the head of intelligence closer to the President (both physically and personally). Under this arrangement, the Director of National Intelligence could focus on the major intelligence issues and serve as an impartial arbiter of intelligence decisions.

However, for a variety of reasons such a step would be a step backward for centralized direction of the intelligence community. The likely outcome of the separation would be a Director of National Intelligence with far less actual power than the present DCI—for the result would be a DNI with no resources trying to establish control over the CIA, the NSA, and the DIA, all of which would have far more resources and influence than the DNI as result of their control of collection and analytical resources. It was acknowledged by the 1975 Murphy Commission that "to function as the President's intelligence adviser, it is essential that the DCI have immediate access to and control over the CIA facilities necessary to assemble, evaluate and reach conclusions about intelligence in all functional fields including political, economic, military and scientific subjects."[2] It is of some significance that during the Cuban Missile Crisis DCI John McCone abandoned use of his Washington office to remain at the Langley headquarters.

Separation of the DCI from the CIA could also retard the flow of information through the intelligence community—adding the Director of the CIA to the heads of the NSA and the Navy as guardians of "their" information. In addition, by creating a position of Director of National Intelligence, the position of Director of the CIA would be sharply lowered in prestige, which would further exacerbate rivalries among the CIA, the DIA, and the NSA as each fought to place itself at the top of the intelligence hierarchy.

The President's intelligence director also needs to have significant control over decisions concerning the development and tasking of technical collection systems and other aspects of CIA activities (particularly covert action and analysis)—control that can only come if those functions are performed by an organization of which he is the head.

The 1992 Boren-McCurdy legislation would have stripped the CIA of any role in the development of technical collection systems. A National Imagery Agency to be established within the Department of Defense would have been made responsible for all aspects of imagery collection and analysis—from determination of collection system capabilities, to tasking and operation of the systems, to processing of the imagery. Similar responsibilities for SIGINT collection and processing were assigned by the legislation to NSA. Such an approach would have established czars for the two major technical collection disciplines. Despite language in the legislation indicating that these czars would be responsible to the Director of National Intelligence, the agency heads' operational control over all aspects of their collection activities would have placed them in positions of unique power and diluted national control of those important assets. Such national control is necessary because the purpose of constructing and operating collection systems is to provide useful political, military, and economic intelligence to *consumers*—including the President, the National Security Adviser and his staff, the Department of State, and several other departments and agencies—not to develop the most advanced collection systems for their own sake, produce the maximum number of high-resolution photographs, or maximize the volume of electronic intercepts.

Instead of assigning responsibilities for procurement decisions and tasking to DOD agencies, any new guidelines or legislation affecting intelligence organizations should be designed to strengthen national control. Rather than the Secretary of Defense making decisions concerning procurement of satellite reconnaissance systems based on the NREC's recommendation, it should be the DCI who makes the decisions—with the Secretary of Defense having the right to appeal to the President. In addition, the DCI should insure that the imagery and tasking authorities act as true arbiters of intelligence requirements and not captives of their military representatives.

Unfortunately, developments since 1992—the transfer of COMIREX's functions to the Central Imagery Office within the Department of Defense and the location of the National SIGINT Committee at NSA—indicate that there will be greater Defense Department, and less civilian, influence in tasking decisions.

Proposals to strengthen the DIA by eliminating the military service intelligence units have been based in part on the argument that the existence of the service intelligence units inhibits the DIA from fulfilling its intended role—that is, to insure that the parochial interests of the military services do not determine the content of intelligence analysis. In addition, it is argued that because of career advancement pressures, the best analysts often stay in the military services rather than work in the DIA.[3]

Under congressional and budgetary pressure, the individual services and unified commands have taken steps to consolidate intelligence operations into single commands or agencies. In addition, DIA control over military service intelligence production has increased. The DIA has also, as noted above, taken over control of military HUMINT operations. However, there would be drawbacks to any attempt to completely eliminate individual service intelligence organizations. As a study team from the Office of the Secretary of Defense noted, such a proposal may not be politically feasible—one can imagine an intense and unified opposition by the JCS to any attempt to strip the military services of their intelligence capabilities. And there is some rationale for having intelligence units responsive to those who most need the information. Thus, although there is reason to fear that letting the Navy estimate foreign naval capabilities could bias the estimate, it is also understandable that a Chief of Naval Operations with responsibility for managing the U.S. naval effort and recommending naval policies would want to have some control over intelligence production concerning naval affairs. Further, the DIA, as an arm of the Defense Department, has its own parochial interests or biases that could influence its product—as indicated by the various disputes the agency has had with the CIA. Eliminating the potentially competing views of the different services might, on some occasions, result in a "unanimous" military intelligence viewpoint not justified by the data.

At this point perhaps the best model of service intelligence consolidation is that of the Navy—which has reduced the six intelligence organizations that existed in September 1991 to two—the Office of Naval Intelligence for all non-SIGINT activities and the Naval Security Group Command for SIGINT collection, with both organizations based in the Washington area. At present the Army and Air Force still maintain separate Assistant/Deputy Chief of Staff organizations in addition to their main intelligence organizations (with the Air Force organization headquartered in San Antonio, Texas) and S&T centers located in Charlottesville, Virginia, and Dayton, Ohio, respectively.

Although the Army and Air Force, unlike the Navy, have consolidated their SIGINT operations with other aspects of intelligence activities (the Army in 1977, the Air Force in 1991), such a consolidation may have some drawbacks. Because SIGINT operations in a consolidated organization will represent the bulk of the budget and manpower it is possible that such activities would be the primary focus of attention to the neglect of other activities. This result could pose a problem if SIGINT became the primary path to advancement in such organizations. When the Air Force Intelligence Command (AFIC) was formed in 1991, consolidating the Foreign Technology Division (FTD) of the Air Force Systems Command, the Air Force Special Activities Center (AFSAC), and the Electronic Security Command (ESC), the Commander and Deputy Commander of ESC became the AFIC Commander and Deputy Commander, while another ESC official was assigned as Commander of the renamed FTD.

THE HUMINT FACTOR

In the aftermath of the Persian Gulf War, discoveries about the nature of the Iraqi nuclear program led one analyst to observe that "in spite of the massive intelligence-gathering means at the disposal of several nations, including overhead reconnaissance and electronic intercepts, there seems to have been serious deficiencies in the general assessment of Iraq's nuclear program."[4]

Some have suggested that such deficiencies were the result of an inadequate devotion to human intelligence and an overreliance on technical collection, particularly imagery and signals intelligence. In addition, it has been suggested that the collapse of the Soviet Union, as well as the increased attention to terrorist and narcotics targets, has sharply decreased the value of the technical collections systems designed principally with the Soviet target in mind.

In late 1992 it was reported that "U.S. intelligence professionals who have been stymied in their attempts to monitor and curb proliferation through satellite intelligence gathering and export controls, are turning anew to developing networks of agents and informants." In particular, the report claimed that the CIA is working "at a frenzied pace" to establish human intelligence networks in hard-to-penetrate countries such as Iraq and North Korea.[5]

Potentially, HUMINT can provide a level of understanding, including of foreign nuclear weapons programs, drug cartels, and terrorist groups, that may be unattainable from technical collection. Human sources can provide not only information on intentions but also an integrated overview of a program (its people, facilities, suppliers, and progress) that could be extraordinarily difficult to piece together by relying on technical collection. Further, human sources can report on what is inside facilities and can acquire and pass on documents and hardware of great value.[6]

Although it is important to acknowledge the potential and demonstrated value of HUMINT—and the value of improving HUMINT collection—in dealing with the full-range of intelligence targets, it is equally important not to overestimate either the uniqueness or feasibility of successful HUMINT operations.

One proposition about HUMINT, repeated ad nauseum and usually taken as self-evident, is that HUMINT can provide information about intentions while technical collection cannot. However, as former DCI Stansfield Turner has written:

> As a general proposition, that is simply not true. Electronic intercepts may be even more useful in discerning intentions. For instance, if a foreign official writes about plans in a message and the United States intercepts it, or if he discusses it and we record it with a listening device, those verbatim intercepts are more likely to be more reliable than second-hand reports from an agent. Not only do agents have biases and human fallibilities, there is always the risk that an agent is, after all, working for someone else.[7]

Furthermore, as desirable as HUMINT may be, it may be impossible to attain sufficiently reliable human intelligence from major targets—whether they be nations (e.g., Iraq and North Korea), terrorist groups, or drug cartels. It should not be forgotten that along with notable U.S. HUMINT successes there have been some significant failures. Thus, it has been reported that the CIA networks in East Germany and Cuba were heavily penetrated by the security services of those nations. Local conditions—the isolation of the country, the thoroughness and brutality of the security services, and a lack of U.S. diplomatic representation—may preclude successful recruitment. Recruiting a source in the Pakistani nuclear program will not be as difficult, probably by several orders of magnitude, as recruiting a source in the North Korean program. Penetration of some terrorist groups and drug cartels may also be extremely difficult because membership may be limited to relatives and those they have known for long periods of time.[8]

Furthermore, the unpredictable nature of international events after the collapse of the Soviet Union reduces the value of intelligence collection programs of limited flexibility. Imagery satellites in low-earth orbit routinely pass over almost every target on earth. The U.S. constellation of SIGINT satellites in geosynchronous orbit can be used to intercept communications from virtually anywhere in the world. HUMINT sources, in contrast, have to be developed over a period of time. As a Joint Chiefs of Staff publication has noted, "HUMINT is not surged easily or with certainty. Relatively long lead times are required to establish human intelligence resources and systems."[9]

Thus, when a crisis in the former Yugoslavia or Somalia develops in a short period of time, what was a low-priority target quickly becomes a high-priority target. Often, the new target may not have been the focus, with good reason, of a high-priority HUMINT effort, and thus such intelligence may be limited for a substantial period of time—including the entire period during which the area is of major concern to the United States.

ECONOMIC INTELLIGENCE VS. INDUSTRIAL ESPIONAGE

Economic intelligence—intelligence concerned with the structure and vulnerabilities of foreign economies, the distribution and availability of key resources, international trade patterns, and the domestic economic and foreign trade policies of foreign governments—has been a concern of U.S. intelligence since at least World War II. In 1948 an Economic Intelligence Committee (EIC) was established under the Intelligence Advisory Committee (IAC). The EIC has continued to operate over the past forty-six years—under the IAC and its successors, including the present National Foreign Intelligence Board. The greater present-day concern with economic intelligence is indicated by the CIA's 1993 decision to produce a daily Top Secret-Codeword economic intelligence report.[10]

The economic intelligence traditionally collected by the U.S. intelligence community has supported policymaker decisions concerning the utility and specifics of economic sanctions, foreign aid programs, energy policy, the stockpiling of key resources, and international trade strategy.

Revelations concerning the economic espionage activities of the French Directorate General of External Security and the intelligence services of other friendly nations as well as the increased focus on economic competitiveness have led to suggestions to expand the scope of the intelligence community's economic intelligence effort. Some have even proposed that the intelligence community begin acquiring the trade secrets, whether industrial processes or marketing strategies, of foreign companies, with the information to be passed to U.S. corporations. In his February 1993 confirmation hearings, DCI James Woolsey acknowledged that industrial espionage was "the hottest current topic in intelligence policy."[11] Former DCI Stansfield Turner has written that "the preeminent threat to U.S. national security now lies in the economic sphere. ... We must, then, redefine 'national security' by assigning economic strength greater preeminence." Turner went on to argue that "the United States would have no compunction about stealing military secrets to help it manufacture better weapons" and that if economic strength is to be "recognized as a vital component of national security, parallel with military power, why should America be concerned about stealing and employing economic secrets?"[12]

However, even the *theoretical* case for U.S. intelligence involvement in industrial espionage—whether employing human or technical collection methods—rests on several dubious propositions. Perhaps the most dubious proposition is that foreign industrial and commercial activities are a threat. Even those with the dimmest memories of economics courses should remember that competition is a means of encouraging better products and that such competition benefits the consumer. In addition, the benefits of economic competition transcend national borders. For example, large sales of a Japanese car in the United States benefit not only the American consumers who purchase it but also U.S. auto parts companies that sell to the Japanese manufacturer and U.S. workers employed at the Japanese manufacturer's U.S. plants.[13]

But aside from the weakness of the underlying assumptions used to justify a policy of industrial espionage, there are both practical and moral problems with the policy itself. Two related problems would be deciding on the targets of U.S. industrial espionage activities and the companies that would benefit from the product of those activities. Even if decisions were made in what was believed to be the national interest, the choices would represent a back-door national industrial policy in which the government deemed which sectors or corporations were worthy of government aid. More likely, decisions would be affected by a variety of political considerations, with political pull being at least as important as any consideration of perceived merit.[14]

Another complicating factor is that there has been a blurring of the line between U.S. and foreign companies. There are U.S. companies with foreign subsidiaries and foreign firms with U.S. subsidiaries. In addition, U.S. corporations may undertake joint ventures with foreign corporations—as AT&T, Motorola, and Apple did in February 1993 with three foreign companies. Such ambiguities would further complicate the decisionmaking process with respect to which companies would benefit from industrial espionage activities.[15]

Yet another obstacle is the intelligence community's desire to protect sources and methods. Industrial espionage could be conducted by HUMINT, SIGINT, and imagery assets—all of which the intelligence community makes significant efforts to protect. There would undoubtedly be concern about disclosing *current* intelligence, derived from U.S. collection operations, to organizations outside the U.S. government, particularly those with no experience in protecting such information.

A fifth reason to question the wisdom of an industrial espionage program is the need to insure the intelligence community's ability to deal with true national security matters—such as proliferation, terrorism, regional crises, and developments in key foreign countries. The intelligence services will also have to find a way to deal with the uncertainty of the post–Cold War world, where the adversaries and intelligence targets can shift rapidly. Given that the intelligence community is experiencing, and will probably continue to experience, budget and personnel cuts, it seems advisable to insure that resources are first available to deal with true national security problems.

There are also questions of legality and morality. Not only might dissemination of such intelligence place government officials in violation of the Trade Secrets Act, but the U.S. government might become the target of civil litigation in U.S. and foreign courts. Plaintiffs could include companies (or their shareholders) who do not receive intelligence that their competitors receive as well as companies whose trade secrets or intellectual property were stolen. In addition, U.S. companies that receive information might be subject to litigation—either in the United States or abroad.[16]

Finally, adopting a policy of industrial espionage would be both hypocritical and immoral. To object to foreign nations stealing U.S. corporate secrets while doing the same would obviously be hypocritical. So would asking a country to adopt a free-trade policy and eliminate tariffs so that a U.S. company could import products that might have been developed using technology stolen from a company of that very country. But the best reason for not adopting such a policy is its clear immorality. However much one might talk about "economic security" or "leveling the playing field" or "commercial intelligence," what is involved is outright theft and the violation of property rights.

The proper role of the CIA is in the area of counter–industrial espionage—to provide information on the industrial espionage activities of foreign intelligence services and undertake appropriate actions to neutralize those activities. In a November 1993 speech, DCI James Woolsey indicated that this would be the CIA's role. He told a group of industrial leaders, "The CIA is not going to be in the business [of] spying on foreign corporations for the benefit of domestic business." However, the CIA would "pay careful attention to those who are spying on American companies and bribing their way to contracts they cannot win on the merits, to the disadvantage of American companies and American workers."[17]

Even the notion of providing intelligence on economic and market trends and emerging technologies to companies or trade associations should be looked upon with skepticism. Such a proposal would seem to rest on the same fallacious notion as that behind the idea of a national industrial policy—that government employees, who would place none of their own resources at risk, have a better understanding of the market and forthcoming technologies than those actually involved in a specific industrial sector. As a senior corporate executive has observed, "If a company needs the CIA to tell them what's going on in their area of business, then they're already in Chapter 11."[18]

SUPPORT TO MILITARY OPERATIONS

In his April 1992 farewell message to NSA employees, outgoing Director William Studeman observed, "The military account is basic to NSA as a defense agency, and lack of utter faithfulness to this fact will court decline." Studeman went on to label Support to Military Operations (SMO) as one of the legs "on which NSA must stand."[19]

One consequence of Operation Desert Storm was that attention to the needs of the military, particularly military commanders, increased dramatically. In the aftermath of that Operation, General Norman H. Schwartzkopf told the Senate Armed Services Committee, "The intelligence community should be asked to come up with a system that will, in fact, be capable of delivering a real-time product to a theater commander when he requests that."[20]

Subsequent to that testimony the Department of Defense issued the final version of its report on *Conduct of the Persian Gulf War*. The report noted "a lack of available assets in disseminating national and theater intelligence" to tactical commanders. "Tactical intelligence dissemination," it went on, "was constrained by a lack of sophisticated and secure communications below division level."[21] In addition, Operations Desert Shield and Desert Storm "placed great demands on national, theater, and tactical imagery reconnaissance systems. The insatiable appetite for imagery and imagery-derived products could not be met."[22]

To correct deficiencies revealed during these operations, the CIA created the post of Associate Deputy Director of Operations for Military Affairs and undertook a number of initiatives designed to insure the ability to disseminate imagery and SIGINT collected by national systems to the theater and military commanders. In addition, at the impetus of Congress, the National Defense Authorization Act for Fiscal Years 1992 and 1993 called on the Secretary of Defense, after consultation with the Director of Central Intelligence, to "prescribe procedures for regularly and periodically exercising national intelligence collection systems and exploitation organizations that would be used to provide intelligence support, including support of the combatant commands, during a war or threat to national security."[23]

The concern that in time of war all U.S. collection systems, tactical and national, be available to support U.S. military forces, and that a dissemination architecture be designed to facilitate the speedy transmission of vital data to the theater, is more than reasonable. However, it is also necessary to recognize that, in the absence of war, much of the intelligence collected, even if military in nature, is used to facilitate the peacetime policies of the United States. Thus, policies that go beyond reasonable consideration of the military's peacetime intelligence needs (including preparing for optimal use of national assets during war) and virtually turn over control of national intelligence operations to the Department of Defense—such as the proposed DIA takeover of imagery tasking—are not prudent.[24]

To elaborate, it is important to distinguish between *military intelligence,* which may have a number of customers, and *intelligence that serves purely military purposes.* Although imagery is largely converted into military intelligence, it does not necessarily follow that the bulk of the military intelligence derived from imagery is only for or predominantly for military use. A satellite image of the Israeli nuclear facility at Dimona or Pakistani-Indian troops confronting each other constitutes military intelligence. But since the United States is hardly likely to become involved in military action against Israel or insert itself militarily into an Indo-Pakistani conflict, the imagery would be of more direct concern to the President, the National Security Council, and the State Department than military commanders. Similarly, the undoubtedly large number of images taken in 1993 of North Korean nuclear facilities, troop concentrations, and other military facilities undoubtedly helped to guide U.S. diplomatic efforts toward avoiding any military conflict and obtaining North Korean adherence to the Nuclear Non-Proliferation Treaty.

REQUIREMENTS AND BUDGETS

Both the end of the Cold War and the national deficit resulted in significant congressional pressure for the intelligence community to reduce personnel and expenditures. Partially as a result of that pressure, the intelligence community plans a 17.5 percent reduction in personnel by the end of the 1997 fiscal year.

It is clear that there are numerous instances in which personnel should be reduced and programs reduced or eliminated. The consolidation at the military service and unified command level of numerous intelligence organizations was undertaken, in part, to reduce unnecessary duplication of administrative and security personnel and costs. In addition, a number of ground-based SIGINT facilities have been closed down, particularly those that had been targeted on the Warsaw Pact. One can point to other programs—the seismic monitoring program run by AFTAC and the Navy's SOSUS, space and airborne ocean surveillance, and submarine reconnaissance programs, for example—where cutbacks would be appropriate.

Also, it is clear that, overall, and at least for the time being, fewer resources can be devoted to monitoring Russia and other former Soviet states—both because of the state of Russian-U.S. relations and the increased availability of open source data. The case probably cannot be made, however, that a dramatic peace dividend can be squeezed out of the intelligence budget without unacceptably reducing the intelligence required by U.S. national security decisionmakers in dealing with a multitude of developments and activities—including events in Russia, the foreign and domestic policies of the PRC, regional conflicts, the proliferation of weapons of mass destruction, and terrorism.

As long as Russia maintains significant military forces, particularly nuclear forces subject to arms control agreements, it will remain a major intelligence target. In addition, the events of October 1993 in Moscow indicate that the Russian future is still uncertain. Advanced information on domestic developments will remain of significant interest to U.S. decisionmakers.

The greatest concern of U.S. decisionmakers in upcoming years is likely to be restricting the spread of advanced military technologies—particularly nuclear, chemical, biological, and ballistic missile technologies—and preventing the use of such technologies as have been acquired. These tasks will require monitoring the pursuit and application of those technologies by a number of countries—including Israel, India, Pakistan, Iran, Iraq, and North Korea. In addition to monitoring within-country activities, attention will have to be directed toward the licit and illicit international supply of various components of those technologies. At times, proliferation intelligence can have a clear payoff. In 1992, on the basis of intelligence concerning Iranian procurement activities, the United States acted to prevent China from selling key technologies to Iran.[25]

China will also remain a significant intelligence target—owing to its expanding military power, its indiscriminate sale of advanced weapons technology, and continued concern over its human rights policies. The possibility that regional grievances and showdowns, such as those between India and Pakistan, will result in war, including nuclear war, will also continue to concern U.S. national security officials. And the threat of terrorism, particularly from groups seeking to undermine the Arab-Israeli peace process, remains.

Besides the need to monitor the proliferation activities of Russia and other targets, the laws of physics and optics will limit the extent to which savings can be realized from the intelligence budget. A substantial part of the intelligence budget is devoted to the development and operation of space reconnaissance systems—particularly imagery systems. Because such systems must operate in low-earth orbit to be effective, a single satellite is in view of a given target for only a short period of time each day. The implication is that repetitive coverage, vital in wartime but also of great value in peacetime, can only be obtained by maintaining a constellation of such satellites. The larger the constellation, the more frequent the coverage and the less the probability that a foreign nation can hide its military activities from the United States. Thus, even if the need for satellite coverage of Russia decreases, cutting back on the number of satellites in orbit would also decrease U.S. ability to monitor Iraq, Iran, and North Korea. The discoveries about the Iraqi nuclear program that came to light during and after the Persian Gulf War indicate a need to conduct more intense technical collection activities against such targets (both in respect to geographic scope and frequency of coverage) in order to reduce the chance of missing important nuclear-related construction activities.

BUDGET SECRECY

Although it may not be possible to effect a major reduction in the intelligence budget, there is one major change that should be made—declassification of budget and personnel figures. Within the executive branch and Congress, only two alternatives are considered—continued secrecy or release of a total budget figure. There appears to be unanimous agreement among those in Congress and the Executive Branch that release of the budgets for specific agencies or programs would jeopardize the intelligence community's ability to perform its mission.

Intelligence officials fear that even providing an official total budget figure could lead to discussions about specific programs as CIA officials were forced to justify their resistance to budget cuts. In addition, they fear that any future requests for increases in the intelligence budget would be met by demands for public justification—including discussions of which intelligence programs would be established or enhanced by the proposed increases. In either case, the details of specific programs would have to be disclosed. And such disclosure, it is argued, would allow targets of intelligence programs—whether North Korea, Iran, or Colombian drug lords—to neutralize U.S. intelligence efforts.

However, the fear that disclosing the overall intelligence budget, or even that of specific agencies and programs, would automatically compromise U.S. intelligence capabilities does not stand up to scrutiny. Unfortunately, that fear has become such a part of the intelligence community's conventional wisdom that it is rarely subject to critical analysis.

There is a significant difference between the amount of dollars spent or the number of personnel and the nature of their activities. There are a multitude of ways to spend $28 billion on intelligence collection and analysis. Different mixes of collection systems (space vs. air vs. ground) and capabilities (imagery vs. signals intelligence) are possible for any given expenditure. Likewise, there are many different ways to employ more than 100,000 people on intelligence missions. To suggest that a foreign nation can divine what information the United States is collecting about it, and how, simply as a result of knowing the total U.S. intelligence budget is absurd.

Moreover, there is a big difference between specifying what intelligence collection capabilities the United States maintains (and at what cost) and specifying exactly how and when those capabilities are used. Consider U.S. imagery satellites. It is officially acknowledged that the United States operates such satellites, and a great deal of information has been published in the press and in books about their capabilities. But that information—and a multitude of official leaks that indicate satellite targets—has not prevented those satellites from providing information of great value to the United States—from the extent of the disaster at Chernobyl in 1986 to Iraqi troop deployments on the eve of Desert Storm in January 1991.

Nor has the information that has appeared on aerial reconnaissance, space surveillance, and ocean surveillance systems—often in official U.S. government publications—prevented those systems from providing valuable intelligence. As indicated by the relevant chapters in this book, one can find details on the numbers, basing arrangements, capabilities, and even some of the targets of those systems in documents available under the Freedom of Information Act, documents intended for public distribution by the General Accounting Office and executive branch agencies, and congressional hearings. Specific systems covered in such documents include the U-2 spy plane, P-3C ocean surveillance aircraft, and

COBRA DANE radars used to monitor Russian ICBM tests and foreign space activities.

There are cases where the details, or even the existence, of entire programs must be classified. For example, the IVY BELLS program, which involved placing listening devices on Soviet underseas cables, required absolute secrecy. Once the Soviets were aware of the program, they were able to retrieve such devices. Likewise, when a collection effort involves technological advances so dramatic that other nations are not likely to be aware that such an effort is possible, and therefore take no precautionary measures (such as encrypted communications), secrecy will also be required.

But cases where total secrecy is required are the exception rather than the rule. Significant aspects of most U.S. intelligence collection programs can be discussed openly without presenting a danger to the collection effort. It is important that there be a far more open debate about the nature of U.S. intelligence activities than has occurred in the past to ensure that unnecessary expenses are eliminated and necessary activities adequately funded. That debate requires specifics, not the vague generalizations that have been the essence of official testimony on U.S. intelligence operations.

NOTES

1. J. Patrick Coyne, Memorandum for the President, Subject: Reorganization of Intelligence and Covert Activities, July 14, 1961, *Declassified Documents Reference System* (*DDRS*) 1981-623B; Peter Szanton and Graham Allison, "Intelligence: Seizing the Opportunity," *Foreign Policy* (Spring 1976): 183–214; Allen E. Goodman, "Reforming U.S. Intelligence," *Foreign Policy* (Summer 1987): 121–36; Allen E. Goodman, "Dateline Langley: Fixing the Intelligence Mess," *Foreign Policy* (Winter 1984–1985): 160–79; Stansfield Turner, "The Pentagon's Intelligence Mess," *Washington Post,* January 12, 1986, pp. D1, D2; Stansfield Turner, "Intelligence for a New World Order," *Foreign Affairs* (Fall 1991): 150–66; U.S. Congress, Senate Select Committee on Intelligence, *Review of Intelligence Organization* (Washington, D.C.: U.S. Government Printing Office, 1991); Presidential Review Memorandum/NSC-11, "Intelligence Structure and Mission," February 22, 1977. The proposed legislation was S.2198, the "Intelligence Reorganization Act of 1992," and H.R. 4165, the "National Security Act of 1992."

2. Commission on the Organization of the Government for the Conduct of Foreign Policy, *Report* (Washington, D.C.: U.S. Government Printing Office, 1975), p. 98.

3. Turner, "The Pentagon's Intelligence Mess."

4. Anthony Fainberg, *Strengthening IAEA Safeguards: Lessons from Iraq* (Stanford, Calif.: Center for International Security and Arms Control, Stanford University, 1993), p. 10.

5. David A. Fulghum, "Advanced Arms Spread Defies Remote Detection," *Aviation Week & Space Technology,* November 9, 1992, pp. 20–22.

6. Rodman D. Griffin, "As Intelligence Needs Change, So Do CIA Recruits' Resumes," *Washington Times,* December 28, 1992, p. A5.

7. Turner, "Intelligence for a New World Order," p. 154.

8. David E. Sanger, "Journey to Isolation," *New York Times Magazine*, November 15, 1992, pp. 28ff.; "Saddam's Nuclear Secrets," *Newsweek*, October 7, 1991, pp. 28–35; Jack Anderson and Dale Van Atta, "Cuban Defector Impeaches CIA Spies," *Washington Post*, March 21, 1988, p. B15; Bill Gertz, "Stasi Files Reveal CIA Two-Timers," *Washington Times*, September 12, 1991, pp. A1, A11.

9. Joint Chiefs of Staff, Joint Pub 2-0, *Doctrine for Intelligence Support to Joint Operations* (Washington, D.C.: JCS, June 30, 1991), p. II-23.

10. Private information.

11. R. Jeffrey Smith, "Administration to Consider Giving Spy Data to Business," *Washington Post*, February 3, 1993, pp. A1, A12.

12. Turner, "Intelligence for a New World Order," pp. 151–52.

13. See Randall Fort, "Economic Espionage: Problems and Prospects" (Washington, D.C.: Working Group on Intelligence Reform, Consortium for the Study of Intelligence, 1993), p. 6. Also see Stanley Kober, "The CIA as Economic Spy: The Misuse of U.S. Intelligence After the Cold War," *CATO Institute Policy Analysis Paper No. 185*, December 8, 1992.

14. Fort, "Economic Espionage: Problems and Prospects," pp. 6–10.

15. Ibid., p. 8.

16. Ibid., pp. 14–15.

17. Bill Gertz, "CIA Chief Rejects Industrial Spying," *Washington Times*, November 24, 1993, p. A3.

18. Quoted in Fort, "Economic Espionage: Problems and Prospects," p. 14.

19. William O. Studeman, "Farewell," April 8, 1992.

20. Molly Moore, "Schwartzkopf: War Intelligence Flawed," *Washington Post*, June 13, 1991, pp. A1, A40.

21. Department of Defense, *Conduct of the Persian Gulf War: Final Report to Congress* (Washington, D.C.: DOD, April 1992), p. 416.

22. Ibid.

23. U.S. Congress, Public Law 102-190, *National Defense Authorization Act for Fiscal Years 1992 and 1993* (Washington, D.C.: U.S. Government Printing Office, 1991), Section 924.

24. U.S. Senate Select Committee on Intelligence, *Review of Intelligence Reorganization*, p. 23.

25. Steve Coll, "U.S. Halted Nuclear Bid by Iran," *Washington Post*, November 17, 1992, pp. A1, A30.

ACRONYMS AND ABBREVIATIONS

AAA	anti-aircraft artillery
AABL	Advanced Atmospheric Burst Locator
AARS	Advanced Airborne Reconnaissance System
ABMA	Army Ballistic Missile Agency
ACC	Air Combat Command
ACE	Allied Command Europe
ACINT	Acoustic Intelligence
ACIS	Arms Control Intelligence Staff, Office of the Director of Central Intelligence
ACOUSTINT	Acoustic Intelligence
ACS, I	Assistant Chief of Staff, Intelligence
ADONIS	AMOS Daylight Near-Infrared Imaging System
AEC	Atomic Energy Commission
AEDS	Atomic Energy Detection System
AFAR	Azores Fixed Acoustic Range
AFIA	Air Force Intelligence Agency
AFIC	Air Force Intelligence Command
AFIS	Air Force Intelligence Service
AFISA	Air Force Intelligence Support Agency
AFMIC	Armed Forces Medical Intelligence Center
AFOSI	Air Force Office of Special Investigation
AFR	Air Force Regulation
AFSA	Armed Forces Security Agency
AFSAC	Air Force Special Activities Center
AFSAC/IRC	Armed Forces Security Agency Council/Intelligence Requirements Committee
AFSG	Air Force Security Group
AFSPACECOM	Air Force Space Command
AFSS	Air Force Security Service
AFTAC	Air Force Technical Applications Center
AGER	Auxiliary General Environmental Research

AGTR	Auxiliary General Technical Research
AIA	Air Intelligence Agency
AIA	Army Intelligence Agency
AIC	Atlantic Intelligence Command
AIOD	Army Intelligence Operations Detachment
AIS	Army Intelligence Survey
ALCOR	ARPA Lincoln C-Band Observable Radar
ALEXIS	Array of Low-Energy X-Ray Imaging Sensors
ALPA	Alaska Long Period Array
ALTAIR	ARPA Long-Range Tracking and Instrumentation Radar
AMOS	Air Force Maui Optical Station
AMSIC	Army Missile and Space Intelligence Center
ANZMIS	Australia–New Zealand Military Intelligence Service
AOB	Air Order-of-Battle
AOMC	Army Ordnance Missile Command
AR	Army Regulation
ARDE	Alanza Revolucionaria Democratica (Democratic Revolutionary Alliance, Nicaragua)
ARIA	Advanced Range Instrumentation Aircraft
ARIS	Advanced Range Instrumentation Ships
ARPA	Advanced Research Projects Agency
ASA	Army Security Agency
ASARS	Advanced Synthetic Aperture Radar System
ASD	Assistant Secretary of Defense
ASIS	Australian Secret Intelligence Service
ASTIB	*Army Scientific and Technical Intelligence Bulletin*
ATARS	Advanced Tactical Airborne Reconnaissance System
ATGM	Antitank Guided Missile
ATS	Advanced Telemetry System
BBC	British Broadcasting Corporation
BGPHES	Battle Group Passive Horizon Extension System
BMEWS	Ballistic Missile Early Warning System
BNE	Board of National Estimates
BRUSA	British–United States Communications Intelligence Agreement
BSTIS	*Biweekly Scientific and Technical Intelligence Summary*
C^3I	Command, Control, Communications, and Intelligence
CAMS	COMIREX Automated Management System
CAPG	Covert Action Planning Group
CARS	Contingency Airborne Reconnaissance System
CASPER	Contact Area Summary Position Report
CCD	Charged Couple Devices
CCF	Collection Coordination Facility

CCP	Consolidated Cryptographic Program
CCPC	Critical Collection Problems Committee
CDAA	Circularly Disposed Antenna Array
CDT	Central Data Terminal
CENTCOM	U.S. Central Command
CERP	Combined Economic Reporting Program
CFI	Committee on Foreign Intelligence
CIA	Central Intelligence Agency
CIC	Counterintelligence Center, Directorate of Operations, CIA
CIG	Central Intelligence Group
CINCLANT	Commander-in-Chief, Atlantic
CINCLANTFLT	Commander-in-Chief, Atlantic Fleet
CINCPACFLT	Commander-in-Chief, Pacific Fleet
CINCSAC	Commander-in-Chief, Strategic Air Command
CIO	Central Imagery Office
CIPC	Critical Intelligence Problems Committee
CIRL	Current Intelligence Reporting List
CIS	Commonwealth of Independent States
CIS	Country Intelligence Study
CISR	Communications Intelligence Supplementary Regulations
CITA	Central Imagery Tasking Authority
CITS	Central Command Imagery Transmission System
CMO	Central MASINT Office
CMS	Community Management Staff
CNC	Crime and Narcotics Center, Directorate of Intelligence, CIA
COIC	Combat Operations Intelligence Center
COMINT	Communications Intelligence
COMIREX	Committee on Imagery Requirements and Exploitation
COMOR	Committee on Overhead Reconnaissance
COMSEC	Communications Security
CORD	Current Operations and Readiness Department, Navy Operational Intelligence Center
COS	Chief of Station
CPAS	Office of Current Production and Analytic Support, Directorate of Intelligence, CIA
CRITICOMM	Critical Intelligence Communications
CROSS	Combined Radio Frequency and Optical Space Surveillance
CSAW	Communications Supplementary Activity Washington
CSE	Communications Security Establishment, Canada
CSS	Central Security Service
CTC	Counterterrorism Center, Directorate of Operations, CIA
DARO	Defense Airborne Reconnaissance Office
DARPA	Defense Advanced Research Projects Agency

DARSC	Defense Airborne Reconnaissance Steering Committee
DCI	Director of Central Intelligence
DCID	Director of Central Intelligence Directive
DCSI	Deputy Chief of Staff for Intelligence, U.S. Army
DEA	Drug Enforcement Administration
DEB	Defense Estimative Brief
DEFSMAC	Defense Special Missile and Astronautics Center
DEPLOC	Daily Estimated Position Locator
DGI	General Directorate of Intelligence, Cuba
DGSE	Direccion General de Seguridad del Estado (Directorate General of State Security, Nicaragua)
DGSE	Direction Générale de la Sécurité Extérieure (Directorate General of External Security, France)
DHS	Defense HUMINT Service
DIA	Defense Intelligence Agency
DID	*Defense Intelligence Digest*
DIE	Defense Intelligence Estimate
DIEM	Defense Intelligence Estimative Memoranda
DIN	Defense Intelligence Network
DIN	*Defense Intelligence Notice*
DIN	Digital Network
DINSUM	*Daily Intelligence Summary*
DIO	Defense Intelligence Officer
DIPPs	Defense Intelligence Projections for Planning
DIRNSA	Director, National Security Agency
DISOB	*Defense Intelligence Space Order of Battle*
DISUM	Defense Intelligence Summary
DITS	Digital Imagery Transmission System
DITSUM	*Defense Intelligence Terrorist Summary*
DMA	Defense Mapping Agency
DMACSC	Defense Mapping Agency Combat Support Center
DMARC	Defense Mapping Agency Reston Center
DMASC	Defense Mapping Agency Systems Center
DMOB	Defensive Missile Order-of-Battle
DMSP	Defense Meteorological Satellite Program
DNI	Director of Naval Intelligence
DOD	Department of Defense
DODJOCC	Department of Defense Joint Operations Center Chicksands
DOE	Department of Energy
DOS	Digital "O" System
DPS	Digital Production Systems
DRD	Domestic Resources Division
DRSP	Defense Reconnaissance Support Program

DS&T	Directorate of Science and Technology, CIA
DSCS	Defense Satellite Communications System
DSD	Defence Signals Directorate, Australia
DSP	Defense Support Program
DSPO	Defense Support Project Office
DSSCS	Defense Special Security Communications System
DST	Directorate for Territorial Surveillance, France
DSTS	Deep Space Tracking System
DVITS	Digital Video Imagery Transmission System
EAL	Economic Alert List
EC	Economic Community
EHF	Extremely High Frequency
EIC	Economic Intelligence Committee
ELINT	Electronic Intelligence
EMP	Electromagnetic Pulse
EPA	Environmental Protection Agency
ESAF	European Special Activities Facility
ESC	Electronic Security Command
EUCOM	U.S. European Command
EUCOMSITS	European Command Secondary Imagery Transmission System
EUDAC	European Defense Analysis Center
EXRAND	Exploitation Research and Development Subcommittee (of COMIREX)
FASTC	Foreign Aerospace Science and Technology Center
FBI	Federal Bureau of Investigation
FBIS	Foreign Broadcast Information Service
FCC	Federal Communications Commission
FDS	Fixed Distributed Surveillance
FICEURLANT	Fleet Intelligence Center, Europe and Atlantic
FICPAC	Fleet Intelligence Center, Pacific
FIPC	Foreign Intelligence Priorities Committee
FISINT	Foreign Instrumentation Signals Intelligence
FIST	Fleet Imagery Support Terminal
FLTSATCOM	Fleet Satellite Communications System
FMEP	Foreign Materiel Exploitation Program
FNLA	National Front for the Liberation of Angola
FOSIC	Fleet Ocean Surveillance Information Center
FOSIF	Fleet Ocean Surveillance Information Facility
FRB	Foreign Resources Branch, Domestic Resources Division, Directorate of Operations, CIA
FRD	Foreign Resources Division, Directorate of Operations, CIA
FSTC	Foreign Science and Technology Center
FTD	Foreign Technology Division

GATT	General Agreement on Tariffs and Trade
GCHQ	Government Communications Headquarters, United Kingdom
GCSB	Government Communications Security Bureau, New Zealand
GDIP	General Defense Intelligence Program
GEODSS	Ground-Based Electro-Optical Deep Space Surveillance
GIUK	Greenland-Iceland-United Kingdom
GMAIC	Guided Missile and Astronautics Intelligence Committee
GOB	Ground Order-of-Battle
GPS	Global Positioning System
GRCS	Guardrail Common Sensor
GRU	Glavnoye Razvedyvatelnoye Upravleniye (Chief Intelligence Directorate, Soviet/Russian General Staff)
HF	High Frequency
HPSCI	House Permanent Select Committee on Intelligence
HQ CSTC	Headquarters, Consolidated Space Test Center
HRC	Human Resources Committee
HRP	Hydroacoustic Recorder and Processor
HUMINT	Human Intelligence
IAC	Indications and Analysis Center
IAC	Intelligence Advisory Committee
ICBM	Intercontinental Ballistic Missile
IC/EXCOM	Intelligence Community Executive Committee
ICMS	Improved CRYSTAL Metric System
ICS	Intelligence Community Staff
IDC	Interagency Defector Committee
IG-CI	Interagency Group—Counterintelligence
IG-CM (P)	Interagency Group—Countermeasures (Policy)
IG-CM (T)	Interagency Group—Countermeasures (Technical)
IGCP	Intelligence Guidance for COMINT Production
IHC	Information Handling Committee
IICT	Interagency Intelligence Committee on Terrorism
IIM	Interagency Intelligence Memorandum
ILD	International Liaison Department, PRC
INFOSEC	Information Security
INR	Bureau of Intelligence and Research, Department of State
INSCOM	Army Intelligence and Security Command
INTELSAT	International Telecommunications Satellite
IPAC	Intelligence Center, Pacific
IPC	Intelligence Producers Council
IRAC	Intelligence Resources Advisory Committee
IROL	Imagery Requirements Objectives List
IRSIG	International Regulations on SIGINT

ISA	Intelligence Support Activity
ISAR	Inverse Synthetic Aperture Radar
ISID	Inter-Services Intelligence Directorate, Pakistan
ITAC	Intelligence and Threat Analysis Center
ITW/AA	Integrated Tactical Warning and Attack Assessment
JAC	Joint Analysis Center
JAEIC	Joint Atomic Energy Intelligence Committee
JCS	Joint Chiefs of Staff
JFS	J Field Set
JIC	Joint Intelligence Center
JICPAC	Joint Intelligence Center, Pacific
JIEP	Joint Intelligence Estimates for Planning
JLREID	Joint Long-Range Estimative Intelligence Document
JMSDF	Japanese Maritime Self-Defense Forces
JPRS	Joint Publications Research Service
JRC	Joint Reconnaissance Center
JSTPS	Joint Strategic Target Planning Staff
KEYSCOM	Imagery Interpretation Keys Subcommittee (of COMIREX)
KGB	Komitet Gosudarstvennoy Bezopasnosti (Soviet Committee for State Security)
KH	Keyhole
KIQ	Key Intelligence Question
LANTDAC	Atlantic Command Defense Analysis Center
LANTFAST	Atlantic Forward Area Support Team
LANTJIC	Atlantic Joint Intelligence Center
LASA	Large Aperture Seismic Array
LASINT	Laser Intelligence
LASS	Low-Altitude Space Surveillance
LAVR	Large Area Vulnerability Report
LIC	Low Intensity Conflict
MASINT	Measurement and Signature Intelligence
MCIC	Marine Corps Intelligence Center
MCL	McClellan Central Laboratory
MGT	Mobile Ground Terminal
MIB	Military Intelligence Board
MIIA	Medical Intelligence and Information Agency
MOTIF	Maui Optical Tracking and Identification Facility
MPLA	Popular Movement for the Liberation of Angola
MRR	Movement for the Recovery of the Revolution, Cuba
NAIC	National Air Intelligence Center
NASA	National Aeronautics and Space Administration
NATO	North Atlantic Treaty Organization
NAVALEX	Naval Electronic Systems Command

NAVFAC	Naval Facility
NAVSPASUR	Naval Space Surveillance
NAVSPAWAR	Naval Space and Air Warfare Command
NCB	National Collection Branch, Domestic Resources Division, Directorate of Operations, CIA
NCD	National Collection Division, Directorate of Operations, CIA
NCIPB	National Counterintelligence Policy Board
NDS	Nuclear Detonation (NUDET) Detection System
NEACP	National Emergency Airborne Command Post
NETCAP	National Exploitation of Tactical Capabilities
NFAC	National Foreign Assessment Center
NFIB	National Foreign Intelligence Board
NFIC	National Foreign Intelligence Council
NFIP	National Foreign Intelligence Program
NFMP	Navy Foreign Materiel Program
NFOIO	Naval Field Operational Intelligence Office
NGIC	National Ground Intelligence Center
NIAM	National Intelligence Analytical Memorandum
NIC	National Intelligence Council
NIC	Naval Intelligence Command
NICB	National Intelligence Collection Board
NID	*National Intelligence Daily*
NIE	National Intelligence Estimate
NIO	National Intelligence Officer
NIPB	National Intelligence Production Board
NIPSSA	Naval Intelligence Processing System Support Activity
NISC	Naval Intelligence Support Center
NISR	National Intelligence Situation Report
NISSTR	National Intelligence Systems for Support of Tactical Requirements
NIT	National Intelligence Topic
NITC	National Intelligence Tasking Center
NJMIC	National Joint Military Intelligence Center
NMCC	National Military Command Center
NMIC	National Maritime Intelligence Center
NMIC	Naval Maritime Intelligence Center
NMICC	National Military Intelligence Collection Center, DIA
NMIPC	National Military Intelligence Production Center, DIA
NMISC	National Military Intelligence Support Center, DIA
NOB	Naval Order-of-Battle
NOIC	Navy Operational Intelligence Center
NOO	Naval Oceanographic Office
NORSAR	Norwegian Seismic Array

NPC	Non-Proliferation Center, Office of the Director of Central Intelligence
NPIC	National Photographic Interpretation Center
NREC	National Reconnaissance Executive Committee
NRL	Naval Research Laboratory
NRO	National Reconnaissance Office
NRP	National Reconnaissance Program
NRPC	Naval Regional Processing Center
NSA	National Security Agency
NSAM	National Security Action Memorandum
NSC	National Security Council
NSCIC	National Security Council Intelligence Committee
NSCID	National Security Council Intelligence Directive
NSD	National Security Directive
NSDD	National Security Decision Directive
NSDM	National Security Decision Memorandum
NSGC	Naval Security Group Command
NSOC	National SIGINT Operations Center
NSPG	National Security Planning Group
NSRL	National SIGINT Requirements List
NSTL	National Strategic Target List
NTIC	Naval Technical Intelligence Center
NTPC	National Telemetry Processing Center, NSA
NUCINT	Nuclear Intelligence
OACS, I	Office of the Assistant Chief of Staff, Intelligence
OAG	Operations Advisory Group
OAS	Organization of American States
OASIS	Operational Applications of Special Intelligence Systems
OEE	Office of Export Enforcement, Department of Commerce
OFA	Office of Foreign Availability, Department of Commerce
OGI	Office of Global Issues, Directorate of Intelligence, CIA
OIA	Office of Imagery Analysis, Directorate of Intelligence, CIA
OIR	Office of Information Resources, Directorate of Intelligence, CIA
OIS	Office of Intelligence Support, Department of the Treasury
OLA	Office of Leadership Analysis, Directorate of Intelligence, CIA
OMB	Office of Management and Budget
ONE	Office of National Estimates
ONI	Office of Naval Intelligence
OPC	Office of Policy Coordination
OPEC	Organization of Petroleum Exporting Countries
OPINT	Optical Intelligence

OR&D	Office of Research and Development, Directorate of Science and Technology, CIA
ORTT	Office of Resources, Trade, and Technology, Directorate of Intelligence, CIA
OSD	Office of the Secretary of Defense
OSI	Office of Strategic Information, Department of Commerce
OSIS	Ocean Surveillance Information System
OSO	Office of SIGINT Operations, Directorate of Science and Technology, CIA
OSS	Office of Strategic Services
OSWR	Office of Scientific and Weapons Research, Directorate of Intelligence, CIA
OTA	Office of Threat Assessment, Office of Intelligence, Department of Energy
OTS	Office of Technical Services, Directorate of Science and Technology, CIA
PACBAR	Pacific Radar Barrier
PACCS	Post-Attack Command and Control System
PACE	Portable Acoustic Collection Equipment
PACFAST	Pacific Forward Area Support Team
PACOM	Pacific Command
PARCS	Perimeter Acquisition Radar Characterization System
PARPRO	Peacetime Aerial Reconnaissance Program
PASS	Passive Space Surveillance System
PCG	Planning and Coordination Group
PD	Presidential Directive
PDB	*President's Daily Brief*
PDD	Presidential Decision Directive
PFLP-GC	Popular Front for the Liberation of Palestine—General Command
PGW	Precision Guided Weapons
PID	Photographic Intelligence Division
PLO	Palestine Liberation Organization
PMEL	Precision Measurement Equipment Laboratory
PNET	Peaceful Nuclear Explosions Treaty
PNIO	Priority National Intelligence Objective
PORTS	Portable Receive and Transmit System
PRC	People's Republic of China
PRC	Policy Review Committee
QRT	Quick Reaction Team
RADINT	Radar Intelligence
RAF	Royal Air Force
RAM	Reform the Armed Forces Now Movement, Philippines

RAW	Research and Analysis Wing, India
RDSS	Rapidly Deployable Surveillance System
RDT&E	Research, Development, Test, and Evaluation
ROFA	Remote Operations Facility, Airborne
RPV	Remotely Piloted Vehicle
RRS	Remote Relay System
RSVC	Reconnaissance Satellite Vulnerability Computer
RTG	Reconnaissance Technical Group
RTS	Reconnaissance Technical Squadron
RWO	Ramstein Warning Office
SAC	Strategic Air Command
SACEUR	Supreme Allied Commander Europe
SAM	surface-to-air missiles
SATRAN	Satellite Reconnaissance Advance Notice
SB	Sluzba Bezpiecezecstwa (Security Service, Poland)
SBSS	Space Based Surveillance System
SCA	Service Cryptological Authority
SCC	Special Coordination Committee
SCE	Service Cryptological Element
SCI	Sensitive Compartmented Information
SCOL	SIGINT Combined Operating List
SDIE	Special Defense Intelligence Estimate
SDS	Satellite Data System
SECOM	Security Committee
SHF	Super High Frequency
SI	Special Intelligence
SIG-I	Senior Interagency Group—Intelligence
SIGINT	Signals Intelligence
SIGSEC	Signals Security
SIOP	Single Integrated Operational Plan
SIPRI	Stockholm International Peace Research Institute
SIRE	Space Imagery Receive Experiment
SIRVES	SIGINT Requirements Validation and Evaluation Subcommittee
SIS	Special Intelligence Service, FBI
SIS	Secret Intelligence Service, United Kingdom
SISDE	Servizio per le Informazione e la Sicurezza Democratica (Democratic Security and Information Service, Italy)
SISMI	Servizio per le Informazione e la Sicurezza Militare (Military Security and Information Service, Italy)
SLBM	Submarine-Launched Ballistic Missile
SMILS	Sonobuoy Missile Impact Location System
SNIE	Special National Intelligence Estimate

SOER	Standing Operational ELINT Requirements
SORS	SIGINT Overhead Reconnaissance Subcommittee
SOSUS	Sound Surveillance System
SOUTHCOM	Southern Command
SOVPACFLT	Soviet Pacific Fleet
SPADATS	Space Detection and Tracking System
SPADOC	Space Defense Operations Center
SPATS	*Strategic Posture Aerospace Threat Summary*
SPAWAR	Naval Space and Air Warfare Command
SPIN	*Space Intelligence Notes*
SPINTCOM	Special Intelligence Communications
SPIREP	*Spot Intelligence Report*
SPOEM	Special Program Office for Exploitation Modernization
SRBM	Short-Range Ballistic Missile
SRC	Strategic Reconnaissance Center, Strategic Air Command
SSC	Space Surveillance Center
SSN	Space Surveillance Network
START	Strategic Arms Reduction Talks
STIC	Scientific and Technical Intelligence Committee
STRATCOM	U.S. Strategic Command
STRATJIC	Strategic Joint Intelligence Center
STS	Space Transportation System
SURTASS	Surface Towed Array Sensor System
SVR	Satellite Vulnerability Report
SVR	Sluzhba Vneshney Razvedki (Foreign Intelligence Service, Russia)
SWINT	Safe Window Intelligence
TAREX	Target Exploitation
TARPS	Tactical Reconnaissance Pod System
TCP	Tactical Cryptologic Program
TDF	Tactical Digital Facsimile
TDI	Target Data Inventory
TDRS	Tracking and Data Relay Satellite
TELINT	Telemetry Intelligence
TENCAP	Tactical Exploitation of National Capabilities
TERCOM	Terrain Contour Matching
TFC	Tactical Fusion Center
TGIF	Transportable Ground Intercept Facility
TIARA	Tactical Intelligence and Related Activities
TID	Technical Intelligence Division
TIP	Travelers in Panama (File)
TK	Talent-Keyhole
TRANSCOM	U.S. Transportation Command

TREDS	Tactical Reconnaissance Exploitation Demonstration System
TRIGS	TR-1 Ground Station
TSD	Technical Services Division, Directorate of Science and Technology, CIA
TSR	Time Sensitive Requirements
TTIC	Technology Transfer Intelligence Committee
UAV	Unmanned Aerial Vehicle
UCLA	Unilaterally Controlled Latino Assets
UHF	Ultra High Frequency
UKUSA	United Kingdom–United States Security Agreement
UNITA	National Union for the Total Independence of Angola
UNO	Unidad Nicarguēnsa Opositora (United Nicaraguan Opposition, Nicaragua)
USACOM	U.S. Atlantic Command
USAFE	United States Air Forces, Europe
USAREUR	United States Army Europe
USCIB/IC	U.S. Communications Intelligence Board/Intelligence Committee
USGS	United States Geological Survey
USIB	United States Intelligence Board
USNAVEUR	U.S. Naval Forces, Europe
USSID	United States Signals Intelligence Directive
USSOC	U.S. Special Operations Command
USSPACECOM	U.S. Space Command
USSS	United States SIGINT System
VHF	Very High Frequency
VKL	Communications Experience Facility, Finland
VOD	Vertical Observation Data
WIS	*Weekly Intelligence Summary*
WISE	Warning Indications Systems, Europe
WSSIC	Weapons and Space Systems Intelligence Committee
WWR	*Weekly Watch Report*

ABOUT THE BOOK AND AUTHOR

Despite the end of the Cold War, intelligence activities continue to be an important component of U.S. national security operations (costing about $28 billion a year). Intelligence information will be vital in formulating and implementing policy on Russia, terrorism and narcotics trafficking, the proliferation of weapons of mass destruction, and the broader international strategic environment. Reliable intelligence is also vital as support for U.S. and UN military operations and inspections.

In this comprehensively updated edition, Jeffrey Richelson has again obtained documents through the Freedom of Information Act to offer readers an extraordinarily detailed look at the organizations that collect and analyze intelligence, at covert actions and counterintelligence operations, and at the means by which the vast intelligence community is managed.

Richelson examines the missions, functions, and organizational structure of all U.S. intelligence operations, including the National Security Agency, the National Reconnaissance Office, Defense Department organizations, military service organizations, intelligence components of the unified military commands, and civilian intelligence organizations as well as the CIA. This new edition explains the major organizational upheaval that has occurred in recent years.

Richelson also explores the details of intelligence work, laying bare a complex range of collection activities—imagery, signals intelligence, nuclear intelligence, human intelligence, open sources, and liaison. He assesses the reports and estimates generated by intelligence-community analysts and discusses the methods used to manage the intelligence community—offices, committees, directives, and regulations. Richelson concludes with his views on current controversies regarding the intelligence community: What makes for an effective organization? What is the value of human intelligence operations? What is the potential for economic espionage?

Jeffrey T. Richelson is an author and consultant. He has written numerous books on intelligence and defense issues, including *America's Secret Eyes in Space, Foreign Intelligence Organizations,* and *Sword and Shield: The Soviet Intelligence and Security Apparatus.*

INDEX